The Zondervan 1983 PASTOR'S ANNUAL

A Planned Preaching Program for the Year

T. T. Crabtree

ZONDERVAN PUBLISHING HOUSE
OF THE ZONDERVAN CORPORATION
GRAND RAPIDS, MICHIGAN 49506

Scripture quotations are from the *King James Version* unless otherwise designated.

Additional translations used are:

American Standard Version © 1929 by International Council of Religious Education, Thomas Nelson & Sons (ASV)

Living Bible © 1971 by Tyndale House Publishers (LB)

New English Bible © 1970 by Oxford University Press (NEB)

New International Version © 1978 by New York International Bible Society (NIV)

New Testament, a New Translation by James Moffatt © 1950 by James A. R. Moffatt, Harper & Brothers

New Testament in Modern English, Revised Edition, by J. B. Phillips © 1972 by J. B. Phillips

Revised Standard Version © 1952 by Division of Christian Education of the National Council of the Churches of Christ in the United States of America, Thomas Nelson & Sons (RSV)

Today's English Version, Good News Bible © 1976 by American Bible Society (TEV)

THE ZONDERVAN PASTOR'S ANNUAL FOR 1983

Grand Rapids, Michigan

This printing, June 1982

Library of Congress Catalog Card Number 71-9126

ISBN 0-310-22661-9

Printed in the United States of America

CONTENTS

SERMONS

MISCELLANEOUS HELPS

Communion Services

Funeral Messages

Wedding Ceremonies

Messages for Older Children and Young People

Indexes

ACKNOWLEDGMENTS TO CONTRIBUTING AUTHORS

Tom S. Brandon	A.M.	January 2, 9, 16, 23, 30
		February 6, 13, 20, 27
Jerold R. McBride	P.M.	January 2, 9, 16, 23, 30
James E. Carter	P.M.	January 5, 12, 19, 26
	A.M.	December 4, 11, 18, 25
T. T. Crabtree	P.M.	February 6, 13, 20, 27
	A.M.	June 26, July 3
		September 4, 11, 18, 25
	P.M.	September 7, 14, 21, 28
	A.M.	October 2, 9, 16, 23, 30
	P.M.	October 5, 12, 19, 26
		December 4, 11, 18, 25
David L. Jenkins	P.M.	February 2, 9, 16, 23
		March 2, 9, 16, 23
		April 6, 13, 20, 27
		Miscellaneous Section
Bill Whittaker	A.M.	March 6, 13, 20, 27
		April 3, 10, 17, 24
		May 1
D. L. Lowrie	P.M.	March 6, 13, 20, 27
		April 3, 10, 17, 24
		August 7, 14, 21, 28
		September 4, 11, 18, 25
Charles R. Wade	A.M.	May 8, 15, 22, 29
		June 5, 12, 19
W. T. Holland	P.M.	May 1, 8, 15, 22, 29
		June 5, 12, 19, 26
		July 3, 10, 17, 24, 31
		October 2, 9, 16, 23, 30
Harold T. Bryson	P.M.	May 4, 11, 18, 25
		June 1, 8, 15, 22, 29
		July 6, 13, 20, 27
		August 3, 10, 17, 24, 31
		November 6, 13, 20, 27
Robert G. Campbell	A.M.	July 10, 17, 24, 31
		August 7, 14, 21, 28
Fred M. Wood	A.M.	November 6, 13, 20, 27
	P.M.	November 2, 9, 16, 23, 30
		December 7, 14, 21, 28
Bennie Cole Crabtree		Sentence Sermonettes

PREFACE

It is with a thankful heart that we send forth this eighteenth volume of the *Zondervan Pastor's Annual* with a prayer that it can be used to bless the life and ministry of pastors around the world.

Professors of preaching have been insisting through the years that pastors should have a planned preaching program rather than an unplanned preaching program. This volume, like those in the past, is sent forth with the hope that it can provide assistance to pastors who are seeking to plan a comprehensive preaching program that will enable them to do a better job of preaching the whole counsel of God.

Dr. Vernon L. Stanfield, an outstanding professor of preaching, has stated in the revised edition of *On the Preparation and Delivery of Sermons* by Dr. John A. Broadus (New York: Harper & Row, 1979) that "Both general and immediate preparation will be easier if there is an overall plan for a pastor's preaching program. Far too many preachers plan one sermon at a time or for one Sunday at a time."

Dr. Stanfield further states, "Planning will give purpose and direction to preaching . . . planning also helps the preacher with sermon preparation . . . planning removes much of the stress and strain of lack of preparation . . . for the pastor to plan his preaching will also help him to plan worship" (pp. 257–60).

Without the valuable assistance of the contributing authors who have assisted me by providing portions of the sermonic material found in this volume, the task would have been impossible.

The manuscripts included come from pastors who truly have a pastor's heart. Each man has a proven performance record indicating his dedication to God and his love for people. The material which is provided offers both variety and freshness as the contributors have put forth a sincere effort to meet the spiritual needs of the congregations to which they minister.

Without reservation I would dedicate this book to my beloved wife, Bennie Elizabeth, who is God's great blessing to my ministry.

I am deeply indebted to an excellent secretary, Mrs. Dale Wiser, who has worked diligently in assisting me with this task.

I would also like to express my gratitude to the ministerial staff and to the congregation of the First Baptist Church of Springfield, Missouri. They are a great folk in the Lord who challenge me continually with the opportunity of correctly interpreting and faithfully proclaiming the whole Word of the Lord from Sunday to Sunday.

It is the prayer of my heart that each minister using this *Annual* will let the Holy Spirit use him in such a manner as to improve on everything that has been suggested. May the Holy Spirit help each pastor to be a good minister, an authentic spokesman for God, as well as an effective evangelist during these days of opportunity.

— T. T. Crabtree, Pastor
First Baptist Church
Springfield, Missouri 65806

A PLANNED PREACHING PROGRAM

Sunday Morning Themes

Celebrating the Life Which Christ Makes Possible—*January*
The New Life That Is Possible Through Christ—*February*
Going to Jerusalem—*March*
Recognizing and Responding to the Living Lord—*April*
The Christian Family Living for Christ in the Present—*May, June*
The Seven Deadly Sins—*July*
Finding Victory Over the Seven Deadly Sings—*August*
Recognizing and Responding to God's Gift of the Holy Spirit—*September*
Today Is the Day of Salvation—*October*
Thanksgiving to God and Thanksliving for God—*November*
God's Affirmative Action—*December*

Sunday Evening Themes

The Central Theme of the Great Apostle—*January*
Is There Any Good News for Those Who Suffer?—*February*
Beneath the Cross of Jesus or Were You There When They Crucified My Lord—*March, April*
Thinking About the Cross—*May*
The Inward Attitudes of the True Disciple—*June, July*
The Master's Recipe for Effective Praying—*August, September*
The Church Which Is His Body—*October*
The Past Speaks to the Present—*November*
Go Tell It on the Mountain—*December*

Wednesday Evening Themes

Concerning Colossians—*January*
What the Bible Says—*February, March, April*
The Christ of John's Gospel—*May, June, July, August*
Amen and Amen—*September, October*
Lessons From a Changed Man—*November*
Lessons From Joseph—*December*

SUGGESTED PREACHING PROGRAM FOR THE MONTH OF JANUARY

Sunday Mornings

The return of January provides the pastor with a time of new beginnings, both for his personal devotions and for his ministry of feeding the sheep of God's flock. A response of celebration and praise for life with all of its opportunities would be appropriate. The suggested theme for the month is "Celebrating the Life Which Christ Makes Possible."

Sunday Evenings

The four Gospels contain the written testimony of inspired writers as they sought to report not only the events in the life of Jesus but the significance of those events.

Paul's epistles were written to exalt Jesus Christ and to explain the meaning of His life and His teachings. He wrote his various epistles to meet great needs in the life of the early disciples. "The Central Theme of the Great Apostle" is the theme of a series of messages based upon five of Paul's major epistles.

Wednesday Evenings

It is suggested that the devotional study of the Book of Colossians be completed and the theme "Concerning Colossians" be used.

* * *

SUNDAY MORNING, JANUARY 2

TITLE: Finding the Lost Book

TEXT: **"And Hilkiah the high priest said unto Shaphan the scribe, I have found the book of the law in the house of the LORD" (2 Kings 22:8).**

SCRIPTURE READING: **2 Kings 22**

HYMNS: **"O Worship the King," Grant**
"Word of God, Across the Ages," Blanchard
"Break Thou the Bread of Life," Lathbury and Gross

OFFERTORY PRAYER:

Heavenly Father, Your Holy Word tells us to bring all the tithes into the storehouse, that there may be meat in Your house. We humbly yet gratefully offer to You our tithes and offerings this day. Thank You for the privilege. May Your name be honored through Christ, our Savior and Lord.

Introduction. During the reign of King Josiah a great discovery was made. Hilkiah the priest announced to Shaphan the scribe, during the time that the temple was being repaired, "I have found the book of the law in the house of the LORD" (2 Kings 22:8).

From that simple statement occurs one of the most interesting experiences in the Old Testament. Not only did it have a message for then, it has a message for now. It has to do with finding the lost book, rediscovering the Bible. This is especially appropriate for the beginning of a new year. Finding the lost book or rediscovering the Bible may be considered in two ways.

I. Rediscovering the Bible historically.

A. *The discovery of the lost book.*

1. The times. Josiah was the grandson of Manasseh, one of the most wicked kings of Judah. During his reign the nation was flooded with idolatry and immorality. The worship of Baal was restored in a land that was filled with the worship of stars, wizards, and enchantments. Violence reigned; the temple of God was neglected. The king and the people had heard the prophets' words, but they rebelled against the God of their fathers.

2. The king. Then along came Josiah. He was eight years old when he began to reign and he reigned thirty-one years. He was righteous before the Lord, loyal to his heritage, and dedicated to God throughout his reign. He was influenced toward the Lord by godly people, so he began to seek the Lord and repair the temple. While this was happening, the lost book was found!

3. The book. The book that was found was called "the book of the law" and was either a part or all of the Book of Deuteronomy. It was God's Word discovered anew! It had been lost for some time under a pile of stones in the temple or in one of the chambers, where it had remained unnoticed for years. Wherever it was, it is quite evident that the people of God had not been reading their Bible as they should.

B. *The dynamic response to its discovery.* Josiah's response is described by the historian in four ways.

1. Josiah heard it read (2 Kings 22:11). This is the first step toward a personal discovery of God's Word: a willingness to read it or hear it read. Josiah's heart was tender and he humbled himself before the Lord.

2. Josiah responded to the message of the book (2 Kings 22:11). He was so moved by what he heard that he tore his clothes in grief and repentance.

3. Josiah read the book to all the people (2 Kings 23:1–2). God spoke to their hearts as He did to Josiah's. They were convicted of forgotten vows, and they renewed the covenant of the nation to the Lord.

4. Revival came in response to finding the book. The temple was cleansed of heathen worship and the land was cleansed of idolatry. Immorality was stamped out. The observance of the Passover was renewed. Rediscovering the Bible brought new leadership, new purpose, and a new spirit of worship to the people.

May we remember that the Word of God is powerful! It kindles fires in our hearts. It leads to life and creates light by which to live. It is God's Word to us!

Also, it may be that many people have lost their Bibles today. A Christian can lose his Bible, not just physically but spiritually. If you are not reading your Bible with meaning, it is as lost to you as was the Word of God to Israel. You may lose your Bible by turning to the goals of wealth, pleasure, ambition, or success. But it can be different! Open your Bible and begin to read it, and a new spiritual day will be yours.

II. Rediscovering the Bible presently.

You can rediscover the Bible in three ways.

A. *Rediscover the Bible authoritatively.* The Bible is not an authority on science or history; it is an authority in spiritual things. It is not just a book of religion; it is divine revelation. It is the book of redemption, the book of divine inspiration. It reveals God to us. It is the Word of God!

It is our final authority in life, the authoritative basis of our faith. Goethe said, "When I go to hear a preacher preach, I may not agree with what he says, but I want him to believe it." We need something to stand on for our faith and practice. The Bible is the answer.

B. *Rediscover the Bible personally.* It has the power to speak to us personally. The Holy Spirit will open the Word to our hearts as we open our hearts to the Word. Jesus did this for the disciples on the Emmaus Road as He explained the Scriptures about His coming. When their eyes were opened, they recognized Him and said, "Did not our heart burn within us, while he talked with us by the way?" (Luke 24:32). He still does that today in our hearts through the Spirit!

C. *Rediscover the Bible practically.* One goal for our lives should be a renewed emphasis on the Bible.

1. Hear it. Proverbs 1:5 says, "A wise man will hear, and will increase learning."

2. Read it. We forget 90 to 95 percent of what we hear. So read the Bible for yourself. Read it with a searching spirit. Read it in faith. Read it for fellowship with the heavenly Father. Read it prayerfully.

3. Study it. We forget 70 percent of what we read. So study the Scriptures personally, with a notebook to take notes on what you discover. Study it in Sunday school. Study it whenever you have an opportunity.

4. Memorize it. Hide it in your heart. Memorize verses, chapters, whole sections of Scripture. Set a goal to commit it to memory.

5. Meditate on it. Of the psalmist it is said, "And in his law doth he meditate day and night" (Ps. 1:2). Get up in the morning thinking about it. Go to bed at night meditating on it.

Conclusion. The Bible becomes a living book to us when we experience its truth and life for ourselves. Bishop E. Berggrav, of the Lutheran Church in Norway, spent most of World War II in a Nazi concentration camp. It was there that he found Christ in the pages of the Bible. His reading it aloud brought the reality of Christ to his life so that his faith was restored and his spirit renewed.

Discover the Bible for yourself. Commit yourself to God's Word this year. It brings new life!

—*TSB*

* * *

SUNDAY EVENING, JANUARY 2

TITLE: Believe and Behave

TEXT: "And be not conformed to this world: but be ye transformed by the renewing of your mind, that ye may prove what is that good, and acceptable, and perfect will of God" (Rom. 12:2).

SCRIPTURE READING: Romans 1:16; 12:2

Introduction. "Believe and behave" is the central theme of the Book of Romans. Paul contends that what one believes has everything to do with how he or she behaves.

And Paul assigns equal importance to both belief and behavior. If one's belief is wrong, his behavior will be wrong. On the other hand, if one's behavior is wrong, his belief cannot be right. In the final analysis, a person's behavior says more about his beliefs than does his verbal testimony or his written creed.

There is a propensity to emphasize one of these truths to the exclusion of the other. To be guilty of this is to have a partial and imbalanced Christianity.

Paul, being a man of a balanced faith, gives equal emphasis to both belief and behavior. The first eleven chapters of Romans deal with belief and the last five with behavior.

In the winter of 57–58 A.D. Paul was in Corinth at the close of his third missionary journey. He was soon to return to Jerusalem with the offering for the poor. A woman named Phoebe, who lived in a suburb of Corinth, was soon to sail to Rome. Paul saw an opportunity to send this letter to the church of Rome with her.

Since there was no postal service in the Roman Empire except for government business, personal letters had to be carried by friends. Paul was not sure he would get away from Jerusalem alive. Desiring to leave a written explanation of the gospel of salvation in the hands of the Christians at Rome, he wrote this letter, which Phoebe delivered safely to the church.

Realizing that this may be his only communication with the church so strategically located in the capital of the world, he stressed what he must have felt to be the two cardinal truths of the Christian faith—the belief that results in salvation and the behavior that results from salvation.

I. The belief that results in salvation (Rom. 1:16).

Paul is anxious to move directly to the theme of his letter; and so with a few brief words of introduction out of the way he proclaims, "For I am not ashamed . . ." (Rom. 1:16). What kind of belief is this that makes possible the reception of salvation?

A. *It is a belief in the unlimited power of salvation* (Rom. 1:16a, b). The apostle has just said that he is proud of the gospel of salvation. He considered it a privilege to preach it. What a strange statement for Paul to make in light of all that had recently happened to him. At Philippi he had been jailed; at Thessalonica he had been expelled; at Berea he was smuggled out; and at Athens he was scorned.

The gospel he preached in Corinth was considered by the Greeks to be "foolishness" and to the Jews it was a "stumbling block." Yet in spite of that, Paul proudly declares the gospel to be "the power of God unto salvation"! The unlimited power of the gospel made Paul triumphant over all the obstacles in his path.

When Paul talks of the "unlimited power of God unto salvation," he speaks from personal experience. At first he hated the Christian faith; his heart was calloused against the call of God. Therefore he marched toward Damascus to arrest and harass those who were followers of Christ.

If ever a man were unbending in his conviction, Paul was that man. Nothing could change him—*until* he encountered the person of Jesus Christ. It was then he discovered that in the gospel of Christ there is the unlimited power of God that can change any man, anywhere, in any condition!

The belief that results in salvation is a belief in the unlimited power of salvation.

B. *It is a belief in the unrestricted availability of salvation* (Rom. 1:16c, d). Paul proclaims that this salvation is available to "everyone that believeth."

Why does Paul say, "To the Jew first"? Because they were in the immediate proximity and had the best religious background for accepting the gospel.

Then he says, "And also to the Greek." The gospel reached Greeks as well as Jews. The Greeks were the intellectuals of the first century and often were cynical. Stoicism and Epicureanism were 400 years old, and in each the excitement had almost gone out of the movements and decay had set in. Greek-Roman religion in the first century was confused and chaotic, with so many gods and deities that cities even maintained "catch-all" shrines to provide for divine emanations that might have been overlooked.

What caused Greeks to become Christians? The answer is revealed in the opening of Paul's address on Mars Hill, "The God who made the world and everything in it, being Lord of heaven and earth, does not live in shrines made by man" (Acts 17:24 RSV). In the place of the randomness that Athens offered, Paul tells of a God who can speak for Himself and is not contained in human thought. This Jesus provides an unrestricted, universally available salvation.

In his letter to the church at Rome Paul says that *salvation is available without restriction because of:*

1. The *need* that requires it. "For all have sinned, and come short of the glory of God" (Rom. 3:23).

Since *all* have sinned, salvation is available to all. It is available without restriction because man has sinned without exception.

2. The *grace* that provides it. "For the wages of sin is death; but the gift of God is eternal life through Jesus Christ our Lord" (6:23).

Salvation is available without restriction not because of the goodness of man but because of the grace of God. If it were available on the basis of our goodness, it could not be available without restriction.

3. The *price* that purchased it. "But God commendeth his love toward us, in that, while we were yet sinners, Christ died for us" (5:8).

How could God "prove his love toward us" through the death of Christ? Because "God was in Christ reconciling the world unto himself" (2 Cor. 5:19). Christ died *for us.* Christ died on our behalf—voluntarily. "I lay down my life . . . no man takes it from me" (John 10:17–18).

A little boy made a boat. He lost it in the street gutter in front of his home. It was swept down a street sewer. Later he saw it in a window of a pawn shop. He saved his pennies and paid $1.00 for his boat. As he left the shop he said, "Little boat, you're mine twice—I made you and I purchased you."

We are God's twice. He made us and He purchased us.

4. The *love* that insures it. Robert Bruce, a disciple of John Knox, died on July 27, 1631. He had come to breakfast and his younger daughter sat by his side.

"As he mused in silence, suddenly he cried: 'Hold, daughter, hold; my Master calleth me.' He asked that the Bible should be brought, but his sight failed him and he could not read. 'Cast me up the eighth of Romans,' cried he, and he repeated much of the latter portion of this Scripture till he came to the last two verses: 'I am persuaded that neither death, nor life, nor angels, nor principalities, nor powers, nor things present, nor things to come, nor height, nor depth, nor any other creature, shall be able to separate us from the love of God which is in Christ Jesus our Lord.' 'Set my finger on these words,'' said the blind, dying man; 'God be with you, my children. I have breakfasted with you, and shall sup with my Lord Jesus this night. I die believing in these words''' (Marcus Loane, *The Hope of Glory* [Waco: Word, 1969], p. 160).

But if this belief has any validity to it at all there is:

II. The behavior that results from salvation (Rom. 12:1–2; 13:1–5; 14:21; 15:1–3).

Belief results *in* salvation—behavior results *from* salvation. In other words, belief saves. Behavior proves that one is saved. Paul points out three areas which this behavior affects.

A. *It is a behavior that affects our conduct* (Rom. 12:1–2).

''I beseech you *therefore*. . . .'' Whenever you see the word *therefore* in Scripture you should ask, What is it ''there for''? It always looks back on what has been said.

Paul is saying, ''In light of the belief that results *in* salvation, I now set forth the behavior that results *from* salvation. Because you have believed, 'therefore' you should behave!''

He does not say ''I command you!'' He says ''I beseech you.'' After all, he *is* speaking to those who had already believed in Christ and thus should of their own volition behave as believers.

There may be many things we cannot do and much we cannot give, but by the grace of God we can behave! So Paul says:

1. This is a conduct that is voluntary—''present *your* bodies'' (v. 1).
2. It is a conduct that refuses to be molded by others.

''Be not conformed . . .'' (v. 2a). ''Don't let the world around you squeeze you into its own mold'' (v. 2a PHILLIPS).

When the world's conduct is unbecoming to a Christian, the true believer behaves like a Christian gentleman. He does not take on the color of his social environment. Like his Savior he is distinctively different from those about him!

3. It is a conduct that comes from within.

''But be ye transformed by the *renewing of your mind* . . .'' (v. 2b). ''But let God remold your minds from *within,* so that you may prove in *practice* that the plan of God for you is good . . .'' (v. 2b PHILLIPS).

Until a man has that kind of genuine belief that results in salvation, he lacks the power within to behave. But when Christ comes into a man's life he is a *new* man. The center of his being is different. The driving power of his life is different.

B. *It is a behavior that affects our citizenship* (13:1–5).

Your citizenship—the way you relate to people in elected positions of authority—may be the greatest testimony you have. In God's economy there is no place for the destructive spirit of rebellion and anarchy.

C. *It is a behavior that affects our concern* (14:21; 15:1–3a).

In chapter 14 Paul states that salvation enables Christians to behave in such a way as to place the concerns of others above our own selfish interests. When a Christian reaches this level of behavior, no longer is the criteria ''Is it right or wrong?'' but rather ''Will it cause my brother to stumble?''

If there be anything at all to our belief in Christ, we shall behave as Christ would. We shall not be out to please ourselves, to prove our point, or to insist on our own way. Rather that Christian love of which Paul speaks in 1 Corinthians

13 will characterize us . . . a love that "Doth not behave itself unseemly, seeketh not her own, is not easily provoked, thinketh no evil" (v. 5).

It is a beautiful milestone in a Christian's pilgrimage when he reaches that point when the spiritual welfare of those around him is more important than the pleasure of pleasing self.

Conclusion. Believe and behave! That's the message of the Book of Romans. "Believe *and* behave"—not "Believe *or* behave." When we capture *both* of these truths to the extent that they are translated into the flesh and blood of our lives, then Paul's letter to the church at Rome has accomplished its purpose both in the church in centuries past and in our time. —*JRM*

* * *

WEDNESDAY EVENING, JANUARY 5

TITLE: The Purpose of Prayer

TEXT: "Continue in prayer, and watch in the same with thanksgiving; withal praying also for us, that God would open unto us a door of utterance, to speak the mystery of Christ, for which I am also in bonds: that I may make it manifest, as I ought to speak" (Col. 4:2–4).

SCRIPTURE READING: Colossians 4:1–4

Introduction. A contemporary minister relates an incident that is familiar to all ministers. It is the experience of the embarrassment to a hostess when a preacher is present at the dinner table and some member of her family begins to eat before grace is said. There is always the quick reprimand and the shocked look on the face of the offender, and then the preacher offers grace in the strained silence. Usually he is grateful that this same family has never watched him trying to restrain his own children until after prayers. Then all is well unless the host or hostess feels called upon to explain.

It is amazing how often the explanation will seem to follow a prepared script. The hostess will say, "We don't always say grace before meals at our house." This has been fairly obvious, but the cornered clergyman butters his roll and waits because he knows there is another line to this script. "But," she adds—and this usually with a rallying smile and somewhat breezily said—"we take it for granted that God knows how grateful we are!"

Why should we pray? God knows how grateful we are. That sounds reasonable enough. That figures, according to the logic of the dinner table. The trouble is that it will not stay at the dinner table. It leaves the table and roams all over the house. And we soon find ourselves saying, "Why pray at all? God knows all that we need." Did not Jesus Himself say that God knew all that we needed before we even asked Him? But the conclusion of Jesus was, therefore do pray. This same line of reasoning led Frederick B. Speakman, in his book *Love Is Something You Do,* to ask the provocative question, "What if God refuses to read His children's mail unless it is addressed to Him?"

This tells us something of the purpose of prayer. We are to pray in order that we might commune with God and share with Him the deepest, most sincere, most heartfelt needs of our lives. We are to pray in order to express to God the gratitude and praise and joy that we feel in Him and in salvation. This Paul expressed in three verses in the concluding chapter of Colossians.

I. The purpose of prayer is seen in the manner of prayer (v. 2).

A. *We are to pray with perseverence.* Prayer is not to be a spasmodic outburst in a moment of emergency but the persistent calling on God for His guidance and blessing.

B. *We are to pray with watchfulness.* This word literally means to be wakeful, to be alert when you pray. Maybe Paul was thinking of the time on the Mount of Transfiguration when the disciples fell asleep, and that it was only when they were awake that they saw Christ's glory.

Prayer should not be reserved just for a time of crisis. We should pray before the crisis comes in order to have the spiritual resources to meet the testing time. Napoleon said that battles are not won on the battlefield; rather they are won at the conference table in the planning meetings before the battle is ever begun. Even so, the crisis does not make the man. He must be a man before the crisis comes. The crisis only proves whether he is a man.

C. *We are to pray with gratitude.*

II. The purpose of prayer is seen in the object of prayer (vv. 3–4).

A. *We are to pray that God will give us an open door of service.* Remember that Paul was in prison when this prayer was offered. There were many things for which one could pray while in prison—release, a favorable outcome to the trial, comfort, rest—but Paul prayed that God would give him an opportunity to minister.

B. *We are to pray that God would allow us to take advantage of our opportunity for service.* To pray for the open door, an opportunity for service, is just half the prayer. We are to pray, too, for the courage and ability to take advantage of the opportunity that is there.

The burden of Paul's prayer was that he might be able to "speak the mystery of Christ." This must be a dominant desire for us, too.

Conclusion. This is the purpose of prayer: We pray that we might commune with God with persistence, watchfulness, and thankfulness in order to have opportunities to witness for Christ and the strength to take those opportunities.

—*JEC*

* * *

SUNDAY MORNING, JANUARY 9

TITLE: Celebrating Supernatural Living

TEXT: "Enlarge the place of thy tent, and let them stretch forth the curtains of thine habitations: spare not, lengthen thy cords, and strengthen thy stakes" (Isa. 54:2).

SCRIPTURE READING: Isaiah 54

HYMNS: "I Stand Amazed in the Presence," Gabriel
"Faith Is the Victory," Yates
"Blessed Assurance, Jesus Is Mine," Crosby

OFFERTORY PRAYER:

Thank You, Father, for the privilege of giving to You for the glory of Your name and cause. The words of Jesus are so true, "It is more blessed to give than to receive." Thank You for this heavenly blessing! Amen.

Introduction. The Christian life is a supernatural life, an exciting adventure that begins with a life-changing, spiritual birth. It begins with faith and continues as a work of faith. Living the Christian life this year can be a celebration!

In Isaiah 54:2, the Lord called for Israel to expand their vision, "Enlarge the place of thy tent, and let them stretch forth the curtains of thine habitations: spare not, lengthen thy cords, and strengthen thy stakes." This is to be done because the Lord was to restore Israel to her former glory.

The prayer of the Christian's heart is for the Lord to stretch his vision, enlarge his faith, and expand his goals. A faith-vision is one in which the Christian visualizes what God intends to do and acts in harmony with it. Hebrews 11 records men and women who had a faith-vision. They saw by faith and obeyed God's call. If we are to experience the adventure of believing God, there are four things we must do.

I. Learn to think supernaturally.

Proverbs 23:7 says, "As [a man] thinketh in his heart, so is he." We become what we think, and we determine the way we think as an act of the will.

How can we change our thought life? First, we can saturate our minds with God's Word and make ourselves available to have the mind of Christ. Next, we can follow the words of Colossians 3:1–2: "Seek those things which are above. . . . Set your mind on things above." Think worthy thoughts, faith thoughts, and thoughts of praise, worship, and thanksgiving. And third, think about the attributes of God, His goodness, greatness, generosity, and glory.

Think supernaturally! Think about who you are spiritually. No longer a servant, but a son. No longer lost, but found. No longer an alien, but a citizen of the kingdom.

Think of your spiritual heritage—the hope of your calling, the riches of His glorious heritage, and the abundant greatness of His power to believers.

Think like children of the King! When we begin to think these thoughts, our vision is stretched. Knowing the Lord for who He is will change our lives.

II. Learn to plan supernaturally.

This involves our personal lives, our families, the church, our business, or whatever appeals to our need for planning.

A. *There is nothing wrong with planning.* Proverbs 16:9 says, "We should make plans, counting on God to direct us." God Himself is a planner. He has a well-thought-out plan for the world from the first day until the last. Psalm 139:16 in the Living Bible indicates divinely detailed planning for our lives.

B. *Let God reveal His vision to you.* This becomes the basis of our faith. Then we set our goals, so that they become His goals for us.

C. *Prepare fully for the fulfillment of His goals.* Our faith will be tested, but God is faithful when we trust Him and obey Him. The Lord confirms His direction for us and He assures us, through prayer, of His will (1 John 5:14–15). This will mean supernatural planning, planning by faith, following God's plans.

D. *Planning by faith means having big plans, God-sized plans.* The plans and goals God gave to people have two consistent elements: a worldwide influence and a lasting impact.

God's goal to Adam and Eve was to "be fruitful and multiply and fill the earth and subdue it" (Gen. 1:28). God's goal to Abraham was not just to have a son, but to start a nation and to be a blessing to all the families of the earth (Gen.

12:1–13). Jesus' goal for the disciples was for them to be witnesses in the power of the Holy Spirit from Jerusalem to the uttermost parts of the earth (Acts 1:8).

God-sized plans are big plans, supernatural plans. If they are small enough for us to do them ourselves, they aren't God-sized, and God will not get involved in them. They are big enough plans when they need God's intervention.

Dr. Joon Gon Kim received a vision from the Lord to have a gathering for Christian training in Korea. His goal was 300,000 delegates, but 323,419 came from seventy-eight countries, including 15,000 pastors and evangelists. The largest evening service was attended by one and one-half million. More than one million registered salvation decisions in one evening. This happened because the Lord touched the heart of one man to believe God for great things!

III. Learn to pray supernaturally.

Supernatural praying is found in John 14:12–14, where it says, "Greater works than these shall ye do. . . ." God gives us the faith to pray for something, and as we pray, He causes our faith to grow and to pray even greater things for Him. "According to your faith, be it unto you" (Matt. 9:29).

Everything we say or do in our lives we can expose to the adequacy of Christ Jesus in us. Christ is alive in every believer making this a reality (Gal. 2:20).

We can never ask God for too much if our hearts and motives are pure, and if we pray according to the Word and will of God. Someone has said, "Whatever we vividly envision, ardently desire, sincerely believe, and enthusiastically act upon will come to pass, if there is a scriptural authority for it.

A Christian organization was praying the Lord to provide miraculously a large sum of money. Within a few days a man announced that he would give the ministry a gift of $1,100,000. This was unquestionably a supernatural provision!

IV. Learn to claim supernatural resources.

We are not ordinary people. Our lives are joined with the One who spoke the world into existence. We belong to Him who has been given all authority in heaven and earth. He dwells in us in all His resurrection power. We can claim Philippians 4:13 for our lives!

Our faith may be small, but like a muscle it will grow with exercise. If you are struggling to trust God for some need, for someone's salvation, or for financial help, then pause to meditate on whatever barrier to your faith you are facing right now. Remind yourself of God's power available to you to accomplish the supernatural. If you are not trusting God, this is sin. Confess your unbelief to Him and claim by faith His supernatural resources.

Conclusion. This is what it means to celebrate supernatural living. This is God's glory for our lives and for the church! — *TSB*

* * *

SUNDAY EVENING, JANUARY 9

TITLE: A More Excellent Way

TEXT: "But covet earnestly the best gifts; and yet shew I unto you a more excellent way" (1 Cor. 12:31).

SCRIPTURE READING: 1 Corinthians 12:29–31; 13:13

Introduction. You can live any way you want to live. This is your right. You are the only person who has the power to determine how you will live. You can be agreeable or disagreeable, a help or a hindrance, an asset or a liability to yourself, your family, your co-workers, and the kingdom of God. But Paul says, "I would show you 'a more excellent way.'" The Christian life was never meant to be a good way or even a better way but rather a more *excellent* way!

Paul had just received a letter from the church at Corinth listing all kinds of problems that had risen in their fellowship for one reason: they were not following "a more excellent way."

The apostle is saying, "In light of all your varied lifestyles and the difficulties and heartaches they have brought upon the church, it seems to me that it is high time you recognize your need of following 'a more excellent way.'"

He declares love to be "a more excellent way." In this First Letter to the Church at Corinth he lists four reasons why love is a more excellent way:

I. Its ministry of healing (1 Cor. 1:10–17a).

A long letter had been written by the church at Corinth to Paul listing several of their problems. But one problem that was not listed was the problem of divisions in the church.

Paul learned of this problem from the relatives of Chloe, a well-known member of the congregation. He is not secretive; he names the source of his information and then deals directly with the problem.

But the fact that he chooses to deal first with this subject proves that of all the problems mentioned he considered this one to be the most critical.

It is to this problem that he immediately addresses himself. And it is to this problem that he applies the healing ministry of love.

A. *The healing ministry of love is realized when Christ is honored* (1:12–16).

In verse 12 of 1 Corinthians 1 we can see what Paul may be saying about each group that wanted to rally around some human personality.

Some said, "I am of Paul." Paul did not take this as a compliment, nor does any preacher. In claiming to follow Paul the theologian they were claiming to be "great theologues."

Others said, "I am of Apollos." These were the "cultured vultures" who worshiped oratory, since Apollos was a prince of preachers.

Still others said, "I am of Peter," the fiery evangelist. This is the "tell-it-like-it-is" crowd.

And the "super Christians" said, "I am of Christ."

In light of these childish divisions, Paul turns to some wholesome humor. He has fun with the situation as he singles out no one else but himself as an example.

In verse 13 he asks, (a) "Is Christ fragmented? Tell me about it." (b) "I haven't noticed any nail prints in my hands. . . ." (c) "Did Christ say in the Great Commission to baptize in the name of the Father and of the Son and of Paul the apostle?"

In verses 14–16 Paul expresses relief that he baptized but a few, lest that make of them his followers.

B. *The healing ministry of love is realized when the gospel is preached* (1:17).

The gospel is the good news about the healing ministry of Christ's love.

Christ is the focal point of the gospel—not Paul or Apollos or Peter or any other man.

II. Its simplicity of language (2:1–2).

Love is never concerned with impressing others with our importance, our knowledge, our intelligence, or our "excellency of speech or wisdom." Love of self is vitally concerned about these things. But not the love that is "a more excellent way."

It is concerned with making as clear and as simple as possible the gospel of Jesus Christ and His power to save.

If any man could have complicated the simple with multisyllable verbiage it was Paul. He certainly had the vocabulary and the intellect to do it. But Paul had been down the empty halls of academe as a Pharisee and found nothing until he encountered the more excellent way of God's redemptive love.

Someone has said, "It is nice to be important, but it's more important to be nice!" Paul had the nicety to speak in love's simplicity of language so that all may understand.

No wonder Paul says, "And my speech and my preaching was not with enticing words of man's wisdom, but in demonstration of the Spirit and of power" (2:4).

The reason he offers for speaking in love's simplicity of language is "that your faith should not stand in the wisdom of men, but in the power of God" (2:5).

As long as my faith stands in the "wisdom of men" it can fall. For there will always be someone wiser than I who can undermine that faith. But when my faith stands "in the power of God" no man on earth and no power of Satan can cause that faith to fall!

III. Its competency for problem-solving (chaps. 5–12).

In these eight chapters, Paul addresses himself to that long list of problems of which the Christians of Corinth had written. The problems of lawsuits, sexual impurity, marriage, eating meat sacrificed to idols, the place of women in the church, abuses of the Lord's Supper, and placing one's piety on parade. In all fairness he deals with one problem at a time. He does not rush through these problems as though they are not serious. Rather he devotes eight chapters to discussing them. But at the end of his discussion he informs them that there is not one problem they have shared that love is not competent to solve.

Especially in the face of life's problems Paul sees love as a more excellent way because of its competence for problem-solving.

A. *The problem of sexual impurity* (5:1–2). He is saying that because you love that person you must deal with him in such a way that he will turn from his sin. And because you love the church you cannot allow the continuance of this problem to "infect it."

Love is a more excellent way because of its competency of solving the problem of sexual impurity. And this applies to any form of sexual impurity. Because when you love someone, you will not use him or her as an object to satisfy your own desires. You will not inflict on that person the guilt and hurt of sexual impurity.

B. *The problem of lawsuits* (6:1–8). Love is a more excellent way to resolve differences than civil lawsuits. Paul states that it is unchristian for fellow believers to take their differences to heathen courts—to rely on those who know nothing of the grace of God to settle their problems. This, he says, can and ought to be solved by Christians in the spirit of Christian love.

C. *The problem of abusing our Christian liberty* (chap. 8). Paul contends that souls are more important than steak. Men are of more value than meat. Lives are more important than our liberty.

When we are tempted to say, "It is my right to do this, or to say that," we must recall the words of Paul, who advocates a more excellent way: "All things are lawful unto me, but all things are not expedient" (6:12a).

There are certain times when we have every right in the world to do a certain thing. But the more excellent way of love reminds us that if using our liberty in such a way will cause one brother to stumble, if it will reflect in the least on the work of our Lord, we should refuse to use that liberty.

D. *The problem of placing our piety on parade* (chap. 12). When the more excellent way of love binds us together as the body of Christ, there is a unity that nothing can sever. We care for one another—we rejoice with one another.

Love is a more excellent way because it removes a competitive, jealous spirit among God's people. It takes piety off parade and puts Jesus Christ on parade!

IV. Its superiority of value (12:31–13:13).

Paul concludes chapter 12 by saying, "And yet shew I unto you a more excellent way." Then he goes into the beautiful love chapter of 1 Corinthians 13 which he concludes by saying, "The greatest of these is love."

Why is love "the greatest of these"? Why is it "a more excellent way"? Because of its superiority of value.

A. *The superiority of love's value is seen in the worth it imports to the gifts of the Spirit* (13:1–3). These gifts have no intrinsic value. The only value they have is the value love imports to them.

B. *The superiority of love's value is seen in the words used to describe it* (13:5–13).

Conclusion. Paul closes his letter in these words, "Let all things be done with *charity*" (16:14); and his final sentence is, "My *love* be with you all" (16:24a).

Love is a more excellent way because of:

1. Its ministry of healing
2. Its simplicity of language
3. Its competency for problem-solving
4. Its superiority of value

—*JRM*

* * *

WEDNESDAY EVENING, JANUARY 12

TITLE: A Witness to the World

TEXT: "Walk in wisdom toward them that are without, redeeming the time. Let your speech be always with grace, seasoned with salt, that ye may know how ye ought to answer every man" (Col. 4:5–6).

SCRIPTURE READING: Colossians 4:5–6

Introduction. The professing Christian not only lives a life of faith toward God and obedient response to the Spirit of God, he also lives in a world that is often hostile to Christ, or worse still, negligent of Christ. The response that is made to this situation is most important for the Christian life and witness.

One response that is often made is identification with the world. In this case, the Christian so closely identifies himself with the world around him that it is difficult to find the difference between a believer and a nonbeliever.

Another response that is sometimes made is withdrawal from the world. In this case, the Christian tries to shut out entirely the world around him and live in his own little private, well-protected world.

Neither of these is the proper response. The proper response is for the Christian to be a responsible witness to the world. He lives in the world. He makes his living in the world. He associates with people of the world. And in all of this he should try to give a responsible witness of his faith to the world. His faith becomes a guiding principle for his life. His encounter with God in worship gives him strength and power for life. His character, growing out of his relationship of faith in God, gives silent but eloquent witness of the meaning of faith and salvation. By his very life he is a salesman for salvation. Elton Trueblood once said that faith lives or dies not by what goes on in churches, but by what, as a result of the churches, goes on outside of them.

That is what the apostle Paul meant by these two verses in the last chapter of his Colossian letter. He urged them to "walk in wisdom toward them that are without," by which he meant those who are outside the Christian fellowship. He had both an offensive and a defensive purpose in mind. The defensive purpose was to protect the good name of the Christian community. The offensive purpose was to go after outsiders and bring them into the Christian fellowship and to faith in Christ. This is still our witness to the world.

I. A witness to the world involves the walk before the world.

A. *We walk with wisdom in our witness.* This could be a gentle warning about the methods of witness that are used. We must use wisdom and discretion in presenting the claims of Christ to those who do not know Him.

B. *We walk with wisdom in our practices.* The kind of life that we live before the world is caught up in the word *walk.* As we walk in the world we are to make sure that the walk we practice is consistent with the talk we make. A man once got down on his knees at a golf tournament as the ball hit by Arnold Palmer rolled close to him. He was checking to see if the ball was the same brand that Palmer had been advertising on television.

II. A witness to the world involves the opportunity with the world.

A. *Our time must be used well.* We are told to "redeem the time," which means literally "to buy up the time." Since we all have the same amount of time, the way that we use time is very important.

B. *Our time should be used for witness.* Every opportunity to witness must be taken. John A. Broadus said that opportunity was like a fleet horse that pauses for one moment by one's side. If one fails to mount him in that moment, he can hear the clatter of his hooves down the corridors of time.

III. A witness to the world involves the talk to the world.

A. *Our speech should be with grace.* As our conduct is marked by grace so should our speech be marked by grace. *Grace* means charm, winsomeness, wit. This is the kind of talk that witnesses for Christ—charming, winsome, gentle, not abusive, loud, coarse, or crude.

B. *Our talk should be well seasoned.* This kind of talk has the ring of reality about it. A Hindu woman became converted and suffered much persecution from her husband. When the missionary asked her what she did when her husband became angry with her, she replied that she cooked his food better. When he complained, she swept the floor cleaner. When he spoke unkindly, she answered him mildly. She tried to show him that when she became a Christian she became a better wife and mother.

C. *Our talk should be directed toward the individual.* As we "answer every man," we are assured that we talk to individuals. Stock answers and memorized replies do not fill the bill. Each occasion should be met with talk personally intended for the individual.

Conclusion. These words of general instruction are important for us. We have in this letter the inspiring assurance of Christ and in these words an invitation to take the initiative in witness for Christ. —*JEC*

* * *

SUNDAY MORNING, JANUARY 16

TITLE: Christ—the Only Hope

TEXT: "For the hope which is laid up for you in heaven, whereof ye heard before in the word of the truth of the gospel" (Col. 1:5).

SCRIPTURE READING: Colossians 1:3–8

HYMNS: "Crown Him With Many Crowns," Bridges
"The Solid Rock," Mote
"Victory in Jesus," Bartlett

OFFERTORY PRAYER:

Even as Jesus sat over against the treasury and observed the giving, so Your eye is upon us at this moment. Deliver us from the fear of giving to the freedom of it. May You be pleased with the gifts we bring! Amen.

Introduction. The key word in today's message is *hope;* and the conviction of truth that is as deep as life and eternity is that Christ is the hope! This year, 1983, is a year to acknowledge this truth.

This is a bold claim, the "only" hope, in that it eliminates other claims to hope. It is a timeless claim because it has been believed for centuries; and it is a responsible claim because to believe it is to accept certain responsibilities. Christ is the only hope!

I. Christ is the only hope for salvation.

A mine shaft collapsed and a rescue team was immediately organized to dig out the entombed men before the air was exhausted. As they approached the doomed miners, they thought they heard a tapping on the rocks. As they paused to listen, in Morse code came the question repeatedly: "Is there any hope? Is there any hope?" Is there any hope for salvation?

A. *Christ is the only hope for a salvation desperately needed.* The Bible says that man has "no hope" and is "without God in the world" (Eph. 2:12). He is spiritually lost, "condemned already" (John 3:18). Not tomorrow, not next year, not at twenty-one, nor at death, but now, already condemned! Man is trapped spiritually in his need.

Furthermore, man is trapped in his sinful nature. "The heart is deceitful . . . and desperately wicked: who can know it?" (Jer. 17:9). Out of the heart of man proceed all types of sin (Matt. 15:19). Man's heart has a nature to sin and to rebel against God and spiritual authority.

Man is trapped, also, in the agonizing results of sin. "The wages of sin is death" (Rom. 6:23). He is trapped in his human weakness and despair. The cry of Paul was, "Who shall deliver me from the body of this death?" (Rom. 7:24). Christ is the only hope!

B. *Christ is the only hope for salvation divinely provided.* In answer to a seeking heart, "What must I do to be saved?" is the reply, "Believe on the Lord Jesus Christ, and thou shalt be saved" (Acts 16:30–31).

The Lord Jesus Christ is the Savior. There is much confusion at this point. Salvation is not in a parent's faith, in religious principles, in a church, in culture, in outward symbols, or in a good life. Salvation is in a person, Jesus Christ!

Jesus Christ is God's provision (1 Tim. 1:15); God's deed (1 Cor. 15:3); and God's gift (Rom. 6:23). He is the living Savior and Lord.

C. *Christ is the only hope for salvation personally received.* What are we to do? How are we to respond? Upon hearing "the hope of the gospel," which is Christ, we are to believe Him. We are to acknowledge the truth of Christ, accept the facts of His life, death, and resurrection, and trust ourselves to Him in personal surrender. John 1:12 says, "But as many as received him, to them gave he power to become the sons of God, even to them that believe on his name."

An Air Force sergeant moved to Sherman, Texas, several years ago. He and his family were saved before they were transferred to another base. He said, "We came to Sherman so poor; we are leaving so rich." Christ is the only hope!

II. Christ is the only hope for life's needs.

Paul spoke of the hope of the gospel "which is come unto you . . . and bringeth forth fruit . . . in you" (Col. 1:6). Christ touches lives now and transforms them. He gives power to live now, not just for heaven. Galatians 2:20 says that "the life which I now live," the Christ-life in us is power, peace, and joy. Many testify to what Christ is doing in their lives today.

J. B. Phillips in his book *God Our Contemporary* writes a chapter entitled, "The Inadequacy of Humanism," in which he describes secular humanism as a bleak and cruel creed. It denies the Christian faith and the need for any moral or spiritual authority outside humanity. Humanism restricts life to this earth; it denies God and says there is no life beyond this one. So it offers no hope to the severely handicapped, no power to guide and strengthen someone defeated by emotional conflicts. It has nothing to offer for the crises of life.

Secular humanism would have been useless some time ago, when in one week's time, it was necessary to minister to two families who lost teen-age sons, to a man whose mother died in her sleep, to the family of a five-year-old girl who died of a brain tumor, and to a wife whose husband was killed in military service.

Secular humanism had nothing to say. It was coldly, cruelly silent. But Christ did! Matthew 11:28 says, "Come unto me, all ye that labor and are heavy laden." John 10:10 says, "I am come that they might have life; and . . . have it more abundantly." And Philippians 4:13 says, "I can do all things through Christ who strengtheneth me."

Christ is the only hope!

III. Christ is the only hope for eternity.

The hope of Christ is an eternal certainty by pointing beyond life now to life forever. Colossians 1:5 says, "For the hope which is laid up for you in heaven. . . ."

A. *The hope of Christ is the hope of His return.* He personally promised it (John 14:3); the angels divinely announced it (Acts 1:11); and Paul the apostle victoriously described it (1 Thess. 4:16). Jesus is personally, powerfully, and suddenly coming again. This is hope!

B. *The hope is the hope of the resurrection.* Christ has abolished death (2 Tim. 1:9–10) and the resurrection is promised as a living fact in 1 Corinthians 15. Death is not the end for the believer because Christ is our hope.

C. *The hope of Christ is the hope of deliverance from judgment.* Hebrews 9:27 says, "And it is appointed unto men once to die, but after this the judgment." Christ bore our judgment at the cross. Though judgment is certain, in Christ we need not fear because we have passed from death unto life.

Conclusion. Christ is the only hope! What a marvelous and audacious claim! Do we believe it? Then we must tell it, proclaim it, share it, witness it, and offer it everywhere we go.

— *TSB*

* * *

SUNDAY EVENING, JANUARY 16

TITLE: When You Have Been Wronged

TEXT: "We are troubled on every side, yet not distressed; we are perplexed, but not in despair; persecuted, but not forsaken; cast down, but not destroyed" (2 Cor. 4:8–9).

SCRIPTURE READING: 2 Corinthians 4:8–10

Introduction. Some people at Corinth did not like Paul. His insistence on Christian morality and his daring to correct those whose lives proved to be a contradiction to their profession had infuriated them. These worldly church members along with the Judaizers joined forces against him.

Apparently Paul had sent a letter between 1 Corinthians and 2 Corinthians which is now lost. It must have been very stern since it stirred up a furor against him.

The person over whom the furor had risen must have been the man who Paul reprimanded in 1 Corinthians (5:1–5) for living with his stepmother. Apparently this man was influential. He persisted in his sin and led an open revolt against Paul, taking some of the leaders with him.

Because of Paul's second letter, the church was brought back into line. They saw the evil of this man and disciplined him.

But in the process, Paul was grievously wronged, both by this man and others in the church. They said Paul had no authority to advise them, that he bore no letters of commendation from leaders in Jerusalem as they did, that his was a weak and unimpressive personal appearance. And they accused him of going back on his word by not coming to Corinth when he said he would.

If ever a man was wronged, Paul was. But because Paul was the Christian he was, we learn from him three basic truths that emerge when one has been wronged.

I. There are lessons to be learned (2 Cor. 2:14).

All is not for naught when you have been wronged. There are lessons to be learned! You can emerge a stronger and wiser person. Paul learned three worthy lessons from his experience of being wronged.

A. *How to triumph over wrong* (2:14a). To "triumph over wrong" does not mean to overcome it or to defeat it. But rather it means to refuse to be defeated and overcome by the wrong done to you. You may not be able to control what others do, but you can control how you respond to the wrong done. There is both a human and a divine side to this victory. If you do your part, God will be faithful to do His part.

1. Human endurance.

"We know how to encourage you to *endure* patiently the same sort of trouble that we have ourselves *endured*" (2 Cor. 1:6 PHILLIPS).

An old mule, thought to be of no further use, was put in a deep ditch, and shovel after shovelful of dirt was thrown down to bury him. The old mule refused to be buried. He would shake the dirt off his back, pack it down with his feet, and gradually but surely stand higher and higher until, after enough dirt had been thrown on him, he simply stepped out of the ditch and galloped away!

2. Divine comfort.

"You can be sure that the more we undergo sufferings for Christ, the more He will shower us with His *comfort* and encouragement" (1:5 LB).

We are not left to face this trial with sheer human endurance alone. There comes to us the comfort of God. Between verses 3 and 7 the noun *comfort* or the verb *comfort* appears nine times.

When there is no one left to comfort, "the God of all comfort" (v. 3) reaches down with divine compassion and comfort.

B. *How to comfort others who are wronged.*

"And why does He do this? So that when others are troubled, needing our sympathy and encouragement, we can pass on to them this same help and comfort God has given us" (1:3 LB).

Experiencing suffering and sorrow can be an experience that will enable us to help others who are struggling with life's hardships.

C. *How dependent we are on God.*

"We felt we were doomed to die and saw how powerless we were to help ourselves; but that was good, for then we put everything into the hands of God, who alone could save us, for He can even raise the dead" (1:9 LB).

We have no information about the terrible experience Paul went through at Ephesus. But he saw that the experience had had one tremendous use—it had driven him back to God. It had proved to him his utter dependence on God.

II. There are attitudes to be displayed (1:13; 2:5–11; 3:1–2).

The real damage that being wronged can do is not the injury it brings but the attitudes it invokes. Seldom does being wronged cripple us. But we can cripple ourselves by our attitude toward those who have wronged us.

Paul portrays the kind of attitude we must display whenever we are wronged.

A. *An attitude of openness.*

"My letters have been straightforward and sincere; nothing is written between the lines!" (1:13 LB).

Some claimed that Paul in his letters did not quite mean what he said. Paul replied that there were *no hidden meanings in his words.* He had maintained an attitude of absolute openness during this entire experience. He had told nothing but the truth, being honest with all involved. In the language of today he had "called an ace an ace and a spade a spade!"

What are you to say when you have been wronged? Just tell the truth! This is not being vindictive or accusative, it is just being open. And an attitude of openness is always the right attitude in trying times.

B. *An attitude of forgiveness* (2:5–11).

When Paul visited Corinth there was a ringleader to the opposition. His short visit had been poisoned by the efforts of one man. This man had insulted Paul.

Discipline had been exercised, but some felt that it had not been severe enough and wanted to impose a still greater punishment. It is then that the greatness of Paul emerged.

Paul said that enough had been done. The man was now penitent, and to exercise still further discipline would do more harm than good. It might even drive the man to despair.

Ours is not to render the sinner harmless by beating him into submission, but to make him a true child of God.

C. *An attitude of innate integrity* (3:1–2).

There is an "infused integrity" and there is an "innate integrity." *Infused integrity* is the reputation we hope to gain by what others say about us. *Innate integrity* is the character that is ours because of the persons we are. One is genuine, the other is counterfeit. One is natural, the other is assumed.

When you have been wronged, display the attitude of innate integrity. You do not need to answer every charge leveled at you. Your own life and character is answer enough.

III. There are ministries to be fulfilled (4:1).

Paul says, "In spite of the terrible wrong that has been done to me, I will not faint—I will not be discouraged and quit—for there are ministries to be fulfilled!"

How many people quit whenever they are wronged! Had Paul done this, he would have quit the ministry long before he reached Corinth!

We cannot allow the criticisms and ill will of others to distract us from our calling—there are ministries to be fulfilled. And the more quickly we begin to fulfill our ministry, the more quickly we shall recover from the wrong done to us.

A. *The ministry of* proclamation *of Jesus Christ* (4:5, 7–11; 5:18–20).

B. *The ministry of* separation *from the world* (6:17). Even when wronged by alleged Christians you have a ministry to be fulfilled. Refuse to allow the wrong others do to you to cause you to give up your faith and to return to the world. You have the ministry of separation to fulfill!

C. *The ministry of* dedication *of possessions* (9:7). It matters not how my Sunday school teacher or class members or any church leader may wrong me; I have a ministry of dedication of possessions to fulfill. My Christian stewardship is not unto men but unto God.

D. *The ministry of* celebration *of sufferings* (12:7b–9). Paul is saying, "If it is the will of God that this suffering stay with me, I will turn my suffering into celebration. It will become a ministry of celebration because my suffering is a living demonstration of Christ's power to sustain."

"I am quite happy about 'the thorn,' and about insults and hardships, persecutions and difficulties; for when I am weak, then I am strong—the less I have, the more I depend on Him" (12:10b LB).

Conclusion. When you have been wronged:

I. There are *lessons* to be learned.
II. There are *attitudes* to be displayed.
III. There are *ministries* to be fulfilled.

Whatever wrongs may have been done or may yet be done to you, you can say with Paul, "Now thanks be unto God, which always causes us to triumph in Christ" (2:14).

—*JRM*

* * *

WEDNESDAY EVENING, JANUARY 19

TITLE: Transforming Friendships

TEXT: "All my state shall Tychicus declare unto you, who is a beloved brother, and a faithful minister and fellow-servant in the Lord: whom I have sent unto you for the same purpose, that he might know your estate, and comfort your hearts" (Col. 4:7–8).

SCRIPTURE READING: Colossians 4:7–18

Introduction. Some of our most meaningful relationships are those we have with friends. We can recall with warm feelings the hours we have spent together and the joys, sorrows, and experiences that we have shared. The Bible speaks highly of friendships: "A man that hath friends must shew himself friendly: and there is a friend that sticketh closer than a brother" (Prov. 18:24).

Friendships help to make life beautiful and enjoyable. Elizabeth Barrett Browning, the poet, asked Charles Kingsley, the novelist, the secret of his life. He thought a moment, then replied, "I had a friend."

One of the most important things we can do in life is to make friends and to cultivate lasting friendships.

When we come to the last section of the letter to the Colossians, we meet a whole host of Paul's friends. These were friends who were with him in Rome. Remember that he was a prisoner. It is sometimes dangerous to be the friend of a prisoner. But these men chose to demonstrate their friendship and loyalty to Paul by staying with him. Some of these names we identify immediately—Mark and Luke, for instance—but others are not so familiar.

In these names and in these references there is a great message to us: the message of transforming friendships. We can see a lot of gospel in the names mentioned here.

I. A transforming friendship can change a life.

A. *It is possible for a life to be changed.* Paul refused to write about his personal problems in this public letter. The bearer of the letter, Tychicus, would fill them in on those details. With him would be Onesimus, who was described as a "faithful and beloved brother" and who was evidently a native of Colosse.

Onesimus was the slave of Philemon, also of Colosse. This slave had stolen something from Philemon and fled to Rome to lose himself in the crowded streets and among the many people. But while there he met someone—Paul—who introduced him to someone else—Jesus Christ. Now this man who once had been a fugitive slave was going back to Colosse with a letter to the Colossian church, but also with a letter to Philemon from Paul. In this letter Paul would appeal to Philemon to take him in and to receive him as a Christian brother.

B. *The friendship that changes a life makes it profitable.* "Profitable" is the meaning of Onesimus' name. He had not been profitable, but now his life was indeed profitable.

II. A transforming friendship can develop steadfastness.

A. *A steadfast friend shares experiences with you.* Aristarchus was a native of Thessalonica who was a Jew by birth. Called a "fellow-prisoner," he willingly shared the bondage of all believers in Christ.

B. *A steadfast friend stays with you.* Aristarchus is seen three times in the New Testament: during the riot in Ephesus at the Temple of Diana when he was captured by the mob (Acts 19:29), when Paul sailed as a prisoner for Rome (Acts 27:2), and here with Paul in Rome. He was a man who stood by Paul in a crisis, always at hand in a time of need.

Someone has described a friend as one who steps in when the whole world steps out.

III. A transforming friendship can build a life.

A. *Lives are sometimes hurt by hasty decisions.* Mark is the next name mentioned. Mark had set out with Paul and Barnabas (he was a relative of Barnabas) on the first missionary journey but soon left them and went home to Jerusalem. Paul refused to take him with them on the second missionary journey. Their missions team broke up over Mark.

B. *Lives can be rebuilt and reclaimed by friendship.* Mark's life was rebuilt. Now Paul had Mark with him in a place of difficult service.

IV. A transforming friendship can weld a heart of loving service.

A. *Loving service can be given to a church.* Paul mentioned Epaphras, who was likely the founder and pastor of the church at Colosse as well as those at Hieropolis and Laodicea. The concern that he had for the people there was manifested as he prayed daily for them that they might stand within the will of God.

B. *Loving service can show a contrast in fidelity.* Luke, the beloved physician, and Demas are mentioned. Demas is mentioned only here, in Philemon 24, and in 2 Timothy 4:10, where the sad and haunting words appear, "Demas hath forsaken me, having loved this present world." In the following verse appear the words, "Only Luke is with me now." Demas and Luke show a contrast in fidelity.

C. *Loving service is willing to share one's home for Christ.* The last name listed is Nymphas in whose house a church met. He shared what he had with Christ and the Christian witness.

Conclusion. Real service to God is that which lasts when all others have gone. There are friendships that lead to Christ and witness to Christ. But overarching this transforming friendship and making it all possible is our greatest Friend—Jesus Christ.

—*JEC*

* * *

SUNDAY MORNING, JANUARY 23

TITLE: The Secret of Facing Need

TEXT: **"My God shall supply all your need according to his riches in glory by Christ Jesus" (Phil. 4:19).**

SCRIPTURE READING: **Philippians 4:4–20**

HYMNS: **"Come Thou Fount of Every Blessing," Robinson**
"All That Thrills My Soul," Harris
"God Will Take Care of You," Martin

OFFERTORY PRAYER:

Praise the Lord for the joy of giving! As the Lord Jesus Christ gave Himself to You, so we too give ourselves to You. We bring to Your altar our hearts and possessions. Use them for Your sake and the salvation of souls. Amen.

Introduction. What does a Christian do when a recession comes and the talk of financial struggles increases? As this message is being prepared, the prime rate in interest reached to 18 percent this week. Inflation continues to spiral upward, and the *Wall Street Journal* reports that personal bankruptcy proceedings are on the increase again. Millions of people are in a "tight pinch" financially and Christians are not immune. However, God does have a word for us!

When you are confronted with special needs for yourself, your family, your job, or your church, what do you do? Paul writes his Philippian letter having some intense needs himself. As a servant of Christ, he is a prisoner in Rome. He acknowledges that he is afflicted (4:12) and that he is under pressure (4:14); he refers to his necessity and to their need (4:15–15).

Paul has learned the secret to facing need. This is a key to celebrated Christian living. There are some specific ways to respond.

I. Be enthusiastic (4:4).

When we have a need, we are not to hide it, deny it, or disregard it; we are to rejoice in it in the Lord. We are not merely to tolerate our need, we are to exult in it. The word *rejoice* is an imperative, a command. It is present tense, urging continual action. It is an attitude of life, "always." It is given double emphasis in the light of the Philippians' difficulties. Our focus is to be on the Lord, not on our need.

It was one of those never-should-have-gotten-out-of-bed days for a certain preacher. He cut his face while shaving. Then his wife burned the toast. When he hurried out to get into his car to drive to an appointment, he had a flat tire.

He finally got his car back on the road and was going a few miles over the speed limit, when a traffic officer stopped him and gave him a ticket for speeding. By that time he was extremely upset, and he made a rather sorry picture as he complained bitterly to the policeman about the kind of day he was experiencing. "I know what you mean," said the officer. "It used to happen to me that way—before I became a Christian!"

II. Be gentle (4:5).

Christians' enthusiasm is not without reason. The word *moderation* means a readiness to listen to reason. It is the attitude of yielding one's rights, thus showing consideration and gentleness to others.

The tendency of the world is to become hard and tough, to demand one's rights; but this is not the Christian response. We are to be gentle toward all men.

III. Be peaceful (4:6–7).

The natural tendency in the time of need is to worry. Every night Americans take 19 million sleeping pills. Worry is not the answer! We can either worry or pray.

God's Word says we are to "be careful for nothing"—not even one thing. This means that it is a sin to worry. Rather, we are to pray.

Peace comes by prayer as a spirit of worship, by supplication for one's personal needs, and by thankfulness for what is happening in our lives. Peace beyond human understanding keeps guarding our inner life. This is the way to respond to need.

IV. Be positive (4:8).

Think positively, not negatively! Think spiritual thoughts. Think high thoughts, true and honest thoughts, thoughts worthy of respect, just thoughts, living by God's standards. Think morally pure thoughts; loving, pleasing, and agreeable thoughts. Carefully reflect on these thoughts and keep practicing them! This is the way the God of peace will bless!

V. Be teachable (4:9, 11).

"Those things, which ye have . . . learned. . . . for I have learned . . ." (vv. 9, 11). The Lord has a purpose for the need in your life.

A. *The Lord uses a need to develop us*. What happens to us is not as important as how we respond to what happens. He is developing spiritual qualities in our lives. In this chapter several strong qualities are discovered: gratefulness (v. 6), joyfulness (v. 10), contentment (v. 11), flexibility (v. 12), and faith (v. 13). What quality is He developing in you?

B. *The Lord uses a need to reprove us*. A need that we have causes us to search our hearts to ask the Lord, "What's wrong?"

C. *The Lord uses a need to test us*. When we have a need and the funds for it are not available, the Lord may be testing us. Whatever our need and whatever God's purpose, we are to thank Him.

VI. Be content (4:10–12).

Contentment is an attitude that none of us possesses naturally. It is something we learn. Paul learned it; he had not always known it. We don't know it either because our natural inclination is not to learn to be content. Rather, it is to complain of our circumstances or to covet what we do not have. Contentment is realizing that God has provided everything I need for my present happiness. The opposite is covetousness, lusting for more and more.

VII. Be expectant (4:13).

"I can do all things through Christ which strengtheneth me." There is no greater verse in all the Bible. When we have the right attitude, there is nothing we cannot do! This verse is positive: "I *can.*" It is personal: "*I* can." It is powerful: ". . . do *all* things." In the face of your need, you can be defeated or you can be expectant of the victory Jesus gives.

VIII. Be generous (4:14–18).

The Philippian church was a generous church, consequently Paul's needs were met (vv. 14, 16, 18).

In the time of our need, we tend to be stingy; but the key to qualifying for verse 19 is the attitude of generosity within us. If we are in "need," then this means that we are to begin giving.

IX. Be fulfilled (4:19).

All our need is supplied and satisfied. God's treatment of the Philippians will correspond to their treatment of Paul. This is the divine principle of giving and receiving.

Conclusion. What about your needs? How are you responding to them? What are you doing with them? We need to take our eyes off the financial page and put them on God. God's Word says, "My God shall supply all your need according to his riches in glory by Christ Jesus" (v. 19). —*TSB*

* * *

SUNDAY EVENING, JANUARY 23

TITLE: Free At Last!

TEXT: "Stand fast therefore in the liberty wherewith Christ hath made us free, and be not entangled again with the yoke of bondage" (Gal. 5:1).

SCRIPTURE READING: Galatians 5:1

Introduction. The "Magna Charta" of spiritual emancipation, the "Declaration of Independence" from salvation by works, and the "Manifesto of Gospel Liberty" are but a few of the phrases that may be used to define the main theme of Paul's letter to the Galatians. If I were to reduce the 149 verses of this letter to three words, they would be "Free at last!"

Freedom is generally assumed to be the birthright of all men, yet man is anything but free. Bondage is more likely to be his lot. For some the cause is psychological, for others economic, and for still others political.

But Paul, with his profound insight into man's basic need, has forever made clear that only in Christ Jesus is man truly free.

For this very reason Paul is determined that every obstacle should be removed from man's path to God. Nothing—not legalism, not moralism, not ritualism—shall be allowed to prevent man from experiencing the freedom that comes only from Christ.

Like the Galatians, ours is the happy experience of knowing that because of Jesus Christ and Him alone we are "free at last!"

I. Free to be saved by faith (2:16).

In this verse Paul is saying, "We are free at last from all bondage to the law and to works."

For the first time in this epistle the word *justify* occurs. Yet it is one of the most significant terms in Paul's theology. It means "to pronounce righteous." That righteousness, by which a man is accepted by God, comes not from the fulfillment of any legal enactments, but by faith.

A. *Which liberates us from bondage to the law.* If the law cannot save, then what is its purpose? "Consequently, it is clear that no one can ever win God's favor by trying to keep the Jewish laws, because God has said that the only way we can be right in His sight is by faith. As the prophet Habakkuk says it, 'The man who finds life will find it through trusting God.' . . . But Christ has bought us out from under the doom of that impossible system by taking the curse for our wrongdoing upon Himself" (Gal. 3:11, 13a LB).

What is the place of the law? The law tells man what sin is and demonstrates what sin is, But most important, the law drives man to the grace of God.

The result of the law is that it shows man his own weakness and drives him to a despair in which he sees that there is nothing left but to throw himself on the mercy and love of God.

By the word *schoolmaster* Paul conceives of the law system as a helper to bring men to Christ. It was God's method of preparing the world for the coming of Jesus.

B. *Which appropriates the saving grace of Christ.*

"For it was through reading the Scripture that I came to realize that I could never find God's favor by trying—and failing—to obey the laws. I came to realize that acceptance with God comes by believing in Christ" (2:19 LB). Paul was certain that, through faith, Jesus Christ had done for him what he could never have done for himself.

Martin Luther was an example of discipline and self-denial. "If ever," he said, "a man could be saved by monkery that man was I." He went to Rome. It was considered to be an act of great merit to climb the Scala Sancta on hands and knees. He climbed upwards seeking that grace that he might win. There came to him the voice from heaven, "The just shall live by faith" (Gal. 3:11). The life at peace with God was not to be attained by this futile effort. It could only be had by casting himself in faith on the mercy of God. It is when we give up our struggle that the saving grace of Christ is ours.

II. Free to grow in grace (Gal. 5:1).

"So Christ has made us free. Now make sure that you stay free and don't get all tied up again in the chains of slavery to Jewish laws and ceremonies" (5:1 LB).

No longer do we serve God as slaves to laws and ceremonies. Rather, we serve Him as people free to grow in grace.

There are those today who have reverted to the error of the Galatians. They teach that we are initially "saved by grace" but that we are kept saved and thus grow by works.

In other words, Christ makes the "down payment," but we must make the "monthly installments" or suffer a divine foreclosure and repossession of our salvation.

Here Paul states that nothing could be further from the truth. In Philippians 1:6 he speaks with certainty: "Being confident of this very thing, that he which hath begun a good work in you will perform it until the day of Jesus Christ."

So we are free to grow in grace:

A. *Because of the continuing work of the Holy Spirit.*

"Surely you can't be so idiotic as to think that a man begins his spiritual life in the Spirit and then completes it by reverting to outward observances" (Gal. 3:3 PHILLIPS).

"Not by might, nor by power, but by my spirit, saith the LORD of hosts" (Zech. 4:6).

Our rate of growth in grace is in direct proportion to the degree to which we allow the Holy Spirit to fill us. When we are saved, the Holy Spirit takes up residence in us—we have all of the Holy Spirit we shall ever get, but He does not have all of us.

There are often areas of our lives that are "off limits" to the Holy Spirit. When this is true, we have arrested our growth in grace. This is why Paul says to born-again believers, "Be *filled* with the Spirit" (Eph. 5:18b).

B. *Because of the* indwelling *presence of Christ* (Gal. 2:20). Paul was dead; his old personality was in the bonds of sin, vainly striving for righteousness by means of works of law.

Elsewhere the change is called the new birth or regeneration; here Paul says: "There lives in me Christ." Christ, the Life, lives in Paul (R. C. H. Lenski, *The Interpretation of St. Paul's Epistles to the Galatians, to the Ephesians, and to the Philippians,* [Minneapolis: Augsburg Publishing House, 1961], p. 116).

Yielding your life to the indwelling presence of Christ is not a once-in-a-lifetime experience. It is something that you must do each day. Paul said, "I die daily" (1 Cor. 15:31) and here (Gal. 2:20) he says, "I am crucified with Christ."

You should begin every day by saying, "Lord Jesus, here is my body for You to use this day. I offer it to You as a garment in which You may clothe Yourself. I do not ask You to help me do anything. I simply step aside and ask You to come and do whatever You will in and through me this day. Amen."

When Christ is in control of your life, Bible reading, prayer, witnessing, and fellowship with other Christians will naturally follow, and you will grow in grace.

III. Free to live as members of God's family (Gal. 3:26, 28–29).

"For now we are all children of God through faith in Jesus Christ. . . . We are no longer Jews or Greeks or slaves or free men or even merely men or women, but we are all the same—we are Christians; we are one in Christ Jesus. And now that we are Christ's we are the true descendants of Abraham, and all of God's promises to him belong to us" (Gal. 3:26, 28–29 LB).

There are five characteristics of God's family:

A. *We are equal* (Gal. 3:28). What does this mean to the church today? It means that none of us have vested rights—no one is above or better than others. It means that the opinion of each person is of great value but of no more value than any other person. It means that the congregation is to be the church. It means that as members of the family of God we are more concerned about our responsibilities to other members than our own individual rights.

It means that because we are members of God's family, we are "kindly affectioned one to another with brotherly love; in honor preferring one another" (Rom. 12:10).

It means that as we reach out to others, as we witness to them and win them, that we do so regardless of their past, their race, or their cultural level. It means that when they become members of God's family, we accept them as our equal.

B. *We are heirs* (Gal. 4:7). Every member of a family is an heir to the father's wealth. We are not servants, laboriously striving to keep the law. We are sons of God, born into His family by grace through faith and thus full heirs to all of His riches.

My Father is rich in houses and lands,
He holdeth the wealth of the world in His hands!
Of rubies and diamonds, of silver and gold,
His coffers are full, He has riches untold.

I once was an outcast stranger on earth,
A sinner by choice, and an alien by birth.
But I've been adopted, my name's written down,
An heir to a mansion, a robe, and a crown.

Refrain: I'm a child of the King, A child of the King:
With Jesus my Saviour, I'm a child of the King.

(*Baptist Hymnal* [Nashville: Convention Press, 1956], p. 270)

C. *We care for and encourage one another* (Gal. 6:1–3).

"If anyone thinks he is too great to stoop to this, he is fooling himself. He is really a nobody" (Gal. 6:3 LB).

Paul states that when a man does slip, the Christian duty is to get him on his feet again. Paul goes on to claim that when we see a man fall into a fault or sin we would do well to say, "There but for the grace of God go I."

D. *We bear the "fruit of the Spirit"* (Gal. 5:22–23).

E. *We are productive* (Gal. 6:4, 9).

"Let everyone be sure that he is doing his very best, for then he will have the personal satisfaction of work well done" (Gal. 6:4 LB).

Salvation by grace does not mean freedom from service but rather freedom to serve.

The more we realize that we are members of God's family not through any merit of ourselves but solely through the grace and love of God, the harder we shall work and the more productive we shall become—not in order to become a member of God's family but because of the thrill of being a member of His family. We are free to live as productive members of God's family.

Conclusion. An old Negro spiritual captures the spirit of Paul's letter to the church at Galatia.

"Way down yonder in the graveyard walk,
Me and my Jesus goin' to meet and talk.

On-a my knees when the light passed by,
Thought my soul would rise and fly.

Some of these mornings bright and fair,
Go-in' meet King Jesus in the air.

Free at last, free at last,
Thank God, I'm free at last!"

—*JRM*

* * *

WEDNESDAY EVENING, JANUARY 26

TITLE: A Reminder for Ministry

TEXT: "And say to Archippus, Take heed to the ministry which thou hast received in the Lord, that thou fulfill it" (Col. 4:17).

SCRIPTURE READING: Colossians 4:17

Introduction. It was Super Sunday, the day for the Super Bowl. I had tried to capture the spirit of the occasion in the Sunday morning service that day. The Children's Sermon had a Super Bowl theme, and the morning message carried the title "Playing in the Faith Bowl." But at the lunch table that day a four-year-old boy said to his parents, "The pastor should have been talking about Jesus and God today instead of talking so much about football."

That was a reminder for ministry.

Paul gave a reminder for ministry also. It is found in the next to last verse in the Book of Colossians. Included in the list of personal greetings and miscellaneous matters with which Paul characteristically closed his letters was this reminder of ministry to Archippus.

We know almost nothing about Archippus. Apparently he was a young man. Some think he may have been Philemon's son or the pastor of the church that met in Philemon's house. It is not really known what church he served, or whether he served in a pastoral ministry at all. So it is not doing any damage to the Scripture to make a general application from this verse to the ministry that we all have as Christians. Whether ministry is the more formal ministry of a pastor, a church staff position, a deacon's ministry, or the ministry that all Christians share, this verse is a reminder for ministry.

I. The reminder for ministry is personal.

A. *Our ministry is personal.* Paul addressed this word to one person—Archippus.

Each one of us who is Christian has a ministry to which he has been called. God calls some of us to special ministries, but all of us have been called to ministry.

B. *Our ministry has precedent.* Jesus assured us that He had come into the world to minister rather than to be ministered to.

God called Moses, Samuel, and Paul, for instance, into special kinds of ministry for His sake. We have good biblical precedent for the ministry that we will perform in Christ's name.

C. *Our ministry is permanent.* In *The Christian Persuader* Leighton Ford told of their airplane setting down at Dakar, West Africa, while the Billy Graham team was en route to the African Crusades in 1960. A French missionary met them for coffee. They found out that he had labored in that Muslim center for ten years. One of the group asked him how many converts he had. He thought and replied that there had been one or two, perhaps three converts. Surprise was registered. If there were only three converts in ten years, why did he stay? He answered that he stayed because Jesus put him there.

II. The reminder for ministry is practical.

A. *Watch what is done.* "Take heed" is the advice given by Paul. In ministry we watch what is done.

There are many things that can be done in Christian ministry, but some of them have priority. Such things as the importance of persons, the ministry of comfort and strength, and personal preparation through prayer and study are always priority items in ministry.

B. *Watch how it is done.* Ministry must be performed in a way that is God-honoring and leads people to faith in God, not praise for the minister.

III. The reminder for ministry is purposeful.

A. *The source for ministry.* This ministry is "in the Lord." This indicates the source of ministry. All ministry is "in the Lord" in that God gives us the place to serve and the call to service, and He has provided the reconciliation which is announced.

B. *The strength for ministry.* Ministry is performed "in the Lord." It is by God's strength that one serves. A spider once spun a large and intricate web. He became proud of the web that he had spun and snapped the filament that hung down from the top since it did not fit into the design he had spun. But in snapping the filament he snapped the anchor of the web and it fell crashing to the floor.

IV The reminder for ministry is pointed.

A. *Ministry must be fulfilled.* "That thou fulfill it" is the pointed advice that is given. Ministry must be fulfilled as God calls us to minister.

B. *Ministry cannot be transferred.* Each one of us has a personal responsibility for his ministry that cannot be transferred to someone else. We must fulfill our own ministry.

C. *Ministry cannot be measured by inaccurate models.* Our models for ministry have too often come from the commercial world or from the athletic arena. We do not consider ourselves to have fulfilled our ministry unless we have "won," whatever form winning may take.

But Jesus gave us a different model by which to judge ministry. It is the model of His own life. Even our apparent failures may become successes in the hands of God. The Cross looked like a failure, but the Resurrection showed it was the fulfillment of God's purpose in the redemption of humankind.

Conclusion. This is our reminder for ministry. Take it. Heed it. Make your ministry as a Christian all that God wants it to be and allows it to be. —*JEC*

* * *

SUNDAY MORNING, JANUARY 30

TITLE: Christian Rewards

TEXT: "Every man shall receive his own reward according to his own labor. . . . If any man's work abide which he hath built thereupon, he shall receive a reward" (1 Cor. 3:8b, 14).

SCRIPTURE READING: 1 Corinthians 3:8–15

HYMNS: "Lead On, O King Eternal," Shurtleff
"Face to Face With Christ My Savior," Breck
"O That Will Be Glory," Gabriel

OFFERTORY PRAYER:

Heavenly Father, cultivate in us the grace of giving. Cause us to know the joy and celebration of giving to You. And teach us Your laws of liberality, for Your glory. Amen.

Introduction. Living the supernatural life is a blessing not only now but also in the future. There is a great difference in the doctrine of salvation for the lost and the doctrine of rewards for the saved. Salvation is by grace, not by works, but rewards are according to the works of the believer. Salvation is a gift; rewards are earned.

First Corinthians 3:8–15 reveals several truths about rewards: (1) Every believer will be rewarded according to his own labor (v. 8). (2) We are laborers together with God, not for salvation but for His service (v. 9). (3) The believer is to build on Christ as his foundation (v. 11). (4) The believer has a choice of two kinds of building materials: gold, silver, and precious stones or wood, hay, and stubble. The first represents eternal materials, the second represents temporal materials. Building with eternal materials results in rewards. Building with temporal materials results in loss at the judgment seat of Christ.

A minister sat at the bedside of a dying friend. As the friend talked of his home-going, tears filled his eyes. Knowing the man was young in the Lord, the minister thought he was afraid to die, and attempted to speak words of encouragement to him. The friend said, "I am not afraid; I am just ashamed to die." He went on to say that Christ was his Savior, but He had to meet Him empty-handed. His life was like "wood, hay, stubble."

It doesn't have to be that way. The Christian can live and die crowned with victory. Christians' rewards are sometimes called a prize, but several times they are called a crown. There are five crowns mentioned in the New Testament.

I. The crown of life (James 1:12).

This is sometimes called "the lover's crown." The believer finds strength to overcome temptation and endure trials through the love of God. Without His love in our hearts, trials can cause us to become bitter and critical and lose the crown of life.

This is also the crown that is received for being "faithful unto death" (Rev. 2:10). All believers have eternal life, but not all believers will be rewarded the crown of life. To receive it, we must love the Lord more than our lives (Mark 8:35). We must live for Christ and endure temptations and trials in the power of the love of God.

II. The crown of rejoicing (1 Thess. 2:19–20)

This is called the soul-winner's crown. The greatest work you are privileged to do for the Lord is to bring others to a knowledge of Christ as personal Savior.

A. *Why win souls?*

1. Because it is wise to win the lost (Prov. 11:30).
2. Because it is a work against sin (James 5:20).
3. Because it is a cause for joy in heaven (Luke 15:10).
4. Because every soul-winner will shine as the stars forever (Dan. 12:3).

B. *How to win souls?*

1. With your life. Others see Christ in you as you respond properly in life situations (2 Cor. 3:2).
2. With your mouth. Verbally witness for Christ, trusting the Holy Spirit to give you power (Acts 1:8).
3. With your giving. Give tithes and offerings that others may preach Christ and so have fruit that may abound to your account (Phil. 4:15–17).

There is rejoicing when the lost are saved. Heaven rejoices (Luke 15:10); the lost soul saved rejoices (Acts 8:39); the whole family rejoices (Acts 16:34); and the sower and reaper rejoice together (John 4:36).

III. The crown of righteousness (2 Tim. 4:8).

This is the crown that is earned by the believer who looks for and loves the second coming of Christ. In light of that Paul could say, "I have fought a good fight" (v. 7a). In the realm of spiritual warfare, Paul won the battle. He could also say "I have finished my course" (v. 7b). In the course of travel, there was no detour of hard places. There was no looking back (Luke 9:61–62); he kept his eyes on Christ (Phil. 1:6). Finally, he could say, "I have kept the faith" (v. 7c). He preached all the counsel of God (Acts 20:24–31).

IV. The crown of glory (1 Peter 5:4).

This is a special reward for the faithful, obedient, God-called pastor. The Chief Shepherd Himself gives it. It is eternal; it "fadeth not away." Yet every beleiver may share in the pastor's "crown of glory" (Matt. 10:41). God will reward you for supporting His chosen servant, through prayer and encouragement and giving freely of self and possessions.

The pastor earns this reward by:

A. *Feeding the church* (1 Peter 5:2).

B. *Taking the spiritual oversight of the church* (v. 2b).

C. *Being an example to the church* (v. 3). He is to walk with God by faith. He is to be a spiritual leader.

V. The incorruptible crown (1 Cor. 9:24–25).

This is the crown for victorious living. In the Greek games, they ran for a corruptible crown; in the Christian race, we run for an incorruptible one.

The key to victory is a disciplined life, whether in the Olympic games or in the Christian life. An athlete denies himself many things his body craves; a Christian must subdue his body or become a "castaway." The New Testament contains rules for believers to win the crown of victory.

A. *The believer must deny self of anything that would weigh him down and hinder him* (Heb. 12:1).

B. *The believer must keep his eyes fixed on Christ* (Heb. 12:2).

C. *The believer must find his strength in the Lord* (Eph. 6:10–18).

D. *The believer must place his all upon the altar of the Lord* (Rom. 12:1–2).

E. *The believer must, by faith, refuse anything that would impede spiritual progress* (Heb. 11:24–29).

There is no way to win this crown and be a spectator to the Christian life. We must enter the race and run to win!

Conclusion. In an old legend, an angel was talking with an aged Christian. Going into a great vault, he brought out a beautiful crown with shining jewels of rare value. He said, "This is the crown I designed for you when you were a youth, but you refused to surrender yourself completely to the Lord; now it is gone."

From the vault he brought another crown. It was beautiful, but not nearly so beautiful as the first one. He said, "This is the crown I designed for your middle age, but you gave those years to indolent discipleship; and now it is gone."

A third time he brought from the vault a crown. This was just a plain gold crown, with no jewels in it. He said, "Here is the crown of your old age. This is yours for all eternity."

Every man shall receive his own reward according to his own labor. What will your reward be?

—*TSB*

* * *

SUNDAY EVENING, JANUARY 30

TITLE: Christian Unity

TEXT: "I therefore, the prisoner of the Lord, beseech you that ye walk worthy of the vocation wherewith ye are called, with all lowliness and meekness, with longsuffering, forbearing one another in love; endeavouring to keep the unity of the Spirit in the bond of peace" (Eph. 4:1–3).

SCRIPTURE READING: Ephesians 4:1–6, 28–32

Introduction. Ephesians has been called "the queen of the Epistles." When John Knox was dying, the book he had most frequently read to him was the Book of Ephesians.

Paul deals with no problems in this letter. All news was good news from the people at Ephesus. So Paul had the joyous privilege of writing a positive letter to encourage them.

The theme of this letter is "Christian unity." Having established many churches and observed them grow, Paul realized that without unity nothing else really matters. And with unity nothing can defeat the church.

In his first three chapters, Paul lays the foundation for Christian unity. In his last two chapters he describes the practical results of unity. And in chapter 4 he deals with the heart and soul of Christian unity.

Thus it is on this fourth chapter we shall focus our attention. It is here that the apostle speaks of: (1) the behavior of Christian unity, (2) the basis of Christian unity, and (3) the benefits of Christian unity.

I. The behavior of Christian unity (Eph. 4:1–3).

Paul begins with behavior because it has everything to do with Christian unity.

Often it appears that *behavior* is more important than *beliefs* in maintaining unity in the church. For example, in our church there are many different beliefs concerning prophecy, the return of Christ, and social practices, and yet there is unity. But I could absolutely destroy this unity by my misbehavior.

Few church splits can be traced to bad theology. But many can be traced to bad behavior.

Thus Paul quickly and directly deals with behavior as an urgent matter of priority.

"I . . . beseech you [to] walk worthy of the vocation wherewith ye are called" (v. 1b).

In case they do not understand what kind of behavior Paul is speaking of, he spells it out. He lists seven characteristics of that kind of behavior that builds Christian unity.

A. *It is compatible with our calling.*

"I beg you to live lives worthy of your high calling" (v. 1b PHILLIPS).

If I am to help bring about Christian unity, I must conduct myself in such a manner as never to reflect on my calling as a Christian. Since I bear the name of Christ, I must never bring that name into disrepute.

B. *It is humble* (v. 2a—"lowliness"). I must not be stuck-up, egotistical, or proud. A very wise person said, "Egotism is the sedative nature provides to deaden the pain of being a fool."

But how does humility come about? It comes from two things:

1. Self-knowledge. Humility depends on honesty; it depends on having the courage to look at ourselves without the rose-tinted spectacles of self-dramatization, self-admiration, and self-love.

2. God-knowledge. Humility comes from comparing our life with the life of Christ. As long as we compare ourselves with others, we may come out of the comparison well. It is when we compare ourselves with Christ that we see our own failure. But God-knowledge plus self-knowledge equals humility.

C. *It is gentle* (v. 2b—"meekness"). A person who is gentle is so God-controlled that he is kind and gracious toward others. He is a person in whom *self* has died and through whom *Christ* in all of His meekness lives. Paul said, "I am crucified with Christ, nevertheless I live, yet not I but Christ lives in me."

D. *It is patient* (v. 2c—"longsuffering"). Chrysostom defines this as the spirit which has the power to take revenge but never does so. Patience is the spirit which bears insults without bitterness or complaint.

E. *It is magnanimous* (v. 2d—"forbearing one another"). As Christians we must be magnanimous toward others and their faults as God has been magnanimous toward us.

"Make allowances for one another" (v. 2d PHILLIPS).

F. *It is loving* (v. 2d—"forbearing one another *in love").* We should never forbear another through sheer grit and determination, but through Christian love.

There are four Greek words for love. But the word used here is the highest. It means that I must love a person so much that nothing he does or says will keep me from loving him and seeking his highest good. Even though he injures and hurts me, I will never feel anything but kindness toward him.

G. *It is peaceable* (v. 3—"endeavoring"). Peace won't happen—you must make it happen.

II. The basis of Christian unity (vv. 4–6).

Behavior is important to Christian unity. But a sound basis is absolutely indispensable! What is the basis, the foundation, on which Christian unity is built? Paul lays seven foundation stones: one body, one Spirit, one hope, one Lord, one faith, one baptism, and one God.

A. *One body* (v. 4a—"There is one body"). Christ is the head and the church is the body. The unity of the church is essential for the work of Christ.

B. *One Spirit* (v. 4b—"and one Spirit").

C. *One hope* (v. 4c—"even as ye are called in one hope"). This is the hope of the ultimate consummation of our salvation in heaven.

D. *One Lord* (v. 5a—"one Lord").

E. *One faith* (v. 5b—"one faith"). Paul is not speaking here of a set of beliefs that may characterize a particular denomination. There is "one faith" by which men come into a saving relationship to Christ as Lord. There may be many "faiths" (denominations), but there is only one faith by which we are saved. And that is faith in Jesus Christ as Savior!

F. *One baptism* (v. 5c—"one baptism"). Just as there is one faith through which all come into saving relationship to Christ, there is "one baptism" through which they make outward demonstration of that inward experience.

G. *One God* (v. 6). There is "one God"—and one God unites us into one family of God. Paul says four things about the one God.

1. He is *Father* of all—that is, He *created* all.
2. He is *above* all—that is, He *controls* all.
3. He is *through* all—that is, He *sustains* all.
4. He is *in* all—that is, He is *present*.

III. The benefits of Christian unity (vv. 28–32).

Quite predictably someone may ask, "Why all the fuss about unity? Does it really make that much difference? What are the benefits of Christian unity?"

The last five verses of this chapter list the benefits of Christian unity. Here we learn that unity in the church *does* make a difference—a *big* difference! Here is what happens when unity prevails:

A. *Conduct is changed* (v. 28). When there is Christian unity, there is a change in conduct. No longer do I ask, "What can I get?" but rather, "What can I share?"

But when we are united in allowing the Holy Spirit to fill us, the hope of heaven to challenge us, and the Lord Jesus Christ to guide us, conduct is changed!

B. *Conversation is clean* (v. 29).

"Don't use bad language" (v. 29 LB).

It is difficult to be in "unity" with God and His people and have a filthy mouth.

There is an ancient proverb that says, "The heart of man is a well and the mouth of man is a bucket, and that which is in the well of the heart can be determined by what is in the bucket of the mouth."

C. *Commitment is deepened* (v. 30). When we live each moment aware that there is but one Holy Spirit by whom we have been born again, we desire to do nothing to grieve Him. One of the benefits of Christian unity is that we reach a level of commitment beyond which we shall not grieve the Holy Spirit.

D. *Conflict is omitted* (v. 31). Unity omits conflicts. And conflicts come from "the sins of the spirit." Paul has dealt with the sins of the flesh (stealing, foul language, etc.). Now he deals with the sins of the spirit—or, as Gertrude Behana calls them, "Christian sins." These Christ identifies as bitterness, anger, clamor, evil speaking, and malice.

When we are one in Christ, we are free from all such disruptive and divisive conflicts.

E. *Kindness is practiced* (v. 32). "Kind" means the exercise of thoughtful consideration.

Conclusion. Clarence McCartney relates that the Roman soldiers on guard at the crucifixion of Jesus were dividing the prisoner's clothes. When they came to His coat, they discovered that it was seamless. To tear it would ruin it. For this reason they decided to keep it intact and cast lots for it.

The seamless robe of Christ has become a metaphor for the unity of the church. Henry Ward Beecher prayed that the church might be one again, like the seamless robe of her Lord. The metaphor is one of great beauty and appropriateness. Strife and divisions within the church have been ugly efforts to tear into pieces the sacred garment of the truth. The Crucified One looks down sadly upon the miserable conflict between those He died to redeem. His look of love and sorrow seems to repeat His prayer, "That they all may be one . . . that the world may believe that thou didst send me" (John 17:21). —*JRM*

* * *

SUGGESTED PREACHING PROGRAM FOR THE MONTH OF FEBRUARY

Sunday Mornings

With every new year there comes an awareness of new things. In the month of February the suggested theme for the messages will be "The New Life That Is Possible Through Christ."

Sunday Evenings

In every pew in every congregation there is at least one person with a broken heart. Part of the function of the pastor-shepherd is to attempt to bind up the broken-hearted. The suggested theme is "Is There Any Good News for Those Who Suffer?"

Wednesday Evenings

Billy Graham often says, "The Bible says. . . ." Every believer needs to know "What the Bible Says." This will be the theme for the Wednesday evenings for the next three months.

* * *

WEDNESDAY EVENING, FEBRUARY 2

TITLE: What the Bible Says About Itself

Introduction. In recent years there has been considerable polarization concerning the Bible and its contents on the part of Christians of all persuasions. Some claim that only parts of it are inspired. Others declare that its thoughts are inspired but not its language. Stilted and theological-sounding terminology has been used to describe certain concepts regarding the Bible and its contents, such as, "verbal inspiration," "plenary inspiration," "inerrancy," and so forth.

Perhaps the safest course to pursue is to let the Bible speak for itself. We are always to be wary of those persuasions which lean toward bibliolatry, or the worship of the Bible as though it were a good-luck charm. The important thing about the Scriptures is that they reveal to man what God is like, and how man can be reconciled to God through His Son Jesus Christ.

I. What the Scriptures are called.

A. *The Word of God* (Heb. 4:12). As the Word of God, the Scriptures are an extension of God's Being (John 1:1). They are more than just what God "said." They are the essence of His nature.

B. *The Word of Truth* (James 1:18). Jesus said, "I am the way, the truth, and the life." God's Word does not merely "contain" truth; it *is* absolute truth. Jesus said, "Ye shall know the truth, and the truth shall make you free" (John 8:32).

C. *The Oracles of God* (Rom. 3:2). Pagans referred to messages from their gods as "oracles." Paul was writing to Roman Christians (many of whom were only recently out of paganism), explaining to them that the messages of the *true* God (which he calls "oracles") were first given to the Jews.

D. *The Word* (James 1:21–23). The "engrafted word" suggests the personification of Jesus Christ, who is "in you" in the person of the Holy Spirit.

E. *Holy Scriptures* (Rom. 1:2). They are "holy" because they are uniquely God's words.

F. *Sword of the Spirit* (Eph. 6:17). As the "sword," they comprise the Christian's defense against Satan. The Holy Spirit makes the Word powerful in the heart of the believer. He "activates" it.

II. How the Scriptures are described.

A. *They are authoritative* (Ps. 19:7–8). Because they *are* the words of God, they contain absolute authority.

B. *They are inspired* (2 Tim. 3:16–17). They are God-breathed, and thus they communicate to man the very personality of God.

C. *They are "sharp"* (Heb. 4:12). "For the word of God is quick, and powerful, and sharper than any two-edged sword, piercing even to the dividing asunder of soul and spirit . . ." (Heb. 4:12). This means that God's Word is incisive like a surgeon's scalpel. It does not "mangle," but opens the heart to reveal its contents.

D. *They are pure* (Prov. 30:5). "Every word of God is pure. . . ." When man tries to "add to" God's Word, he destroys its purity. It is the design of Satan to tamper with God's Word, to make man doubt it and twist its truth.

III. How the inspiration of the Scriptures is proved (Heb. 2:1–4).

A. *They were first spoken by the Lord (thundered from Mt. Sinai).*

B. *They were confirmed by those who heard them.*

C. *They were accompanied by signs and wonders.*

D. *They were corroborated by the gifts of the Holy Spirit, and the coming of the Spirit in power on the Day of Pentecost.*

IV. How the Scriptures are understood.

A. *By illumination provided through the indwelling ministry of the Holy Spirit* (1 Cor. 2:10–14).

B. *By searching them.* "Search the scriptures; for in them ye think ye have eternal life: and they are they which testify of me" (John 5:39).

C. *By reasoning* (Acts 17:2). Paul "reasoned" with the Jews in the synagogues. Through the prophet Isaiah, the Lord God challenged: "Come now, and let us reason together, saith the LORD: though your sins be as scarlet, they shall be as white as snow; though they be red like crimson, they shall be as wool" (Isa. 1:18).

D. *By human help* (Acts 8:27–35). With his limited understanding, the Ethiopian was searching the Scriptures. God provided "human help" in the coming of Philip to interpret the meaning of the Scriptures to the searching heart of the Ethiopian.

V. How the Scriptures should be received.

A. *Let them dwell in us richly* (Col. 3:16); that is, let them be alive and effective in our lives.

B. *Search and study them daily* (Acts 17:11). A daily reading and studying of God's Word is a marvelous habit to form.

C. *Hide them in our hearts* (Ps. 119:11). They provide a "reserve power" with which to combat sin and temptation. Furthermore, when we "hide them in our hearts," God will bring them to our remembrance at the time of need.

D. *Delight in them* (Ps. 1:2).

E. *Teach them to our children* (Deut. 11:19). This means *not* just in church, but in the home as well.

Conclusion. Through the Word of God man learns of his sin nature and his need for salvation. Because the Word of God is alive and powerful, it is used of the Spirit to probe relentlessly into our hearts. The spiritual nourishment it provides brings about spiritual growth and releases within us a marvelous defense mechanism against sin.

—DLJ

* * *

SUNDAY MORNING, FEBRUARY 6

TITLE: Where Is Jesus?

TEXT: "So then after the Lord had spoken unto them, he was received up into heaven, and sat on the right hand of God" (Mark 16:19).

SCRIPTURE READING: Mark 16:14–20

HYMNS: "How Great Thou Art," Hine
"Glorious Is Thy Name," McKinney
"Jesus Shall Reign Where'er the Sun," Watts

OFFERTORY PRAYER:

"Bless the Lord, O my soul: and all that is within me, bless his holy name. Bless the Lord, O my soul, and forget not all his benefits." This is our prayer of recognition of Your many blessings and our prayer of release to You of our gifts of self and money. To Your Name be all glory! Amen.

Introduction. New life in the church is desperately needed today. The hope of the church is Christ Himself. The basic question is, Where is Jesus? The answer to this question enables us to praise Jesus Christ for His position now in God's eternal plan. Mark 16:19 says, ". . . he was received up into heaven, and sat on the right hand of God." Luke 24:50–51 says, "And he led them out as far as to Bethany, and he lifted up his hands, and blessed them. And it came to pass, while he blessed them, he was parted from them, and carried up into heaven." Acts 1:9–11 describes this scene: "And when he had spoken these things, while they beheld, he was taken up; and a cloud received him out of their sight. And while they looked stedfastly toward heaven as he went up, behold, two men stood by them in white apparel; which also said, Ye men of Galilee, why stand ye gazing up into heaven? this same Jesus, which is taken up from you into heaven, shall so come in like manner as ye have seen him go into heaven." Two questions need to be answered.

I. Where is Jesus?

A. *His ascension was His home-going*. It was His going back to His Father. It was the restoration of the glory He possessed before the world was; as John 17:5 says, "And now, O Father, glorify thou me with thine own self with the glory which I had with thee before the world was."

Jesus longed to be there. He described Himself as the householder who was to go into a far country from which He would return to reward His servants (Matt. 21:33). He talked about being "lifted up" (John 12:32); He talked about preparing a place for us (John 14:3); and He announced, "I go unto my Father" (John 14:12, 28; *see also* 16:5, 7).

B. *He is exalted to the Father's right hand*. Mark 16:19 says, ". . . and sat on the right hand of God." In Acts 2:33 Peter proclaims His "being by the right hand of God exalted." In Philippians 2:9–11, Paul beautifully concludes, "Wherefore God also hath highly exalted Him. . . ." These are powerful Scriptures. However, Ephesians 1:19–23 even more fully describes where Jesus is and what it means. He is at the Father's right hand, "far above all principality, and power, and might, and dominion, and every name that is named. . . ."

This describes His victory. His work was finished. He was ready to sit because He had done all the Father had told Him to do. He experienced victory over Satan, sin, the world, the flesh, and death.

This is also His new position. It describes His sovereignty and superiority. It describes His authority. He is Lord of all, Lord of heaven and earth, the highest authority of all.

It is also a position of ministry. From where He is, what is He doing? This is the second important question.

II. What is He doing?

What kind of ministry is Jesus performing today?

A. *His is a drawing ministry*. According to John 12:32 He is drawing all men to Himself. This is His saving ministry (Acts 4:12). He is not dragging men to Himself, He is magnetically drawing them.

He is doing this right now in the world, through His Spirit, through His love, through His Word, and through His people. So, from heaven He is drawing on earth!

B. *His is an interceding ministry*. He stands between us and the Father. Romans 8:34 says, "Who is he that condemneth? It is Christ that died, yea rather, that is risen again who is even at the right hand of God, who also maketh intercession for us." First John 2:1–2 teaches that Jesus Christ is our Advocate, our heavenly lawyer, our Counselor. He represents us before the Father. Satan accuses us to the Father and the Father to us, but Jesus represents our case before the Father. What hope and encouragement this is!

C. *His is a directing ministry*. Ephesians 1:22–23 indicates that God "hath put all things under his feet, and gave him to be the head over all things to the church, which is his body, the fulness of him that filleth all in all." He is the Head of the body; and as the head leads the body, so Christ leads the church. He tells the church what to do.

As the Head He does two things for the church.

1. He gives the gift of the Holy Spirit, then and now (Acts 2:33, 38).
2. He gives spiritual gifts to believers, by which He directs the minis-

try of the church (Rom. 12:6). We are empowered by the Spirit to exercise the spiritual gift that is ours, in relation to other members of the church—all under Christ's direction.

D. *His is a building ministry.* Matthew 16:18 states, "I will build my church"; and Acts 2:47 describes saved people being added to the church. Acts 6:7 reveals that the Lord is not satisfied just in adding to His church, He is multiplying it. This is His work and desire today for His churches!

E. *His is a preparing ministry.* He is doing something in heaven. John 14:2 says He is preparing a place for us, a heavenly home. When He gets our home ready, He will call us to heaven. In fact He will come for us and take us all to heaven.

F. *His is a sharing ministry.* His desire for us is expressed in John 17:24: "Father, I will that they also, whom thou hast given me, be with me where I am; that they may behold my glory, which thou hast given me: for thou lovedst me before the foundation of the world." The reality of this desire is expressed in Ephesians 2:5–6, where we sit with Him, and in Romans 8:28–30, where not only is He glorified, but we are too! Also, in Ephesians 1:19–22, not only does He have authority, but we also are given authority. His victory is our victory! "As he is, so are we in this world" (1 John 4:17). All He has, we share with Him. All He does, we do with Him. His new position and ministry in heaven is our new position and ministry on earth!

Conclusion. Christ's new position is the basis of knowing victory in our Christian life. We are in Him. We are identified with Him. This means victory over the world and every circumstance.

— *TSB*

* * *

SUNDAY EVENING, FEBRUARY 6

TITLE: How Do You Face Trouble?

TEXT: "Then Job arose, and rent his robe, and shaved his head, and fell upon the ground, and worshiped. And he said, 'Naked I came from my mother's womb, and naked shall I return; the LORD gave, and the LORD has taken away; blessed be the name of the LORD'" (Job 1:20–21 RSV).

SCRIPTURE READING: Job 1:13–22

Introduction. Is there any good news for those who suffer? In times when trouble strikes, we need to take an inventory to see if there is any good news that can cheer our hearts and help us bear the burden of pain.

Trouble and suffering are facts of life that all of us must cope with sooner or later. There are incurable diseases that will afflict those near and dear to us as well as us personally. There are financial disasters that are experienced by some that make it impossible for them to recoup their fortunes. There are domestic tragedies that cannot be remedied. There are fatal accidents on life's highways. There are dead-end streets where all hopeful expectations are brought to a full stop. There are wars and rumors of wars that create anxiety and bring about much suffering.

How is a follower of Jesus Christ to cope with suffering and trouble?

When trouble comes, some turn to religion; it deepens and strengthens their faith. Others turn away from religion in disappointment and despair. Still others turn against religion in hate and cynicism.

How does one cope with pain and trouble? Some bluster and bluff and cuss. Some develop a headache and take an aspirin. Some take to alcoholic drinks or resort to drugs which enable them to escape from the pain of reality. Some pray and trust God.

What will you do when trouble comes? Will you turn to God? Will you run from God? Will you turn against God?

Jesus was concerned about all who suffered.

Let us take a look at Job, who is an illustration of how a man coped with trouble in times before Christ ever came.

I. The character of Job (Job 1:1, 8).

Job is a dramatic illustration of one who experienced undeserved suffering. He is a dramatic illustration of how the innocent can suffer.

A. *Job was a blameless man.* He was blameless in the eyes of God, in the eyes of others and in his own eyes.

B. *Job was upright.* This means that he was straight and genuine and right in his relationships.

C. *Job feared God.* He was a reverent worshiper of God as he understood Him.

D. *Job was a man who turned away from evil.* There was no compromise in his life.

II. The position of Job.

Job lived in a time when it was commonly believed that if one was good and did good, he would be happy and prosperous. Job was a good man, and he was also happy and prosperous.

A. *There was none other like him.* He was the best of the best.

B. *Job enjoyed great wealth.*

C. *Job had a wonderful family.*

D. *Job was a priest in his own household* (1:5).

E. *Job was the epitome of success and happiness.*

III. Job's calamity and suffering.

Suddenly Job experienced great suffering and catastrophe that was unexpected, undeserved, and unexplained.

A. *Job suffered the loss of his property* (1:14–17).

B. *Job experienced the pain of the tragic death of his children* (1:18–19).

C. *Job experienced the loss of his health* (2:7–8).

D. *Job experienced bad counsel and advice from his wife* (2:9).

E. *Job experienced the pain of sincere friends who blundered in their efforts to assist him in his time of hurting.*

It should be recognized that Job was fortunate in some respects.

1. His friends did come to him. This involved great effort on their part.

2. They sat in silence with him for seven days. Sometimes silence can be of great support to one who is suffering.

3. They gave the best advice that they knew to give Job. Basically they said to him, "Job, acknowledge your sinfulness. Admit your hypocrisy. Confess your secret sins." Job's friends were philosophers and thinkers, and they came offering to him the best solutions for the complex problems he faced that the world had to offer at that time.

Job and his friends believed that suffering was the result of sin and that if one suffered it meant that he was a sinner.

In the midst of his pain, Job held on to his personal conviction regarding his personal integrity. He was convinced that he did not deserve the suffering that he was experiencing. His suffering was totally out of proportion to any sin of which he might have been guilty.

We learn from the Book of Job as we study it in its entirety that suffering is not always the result of sin that has been committed by the sufferer.

Another thing that we learn from the Book of Job is that often God is blamed for tragedies and catastrophes and hurts for which He is not responsible.

Job's friends came to him with the suggestion that his sufferings were the unavoidable consequence of some great flaw in his character and in his beliefs and conduct. Job was patient in the sense that he held on to his sense of integrity and denied that his sufferings were due to some great sin in his life.

When suffering comes to us, we must hold on to the conviction that God is love and that God is good. We must believe that God always acts in conformity with His good character.

Conclusion. How will we handle trouble? Will it bring us closer to Christ? Will it turn us away from Christ? Will it turn us against Christ?

There are several suggestions that could be helpful for us in the present as we think in terms of the possibility of great suffering in the future.

First, let's get acquainted with Christ as Savior and Teacher and Friend and Helper. Let each of us study Jesus Christ as he dealt with the pain and the suffering of others. Let us be assured that He is the same yesterday, today, and forever.

Before suffering comes let's develop some of the great resources that will assist us should catastrophe come. In the same way that we would take out insurance against liability or tragedy, let's take out some spiritual insurance.

1. We need to develop the daily habit of a quiet time in which we let God speak to us from His Word.

2. Prayer should become a daily conversation with God in which we not only speak to Him but let Him talk to us.

3. The habit of participating in public worship will give to us the inward resources that will help us when suffering comes.

4. Developing genuine Christian friendships with other members of the family of God allows them to be the medium of God's ministry to us when trouble comes.

5. We must expect the angels of God to come in our time of need.

In the meantimes let us not be in an agony of anxiety about what trouble may come in the future. Let's determine to live now for the highest and best as we understand it under the leadership of the living Christ and in the power of the Holy Spirit.

— TTC

WEDNESDAY EVENING, FEBRUARY 9

TITLE: What the Bible Says About God

TEXT: "The LORD is righteous in all his ways, and holy in all his works. The LORD is nigh unto all them that call upon him, to all that call upon him in truth" (Ps. 145:17–18).

SCRIPTURE READING: Psalm 145

Introduction. It is impossible to define God. To do so is to limit Him. A definition suggests a sphere of function or being for something. It *is* possible, however, to *describe* God. And the sourcebook from which we arrive at a description is the Bible. Thus it is appropriate to entitle this study, "What the *Bible* Says About God"—for that is all that matters.

I. The nature of God.

A. *God is a Spirit* (John 4:24). Man has always tended to depend upon some tangible evidence for the existence of God. It is a ministry of the Holy Spirit to enable man to grow in his understanding and concept of God as "Spirit."

B. *God is one* (Deut. 6:4). Monotheism was the great distinctive of Judaism. Polytheism was the curse of the ancient world. Even though God has expressed Himself to man in a multiplicity of ways, He is still one God.

C. *God is personal* (John 17:1–3). Man can "know" (experience) *not* an "impersonal Force" or an "Absolute Power," but a God who has personality and identity with man.

D. *God is trinitarian.* Though God is one Person, He reveals Himself to man as bearing three relationships (Gen. 1:1–3, 26; Matt. 3:16–17). As the "Father," He is infinite in love, power, and wisdom. He is the Creator who had divine purpose in all that He did. As the "Son," He is the revealer of God, the key to man's knowledge of God and history. As the "Holy Spirit," He manifests Himself spiritually to man. He "came upon" men in the Old Testament, enabling them to prophesy and perform mighty works. He was the agent in Jesus' conception, present at His baptism and during His temptation in the wilderness. He empowers and indwells believers and convicts the unsaved.

II. God's natural attributes.

A. *He is infinite* (1 Kings 8:27). There is no limit to His being.

B. *He is omnipotent.* He has all power and can do anything in keeping with His nature and purpose. The only limits to His power are self-imposed. He cannot lie or act contrary to His own laws, character, and purpose.

C. *He is omnipresent.* He is present at all times—in all parts of His creation and universe. He is limited neither by time nor space, but is a free, personal Spirit.

D. *He is omniscient.* He has all knowledge, knows all things simultaneously. His knowledge is immediate without processes of thought or reason. God's foreknowledge is a part of His omniscience.

E. *He is changeless* (immutable). He is the One in whom there "is no variableness, neither shadow of turning" (James 1:17).

III. God's moral attributes.

A. *God is capable of hatred of evil and of those things which oppose and seek to interrupt His divine purposes.*

B. *God is impartial* (1 Peter 1:17). He does not show "respect of persons."

C. *He is longsuffering* (Exod. 34:6). God's longsuffering attitude toward sinful man is one of His most amazing characteristics.

D. *He is love* (1 John 4:8, 16). God does not "possess" love; He *is* love. Love is the essence of His nature and His character.

E. *God is capable of showing vengeance* (Deut. 32:35; Rom. 12:19). God's vengeance, unlike man's, is not a calculated retaliation because of personal hurt. Man's refusal to respond to the loving appeal and invitation of God ultimately releases God's judgment.

IV. The roles of God.

A. *He is Creator* (Gen. 1:1). He is the one who conceived and made all things.

B. *He is Judge.* God judges man through His Word, by His Spirit, by His perfect and holy nature.

C. *He is man's Shepherd* (Gen. 49:24; Ps. 23; John 10:11, 14). One of the most beautiful descriptions of Jesus in His relationship toward and concern for man is that of Shepherd.

Conclusion. Man's intellectual limitations would make it impossible for him ever to exhaust his descriptions of God. Every day lived as a member of His family produces new insights and discoveries concerning Him. We can say with Paul: "O the depth of the riches both of the wisdom and knowledge of God! how unsearchable are his judgments, and his ways past finding out!" (Rom. 11:33).

—*DLJ*

* * *

SUNDAY MORNING, FEBRUARY 13

TITLE: Where the Spirit of the Lord Is

TEXT: "And when the day of Pentecost was fully come, they were all with one accord in one place. . . . And they were all filled with the Holy Ghost . . ." (Acts 2:1, 4).

SCRIPTURE READING: Acts 2:1–21

HYMNS: "All Hail the Power," Perronet
"Breathe on Me," Hatch
"Sweet, Sweet Spirit," Akers

OFFERTORY PRAYER:

Father, as we give to You and to Your church this morning, we give in the spirit of Your Word that says, "For ye know the grace of our Lord Jesus Christ, that, though he was rich, yet for your sakes he became poor, that ye

through his poverty might be rich." May Your work be enriched by the gifts You enable us to give. For Your glory, we pray. Amen.

Introduction. In Acts 2 is recorded an awesome event that occurred in history that means that the church will never be the same. It happened just as definitely as Jesus' birth and resurrection. It was the coming of the Holy Spirit into the life of the church. The believers were never the same following Pentecost. The church really became the church at Pentecost.

We will never need Pentecost again as such, just as we will never need Bethlehem again or Calvary as an historical event. But we will need the Person of Pentecost, the Holy Spirit, in control of our lives and the church.

This is a fascinating chapter of Scripture! It has much to teach us as a church if we would know the Spirit of Pentecost. Where the Spirit of the Lord is, there is something spiritually special. This is the story of Acts. This is the story of the church through the centuries. This is its message to us today.

Where the Spirit of the Lord is, there are four results.

I. There is the presence of the Lord.

There was a sudden and strange awareness of some supernatural events happening. There was a sudden sound from heaven, like a rushing, mighty wind. It filled the house where the disciples were sitting. There was an appearance of cloven tongues, like fire, upon each of them. They were all filled with the Holy Spirit. Strange, supernatural things began to happen. They began speaking in languages not previously learned. The crowd heard these events and were drawn together. They heard them speak and were amazed and marvelled. A very special moment in God's eternal plan was occurring.

It was the coming of the Holy Spirit. It was the manifestation of the presence of the Lord at Pentecost; the Holy Spirit entered into a new temple. The tabernacle was just an empty tent until Exodus 40:34: "Then a cloud covered the tent of the congregation, and the glory of the LORD filled the tabernacle." The temple of Solomon was an empty building until 1 Kings 8:10–11, ". . . the cloud filled the house of the LORD . . . for the glory of the LORD had filled the house of the LORD." Now in the New Testament, the Lord was filling a new temple, not one of skins and tapestries, nor of stones and ornaments, but His new temple, the church. Christ is the foundation, and born-again believers are the living stones.

On the Day of Pentecost, the Holy Spirit came to indwell the church, all believers, just as the shekinah glory of God filled the tabernacle and the temple with the glorious presence of the Lord! He indwells the church because He dwells in every believer, personally and individually (John 14:17; 1 Cor. 6:19; Eph. 2:21–22).

Where the Spirit of the Lord is, there is a manifestation of His power and an awareness of His holiness in relation to sin. This is what the "mighty wind" and "tongues like fire" represent. It is personal to those who sense that something wonderful is happening. It is perplexing to many who do not know the Lord.

II. There is power for evangelism.

The Day of Pentecost reveals that the Holy Spirit uses and blesses two primary methods of evangelism.

A. *The first is personal witnessing.* Acts 1:8 says, "Ye shall receive power, after that the Holy Ghost is come upon you: and ye shall be witnesses unto me. . . ." Acts 2:4 says, "They were all filled with the Holy Ghost, and began to speak with other tongues." Then verse 11 says, "We do hear them speak in our tongues the wonderful works of God."

The fullness of the Spirit was not given for their spiritual uplift; it was given to make them powerful witnesses and to equip them for service. All of us do not have the gift of evangelism, but every Christian is a witness! Being filled with the Spirit precedes personal witnessing (Acts 4:31).

B. *The second is powerful preaching*. Acts 2:14 refers to Peter's preaching, when he stood up and lifted up his voice. He preached powerfully with the Spirit in control.

1. Such preaching leads people to repentance (2:37).
2. Such preaching is anointed preaching (2:4).
3. Such preaching is bold preaching (2:22–24, 36).
4. Such preaching is Christ-honoring preaching (2:22–24).

The Lord's Spirit still honors these ways of evangelism.

III. There is the victory of harvest.

Pentecost was called the Feast of Harvest and celebrated the summer harvest. It was on that day that the Holy Spirit harvested 3,000 souls. The number itself was significant in that it was exactly that many who were killed on the day the law came down from Mt. Sinai, and the people were worshiping the golden calf. The letter kills; the Spirit gives life.

This is the age of the Spirit. He is still harvesting souls. We are still under the order of Pentecost. George Whitefield saw 30,000 converted in his revivals in America. In the 1858 revival, conversions numbered 50,000 per week. Today, through Billy Graham's ministry, hundreds of thousands have come to Christ. The harvest of the Holy Spirit is seen throughout the world! And it will come today just as it did then.

IV. There is a pattern for doing God's work.

The marks of a church that is doing things God's way are found in Acts 2:41–47.

A. *Atmosphere*. They possessed a "fear," a reverence of the Lord, an awareness that God was at work.

B. *Activities*.

1. Teaching (v. 42).
2. Fellowship (vv. 42, 46).
3. Breaking of bread (vv. 42, 46)—fellowship meals and the Lord's Supper.
4. Prayers (v. 42).

C. *Attitudes*.

1. Generosity (vv. 44–47).
2. Oneness of spirit (v. 46).
3. Gladness (v. 46).
4. Praise (v. 47).
5. Favor (v. 47).

D. *Additions* (vv. 41, 47). The Lord adds to the church saved people. The church grows and there is the spirit of excitement and enthusiasm.

Conclusion. It is not the size of the church that counts, but the spirit! Lord, touch us with the freshness of Your Spirit. Work Your work in us and through us for Your glory!

— *TSB*

* * *

SUNDAY EVENING, FEBRUARY 13

TITLE: Is There a Connection Between Sin and Suffering?

TEXT: **"Then his wife said to him, 'Do you still hold fast your integrity? Curse God, and die.' But he said to her, 'You speak as one of the foolish women would speak. Shall we receive good at the hand of God, and shall we not receive evil?' In all this Job did not sin with his lips" (Job 2:9–10 RSV).**

SCRIPTURE READING: **Job 2:11–13**

Introduction. When calamity struck the house of Job, his friends came at great trouble and inconvenience to comfort and counsel him.

Job's friends held to the traditional thoughts of their day, and in many respects the thoughts of our day. They believed that God always rewards righteousness. They believed that God always punishes wickedness. They perceived that righteousness always pays off with peace, prosperity, popularity, plenty, and permanence.

They believed that wickedness would always be punished and that very shortly. They saw God as a judge. They understood Him somewhat in terms of His being a prosecuting attorney or a policeman. They believed God to be an executioner. They believed that God's law was self-operating and self-executing, and that if you found yourself in great pain and suffering, it was proof positive that you were a great sinner.

The writer of the Book of Job challenges all of our simple solutions to the complex questions that plague us when pain and trouble come. The easy answer is usually the incorrect answer.

While recognizing that sin will eventually result in suffering, when you study the Book of Job, you cannot help but come to the conclusion that all suffering is not the direct result of sin that has been committed by the one who is experiencing pain. Job himself is an excellent illustration of this.

I. Job was a very good man who did not deserve to suffer as he was suffering.

A. *He suffered the loss of all of his worldly property.*

B. *He suffered the loss of his children.*

C. *He suffered the absence of a sympathetic, understanding wife.* We need to recognize that she was suffering from deep depression when she came to him and gave him advice that was really a suggestion that there was a way by which he could commit suicide and get out of his pain.

D. *Job suffered the unsympathetic misunderstanding of his sincere friends.*

E. *Job suffered indescribable pain.*

Is there a connection between sin and suffering? The answer could be yes, and the answer could just as well be no.

II. The suffering of Job is ascribed to Satan (Job 2:7–8).

Job did not know that his pain and suffering had been brought upon him by the activity of Satan.

Job's friends did not know that Satan was responsible for the suffering that Job was experiencing.

Both Job and his friends believed that sin always produces suffering. Consequently, his friends concluded that because Job was suffering, this indicated that he was a great sinner. Job knew in the deepest part of his being that he had not sinned in a manner that would provoke God to pour out such suffering upon him.

In the midst of his pain, as he suffered indescribably, Job gave voice to some very painful and pointed questions:

1. How can a man be just before God?
2. How can I stand before God?
3. Why does God not come to me in my time of pain?
4. Why will God not listen to my pleas?
5. Why does God let things like this happen?

Job was plagued with the pain and the agony that many experience when undeserved suffering threatens their very existence. If God is all powerful, why do these things happen? If He is love, why does He permit some things to happen?

The traditional answer during the days of Job was that God does good for the good and bad for the bad.

There are many in the present day who hold to these ancient thoughts. The other side of the coin is that many of us expect favored treatment by God because of our virtues and our high self-esteem. Many become indignant with God because of suffering and want to know what they have done to deserve such.

To the problem of why the innocent suffer, the Book of Job gives no complete and satisfactory answer.

III. The painful problem of undeserved suffering.

From before the days of Job up to the present, men and women have grappled with the painful problem of suffering. We have come to recognize that while sin will produce suffering, not all suffering is due to some sin that has been committed by the one who is suffering.

Pain and suffering come upon us from all directions. Natural disasters produce suffering. Many suffer because of historical decisions made by the different countries of the world. Ancestral choices bring pain upon descendants.

The Hindus and Buddhists have built their whole philosophy upon the question of the responsibility for pain and suffering. They believe that pain is inevitable because of evil deeds and conduct in a previous existence. Reincarnation is a basic belief in this system of thought, and consequently, present-day pain is explained. Kind and benevolent behavior is encouraged to improve one's lot in a future existence.

We can receive much light for the problem of pain through medical science. One physician has said, "We differentiate between pain that serves a useful purpose and pain that serves no useful purpose. An example of pain that serves a useful purpose is like a lump in the breast for cancer, a pain in the back indicating a herniated disc, or difficulty in chewing indicating an abcessed tooth.

"Some pain serves no useful purpose, for instance, a muscle-tension headache. It is a job for the doctor to differentiate between pain that serves a useful purpose and pain that is useless.

"There are some choices as we face the problem of pain.

1. We can ignore pain. This may not be appropriate because pain may be a warning from the body concerning a problem.
2. We can investigate the causes of pain.
3. We can do something about the pain.

"The pain is best managed by a team approach, that is, in a hospital where you can use a team combination of a physician, a physical therapist, and even a psychologist. There are forms of both physical and emotional pain. In the old days we used to say that one should offer up pain to the Lord, but now there is more treatment of pain, yet some pain still cannot be alleviated."

Dr. Norman L. Geisler has written a book dealing with the problem of pain and the results of evil (*The Roots of Evil,* Zondervan Publishing House, 1978). In this splendid book we are told that much pain comes directly from our own free choices. It also comes upon us indirectly from the exercise of our freedom. We experience pain also because of the free choice of others. We experience some pain because of the good choices that other people make, but in which accidents are involved. He calls our attention to the fact that some suffering comes because of the activity of evil spirits (Job 1:6; Matt. 17:14–19; Mark 5:1–13).

Some physical pains or evils may be God-given warnings of greater physical harms. Not all pain is bad. Some physical suffering may be used by God to warn us against moral evils. C. S. Lewis is quoted as saying, "God whispers to us in our pleasures, speaks in our conscience, but shouts to us in our pain; it is his megaphone to rouse a deaf world."

Some pain and suffering may be permitted as a condition of producing spiritual refinement in our hearts and lives (Rom. 8:28).

Conclusion. There is no final answer. There is no satisfactory solution to the problem of pain and suffering in the present. Our great hope and our steadfast faith must be in God, who throughout all the record of His self-revelation in the Scriptures reveals Himself as the God who is for life and for health and for relief from pain. Heaven is described as a place where God ". . . will wipe away every tear from their eyes, and death shall be no more, neither shall there be any mourning nor crying nor pain any more, for the former things have passed away" (Rev. 21:4 RSV).

Heaven is to be thought of not only as a destination but as a way of life. God is at work in the world to bring heaven into the present for those who will trust Christ and obey Him.

We can trust God to help us with the problem of pain and suffering. We can believe that He hurts when we hurt. We can believe that He weeps for us when we weep.

We can look forward by faith to the day when pain shall be no more.

—*TTC*

* * *

WEDNESDAY EVENING, FEBRUARY 16

TITLE: What the Bible Says About the Trinity

Introduction. The doctrine of the Trinity is a distinctive mark of Christianity. Though there are "triads" of divinities in many of the world religions and philosophies (such as the Egyptian triad of Osiris, Isis, and Horus—corresponding to the human family of father, mother, and child), none of these carries any similarity to the Christian teaching concerning the Trinity. It must be understood, however, that it is not possible to "prove" the Trinity from the standpoint of human reason. The trinitarian nature of God comes to man by divine revelation. It is interwoven throughout the Old and New Testaments. Thus the Bible presents God as a rational Spirit Being who is infinite in His attributes of love, holiness, wisdom, power, majesty, justice, truth, and goodness. It also presents Him as One who externally exists in three Persons, yet one in substance and in purpose.

I. There is one God.

A. *In the Old Testament, He is revealed in the Shema* (Deut. 6:4–5), *with which every Jewish synagogue service is opened; in the Decalogue* (Exod. 20:3); *and by the prophets* (Isa. 45:5–6).

B. *In the New Testament, He is revealed in the words of Jesus* (John 10:30), *the words of James* (James 2:19), *and the words of Paul* (1 Cor. 8:4–6). He is described as the Father "of whom are all things" (v. 6) and in whom "we live, and move, and have our being . . ." (Acts 17:28).

C. *Adam and Eve believed in one God; but sin gave birth to polytheism because, in his guilt, man manufactured gods whom he could appease.* Sinful man feared demonstrations of natural power, so he worshiped the storm, the wind, fire, the sun, etc. Today, Satan manipulates material things in our lives until they become gods.

II. The one God exists as three Persons.

A. *The first inference of the Trinity is discovered in Genesis 1:1, when Moses used the plural form of the divine Name:* "In the beginning God *(Elohim)* created the heavens and the earth." Our God is so great in His being and in His attributes that to limit Him to one expression or manifestation of Himself is to ignore His majesty and power.

B. *Several passages employ certain repetitions of the name of God which apparently distinguish between "God" and "God"* (see Ps. 45:6–7; 110:1 [messianic references]; Hos. 1:7). There are other remarkable passages which refer to the Angel of Jehovah (Gen. 16:7–14; 22:11–16; Exod. 3:2–5; Judg. 13:20–22).

C. *The amazing fact of the New Testament is the way in which it presents the doctrine of the Trinity without any struggle or controversy.* The teaching of Jesus is trinitarian throughout. He speaks *to* the Father and *of* the Holy Spirit, and He does so without apology and without explanation (see John 14:16–17; 15:26).

D. *Paul gives an apostolic benediction in 2 Corinthians 13:14, which is a prayer directed to Christ for His grace, to the Father for His love, and to the Holy Spirit for His fellowship.* Here, the Deity and equality of each person of the Godhead are taken for granted. God exists as three Persons, and each of the three is equal in power and glory, being one in substance.

E. *It is also important to note, in the Great Commission (Matt. 28:19–20), that Jesus instructed His followers to go into all the world "baptizing them in the name* [*not* names] *of the Father, and of the Son, and of the Holy Spirit.*" This is another indication of the unity and oneness of the Trinity.

Conclusion. *The Father is God.* On many occasions, Jesus prayed to God the Father (Mark 14:36; John 11:41; 17:11; et al.). In 1 Corinthians 8:6, Paul declares: "To us there is but one God, the Father, of whom are all things." Again, Paul identifies himself as "an apostle . . . through Jesus Christ and God the Father" (Gal. 1:1 RSV).

The Son is God. John wrote, "In the beginning was the Word, and the Word was with God, and the Word was God. . . . And the Word became flesh . . ." (John 1:1, 14 RSV). "For in him [in Christ] dwelleth all the fulness of the Godhead bodily" (Col. 2:9). Hebrews 1:3 contains one of the strongest statements in the New Testament in declaring the deity of Jesus. He is said to be the exact expression of the substance of God. What is substance? It is whatever is necessary to be God. The Son is declared to be the exact expression of that substance. Also, the attributes of Deity ascribed only to God are ascribed to the Son: holiness (John 6:69; Heb. 7:26); immutability (Heb. 1:11–12; 13:8); omnipotence (Matt. 28:18); omniscience (Matt. 9:4; John 16:30); life (John 1:4; 11:25; 14:6); eternity (John 1:1; 8:58; 17:5; Heb. 1:8); omnipresence (Matt. 28:20); judgment (Matt. 25:31–46); creation (John 1:3, 10; Col. 1:16–17).

The Holy Spirit is God. Peter declared it in his word to Ananias (Acts 5:3–4); Paul stated it (1 Cor. 2:11); and Jesus alluded to it in the Great Commission (Matt. 28:19–20) that the Holy Spirit is equal with the Father and the Son as Deity.

— *DLJ*

* * *

SUNDAY MORNING, FEBRUARY 20

TITLE: The Living Christ in the Church

TEXT: ". . . Silver and gold have I none; but such as I have give I thee: In the name of Jesus Christ of Nazareth rise up and walk. . . . And his name through faith in his name hath made this man strong . . ." (Acts 3:6, 16).

SCRIPTURE READING: Acts 3:1–18

HYMNS: "There Is a Name I Love to Hear," Whitfield
"Because He Lives," Gaither
"The Church's One Foundation," Stone

OFFERTORY PRAYER:

Praise be to Your name for Your bountiful gifts. We acknowledge them with thanksgiving, and present our gifts to You in joy and praise. Thank You for the privilege of giving. In Jesus' name. Amen.

Introduction. Lenin's embalmed remains lie in a crystal casket in a tomb in Red Square in Moscow. On the casket it says: "He was the greatest leader of all peoples, of all countries, of all times. He was the Lord of the new humanity. He was the saviour of the world." All that Lenin did was in the past tense, but we have a living Christ.

How do we know that Jesus Christ is a living Person and power among us? For the Jerusalem church, the healing of the lame man signified the power of the living Christ and that He was present among them. How about us? Do we see lives being changed miraculously? Are things happening among us that amaze us and fill us with wonder? The strong emphasis of the Book of Acts is the reality of the living Christ in the church. Notice three lessons from Acts 3.

I. The lesson of a crippled society and what can be done about it.

Here is a lame man who was crippled from birth. He was carried by someone daily to the gate Beautiful. He begged from the crowds of worshipers who passed this prominent place. It was here that a great event happened.

He saw Peter and John approaching the gate, so he begged from them. Why Peter and John? Only God can answer that. Peter's words changed his life! "Silver and gold have I none; but such as I have give I thee: In the name of Jesus Christ of Nazareth rise up and walk" (v. 6).

Peter also took him by the hand and lifted him up. He was immediately healed. He leaped up, stood, walked, leaped, and praised God! He had been made whole; a cripple had been healed.

The truth is that all of us are cripples. All of us need healing. We are crippled spiritually. We have all sinned (Rom. 3:23); we are like sheep who have gone astray (Isa. 53:6); and we perish spiritually (Luke 13:3). We are like the man at the gate, helpless and powerless. It is to be a spiritual cripple to be without Christ, now and forever. Salvation is man's basic need.

Society is crippled also, with its crippled marriages, morals, and relationships. Ours is a society crippled with immorality. The sin of homosexuality is a way of life for thousands. Society is being flooded with pornography. Some people are crippled by alcohol, and the age of problem drinkers continues to get younger. Some are crippled with negative attitudes, anger, hate, resentment, bitterness, and unforgiveness. Only Jesus Christ can bring us what we need.

II. The lesson of divine authority and how to appropriate it.

Verses 6 and 16 say, "In the name of Jesus Christ of Nazareth" and "his name through faith in his name." Jesus said to His disciples, "Whatsoever ye shall ask in my name, that will I do, that the Father may be glorified in the Son" (John 14:13). So Peter speaks in the name of Jesus Christ.

There is power and authority in Jesus' name! The answer to our crippled generation is the name of Jesus Christ, not silver and gold. And Peter evidences the discovery of a newfound authority, Jesus' name.

Jesus was given all authority in heaven and earth (Matt. 28:18). His authority is described in Ephesians 1:19–23. This authority was shared with the apostles to demonstrate Christ's power. And according to Ephesians 1, all believers share the privilege of this authority. All that we do should be done in the awareness of spiritual authority. We have the authority to call people to salvation. We have the authority to pray victoriously. We have the authority to resist the devil and to put him to flight. We have the authority to enforce Christ's victory in life and home and church and nation.

This is not spiritual authority that is to be taken lightly; it is to be exercised by believers who are filled with the Spirit, living cleansed lives, and walking by faith. There is power in the church when believers appropriate this authority.

III. The lesson of a living message and its reliance for our times.

Peter explains that the miracle was God's work, the living Christ at work. What makes this first-century message relevant to twentieth-century times?

A. *The message of the responsibility for Christ's death* (vv. 13–14). The apostles stressed the fact that the Crucifixion was the greatest crime in human history. The fact is, all of us are responsible for Christ's death.

B. *The message of the resurrection of Christ from the dead* (v. 15). Without the Resurrection there is no hope, no salvation, no church, and no living Christ!

C. *The message of the power of Christ's presence* (v. 16). This is the secret of the Christian life and the source of power in the church.

D. *The message of repentance and new life* (v. 19). Repentance is a forgotten message in our generation, but there is no new life without it.

E. *The message of revival from the Lord's presence* (v. 19c).

F. *The message of the return of the Lord* (v. 21). The message of the early church was the second coming of Jesus Christ. His coming was always in the consciousness of the first believers.

G. *The message of response to God's message* (vv. 22–26). It is a simple message: hear and be blessed (v. 22), or refuse to hear and be destroyed. There are untold blessings in responding to Christ; there is spiritual ruin in rejecting Him.

Conclusion. Whenever this message is preached, something happens! The Book of Acts is living proof of the living Christ in the church. He means hope for a crippled society, authority for the people of God, and a message for all times. Appropriate this reality to your life by faith. This is new life in the church!

— *TSB*

* * *

SUNDAY EVENING, FEBRUARY 20

TITLE: The Management of Pain

TEXT: ". . . a thorn was given me in the flesh, a messenger of Satan, to harass me, to keep me from being too elated" (2 Cor. 12:7 RSV).

SCRIPTURE READING: 2 Corinthians 12:7–10

Introduction. From the cradle to the cemetery, much that we do is done in order that we might avoid pain.

Those of us who watch the television commercials cannot help but notice how many of these are offering suggestions concerning the best possible management of pain. Some of the suggestions are both insulting and revolting. It is often suggested that one should sidestep pain and escape through some form of drink or drug. Yet those who cope with pain through alcohol or some other form of drug will find that their pain increases rather than disappears.

There are some who seek to manage pain through radical endurance. They are the successors of the Stoics who believe that one must "grin and bear it."

Many of the peoples of the world live where excellent medical services are available, and they use the services of physicians and nurses and hospitals to cope with the problem of pain.

The Hindus and the Buddhists believe that pain or suffering is inevitable and inescapable because, according to their beliefs, suffering is due to evil deeds and cruel behavior in a former life. It must be endured so as to improve one's lot in a future existence.

How will you manage pain when it comes to disturb you and perhaps to threaten your very being?

I. Paul experienced great pain (2 Cor. 12:7–9; Gal. 4:12–13).

There have been various suggestions concerning what Paul's "thorn in the flesh" really was.

A. *Some have speculated that it was a form of reoccurring malaria which produced serious headaches.*

B. *Some speculated that it was a form of epilepsy, and this is based on Paul's account of his conversion experience and his being struck blind.*

C. *Some have thought that it was a painful and repulsive eye trouble* (cf. Gal. 4:15; 6:11).

D. *There can be no question that Paul experienced terrible persecution and great suffering as a result of it* (2 Cor. 11:24–27). Paul was no stranger to pain.

II. Paul perceived his pain as coming from God.

At first glance you would think that this thorn in the flesh was actually the result of Satan's activity. Paul interprets it as coming from God in order to produce a benevolent spiritual effect in his life.

A. *Paul's thorn in the flesh did not come as a punishment for sin.*

B. *Paul's thorn in the flesh served to prevent him from becoming proud, arrogant, and self-sufficient.*

III. Paul recognized that Satan uses pain to hurt and to hinder.

A. *He speaks of his thorn in the flesh as "a messenger of Satan."*

B. *Paul was harrassed and buffeted by pain.*

C. *Satan uses pain to create doubt in the mind of the sufferer concerning the goodness of God.* Satan seeks to create depression by injecting doubt into our minds concerning the character and the behavior of our Father God.

D. *Satan seeks to foster bitterness and hate because of pain.* We must beware of the strategies of the Evil One; he is out to destroy us because he is the enemy of God and our enemy as well (1 Peter 5:8–9). If Satan can cause us to become angry at God and to react with bitterness and hostility toward either God or others, he is leading us in a path of self-destructiveness.

IV. Paul prayed for the removal of the thorn.

A. *Paul was a man of great faith and prayer.* He believed in bringing every problem before God's throne of grace for help and mercy.

B. *Three times he prayed for relief from the agony of this painful thorn.* By way of parenthesis, we should be reminded that our Lord prayed three times for the removal of the cup of suffering in the Garden of Gethsemane as He faced the agony of crucifixion on the following day. The Scriptures say that the angels came and ministered to Him, but the cup was not removed.

C. *Paul's persistent prayer for the removal of the thorn was not granted.* When you pray for relief from the pain that plagues your body and seemingly there is no answer, what will you do? You will not be able to ignore pain, because pain is no illusion.

V. Paul used all possible proper resources for the management of his pain.

A. *Luke was a physician and was Paul's traveling missionary partner through Asia Minor and in many of the journeys from then until he suffered martyrdom in Rome.*

B. *Paul accepted pain as something that was permitted by the will of God even when he could not understand it.*

C. *Paul offered thanksgiving to God in the midst of his sufferings and pain.* This does not mean that he always thanked God for the sufferings; but in the midst of his pain and suffering, he sought for that for which he could be thankful. His words to the Thessalonian believers are appropriate at this point, "Rejoice always, pray constantly, give thanks in all circumstances; for this is the will of God in Christ Jesus for you" (1 Thess. 5:16–18 RSV). To search for something to be thankful for in the midst of great pain, creates a positive way of thinking and an open mind and heart through which God can minister to us in our times of need.

D. *Paul made the most and best of each day.* He tried not to let yesterday distress him in the present. He attempted not to worry about tomorrow.

E. *Paul did not let bitterness rule and ruin him when pain throbbed through his body.* A dramatic illustration of the manner in which he dealt with pain is revealed in his experience in the Philippian jail when, following a cruel beating, he and Silas "were praying and singing hymns to God, and the prisoners were listening to them" (Acts 16:25 RSV).

F. *Paul believed that through Jesus Christ it was possible for one to be on top of the painful circumstances of life* (Phil. 4:13).

Somewhere along the way we have gotten the false impression that if you are good and try to do right that God will give you an exemption from pain and suffering and trouble. This is unrealistic. It is unbiblical. It is contrary to the experience of the great saints.

Conclusion. Jesus came to help men cope with pain. We have no record in the Scriptures of Jesus turning away from those who were in pain. He healed the sick. He gave sight to the blind. He gave hearing to the deaf. He enabled the lame to walk. He cooled the fevered brow of Peter's mother-in-law. With faith in His love and kindness, we are to face pain.

We can be assured that the blessings of God will rest upon the doctors and modern medical facilities, and we should seek the services of these as we cope with pain.

Jesus came also to help us cope with the pain of being fallen creatures, mistake-makers, sinners who are lost from the Father God and who do not know the way home. Jesus came to help us cope with our incompleteness and our spiritual deadness toward God. Jesus came to help us avoid the pain of missing heaven when this life is over. He died on a cross and conquered death and the grave in order that He might prepare for us a home in heaven.

Let us trust Him to help us overcome all of the pain associated with being human beings, and let us rejoice in the fact that there will come a day when there will be no more pain.

— *TTC*

WEDNESDAY EVENING, FEBRUARY 23

TITLE: What the Bible Says About the Three Stages of Man

Scripture Reading: Romans 7

Introduction. In Romans 7 Paul describes man as being either natural, carnal, or spiritual. The *natural man* is the unsaved man who can rise no higher than his intellectual, moral, or volitional powers can lift him. The *carnal man* is a saved man who is still dominated at least partially by the power of sin, and who lives under the control of the old nature of Adam within him. The *spiritual man* is the believer whose life is controlled by the Holy Spirit.

I. The spiritual man (vv. 1–6).

A. *Paul says first that the spiritual man shows that he is delivered from the law*. He illustrates this with the marriage relationship, showing how valid and how vital are the claims of the law up to the time of death.

B. *How is this fact—that the power of the law ends at death—revealed in the life of the spiritual man?* He is no longer "trying" for victory any more than he is "trying" to be saved. The spiritual Christian has discovered a more thrilling way to victory in his life. Because of his identification with Christ in His death, the claims of the law are broken (v. 4).

C. *The spiritual man has also discovered a more thorough way to victory.* The failure of the flesh no longer overpowers him (v. 5). Paul is saying that when we were "natural men," "unregenerate," "the motions of sins" or the sinful passions were aroused and excited by the law. For the law told man what sin is without providing for him the power to overcome it.

D. *Note Taylor's translation of verse 6:* ". . . and now you can really serve God; not in the old way, mechanically obeying a set of rules, but in the new way, with all of your hearts and minds" (LB).

II. The natural man (vv. 7–13).

A. *In these verses, Paul tells us that if the spiritual man is delivered from the law, then the natural man is doomed by the law.* As a "natural man," Paul discovered that the law of God exposed the hidden nature of sin in his life. The law did this in two ways. First, it showed him his sinful nature (v. 7). He saw, because of the law, a hideous caricature of what he was without God in his life. Second, the law activated his sinful nature (vv. 8–9). Paul is saying that before the law came, there was freedom from an accusing conscience, a kind of "false peace" brought about by his ignorance of sin. The coming of the law changed all of this. Its straight edge revealed the crookedness in his human nature. As the summer sun shines on a vacant lot and warms the soil, it causes the hidden seeds to spring to life, covering the lot with weeds. So the law of God, shining on the human heart, caused the latent seeds of sin to germinate and to reveal themselves.

B. *The law of God also shows us the seriousness of sin.* All sin is against God; thus it demands eternal damnation and condemnation. There are at least fifteen words in the Old Testament for "sin," and they cover the entire spectrum of all possible kinds of wrong attitudes toward God *and* man. There are about as many words in the Greek New Testament also which cover the various facets of sin. When you take all of these words for sin, you have something of an idea of what God thinks about sin in all of its forms.

C. *As we have alredy intimated, we have seen that the law cannot save.* Salvation is alone the glorious prerogative of God's incomparable grace. Paul found, as a sinner, his best efforts to win salvation were totally unavailing. There stood before him a law which was "holy, and just, and good." It was an uncrossable barrier which he could not deal with. The best moral efforts he could muster shriveled up and died before the unrelenting searchlight of God's perfect law.

III. The carnal man (vv. 14–18).

A. *If the spiritual man is delivered from the law by the grace of God, and the natural man is doomed by the law, by the same token, the carnal man is defeated by the law.* Between what the law demands and what the flesh can produce, there is "a great gulf fixed." The temptation of the carnal man (the saved but defeated Christian) is continually to revert to human effort and good works as a means of meriting God's approval.

B. *The word* carnal *describes, then, a Christian who, though saved, is still in bondage to the power of the flesh.* In verses 15–17 Paul shows us the conflict in potentialities which exists in the carnal Christian. There is a "clash" within the carnal man because of the old, Adamic nature and the new nature of God existing side by side.

C. *Taylor translates verse 18:* "I know I am rotten through and through so far as my old sinful nature is concerned. No matter which way I turn I can't make myself do right. I want to but I can't" (LB). Paul describes a conflict within the believer so great that one is almost pulled apart at times. The answer lies only in one's daily submission to the Holy Spirit.

Conclusion. In the last verse of Romans 7, Paul gives us a preview of what is to come in chapter 8. He asks the question in verse 24: "Who shall deliver me . . . ?" And in answer, like a wondrous revelation bursting in upon his discouraged soul, he exclaims, 'O thank God!—He will! through Jesus Christ, the Anointed One, our Lord!" (AMPLIFIED). —*DLJ*

* * *

SUNDAY MORNING, FEBRUARY 27

TITLE: Heart Cry for Revival

TEXT: **"Why hast thou then broken down her hedges, so that all they which pass by the way do pluck her? . . . Return, we beseech thee, O God of hosts: look down from heaven, and behold, and visit this vine" (Ps. 80:12, 14).**

SCRIPTURE READING: **Psalm 80**

HYMNS: **"God of Grace and God of Glory," Fosdick**
"Lord, Send a Revival," McKinney
"Rise Up, O Men of God," Merrill

Offertory Prayer:

Worship the Lord in the beauty of holiness. Give unto the Lord the glory due unto His name. We offer ourselves, our time, our hearts, and our gifts of money to the glory of Your name. Cause Your work to grow and Your church to glow, as we give in Jesus' name. Amen.

Introduction. There is a truth in Psalm 80 that is urgently important to every life. It is a word from God, which will help us to understand events in our times. It will result in a heart cry for revival. New life in the church is related to this heart cry. There are three words that will pinpoint this truth.

I. Hedges.

Verse 12 says, "Why hast thou then broken down her hedges . . . ?"

A. *The powerful place of "hedges."* At the heart of this truth is a biblical understanding about hedges. In the Bible there are hedges about three things: a hedge about a nation (Ps. 80:12; Ezek. 13:5), a hedge about a family (Job 1:10), and a hedge about a person (Hos. 2:6).

God's hedge is His invisible wall of protection that He builds around a nation, family, person, church, and possessions when we are willing and obedient to Him. A hedge was protection for a vineyard and a property marker for the owners.

In the New Testament, Jesus prayed for Peter and in essence built a hedge of protection around him (Luke 22:31–32). He also prayed a prayer of protection for His disciples (John 17:11, 15). Paul prays for those under his spiritual care. Second Corinthians 10:4–5 describes powerful truths for this kind of protection.

B. *The perturbing problem about hedges.* Verse 12 speaks about "broken-down hedges." Something happened to the "hedge" of Israel. They were confronted with enemies like a wild boar is to a vineyard (v. 13).

There are enemies today like "wild boars" running rampant throughout the world, the nation, our own particular area. George Gallup says the United States is suffering a critical moral crisis. Street crime, alcohol and drug abuse, and spiritual illiteracy are confronting the nation. But there is more. An irreverent spirit, sexual immorality, destruction of marriage and the family, teen-age pregnancies, violence, and murders—all threaten America. Something is happening in America. The hedges are breaking down.

Who breaks down the hedges? Verse 12 says it is God who does it. Why does He do this? For three reasons:

1. To bring judgment to His people (Isa. 5:5).
2. To arouse us into spiritual alertness.
3. To call us to confess and forsake our sins. A holy God demands a holy life.

II. Hope.

The second word is *hope*. Is there any hope for the "hedges" to be rebuilt? Yes, there is, if we understand the ways that God builds a "hedge." How does He do this?

A. *He builds a "hedge" through godly people*. Ezekiel 22:30 says, "And I sought for a man . . . before me for the land. . . ." Job was a godly man (Job 1:5). He was "perfect," not without sin but wholeheartedly given to pleasing

God. He was "upright," that is, all his relationships were right—with God, with self, and with others. He "feared God," reverently trusted Him, and "eschewed evil," hated evil and turned away from it. His outward walk was like his inward relationships!

B. *He builds a "hedge" through the Word of God.* Ezekiel 13:1ff. teaches this. Ezekiel was speaking against the prophets of Israel. They had not regained the hedge. They followed their own mind and saw nothing (v. 3). They lacked the vision that the Lord gives to His prophets. This teaches that the hedge is built by the Word of God through true servants of the Lord. As prophets of God preach the Word and lift up God's standard, God's hedge is built around one's life, family, church, city, or nation.

C. *He builds a "hedge" through prayer.* Ezekiel 22:30 says, "And I sought for a man among them, that should make up the hedge, and stand in the gap before me for the land, that I should not destroy it: but I found none." God's hedge is built through intercessory prayer.

Soon after the colonists came to America, the people turned from God, and the nation experienced a moral slump. Greed pervaded the people's lives, churches were poorly attended, and European atheism filled the vacuum.

In New England, some people began to pray for revival. In 1734, in Northhampton, Massachusetts, Jonathan Edwards preached his sermon "Sinners in the Hands of an Angry God"; and in one service hundreds of people repented of their sins and turned to the Lord. Unbelief was diverted, righteous living returned, and in a short time one-sixth of the population was won to Christ. Churches were filled with worshipers.

Again in 1849 revival came in answer to prayer. This has always been the way the Lord has worked. God builds the hedges of protection when we pray!

III. Heart cry.

Upon the awareness of what is happening, there arises out of the heart of the psalmist a heart cry for revival. "Return, we beseech thee . . . look down . . . behold, and visit this vine." Hear the heart cry of those who care, "Lord, visit this vine" (v. 14). Lord, visit this nation! You purposed for it to be blessed. Now You have broken down the hedges that protect it. Lord, visit this vine. Turn us again! This is the heart cry!

Lord, visit Your church! You birthed it. You are building it. It belongs to You. It exists for Your purpose. This is our heart cry for revival and for souls.

Lord, visit our families! Many are suffering. We need help. The hedge is breaking down about our families. Visit our homes with revival!

Lord, visit our lives! Get our attention. We are being overcome with evil. We have sinned. Protection is gone. Lord, visit our lives!

Conclusion. A young ministerial student was preaching in a church one Sunday evening. The elderly pastor had seen some glorious outpourings of the Spirit in his early years. He said longingly that he and his wife had prayed every morning and evening for ten years to see one more mighty moving of the Spirit.

The young student had hardly started preaching when a woman began to weep, and then another and another. Soon the entire congregation was on its knees. In the midst of prayer and weeping, people were finding Christ as Savior, old animosities were being healed, broken families were being united, and new spiritual commitments were being made. The pastor moved slowly down the aisles, saying softly, "He did it one more time."

Lord, visit this vine!

—*TSB*

* * *

SUNDAY EVENING, FEBRUARY 27

TITLE: The Mystery of Pain and Suffering

TEXT: "Do you think that these Galileans were worse sinners than all the other Galileans, because they suffered thus?" (Luke 13:2 RSV).

SCRIPTURE READING: Luke 13:1–5

Introduction. There are some who see no mystery about the problem of suffering. They believe that suffering is the result of an inevitable law that every cause produces an effect. They would reason that suffering is due to some great sin that the sufferer has committed.

The Christian has a problem with suffering that the non-Christian does not have. Christianity proclaims that God is love and that He loves the whole world. If this is true, why does He permit undeserved suffering? If God loves us and if He has all power, then He should protect us from pain and suffering. Some have sought to solve this problem by saying that the person who suffers has been guilty of some sin that has brought the judgment of God upon him. This simplistic solution to a complex question is unsatisfactory and incorrect.

Between our entrance into life and our exit from life, there is pain and suffering on all sides. There are many forms of suffering in the world: physical, mental, emotional, spiritual, visible, invisible, recognized, and unrecognized suffering.

There is much suffering in the world because of natural disasters. Many suffer because of historical events and decisions that were made in the past. Many suffer because of choices made by their ancestors. It must also be recognized that much suffering comes to us because of our personal choices and through the choices of others.

What are the teachings of Jesus about pain and suffering? Does Jesus have any good news for those who suffer?

I. Jesus would insist that we reject the thought that all suffering comes from God.

Jesus lived in a time when men were making false diagnoses of the problems that they confronted in daily life. Because they believed that sin resulted in suffering and that God was a just God who would punish the wicked, they reasoned that all suffering was due to the anger of God. The end result of this incorrect way of thinking served to deprive the believer of the comfort and encouragement that he needed in times of weakness, pain, and insecurity.

The end result of this simple but inaccurate solution for the mystery of suffering served to deprive the sufferer of the help that he so desperately needed when it seemed as if his world had caved in and that the heavens had collapsed upon him.

It is recorded in John 11 that Jesus wept in the presence of sorrow when

Mary and Martha were grief-stricken over the death of their brother Lazarus. We must have faith to believe that He weeps with us when we experience the pain of sorrow. The fact that our Lord ministered to those whose bodies were racked with pain and whose minds were tormented with insecurity should encourage us to believe that He comes to us in the midst of our sufferings. The prophet had proclaimed concerning the suffering of the people of God that God related to them with sympathy and compassion and helpfulness: "In all their affliction he was afflicted, and the angel of his presence saved them; in his love and in his pity he redeemed them; he lifted them up and carried them all the days of old" (Isa. 63:9 RSV). We must reject every suggested solution to the mystery of suffering which deprives us of the benevolent presence and grace of our loving God.

II. Jesus rejected the doctrine that all suffering was due to sin committed by the sufferer.

Jesus lived in a time in which men had a very simple solution to the problem of suffering. They believed that if a person suffered, either he or his parents had sinned. They were concerned about fixing responsibility for suffering.

Jesus categorically denied that suffering can be traced directly to some sin in the life of the sufferer.

Many of us have responded to unexpected and undeserved pain with the question, "What have I done to deserve this?" Often when we witness the undeserved suffering of others, we ask the question, "Why does a good person have to suffer while others are spared?"

To explain the problem of pain as always being the result of some sin that has been committed by the sufferer is inaccurate and contradicts the teachings of Jesus Christ (Luke 13:1–5).

In the Scripture passage under consideration, Jesus calls attention to the fact that some suffering is due to the cruelty of others, while some suffering may be due to the faulty construction of a tower that collapsed.

III. Jesus would have us reject the idea that pain is an illusion.

There are those who beleive that there is no such thing as pain, that it is a mere illusion; and they suggest that we use our minds to eliminate the negative thoughts which produce pain.

A. *It is true that many of our ills are in our minds.* Psychosomatic illness afflicts many people. Much suffering could be eliminated if we would think correctly and eliminate negative and destructive ways of thinking, and instead fill our minds and hearts with positive and affirmative thoughts.

B. *To make pain an illusion is a form of escape from reality that will ultimately disappoint and lead to tragedy.* Many have suffered indescribable pain and anguish because they accepted this inadequate and inaccurate solution to the mystery of pain and suffering.

If one holds to this solution with great rigidity, he could be guilty of murdering those near to him; and it is possible that he may commit suicide, that is, reduce the length of his life by refusing to secure proper medical attention.

IV. Jesus would lead us to reject the idea that present suffering is due to evil done in a previous existence.

In many parts of the world, it is beleived that we have no personal responsibility for the suffering that we endure in this life. Rather, it is believed that suffering and pain in the present is due to a life of evil and selfishness and cruelty in a prior existence before birth into one's present life.

To believe that pain in the present is due to evil done in a previous existence leads to an attitude of fatalism and helplessness.

It is interesting that those who hold to this philosophy of life know nothing about the joy that can be experienced as a result of God's forgiveness.

Conclusion. There is no one simple solution that is always satisfactory regarding the mystery of pain and suffering.

We can be assured that our Father God will not permit pain to come into our lives which we will be unable to endure with His help.

Our Father God is no stranger to suffering. His heart has hurt with the hurt of all mankind.

Our Savior was and is no stranger to suffering.

1. Our Savior suffered the pain of misunderstanding.
2. Our Savior suffered the pain of loneliness.
3. Our Savior suffered the pain of cutting criticism.
4. Our Savior suffered the pain of rejection.
5. Our Savior suffered the pain of public humiliation.
6. Our Savior suffered the pain of crucifixion on a cross.
7. Our Savior suffered the pain of death on a cross.

Because our Savior has experienced pain and suffering, He is able to sympathize with us in whatever life may bring to us (Heb. 2:18).

How can we cope with the mystery of pain and undeserved suffering?

Let us recognize and grasp the truth that God loves us and that He cares and wants to help us.

Let us remember that our Lord Himself has suffered.

Let us respond to His precious promises to be with us even unto the end of the ages.

Let us secure medical services, and let us pray for our physicians and for all of those who give themselves to the healing ministry.

Let us make the most and the best of each day as we live one day at a time.

— *TTC*

* * *

SUGGESTED PREACHING PROGRAM FOR THE MONTH OF MARCH

Sunday Mornings

As we approach Easter, a series of messages regarding the determination of our Lord to face the ordeal of Crucifixion to reveal the love of God for sinners can be helpful to believers and nonbelievers alike. "Going to Jerusalem" is the theme for a series of messages for the Sunday mornings.

Sunday Evenings

"Beneath the Cross of Jesus" is the suggested theme for a series of biographical messages regarding the people who were present when Jesus was dying on the cross. All of us were there as well as these whom we will study. "Were You There When They Crucified My Lord?" would also be a good theme for these messages.

Wednesday Evenings

Continue with the theme "What the Bible Says."

* * *

WEDNESDAY EVENING, MARCH 2

TITLE: What the Bible Says About Things That Accompany Salvation

TEXT: **"But, beloved, we are persuaded better things of you, and things that accompany salvation, though we thus speak" (Heb. 6:9).**

SCRIPTURE READING: **Hebrews 6:9–12**

Introduction. A fallacy that has stopped the spiritual growth of countless Christians is the concept of salvation as a termination point rather than a point of beginning. It is almost as if some people, when they are saved, look back upon that experience and say, "Whew! I got *that* attended to; now I can settle down to the business of living!" And they build a fence around their Christianity and pay periodic visits to it, but by and large they live their lives as *they* want to.

In this Hebrews passage, the author is talking *not* about what *constitutes* salvation; rather he is recalling what *manifests* or demonstrates a genuine salvation experience—both to the individual himself and to those who observe. In gleaning through the Epistle to the Hebrews, one can discover four major accompaniments to one's salvation.

I. First, there is the gift of assurance (Heb. 6:17–20).

A. *Very often a pastor hears someone say: "Pastor, there are times when I seriously doubt that I have ever been saved!"* And the look on the person's face indicates that those are not idle words, for the distress and uncertainty are plainly seen. And usually the person will add: "You see, I don't *feel* the way I used to feel about my faith and my relationship to God." What people who doubt their salvation do not realize is that there are few things in the world more undependable than one's feelings. Therefore, because of the inconsistency of our feelings, Satan delights in attacking us at this point.

B. *In Hebrews 6:17–20, we are taught that the security of our salvation rests exclusively upon the faithfulness of God, not of ourselves.* Two things are underscored in this passage which form the basis for the assurance of one's salvation. First, *the Word of God* (v. 18). One's confidence in a fellow believer may be shattered because of his human weakness. But God's Word never changes. It is alive with the breath of God. Jesus said, "Heaven and earth shall pass away, but my words shall not pass away" (Matt. 24:35). Second, *the mission of Jesus in heaven right now* for the Christian is further assurance that we are eternally secure in the grace of God. For Jesus functions now as our High Priest (v. 20). He is there to intercede for us, to represent us before the Father in heaven.

II. Second, a vital accompaniment to salvation is the awakening of spiritual appetite (Heb. 5:12–14).

A. *In this passage, the writer tells us that* milk *is important for children.* It contains certain ingredients which are necessary to the development of young bodies. It contributes to the growth and development of the bone structure, enabling one to learn to stand erect and walk. But then there comes a time in the growth development when there must be a supplement to the milk diet. The individual needs the strength that comes from *meat.* The milk supplied the calcium for his teeth; now he is equipped to chew the meat. The "meat" represents all of the other foods which a child begins to take into his body after he passes through the stage of requiring milk only.

B. *The spiritual analogy is obvious.* There is that time in the spiritual development of the believer that he must have the "milk" of God's Word. He would choke on the strong "meat" of the Word in the early days of his Christian life. But it is not long until the "milk" of the Word provides the bone structure and the teeth, and he is ready for the "strong meat" of the Word of God.

III. A third thing which accompanies salvation is a longing for association with God's people (Heb. 10:25; 13:7, 17).

A. *Three times in the Hebrews letter "association" is referred to:* first, the writer speaks of "not forsaking the assembling of [yourselves] together," then about "remember[ing] . . . those who spoke to you the word of God" (RSV) and "obey[ing] your leaders . . . [who] are keeping watch over your souls" (RSV). What he is saying is that we are not to stop coming together in Jesus' name. We are to follow the admonishments and exhortations of those whom God has set over us as teachers and shepherds, and we are to show appreciation and thanksgiving for those whom God used to speak to us His Word.

B. *Then, in 13:1, we are told to "Let brotherly love continue."* This cannot be done effectively or consistently unless we assemble together with our brothers and sisters in Christ. This is why the Lord's Day in the Lord's house should be meaningful to the people of God. Not only do we receive strength, but we are provided opportunity to share strength in Christ with each other.

C. *Third, we are told to "strive for peace . . . ,* [avoid] bitterness" (12:14–15). The way some Christians act when they come to God's house is disgraceful, for they sow discord and are hurtful and snobbish. But when Christ is alive and Lord in one's life, there is an attractiveness and a winsomeness which acts as a magnet and draws those who are lonely and confused. It makes the

Christian anxious for the Lord's Day to come, so that he can be in the Lord's house and fellowship with the people of God. "Forsaking the assembling" of ourselves together becomes a symptom of spiritual regression.

IV. A fourth accompaniment to salvation is a determination to adhere, or a refusal to turn loose that which is essential in the growth and development of one's spiritual life (Heb. 4:14; 12:3).

A. *Throughout the Epistle to the Hebrews, the clearest emphasis falls upon* faith—not faith simply as "trust," but rather as a steadfast fidelity and loyalty to what has been known, heard, seen, and experienced of God. It is a quality of faith that *holds fast* (4:14). How tragic that some Christians are like clouds in the sky, driven by the wind first this way and then the other. There is no dependability or stability in their faith.

B. *Then, there is a quality of faith that* persists (12:3). There come those trying times in all of our lives when we feel like "throwing in the towel," giving it all up. But true faith persists; it "keeps on keeping on" even in the face of overwhelming difficulties. The believer may indeed be "down" occasionally; but he must rise again, tenaciously and perseveringly. God gives us strength to do this.

Conclusion. There are other things, surely, which should accompany one's salvation. But these are basic: assurance, appetite, association, and adherence or perseverance. Are these things present and operative in *your* life? What is the state of your spiritual health? Are you failing to grow in the faith because these "accompaniments" to your great and free salvation are dormant and inoperative in your life?

—*DLJ*

* * *

SUNDAY MORNING, MARCH 6

TITLE: Going to Jerusalem

TEXT: "When the days drew near for him to be received up, he set his face to go to Jerusalem" (Luke 9:51 RSV).

SCRIPTURE READING: Luke 9:22–27, 51

HYMNS: "Hail, Thou Once Despised Jesus," Bakewell
"Jesus, I My Cross Have Taken," Lyte
"Living for Jesus," Chrisholm

OFFERTORY PRAYER:

Our Father, we praise You for the gift of life. Your creative power brought us into being and daily sustains us. We thank You for Jesus, who paid the wages of sin and whose resurrection makes possible our victory over death. May You find us walking in His steps, obedient to Your will, and willing even to die if that sacrifice should be needed. Accept our gifts as an expression of our love for the gift of Christ, our Savior and Lord. In His name we pray. Amen.

Introduction. Each year thousands of pilgrims make their way to Israel and the holy city of Jerusalem. For many it is the fulfillment of a lifetime to say, "I walked today where Jesus walked." A journey to Jerusalem can be a rewarding travel experience. Today we begin a *spiritual* journey to Jerusalem, walking with Jesus through those crucial hours surrounding the Crucifixion and Resurrection. Observe carefully the individuals on the journey—we shall see ourselves!

An author's repeated use of a phrase may be his intention to convey something special. The Gospel of Luke is one of the best-written books in the New Testament, and Luke uses a favorite phrase several times in chapters 9–20: going to Jerusalem (9:51; 13:22; 17:11; 18:31; 19:28). This is more than a literary device. Luke notes a decisive turn in the ministry of Jesus. At Jerusalem God's chosen people will have their hour of decision. Jesus' journey gives meaning to the Easter event and our response to God's work in Christ.

I. An act of courage.

A. *Jerusalem—the hot spot.* Jerusalem was the center of Jewish life and religion. As such it was the center of growing animosity to this itinerant Nazarene. The decision to "set his face to go to Jerusalem" was a deliberate choice to enter the storm. Jesus demonstrated true courage. On an earlier occasion when Jesus announced His intention to go to Bethany and the home of Lazarus, the disciples warned Him, "Rabbi, the Jews were but now seeking to stone you, and are you going there again?" Jesus replied, "If any one walks in the day, he does not stumble" (John 11:8–9). He knew what He was facing. Jesus' journey to Jerusalem was not the irresponsible action of a blind fanatic. He knew the risks yet faced them courageously. Christian commitment does not shrink from involvement in the hot spot.

B. *Our example.* Jesus is the continuing example and inspiration for us to face life and its difficulties with courage. "Let us run with perseverance the race that is set before us, looking to Jesus the pioneer and perfecter of our faith, who for the joy that was set before him endured the cross, despising the shame, and is seated at the right hand of the throne of God" (Heb. 12:1c–2).

II. Commitment to the will of God.

A. *Doing the Father's will.* The journey to Jerusalem was part of Jesus' desire to do the Father's will. At age thirteen this desire was expressed: "Did you not know that I must be in my Father's house?" (Luke 2:49). His prayer in the garden sumarized His entire life: ". . . not my will, but thine, be done" (Luke 22:42). Dwight L. Moody once heard a preacher declare the world had yet to see what God could do with a person completely dedicated to His will. Moody determined to be such a person—and the world has felt the impact. What could be done through us if we had a similar commitment to do God's will?

B. *A willing offering.* Some view the will of God as a decision forced on us. God did not send Jesus to the cross. The content of His message and the nature of His person made it inevitable. Sin and holiness conflict; good men have a hard time in this world. Jesus knew this but still remained willing to give Himself. Isaiah prophesied: ". . . he makes himself an offering for sin" (Isa. 53:10). The word *offering* comes from Leviticus and the sacrificial system. Christ is our sin offering. He freely gave Himself for our sins to free us from sin and death. It was written of Christ, "Lo, I have come to do thy will. . . . And by that will we have been sanctified through the offering of the body of Jesus Christ once for all" (Heb. 10:9–10).

III. Lose life to find life.

A. *Take up the cross.* Christ's offering brought life; and in order to possess that life, we must offer our lives. In a few weeks we will celebrate the event which climaxed Christ's journey to Jerusalem. Do not forget that the Crucifixion preceded the Resurrection. The discovery of life comes in the loss of life. We must do God's will and give our lives. Jesus said, "If any man would come after me, let him deny himself and take up his cross and follow me" (Matt. 16:24). There can be no life without that courageous decision.

B. *Lent—a journey to Jerusalem.* We are now in the midst of Lent, the forty days preceding Easter. Say "Lent" to some people and they think of a speck of dust on clothes. For others these are days of spiritual preparation, renewal, and dedication. Lent corresponds to Christ's journey to Jerusalem. On His way to Jerusalem Christ tried to lead the disciples into God's will and enable them to give themselves. The Master Teacher taught crucial lessons about values and motives.

Conclusion. Will you join me on that kind of pilgrimage? A journey to know God's will and to do it. Will you make the commitment to follow Him wherever He leads, even into the hottest spot? You need not fast (although some need to) but do put Jesus first. Set your face toward Jerusalem, remembering the words of Him who goes before you: "Whoever would save his life will lose it, and whoever loses his life for my sake will find it." —*BW*

* * *

SUNDAY EVENING, MARCH 6

TITLE: The Face of Fortune: Barabbas

TEXT: "Now at that feast the governor was wont to release unto the people a prisoner, whom they would. . . . Then released he Barabbas unto them: and when he had scourged Jesus, he delivered him to be crucified" (Matt. 27:15, 26).

SCRIPTURE READING: Matthew 27:15–26

Introduction. Pilate presented Barabbas to the crowd as an alternative. By doing this he sought to escape his responsibility in the ordeal. His training in Roman justice made it difficult for him to condemn an innocent man.

The offer of Pilate takes on special significance if both of these men had the same name. Many scholars believe that the full name of Barabbas was Jesus Barabbas. There is some manuscript evidence for this. So, the crowd had to choose between Jesus of Nazareth and Jesus Barabbas.

When considered as an individual, the face of Barabbas is truly the face of good fortune. Never did a better thing happen to a man on the day of his expected death. Jesus of Nazareth probably died on the cross that had been prepared for Jesus Barabbas. When the Sabbath came, Jesus was lying dead in the tomb of Joseph, and Barabbas was sleeping in his own bed. This graphically sets forth the central truth of the gospel, "Christ died for us."

I. An undeserved fortune.

Barabbas was worthy of death. Justice had finally caught up with him. But are we not all deserving of death when we are measured by God's perfect standard of righteousness?

A. *Because of wasted opportunities.*

"Barabbas" means "son of a father." This probably indicates that he was the son of a rabbi. His full name then would have been Jesus, the Son of the Rabbi. Growing up in the home of a rabbi would give him the opportunity to know the things of God. It would bring many special opportunities spiritually. But he had failed to take advantage of the opportunities.

Does that sound like your story? You may not have grown up in a minister's home, but God has graced you with special opportunities.

B. *Because of the broken law.*

Barabbas had broken the law of man and the law of God. He had been a terrorist against the Roman government. He was a devoted member of the Zealots, who were committed to the overthrow of Roman rule. In the process of pursuing this goal, he had broken many of the laws of God.

He had been guilty of breaking almost all of the second table of the Ten Commandments. Disobedience to parents, murder, stealing, lying, and covet-eousness were characteristics of his life.

Surely, if Jesus was going to die in the place of someone, it would not be someone like Barabbas. But in the providence of God, it was for such an undeserving one so that the great truth of grace in the gospel might be revealed. "But God commendeth his love toward us, in that, while we were yet sinners, Christ died for us" (Rom. 5:8). He died for sinners!

II. An unsought fortune.

A. *For Barabbas.*

As Barabbas lay in his cell awaiting his crucifixion, it never occurred to him to ask someone to take his place. His assumption was that his crimes had caught up with him. No one was more surprised than Barabbas with the outcome.

He must have first received the news of his release with some skepticism. He may even have thought it to be a prank by the soldiers. But it was true. Without any request from Barabbas, without an appeal from his broken-hearted parents, Jesus Christ died in the place of Barabbas.

B. *For the sinner.*

Jesus Christ did not die for us in response to any appeal on our part. Indeed, instead of sinners asking Him to bear their sins to the cross, they were busy rejecting Him. "He came unto his own, and his own received him not" (John 1:11). The only explanation that can be found for this great deed is in His love. He died for us because He wanted to.

III. The unrestricted fortune.

A. *The freedom of Barabbas.*

All Barabbas had to do was walk out of the jail, and he was a free man. Since Jesus was dying in his place by the decree of Pilate, the Roman law had no claim on him. His debt to society was paid.

It must have taken Barabbas a good while to realize what had really happened. He may have continued to hide every time he saw a Roman soldier coming. He may still have expected some word that it was not really true. But it was! Barabbas had the good fortune to receive unrestricted freedom at the expense of another man.

B. *Freedom through the gospel.*

Forgiveness must be God's greatest gift to man. It involves God's canceling all of the debt of our sin. But we must never forget that God is free to cancel the debt only because Christ paid it. "He himself bore our sins in his body on the tree, so that we might die to sin and live to righteousness. By his wounds you have been healed" (1 Peter 2:24 RSV). "In whom we have redemption through his blood, the forgiveness of sins" (Eph. 1:7).

This means that we can know freedom from condemnation, freedom from guilt, freedom from the stains of sin—all through the death of Jesus Christ. No wonder Paul exclaimed, "God forbid that I should glory, save in the cross of our Lord Jesus Christ . . ." (Gal. 6:14).

Conclusion. Barabbas accepted the death of Jesus in his place. He gladly walked out of the jail to allow Jesus to die in his palce. I do not know whether it ever meant anything more to him or not. It should surely mean more to us.

Dr. Charles Allen shares a story from William L. Stidger about a young lad he had baptized as a baby. The boy grew up, and when World War II began, he joined the Navy. One night his ship came into Boston, and the lad visited his former pastor and friend. During their visit together, Dr. Stidger said, "Bill, tell me the most exciting experience you have had thus far." The boy seemed to hesitate. It wasn't that he had difficulty in selecting the most exciting experience. Rather, the experience he had in mind was so wonderful and sacred that he had difficulty in putting it into words.

He was the captain of a large transport and, along with a convoy, was making his way across the Atlantic. One day an enemy submarine rose in the sea close by. He saw the white mark of the torpedo, coming directly toward his transport loaded with hundreds of boys. He had no time to change course. Through the loudspeaker he shouted, "Boys, this is it!"

Nearby was a little escorting destroyer. The captain of the destroyer also saw the submarine and torpedo. Without a moment's hesitation, he gave the order, "Full speed ahead!" Into the path of the torpedo the tiny destroyer went and took the full impact of the deadly missile midship. The destroyer was blown apart and quickly sank; every man of the crew was lost.

For a long time the boy remained silent. Then he looked at his beloved pastor and said, "Dr. Stidger, the skipper of that destroyer was my best friend." Again he was quiet awhile, then slowly, he said, "You know there is a verse in the Bible which has special meaning for me now. It is, 'Greater love hath no man than this, that a man lay down his life for his friends.'"

O, but we were not His friends when Christ lay down His life for us. We were His enemies, yet He took our place upon the cross. Will you not receive such a One as your Savior and Lord tonight? —*DLL*

* * *

WEDNESDAY EVENING, MARCH 9

TITLE: What the Bible Says About Prayer

TEXT: "And when you pray" (Matt. 6:5 RSV).

SCRIPTURE READING: Matthew 6:5–13

Introduction. What *is* prayer? To say that prayer is simply "communication with God" is an oversimplification. Prayer is the sincere desire of the soul of man expressed toward God. Prayer is the means whereby the creature establishes an intimacy with the Creator. Prayer creates an awareness of God's constant nearness to His people.

Prayer is also the means whereby the unbeliever, recognizing his sinfulness and need for salvation, reaches out by faith to receive God's gift of eternal life. Prayer is the expression of praise to God, as well as the medium through which petitions are made on behalf of human need.

Prayer is dealt with, described, and illustrated throughout the Bible. The greatest and most profound demonstration of prayer is depicted in the earthly life of Jesus, who is often portrayed praying to His heavenly Father.

I. General requirements for effective prayer.

A. *A forgiving spirit* (Matt. 6:14). Why is forgiveness on man's part so difficult? Man's nature is to be retaliatory, to seek vengeance. To truly forgive as Christ taught us is to relinquish all tendencies to "get even" with those who have wronged us. An unforgiving spirit overwhelms a person and creates a barrier which makes it impossible for God's forgiveness to enter. Actually, *our* forgiveness toward others is but the *outgoing* of God's forgiveness expressed toward *us*—like the ebb tide!

B. *Simplicity* (Matt. 6:5–6). Prayer, for the Pharisees, was a performance for the sake of those around them. These words of Jesus do not constitute an indictment against public prayer, *if* we realize that public prayer should be *one* of God's children leading as *each* heart silently joins in the prayer, affirming and enforcing the prayer being prayed audibly. "Entering the closet" may be more symbolism than a literal act, suggesting the closing out of the interfering world while one communicates with God. This can be done anywhere, even in the midst of the busy marketplace.

C. *Humility and repentance* (Luke 18:10–14). Both the Pharisee and the publican (or tax collector) in this story could represent lost men. The publican prayed the only prayer that God can hear from the sinner—a prayer of confession, admission of sin, a cry for mercy. The prayer of the Pharisee describes the person who considers himself "good" and therefore a credit to God and to His kingdom. This person considers his good works the price of his admission into the kingdom of God.

D. *Unity of believers* (Matt. 18:19–20). The explanation of this apparent "blank check" from God is in verse 20. The realization and recognition of God's presence *with* us will position our prayer requests within His will. Prayer is *never* like "rubbing an Aladin's lamp" in order to bring forth some "divine genie" to do our bidding. Prayer, in its petitionary nature, is primarily seeking the will of the heavenly Father.

E. *Intensity* (Matt. 7:7–11). Again, the thrust of this prayer promise is concerning the finding of God's will. Never is it necessary to beg of cajole God. It is our slowness of heart and spiritual immaturity that make it necessary for us to spend time searching for His will. But *as* we "ask, seek, and knock," the very exercise of our faith has a cleansing and nourishing effect on us, preparing us to receive the answer in accord with God's will, and not with our wishes.

F. *Unceasingly* (1 Thess. 5:17). "Pray without ceasing." Let your communication line remain open constantly between you and God. A Christian's attitude of life should be an expression of communication with God. This tends to create a beautiful and cherished "naturalness" about one's prayer life.

II. Personal requirements for effective prayer.

A. *Purity of heart* (Pss. 24:3–5; 66:18–19). God, through the ministry of the indwelling Holy Spirit, reveals sin when it exists in the lives of His people. If, after that, we do not deal with it, then our prayers are aborted. "The hill of the Lord" and "his holy place" describe the experience of personal confrontation of communication with God. "Clean hands" would suggest that my actions are open for God to see; and "a pure heart" would indicate that all sin is confessed.

B. *Faith* (Matt. 21:22). Sadly, every Christian who "prays" does not believe in his heart that God answers prayer. To truly believe with the intensity of faith Jesus describes requires the cultivation of the gift of faith God gives to each believer in embryonic form.

C. *In Christ's name* (John 14:13). "And whatsoever ye shall ask in my name, that will I do. . . ." This is not just an "evangelical formula" we use to close our prayers. It is a recognition that in Christ "all things consist"—that is, all good things have their source in Him. "His name" represents all that He is.

D. *According to God's will* (1 John 5:14). "And this is the confidence that we have in him, that, if we ask anything according to his will, he heareth us." This, indeed, is the ultimate secret to effective prayer.

III. The constituent parts of prayer.

A. *Adoration* (Ps. 103). What does adoration of God do for one? It decimates self and exalts God.

B. *Confession* (1 John 1:9). Confession of sin is the key which opens the door to a continuing, unbroken fellowship with God.

C. *Thanksgiving* (Phil. 4:6). The sin of ingratitude is perhaps the most common sin among Christians. Too often we take God for granted.

D. *Supplication* (1 Tim. 2:1–3). "Supplication" describes a humble and earnest request before God.

E. *Intercession* (James 5:15). There are many kinds of "sickness" (which means "unwholeness"). We are to intercede for those who are sick, for one can be so far from God that he cannot pray for himself.

Conclusion. Prayer should and *must* be an integral part of every Christian's life. We should engage in secret (private) prayer (Matt. 6:6); in family prayer (Acts 10:2, 30); in group prayer (Matt. 18:20); and in public prayer (1 Cor. 14:14–17).

— *DLJ*

SUNDAY MORNING, MARCH 13

TITLE: Consequences of Bad Religion

TEXT: "So the chief priests and the Pharisees gathered the council, and said, 'what are we to do?' . . . So from that day on they took counsel how to put him to death" (John 11:47, 53 RSV).

SCRIPTURE READING: John 11:45–53

HYMNS: "Great Redeemer, We Adore Thee," Harris
"I Stand Amazed in the Presence," Gabriel
"Am I a Soldier of the Cross?" Watts

OFFERTORY PRAYER:

Our heavenly Father, we thank You for the promise of Your presence where two or three are gathered in Your name. We ask Your blessings on our worship this day in the desire that a new encounter with You will empower us for greater service. Forgive us of all that makes our worship a religious performance rather than a spiritual fellowship. Liberate us from an inordinate attachment to religious tradition so that we can be responsive to the free work of the Spirit. We are grateful for the opportunity to give in support of Your mission as it is fulfilled through this fellowship. We pray that our gifts are a true indication of greater sacrifice. Confront us again with the pattern of the Macedonians who "first gave themselves." In Jesus' name we pray. Amen.

Introduction. Christ died during Passover week in Jerusalem. It was the high holy week of the year for the Jewish people. Jerusalem was crowded with religious pilgrims. It does not take much reading of the gospel narratives to realize Jesus was crucified by religious people. The voices that shouted "Crucify Him!" had frequently prayed in the temple. The Cross is an example of the evil which can be accomplished by bad religion.

I. Religion and the Cross.

A. *Jerusalem—the Holy City.* Mark records an impressive list of religious leaders who participated in the crucifixion of Christ. The Sadducees were the priestly party whose work and interest focused on the temple. They loved a smooth, formal worship service; pomp and ritual was their thing. The Pharisees were the legalists whose pride in keeping the fine points of the law separated them from "sinners." The scribes interpreted and preserved the law. The chief priests officiated at worship and spoke the words of forgiveness. Completing the group were the elders—community leaders and various rulers. All of these leaders mingled with a crowd of zealous Jews, many of whom journeyed many miles for the annual Exodus deliverance celebration.

It was not the down-and-out group who crucified Jesus. The up-and-in crowd did it—honest, hard-working, religious people.

B. *The Jerusalem—Rome connection.* The ease with which these religious leaders became a party to evil was partly a result of an unhealthy connection between them and the state. The Romans controlled the Sanhedrin; the High Priest was a Roman appointee who acted at the bidding of the Roman officials.

One of the chief priests expressed their dilemma: "What are we to do? . . . If we let him go on thus, every one will believe in him, and the Romans will come and destroy both our holy place and our nation" (John 11:47–48).

The equivalent of the church had kneeled before the state. God was no longer acknowledged as supreme authority. The alliance never paid off. The power with whom they cooperated turned on them in 70 A.D. and destroyed Jerusalem and the temple. Only evil can come from an unhealthy connection between church and state. A free church in a free state is the ideal. The church is to exercise her prophetic role and call the state to fulfill her duty to responsibly use authority granted by God.

Out of self-interest Caiaphas said it was better for Jesus to die for the nation than for the entire nation to perish (v. 50). Jesus did die for the nation but for an entirely different reason. "Righteousness exalts a nation, but sin is a reproach to any people" (Prov. 14:34). Only through the death of Christ can a nation have the reproach of sin replaced by the righteousness of God.

II. Lost concern for people.

A. *People or place.* The resurrection of Lazarus was the immediate experience which precipitated this religious conspiracy. Some believed while others "went to the Pharisees" (John 11:46). New life for the dead was not as important as preserving "our holy place." Stones and mortar took priority over sin and mortality. The people whom God called to be "a light to the nations" had replaced their world vision with concern for "our nation." Religion is an evil force when it becomes an institutional caretaker and loses concern for people. Missionary Billie Pate said, "The church must translate its heart from the empty cavity of brick and mortar to the throbbing marketplace of human need. Too long it has lifted the cup of cold water to its own lips."

B. *Rules or right.* One Sabbath day Jesus entered the synagogue and a man with a withered hand was among the worshipers. The religious authorities "watched him, to see whether he would heal him on the sabbath, so that they might accuse him" (Mark 3:2). The Lord is in the business of putting things right; religious rules are of secondary importance. Evil religion is concerned for the status quo. The "Old Time Religion" which some yearn for may be only an emotional, actionless, and archaic relationship to God which is foreign to the abundant life Jesus imparts.

III. Something greater than religion.

Jesus once answered the criticism of the Pharisees by declaring: "I tell you, something greater than the temple is here" (Matt. 12:6). Heaven will have "no temple in the city, for its temple is the Lord God the Almighty and the Lamb" (Rev. 21:22). Someone said, "One man's religion is another man's burden." Religion had become a burden in Jesus' day. The religion of the Pharisees brought despair and futility. Christ offered joy, hope, life. He offered Himself instead of a religion. He calls all to accept Him rather than a creed or dead religion. Caiaphas and his religious conspirators thought they had put an end to the Nazarene. Instead his death let life loose for all the world.

German pastor Martin Niemöller tells of "the sermon of the gallows: There was in front of my cell window in the Dachau concentration camp a gallows, and I often had to pray for those who were hanged on it, poor souls. This gallows put a question to me: What will happen when one day they will put *you* to this test and lay the rope around *your* neck? Will you then with your last breath cry out, 'You criminals, you think you are right in executing me as a criminal, but there is a living God in heaven, and he will show you!''? And then the second question followed: What do you think would have happened if Jesus had died that way, cursing his enemies and murderers? You know the answer: Then you would be rid of him; for there then would be no gospel, no good tidings of great joy, no salvation, no hope! Not for anyone, not for you! But—thank God—he, Jesus, died otherwise, differently, not cursing his murderers, but praying on their behalf: 'Father, forgive them; they know not what they do!' They *could not* get rid of him, for he held on and kept them in his forgiving love; and his Father heard his prayer and was well pleased with his Son. So there *was* no escape. This death worked too well—and there *is* no escape—this death marks his final victory: 'I have overcome the world!' How? By overcoming hatred with love, evil with doing good!'' (Clyde Fant, Jr. and William Pinson, Jr., eds. *20 Centuries of Great Preaching,* Vol. X [Waco: Word Books, 1971], p. 249).

Conclusion. Look at the Cross. Religious people did it! The right lost out to rigid rules; self-interest prevailed over service to others; religion took the place of a relationship with God. Evil was the result, but Jesus triumphed over the evil and lives. To all who receive Him comes faith that conquers and changes the world, putting good in the place of evil. —*BW*

* * *

SUNDAY EVENING, MARCH 13

TITLE: The Face of Favor: Simon of Cyrene

TEXT: ''And they compel one Simon a Cyrenian, who passed by, coming out of the country, the father of Alexander and Rufus, to bear his cross'' (Mark 15:21).

SCRIPTURE READING: Mark 15:15–25

Introduction. ''Were you there when they crucified my Lord?'' Simon of Cyrene was. As you study the faces beneath the cross you will discover the face of this favored man. At first he was there unwillingly, but in time he would be grateful for the favor. He carried the cross of Jesus to the place of crucifixion.

This Simon was born into a dedicated Jewish home in the North African city of Cyrene. His parents expressed their faith at his birth by giving him the name of Simon. Simon was one of the famous sons of Jacob the partriarch.

As he grew into manhood, Simon dreamed of going to the Holy City of Jerusalem to observe a Passover. Such a pilgrimage was the aspiration of all the faithful Hebrew people scattered across the world. Finally, the dream of Simon of Cyrene was realized. His heart beat wildly with excitement as he entered the Holy City for the first time. When he arrived in Jerusalem, he found the city greatly disturbed by rumors. Everyone was talking about the Teacher from Galilee. There was a sharp division among the people over Him. Some felt certain that He was the long-awaited Messiah, but others considered Him a false prophet. There were reports that the leaders of the people were plotting His death.

On the day of the great Passover, Simon came upon a strange spectacle as he entered the city. He saw a noisy crowd clustered around a band of soldiers. In the midst of the soldiers was an obviously weary man bearing a Roman cross. Most of the crowd was heckling the condemned man. The soldiers were prodding Him to hasten His step . . . His steps were just too slow. To any observer it was obvious that the man was about to fall beneath the weight of the cross. When he saw what was happening, Simon decided not to get involved and to just pass by.

Just then the soldiers decided that they had had enough of the slow pace of the tired criminal. They wanted to get their assignment over with. They looked around for someone to carry the cross, and their eyes fell on Simon. One of them grabbed Simon. "You!" he growled. "You take this cross out to the hill." Because he was a Jewish man, Simon was powerless to refuse. The Roman soldier had the power to conscript any non-Roman any time he pleased. Reluctantly and with a great sense of embarrassment, Simon shouldered the cross and followed the soldiers to Golgotha.

It might have been the outcry of the women that caused Simon to take a second look at the condemned man. Somewhere along the way he became aware that he was bearing the cross of Jesus of Nazareth.

It is easy for us to see that the soldiers unknowingly bestowed a real favor on Simon. Any of us who know Him would have been glad to carry the cross. Yet, in a real sense the opportunity to bear His cross is always with us. The cross symbolized all of the shame and reproach attending the life and death of our Lord. The cross was what it cost our Lord to do the will of His Father. If we choose to walk in His ways, we too will bear the cross. This event changed the life of Simon forever. What a favored man!

I. The favor of cross-bearing may be hidden.

No doubt Simon saw nothing good in the ordeal at first. At best, he viewed it as a nuisance and inconvenience. Bearing the cross took time away from other activities he had planned for this special day. He had not planned on such an interruption.

Probably his resentment went even deeper. He must have felt a deep surge of resentment which he had to endure silently. Being treated like a common slave on what was to be the greatest day of his life was just too much. Would some of the people think that he was a disciple of Jesus, or might someone think that it was his cross? What if he met one of his friends on the way? Cross-bearing never seems to be a favor at first.

What was your first reaction to cross-bearing? Were you surprised that others would treat you in such a manner simply because you were a Christian? How could anyone question your motives and accuse you so wrongly? Jesus knew that this would be a problem for His disciples, so He gave thorough and frequent instructions on the matter. He instructed His disciples to rejoice whenever they bore the shame of the cross.

The favor is the reason for the joy. The favor may be hidden to the natural eye, but it is seen by those who walk in the Spirit. The apostle Paul describes such suffering as a "gift." It is a favor from the Lord to be able to suffer shame with Him.

II. The favor of cross-bearing should be acknowledged.

So much is implied in the New Testament about this man Simon of Cyrene. We must allow our "sanctified" imagination to fill in the details.

A. *In public commitment*. We are not told when Simon actually became a disciple of Jesus. The fact that his name is given here can be taken as proof that the story of his conversion to Jesus Christ must have circulated widely among the early Christians.

It probably happened on the Day of Pentecost. Luke reports that men from Cyrene were among the three thousand converts that day. The manner in which Jesus died must have impressed Simon. Jesus had a remarkable look of peace on His face throughout the ordeal. There was absolutely no evidence of fear. The only time He said anything, it was either to pray to God or to help someone. He never appealed to the soldiers for mercy nor accused them of injustice. Then the report of His resurrection had been circulating throughout the city. Simon had been thinking about the Man and His death for fifty days. As he heard Simon Peter, a disciple who had faltered during the ordeal because of fear, declaring boldly that this same Jesus is both Lord and Christ, it was too much. There was a compulsion in the heart of Simon that made him believe. He stepped out from the crowd and willingly accepted baptism in water at the hand of one of the apostles. This was a public acknowledgment that bearing the cross was a favor. He was ready and willing to bear any shame for this Jesus.

B. *In active service*. Simon of Cyrene translated this public commitment into active service. It is probable that he is the Simon who became a leader in the great missionary movement in Antioch. He continued his identification with Jesus in aggressively seeking to make disciples for Him.

Are you holding back from this public identification with Jesus Christ? Have you been afraid of the consequences? Do you consider the potential cost too high? Simon had no choice the first time he was identified with Him, but what he learned about Jesus made him a willing cross-bearer! He learned that it is truly a privilege to bear His cross. You, too, should make a public acknowledgment.

III. The favor of cross-bearing can be shared.

Simon of Cyrene led his two sons to be cross-bearing Christians. He shared the privilege with them. We are not given the details, but we are given the names of Alexander and Rufus. The inclusion of their names indicates that they had become well known among the early Christians.

The Gospel of Mark was written to be used as a gospel tract in the city of Rome. When Paul wrote a letter to the Roman church, he sent greetings to Rufus and his beloved mother (Rom. 16:13). Could his relationship to Rufus and his mother date back to Paul's ministry with the church in Antioch? There is a tradition that Rufus became an effective church leader and that his brother Alexander suffered martyrdom for the cause of Christ. And it all began with Simon bearing the cross.

At first, it seemed like the worst thing that could ever happen to him, but it became life's greatest blessing. It changed his life and the life of his family. It was truly a favor.

If you bear the cross of Christ, you will influence others. Would it not be wonderful to influence your own sons and daughters to bear their cross after Christ?

Conclusion. We sing "Must Jesus bear the cross alone and all the world go free? No, there is a cross for everyone, and there is a cross for me." Dr. Broadus says that the original version of the hymn read, "Must Simon bear the cross alone, and other saints go free? Each saint of thine shall find his own, and there is one for me.'' Surely, the hymn writer says things as they are. There is a place beneath the cross for me.

You find this place of favor willingly. The cross will not be forced on you. You must make a commitment of life to Jesus Christ publicly and continuously. You must be willing to bear any shame or suffer any loss in His service. Will you join Simon of Cyrene beneath the cross? —*DLL*

* * *

WEDNESDAY EVENING, MARCH 16

TITLE: What the Bible Says About Vengeance

TEXT: **''Not . . . seven times, but seventy times seven'' (Matt. 18:22 RSV).**

SCRIPTURE READING: **Matthew 18:21–22**

Introduction. Peter's question, ''How often shall my brother sin against me, and I forgive him? As many as seven times?'' and our Lord's answer, ''Not seven times, but seventy times seven'' reflect man's struggle with the problem of vengeance. Because man's nature is to be independent, he finds that it is an instinctive reaction from within to fight back, to lash out at those whom he feels have infringed upon his ''rights.''

Jesus, of course, had a great deal to say about this in the Sermon on the Mount, radiating from His basic and startling command, ''Love your enemies!'' That was a totally unheard-of attitude toward one's enemies, even among the most religious in Judaism. The exhortation of the rabbis was rather, ''Love your friends and *hate* your enemies.''

The apostle Paul, then, expanded on Jesus' theme in Romans 12:14–21. In rapid-fire succession he provided a list of exhortations which deal, both directly and indirectly, with a Christian's attitude toward vengeance.

I. First, ''Bless them which persecute you: Bless, and curse not'' (Rom. 12:14).

A. *Taylor translates this verse, ''If someone mistreats you . . . , don't curse him; pray that God will bless him.''* This is the Christian principle of ''heaping coals of fire upon another's head.'' This is the true spirit of Christianity. On the cross, Jesus prayed for those who were crucifying Him. In so doing, He demonstrated the proper attitude of a Christian toward his enemies.

B. *To despise or retaliate against those who despitefully use us is to push them farther away from God.* It is more likely that we will win them to faith in Christ—or if they are Christians, to a repentance of their wrong-doing—if we disarm them with our love rather than castigate them with our vengeance.

II. Second, ''Rejoice with them that do rejoice, and weep with them that weep'' (v. 15).

A. *What is the principle demonstrated in this exhortation?* It is all ''giving out.'' When something good happens to your fellow Christian, do you truly enter into his joy, or is there a tinge of jealousy because that good thing did not happen to *you?*

B. *"Weep with the weeping ones."* Are you able to feel deeply and meaningfully with another in his sorrow? Or are you inclined to pass judgment on him with the flippant remark, "Well, he got what he deserved!" To truly "weep with the weeping ones" in the Christian sense means to enter into their sorrow, to empathize with them. Jesus did this when He wept at the graveside of Lazarus, though he knew that in a few moments He would turn that scene of sorrow into joy.

III. Third, "Be of the same mind one toward another. . . . Condescend to men of low estate" (v. 16).

A. *Paul is not saying that we should be uniform, or that we must agree with others in every respect.* Rather, he is saying that we must make allowances for one another. We are not to sacrifice the harmony and good spirit of the body of Christ just to win a point. This kind of stubbornness is most often the result of pride.

B. *The word* condescend *in this verse does not mean to "look down upon," as it has largely come to mean in our modern usage.* Rather, it means, literally, "to be carried away with." It suggests that we are to deliberately seek out the lowly and the meek. In so doing, we deal a death blow to sinful pride in our lives and in our attitudes.

IV. In verses 17–21, Paul has marked out for us four distinct methods by which we can accomplish victory over vengeance.

A. *First, "Recompense to no man evil for evil"* (v. 17a). In other words, "never return injury for injury." To retaliate is a part of unregenerate human nature. To turn the other cheek and to reward good for evil is divine.

B. *Second, "Provide things honest in the sight of all men"* (v. 17b). Goodspeed translates it, "See that you are above reproach in the eyes of everyone." The Christian is to be scrupulously honest in all of his dealings with his fellowman. Nothing will provide more "ready ammunition" for the unbeliever in his attacks against the Christian faith than inconsistency or questionable principles in the lives of Christians whom he observes.

C. *Third, "If it be possible, as much as lieth in you, live peaceably with all men"* (v. 18). Paul was a realist; he knew from personal experience that the gospel would be resisted with great violence wherever it was preached with power. Whereas it is not always possible to live peaceably with all men, the *initiative* in disturbing the peace or disrupting relationships with others should never lie with the Christian whose life is in tune with his Lord.

D. *Finally, in verses 19–21, Paul sets out his fourth principle: opposition, hatred, and persecution are to be repaid with good.* One of human nature's greatest temptations is to "pay back"—to "get even" with that person who has wronged us. This is not the way Christ taught His followers.

Conclusion. It is not necessary for the Christian to avenge himself because he belongs to God, and God is going to protect His own property! Instead, we are to love our enemies—not just with our words, but with our *deeds*. We are to actively express the Christian attitude of concern and "agape" love toward them.

Nowhere did Jesus promise us that the world would be kind to us. On the contrary, He said, "In the world ye shall have tribulation." But quickly He

added, "But be of good cheer; I have overcome the world" (John 16:33). Only in His strength can we overcome these unchristian attitudes which issue forth in acts of vengeance.
—*DLJ*

* * *

SUNDAY MORNING, MARCH 20

TITLE: Keeping Warm At the Fire of the Enemy

TEXT: **"Peter followed at a distance; and when they had kindled a fire in the middle of the courtyard and sat down together, Peter sat among them" (Luke 22:54b–55 RSV).**

SCRIPTURE READING: **Luke 22:31–34, 54–62**

HYMNS: **"Stand Up, and Bless the Lord," Montgomery**
"In the Hour of Trial," Montgomery
"Jesus, and Shall It Ever Be," Grigg

OFFERTORY PRAYER:

Loving Father, we are thankful for every blessing of life. We thank You for health and strength; we are grateful for meaningful work, and praise Your name for the love of family and friends. We acknowledge that every good and perfect gift comes from You. Forgive us for unfaithful stewardship of our relationships and our possessions. Open our eyes to the needs of others and especially those without Christ. We offer these gifts out of our abundance to send the gospel to others. May the glory of the Lord fill this house of worship today and send us forth with gladness. In Jesus' name we pray. Amen.

Introduction. A spiritual defeat in the life of an apparently strong Christian usually elicits the comment: "I would have expected that to happen to anyone but him." Peter's denial while keeping warm at the enemy's fire creates a similar surprise. Peter was such a strong individual with qualities that make a great leader and dynamic Christian.

I. Peter: a person of strength.

A. *Strength of leadership.* Whenever the disciples are listed, Peter's name comes first. This surely reflects the disciples' view of his leadership. Peter was one of the inner circle of disciples privileged to share in special experiences with Jesus, such as the Transfiguration. On the Day of Pentecost it was Peter who stood to preach.

B. *Strength of spirit.* Peter possessed no timid spirit. He was a bold spiritual adventurer. Once he tried to walk on water, and later he ran to the tomb.

C. *Strength of body.* As a fisherman his muscles were developed by casting large nets and rowing boats. He showed his physical strength in the garden—strong enough to take on the entire mob.

In spite of all these qualities, Peter denied the Lord. "Therefore let any one who thinks that he stands take heed lest he fall" (1 Cor. 10:12 RSV). No Christian is immune from the "flaming darts of the evil one" (Eph. 6:16 RSV).

II. Peter: vulnerable to sin.

A. *Blind to his weakness*. Peter was a typical person. He had strengths and weaknesses, but it seemed the disciple was blind to his weaknesses. Peter confidently told the Lord, "I am ready to go with you to prison and to death" (v. 33). A noble expression and a wonderful assurance—apparently uttered in ignorance of the inner self's potential for succumbing to sin's temptation.

Victor Hugo wrote: "I feel two men struggling within me." Paul also had a realistic view of the tension between good and evil which rages in every soul: "My own behavior baffles me. For I find myself not doing what I really want to do but doing what I really loathe. . . . It must be that sin has made its home in my nature. . . . It is an agonizing situation, and who on earth can set me free from the clutches of my sinful nature?" (Rom. 7:15–24 PHILLIPS).

B. *Satan attacks the vulnerable spot*. Jesus warned Peter of Satan's impending attack that "he might sift you like wheat" (v. 31). The Evil One caught the strong disciple in a vulnerable moment—surrounded by the enemy and separated from the other disciples. He will sift us until he finds the most vulnerable place at which to hurl his temptation.

Our fight is not against "flesh and blood" but "against the world rulers of this present darkness, against the spiritual hosts of wickedness" (Eph. 6:12 RSV). Jesus taught us to pray for deliverance from the Evil One (Matt. 6:13 RSV). We say with Paul: "I thank God there is a way out through Jesus Christ our Lord" (Rom. 7:25 PHILLIPS).

III. Peter: the pressure to conform.

A. *The pressure of men*. What was the vulnerable spot for Peter? He let himself be guided by those around him. Is this entirely wrong? A healthy concern for what others think is an asset. Nothing should be done to place a stumbling block in another's path nor to offend our brother. Peter went beyond this to permit his actions to be molded by those around him. A dialogue between Jesus and Peter, recorded in Matthew 16, illustrates this peer pressure. Jesus talked about His coming rejection and death. Peter strongly reacted, "God forbid, Lord! This shall never happen to you" (v. 22 RSV). Peter's concept of the Messiah did not contain any idea of the Suffering Servant. Peter subscribed to the popular concept of the victorious Messiah conquering the Romans and reestablishing the throne of David. Jesus rebuked him: "Get behind me, Satan! You are a hindrance to me; for you are not on the side of God, but of men" (v. 23 RSV).

Peter exhibited this tendency to reflect prevailing pressure on a later occasion, which Paul described in Galatians 2. "For before certain men came from James, he [Peter] ate with the Gentiles; but when they came he drew back and separated himself, fearing the circumcision party" (v. 12 RSV). Peter knew the Lord was no respector of persons, but he was afraid to resist the pressure of a strong group in the church. Peter was a strong man but not strong enough to stand against the values of immature Christians—even though they were against God.

B. *The pleasure of God*. In the face of compromising peer pressure what are we to do? Paul expresses what is pleasing to God: "Do not be conformed to this world but be transformed by the renewal of your mind, that you may prove what is the will of God, what is good and acceptable and perfect" (Rom. 12:2 RSV).

Two distinguished statesmen delivered addresses before a British university. Benjamin Disraeli said: "If you would succeed, know the temper and spirit of the times in which you live and act accordingly." William Gladstone said: "Do not drift with the age. Have fixed principles and stand by them." At the enemy's campfire Peter took the first course of action and lived to regret it.

Conclusion. In the days following Jesus' resurrection, some of the disciples had breakfast with the Lord beside the Sea of Galilee (John 21). Three times Jesus asked Peter if he loved Him and then told Peter he would have to suffer for Him. Peter pointed to John and asked, "Lord, what about this man?" Jesus responded, "If it is my will that he remain until I come, what is that to you? Follow me!" The tension was still present; it was still difficult to face the will of God.

The same crucial question which Peter faced encounters us: "What will you do with Him who is called Christ?" You can't pass the decision off to someone else. You must decide. The pressure of others will offer convenient options. The warmth of the enemy's fire will be appealing. May the Lord hear us say: "Yes, I know Jesus—He is my Lord!" —*BW*

* * *

SUNDAY EVENING, MARCH 20

TITLE: The Face of Failure: Simon Peter

TEXT: "And as Peter was beneath in the palace, there cometh one of the maids of the high priest: and when she saw Peter warming himself, she looked upon him, and said, And thou also wast with Jesus of Nazareth. But he denied saying, I know not, neither understand I what thou sayest. And he went out into the porch; and the cock crew. And a maid saw him again, and began to say to them that stood by, This is one of them. And he denied it again. And a little after, they that stood by said again to Peter, Surely thou art one of them: for thou art a Galilean, and thy speech agreeth thereto. But he began to curse and to swear, saying, I know not this man of whom ye speak. And the second time the cock crew. And Peter called to mind the word that Jesus said unto him, Before the cock crow twice, thou shalt deny me thrice. And when he thought thereon, he wept" (Mark 14:66–72).

SCRIPTURE READING: Mark 14:53–72

Introduction. Any of us could have done what Peter did. Failure as a disciple does not require special weakness or skill. A careful record was kept of Peter's failure to remind us of this. This chief apostle was present at the cross as a failure.

Let us review the facts as we know them about Peter so that we can put his failure into proper perspective. He joined the followers of Jesus very early when his brother, Andrew, brought him to Jesus. He forsook a fishing business in order to become a "fisher of men." Jesus chose him to be one of the twelve apostles, and later included him in the "inner circle." He was present at the Transfiguration of our Lord and was an "eyewitness" of most of His miracles. He had received personal instruction from the Lord on a daily basis for over three years when he failed.

He had not always been a failure. He was the one who gave the bold confession which so thrilled the heart of the Lord Jesus. Peter had never been without words before. But now under the pressure of the circumstance, when faced with the inquiry of the group in the courtyard of the high priest, he cracked. He openly, shamefully, denied three times that he knew the Lord. Though he had loved the Lord, he denied Him.

Most of us who have been in the way of discipleship very long can identify with Peter. We know the pain of failure. Let us learn from the experience of the "big fisherman."

I. The shame of our failure.

Failure is always shameful, but is especially so when it is found in the life of one so privileged.

A. *The failure represents a misjudged evil.*

Peter had no intention of failing. His intentions were to be faithful to the Lord regardless of what might happen. He gave a sincere expression of these intentions in the Upper Room as they observed the Passover. However, in making his spiritual calculations, Peter misjudged the power of the Evil One. Jesus sought to sober his calculations by reminding Peter that Satan had made a request to sift Peter, but Peter ignored the warning. He felt sufficient in his own strength for any power that might rise against him.

Wise men are careful to measure the strength of their enemy. Men who succeed in discipleship are always mindful that the enemy is like a "roaring lion seeking whom he may devour." Peter learned this the hard way.

B. *The failure represents a mistaken concept of self.*

Peter did not know himself as well as he thought. Peter could not do all that Peter *thought* Peter could do. There was still present in him more of old Simon than he wanted to admit.

The words of dedication spoken by Peter in the Upper Room did not come from his faith in God, but rather from his faith in himself. They were the bold claims of a self-sufficient man. The man best prepared for the way of discipleship is the one who confesses with another apostle, "In my flesh there dwelleth no good thing." Our only hope of avoiding failure is by utterly depending on the Lord and His strength.

C. *The failure involves a denial of Christ.*

It happened three times. As Peter sought to be inconspicuous in the courtyard, he was discovered. Three times he was asked if he was not a follower of Jesus, who was then on trial. Each time Peter's response was the same. He denied that he had ever known the Lord. Because he suspected that his denial was not convincing the crowd, the third time even included a religious oath and curses. Could anything be worse than a disciple who has received so much denying the Lord?

Many of us have done the same shameful thing. It may have been by our words or by our deeds, but we denied Him. Usually the circumstance under which we did it was not nearly so threatening. To fail our Lord is a shameful deed regardless of the circumstance.

II. The sorrow over our failure

A. *A sign of repentance.* True disciples weep over their failures. They are never proud or boastful about such shameful matters. Peter's sorrow began the moment he heard the crowing of the rooster. This reminded him of the words of warning the Lord has spoken to him. Then there was the look that he received from Jesus as he remembered. The look must have been filled with sorrow and hurt. It sent the Big Fisherman out into the night to express his sorrow with tears. He was not sorry that he had been caught in his deed, but rather he was sorry for what he had done and for what it had done to the Lord Jesus.

There is no real repentance without this type of sorrow. Such sorrow is a proper response when you know that you have failed.

B. *A step toward recovery*. The Scriptures assure us that God is nigh to those of a "broken and contrite heart." If Peter had approached the whole ordeal with the same broken spirit that he had when he came out of it, he would never have failed. But he was soon to discover that his tears were not in vain. Our forgiving and compassionate God takes note of such tears of sorrow. They are a true step toward spiritual recovery.

III. The solace after our failure.

The experience of Simon Peter is good news for every failing disciple. Our failures do not have to be final.

A. *The solace of forgiveness*. Tears of repentance will bring us to the solace of forgiveness. Thomas wrote a poem about God commissioning one to find the world's greatest treasure. Finally, he comes with a tear of repentance which proves to be the most precious thing earth can produce.

Martin Luther wrote, "No article of the creed is so hard to believe as this: I believe in the forgiveness of sins. But look at Peter. If I could paint a portrait of Peter, I would write on every hair of his head forgiveness of sins."

How do we know that he was forgiven? When Jesus came back from the grave, He sent a special message to His disciples. He gave the woman who carried the message special instructions to see that the message was given to Peter personally. Our Lord forgave Peter fully, and He will forgive us when we fail.

B. *The solace of fellowship*. Much of the sorrow related to failure comes from the broken fellowship. Knowing that you have disappointed Him makes you so uncomfortable in His presence. But when He forgives, then you begin to enjoy His company again. Peter found this to be true in the time he spent with the Lord after the Resurrection. The fellowship was restored. He was not banished forever as he thought he might be.

Conclusion. How you handle your failures is so important. For Peter the shameful failure became a positive experience as he allowed his heart to be broken, and sought another opportunity. The record of his ministry in the Acts of the Apostles is evidence enough of what a failure can become. How are you handling your failures? —*DLL*

* * *

WEDNESDAY EVENING, MARCH 23

TITLE: What the Bible Says About Stewardship

TEXT: "Turn in the account of your stewardship, for you can no longer be steward" (Luke 16:2 RSV).

SCRIPTURE READING: Luke 12:13–34

Introduction. There is no area of sensitivity within man more acute than that area which involves his possessions, his money, his personal fortune, whether it be large or small. He may be open about every other part of his life, but the moment the question concerning his possessions arises, he becomes very defensive. Nonetheless, some of the most piercing and pertinent parables and sayings of Jesus dealt with the subject of the stewardship of one's possessions. Jesus knew the joys which awaited that disciple when this last bridgehead of commitment was established in his life—when he made a full and complete surrender of his *all* to God, including the stewardship of his possessions.

Luke 12:13–34 contains one of Jesus' clearest commentaries on the subject of stewardship. He began with a parable, a story illustration of the truth He was attempting to drive home to their hearts. And this particular story was precipitated by a dramatic little incident that arose involving two brothers. Evidently their father had died, and the estate had not yet been divided in a way that was agreeable to one brother in particular. For he made a request of Jesus: "Master, speak to my brother, that he divide the inheritance with me."

Then note verse 15: "He said unto *them.*" No doubt the disciples and the crowd listened carefully to Jesus; but most likely He directed His remarks specifically to these brothers. First, He stated a principle: "Take heed, and beware of covetousness: for a man's life consisteth not in the abundance of the things which he possesseth." Then, after he had secured the attention of the brothers, he began to relate a story about a rich man. Traditionally we have taken this man to be an unbeliever, who worshiped the god of materialism. He may have been. Or he may have been a believer, but a carnal, ego-centered, materialistically oriented Christian.

I. The first implication Jesus made as He related this story is that there is a danger in developing a false sense of security in one's life.

A. *Here we see a man who has become a success in his work.* He may have been a gentleman farmer with a palatial home, with excellent barns and outbuildings, impeccable fields symmetrically and beautifully tilled and planted. And we say, "What a fortunate man! Ah, to have *one year's income* from that man's possessions! It would take the pressure off, and I could breathe again!" What is it? We think all too often of the sense of security in the relief from financial strain. And we rationalize that it is good to be rich.

B. *Yet Jesus said that it is one of the hardest things in life for a rich man to keep his riches* and *God in a proper relationship and in proper perspective.* This is true because the possession of wealth so often gives man a false sense of security. Jesus spoke of "the deceitfulness of riches" in Matthew 13:22. When a man comes to possess riches, he often is deceived about his position in life. He begins to rely on his riches and position in life, rather than on God. Therefore, anything that gives man a sense of security other than God is false and desperately fickle.

II. The second tragedy in this story Jesus told was the foolishness of planning without God.

A. *In the midst of all his false security, this man, who had pushed God aside, made some clever and even admirable plans.* In spite of his wealth, he was a prudent and practical-minded man. He took great pains to insure against every contingency. His plans included not only the present, but the far-distant future as well. He did not intend to play the miser and make himself miserable trying to get more and more. He was going to retire and enjoy life! So he made careful and detailed plans to enjoy the wealth he had accumulated.

B. *But alas! he had failed to recognize that there was a sovereign God who might very well have other plans for him!* In short, this man had not consulted God, and his plans exploded because he had considered himself, and himself only. It is a weakness of man to try to master his circumstances and become lord of his own destiny. In so doing, he presumes upon God, treating Him as though He were a genie in an Aladin's lamp.

C. *To this clever planner and schemer God said, "Thou fool!"* Caesar Borgia of Italy was a great schemer and successful planner; he was a subtle diplomat. He made shrewd and careful plans to achieve, on the death of his father, Alexander, a *coup d'état* that would result in his being master of Italy. He told Machiavelli that he had prepared for every eventuality on his father's death. But one thing destroyed all his schemes. When his father died, Caesar Borgia was ill and not one of his plans could be put into action. He had planned so cleverly, but God said, "Thou fool!" He had other plans.

III. The third tragedy in this story is the tragedy of having no riches of soul toward God.

A. *On that night when God called for the soul of this rich farmer, he had no riches toward God.* Jesus explicitly draws our attention to this: "So is he that layeth up treasure for himself, and is not rich toward God" (v. 21). God looks for riches in the heart and soul of man. From the world's point of view, the rich man had been a success. But how pathetic was his life as it was viewed in the light of eternity.

B. *When Jesus finished the parable, He turned to His disciples and gave them an even deeper interpretation of what He had been trying to say.* He spoke of the folly of anxiety and worry concerning material things. He illustrated with the birds whom the Lord God feeds, with the lilies of the field whom God adorns with such beauty. The birds are here for such a brief time, and the lilies flourish in a day, and tomorrow are burned in the oven. Then Jesus asked His disciples, "How much more will he clothe you, O ye of little faith?" (v. 28).

Conclusion. Then Jesus struck the nerve center of this whole matter of stewardship when He said, "But . . . seek ye the kingdom of God; and all these things shall be added unto you. Fear not, little flock; for it is your Father's good pleasure to give you the kingdom. . . . For where your treasure is, there will your heart be also" (Luke 12:31–32, 34). —*DLJ*

* * *

SUNDAY MORNING, MARCH 27

TITLE: A Man Passing Through the Crowd

TEXT: "And they compelled a passer-by, Simon of Cyrene, who was coming in from the country, the father of Alexander and Rufus, to carry his cross" (Mark 15:21 RSV).

SCRIPTURE READING: Mark 15:16–32

Hymns: "O Sacred Head, Now Wounded," Gerhardt
"At the Cross," Watts
"Lead Me to Calvary," Hussey

Offertory Prayer:

Lord, You know our hearts and are aware of the motivation for our presence here today. Even as You see our sin, we pray You will bless us with a new transfusion of Your love, forgiveness, and power. We know You see the amount of our gifts only as it reflects our capability and commitment. We love You and rejoice in the changes You have made in our lives. In Jesus' name. Amen.

Introduction. "And they compelled a passer-by, Simon of Cyrene . . . to carry his cross." A man passing through the crowd was suddenly thrust to center stage of the drama of redemption. Can you imagine the shock and shame Simon of Cyrene experienced? A proud Jew involved in the ugly proceedings of a crucifixion—a site reserved for criminals and slaves. They "compelled" him into service. Did Simon resist? It was useless resistance for Roman authorities could exercise this selective service on the spur of the moment.

Although Simon recoiled at this demand, the experience led to a complete turnabout of his life. Not only did Simon bring relief to the weak and emaciated body of Jesus, his walk to the place of the skull took him to the source of real life.

I. A Cyrenian with character.

Simon was probably a dedicated Jew. Acts 6:9 notes the Cyrenian Jews had their own synagogue in Jerusalem. Simon's presence in Jerusalem could indicate his commitment to the faith of Abraham, Isaac, and Jacob.

He was "coming in from the country." This very likely means he was an immigrant from North Africa who lived in the farming districts near Jerusalem. Cyrene was noted for its farming. As a farmer, Simon was accustomed to hard work and his body probably gave evidence of physical strength and endurance. The soldiers did not have time to waste to lay the cross on a man unused to toil and hardship.

Simon was "passing by"—going about his business. No doubt he had left home early that morning and had many things to do and "miles to go and promises to keep before I sleep." Simon was a marked contrast with the unruly mob moving from Pilate's palace to Calvary. They had been easily distracted from meaningful work and gave shouts of allegiance to whomever could arouse their emotions. This Cyrenian with character was on his way to accomplish something.

II. Caught in the clutches of circumstance.

A. *The innocent suffer*. Simon's determined and purposeful journey was interrupted by circumstances not of his own choosing. He had another's burden thrust on him. He was caught in the clutches of circumstance. Some of our failures and disappointments come as a result of our own selfish sowing, unwise decisions, or hasty judgment. At other times we are caught in the consequences of another's sin. Simon typifies the sufferings of good people throughout all time. His experience illustrates the widening circle of influence individual decisions have on others. "No man is an island." It is not just *my* business what I do.

B. *More than conquerors.* Simon's experience is an assurance of God's special concern for those who have to bear burdens they did not choose. Jesus said, "Come to me, all who labor and are heavy laden, and I will give you rest" (Matt. 11:28 RSV).

In Viet Nam a grenade exploded near Max Cleland, causing the loss of both legs and an arm. He courageously faced this tragic circumstance and in 1977 was made head of the Veteran's Administration. Cleland testifies, "There is help available from God when we need it most." He closes many of his speeches and interviews with the prayer written during the Civil War by a Confederate soldier:

> I asked God for strength, that I might achieve,
> I was made weak, that I might learn humbly to obey.
> I asked for health, that I might do greater things,
> I was given infirmity that I might do better things.
> I asked for riches, that I might be happy,
> I was given poverty, that I might be wise.
> I asked for power, that I might have the praise of men,
> I was given weakness, that I might feel the need of God.
> I asked for all things, that I might enjoy life,
> I was given life, that I might enjoy all things.
> I got nothing that I asked for—
> but everything I had hoped for.
> Almost despite myself, my unspoken prayers were answered.
> I am, among all men, most richly blessed.

With Christ we can conquer the circumstances of life (Rom. 8:37).

III. Converted at the cross.

Mark identifies Simon as "the father of Alexander and Rufus." These were men known to the readers of the gospel, evidently active in the fellowship of believers. In Romans 16:13 Paul sends greetings to "Rufus chosen in the Lord." Is this the same individual—Simon's son? Is this scriptural evidence that Simon was converted and established a Christian home out of which came two saved boys who became leaders in the church? I think so. Compelled to carry the cross, Simon fell under the Lord's comparison. Did they talk as the procession made its way to Calvary? Bitterness turned to belief; hatred became hope; shame moved to salvation. He heard Jesus pray repeatedly, "Father, forgive them for they know not what they do." Simon saw Jesus willingly give Himself and slowly the hope of the prophets dawned into reality—"He was wounded for our transgressions, he was bruised for our iniquities; upon him was the chastisement that made us whole, and with his stripes we are healed" (Isa. 53:5 RSV).

Conclusion. Arthur Blessett, chaplain of Sunset Strip, California, carried a ninety-pound cross across America and across many countries of the world. Speaking at a national conference, he related the experience of carrying the cross across the newly opened border between Israel and Egypt soon after the historic Camp David peace treaty was signed. The Arab commander at the border asked for a piece of his cross. Jesus said, "If any man would come after me, let him deny himself and take up his cross and follow me" (Mark 8:34 RSV). You may be passing by today. A person in the crowd. A jeweled cross may hang around your neck. Have you taken up the cross? The way of the cross leads home—to forgiveness of sin, abundant life, the defeat of death. Simon of Cyrene—a man passing through the crowd—found it to be so. So can you! —*BW*

SUNDAY EVENING, MARCH 27

TITLE: The Face of Faithfulness: John

TEXT: "Now there stood by the cross of Jesus his mother, and his mother's sister, Mary the wife of Cleophas, and Mary Magdalene. When Jesus therefore saw his mother, and the disciple standing by, whom he loved, he saith unto his mother, Woman, behold thy son! Then saith he to the disciple, Behold thy mother! And from that hour that disciple took her unto his own home" (John 19:25–27).

SCRIPTURE READING: John 19:17–27

Introduction. Christianity began with a group of men gathered by Jesus, but at the cross it looked like a woman's movement. Of the twelve men Jesus made apostles, only one was faithful to the end. Four faithful women stood with this one man until the end. Is it not a marvel that there were so few?

The faithful women had good reason to be there. One of them was the beloved mother of Jesus. She had a sister who stood by her side through the ordeal. Mary Magdalene was another of the four, and with her was the wife of Cleophas. But it is John on whom we want to fasten our attention. His face beneath the cross is the face of faithfulness. He represents that quality that our Lord placed so much value on. A study of John's presence at the cross should help you in your pursuit of faithfulness.

I. The extent of faithfulness.

Years later, John was taking a letter from the risen Lord to the church in Smyrna. In the letter, the Lord admonished that suffering church, "Be thou faithful unto death" (Rev. 2:10d). John would know about this type of faithfulness. It is the quality of faithfulness each of us needs.

A. *Faithfulness until death.* The words could be understood to mean, "Be faithful for all of your life." It would be a word calling for faithfulness regardless of what life might bring. John had this kind of faithfulness. It is the kind that a couple promises to each other in the marriage ceremony. It is "until death do us part." It is interesting to ask a couple as they approach marriage, "Under what circumstances will you seek a divorce?" Their answers are always revealing. Some confidently reply, "Under no circumstances." As a pastor, I like that response, but I am fully aware they will be surprised by some of the difficulties that will test this commitment to faithfulness.

The cross did not force John away from his commitment to Jesus. He intended to be faithful unto the end of life.

B. *Faithfulness unto death.* When the Lord admonished Smyrna, this is probably what He meant. "Faithfulness unto death" meant primary faithfulness even at the expense of life.

The extent of the danger facing John is debated by the scholars. However, it is evident that the other apostles thought that there was danger at the cross. Anyone who has followed the rage in a mob knows that with a mob on the loose no one is safe. Jesus was on the cross because of such a mob movement. The danger to John must have been real. Yet he was ready to face even the possibility of death because of his desire to be faithful to the Lord. Even if it cost him his life, he would not run. This is the quality of faithfulness that the Lord wants in each of us. If our faithfulness has limitations, then it is flawed.

II. The inspiration for faithfulness.

Why did John stand beneath the cross while the others hid in fear? If we can know this, we will know the real secret of faithfulness.

A. *Not a sense of duty.* Could it have been a sense of duty that brought John to stand beneath the cross? It must be admitted that such a sense of duty will aid in maintaining faithfulness in hard times. It will keep a soldier in his place of danger when others might flee. It will keep a son or daughter faithfully attending to the needs of their aging parents. But the Christian secret of faithfulness goes much deeper than a sense of duty.

B. *The love of Jesus.* John gives us a clue to why he was there by the way he identified himself. He is the disciple "whom Jesus loved." His presence at the cross was a response to that love. Jesus loved all of the apostles just as much as he loved John, but this man seemed to have a special capacity to receive that love. He had a special awareness of that love. He seemed to know better than the others that Jesus was bound to His cross by His love for them. If Jesus would do what He was doing out of love, could not John stand by the cross through the ordeal? Gratitude and love compelled him to do it.

This is the secret of Christian faithfulness. It will keep a man faithful in his service. It will keep a person faithful through all kinds of persecution. It will make a survivor out of you. If you are wavering in your commitment, then you need to be refreshed by a fresh awareness of how much you are loved by Jesus. It is faithfulness unto Him!

III. The reward for faithfulness.

The experience of faithful John illustrates beautifully the rewards which faithfulness to Christ will bring.

A. *The approval of Christ.* Without speaking a word of approval to John, Jesus gave His approval to him for his faithfulness. It must have been conveyed to him by a look from the cross. Can you imagine the difference in the look John must have received from that which Peter received in the moment of his denial? The look Peter received sent him into the night weeping in shame, but the look John received sent him home to take care of the mother of Jesus. While John does not describe that look, my imagination lets me see the look of gratitude that Jesus must have conveyed to John. He, along with the women, was the one bright spot in the sea of darkness.

Jesus promised that faithfulness to Him will result in a final and blessed, "Well done, thou good and faithful servant."

B. *The trust of Christ.* His trust is the greatest reward for faithfulness. John received this trust in a special gesture by Christ from the cross. As Jesus came to death, He felt a special responsibility for the care of His mother. As the broken-hearted mother stood by the cross, her first-born Son made provisions for her needs. He said to her, "Woman, behold thy son!" Then he said to the disciple, "Behold thy mother!" John reports, "and from that very hour that disciple took her unto his own home." Tradition tells us that Mary had other children, but it was John who cared for her until her death years later in the city of Ephesus. Jesus trusted John with a very special assignment.

Our Lord taught that this is the primary reward for faithfulness. "Thou hast been faithful over a few things, I will make thee ruler over many things'' (Matt. 25:23b). Can anything be greater than the Lord of glory trusting you with a special assignment? Those assignments are reserved for those who have proven themselves to be trustworthy through their faithfulness.

Conclusion. This is a word for those who are undergoing trials. It may be that you feel yourself to be standing in a most difficult place. What do you do? ''Be thou faithful unto death.'' Do it because of His love for you! You will find the rewards for such faithfulness to be more than enough. Won't you take a place of faithfulness with John beneath the cross?
—*DLL*

* * *

WEDNESDAY EVENING, MARCH 30

TITLE: What the Bible Says About Death

TEXT: ". . . for in the day that you eat of it you shall die" (Gen. 2:17 RSV).

SCRIPTURE READING: Revelation 21:1–4

Introduction. The fact there are so many different ideas concerning what happens to the soul of a person when he dies indicates the desire on man's part to understand the phenomenon of death. We hear and use such expressions as ''the 'other' life,'' ''life in the next world,'' ''life after death,'' and ''life on the other side.'' Does the Bible speak conclusively about this question? Yes! And the scriptural answer provides the abiding hope for the Christian, particularly as he or a loved one approaches the death experience.

I. What is death?

A. *Death is the consequence of sin* (Rom. 5:12). When Adam and Eve sinned in the Garden of Eden, death became their companion. They died spiritually, in that they broke spiritual relationship with God. The vital fellowship and relationship with Him which they had enjoyed in the Garden was broken, dead. Also, the principle of death became operative in their physical lives: they started to die physically. The inevitable deterioration of the physical body is a result of sin.

B. *Death is the lot of all men* (Heb. 9:27). The death experience is inescapable with man. Man is dying (progressively) and he shall die (terminally).

C. *Death terminates earthly life* (Eccl. 9:10). The death experience proves the transitoriness of physical existence.

D. *Death is described as ''return to dust''* (Gen. 3:19), *the removal of breath* (Gen. 25:8), *and as a ''departure''* (Phil. 1:23). An amazing discovery for the Bible student is the difference in the attitudes of Old Testament and New Testament saints in regard to death. The coming of Christ and His teachings clarified the death experience for the Christian in a remarkable way.

E. *Recognition after death: the departed recognized by the living* (Matt. 17:1–8). This was a ''spiritual recognition'' of Moses and Elijah on the part of Peter, James, and John. There is a greater knowledge of all things in heaven (1 Cor. 13:12). All of the mysteries and perplexities of this earthly life will be cleared in heaven.

II. The state of the dead.

A. *Before the resurrection of Christ, the dead apparently went to "Sheol."* In the story of the rich man and Lazarus which Jesus told, the rich man was tormented in flames and was able to look across a gulf and see Lazarus in "Abraham's bosom" (another expression for Paradise). Jesus told the thief on His right, as He was dying on the cross, "Today shalt thou be with me in paradise" (Luke 23:43).

B. *After the resurrection of Christ, and throughout the epistles of the New Testament (patricularly those portions written by the apostle Paul), a believer who dies is said to be "absent from the body, and . . . present with the Lord" (2 Cor. 5:8).* Death is also regarded in the New Testament as "sleep," referring to the body, not to the soul, which goes immediately to be "with the Lord." John, in the Revelation, describes believers who die as being "happy" because they are able to "rest from their labours," knowing that "their works do follow them" (Rev. 14:13).

C. *Paul considered death for the believer to be an experience of "gain"* (Phil. 1:21) *instead of loss.* It meant for him the final victory over "self" and temptation.

D. *In speaking of his "departure," Paul anticipated the "crown of righteousness" which awaited him—and not him only, but all those who "love his [Christ's] appearing"* (2 Tim. 4:8). Paul's attitude toward death was not a morbid desire to escape from life; rather he knew that the joys awaiting him after this life were far and beyond anything he could ever imagine or conceive.

III. The Christian attitude toward death.

A. *Paul said, "I am in a strait betwixt two [tight spot between two ideas], having a desire to depart, and to be with Christ; which is far better: nevertheless to abide in the flesh is more needful for you"* (Phil. 1:23–24). Again, this was not "escapism" on Paul's part. Paul lived in such constant and close communion with his Lord that he actually longed to be with Jesus. At the same time, however, he felt the pressing responsibility God had given him in regard to the establishing of these churches and the strengthening of these new Christians in the faith. Thus he was "needed" in this life and would find joy fulfilling the purpose God had for him.

B. *Paul also set down for the Thessalonian believers (and us) the Christian attitude toward the death of loved ones* (1 Thess. 4:13–14). He attached the certainty of the resurrection of the dead to one's belief and assurance that Christ had been rasied from the dead.

Conclusion. While physical death is not a pleasant anticipation while one is in the midst of life, yet to God, in regard to His children, it is a glorious homecoming. Jesus said to His disciples, "In my Father's house are many mansions . . ." (John 14:2). He has gone "to prepare a place" for us, and He will come again to receive us. (vv. 3–4). Death is no longer an enemy to the believer in the Lord Jesus Christ. It is simply a blessed transposition from an earthly life of imperfection and incompletion to one of perfection and eternal joy. —*DLJ*

* * *

SUGGESTED PREACHING PROGRAM FOR THE MONTH OF APRIL

Sunday Mornings

"Recognizing and Responding to the Living Lord" is the theme for these messages, which exalt the Christ who died on a cross and who conquered death and the abode of the dead.

Sunday Evenings

Continue with the theme "Beneath the Cross of Jesus" or "Were You There When They Crucified My Lord?"

Wednesday Evenings

Complete the series of messages using the theme "What the Bible Says."

* * *

SUNDAY MORNING, APRIL 3

TITLE: The Sound of a Familiar Voice

TEXT: "Jesus said to her, 'Woman, why are you weeping? Whom do you seek?' Supposing him to be the gardener, she said to him, 'Sir, if you have carried him away, tell me where you have laid him, and I will take him away.' Jesus said to her, 'Mary.' She turned and said to him in Hebrew, 'Rabboni!' (which means Teacher)" (John 20:15–16 RSV).

SCRIPTURE READING: Luke 8:1–3; John 20:1–18

HYMNS: "This Is the Day the Lord Hath Made," Watts
"The Head That Once Was Crowned," Kelly
"Christ, the Lord, Is Risen Today," Wesley

OFFERTORY PRAYER:

Lord God, Author of life and Conqueror of death, we rejoice in the privilege of worship. On this Resurrection Day we thank You for the signs of new life which abound in Your beautiful creation. We thank You even more for new persons—saved from sin and given abundant life. We pray for guidance and strength in bearing each other's burdens. Help us to minister to each other. May no breach of fellowship make our offerings unacceptable. Pierce our hearts with the probing light of the Spirit so that we shall see ourselves as You see us. Convict us of the need to forgive as we have been forgiven, to love as we have been loved, and to give as we have been given. We pray this in Jesus' name. Amen.

Introduction. Each of us can recall moments when the sound of a familiar voice was an especially meaningful experience. It might have been a long-distance call from soneone special, the voice of an old friend in a crowd of strangers, a tape recording of a son away from home, or words of assurance following surgery. The sound of a familiar voice is powerful medicine. I doubt if any of us have experienced the feeling Mary Magdalene had when she heard the familiar voice of Jesus in the garden of His burial! This was not their first encounter. Jesus had spoken important words to her in the past. He still speaks and waits for us to hear and respond.

I. The word of conversion.

A. *Life in need of change.* Mary first heard the Lord speak the word of conversion. Luke records, "Mary, called Magdalene, from whom seven demons had gone out" (Luke 8:2 RSV). This woman, possessed by evil, had lived a life of torment and suffering. Tradition says she was a prostitute. That label may have fixed itself on her because of the extremely wicked town from which she came. The people knew Mary; they had seen how the devil had used her and captivated her body and made her a public shame.

I wonder what happened at the first meeting between Mary and Jesus. The divine Son of God face-to-face with a demon-possessed woman! Did she cry out in scorn at Jesus, as others had? Did she cower in fear in a dark corner, afraid of His power? The circumstances do not matter. What is significant is that this woman, so desperately in need of transformation, met the Master and heard the word of conversion: "Be whole!"

Is your life in need of change? What kind of demon possesses you? The demon of selfishness? Fear? Hate? An anonymous poet expresses our longings:

Oh, I wish there were some wonderful place
Called the Land of Beginning Again
Where all our sins and mistakes
Could be laid aside like a shabby old coat
And never be put on again!

There is such a place! The place where you meet Jesus. He can change your life just as He did the life of Mary Magdalene.

B. *The power of the Resurrection.* It is significant that Mary was the first person to see the Risen Lord. She had one of the more dramatic conversion experiences. God is telling us something here about resurrection and conversion. Without Christ's resurrection there can be no conversion. Paul wrote to the Philippians of his desire to "know him, and the power of his resurrection" (3:10). It is the resurrection power that changes people. A dead Christ can change no one. The Corinthians were told: "If Christ has not been raised, your faith is futile and you are still in your sins" (1 Cor. 15:17 RSV).

The power of sin nailed Jesus to the cross; the power of God raised Him. That same power continues to work, and if you will repent of sin and trust Jesus, His power will change you today.

II. The word of appreciation.

A. *Involved in ministry.* Following her conversion, Mary Magdalene assumed a place of service in the disciple band. She, in cooperation with others, traveled with Jesus and the disciples and "provided for them out of their means" (Luke 8:3 RSV). We are not told the exact nature of Mary's ministry. She might have washed their clothes, helped with the food, and provided funds for needs in the group. Her ministry was a result of the love she had received from Christ.

Conversion should result in committed service. "For we are his workmanship, created in Christ Jesus for good works, which God prepared beforehand, that we should walk in them" (Eph. 2:10 RSV).

B. *Appreciation for service.* How often Jesus must have said to Mary, "Thank you, Mary!" She frequently heard the word of appreciation for her service; and if the Lord said it to Mary, He will say it to us. If the Lord noticed the widow's mite and offered praise for her faithfulness, He notices what we do. He appreciates our ministry, whether great or small.

I sometimes hear the elderly and homebound express the sentiment of feeling forgotten and unappreciated. They have faithfully served in the past but now are no longer able. Some of them may be forgotten by the church, but the Lord remembers. He appreciates every labor, and in eternity they will hear His word of appreciation: "Well done, good and faithful servant; . . . enter into the joy of your master" (Matt. 25:21 RSV).

III. The word of commission.

A. *Go tell.* The third word Jesus spoke to Mary was the word of commission. When Jesus lovingly spoke her name, Mary said, "Master," and grasped the Lord in adoration. Jesus said, "Do not hold me." It was not a time of worship. The Resurrection is not a doctrine to hold selfishly but an experience to share in an unselfish way. We are not to hold on to it but give it away. Mary Magdalene obviously understood for she "went and said to the disciples, 'I have seen the Lord'" (v. 18).

A newspaper had this interesting editorial about Easter: "Easter is usually a quiet occasion. . . . Millions of Americans make a special effort to go to church on Easter Sunday. Easter is a wholesome kind of holiday. It gives all of us an opportunity to recuperate in a small measure from the harassments of daily life." That is not what the Lord intended. The Resurrection is the impetus to enter the harassments of life and change the world. It is ironic that the big event at Easter now is in church. We prepare pretty eggs, buy flowers, dress up, and go to church. Jesus said the big event ought to be outside the church—go tell!

B. *Every disciple telling.* Mary's commission illustrates the Lord's desire to use every disciple to share the Resurrection news. The Lord's appearance to Mary sent a shock wave throughout the disciple band—a woman, and with her past, by herself (Jesus usually demanded two witnesses). Isn't that like Jesus? The person others consider unlikely is the one He uses. The ingredient that makes the difference is love. He will use any of us to tell the Good News.

Conclusion. Jesus still speaks. His voice can be heard today. Are you listening? "Behold, I stand at the door and knock; if any one hears my voice and opens the door, I will come in . . ." (Rev. 3:20 RSV). Mary speaks of conversion, appreciation for service, and commissioning us to tell the world—He lives! —*BW*

* * *

SUNDAY EVENING, APRIL 3

TITLE: The Face of Folly: Judas

TEXT: "The Son of man goeth as it is written of him: but woe unto that man by whom the Son of man is betrayed! it had been good for that man if he had not been born" (Matt. 26:24).

SCRIPTURE READING: Matthew 26:14–16, 47–50; 27:3–10

Introduction. Judas played the part of a fool. When he placed the kiss of betrayal on the face of the Lord Jesus, he acted foolishly. This is the consensus of history. Dante pictured Judas in the very bottom of hell. He saw him as being isolated from all other sinners, and in the grip of the most horrible torment.

Jesus said, "The Son of man goeth as it is written of him: but woe unto that man by whom the Son of man is betrayed! it had been good for that man if he had not been born." Surely, anything that would completely negate the value of life must be foolish. Yet this is how Jesus spoke of the act of Judas.

Judas felt that he had played the fool after it was over. He felt the only appropriate response was to end his life in suicide.

What was so terrible about the crime of Judas? Actually, it is different only in degree from the sin which many people commit. It is a matter of rejecting the claims of Christ and handing Him over to His enemies. Let us look at this face of folly beneath the cross.

I. The decision of the fool.

A. *The basis of the decision.*

We must go back to the beginning to understand the decision of Judas. Judas was the only one of the Twelve from Judea. He was the only southerner in the group. Evidently, he joined the company of Jesus with burning hopes for a glorious and powerful earthly kingdom. While some of the others were able to move from this kind of hope to an acceptance of Jesus as a different kind of Messiah, Judas could never make the change.

He made the final decision at a dinner meeting at which Mary broke the alabaster box and anointed the body of Jesus. It was just too much for Judas. He spoke up to rebuke this gesture as being a waste. But Jesus quickly moved to Mary's defense. Up to this time Judas had served as the keeper of the funds for the Twelve, and John tells us that he had been stealing from them. Out of this experience Judas went to the enemies of Jesus with an offer to deliver Him to them for a reward. With the priests he agreed to do it for thirty pieces of silver. His decision seems to have been based on the profit principle. He was ready to salvage anything he could out of the situation.

If you have been rejecting the claims of Christ, what is the basis of your rejection?

B. *The nature of the decision.*

Luke reports that "Satan entered into him." Surely, this means that Satan was responsible for the temptation to betray Jesus; and when Judas yielded to the temptation, Satan took possession of his life. The man who makes this kind of choice should not take all of the credit. He has responded to a satanic temptation and has become the tool of the Adversary of God. This gives profound spiritual and eternal significance to the decision.

II. The deed of the fool.

A. *He spurned genuine love.*

Jesus loved Judas and expressed that love. It was His love for Judas that prompted Him to choose him to be one of the Twelve. It was His love which reached out to Judas at that last Passover. At that dinner Jesus dipped a piece of unleavened bread into the bowl of herbs and handed it to Judas. This was a gesture of special friendship and love. Judas knew what it meant. At that same moment, out of love, Jesus warned him of the consequences of the course of action he was taking. Even in the garden as Judas betrayed Him, Jesus expressed warmth toward him, saying, "Friend."

Judas chose to commit his deed with an expression of love and friendship. He rejected this great love with the kiss of betrayal. Is it not the deed of a fool to spurn such love?

B. *He acted with knowledge.*

Judas had both eyes open to the truth. He knew what he was doing. He understood who Jesus was but wanted no part of that type of Messiah. He had enjoyed three years of helpful instruction from the Master. He had been confronted with the best evidence about the mission of Jesus into the world. He just could not find a place in his life for that kind of Messiah.

How much do you know about Jesus? You may actually know more than Judas. You have the advantage of two thousand years of Christian history. You know the outcome of the cross ordeal. If you refuse Him a place in your life, you, too, are sinning against knowledge.

C. *He aligned himself with the enemies of Jesus.*

Did Judas seek to express his inner resentment through the betrayal? Many scholars so understand his act. They see the frustrated ambition of Judas behind the deed. He would get even by turning Him over to His enemies. Whatever the motivation, it made Judas one with the enemies of Jesus and resulted in the death of Jesus.

What are the attitudes and actions you have taken toward the Lord Jesus?

III. The destiny of the fool.

A. *Temporarily . . . despair.*

The folly is seen best when you consider the end. When Judas realized that Jesus was going to be crucified, he went back to the priests with deep regrets. He wanted to return the money he had taken, but they mocked him. In despair, he cast the silver coins on the floor and rushed out to end it all. Suicide—as it usually is—was the ultimate gesture of despair. It was his way of saying, "Nothing can ever bring meaning to my life. My life is no longer worth living."

Allowing Jesus Christ to be Lord of your life is the only thing that puts you in touch with God's ultimate purpose for you. Any other center for your life will fail. Judas had rejected the only One who could give meaning and purpose to his life.

B. *Eternally . . . his place.*

Judas went to "his place," according to Luke in the Acts. From a comparison of Scriptures we discover that "hell" is "his place." When fully considered, this is not surprising. Heaven is to be the place where men worship and serve God through the Lord Jesus forever. Surely a man who has rejected the claims of Christ on earth, and has betrayed Him into the hands of His enemies, would not want to go to such a place. The only place for such a man is a place of eternal separation from Jesus Christ. This is exactly the nature of hell. Hell is the logical end of a life without Christ.

The destiny is directly related to the decision and the deed. If the decision is different, the destiny will be different. When you consider the end of Judas, surely you will have to agree with Jesus that it would be better if he had never been born. He acted like a fool. Do you dare consider where your decisions and deeds are leading?

Conclusion. Judas kissed Jesus in order to hand Him over to His enemies. There is another way to kiss Him. It was customary in that day for a man to bow before a king and to kiss his ring. The ring symbolized his authority, and the kiss symbolized submission to him. This is the reason that the psalmist wrote, "Kiss the Son, lest he be angry, and ye perish from the way, when his wrath is kindled but a little. Blessed are all they that put their trust in him" (Ps. 2:12).

The man who kisses the Son in submission to His authority is no fool. His life takes on an excitement that will last for eternity. How will you kiss the Son? Will it be the kiss of the fool or the kiss of a wise man? —*DLL*

* * *

WEDNESDAY EVENING, APRIL 6

TITLE: What the Bible Says About the Devil

TEXT: "Be sober, be watchful. Your adversary the devil prowls around like a roaring lion, seeking some one to devour" (1 Peter 5:8 RSV).

SCRIPTURE READING: Matthew 4:1–11

Introduction. We know that the sin of pride had its origin in the Devil, and yet he has no ego problem. By that, we mean that it is not the Devil's desire that we study about him and thus become aware of his person and his tactics. He would much rather "work behind the scenes" and keep alive the fallacy that he is a "red-skinned creature with horns, a forked tail, a pitchfork, with smoke perpetually coming out of his nostrils"! This caricature of Satan gives rise to the sinister persuasion that he is not a real person at all, but a mythological or fictional character who only represents an evil influence in the world. However, the Bible clearly describes the Devil and carefully outlines his strategy.

I. The origin of the Devil.

A. *Satan was created as a being.* The fact that all things that are in heaven and in earth, "visible and invisible, whether they be thrones, or dominions, or principalities, or powers," were created by Christ and for Christ is stated in Colossians 1:16.

B. *The time of the creation of the angelic host is not stated beyond the fact that their creation probably preceded all material things as we know them, and were themselves preceded by that eternity of existence on the part of God* (John 1:1–2).

C. *Among all the heavenly host, Satan's creation alone is mentioned in particular* (Ezek. 28:15). This fact suggests the supreme place that Satan held in relation to all the invisible creatures of God. (For a symbolic portrayal of Satan, read Ezekiel 28:11–19.)

II. The personality of the Devil.

A. *Satan exercises all the functions of a person.* Isaiah describes him as having completed his course and having been judged at the end of time, addressing him under the heavenly title of "Lucifer, son of the morning," and seeing him as fallen from his primal state of glory (Isa. 14:12–17). In verses 13–14 there are listed five ways in which he set his own will against God's.

B. *Because of his sinister and deceitful nature, he gained the title of "serpent" in the Garden of Eden* (Gen. 3:1–15). Every word spoken there and the design of Satan's strategy revealed are evidence of his personality (cf. 2 Cor. 11:3, 13–15; Rev. 12:9; 20:2).

C. *Further indication of Satan's personality is the fact that he apparently has access to God* (cf. Job 1:6–12; 2:1–13; Luke 22:31; Rev. 12:10). He also has access to men (Eph. 6:10–12; 1 Peter 5:8); thus he exhibits every feature of a true personality. Further insight into his personality is discovered in his temptation of Jesus (Luke 4:1–13).

III. The power of the Devil.

A. *Though morally fallen and now judged in the Cross* (John 12:31; 16:11; Col. 2:15), *Satan has not lost his position, and he has lost but little of his power.*

B. *His personal strength cannot be estimated.* It is said of him that he had the power of death (Heb. 2:14), but that power has been surrendered to Christ (Rev. 1:18). He had the power of sickness in the case of Job (Job 2:7), and was able to "sift [Peter] as wheat" in a sieve (Luke 22:31; 1 Cor. 5:5). He is said to have weakened the nations, made the earth to tremble, to have shaken kingdoms, to have made the earth a wilderness, destroying the cities thereof, and not to have opened the house of his prisoners (Isa. 14:12–17). Against the power of Satan not even the archangel Michael would contend (Jude 9).

C. *But there is victory over Satan for the Christian through the power of the Spirit of God and the blood of Christ* (Eph. 6:10–12; 1 John 4:4; Rev. 12:11). Satan's power and authority are exercised always and only within the permissive will of God.

IV. The work of the Devil.

A. *Isaiah 14:12–17 is only one of the many passages bearing on the work of Satan.* This passage reveals Satan's original and supreme purpose. He would ascend into heaven, exalt his throne above the stars of God, and be like the Most High. To be like the Most High was the supreme motive of Satan, and it guides all of his activities. This was behind his approach to Adam and Eve (Gen. 3:5); and they, by adopting Satan's ideal, became self-centered, self-sufficient, and independent of God. This attitude has been transmitted to all men to the extent they are called "children of wrath" and must be born again.

B. *Satan does all in his power to keep the unsaved from being delivered from the power of darkness and translated into the kingdom of God* (Col. 1:13). To do this, he will even promote extensive religious systems (2 Cor. 11:13–15; 1 Tim. 4:1–3). Such satanic delusions are now in the world and multitudes are being deceived by them. These false systems are always to be tested by the attitude they take toward the saving grace of God through the blood of Christ (Rev. 12:11).

V. The destiny of the Devil.

A. *As the Word of God is explicit in regard to the origin, personality, power, and work of Satan, it is equally clear regarding his destiny.* A perfect judgment of Satan has been secured through the Cross (John 12:31; 16:11; Col. 2:14–15), but the execution of that sentence is yet future. It was predicted in the Garden of Eden (Gen. 3:15).

B. *Satan will be cast out of heaven* (Rev. 12:7–12) and will be confined to the abyss, which will make it impossible for him to be active and to continue to deceive the nations.

C. *Finally, Satan will be cast into the lake of fire to be tormented day and night forever* (Rev. 20:10).

Conclusion. Many believe that Satan does not really exist and that the supposed person of Satan is no more than an evil principle, or influence, which is in man and in the world. This conception is proved to be wrong by the fact there is the same abundant evidence that Satan is a person as there is that Christ is a person. Scripture, which alone is authoritative on these matters, treats Satan as a person as much as Christ. If the personality of Christ is accepted on the testimony of the Bible, then the personality of Satan must also be accepted on the same testimony.

— *DLJ*

* * *

SUNDAY MORNING, APRIL 10

TITLE: Life in the Son

TEXT: "And this is the testimony, that God gave us eternal life, and this life is in his Son. He who has the Son has life; he who has not the Son of God has not life" (1 John 5:11–12 RSV).

SCRIPTURE READING: 2 Timothy 1:12; 1 John 5:9–12

HYMNS: "I Know Whom I Have Believed," Whittle
"Blessed Assurance, Jesus Is Mine," Crosby
"Standing on the Promises," Carter

OFFERTORY PRAYER:

Father, we thank You that because of Jesus we can be part of the family of God. Thank You for loving us and wooing us through the Holy Spirit. Lord, we believe; help our unbelief. Forgive us of sin which puts a cloud of doubt before our conversion. Cleanse us, and in the joy of our closer relationship may we be zealous to witness and willing to serve. May these gifts we now present come from cheerful givers, who have assurance the offering will be used to bring others to You. May Your name be glorified in this worship. In Christ's name. Amen.

Introduction. The words of Gaither's hymn confidently express the basis of our Christian hope:

> Because He lives, I can face tomorrow;
> Because He lives, all fear is gone;
> Because I know He holds the future,
> And life is worth the living just because He lives.
> — *William J. Gaither*

After the spiritual high of Resurrection Sunday some might ask, "Where do we go from here?" Because Christ lives, we can be sure of some certainties which change our lives into a daily experience worth living. Paul indicated his confidence when he wrote, "I know whom I have believed." Today and on the three Sundays to come we will examine four gifts every Christian possesses as a result of the living Christ. Each of these gifts is described in the Epistle of 1 John. The key word in this brief document is *know*—the word is found thirty times in 105 verses. John was certain of the gifts that came with Christ. The first gift of which we can be certain is life in the Son—"God gave us eternal life, and this life is in his Son."

I. God gives life.

A. *Life in the Son*. It is not God's will for anyone to perish; He wants each person to live. We will find fulfillment in Jesus, who said, "I am the resurrection and the life; he who believes in me, though he die, yet shall he live, and whoever lives and believes in me shall never die" (John 11:25–26). The resurrection of Jesus assures us of life. No "resurrection spirit" can give us victory over death. Paul asked, "O death, where is thy victory? . . . thanks be to God, who gives us the victory through our Lord Jesus Christ" (1 Cor. 15:55, 57). Lofton Hudson wrote that "death, for many, if not most modern Western men and women, is a four-letter word—obscene, vulgar, nasty, not to be used on stage or in polite society" (R. Lofton Hudson, *Persons In Crises* [Nashville: Broadman Press, 1969], p. 110). Jesus' death and resurrection have changed the face of death. Death need not be the grim reaper but the doorway into eternal life—life in the Son.

B. *New quality of life*. The life God gives in Jesus is more than living forever. He imparts a new quality of life. The words *eternal life* refer to the life of the new age, the very life of God at work within us now. Jesus said, "I have come that men may have life, and may have it in all its fullness" (John 10:10 NEB). An extraordinary quality of life is available in Jesus. It is possible to be dead while alive for all who are without Jesus Christ are "dead in trespasses and sins" (Eph. 2:1). Jesus promised, "He who hears my word and believes him who sent me, has eternal life; . . . has passed from death to life" (John 5:24). Life in the Son is more than just living—it is life with quality.

II. Do you have life?

A. *Received through faith*. The gift of life comes to one who "has the Son," and the Son must be received through faith. "I write this to you who believe in the name of the Son of God, that you may know that you have eternal life" (1 John 5:13 RSV). Faith was the essential element to which Jesus responded. Four men lowered a paralytic through the roof into the house where Jesus was teaching. "When Jesus saw their faith, he said to the paralytic, 'My son, your sins are forgiven'" (Mark 2:5).

Faith is a common ingredient of daily existence, yet many claim they cannot have faith in Christ. Huxley once wrote: "Theology claims the just shall live by faith. Science says the just shall live by verification." Yet the scientist believes in a logical universe. He believes in principles used to verify presumptions. What is a theory? It is something *believed* to be right but unproven. We believe in education, democracy, ourselves. Belief is common; why not believe the best and have life in the Son?

B. *Lost because of unbelief*. If this uncommon life comes to those who believe in Jesus, those who refuse to believe are lost—"he who has not the Son of God has not life." Can the good man be lost? Yes. Can the church-going person be lost? Yes. Can the lovable, generous neighbor who has simply delayed her commitment to Christ be lost? Yes. Faith in Christ is the crucial test—"he who does not believe is condemned already, because he has not believed in the name of the only Son of God" (John 3:18).

Brethren, see poor sinners round you
Slumbering on the brink of woe,
Death is coming, hell is moving,
Can you bear to let them go?
. . .
Tell them all about the Saviour,
Tell them that He will be found.
— *George Atkins*

Realizing life is only in the Son should motivate us to "rescue the perishing, care for the dying, snatch them in pity from sin and the grave."

III. Life—for keeps!

A. *Trust God's testimony.* Remember how as a child you responded to a person's gift by saying, "Is this mine, for keeps?" Life in the Son is a present and permanent possession. God is the basis of this security. A personal testimony about new life is great but "the testimony of God is greater. . . . He who believes in the Son of God has the testimony in himself" (1 John 5:9–10 RSV). To doubt the certainty of life on the basis of the requirements set forth by God is to make God a liar. If you have done what God said to do, then trust His word and rejoice!

B. *He keeps us.* Paul's confident word to Timothy included a testimony of God's keeping power. "I know whom I have believed, and am persuaded that he is able to keep that which I have committed unto him against that day" (2 Tim. 1:12). The word *keep* means "guard" and includes the image of a garrison of heavenly troops protecting the individual. Alexander Whyte, the Scottish preacher, once asked a friend, "How are you keeping?" The friend answered, "Doctor, I'm not keeping; I'm being kept" (Lloyd John Ogilvie, *Life As It Was Meant to Be* [Ventura, California: Regal Books, 1980], p. 62). Christ is able to keep us and present us one day at the throne of glory. Because He was able to defeat death, I know He is adequate for everything in this life and the next.

Conclusion. I share the sense of mystery about which Daniel Whittle wrote:

I know not why God's wondrous grace
To me He hath made known,
Nor why, unworthy, Christ in love
Redeemed me for His own.

I do know I believe Christ. Life in the Son is real. Life is worth the living because He lives.
— *BW*

* * *

SUNDAY EVENING, APRIL 10

TITLE: The Face of Forgiveness: the Thief

TEXT: "And one of the malefactors which were hanged railed on him, saying, If thou be Christ, save thyself and us. But the other answering rebuked

him, saying, Dost not thou fear God, seeing thou art in the same condemnation? And we indeed justly; for we receive the due reward of our deeds: but this man hath done nothing amiss. And he said unto Jesus, Lord, remember me when thou comest into thy kingdom. And Jesus said unto him, Verily I say unto thee, To day shalt thou be with me in paradise" (Luke 23:39–43).

SCRIPTURE READING: Luke 23:26–43

Introduction. Everything about the death of Jesus was designed to bring Him suffering and shame. His being crucified between the two thieves was for the purpose of humiliating Him. His enemies wanted Him presented as a common criminal dying with His kind. As usual, He took the evil designs of His enemies and turned them into something good. The presence of these condemned men provided Him with an opportunity to demonstrate His grace and forgiveness.

Though the two thieves came to the cross from a common background, and had perhaps been companions in sin, they responded to their situation differently. While at first both of them joined the crowd in ridiculing Jesus, soon one of them made a dramatic change in his response to Jesus. The manner in which Jesus submitted to the abuse being placed upon Him convicted the thief. It convicted the thief of his own guilt and of the innocence of Jesus. He knew that death was justly deserved by both him and his companion with their guilt. In his deepest heart he also knew that Jesus was innocent of the charges brought against Him. It was obvious that this Man was just different. He was out of place under the condemnation of the cross. The prayer Jesus was praying probably made an impression. Jesus kept praying, "Father, forgive them; for they know not what they do." How could a man have such confidence in God in such circumstances? There was just something about the way He said the word "Father." Then, surely He must be different to have such a forgiving attitude toward those who are heaping all of this upon Him. All of these impressions led to the appeal of the thief.

"Jesus, Lord, remember me when thou comest into thy kingdom." It was not a very strong appeal, but it was directed to the right person—Jesus. Underneath such a request was an unspoken request for forgiveness. Before he could be remembered in such a kingdom, it would surely be necessary for Jesus to forgive and forget his transgressions.

This simple prayer brought just that—full and free forgiveness. "To day shalt thou be with me in paradise." "Today" stood in contrast to some far-off day of a coming kingdom. He will be more than "remembered." He will *be with* Jesus in the dwelling place of God. The little word *truly* is a translation of the word *amen* in the Greek. The word was the open response of Jesus that granted the request—"May it so be." In doing this, Jesus assumed responsibility for all of the sins of the thief, and granted him this full and free forgiveness.

This incident provides us with a beautiful example of divine forgiveness. Forgiveness is the removal of our sins in such a way that they are no longer a factor in God's dealings with us. We have no greater need than the need to be assured of God's forgiveness.

I. The fullness of the divine forgiveness.

A. *God's forgiveness is full in that He forgives all kinds of sins.* This man brought to the cross guilt for many different types of sins. His sins may have begun in his own home. He was probably leaving behind a broken-hearted father and mother whose warnings and appeals had been spurned. This man may have broken all of the Ten Commandments along the way.

When I find people burdened with guilt, I often ask them, Have you ever done anything which you feel that God cannot forgive? I am constantly surprised by the things people present to me which they feel God cannot forgive: for one person it is adultery, for another homosexuality, for another divorce, for another stealing, and I could go on. The account of this thief's forgiveness is included to say to us that God forgives all kinds of sins.

B. *God's forgiveness is full in that He forgives all sins, regardless of their number.* Can a man accumulate so many sins that God could not forgive them all? Is there a certain number of sins that mark the limit to the divine forgiveness? The forgiveness of this man stands as a witness to the fullness of God's forgiveness. God has no more difficulty in forgiving a multitude of sins than He does in forgiving one sin. For God to forgive any sin required the sacrificial death of His Son, and when He died on the cross He died for all. Being the Son of God, His death has merit enough to cover all our transgressions.

The prophet Isaiah saw this when he cried, "Come now, and let us reason together, saith the LORD: though your sins be as scarlet, they shall be as white as snow; though they be red like crimson, they shall be as wool" (Isa. 1:18). John assured us, "If we confess our sins, he is faithful and just to forgive us our sins, and to cleanse us from all unrighteousness" (1 John 1:9). The term "all unrighteousness" reminds us of the fullness of divine forgiveness.

II. The freeness of God's forgiveness.

This incident exposes more erroneous thinking about how a man receives forgiveness than any other incident in the Bible. Doubtlessly, the Holy Spirit caused Luke to include this for that very reason. God forgives men freely. There was no other way this condemned man could have known forgiveness.

A. *Divine forgiveness is extended apart from good works.*

This man had no opportunity to do any good works. Again and again I encounter people who have the feeling that if they will just do enough good works, God will forgive their transgressions. When they feel pangs of guilt concerning the sins of the past, they redouble their efforts to cover their sins with a multitude of good works. God forgave this thief though he did not perform any deed of mercy or extend one hand of kindness. He received the forgiveness of his sins from Jesus as a free gift.

B. *Divine forgiveness is extended apart from religious affiliation or ordinances.*

There was no opportunity for this man to be baptized, so baptism is not necessary to wash away our sins. There was no opportunity for this man to receive communion, so such an ordinance must not be necessary to receive God's forgiveness. This man did not have opportunity to affiliate with any religious group or institution, so such affiliation must not be necessary for divine forgiveness. Forgiveness is given as a free gift apart from the religious trappings.

C. *Divine forgiveness comes through repentance.*

Repentance is expressed in the acknowledgment of one's sins. This man openly acknowledged his guilt and his worthiness of the condemnation that had befallen him. This is a most difficult thing to do. It is coming to the place where you can sincerely admit, "I have sinned. I am the sinner." This is absolutely essential, for God cannot forgive a sin that you will not acknowledge.

D. *Divine forgiveness comes by faith.*

After the acknowledgment of the sin in repentance, there must be the turning to Jesus for forgiveness. This means that you must do what the thief did. You must ask Jesus for it. Though he did not express it in exact words, Jesus knew what the man meant and wanted. This was faith!

Freeness of forgiveness makes it possible for all men to be forgiven at any place and any time in life. Though this experience surely does not encourage a man to wait for deathbed repentance, it surely does encourage us to beleive that it is never too late to turn to Christ. God forgives freely and fully.

Conclusion. God is a God of forgiveness. He will abundantly pardon. In the death of His Son upon the cross, God made full provisions for the forgiveness of your sins. Jesus willingly and gladly took all of your sins to the tree. Now, God awaits your coming to receive this forgiveness which He freely offers. Will you, like the thief, ask Him to forgive your sins and to become the Lord of your life? —*DLL*

* * *

WEDNESDAY EVENING, APRIL 13

TITLE: What the Bible Says About Demons

TEXT: "For he said to him, 'Come out of the man, you unclean spirit!'" (Mark 5:8 RSV).

SCRIPTURE READING: Mark 5:1–20

Introduction. The subject of demons has run the gamut in peoples' thinking. There are those who become obsessed with the study, allowing their imaginations to run away with them. They see "demons" everywhere. Some become self-appointed "exorcists," and set about to rid their world of these emissaries of Satan. They tend to ascribe everything evil to demonic activity. At the other extreme, there are those who deny the existence of demons, relegating them to ancient mythology or to an earlier era of ignorance and superstition.

The ancient Greeks believed that demons were the souls of evil people who had died. Others have believed that demons are the disembodied spirits of a race of people who existed before Adam and Eve were created. The Scriptures, however, make no mention of such a race.

It is the general consensus of conservative theologians that demons are the angels who revolted with Satan (note the close relationship between Satan and angels in Matt. 12:24 and 25:41). They are also referred to as "unclean spirits" (Mark 9:25). Whereas the King James Version of the Bible refers to them as "devils," the proper translation of the Greek word is "demons." There is *one* Devil, but apparently *many* demons.

I. The nature and activity of demons.

A. *Demons do not appear to be omnipresent; each demon can be in only one place at any given moment.* The incident near Gadara when Jesus allowed the demons which had inhabited the wild man to enter the swine shows that they can be confined and would indicate their lack of omnipresence (Mark 5:1–13. *See also* 2 Peter 2:4). Though they possess a high degree of intelligence by virtue of their long existence and experience, they are not omniscient.

B. *They are promoters of a system of doctrine* (1 Tim. 4:1–3; *compare with* 1 John 2:19; 4:3; *also* 2 Cor. 11:13–15). The doctrine of demons includes a works salvation (1 Tim. 4:3–4), and the denial of the divinity of Jesus (1 John 2:22–23).

C. *They are agents of destruction, particularly of the bodies and souls of men (see* Matt. 9:33; 12:22; Mark 3:10; Luke 13:11, 16; Acts 8:7).

D. *They are promoters of delusion* (Rev. 12:9). One of Satan's basic designs is to deceive, and it appears that his emissaries, the demons, carry out that design. Daniel 10:13, 20 seems to relate this activity particularly to the governments of the world.

II. The phenomenon of demon possession.

A. *Though it is clear in the Scriptures that there is such a thing as demon possession (Jesus and His disciples dealt with it, as did other first-century Christian leaders), not every expression of evil can be termed such.*

B. *Because believers are "not [their] own . . . [but] are bought with a price"* (1 Cor. 6:19–20), *they are God's property.* God is greater than Satan or his demons; therefore, neither Satan nor his demons can have ultimate or final victory over believers. They may, however, influence and harass them. We can be sure, however, that Satan would destroy *every* believer if he could.

C. *The Bible seems to indicate that a believer may be delivered to Satan "for the destruction of the flesh," but the spirit will "be saved in the day of the Lord Jesus"* (1 Cor. 5:5). Whatever relationship Satan or his demons may have to a believer during this earthly life, it cannot be permanent or eternal.

III. The defense against demon power.

A. *It is never wise for Christians to dabble in or flirt with the occult, even on a superficial or entertainment level.* God warned His ancient people about this (Deut. 18:10–11; see also the account of the "book burning" in Acts 19 in regard to the Ephesians). Though astrologers, horoscopes, palm readers, et al., may be "make-believe," still they represent eras in which satanic influence was openly recognized and even deferred to. Even today there are Satan worshipers and cultic practitioners among us.

B. *Even more practically, Paul states: "Let not the sun go down upon your wrath: Neither give place to the devil"* (Eph. 4:26–27). The Bible does speak of a righteous anger or indignation—Paul forbids prolonging it. The indication is that wrath in excess will give opportunity for Satan to gain an advantage in a believer's life.

C. *The Christian should always rely on the presence of the indwelling Holy Spirit in his life, acknowledging that "greater is he that is in you, than he that is in the world"* (1 John 4:4).

Conclusion. In the light of these facts, every believer in the Lord Jesus Christ should be *alert* (1 Peter 5:8). He should take care that he is clothed with the whole armor of God (Eph. 6:13–18). He should always recognize that his body is the temple of the Holy Spirit, and that he should strive to keep himself physically, mentally, and spiritually strong (Rom. 12:2; 2 Cor. 10:5; Phil. 4:8).

—DLJ

SUNDAY MORNING, APRIL 17

TITLE: Living at a New Address

TEXT: "You know that he appeared to take away sins, and in him there is no sin. No one who abides in him sins" (1 John 3:5–6 RSV).

SCRIPTURE READING: 1 John 1:5–9; 3:5–10

HYMNS: "There Is Power in the Blood," Jones
"I Need Thee, Precious Jesus," Whitfield
"Grace Greater Than Our Sin," Johnston

OFFERTORY PRAYER:

Lord God, whom we have come to know in Jesus Christ, we are grateful for this new week. May our worship this Lord's Day be in the right spirit and consistent with the truth revealed in Jesus. We ask Your forgiveness of those things we ought not to have done this past week as well as the failure to do the good we knew about. We desire power over sin, so lead us into the relationship in which that is possible. Motivate us to give with the assurance Paul possessed: "My God will supply every need of yours according to his riches in glory in Christ Jesus." In Jesus' name. Amen.

Introduction. Being a Christian could be described as living at a new address. A Christian is a person who has moved from the house whose landlord is sin into a new home with Christ. This new relationship to sin is the second gift made possible by Christ's victory over death.

I. The living Christ brings death to sin.

A. *A remedy for sin* (1 John 3:5). Mankind has always sought relief from the crushing weight of wrong. Sin brings guilt, death, and shame. How can the sin problem be handled? One approach is to place the blame on someone or something else. Adam played this ancient game called "pass the buck." Some people attempt to handle sin by personal deeds in an effort to balance the scale, but new sins keep upsetting the balance. Presentation of a sacrifice to appease the offended individual is another futile effort. John declares the absolute remedy for sin: "He appeared to take away sins, and in him there is no sin," (RSV). The angel prophesied Jesus' work: ". . . he shall save his people from their sins" (Matt. 1:21). John the Baptist introduced Jesus as "the Lamb of God, who takes away the sin of the world!" (John 1:29 RSV). "For our sake he made him to be sin who knew no sin, so that in him we might become the righteousness of God" (2 Cor. 5:21 RSV). Jesus' critics were right—"only God can forgive sin." His death and resurrection are the only adequate remedy for sin.

His resurrection assures us of this. Since death is the wages of sin, a dead Christ would be powerless over sin. "If Christ has not been raised, your faith is futile and you are still in your sins" (1 Cor. 15:17 RSV). His resurrection means victory over sin and death.

B. *Defeat of the Devil.* Sin is a work of the Devil; "for the devil has sinned from the beginning" (1 John 3:8 RSV). Jesus came to defeat the work of this prince of darkness. When the seventy returned from their successful witness assignments, Jesus exclaimed, "I saw Satan fall like lightning from heaven. . . .

I have given you authority . . . over all the power of the enemy'' (Luke 10:18–19 RSV). The Christian has power to resist and defeat the Devil's temptations. Satan continues his slanderous work of deception, but King Jesus is more powerful than the prince of evil.

II. Sin in a Christian's life.

A. *A Christian is not perfect* (1 John 1:8). The assurance of victory over sin and Satan is quickly countered by the evidence of sin in the life of professing Christians. How are we to reconcile this reality with the truth, ''No one who abides in him sins''? Power over sin does not mean sinless perfection, and the Christian who claims to have reached such a state is guilty of self-deception. ''If we say we have no sin, we deceive ourselves, and the truth is not in us. . . . If we say we have not sinned, we make him a liar, and his word is not in us'' (1 John 1:8, 10 RSV).

B. *A different pattern of life* (1 John 3:6–10). On the surface it appears that the apostle contradicts himself. In chapter 1 he admits sin in the Christian life; in chapter 3 he declares, ''No one born of God commits sin'' (v. 6). The verbs in this section are in the perfect tense and refer to continuous, habitual action. ''No one who practices sin has ever seen Him or come to know Him. . . . Whoever practices sin belongs to the devil . . .'' (vv. 6, 8 WILLIAMS). A genuine Christian exhibits a new pattern in his life. New desires, direction, and destiny are clearly evident. He lives at a new address (2 Cor. 5:17).

III. Victory over sin.

A. *Walk in the light* (1 John 1:7). The way to daily victory over the pull of the old life is to ''walk in the light.'' This dynamic relationship is expressed in a favorite phrase of John's, ''abide in him'' (2:6, 14, 24, 28; 3:6, 24; 4:13, 16). The closer we are to the Lord the farther we will be from sin.

B. *Continual confession and cleansing* (1 John 1:9). When sin occurs, confess it to the Lord and accept His cleansing. His grace is greater than our sin. He will forgive and clean out the sin.

Conclusion. An old gospel song expresses what every Christian has experienced:

> It's different now,
> Since Jesus saved my soul.
> It's different now,
> Since by his blood I'm whole.
> From Satan he rescued me,
> And now I am set free.
> Oh, it's different now!

Have you moved to that new address? —*BW*

* * *

SUNDAY EVENING, APRIL 17

TITLE: The Face of Faith: the Centurion

TEXT: ''Now when the centurion, and they that were with him, watching

Jesus, saw the earthquake, and those things that were done, they feared greatly, saying, Truly this was the Son of God" (Matt. 27:54).

Scripture Reading: Matthew 27:45–56

Introduction. The centurion represented the best of Roman men. They rose through the ranks to be commander over one hundred men. Those who appear in the New Testament are presented as strong and good men.

This unnamed centurion witnessed all of the tragic events connected with the death of our Lord. He was probably present at the arrest and the trial; we know that he was at the cross. What he saw and heard had a profound effect on him.

It was just after the earthquake that he made his confession. He exclaimed, "Truly this was the Son of God." He had become a man of faith in Jesus Christ. This is the confession that God wants to hear from each of us. If we will look closely at this "face of faith" beneath the cross, perhaps we, too, can join him in his confession.

I. The evidence for faith.

This noble man changed his mind about Jesus in a relatively short time. He set out to help the Jews rid themselves of a nuisance and ended up confessing the nuisance to be none less than the Son of God. What were the evidences that changed his mind?

A. *The manner of Christ's suffering.*

Never had the commander seen one human being undergo so much abuse. He had been harassed, beaten, mocked, whipped, spat on, and now crucified. But not once did the victim ever lose His poise or react in anger.

Even as the soldiers nailed Him to the tree, He was meek and submissive. The only words that escaped His lips were a prayer, "Father, forgive them; for they know not what they do." Observing all of this gave the centurion a strange feeling. What kind of man was this? Surely He must be more than human!

B. *The love for enemies.*

It was obvious that the crowd hated Jesus. The relentless barrage of accusations and mockery even as He died was evidence of this. But their ridicule got no like response from Him. The only response He ever made was the prayer, "Father, forgive them." He was obviously concerned about the welfare of the crowd that was causing His death. What love! This impressed the centurion! This caused him to wonder about the judgment of the crowd and Pilate. Did One with such love deserve to die?

C. *The physical phenomena.*

It was a strange day. After Jesus had been on His cross about three hours, a strange darkness came over the land. Even though it was high noon, there was no sun to be seen. As the centurion stood near the cross during the darkness, he heard Jesus utter a strange, eerie cry, "My God, my God, why hast thou forsaken me?"

About three o'clock the darkness lifted, and the victim died. But then the whole countryside began to shake with an earthquake. The centurion sensed that there was a connection between the death of Jesus and the earthquake. Surely, He was not a criminal!

D. *The manner of His death.*

Death came to Jesus in a strange way. This soldier had seen many men die in the course of his duty. He knew that death by crucifixion usually followed a certain pattern. But in this case, just before death, the victim gave a loud cry, "It is finished." It was like a shout of triumph. Then, quietly He prayed again, "Father, into thy hands I commit my spirit." Then He was dead. He died as though He were the one in charge. He died with a quiet trust in God.

The evidence was just too much for the Roman. He knew in his heart that this Man was more than a man. So, he exclaimed, "Truly this was the Son of God." We have more evidence than the centurion, for we know of the glorious Resurrection and continued work of Jesus. Look at the evidence carefully and it will lead to faith.

II. The evidence of faith.

We have two separate accounts of the confession of the centurion. According to Luke, he declared, "Certainly this was a righteous man." Matthew reports that he confessed Jesus to be the Son of God. Doubtlessly both reports are true.

A. *The act of confession.*

The act itself reveals faith. This is the only voice heard at the cross that has anything commendatory to say about Jesus. It is one thing to have some impressions in your heart, but another thing to verbalize those impressions. It is the nature of true faith to confess. If you have never confessed, there is a serious question about your faith.

B. *The substance of the confession.*

What the centurion confessed is the real evidence, however. He confessed the righteous character of Jesus. This contradicted the judgment of the world. This is in itself a rather strong confession.

But then he confessed the uniqueness of Christ, "Truly this was the Son of God." Scholars still debate about how much the soldier understood, and whether or not he meant to confess the deity of Christ. Surely, the gospel writer included this because he saw this as being the logical end of this life and death. Matthew and Luke put it at the climax of the whole story. Without trying to make a theologian out of the soldier, let's accept his confession for what it says. He had come to believe in the uniqueness of Christ, that He was the Son of God.

We see faith beneath the cross, but it is in the heart of a Gentile soldier.

Conclusion. Dr. Russell Bradley Jones tells about an old English farmer who went to London and visited one of the great art galleries of the city. There he was attracted by a painting of the Crucifixion scene. He sat before it, studying each detail with intense interest. At last, forgetful of his surroundings, he cried out, "Bless Him! I love Him!" Others nearby, startled by his words, came to see what was wrong with the old man. From different parts of the gallery they gathered around him. They saw the tears flowing down his bronzed cheeks. They, too, looked at the painting of the Crucifixion. After awhile, one man in the group, with tearful eyes, reached for the farmer's hand and said, "And I love Him too!" Then another and another and still another took the old man's hand, until there was a sizable group of sobbing believers rejoicing at the foot of the picture of Christ's crucifixion, saying, "We love Him too!"

Will you join the centurion beneath His cross in the confession, "Truly this man is the Son of God."

—DLL

WEDNESDAY EVENING, APRIL 20

TITLE: What the Bible Says About Hell

TEXT: "The rich man also died and was buried; and in Hades, being in torment . . ." (Luke 16:22 RSV).

SCRIPTURE READING: Matthew 25:41–46

Introduction. In common usage, "hell" designates the place of future punishment for the wicked. Satan hates the doctrine of an eternal hell. As a result, we have many groups today (some purportedly evangelical) who either deny the existence of hell or else make it a place of annihilation. Satan has even used mythology to discredit the existence of hell in modern minds—such as the Wagnerian "Mephistopheles" from *Faust;* the "River Styx"; Pluto, who is conceived to be the ruler of this region in the depths of the earth (Dante's *Inferno*), and so on.

I. Descriptions of hell.

A. *Hell is described as a place of everlasting fire* (Matt. 25:41) *and eternal punishment* (Matt. 25:46).

B. *Jesus also called hell a place of "outer darkness"* (Matt. 8:12). The "children of the kingdom" to whom he referred apparently were Jews who, because of natural birth, considered themselves automatically children of the kingdom of God.

C. *Paul referred to hell as a place of everlasting destruction* (2 Thess. 1:9).

D. *Perhaps the most common description of hell is found in John's Revelation:* "And the beast was taken, and with him the false prophet that wrought miracles before him, with which he deceived them that had received the mark of the beast, and them that worshipped his image. These both were cast alive into a lake of fire burning with brimstone" (Rev. 19:20).

II. The reason for hell's existence.

A. *Jesus clearly taught that hell was prepared "for the devil and his angels"* (Matt. 25:41). The inference is that human beings who go there must choose the philosophy and lifestyle of Satan's kingdom over against the invitations of God.

B. *Hell exists for the wicked:* "But the fearful, the unbelieving, and the abominable, and murderers, and whoremongers, and sorcerers, and idolaters, and all liars, shall have their part in the lake which burneth with fire and brimstone: which is the second death" (Rev. 21:8).

C. *Hell also will be populated with those who are disobedient:* "But unto them that are contentious, and do not obey the truth, but obey unrighteousness, indignation and wrath, tribulation and anguish, upon every soul of man that doeth evil, of the Jew first, and also of the Gentile" (Rom. 2:8–9).

D. *Hell was also prepared for the "fallen angels":* "For if God spared not the angels that sinned, but cast them down to hell, and delivered them into chains of darkness, to be served unto judgment" (2 Peter 2:4).

E. *Hell will await those who reject the gospel:* "Verily I say unto you, It shall be more tolerable for the land of Sodom and Gomorrah in the day of judgment, than for that city'' (Matt. 10:15).

III. The punishment of hell.

A. *The punishment of hell will be eternal, everlasting:* ''. . . shall be tormented day and night for ever and ever'' (Rev. 20:10).

B. *It will be a bodily punishment:* ''And if thy right eye offend thee, pluck it out, and cast it from thee: for it is profitable for thee that one of thy members should perish, and not that thy whole body should be cast into hell. And if thy right hand offend thee, cut it off, and cast it from thee: for it is profitable for thee that one of thy members should perish, and not that thy whole body should be cast into hell'' (Matt. 5:29–30). The ''body'' indicated here doubtlessly will be of spiritual proportions, since ''flesh and blood'' bodies would not be able to exist in an eternal state, either in heaven or in hell.

C. *Apparently the punishment of hell will vary in degree, and in accord with the opportunity one had to avoid hell:* ''Woe unto you, scribes and Pharisees, hypocrites! for ye devour widows' houses, and for a pretence make long prayer: therefore ye shall receive the greater damnation'' (Matt. 23:14).

D. *The punishment of hell will be unchangeable, doing away with the possibility of ''a second chance''* (see Luke 16:22–31).

IV. Condition of the inhabitants of hell.

A. *They will possess memory of events, people, and opportunities in the earthly life* (see Luke 16:23, 25).

B. *They will cry for release* (see Luke 16:24).

C. *Even in hell, there is no escape from the sovereignty of God.* (Ps. 139:8).

V. Major words for ''hell'' in the Scriptures.

A. *Sheol occurs sixty-five times in the Old Testament and is translated thirty-one times ''hell'' and three times ''pit.''* The general idea is ''the place of the dead,'' not the grave, but the place of those departed from this life. It is used both for the righteous and the wicked (*righteous:* Ps. 16:10; 30:3; Isa. 38:10, et al.; *wicked:* Num. 16:33; Job 24:19; Ps. 9:17, et al.).

B. *Hades—one of the New Testament terms rendered ''hell''—is similar in significance to the Old Testament ''sheol.''* It refers to the underworld, or the region of the departed. It occurs eleven times in the New Testament and is rendered ''hell'' every time with one exception (1 Cor. 15:55, ''grave''). Jesus associated judgment and suffering with the condition of the inhabitants of ''hades'' (Matt. 11:23).

C. *Gehenna—''the valley of Hinnom''—was a place where the Jewish apostasy, the rites of Molech, were celebrated* (1 Kings 11:17). It was converted by king Josiah into a place of abomination where dead bodies were thrown and burned (2 Kings 23:13–14). The word occurs twelve times in the New Testament and in every case denotes the eternal state of the lost after the Resurrection. Christ's descent was into ''hades'' (intermediate state) and not into ''Gehenna.''

Conclusion. Because of the movement in the Scriptures between the literal, symbolic, and figurative in regard to the descriptions and teachings about hell, there exist on the part of sincere students of the Bible many differing interpretations and understandings. Of one thing we can be certain: hell is eternal and is chiefly and most horribly to be considered a place of separation from God. In the final analysis, everything else is incidental. —*DLJ*

* * *

SUNDAY MORNING, APRIL 24

TITLE: What the World Needs Now Is Love

TEXT: "See what love the Father has given us . . ." (1 John 3:1a RSV).

SCRIPTURE READING: 1 John 3:1a, 11–18; 4:7–12

HYMNS: "Love Is the Theme," Fisher
"I Love Thee," Anonymous
"The King of Love My Shepherd Is," Baker

OFFERTORY PRAYER:

Our heavenly Father, we praise You for loving us "while we were yet sinners." We realize the extent of Your love by the gift of Jesus and His death on the cross. We praise You for Your continuing love, active in temptation and trial, forgiving and fortifying us. Remind us that to whom much is given much is required. We ask You to impart comfort to the bereaved and healing to the ill, power to the spiritually weak, and joy to the despondent. We present our gifts in the hope that they will be used to help our church minister to people in need. We give in order to share Your love, which we have so generously received. We pray this in Jesus' name. Amen.

Introduction. A basic need of every person is the need to be loved. The lyrics of a popular song reflect this world-wide longing—"what the world needs now is love." God has met this need in Christ. Because of Jesus, a new kind of love is possible and is at work in our world.

I. See the Father's love.

A. *God loves us* (1 John 3:1). When Martin Luther's translation of the Bible was being printed, a piece of type fell to the floor. The printer's daughter later found the section, which said, "For God so loved the world that he gave." Excitedly, she showed it to her mother. Her mother said it didn't make any sense. "Gave what?" The girl responded, "Oh, Mama, it doesn't matter. If God loves me enough to give me anything, I don't have to be afraid of Him." Many think of God as harsh, judgmental, or indifferent toward the world. The truth is, He loves us. "God is love" (4:8).

B. *The gift of love* (4:9–10). How do we know God loves us? "In *this* the love of God was made manifest among us, that God sent his only Son into the world, so that we might live through him" (v. 9 RSV). The Cross is God's bold demonstration of love. Because He loved us, He suffered the shame and pain. Because He loved us, the awful separation of sin was experienced. Love took Him into the darkness of death.

Bennett Cerf tells of an eight-year-old girl in a Pennsylvania orphanage. She was painfully shy, unattractive, and generally shunned by the other children. The orphanage directors regarded her as a problem child. A rule of the home required the directors' approval of any written communication prior to mailing. One afternoon the girl was seen hiding a letter in the branches of a tree that hung over the wall. The letter was seized and opened. It read: "To anybody who finds this: I love you." Our Lord Jesus was driven by a loveless world outside the city wall. He hung on the cross, a message from God to the world—I love you!

II. The example of Christ.

A. *Inclusive and active* (1 John 3:16–18). The pattern of Christ's love is to be lived out in the Christian's life. "By this we know love. . . ." By what? The example of Christ—the perfect pattern of love. The way to respond to others is to walk in His steps. His love included all people and was active in their lives.

A small boy in Texas has a rare disease which prohibits anyone from touching him. He lives in a sealed environment and has never felt the actual touch of those who love him. Jesus faced many "untouchables" in His day. No one wanted to touch the lepers. When they went out in public, they cried out "unclean" and people avoided them. Jesus touched the lepers; they needed His love. The Samaritans were excluded and considered social untouchables. Jesus ministered to the Samaritan woman and honored every Samaritan in the story of the Good Samaritan. Jesus had fellowship with the religious untouchables, people who did not scrupulously keep the law and were regarded as ceremonially unclean. Jesus loved people. Each person was of value and full of potential. That kind of love is the pattern for every Christian. "Beloved, if God so loved us, we also ought to love one another" (4:11). Can His love be seen in us?

We ask, "Who is our brother?" When in love we seek people in need, we discover our brother. We naturally tend to love those who love us or share our values. We demand change before we give love. *Agape* love includes every person and is actively involved in an effort to share Christ's love with them.

B. *Exclusive and eternal* (2:15–17). The love of Christ is not gullible nor naïve. Love of God, who is holy, means one cannot love the things which are against Christ. We love sinners but do not love the sin. "Do not love the world . . . [nor] the lust of the flesh and the lust of the eyes and the pride of life" (vv. 15–16 RSV). Christ's love is exclusive.

His love is also eternal—"he who does the will of God abides for ever." To receive Christ by repentance and faith is to do the will of God and become united with the love of God. Paul affirmed that nothing could "separate us from the love of God in Christ Jesus our Lord" (Rom. 8:39).

> God's boundless love and arching sky
> Above us when we wake or sleep,
> Above us when we smile or weep,
> Above us when we live or die.
> . . .
> God's endless love! What will it be
> When earthly shadows flee away,
> For all Eternity's bright day
> The unfolding of that love to see!
> —*Maltbie D. Babcock*

Conclusion. Probably no word in our vocabulary is as misunderstood as *love*. We apply it to food and clothing tastes, to sensual relationships, and to religious experiences. My four-year-old asked me one day, "Daddy, how do you spell love?" I told her the four letters, which she proudly printed on a special note to those she loved. The spelling of love in our life is infinitely more complex. In Christ the true meaning is available, and the world desperately needs this love now. Can they see it in us? —*BW*

* * *

SUNDAY EVENING, APRIL 24

TITLE: The Face of Fear: Joseph

TEXT: "And after this Joseph of Arimathea, being a disciple of Jesus, but secretly for fear of the Jews, besought Pilate that he might take away the body of Jesus: and Pilate gave him leave. He came therefore, and took the body of Jesus. And there came also Nicodemus, which at the first came to Jesus by night, and brought a mixture of myrrh and aloes, about an hundred pound weight" (John 19:38–39).

SCRIPTURE READING: John 19:38–42

Introduction. The cross of Christ changed two cowards. They came to the cross bound by fear, but left with a life filled with courage. Since no one likes to give in to cowardly fears, this was a great moment for them.

Many of us find it easier to identify with Joseph and Nicodemus than with anyone else at the cross. We have known what it is to be silent when we should have spoken, to keep our relationship with Christ a secret when it should have been declared.

In many ways Joseph is a man of worthy and commendable character. He is so presented on the pages of the New Testament. Each of the gospel writers tells of his part in the burial of Christ. They tell us that he was a successful businessman who occupied a place of leadership in the community. Luke tells us that he was a "righteous" and "good" man. He was also a part of that remnant that looked for the kingdom of God. In spirit, he was akin to Simeon and Anna who appeared early in the life of Jesus.

He was probably a member of the Sanhedrin along with Nicodemus. This placed him in a unique position to act on behalf of Jesus. Since the decision by the Sanhedrin was unanimous, evidently Joseph and Nicodemus absented themselves from the important meeting. This would be easier than to speak up for Him. They would not have to make known that they were "disciples" of Jesus.

Yet after Christ's death they could keep their secret no longer. The Cross overcame their fear and allowed them to act in a responsible way. It took courage for Joseph to ask for the body of Jesus and to bury it in his own tomb. This was surely a public sign of friendship and support for the dead Christ.

I. The cause of fear.

John analyzes Joseph like this, ". . . being a disciple of Jesus, but secretly for fear of the Jews." Yet the Jews did not cause the fear; their presence simply caused it to be revealed. What caused it?

A. *Valuing position before men more than position before God.*

The riches and the position on the Sanhedrin had come to mean too much to

Joseph. They were the products of a lifetime of effort. He could not just cast them away without thought. What would it mean to lose them? Surely a bold confession of Christ Jesus would mean the loss of these. He would lose his position on the Sanhedrin, and it would probably affect his business adversely. This was at the root of the fear that silenced him. Such a value system has bound many a man with fear.

What impact does your value system have on your relationship to Jesus Christ? The person who is prepared to give a bold witness to Jesus must be ready to "set his affections on things above."

B. *Valuing the praise of men more than the praise of God.*

Having the approval of men can become very important; to lose the approval of others can become a major crisis. This was the reality that faced Joseph. If he made an open stand for Christ, the price would be high. The loss of the approval of others would be immediate. "What others think" can cause us to do many hurtful things.

You probably do not need to fear a physical attack if you become a Christian. You might have to face ridicule from your peers or from some member of your family. But which is more important, having their approval or the approval of God?

II. The cost of fear.

Here we must read between the lines, and attempt to put ourselves in the situation of this Jewish businessman.

A. *The opportunity for fellowship with Jesus.*

This opportunity was lost forever. Joseph missed seeing many of the miracles, hearing many of the lessons, and sharing the conversation with Jesus. He, too, could have walked with Peter and the others in His company. Is fear keeping you from this?

B. *The assurance of eternal life.*

There may be room for debate about whether or not a person can have eternal life and be a "secret disciple." Regardless of what position you take in the debate, surely you will agree that there can be no real assurance of salvation. Fear brings only torment, guilt, and self-accusation. Joseph must have been ashamed to face himself in the mirror when he considered his cowardly actions toward Christ. Assurance comes with a bold confession of Jesus as Lord (Rom. 10:9–10).

III. The cure for fear.

A. *The Cross cures our fears by revealing the end of fear.*

As Joseph and Nicodemus saw Jesus hanging on the cross, they could see the end of cowardly actions. Deep within they knew their silence had played a part in this terrible tragedy. Such cowardly fear hangs "right" on a cross and places "wrong" on a throne.

Realizing what their silence had done prompted them to take action. Do you realize that the body of Jesus might have been thrown in the trash heap or buried in a common grave with the thieves if these two had not acted? Have you ever considered the end of your fearful way of life?

B. *The Cross cures our fears by revealing the love of God to us.*

Nicodemus probably remembered his first meeting with Jesus. In the protective shadows of the night, Jesus had said to him, "And as Moses lifted up the serpent in the wilderness, even so must the Son of man be lifted up, that whosoever believeth in him should not perish, but have eternal life" (John 3:14–15). As Nicodemus and Joseph saw Him hanging there, Nicodemus may have shared this with Joseph. They could see just how far He was willing to go for them.

How could they be silent before such love? How can you? This kind of love casts out fear.

Conclusion. In the light of the love of the Lord Jesus Christ, I call you to action. I call on you to cast aside your secrecy and your fears, and to boldly declare Him as your Lord. Let all the world know that you rest your hopes of eternal life on Christ alone. He promises, "Whosoever . . . shall confess me before men, him will I confess also before my Father which is in heaven. But whosoever shall deny me before men, him will I also deny before my Father which is in heaven" (Matt. 10:32–33).

—DLL

* * *

WEDNESDAY EVENING, APRIL 27

TITLE: What the Bible Says About Heaven

TEXT: "In my Father's house are many rooms . . ." (John 14:2 RSV).

SCRIPTURE READING: Revelation 21:1–4; 22:1–5

Introduction. Heaven is a blessed anticipation for all believers. It is natural, therefore, to have a healthy curiosity to know what heaven is really like. Understandably, the Scriptures are highly symbolic in their descriptions of heaven. This is true because the Bible must use "earthly words" to describe a celestial place. Most of what the Bible says about heaven must be understood in its symbolical and figurative setting. The writers, under the inspiration of the Holy Spirit, were simply using the most exquisite language at their disposal to describe heaven. Some would concentrate on those characteristics of heaven that parallel the material and physical nature of earth, such as, the "streets of gold," "walls of jasper," and "gates of pearl." Heaven is a place where spirit beings dwell; material things are of no significance there. Thus, the purpose of this study is to emphasize the spiritual nature of heaven and not necessarily its "physical" properties.

I. The inhabitants of heaven.

A. *God is there.* "And hearken thou to the supplication of thy servant, and of thy people Israel, when they shall pray toward this place: and hear thou in heaven thy dwelling place: and when thou hearest, forgive" (1 Kings 8:30).

B. *Christ is there.* "Neither by the blood of goats and calves, but by his own blood he entered in once into the holy place, having obtained eternal redemption for us. . . . For Christ is not entered into the holy places made with hands, which are the figures of the true; but into heaven itself, now to appear in the presence of God for us" (Heb. 9:12, 24).

C. *The Holy Spirit is there.* "Whither shall I go from thy spirit? or whither shall I flee from thy presence? If I ascend up into heaven, thou art there: if I make my bed in hell, behold, thou art there'' (Ps. 139:7–8).

D. *The angels are there.* ''Take heed that ye despise not one of these little ones; for I say unto you, That in heaven their angels do always behold the face of my Father which is in heaven'' (Matt. 18:10).

E. *God's people are there.* ''But ye are come unto mount Zion, and unto the city of the living God, the heavenly Jerusalem, and to an innumerable company of angels, To the general assembly and church of the firstborn, which are written in heaven, and to God the Judge of all, and to the spirits of just men made perfect'' (Heb. 12:22–23).

II. The negative characteristics of heaven.

A. *In heaven there will be no marriage, thus apparently no family unit relationships as we know them on earth* (Matt. 22:30).

B. *There will be no death there, no termination of existence and relationships* (Luke 20:36).

C. *''Flesh and blood'' bodies will not inhabit heaven* (1 Cor. 15:50).

D. *There will be no corruption there; that is, nothing will deteriorate or pass away in heaven* (15:42, 50).

E. *There will be no weariness in heaven.* A part of the curse connected with Adam's sin in the Garden of Eden was the fact that he would ''toil'' in order to make his bread, which is suggested by ''the sweat of thy face'' (Gen. 3:17–19). Heaven's inhabitants will not grow tired (2 Cor. 5:1–10).

F. *There will be no pain in heaven* (Rev. 21:4); *nor will there be any night* (22:5), *wicked people* (22:15), *sorrow* (7:17), *or end* (Matt. 25:46).

III. The positive characteristics of heaven.

A. *Heaven will be a place of ceaseless and unending joy* (Luke 15:7, 10), *rest* (Rev. 14:13), *and peace* (Luke 16:25).

B. *Heaven will be characterized by righteousness* (2 Peter 3:13) *which, along with love, is the emanating nature of God.*

C. *In heaven there will be opportunity for service* (Rev. 7:15). It will not be a place or a state of barren inactivity. Its inhabitants will not ''float about on a fleecy white cloud, strumming a harp,'' as heaven is so often caricatured.

D. *Heaven will be a place of reward* (Matt. 5:11–12). God will give proper commendation to those who have been faithful to Him.

E. *God's people will receive an inheritance in heaven* (1 Peter 1:3–5), *which underscores our sonship and heirship with Christ.*

Conclusion. Because of this ''foretaste'' of heaven given believers in the Scriptures (Acts 7:55–56), we should earnestly anticipate our eternal state (2 Cor. 5:2, 8), realizing that it will be a state of existence far superior to any we could conceive on earth. We should ''look for'' the coming of the new heavens and new earth (2 Peter 3:12–13), realizing that it will be ''far better'' than now (Phil. 1:23–24). At the same time, we should rejoice in the fact that our ''treasure'' is safe there (Luke 12:33). *—DLJ*

* * *

SUGGESTED PREACHING PROGRAM FOR THE MONTH OF MAY

Sunday Mornings

Marriage and the family are experiencing great stress in the present day. The church has a vital stake in the husband-wife relationships and in the parent-child relationships of those who constitute its membership. Every possible assistance needs to be given. The suggested theme for these messages is "The Christian Family: Living for Christ in the Present."

Sunday Evenings

The suggested theme is "Thinking About the Cross." As Christians, we live under the inspiration of a crucified but risen Savior. God's gift to us upon the cross motivates us to unselfish service.

Wednesday Evenings

The suggested theme is "The Christ of John's Gospel." We will begin a series of expository studies in the Gospel of John that focus on John's unique portrayal of the Christ.

* * *

SUNDAY MORNING, MAY 1

TITLE: The Spirit Within and the World Without

TEXT: "Little children, you are of God, and have overcome them; for he who is in you is greater than he who is in the world" (1 John 4:4 RSV).

SCRIPTURE READING: Acts 1:8; 1 John 3:23–4:4; 5:4–5

HYMNS: "Come, Thou Almighty King," Anonymous
"Breathe on Me, Breath of God," Hatch
"Seal Us, O Holy Spirit," Meredith

OFFERTORY PRAYER:

Our Father in heaven, we adore You and come to worship. We are not ashamed of the Good News of Jesus, for through it we have come to possess abundant life. We thank You for the power of Your daily presence. Help us to walk by faith and not by sight. We pray that You would forgive us of giving into Satan's deception and trying to cope with our world with only our own ability. Thank You for keeping us unto this day. We are glad we can give to tell the news of life in Christ. Magnify our gifts, and bring in the lost and lonely. We pray this in the name of Jesus, who pleads our cause at the throne of grace. Amen.

Introduction. With what do you associate the word *power?* The power of a river—constructive when harnessed at a dam but very damaging in a rampaging flood? The power of atomic energy, capable of leveling Hiroshima or fueling a mighty ship? The powerful influence of a government leader? The power of peer pressure? *Power* can be defined as "the means to achieve the assignment." It is frustrating to be placed in a leadership position without the power to lead. An automobile without a motor is good only for display or imagination.

A Christian is to be more than a showpiece of morality. Christians are called to be salt and light in the world, a preserving and uplifting influence among men—God's change-agents in the world. Is there power to accomplish this? Jesus gives assurance the power is available: "You shall receive power when the Holy Spirit has come upon you" (Acts 1:8 RSV). The Spirit within is the power to face the world without. This gift of victorious power is affirmed in 1 John: "He who is in you is greater than he who is in the world" (4:4).

I. The Spirit within.

A. *The Spirit assumes residence* (1 John 3:23–24). There is much controversy over the person and power of the Holy Spirit. The debate causes many Christians to completely ignore this vital area of relationship to God. Paul warned that in the last days there would be many "holding the form of religion but denying the power of it" (2 Tim. 3:5 RSV).

The beginning realization of God's power is the fact the Spirit assumes residence in the Christian at the moment of repentance and faith. Obedience to the commandment of faith opens the door for the Spirit's entry. It is impossible to be a Christian without the Holy Spirit. The Spirit convicts of sin. The Spirit turns us toward God. "The Spirit of life in Christ Jesus has set me free from the law of sin and death" (Rom. 8:2 RSV). Jesus promised to send the Comforter and to be with us always. The only way His promise can be fulfilled is by the Holy Spirit—"Christ in you, the hope of glory" (Col. 1:27).

B. *The sign of the Spirit* (1 John 4:2). Someone asks, "How can I be sure the Spirit is within? Is there a certain sign?" The only sign is the confession of faith in and commitment of life to Jesus. "By this you know the Spirit of God: every spirit which confesses that Jesus Christ has come in the flesh is of God" (RSV). Jesus said the Spirit "will bear witness to me" (John 15:26), and "He will glorify me" (16:14).

II. The world without.

A. *Antichrist at work* (1 John 4:3). In opposition to the Spirit's work within us is the spirit of antichrist. The antichrist is not just a powerful evil to be revealed in the end times. The antichrist "is in the world already." The flesh and the Spirit are in conflict. "The god of this world" (2 Cor. 4:4) opposes Christ. Our "adversary the devil prowls around like a roaring lion, seeking some one to devour" (1 Peter 5:8 RSV).

B. *Test the spirits* (1 John 4:1). The spirit of antichrist is a master at deception—"even Satan disguises himself as an angel of light. So it is not strange if his servants also disguise themselves as servants of righteousness" (2 Cor. 11:14–15 RSV). Supernatural phenomena can be performed by the Devil. Just as important as faith in Christ is the commitment to "not believe every spirit." Gullible Christians will find themselves "carried about with every wind of doctrine" (Eph. 4:14). Every teaching should be subjected to the standard of Christ's Word. The Spirit within leads in this search for truth.

III. The Spirit overcomes.

A. *His power is greater* (1 John 4:4). The Word assures us of victory in this conflict with the spirit of antichrist. The Holy Spirit within is greater than he who is in the world. Second Kings 6 records the dramatic account of Elisha before the troops of Syria. Elisha's servant exclaimed in fear, "What shall we do?" That same debilitating fear grips us as we face problems, sin, and an uncertain future. Elisha said, "Fear not, for those who are with us are more than those who are with them" (v. 16 RSV). The prophet prayed, "O LORD, I pray thee, open his eyes that he may see" (v. 17). The young man's fear was overcome when he saw the mountain full of the Lord's army. We need a fresh vision of the spiritual resources within us. Nothing nor anyone is greater than the Lord.

B. *Appropriate the power* (1 John 5:4–5). The unbeliever says, "Seeing is believing." God says, "Believing is seeing!" The same Lord we trust to save us from hell is adequate for life, but His power is limited by lack of faith. "This is the victory that overcomes the world, our faith" (v. 4 RSV).

The Spirit is within us, but does the Spirit control us? We have faith in Jesus, but do we live by the faith of Jesus (Gal. 2:20)? Paul's injunction to "be filled with the Spirit" (Eph. 5:18) refers to the continual control of the Spirit in the believer's life. It involves avoidance of sin and commitment to God's will. The extent of our victory in the world without depends on the Spirit's control within.

"Now the Lord is the Spirit, and where the Spirit of the Lord is, there is freedom" (2 Cor. 3:17 RSV). Freedom to be what God wants us to be. Freedom to love as Christ loves. Freedom to courageously resist temptation and sin. Freedom to witness without fear or intimidation. The Spirit within sets us free to win the world (Acts 1:8).

Christ Jesus "was crucified in weakness, but lives by the power of God" (2 Cor. 13:4 RSV). Appropriate that power!

Conclusion. During the past month we have focused on the gifts which are ours as a result of knowing the living Christ. We can be sure of life in the Son, forgiveness and control of sin, the love of God, and the ability to love others. The Spirit within, the last of these gifts, makes possible all the others. Today I know I have believed and experience "the Spirit himself bearing witness with our spirit that we are children of God" (Rom. 8:16). Do you have that confidence? Have you received God's love in Christ?

Come Holy Spirit,
Dark is the hour—
We need your filling,
Your love and your mighty power;
Move now among us,
Stir us, we pray.
Come, Holy Spirit,
Revive the church today!

—*John W. Peterson*
Singspiration, Inc. 1971

Respond now to the Spirit.

—*BW*

* * *

SUNDAY EVENING, MAY 1

TITLE: The Necessity of the Cross

TEXT: "Was it not necessary that the Christ should suffer these things and enter into his glory?" (Luke 24:26 RSV).

SCRIPTURE READING: Luke 24:13–35

Introduction. This message is not addressed to those who are offended by the cross, nor to unbelievers, nor to those wise in their own conceits who think it foolish. Rather, it is addressed to those who might share, to some degree, in the attitude of those two sad-hearted disciples to whom Jesus appeared on the road to Emmaus. They loved Him. They knew He had died. But they did not see why His death was necessary. Why did He have to die? The unrecognized Christ who walked beside them lovingly described them as "foolish men, and slow of heart to believe" (v. 25) and asked, "Was it not necessary that the Christ should suffer these things and enter into his glory?" (v. 26).

To consider His question in our own context, the cross was necessary from two points of view, God's and man's.

I. From God's point of view the cross was necessary.

A. *The cross was necessary to reveal God's evaluation of human life.*

In Jesus' day human life was cheap. Unwanted children were disposed of. A slave might be killed by his master, and no questions were asked. Despots like Nero lighted their gardens with human torches. Human life is cheap in our day also. This is what makes war possible. This makes poverty and slums and economic injustice possible. Sin is rife and life is cheap. This is the attitude of a sinful world.

But life is not cheap. In God's sight life is supremely valuable. The death of His Son on the cross demonstrates this. Human life is not cheap when God was willing to give His only Son to die to save it.

B. *The cross was necessary to reveal the very essence of God's character.*

"God is love" (1 John 4:8b). Again John says, "Herein is love, not that we loved God, but that he loved us, and sent his Son to be the propitiation for our sins" (4:10). We could never see that without the cross. "But God commendeth his love toward us," Paul tells the Romans, "in that, while we were yet sinners, Christ died for us" (5:8). The cross reveals God in His limitless love, His boundless mercy, and His pardoning grace.

The cross reveals God not as a God of vengeance, nor as a despotic ruler, nor as a merciless judge, but as a loving Shepherd taking the trail of suffering and death to find the sheep that was lost. God is a suffering Father who longs for His prodigal son to return from the far country, and who receives and forgives him when he turns his steps toward home.

C. *The cross was necessary to reveal God's estimate of sin.*

Only as we look at the cross can we realize how awful sin is in God's sight. To many sin is cute, chic, in good taste; but to God sin is a horrible thing.

We call our sins mistakes, weaknesses, slips, complexes. Even when we use the word, we use it lightly, emptied of its real meaning. What is sin? It is sin that takes the holy God, incarnate in the flesh, and treats Him as no beast should ever be treated. It is sin that takes the sinless Jesus and strips Him, lashes Him, spits upon Him, pierces Him with nails, and then laughs at Him.

How bad is sin? Sin is so bad that only the shed blood of the Son of God could do anything about it. A pastor was waiting in a hospital with an anxious father whose little girl was in surgery. Presently, the surgeon came in and described the surgery he had just done. The incision went more than halfway around the little body. A rib had been removed. A nerve had been deliberately clipped. After the surgeon left, the father turned to his pastor and said, "If it took all that to make her well, my baby must have been terribly sick." If it took the death of God's Son to heal, this world must have been terribly sick. The world was and is terribly sick. Only the blood of Christ can heal it.

II. From man's point of view the cross was necessary.

Apart from Christ's death on the cross, we have no salvation; and apart from His sacrifice for our sakes, no hope. The cross is necessary for us. It is the power of God (1 Cor. 1:18).

A. *The cross is the power of God to challenge our sinful hearts.*

Jesus said: "And I, if I be lifted up from the earth, will draw all men unto me" (John 12:32). Nothing but the cross could have such arresting, lifting power. Paul speaks of Christ in the most personal terms when he refers to Him as "the Son of God, who loved me, and gave himself for me" (Gal. 2:20b).

To have someone willing to die for us is an arresting experience; and when someone does so, the experience can be traumatic. A hunter and his dog became temporarily separated. As the hunter was trying to cross a swift stream in a flimsy boat, the boat capsized. Coming up at that exact moment, his dog immediately plunged into the swirling waters to go to the aid of his master. The hunter was caught up into the limbs of a tree floating downstream and eventually made it to shore, but the dog was not so fortunate. His master stood helplessly on the riverbank and watched his faithful dog drown. Later he said, "It is a challenging thing to have someone die for you—even a dog." But consider this: It was *the Son of God* who loved us and gave Himself up for us.

B. *The cross is the power of God to atone for our sins.*

The New Testament is most emphatic on this point. The New Testament has no fine-spun theories about the Atonement. It presents the Atonement—plain! repeated! emphatic! Paul says, "Because we thus judge, that if one died for all, then were all dead" (2 Cor. 5:14b). "Who gave himself for us, that he might redeem us from all iniquity" (Titus 2:14a). The writer of Hebrews tells us, "Without shedding of blood is no remission" (9:22b). In his first epistle John says, "And he is the propitiation [expiation] for our sins: and not for ours only, but also for the sins of the whole world" (2:2). But no one states this more clearly than Peter in his first epistle: "Who his own self bare our sins in his own body on the tree" (2:24a).

C. *The cross is the power of God to change us.*

In that great passage in the fifth chapter of 2 Corinthians, Paul comes to this conclusion: "Therefore if any man be in Christ, he is a new creature: old things are passed away; behold, all things are become new" (v. 17).

As an English Methodist minister was coming out of his church one day, he saw a young workman staring incredulously at a large crucifix. Seeing the minister, the young man said, "I don't see what good it did the Father that His Son should die like that." The minister tried to show him that he had missed the point completely. He replied, "It wasn't for the good of the Father; it was for the good of undone sinners our Lord went to the cross.'' Paul puts it exactly: ''For he hath made him to be sin for us, who knew no sin; that we might be made the righteousness of God in him'' (2 Cor. 5:21).

Conclusion. Let us never question God's ways or God's love. The cross was necessary for Him, it is for us. ''Hallelujah for the cross!'' — *WTH*

* * *

WEDNESDAY EVENING, MAY 4

TITLE: The Greatness of Christ

TEXT: ''And the Word was made flesh, and dwelt among us, (and we beheld his glory, the glory as of the only begotten of the Father,) full of grace and truth'' (John 1:14).

SCRIPTURE READING: John 1:1–18

Introduction. The Gospel According to John begins with a song, like the overture to a great symphonic composition. The themes are stated with stunning force. The dominant note in 1:1–18 is the greatness of Jesus Christ. These verses are often called ''The Prologue.'' They are a poetic portrait of Jesus Christ.

This hymn was composed by John under the divine inspiration of the Holy Spirit. The poem is a marvel in word choices—beginning, word, life, light, witness, glory, grace, and truth. It is also a marvel in arrangement—the Word and God (vv. 1–5), the Word and the world (vv. 9–13), the Word and the flesh (vv. 14, 16–18). So John commences his story of Jesus not with a narrative about birth, wise men, or John the Baptist. He begins it with a song of praise. It is a hymn worthy of our study. Let us examine the teachings of the hymn about Jesus Christ.

I. Jesus is the eternal Christ.

A. *Jesus has coexistence with the Father.* ''In the beginning was the Word, and the Word was with God'' (v. 1a). ''All things were made by him; and without him was not any thing made that was made'' (v. 3). There has never been a time when Jesus was not. Finite human beings have difficulty understanding this profound truth, for in our world there is a beginning and an end. He is the eternal Christ.

B. *Jesus has coequality with the Father.* ''And the Word was God'' (v. 1b). Though there is a distinction between the Father and the Son, there is not independent existence as if there were two wholly separate divine beings, God and Jesus in coexistence. Whenever you look at Jesus, you observe the essence and being of God.

II. Jesus is the incarnate Christ.

A. *The Incarnation is a reality.* ''And the Word was made flesh, and dwelt among us, (and we beheld his glory, the glory as of the only begotten of the Father,) full of grace and truth'' (v. 14). The term *flesh* suggests human nature. Jesus did not cease to be God when He became a man, and He did become fully human. He became the God-man.

The reality of the Incarnation may be seen in the expression ''dwelt among us.'' Literally, it could be translated, ''tabernacled among us.'' In days of old God dwelt in a tabernacle in the midst of Israel. God came to live among human beings in the human form of the Son of God.

B. *The Incarnation has a significant meaning*. To acknowledge that Jesus became a man is to recognize that He can understand us. ''For we have not an high priest which cannot be touched with the feeling of our infirmities; but was in all points tempted like as we are, yet without sin'' (Heb. 4:15).

III. Jesus is the enabling Christ.

A. *Jesus makes Himself available*. ''That was the true Light, which lighteth every man that cometh into the world. He was in the world, and the world was made by him, and the world knew him not. He came unto his own, and his own received him not'' (John 1:9–11). Jesus made Himself available to many people. Oddly enough, many chose not to receive the Lord. One of the hardest truths to understand is that people reject the eternal Christ.

B. *Jesus gave the power to become His child*. ''But as many as received him, to them gave he power to become the sons of God, even to them that believe on his name'' (v. 12). If one makes himself or herself available to the Lord, the Lord will give the status of a child of God. The entrance into God's family does not depend upon heredity or inheritance, personal resolution, or environment. Life in God's family is imparted by the power of God.

Conclusion. Don't miss the theme of this hymn. It focuses on the greatness of Christ. This Christ is speaking to you today. Listen, God is speaking! —*HTB*

* * *

SUNDAY MORNING, MAY 8

TITLE: The Gospel for Women

TEXT: "Oh, Jerusalem, Jerusalem, killing the prophets and stoning those who are sent to you! How often would I have gathered your children together as a hen gathers her brood under her wings, and you would not!" (Luke 13:34 RSV).

SCRIPTURE READING: Luke 13:34–35; 15:8–10

HYMNS: "God, Give Us Christian Homes," McKinney
"Oh, Master, Let Me Walk With Thee," Gladden
"Oh, God in Heaven," Martin

OFFERTORY PRAYER:

Eternal and always-caring God, we pray today out of hearts made grateful by our love for our mothers. We thank You for providing such remarkable help for us in our mothers' love and patience and confidence in us.

We have been graced by our mothers' watchcare over us and by their prayers for us. We have also been graced by Your salvation, which we have not earned but, like our mothers' care, is given freely and abundantly.

As we give our offerings today, we are giving because to us has been given more than we can ever repay or ever acknowledge. Amen.

Introduction. What do these two texts have in common? They both describe the compassion of God in feminine terms. Has it ever occurred to you that Jesus understood God in a feminine as well as a masculine dimension? Most often Jesus taught us that God is Father . . . a loving, caring, patient Father, who desires the good things of life for His children, who put the kingdom of God first in their lives. But Jesus also used, at least twice, feminine analogies to illustrate the nature of God toward His people.

Perhaps He took His cue from Genesis 1:27. Or, perhaps He simply believed that the marvelous fullness of the nature of God required a variety of human analogies to help us understand God's greatness, His compassions, His will for the people of the earth. It is well known that Mary, as the virgin mother, provides the image of mothering warmth for Catholic peoples, almost to the point of deification. But we need not go to extra-biblical sources to find the mothering, feminine concerns in the nature of God. Jesus Himself provides them for us in the two passages before us.

I. God as a mothering hen (Luke 13:34).

Jesus knew that His destiny could not be worked out unless He went to Jerusalem. But He knew that the record for God's men in Jerusalem was not good. With just a hint of satire in His voice, He insisted to His disciples that He must go on to Jerusalem for, "It cannot be that a prophet should perish away from Jerusalem" (Luke 13:33 RSV). (Cf. Jesus' story in Luke 20:1–20.) But in spite of Jerusalem's record with the prophets, Jesus loved that wayward city. In a voice clouded with deep sorrow and pathos, He cried, "How often would I have gathered your children together as a hen gathers her brood under her wing."

The Jews were a displaced and scattered people in Jesus' time. They belonged with one another, but conquest and the judgment of God for their sin had left them scattered across the Roman Empire. Jesus yearned to bring them together in his messiahship. Jesus knew also that the storm was gathering. It would not be long until another judgment would fall upon Jerusalem, and in that storm Jerusalem would be lost to the Jews for all the centuries until now. So Jesus used the feminine image of a mothering hen who protects her scattered chickens.

II. God as a seeking mother (Luke 15:8–10).

In the famous trilogy of parables concerning the nature of God, Jesus speaks of the woman seeking her lost coin, of a shepherd seeking a lost sheep, and a father seeking a lost son. The woman had lost one of her ten coins. It was a serious loss. Perhaps it was a treasured coin that had been given to her in her dowry. Its value was more than what it could be used to buy. It stood for all the good memories of her life and her hopes for her own children. Or perhaps it was a coin which represented savings for a treasured purchase for her family. In any case, the coin was lost. It had slipped through the cracks, but she would not give up until she had found it. God is as this seeking mother, wanting good things for His children. Those things which help provide for His family He will search for until He can bring it to them. Or if the coin represents the children, then let it be said that even when we are one of many, each one is important. The mother did not say, "Well, I've lost only one; I have nine left." She was not satisfied until the treasure was complete. So with God. We may appear to be one of many and not worth very much to some who would set a value on our lives, but to God we are valuable. We are worthy of the search. No one of us can slip through the cracks of human concern without God's knowing and beginning the search.

III. In addition to the feminine analogies for the nature of God it is instructive to note how Jesus regarded women.

Jesus' respect for women does not seem so radical today, but in His day Jewish men prayed, "Praise be to God that He has not created me a Gentile. Praise be to God that He has not created me a woman. Praise be to God that He has not created me a slave or an ignorant man." The Manichaens, one of the most popular mystery religious groups of Rome, prohibited women from membership. The place of women most often in pagan religions was as temple prostitutes. But Jesus changed all that.

A. *A woman's place* (Luke 10:38–42). It was believed by the Jews that a woman was not worthy to handle the Law. Her place was as a house servant. But in this remarkable incident Jesus clearly indicates that a woman's place is not only in serving, but in learning. One of the highest evidences of respect that someone can give another is to take his or her mind seriously and attempt to teach truth. Jesus taught Mary. Notice also that Mary was not a mother, so he was not teaching her for her children, but for herself. For her mind's sake she was taught.

B. *A woman's sin* (Luke 7:36–50). There is no double standard with Jesus. The woman was accepted. Her repentance and sorrow were great—she wept; she brought an expensive gift. She was greatly forgiven (v. 47). Those who have hit bottom know how to praise God most fully.

C. *A woman's gift* (Luke 21:1–4). It was a poor widow whose gift of two copper coins surpassed the rich gifts of those who had more left than they gave. Jesus praised the woman for her willingness to be generous with what she had.

D. *A woman's distress* (Luke 21:20–24). In warfare it seems that women are particularly brutally used. Our Lord's compassion for women in the days of the destruction of Jerusalem serves as a model for all men.

E. *A woman's witness* (Luke 23:55–24:11). Who had the love required to go visit the sepulcher and bathe the dead body of the Savior with spices and ointment? Who was it who first had the courage to go and see if anything could be done for Jesus with the Roman soldiers everywhere around? To what human voice was it given to be the first to say, "Jesus is risen from the dead"? It is true that the disciples thought they were hearing an "idle tale" (v. 11). But that only reveals men's reluctance to hear what God had ordained should be told to them by the women.

Conclusion. It should be no cause for wonder then that Paul could say, "There is neither Jew nor Greek, there is neither slave nor free, there is neither male nor female; for you are all one in Christ Jesus" (Gal. 3:28 RSV). The gospel for women is that God cannot be fully understood without the feminine dimension. He came to seek and to save that which was lost, both men and women. God's respect for persons goes equally to male and female. The gospel for women is that a woman's place can be as a student, that a woman's sin can be forgiven, that a woman's gift can be received, that a woman's distress can be felt, that a woman's witness can be true.

And what of us? Like children lost in a storm or like a coin which has slipped through the cracks of life, God, the mother, would draw you to Himself, for He will seek you until you are safely under His wing. —*CRW*

* * *

SUNDAY EVENING, MAY 8

TITLE: The Theology of the Cross

TEXT: "For while we were yet weak, in due season Christ died for the ungodly. For scarcely for a righteous man will one die: for peradventure for the good man some one would even dare to die. But God commendeth his own love toward us, in that, while we were yet sinners, Christ died for us" (Rom. 5:6–8).

SCRIPTURE READING: Romans 5:1–11

Introduction. When we look at the cross it is easy to become preoccupied with the details of the "agony and bloody sweat," the mocking rabble, and the darkened skies. While we should never forget what was done to our Lord by men that day, the significance of the cross lies in what Jesus did for men. An ancient saint said, "All that He asked to save the world was a cross."

Paul turned again and again to the Cross and made it central in his theology because it was the instrument of the amazing act of love and self-giving which sets men free. Paul preached Christ as crucified because on the cross He finished His work as Mediator between God and man. Paul tells the Galatians: "But far be it from me to glory, save in the cross of our Lord Jesus Christ, through which the world hath been crucified unto me, and I unto the world" (6:14).

As we seek to understand "the theology of the Cross," let us think in the broadest terms possible beginning at the outer rim of the circle and moving in toward the center.

I. The cross conceived.

Three questions cry out for an answer.

A. *When?*

The cross was no afterthought with God. It was the plan of the ages. To the Ephesians Paul speaks of God's having chosen us "in him before the foundation of the world" (1:4b). Exactly what that may or may not mean, it surely tells us that God was not "slipped up on" when man fell into sin. His plan of the ages was ready. It centered around a cross. The cross is the eternal fact—the Lamb of God slain from the foundation of the world. From the beginning of Jesus' ministry, having come from the Father, death was in the air; and its form was the form of a cross.

B. *Where?*

Where was the cross conceived? The answer is in the mind and heart of a Father-God, conceived in love. If the cross is the symbol of our resistance and rebellion, it is also light on the heart of God. The cross does not make God love us; it is the outcome and measure of His love to us.

In the Old Testament we see prototypes or foreshadowings of the cross. There was the sin offering, the scapegoat, the Day of Atonement. But when "the fullness of the time" came, these were fulfilled.

C. *Why?*

There were two reasons why Jesus died on the cross.

1. He died because of our sins, "the just for the unjust, that he might

bring us to God'' (1 Peter 3:18b). Such sinners were we that God's Son had to die in our place.

2. He died because of God's love for us. The heart of the gospel is this: ''God so loved the world, that he gave his only begotten son . . .'' (John 3:16). Moved by love, God sent His son to take His place as a man with men. Conceived in earthly terms the cross is not a sign of God's majesty and power, but an unforgettable reminder of the lengths to which He will go to bring men to Himself.

II. The cross achieved.

We will never understand the mystery of the cross, nor agree on our ideas of the Atonement; but we will not go far astray if we remember one thing: *God did it!* Paul tells the Corinthians: ''God was in Christ, reconciling the world unto himself'' (2 Cor. 5:19a). ''Do you see that man writhing in agony on a cross?'' Paul is asking. ''That is God doing that.''

But you say, ''I thought He was crucified as a result of the treason of Judas, the jealousy and blindness of the high priests, and the weakness of a Roman governor.'' There is truth in this, but it is not the whole truth. Emil Brunner says, ''The cross was the consequence of Judas' treason, of the jealousy and blindness of the high priests, of the human fears of the Roman governor. Yet it was God's work (*I Believe in the Living God* [Philadelphia: Westminster Press, 1961], p. 33).

God is not defeated by the sins of men. The cross at the heart of our faith assures of this. God did not condone the cross, but He took it and wrought it into His final design, which was and is the saving of the world. George W. Cornell, a reporter and theologian, describes what God did this way: ''There on the cross, Christians believe, a loving God was a stand-in for all mankind, substituting himself for man, taking on himself in some mysterious way the result of man's pervasive sin, as demanded by his consistent moral order, so that sinners could be accepted without sin's consequences'' (*The Way and Its Ways* [New York: Association Press, 1963], p. 141).

The Old Testament foretold His coming and that He would suffer. ''In the fullness of time'' He came. His birth is the centerpiece of history. His life was perfect. He could die for our sins since He had no sins of His own. His atonement was perfect and complete, superseding all that foreshadowed it (see Heb. 9:11–12).

III. The cross perceived.

The world agrees on the historical fact that nearly 2,000 years ago, in a tiny province of the Roman Empire, an itinerant Jewish prophet named Jesus was crucified on a Roman cross, but the world does not agree as to what that event means.

A. *Some, like the Greeks, seek after wisdom.*

To them the preaching of the cross is so much foolishness. But, as Paul reminds the Corinthians, ''the world through its wisdom knew not God'' (1 Cor. 1:21).

B. *Some, like the Jews, are offended by the cross.*

It is to them a stumblingblock (1 Cor. 1:23). In Galatia Paul felt the pressure to tone down, to dilute the gospel. If he would only yield on one point, and agree with the Judaizers that not only faith but also the old Jewish rites were necessary to salvation, then his troubles and persecutions would be over. "Then," as Paul put it, "is the offence of the cross ceased" (Gal. 5:11b). And that *is* the offense of the cross—its exclusiveness. There is no other way.

C. *Some, like the modern sophisticates, rebel at the idea of the cross.*

In what is perhaps his best-known play, a modern playwright has made his chief character greater than God because, whereas his chief character can love, God cannot, but is nothing but a destroyer. This is quite in contrast to what is revealed to us on the cross. The love the crucified Christ released on the world is not the love of man, but the love of God for man. God is the lover, man is the beloved. No doubt this playwright got hold of the wrong God and the wrong man.

D. *Some, like genuine Christians, do perceive what the cross is and what it means.*

One of two things happens when a person really sees what the cross is and what it means.

1. One result is *unbelief.* When God meets us in the fullness of His love, we don't want Him because His demands are too high; and we join those who cried long ago, "Away with him; let Him be crucified."

2. The other result is *conviction for sin.* It is only as we see God, in His mercy, taking our place that we see ourselves as we are in all our poverty and nakedness, our sin and wickedness.

IV. The cross received.

When we do see, when we do understand, what will we do? Will we accept the love the Crucified offers us? The cross stands with open arms to welcome every sinful soul. It is the door through which the Father welcomes the prodigal back to the family and home.

To receive the cross is to receive, enter into, and follow a new way of life. This is the only way to follow Jesus. As He Himself said, "If any man would come after me, let him deny himself, and take up his cross daily, and follow me" (Luke 9:23). The cross is not devotion to some form of asceticism. It is the constant refusal to gratify our self-life, the perpetual dying to pride and self-indulgence in order to follow Christ in His redemptive mission for the salvation of all mankind. "Take up his cross daily," Jesus says. The cross means sharing the suffering of Christ to the last and to the fullest.

Conclusion. Let us gaze upon the cross for there love goes on beyond all reason. There love convinces beyond all argument. There love brings home the truth to us until, all doubts and questions silenced, we want only to worship and adore.

Let us thank God, as we say with the poet:

I know not how that Calvary's cross
  A world from sin could free;
I only know its matchless love
  Has brought God's love to me.*

— *WTH*

* * *

---

*Harry Webb Farrington as quoted in *The Questing Spirit,* Luccock & Brentano, Editors, New York, Coward-McCann, Inc., 1947, p. 316.

WEDNESDAY EVENING, MAY 11

TITLE: When Religion Gets Sick

TEXT: "And when he had made a scourge of small cords, he drove them all out of the temple, and the sheep, and the oxen; and poured out the changers' money, and overthrew the tables; and said unto them that sold doves, Take these things hence; make not my Father's house an house of merchandise" (John 2:15–16).

SCRIPTURE READING: John 2:13–25

Introduction. A famous preacher once asked, "What is worse than having no religion?" Then after a pause, he answered his own question, "Having no religion is bad, but having the wrong kind of religion is even worse." Wayne E. Oates, in a provocative book entitled *When Religion Gets Sick,* proposed the possibility of allowing religion to get sick. Having a sick religion may be worse than having no religion at all.

Jesus was concerned with sick religion. His concern is reflected in the event of driving the moneychangers out of the temple. Much of Judaism had gotten sick. The Great Physician sought to bring healing.

Religion can get sick. Not all things that go under the name "religion" are good. What did Jesus see in the temple which caused for such aggressive action?

I. The lost sense of awe and respect for God.

A. *The Jews had lost the profound sense of awe and respect for God.* Look carefully at what Jesus observed when He visited the temple. Many Jewish patrons were coming and going. They had little respect for what took place in the temple, namely a communion with God. They bought and sold animals, and they exchanged money as if the court of the Gentiles was a marketplace.

God had intended the temple to be a meeting place for human beings and Himself. He had not intended the temple to be a den of thieves. He wanted it to be a place of prayer.

B. *Christians can often lose their sense of awe and reverence for God.* As people go about the routine of Bible study and church attendance, they can lose sight of reverence for God. The Lord, His church, and His Book can become rather ordinary objects and routines. The Lord Himself can be viewed as a common person.

The anger of Jesus is aroused when He sees a lost sense of awe and reverence for His Father. Religion can get sick when the sense of the wonder of God departs from a person or a group of people.

II. The lost sense of the cost of religion.

A. *The Jews had lost sight of the cost of serving the Lord.* The presentation of the animals in temple sacrifice represented a commitment on the part of the worshiper. God wanted the Jews to present the best animal out of their flocks. This would mean that they gave their best to God.

When Jesus walked into the temple, He saw that religion had been made cheap. People were told, "Leave your animals at home, and buy one in the temple." Purchasing the animal from the temple merchants cheapened the sacrificial system. This brought anger to the Master.

B. *Modern Christians have lost sight of the cost of commitment.* Following Christ and belonging to a church have become cheap. Dietrich Bonhoeffer, the great German pastor from World War II, said that when Jesus calls a man to follow Him, He calls him to die to himself. Nothing short of total commitment will satisfy the Savior.

III. The lost sense of the outsider.

A. *The Jews had lost the sense of need of the Gentiles.* The place where the moneychangers and merchants transacted business was in the court of the Gentiles. This was a place within the temple precinct where Gentiles, outsiders, could come and learn of the Lord. Most of the Jews in Jesus' time were not concerned for the Gentiles. They were concerned for their rituals but not for the mission God had given them. This mission was to be a blessing to the nations.

B. *Modern Christians can lose the sense of the outsider.* The church can easily become an exclusive club with a preoccupation for its membership. Religion gets sick when people turn inward and do not look outward for the sinners.

Conclusion. How is the health of your Christian expression? If you do not mind, let's have a check-up. Is there a great thrill over the greatness and grandeur of God? Or are you taking shortcuts? Are you asking for the minimal requirements? Then, what about your concern for others? Let's keep our religion healthy and growing. —*HTB*

* * *

SUNDAY MORNING, MAY 15

TITLE: Healthy Families Are No Accident

TEXT: "Judge not, that you be not judged. . . . So whatever you wish that men would do to you, do so to them . . ." (Matt. 7:1, 12 RSV).

SCRIPTURE READING: Matthew 7:1–14

HYMNS: "Oh, for a Faith That Will Not Shrink," Bathurst
"For All the Saints," How
"Come, Come, Ye Saints," Clayton

OFFERTORY PRAYER:

Father, in Your Word You have taught us that if we would know Your presence, we must be still. So in this quiet moment we would be still before You. Sometimes we are so broken by our doubts that we live with an empty spirit and don't know quite how to find You. You promised that if we will quit talking for awhile and let our eyes teach us and allow our ears to listen and our hearts to respond, that You will speak to us again and our doubts can be enveloped within a hope and confidence that come from You.

We bring our offerings this morning . . . not so we can buy assurance from You, nor in a vain attempt to pay You for those times You were clearly present with us. Our gifts are signs of our love even when we, for awhile, may have lost sight of the way. We wait upon You and worship today, through Jesus our Lord. Amen.

Introduction. A healthy family is no accident, and it is usually a happy family. But happiness is not what I'm talking about this morning. Happiness can be too much a goal for us. Happiness is not something we find at the end of the rainbow. It is what happens to us along the way to building a meaningful, purposeful life.

Families, like people, get sick sometimes. We're not always healthy. But when we get sick, we want to get well. Sometimes it's harder for sick families to get well than it is for sick bodies to heal because it's hard for us to admit that our families are sick. Sick families can get well, but it doesn't happen automatically. It happens only when people are determined to do something about it. In our text from the Sermon on the Mount, we have some exciting truths that can be applied to family life.

I. Healthy families are the result of deliberate choices (vv. 13–14).

Jesus said it clearly: God's way is not easy to find, nor is it easy to walk in it once we find it. There are easier ways to live than to live God's way. The traffic that moves in the direction of the world follows a crowded way. People who have never quit justifying their choices by saying, "Oh, everybody's doing it," are walking on that well-traveled thoroughfare.

But Jesus' Word is clear. If you want to find life, then you will often be on a lonely road. That's one reason churches are so important to Christian families. If we had to live out our lives isolated from one another, we really would feel isolated in this world. We gather together in the church not because we're perfect, and not because we're always what we ought to be, but because we understand the ground rules and we know when we're in foul territory. The world doesn't even know there is an out-of-bounds. They live bouncing off one wall to the other, never quite understanding why their lives keep getting shaken out of joint.

We know that our church has many healthy families, but we also know that there are many of us who are really hurting. As a church we are here to help one another, not only when we're well, but also when we're sick. But the church must be more than a hospital; Christians are supposed to eventually get well. In order to be well you must make deliberate choices to that end. It isn't easy. It's costly. Sometimes you have to go against the current to escape the easy flow the world offers you. Step out and feel the breeze that comes when you're all alone, trying to be a family that's willing to be used of God to be different and healthy.

II. Healthy families are built on thoughtful behavior toward one another (v. 12).

This is the golden rule for families. It is perhaps the most important word. A free translation might be, "So whatever you wish that your husband would do for you, do that for him. Whatever you wish that your wife would do for you, do that for her. Whatever you wish that your children would do for you, do that for them. And whatever you wish that your parents would do for you, do that for them."

A healthy family is not a fifty-fifty proposition. It's more like 100 percent on the husband's part and zilch on the wife's part. It's 100 percent on her part and zip on his. It's 100 percent on both parts when you can manage it. And by the grace of God you learn to manage it. If you want more attention from your husband, give him more attention. If you want more love and affection from your wife, then ask yourself, How can I be easier to love and to be affectionate with? And then give affection as you would like to receive it. If you're a child in your family, ask yourself, How would I like for my children to treat me when I am a parent? What kind of children do I want to have? That will help you every time to know how to relate to your parents!

The saddest thing about child-parent relationships is that the things we miss most in our parents are often the very things that are the hardest for us to give to our children. Parents, touch your children, hold them, be proud of them, believe in them, even if your parents weren't able to do that for you. It is not how you're done unto, but how you *wish* you'd been done unto. We've all got scars. Some are more visible than others, but you don't have to inflict the same ones that were inflicted on you if you will stop and cry out to God, "Oh, God, forgive whoever hurt me and let me down, but don't let me do the same. Remind me that I am loved, that You love me. Remind me that I am important. I belong to You. And now, out of who I am before You, let me give myself to the man or woman or children who are special and important to me. You have given them to me. I will treasure them as You have treasured me."

III. Healthy families are honest with one another (vv. 1–5).

When a husband and wife refuse to judge one another, they are on their way to a healthy family. Parents are to respect one another and their children. Criticism and judgmentalism are not to be known in a Christian family. Parents who put their children into competitive modes, judging one child over the other, create heartache that never can be fully measured. Long after the parents are dead that kind of mishandling of life will continue to exact a price. This verse means that we are not to set ourselves up as though we're perfect and the others in the family are somehow unworthy. You can't hide logs in your eye. You never will be healthy until you admit: Yes, that's a log in my eye; let's get it out so we can work on the speck in yours. Parents who understand this do better with their children. And children who understand this don't have to judge their parents as harshly as they might otherwise.

IV. Healthy families are more interested in giving than getting (v. 2).

We usually interpret this verse in terms of money, but it also has to do with loving and caring and being a family. We say you can't outgive God. Nor can you outgive a wife or children or parents who are really gifted by you—with no strings attached. You give your heart and you allow that gift to be loved; soon it begins to bring back the same that you sent it out to do.

V. Healthy families are protected by faithfulness (v. 6).

This verse has generally been used to describe how Christian witnessing ought to be done, but perhaps it has even more to do with marriage. A husband and wife are not to take the precious gift of their sexuality and cast it out before "dogs" or "hogs." Beware, because if you do, they will turn and trample you underfoot as they attack you. Healthy families are protected by fidelity and trustworthiness. You cannot get so modern or so sophisticated that you are permitted to ignore that admonition. Treasure your sexuality. Used within marriage it is indeed holy and as precious as pearls. But nothing can tear a family so apart as giving that which belongs only to one another to any other.

IV. Healthy families are enriched by prayer (vv. 7–11).

A. *If your family isn't healthy, don't abandon it anymore than you would abandon a child who had gone to the hospital sick.* Just because you're sick doesn't mean you're dead. Just because you're ill doesn't mean you can't get well. Prayer changes us and makes us ready for what God is ready to do in our lives.

B. *If you're healthy, don't be proud, be grateful.* Make your prayer one of thanksgiving and sensitivity to improve your decision making, your thoughtfulness, your honesty with one another, your willingness to give, and your fidelity. Be thankful for what God is doing in your family to help you remain strong against the evil which is all around you and threatens your most precious possessions.

C. *Don't insist that everyone around you pray just as you pray.* Some Christian homes would be healthier if no one would insist that everybody be spiritual in the same way as he or she is. It's important to share your prayers together. Every child ought to hear his father and his mother pray. But don't miss what God can do in each individual life by trying to make everybody fit one particular spiritual mold.

Conclusion. Healthy families are no accident. It takes everybody giving his best. Each member of the family has a part in determining how healthy your family will be. — *CRW*

* * *

SUNDAY EVENING, MAY 15

TITLE: The Word of the Cross

TEXT: "For the word of the cross is to them that perish foolishness; but unto us who are saved it is the power of God" (1 Cor. 1:18).

SCRIPTURE READING: 1 Corinthians 1:18–25

Introduction. On the horizons of history many mountain peaks tower high. There is Mount Sinai, where God's people, Israel, received the law. There is Mount Tabor, where "the stars in their courses fought against Sisera" (Judg. 5:20). There is Mount Carmel, where Elijah defeated the prophets of Baal, and God answered by fire. There is Mount Hermon, the probable mountain of the Transfiguration. But towering above them all is Mount Calvary where Jesus was crucified. No mountain towers so high in its influence over the hearts and minds of men as that skull-shaped knoll "without a city wall."

Paul tells the Corinthians: "For the word of the cross is to them that perish foolishness; but unto us who are saved it is the power of God" (1 Cor. 1:18). Dr. Moffatt translates the initial phrase of our text, "the story of the cross," but the meaning in each case is the same. The gospel is essentially the story of the cross and that story is God's word to man. This is God's most tender message to the world.

"The Word of the Cross" has never lost its power. The Cross was a divine event. How so?

I. The cross is God's supreme declaration to men.

God has many ways of speaking to men, but His supreme way is in the cross (Heb. 1:1–2).

A. *The cross is God's declaration of man's guilt.*

Here the sin debt of the human family is fully computed, the bankruptcy of man is vividly declared. Christ's death, the most undeserved and cruelest conceivable, epitomized the tragic condition of humanity. And remember, "Christ died for our sins according to the scriptures" (1 Cor. 15:3b). The great Catholic scholar John M. Oesterreicher says: "Anyone who denies his part in the crucifixion, also thereby excludes himself from any need of, or share in, the redemption" (quoted by George W. Cornell in *The Way and Its Ways* [New York: Association Press, 1963], p. 135).

We might moralize and philosophize about sin, but the only way to see what it really is, is to see what it does. A man was driving while drunk with his wife and two little children in the car. Though his wife pleaded with him to slow down, he would not heed. He wrecked the car and killed his wife and two little children, yet he was not even seriously injured. Two days later as he saw those three caskets side by side in the funeral home, he said, "Never did I realize how awful my sin is until I see now what it has done." Before the gaze of a sin-wrecked world God raises the cross of His Son, and the first declaration of that cross is: "Guilty!"

B. *The cross is God's declaration of man's helplessness.*

If man could have atoned for his sin and guilt in any way, there would have been no necessity for the cross; but he could not. Jesus died on the cross because man had been rendered helpless by his sin. Morality and good works are not enough to settle man's debt of sin.

As the Israelites, bitten by the fiery serpents in the wilderness, had to confess their helplessness by looking to the uplifted brazen serpent, so must we confess our helplessness by looking to the uplifted Christ. Every man is not only guilty before God, but helpless to do anything about it. The cross is the power of God offered to powerless sinners.

C. *The cross is God's declaration of His justice.*

The nature of man's sin called for the most drastic action. That drastic action was God's taking the penalty of our sin upon Himself through the death of Christ on the cross. If God was to blot out our sins and remember them no more, He was faced with a problem. How could the law be satisfied and His forgiving mercy be made possible all at the same time? The law says, "The soul that sinneth, it shall die" (Ezek. 18:4b) and "The wages of sin is death" (Rom. 6:23). There was only one way possible and that was for someone who had no sin of his own to die in our place. Only the sinless Son of God ever met that requirement; and He died for us.

D. *The cross is God's declaration of His love.*

Man's sin without God's love would not have sent Jesus to the cross. God could have dealt with our sin some other way. Had it not been for God's great love, He could have destroyed sin by destroying all sinners. But love sought to save sinners from their sins. The cross was the only remedy. As the cross measures the enormity of our guilt, it also measures the depths of His love.

Pilate wrote the title over the cross: "JESUS OF NAZARETH THE KING OF THE JEWS" (John 19:19). He should have written: "For God so loved the world" (John 3:16). The cross of Christ stands as a supreme declaration of God's love for a guilty world.

II. The cross is God's supreme offer to man.

A. *By the cross God in His love offers His hand to men in their sin.*

"The Word of the Cross" is the word of life. Its message is the message of salvation to all who believe.

Botanists tell of a certain plant in the West Indies called the manchaneel. It exudes a substance extremely poisonous to the touch of man, producing a most terrifying rash and skin eruption. Fortunately, in this same locality, there is a plentiful and effective antidote. The remedy is the life sap of a certain fig which is secured by bruising the body of the fig tree. All men have sinned. We have touched the poison plant of sin, but by faith we may each have access to the tree of healing. The cross is that tree of healing.

B. *In the Bible God's offer of His love and healing is made plain.*

The captain of an old sailing vessel lay dying in his cabin. Knowing that they were too far from port to reach it before he died, he asked if any member of the crew had a Bible. The cabin boy, the only crew member so equipped, was brought to the captain. Looking at the boy with the Bible in his hand, the dying man asked, "Son, can you find something in that book that will help an old sinner who is soon to meet his Maker?" Turning quickly to the fifty-third chapter of Isaiah, the lad read it through slowly. The old "sea dog," who had listened intently, said, "That's pretty, but I'm not sure I understand what it means."

Then this boy, with his mother's Bible in his hand, became the old man's teacher. "Sir," he said, "if you will repeat after me as I read again, I believe you will understand." He read the chapter again, changing only one word: "Surely he hath borne *my* griefs, and carried *my* sorrows. . . . But he was wounded for *my* transgressions, he was bruised for *my* iniquities; the chastisement of *my* peace was upon him; and with his stripes *I* am healed." Suddenly, the old man, who had been following with a weakening voice, broke in to say, "Wait a minute, lad, I think I have it. He was wounded for *my* transgressions and with *His* stripes *I* am healed. That's it! I see it all now, lad! Jesus took my place on the cross; and He offers me salvation." He had caught the message of the cross, and accepting its offer, he had experienced the saving power of the cross of Christ.

III. The cross is God's supreme power among men.

A. *The cross endures.*

The cross of Christ knows no failures. For many centuries the forces of hell have loosed all their fury against it, but it stands, the mightiest power among men.

B. *The cross attracts.*

"The Word of the Cross" is still the most attractive message proclaimed by men. Rhetoric and philosophy and the wisdom of men grow tasteless and stale, but the sincere proclamation of the simple story of the cross remains wondrously new and continues to attract our interest and attention (see John 12:32).

C. *The cross has power.*

The cross has drawing power. It has lifting power. It is the spiritual magnet of the world. The cross draws us from empty creeds and lifts us up out of our sins.

D. *The cross is timeless.*

It is timeless in its appeal. "The Word of the Cross" is old, yet new in its fulness and finality, its urgency. It will attract men when all else fails.

E. *The cross changes men.*

It transformed Simon the fisherman into Peter the rock, the prince of the Apostles. It changed Saul, the persecutor of the church, into Paul, the apostle to the Gentiles. In a garden in Milan, Aurelius Augustine of Thagasta was mightily converted and became the saintly scholar of the fourth century. The roguish and dissolute son of Pietro Barnadone became the beloved Francis of Assisi. After having his heart "strangely warmed" in a meeting at Aldersgate Street, John Wesley was used of God to turn England upside down. In a country Baptist church in Clay County, North Carolina, George W. Truett was converted and became one of the most effective preachers the Anglo-Saxon race ever produced.

Conclusion. No other religion can have the power of Christianity, because no other religion is built around a cross, with its message of man's guilt and helplessness and God's redeeming love. Let us preach Christ and Him crucified (1 Cor. 2:2). — *WTH*

* * *

WEDNESDAY EVENING, MAY 18

TITLE: Passport to the Kingdom

TEXT: **"Jesus answered, Verily, verily, I say unto thee, Except a man be born of water and of the Spirit, he cannot enter into the kingdom of God" (John 3:5).**

SCRIPTURE READING: **John 3:1–21**

Introduction. In order to travel from one country to another, a person must have a passport. Irrespective of how notable a person you are, a passport is a necessity for entrance into a foreign country. It qualifies you for a visit.

Jesus was visited by Nicodemus, a leading Pharisee of his day. Probably he wanted to know more of Jesus' concept about the kingdom of God. The Lord made the concept of the new birth clear to Nicodemus. To enter the kingdom of God, a person must have an experience of regeneration. Upon having a new birth the person will be initiated into life in God's kingdom.

People who desire God's kind of life need to be born again. The new birth could be compared to a passport. With a passport you may go into another kingdom. Likewise, with the new birth you may enter the kingdom of heaven. Let us examine some great facets of the new birth.

I. The new birth is a mandate.

A. *Look at the person who came to Jesus.* "There was a man of the Pharisees, named Nicodemus, a ruler of the Jews" (John 3:1). Nicodemus had many commendable qualities.

1. He was a Pharisee. They were the religious people of Jesus' day who worked meticulously at interpreting and keeping God's laws. Their religion was mainly one of external rules, but they were moral, upright people.

2. Nicodemus was a ruler of the Jews. Probably this meant that he was a member of the Sanhedrin. This was a group of seventy outstanding religious leaders.

3. Nicodemus acknowledged that Jesus had unusual powers from God. "Rabbi, we know that thou art a teacher come from God: for no man can do these miracles that thou doest, except God be with him" (v. 2b). This person who came to see Jesus had a lot of commendable virtues—Pharisee, religious ruler, and one who acknowledged that Jesus possessed a gift from God.

B. *Look at the words of Jesus to Nicodemus.* Jesus went abruptly to the need of Nicodemus. Without being impressed with his credentials or his compliments, Jesus said, "Verily, verily, I say unto thee, Except a man be born again, he cannot see the kingdom of God" (v. 5). Jesus gave a mandate to Nicodemus. This mandate was to be born again. "Marvel not that I said unto thee, Ye must be born again" (v. 7). There is no other way to enter the kingdom. The new birth is a mandate.

II. The new birth is a miracle.

A. *Think about what Nicodemus thought.* When Jesus mentioned the expression "born again," Nicodemus thought of a physical birth. He questioned, "How can a man be born when he is old? can he enter the second time into his mother's womb, and be born?" (v. 4). Nicodemus acknowledged the mandate, but he was confused about the new birth as a physical birth. To go through the physical birth again would be an impossibility.

B. *Think about what Jesus meant.* The Lord was not talking about a physical birth. He was talking about the miracle of a new beginning. For Nicodemus to change would have required a miracle. To be born again means to allow God to come into your life and begin the change. That is a miracle indeed!

III. The new birth has a means.

A. *Listen to the questions of Nicodemus' conversation with Jesus.* This Pharisee asked two times, "How?" (cf. vv. 4, 9). Without a doubt Nicodemus wanted to know how he might have the new birth.

B. *Listen to the answers of Jesus.* Jesus answered Nicodemus' question. He taught Nicodemus that the means of experiencing the new birth was faith. "And as Moses lifted up the serpent in the wilderness, even so must the Son of man be lifted up: That whosoever believeth in him should not perish, but have eternal life" (vv. 14–15). To believe means to open one's life to God. When one opens his life to God, the new birth occurs.

IV. The new birth has manifestations.

A. *Nicodemus was asked to observe the wind.* Jesus used an illustration about the wind: "The wind bloweth where it listeth, and thou heareth the sound thereof, but canst not tell whence it cometh, and whither it goeth; so is every one that is born of the Spirit" (v. 8). The wind blows. It can be seen. Likewise, when the Lord comes into a life, there are some noticeable changes.

B. *Jesus wants people to observe the result of the new birth.* Human beings change when they open their lives to God. Attitudes and actions change. People become children of God.

Conclusion. Do you want to go to the kingdom of God? The only means of entrance is the new birth. Open your life to Christ, and He will change your life.

— *HTB*

SUNDAY MORNING, MAY 22

TITLE: Friends of the Family

TEXT: "Every one then who hears these words of mine and does them will be like a wise man who built his house upon the rock" (Matt. 7:24 RSV).

SCRIPTURE READING: Matthew 7:24–29

HYMNS: "Word of God Across the Ages," Blanchard
"Built on the Rock the Church Doth Stand," Grundtrig
"At the Name of Jesus," Noel

OFFERTORY PRAYER:

Father, these people around us are people You love, and they love one another as You taught them to do. There are many reasons we love and praise You. Help us today to see that many of Your best gifts to us are the people You put in our lives. We are Your people, and You have made us to be friends. May our friendships always strengthen one another and never be used to bring harm to each other or to Your work in the world.

Oh, great God of gifts, we bring our gifts today to You. Much of what we have and can now give is made possible through the help and encouragement of the friends You have given to us. Help us to be worthy friends to others. In Christ's name. Amen.

Introduction. It was front-page news. Two Arlington, Texas, houses, which had been built overlooking the Trinity River, lost their backyards when they began to slide down into the valley. There had been heavy rains for several days. Flooding had occurred in the low-lying places. The people who lived on the cliff probably felt secure from the flood, but they had not counted on the silent erosion of their entire backyards. It isn't too difficult to feel what they must have felt as all the work and dreams they had invested in those houses went sliding down into the river. They were forced to leave their homes in fear that next it would be the back porch and then the back half and then all the house that would disappear into the river bottom.

There are enemies, often unseen ones, that eat away at the foundations, not only of our houses, but of our homes. It's not simply the financial investment we have in our houses that is threatened; our families are vulnerable. To paraphrase our Lord's famous word concerning life, "What shall it profit a man or a woman to gain everything and lose his or her family?" But just as surely as there are enemies of the family (cf. June 5, 1983, sermon), which our Lord's parable brings to mind, there are also friends for the family suggested here. The power of our Lord's message was not only what He taught us to fear, but what He taught us to embrace. He not only taught us what to do, He helps us to see how we are to go about doing what we really want to do. In our text Jesus gives us the clues we need for building healthy families.

I. The words of Jesus are friends to the family (v. 24).

Jesus says in this passage that if we hear His words and do them, then we will be like a wise man who built his house upon the rock. Look back on the words of Jesus and you will discover that these words, which we almost always take as admonitions for personal ethics, are also perceptive words for building healthy families. It is not only the words of our Lord, but the words of all Scripture that give us a strong authority base for making decisions in our families. Some families make decisions about what they will allow their children to do by calling up the neighbors to find out what they are going to let their children do. Many families decide their priorities in purchashing by watching what their neighbors buy.

People who decide what is appropriate and what is inappropriate by simply taking the popular temperature are going to be in trouble quickly. They are like the man who built his house upon the sand. Every wind and storm that comes shakes them to their foundation; but those who build their families upon the written Word of God have a strong foundation for the building of their lives together. Permit a quick warning. If you build your home upon the Word of God, then you must be careful to interpret the Word correctly. Scripture can be interpreted out of context and give power to a husband to be a tyrant without reminding him of his responsibility to love his wife as Christ loved the church. The proper use of the Word of God is not as a hammer to beat other people down, but to bring about thoughtful concern for one another, sacrificial compassion for each member of the family, and to provide the family with the authority base where issues can be examined and careful, moral, loving decisions made.

Here are four words Jesus gave us that have particular application to the family.

A. *Forgiveness.* In Matthew 6:12 Jesus says that when we pray we are to pray to be forgiven in the same manner that we have forgiven those who have sinned against us. In Matthew 18:22, Jesus says you are to forgive, not seven times, "but seventy times seven." There is nothing more devastating to a home than old hurts and offenses which have not been forgiven. If you will pay attention to forgiveness and forgive even when it isn't easy to forgive, you will discover that your family will be able to withstand the storms. It is especially important that we forgive our parents for the times they were not able or willing to be the parents we needed them to be. There are families that still are broken apart because of misunderstandings related to wills and inheritances. The ironic truth is that those who are hurt most by an unforgiving spirit are not those who are unforgiven, but those who will not forgive (cf. 5:21–24).

B. *Love.* In Matthew 5:43–46 Jesus makes it clear that love among His followers is to include the enemy as well as the friend. But it is sadly true that sometimes we find it difficult to love even within the family. Jesus gives us the direction we need. The apostle Paul picked up on Christ's strong example of love in Ephesians 5:25. A husband is to love his wife as Christ loved the church and gave Himself up for her. When Christ lives in us, we begin to discover resources for a love which can give itself away. A prayerful remembering of how our Lord has loved us will create in us the energy to love those around us. The best definition of this kind of love is found in 1 Corinthians 13. Here you will discover excellent guidelines for doing loving actions within the family.

C. *Faithfulness* (Matt. 5:27–30). The fabric of the family is a tightly woven material. Foreign matters introduced into the love relationship tear it apart. Jesus called the Christian family to fidelity one to the other and a love that keeps the eyes focused on one another. The physical love relationship between the mother and the father is absolutely essential for a healthy family. Indeed, the best gift a father can give his children is to love their mother.

D. *Nothing is to come before God* (22:37). This word from our Lord should protect us from making of the family an idol for worship. Because the family is so significant and is capable of bringing so much happiness, we are sometimes tempted to worship our families and elevate them to a place which only God ought to have. Matthew 10:37–39 lays upon those who would follow Christ the absolute primacy of our allegiance to God that comes before other allegiances in life, including that of loyalty to our families. As important as the family is to Christian life, it is not the ultimate for us.

II. The fellowship of the church is a friend to the family (7:24).

When Jesus described the founding of His church, He spoke of building it upon a rock (16:18). As we consider Jesus' comment about the wise builder who built on the rock, we remember that He took His own parable to heart. The house He built—the church—is the second great friend to your family. It is the place where the words of Christ and the word of Scripture are taken seriously and authoritatively. A man who had not been as active as he ought to have been in his church said to his pastor, "This church has been a great gift to my family. Even in those times when I wasn't doing what I should have been doing, the church ministered to my children. The reason my children are what they are today is because of the adult friends and the peers of my children who knew them and cared for them within the life of this congregation. The church has been the most important institution for my family."

A. *In the many relationships a church makes possible to its families, it provides needed support.*

1. Younger families are helped by the witness of older families. Older families become a model for the younger families. This witness helps younger families to make decisions and plan how they want to raise their children and build their families.

2. Older families are helped by the knowledge they are providing guidance for younger families. When a family knows that there are younger families who believe in them and admire them, it gives them encouragement to be faithful to the Lord and to the task of building the finest families they can.

3. All families are helped by their peer families. Knowing that you are part of a whole body of people who are struggling with the same concerns you struggle with will often give you courage to not give up.

4. Unusual families have a place in the larger family of faith—the church. There are families in the church who have handicaps. Perhaps there are children who are mentally or physically impaired. Their faithful witness to Christ and the network of support offered to them by the larger family of faith increases health on both sides. There are individuals in the church who never have their own family. The only family they ever are given is the family that the church becomes to them. Then there are the families that are broken by death or by divorce. The church stands beside them as the hurts are healed and as God helps them to begin again.

5. Families need friends for their family who have the same goals. We tend to take on the goals, standards, attitudes, and ambitions of our friends. Friends shape our futures. One of the best gifts a church can give to a young couple is to provide them a place where they can make close friendships with four or five couples their age with whom they may be able to develop life relationships that will be a bulwark of encouragement and support for them through the years.

B. *In the corporate worship of God the church teaches families how to worship as a family.* When a family is on vacation, they stand in awe before the Rocky Mountains or are amazed by the power and sweep of the ocean. Yet it is the worship that they have done as a family Sunday by Sunday which gives a context for them to praise God and rejoice in His creation. In moments like that families can join hands and quietly pray and thank God for what He has done. Children who know how to worship in church and outside in the beauty of God's world learn something special of the transcendent dimension that overarches all of life. Happy is the family, when tragedy comes to their door, that has learned how to worship and thereby learned to put in context both the good and the evil which comes to life.

III. There are other friends the family has in a community.

Christian people will want to support good schools and teachers who care. A stable community and honest government are the products of people who are willing to be involved. The libraries, medical resources, marriage enrichment opportunities, and cultural activities in a community are all important to the health of family life in the city. Christian people are doing God's work for families when they reinforce positive and healthy attitudes in their local communities.

Conclusion. A healthy family is no accident. You must build it well. Build it on the rock which is our Lord Jesus Christ. Make friends for your family who will stand you in good stead all the days of your life. There is no better place to do that than under the authority of God's Word, in the fellowship of His church, and in a community where people encourage one another in healthy living. —*CRW*

* * *

SUNDAY EVENING, MAY 22

TITLE: Glorying in the Cross

TEXT: "But God forbid that I should glory, save in the cross of our Lord Jesus Christ" (Gal. 6:14a).

SCRIPTURE READING: Galatians 6:11–18

Introduction. Paul's argument in Galatians is that if these Gentile Christians submit to circumcision as a symbol of their commitment to the Jewish law, they have made of no effect the cross of Christ. That would be dependence upon law and not grace for salvation. This is not the gospel of Christ, but another gospel, a gospel different in both identity and kind (1:6–7). This thought is at the heart of our passage. It is summed up in our text: "But God forbid that I should glory, save in the cross of our Lord Jesus Christ" (v. 14a). Paul's glorying was in the cross. This was true in four respects.

I. Paul gloried in the cross as the test of motivation (vv. 12–14).

What were the motives of these Judaizers? What was the motive of Paul?

A. *Their first motive was human pride.*

"As many as desire to make a fair show in the flesh, they compel you to be circumcised" (v. 12). Paul is saying, "They would make capital out of your compliance; they would boast of having won you over to carnal rites.'' The teaching of the Judaizers was only a pious form of human pride.

B. *Their second motive was fear.*

''. . . They compel you to be circumcised; only that they may not be persecuted for the cross of Christ'' (v. 12b). In effect Paul is saying, ''Those who would force circumcision upon you have no sincere faith in its value. Their motive is quite different. They hope thereby to save themselves from persecution for professing the cross of Christ.'' Both Judaism and the Roman authorities would tolerate a Christianity that was only a sect of the Jewish religion. But the cross set the Christians apart in such a way as to bring persecution from both Jews and Romans.

C. *Their third motive was selfishness or worldliness.*

Paul says, ''For not even they who receive circumcision do themselves keep the law; but they desire to have you circumcised, that they may glory in your flesh'' (v. 13). Paul is saying, ''Look at their inconsistency. They advocate circumcision and yet they themselves neglect the ordinances of the law. Their motives are those of worldly men. Their basic motivation is selfish. They want to be able to boast of the number of Gentiles to be circumcised as a result of their efforts.''

D. *Paul's motive was pure and true to the gospel.*

He says, ''But God forbid that I should glory, save in the cross of our Lord Jesus Christ'' (v. 14a). He was saying, ''The offense of the cross shall be my proudest boast.'' Paul makes nothing of his impeccable credentials as a Jew. He could describe himself as ''a Pharisee, a son of Pharisees'' (Acts 23:6b). In writing to the church at Philippi, Paul gives his entire pedigree (3:4–6). From the Jewish standpoint these were real credentials. How did he regard them? As ''refuse.'' He says, ''Howbeit what things were gain to me, these have I counted loss for Christ'' (Phil. 3:7). Paul gloried only in the cross. Could he be in one of our services today he would, no doubt, gladly sing with us:

> In the cross of Christ I glory,
> Tow'ring o'er the wrecks of time,
> All the light of sacred story
> Gathers round that head sublime.*

II. Paul gloried in the cross as the means of separation.

''But God forbid that I should glory, save in the cross of our Lord Jesus Christ, by whom the world is crucified unto me, and I unto the world'' (v. 14). The Jews spoke of ''the offence of the cross,'' ''the scandal of the cross.'' The cross was a means of separation. Some Jews might have accepted Jesus as the Messiah, but a crucified Messiah, a Savior on a cross—they would have none of it.

The Jews would say, ''Why did God permit this wonderful being to experience the suffering, the degrading, agonizing penalty of the cross?'' The apostles answered that the Crucifixion was a part of the experience of the Messiah described and predicted in the Old Testament. Preaching in the temple courts after the healing of the man, ''lame from his mother's womb,'' Peter said, ''But the things which God foreshadowed by the mouth of all the prophets, that his Christ

---

*John Bowring, *Baptist Hymnal,* Walter Hines Sims, ed. (Nashville: Convention Press, 1956) No. 100.

should suffer, he thus fulfilled'' (Acts 3:18). But, for the most part, the Jews would not accept this, nor would many of the Gentiles. To Jews the cross was a stumblingblock and to the Gentiles foolishness. To Paul the cross was God's means of salvation. The breach was irreconcilable. The cross was the means of separation.

In personal terms Paul said of the cross, ''Through which the world hath been crucified unto me, and I unto the world'' (Gal. 16:14b). Paul always regarded his acceptance of the crucified Christ as having ended his life in the world and begun a new life in Christ. To him the world's appeal and prizes are dead. Earlier in the epistle Paul states clearly: ''I have been crucified with Christ; and it is no longer I that live, but Christ liveth in me: and that life which I now live in the flesh I live in faith, the faith which is in the Son of God, who loved me, and gave himself up for me'' (2:20). The cross is primary. All other things are secondary. Paul made his boast in Christ and Him crucified. ''The world hath been crucified unto me.'' He speaks of this as an accomplished fact. It is as if he said, ''What is the world to me now? What are all the things of which I once boasted? They are crucified.'' But turn that coin over.

Paul says, ''Through which the world hath been crucified unto me, and I unto the world.'' This is the other side of the matter. If Paul has bidden farewell to the world, the world, on its part, has taken its measure of Paul. It had no use for him. His lifework was a continuous protest against the world spirit. Thus Paul, like his Master, was ''despised and rejected of men.'' And for what reason? It was Christ crucified. The cross was the means of separation. It was for Paul. It is for us.

III. Paul gloried in the cross as the way of salvation.

Paul continues, ''For neither is circumcision anything, nor uncircumcision, but a new creature'' (v. 15). ''But a *new creature!*'' Externals do not count. What does count is being a new creature in Christ Jesus, having a new heart. This is the way of salvation, the only way, the way of the cross. Jesus said, as He was on that last journey to Jerusalem, ''Whosoever doth not bear his cross, and come after me, cannot be my disciple'' (Luke 14:27). ''The cross stands for death. In principle it is death to self in the act of surrender to Christ. It is the denial of the self that would have its own being apart from God and others. Although it is death, it is also life. The cross is life through death. It is finding a new way of life by rejecting the way of self-love, self-trust, and self-assertion'' (Frank Stagg, *Studies in Luke's Gospel* [Nashville: Convention Press, 1967], p. 99). The cross is God's way of salvation. There is no other.

Galatians 6:15 is one of Paul's summarizing sentences: ''For neither is circumcision anything, nor uncircumcision, but a new creature.'' The only thing that really matters is ''a new creation,'' that is, men and women made new by the transforming power of God's Spirit.

IV. Paul gloried in the cross as the touchstone of Christian unity.

A faithful pastor has said, ''I have little time for ecumenism, the four-dollar word for church union, with the proposition, 'You surrender a little of what you believe and I will surrender a little of what I believe and by and by we will get together.' Let me say frankly and bluntly, that until, by the Scriptures, it is shown me that I am in error, I will not give up one jot nor one tittle of what I believe, but I will meet any man at the foot of the cross. That is the touchstone. The man who trusts in the redeeming merits of Christ's death on the cross for his sins, and only in that, is a Christian; and the one who does not is not a Christian. The man who throws himself like an empty rind upon the grace of God, made possible by the cross, is my brother in Christ; and I care not what the other factors may be."

Listen to Paul again in verse 15: "For neither is circumcision anything, nor uncircumcision, but a new creature." He is willing to accept Jews and Gentiles alike. It makes no difference. He blesses all who agree to live by this principle.

But the key phrase here is in verse 16 where Paul says, "And as many as shall walk by this rule, peace be upon them, and mercy, and upon the Israel of God." The "Israel of God" is in implied contrast to the "Israel after the flesh." It stands here not for the faithful converts from the circumcision alone, but for the spiritual Israel generally, the whole body of believers whether Jew or Gentile.

The entire argument of Galatians is against making two groups of believers —Jewish and Gentile. Paul's clear position is that Jews and Gentiles are one in Christ (3:28). Thus the true "Israel of God" is a bold way of stressing this truth. Paul pronounces a benediction of "mercy and peace" on a third race of men—neither Jews nor Gentiles, but Christians. The cross is the touchstone of Christian unity.

Conclusion. The Cross is not simply an event of nearly 2,000 years ago; it is a spiritual fact now. We are involved. Jesus' choice of the cross as God's way to redeem mankind has been vindicated by thousands who, like Paul, have gloried in the cross. What about you and me? — *WTH*

* * *

WEDNESDAY EVENING, MAY 25

TITLE: A Meeting With the Master

Text: **"Now Jacob's well was there. Jesus therefore, being wearied with his journey, sat thus on the well: and it was about the sixth hour. There cometh a woman of Samaria to draw water: Jesus saith unto her, Give me to drink" (John 4:6–7).**

Scripture Reading: **John 4:1–42**

Introduction. One of the significant features of Jesus' ministry was His meeting with people. Leonard Griffith examined many of these encounters with his book *Encounters with Christ: The Personal Ministry of Jesus*. Griffith emphasized in this work that the church needs to look at the personal interest of Jesus in the individual. The Lord was not so preoccupied with the multitudes that He lost concern for the individual.

Jesus had individual meetings with many people. One of the most significant meetings of the Lord was with a sinful woman at Jacob's well. Let us examine some fascinating facets of this famous interview.

I. The perplexing problems.

The meeting of Jesus with the woman of Samaria was full of problems. To understand the difficulties one must understand some geography and history of Israel. The pious Jew would not go through the land of Samaria. Following the northern kingdom of Israel's captivity in 722 B.C. by the Assyrians, the land was inhabited by Israelites and foreigners. They intermarried; therefore, the pious Jews avoided the land of Samaria. Regarding Jesus, John recorded, "And he must needs go through Samaria" (v. 4). It was necessary for Jesus to go to Samaria.

Various barriers existed for Jesus and the woman.

A. *There was an ethnic barrier*. Jews were somewhat tolerant of other races, but the Samaritans were contemptible to the Jews. When the woman met the Lord, she emphasized this barrier: "How is it that thou, being a Jew, asketh drink of me, . . . a woman of Samaria?" (v. 9).

B. *Another problem was the sex barrier*. Rabbis were forbidden to greet a woman in public. Yet Jesus crossed this barrier. Not only did the Lord cross this barrier, but He chose to talk with a notoriously immoral woman.

C. *Then there was the religious barrier*. The Samaritans worshiped at Mount Ebal. They used the first five books of the Old Testament. The Jews worshiped at Mount Gerizim. There was a wide religious gap between the Jews and Samaritans. All kinds of barriers stood between the woman's meeting with Jesus. It had little promise of meaning.

II. The Master's proposal.

Jesus had the interpersonal skills of overcoming these barriers. Let us follow the strategy of the Master in how He made the meeting with the woman meaningful.

Jesus asked for a common necessity (vv. 7–9). When the woman came to the well, He asked for a drink: "Give me to drink" (v. 7b). Jesus was thirsty, and the woman was thirsty. Even though the two were different in race, sex, and religion, both had a common need to drink.

A. *Jesus aroused her curiosity* (vv. 10–15). After He talked about His and her physical thirst, He mentioned something about "living water." Immediately the woman began to ask questions. "From whence then hast thou that living water?" (v. 11b). The woman realized that Jesus was speaking of another type of water.

B. *Jesus awakened her conscience* (vv. 16–25). The woman did not grasp everything about the living water, so Jesus appealed to her conscience. "Go, call thy husband, and come hither" (v. 16b). Jesus wanted the woman to see that He knew the errors of her life. With her conscience awakened, the woman wanted to talk about her relationship with God. "Sir, I perceive that thou art a prophet. Our fathers worshipped in this mountain; and ye say, that in Jerusalem is the place . . . to worship" (vv. 19–20).

C. *Jesus acknowledged Himself as the Messiah* (v. 26). Skillfully and masterfully Jesus led the woman to the fact that He was the Messiah. At the appropriate moment He made the messianic disclosure, "I who speak to you am he" (RSV).

III. The woman's proclamation.

After the interview with Jesus, the woman left for the city of Samaria. She told the people about the Lord. "Come, see a man, which told me all things that ever I did: is not this the Christ?" (v. 29).

The woman had been changed because of her encounter with the Christ. A careful study of her attitude and actions reflect a radical change in character.

The woman also had a new concern for her life. She left the waterpots and went into the city. Her primary concerns had been the sensual things of life. After her life-transforming experience, she was concerned for the spiritual condition of an entire village.

Conclusion. Why don't you have a meeting with the Master? Let Him tell you about His character and His ability to change people. — *HTB*

* * *

SUNDAY MORNING, MAY 29

TITLE: The Family Deals With Death

TEXT: **"'Lord, if you had been here, my brother would not have died.' When Jesus saw her weeping, and the Jews who came with her also weeping, he was deeply moved in spirit and troubled; and he said, 'Where have you laid him?' They said to him, 'Lord, come and see.' Jesus wept" (John 11:32–35 RSV).**

SCRIPTURE READING: **John 11:1–4, 17–37**

HYMNS: **"A Mighty Fortress Is Our God," Luther**
"What Wondrous Love Is This?" American Folk Hymn
"Because He Lives," Gaither

OFFERTORY PRAYER:

Heavenly Father, we thank You for our families, for they help us grow to be the people we have the potential to be. Especially in times of grief and heartache we turn to our families for strength and comfort. It is because our love for one another is so important to us that death can be so painful when one is gone from us. It would be even harder for us, Lord, if we didn't know that You know what we feel and are present with us in it. As we bring our gifts to You, we remember that You first loved us and gave Your Son. Amen.

Introduction. On this memorial Sunday we have a good opportunity to talk about how families can deal with death. Everyone who has gone through the dying process with a loved one is grateful for the support that a family brings. In the text before us, a family is brought to its knees by the death of the brother, Lazarus. The dynamics of the family relationships are evident to the sensitive observer. Martha's statement of fact in verse 21 calls from Jesus, not an apology for being late, but the answer of faith, "Your brother will rise again." (v. 23 RSV). Martha is the practical, no-nonsense keeper of the house (cf. Luke 10:40), but Mary is the contemplative, sensitive sister whose heart worships her Lord (cf. Luke 10:39; John 11:2). Mary says the same word as Martha did to Jesus, "Lord, if you had been here, my brother would not have died" (v. 32 RSV). But this time there is no theological answer; there is only the entering into her suffering: "Where have you laid him?" (v. 34) and Jesus' tears! To each person's grief Jesus was fully present, and He is present to help us in our need.

As a family is faced with death, it is helpful to remember:

I. Death is always more than it appears to be.

It is obvious that death is sorrow and pain, emptiness and loneliness, frustration and helplessness. Patiently a family needs to work with each other to admit the depth of the sorrow, the extent of the pain, the aching emptiness, and the fear of loneliness. There may be a sense of guilt which will deeply frustrate those who wish they could have been more helpful or had been more attentive.

But people of faith can begin to see also that death is more than the obvious; it is something God can use. Jesus makes the remarkable statement in verse 4 that God can be glorified in the illness and death of Lazarus. It is easier to see that being true for Lazarus, since Jesus raised him from the dead a few days later, than it is for us, who place our loved ones in the grave and by faith must await the resurrection in God's own time. But the quiet testimony of many Christians has been that in the midst of their deepest loss, God has been able to bless and comfort them and bring glory finally to His great name. Surely this is what Paul had in mind in Romans 8:28–29. These do not say that everything that happens to us is good. But they do say that God is willing to work with those who love Him and are willing to work with Him so that everything that comes to us, whether good or bad or indifferent, can be worked out for good. The picture is of God as a great salvager of life's wreckage. In the junkyards of life God moves here and there salvaging what He can so that out of our darkness, grief, and pain, He can create a very special good thing—more and more brothers and sisters who are "conformed to the image of his Son."

II. There is a Christian answer to the taunts of death.

Jesus flings His confidence against the doubts of death. He goes up against the despair of death with the word of great hope (vv. 25–26).

Jesus says there is life on the other side of death. There is no tentativeness in His affirmation. It is the Son's great answer to Job's ancient question, "If a man die, shall he live again?" (Job 14:14). Jesus says that death never will have the final victory for "he who believes in me, though he die, yet shall he live" (John 11:25 RSV).

But the Christian answer to death is not simply the words of Jesus, but the Word who is Jesus. The way of the Christian faith is not God shouting words at us from heaven, but God becoming flesh and entering into our lives, incarnating Himself, and becoming visible to us as flesh of our flesh (1:14). As Jesus Himself walks into the family of Lazarus, Mary, and Martha, He "fleshes out" the eternal God of John's prologue (1:1–14).

Note, however, the necessity of belief in verse 25. To believe in Jesus means that He becomes the Lord God in your life. It is only as you place your life in faith before Him, trusting that He is indeed God's power to deliver us, God's grace to save us, that you are delivered from the worst death can do.

III. Friends can help.

In verse 31 we see a picture of the common experience of all mankind. Mary is surrounded by the friends from her village, and they are seeking to console her. Friends know that even though they cannot do everything, they can do something, and what they can do they must. The one the sisters really wanted to see was Jesus for He was the one who could have kept it from happening.

In the Christian family of faith Jesus often makes His presence known to a family through the love of those who come in His name and offer their hands and hearts on His behalf. In a study by David Haun in 1976, entitled "Help for the Sorrowing . . . a Study in Grief and Bereavement" (Stillwater, Ok.: Oklahoma State University, 1976), it was discovered that one of the most meaningful helps to families in times of grief is the action of their friends as they came to assist them in their grief. The kinds of things that help most are simple activities, they reported, such as, assisting in house care, taking care of the children, standing by to answer the door or phone or to welcome visitors and accept the food that is brought to the house. In almost every instance, the acts of service that were recalled by the bereaved were those which do not require expertise on the part of the volunteer, but simply a desire and willingness to help.

In a church that cares for one another it is never simply the minister who is able to help the family. It is the community of faith which surrounds the grieving hearts and communicates Christ's love.

IV. There is the presence of God through all that comes to us, including death.

God knows about dying. He warned us from the beginning that to walk away from Him would cause us to become vulnerable to dying. Once sin and disobedience had been chosen for the race He did not abandon us to our fate and walk away in disgust. He shoulders our grief upon His own back and bears the burden with us. The cross on which our Savior died became God's painful response to Satan's question in the garden, "Did God say . . .?" (Gen. 3:1). A heartbroken mother cried out in her grief at the loss of her only son, "Oh, where is God when I need Him most?" A friend standing close by replied, "I suppose He's in the same place He was when He lost His son."

The truth of God's grieving is nowhere more clear than in the text before us (vv. 33–36). At this point there are no words of explanation, no call to courage and great faith. There is simply the grief which He shares with them as He walks weeping toward the place where they had laid Lazarus. The Greeks would read John's gospel in disbelief. To them God is the unmoved Mover. He is above our petty emotions. He cannot be touched by our sorrow and pain. But John's gospel is clear: God is not apathetic; He is empathetic with His people.

Martin Luther knew the terrible grief that only a parent can know when his child is dead. A daughter, Magdalena, died in Luther's arms when she was fourteen. He said, "Du liebes Lenichen, you will rise and shine like the stars and the sun. How strange it is to know that she is at peace and all is well, and yet to be so sorrowful!" (Roland Bainton, *Here I Stand* New York: Abingdon Press, 1950). As Martin Luther, we ourselves grieve with all our hearts, and we are somehow comforted because we know our Lord's grief was real. We need not be ashamed nor feel guilty when our hearts are breaking within us. But because we know our Lord's power over death, we do not have to grieve as those who have no hope. We can paraphrase Paul's words: "Grieve, not as those who have no hope, but for goodness' sake, grieve when you have something worth grieving about!" (cf. 1 Thess. 4:13). Christians know that God is present with us when we grieve not only at death, but at times of separation, divorce, retirement, the loss of a job, the loss of a good friend, or the loss of place when we move.

V. The funeral service should bear witness both to the grief and the victory which Christians know.

Dwight L. Moody said that when he was called on to preach his first funeral sermon, he went to the Scriptures to find what Jesus said at funerals. To his amazement he found that Jesus had no funeral sermons. Jesus broke up every funeral He ever attended. Jesus does turn our grief into victory. The resurrections that Jesus gave to others were signs of the great resurrection which was to come in His own life. His own resurrection became the undeniable sign of God's victory over death which He freely gives to those who trust Him. He is, as He said, "the resurrection and the life" (v. 25).

Since we must wait for God's own time to be reunited with those who have gone on to be with Him, our loss and loneliness are not feigned; but over against our pain He places His promise, "though he die, yet shall he live" (v. 25).

Conclusion. In the study by David Haun mentioned above, those who had gone through grief suggested to others that the greatest help they could have in going through death and dying with a loved one was to develop a meaningful religious faith. There were other suggestions such as keeping busy, remembering the good things, understanding the various stages of grief, and accepting death as a normal part of life; but these were all secondary in their minds to the strength which they found in a vibrant faith in God. When the waves of grief flow over you, remember the words of Fanny Crosby, "Down in the human heart, crushed by the tempter, feelings lie buried that grace can restore; touched by a loving heart, wakened by kindness, cords that are broken will vibrate once more." — *CRW*

* * *

SUNDAY EVENING, MAY 29

TITLE: The Triumph of the Cross

TEXT: **"And you, being dead through your trespasses and the uncircumcision of your flesh, you, I say, did he make alive together with him, having forgiven us all our trespasses; having blotted out the bond written in ordinances that was against us, which was contrary to us: and he hath taken it out of the way, nailing it to the cross; having despoiled the principalities and the powers, he made a show of them openly, triumphing over them in it" (Col. 2:13–15 ASV).**

SCRIPTURE READING: **Colossians 2:8–15**

Introduction. Basically there are three great teachings in Colossians.

A. *The incarnation of Jesus Christ.*

He was a real human being of flesh and blood and bones, and not an apparition as some of their false teachers had said. He was God in all that God is and not just an intermediary being as others had taught them. The high water mark of the New Testament is this: "For in him dwelleth all the fullness of the Godhead bodily" (2:9).

B. *The supremacy of Jesus Christ.*

He is supreme in creation and over all created beings (1:15–16); He is supreme in the church (1:18); and He is supreme over all principalities and powers (2:10, 15).

C. *The crucifixion of Jesus Christ and the meaning of it.*

In two ways these heretical teachers had attacked the Christian teaching of redemption through the death of Christ on the cross.

1. "Christ did not have an actual physical body," some of them said. "He only appeared to have." Therefore they maintained that the Crucifixion was not an actual event but only a nonhistorical apparition.

2. Others among these heretics said, "Christ had a real physical body, but He was not God's Son. An *Aeon,* called 'Christ,' came upon Him at His baptism and departed from Him on the cross. Hence," they contended, "the Crucifixion, though a historical event, had no saving power."

It was largely to refute these views that the Epistle to the Colossians was written. Thus, the teaching about the Crucifixion is the main thrust of this epistle. The heart and center, the foundation stone of the Christian religion is this: we are redeemed "through the blood of his cross" (1:20). Through the death of His Son on the cross, God has triumphed over sin and death and the Devil.

Our text presents a fact and the far reaches of that fact. Let us notice these in that order.

I. The fact is this: the triumph of the cross.

Notice the phrases Paul piles upon one another to emphasize this: "Having forgiven us our trespasses . . . having blotted out the bond . . . having despoiled the principalities and powers, . . . he triumphed over them in it" (that is, in the cross).

A. *The triumph of the cross is a historical fact.*

That Christ died an actual death on the cross cannot be disputed. "The blood of his cross" (1:20) was an actual, witnessed, historical event (John 19:34). "Christ died for our sins according to the scriptures" (1 Cor. 15:3b).

B. *The triumph of the cross is a theological fact.*

This is a fact of great significance. In his first epistle John tells us: "The blood of Jesus . . . cleanses us from all sin" (1:7b). Look at Jesus in the Garden of Gethsemane, with the shadow of the cross falling across His very being. What did He do with it! He laid hold of it. He wrestled with it. He lifted it up in His mighty passion. He transformed it. He made it an instrument of redemption.

The communion ritual of the United Methodist Church has this idea. It tells us that Jesus Christ suffered "death upon the cross for our redemption, and made thereby the offering of himself, a full, perfect and sufficient sacrifice for the sins of the whole world."

C. *The triumph of the cross is a spiritual and personal fact.*

"And you, being dead through your trespasses . . . , you, I say, did he make alive together with him having forgiven all our trespasses" (Col. 2:13). This triumph of the cross becomes a personal victory in our lives when by faith in Christ we accept what He has done for us on that cross. That is the fact of our text, "The Triumph of the Cross."

II. The scope: the vast reaches of that fact.

This fact has both a legal and a spiritual aspect.

A. *The legal aspect of the triumph of the cross.*

Verse 14 tells us that the sentence of our condemnation was the sentence of death. That sentence has been taken from us, satisfied by another, canceled forever. By the cross three things have been done about this sentence of death.

1. "Having blotted out the bond . . . that was against us, which was contrary to us." The debt is canceled, marked paid like a canceled check; and we have peace with God.

2. ''He hath taken it out of the way.'' It's gone, thank God! That sentence is over our heads no longer. It is removed! How could it be taken from over us? The perfect law of God must be satisfied. Nothing can thwart it, escape it, or rewrite it.

3. ''Nailing it to the cross.'' What does that mean? It was customary for the Romans to nail the crime for which one had been condemned on the cross of the one being crucified just above his head. Over Jesus' head Pilate wrote: ''JESUS OF NAZARETH THE KING OF THE JEWS.'' (John 19:19b). But that was not the real indictment. Had Pilate known, he could have written: ''Crucified for the sins of men.''

B. *The spiritual aspect of the triumph of the cross.*

Listen to Paul: ''Having despoiled the principalities and the powers . . . , triumphing over them in it'' (that is, in the cross). What appeared to be the defeat of God and the triumph of the powers of darkness proved instead to be the triumph of God and the doom of Satan and sin. The cross was God's field of victory, the implement of His triumph.

Conclusion. Let us ask this question in closing: ''What is or what should be the significance of this great fact, 'The Triumph of the Cross' for our own personal lives?''

A. *Negatively.*

We ought not to serve those things from which we were set free by the cross. ''We who died to sin, how shall we any longer live therein?'' (Rom. 6:2b).

B. *Positively.*

We ought to follow and do and think and say those things worthy of a life redeemed by His blood. This is the way to victory.

At the sign of triumph
Satan's host doth flee,
On, then, Christian soldiers,
On to victory.

— *WTH*

* * *

SUGGESTED PREACHING PROGRAM FOR THE MONTH OF JUNE

Sunday Mornings

We continue the series using the theme "The Christian Family: Living for Christ in the Present."

Sunday Evenings

"The Inward Attitudes of the True Disciple" is the suggested theme for a series of messages based on the Beatitudes, which are found in the beginning of the Sermon on the Mount.

Wednesday Evenings

Continue the series of devotional messages based on the Gospel of John using the theme "The Christ of John's Gospel."

* * *

WEDNESDAY EVENING, JUNE 1

TITLE: Audience Response to the Preacher

TEXT: "From that time many of his disciples went back, and walked no more with him" (John 6:66).

SCRIPTURE READING: John 6:1–71

Introduction. Preaching plays an important role in the life of a church. Congregations demand helpful sermons. They also demand thorough preparation, effective delivery, and decisions from the sermon. The congregation has a right to expect efficiency from the preacher. There is another demand, however. This demand comes from the preacher. He demands a responsive, listening audience. Thomas Jessup, in his book *Effective Religion,* said: "There are two demands of effective religion—a good preacher and a good congregation."

The hearing of an audience plays an important part in a sermon. Jesus told a parable about how people listened to Him. He told of a sower who was sowing seed. Some seed fell by the wayside, some amid thorns, others on rocky soil, and still others on good ground. The point of the parable was how people listened to a sermon. From this parable we could say that every sermon has a response of some kind.

Jesus was a masterful preacher. When He preached, people responded. Let us notice the different responses to His sermons.

I. The religious leaders: rejection.

A. *The Jews resented the Lord's message.* "The Jews then murmured at him, because he said, I am the bread . . . of life; he that cometh to me shall never hunger; and he that believeth on me shall never thirst" (vv. 35, 41). Jesus had referred to the experiences of the Israelites when God fed them with manna. God gave them life, for life was in the bread. Jesus then applied the bread to Himself.

B. *The Jews rejected the Messenger.* To resent the message is to reject the messenger. "And they said, 'Is not this Jesus, the son of Joseph, whose father and mother we know? how is it then that he saith, I came down from heaven?'" (v. 42). The Jews regarded Jesus only as the son of Mary and Joseph. They judged the Lord by external standards.

God's greatest message and messenger came through a Galilean carpenter. The Jews denounced both His message and Him. Within every audience there will be those who will resent God's message and reject His Son.

II. The crowds: dropouts.

A. *Jesus was popular with the crowd at the beginning of His ministry.* People were attracted to Jesus. They heard His unusual sermons. They watched Him perform many miracles. They enjoyed the benefits of His multiplying the loaves and fishes. People often act on impulse.

B. *The crowds began to depart from Jesus.* "From that time many of his disciples went back, and walked no more with him" (v. 66). Why did these people leave? They left because they found the way of Jesus to be too difficult. "Many therefore of his disciples, when they had heard this, said, This is an hard saying; who can hear it?" (v. 60). The word for "hard saying" is *skleros*. It does not mean hard to understand but hard to accept or to live. The crowds knew the claims of Christ, and they were not willing to accept and follow them.

People have not changed. They are continuing to respond to Jesus by dropping out. Of course this does not destroy the idea of the security of the believer. It just discloses the reality or pretense of a person's faith.

III. The apostles: dedication.

A. *Jesus posed an important question to the disciples.* "Then said Jesus unto the twelve, Will ye also go away?" (v. 67). There were only two alternatives. Either the disciples could go away, or they could stay. By their response to His question Jesus tested the dedication of the apostles.

Disciples are always put to the test. The passing of time and various life situations will disclose the reality of commitment.

B. *Peter answered the Master with a demonstration of dedication.* "Then Simon Peter answered him, Lord, to whom shall we go? thou hast the words of eternal life" (v. 68). Peter affirmed the fact that there was no one else to whom the disciples could turn for life. Only Jesus could satisfy their deepest longings.

Conclusion. The sermon is almost over. You will make a response to this sermon. Either you will say, "It was good" or "It was bad." But that is not your only response. Jesus has been presented. Various responses to Jesus have been cited: rejection, dropouts, dedication. What will be your response? —*HTB*

* * *

SUNDAY MORNING, JUNE 5

TITLE: Enemies of the Family

TEXT: "Look carefully then how you walk, not as unwise men, but as wise, making the most of the time, because the days are evil" (Eph. 5:15–16 RSV).

SCRIPTURE READING: Ephesians 5:1–6:4

HYMNS: "Jesus Calls Us O'er the Tumult," Alexander
"When We Walk With the Lord," Sammis
"God Will Take Care of You," Martin

OFFERTORY PRAYER:

Dear Lord, we want our families to be healthy. We want them to bring joy to our lives, strength to our church, and glory to You. We know that sometimes we fail to obey You and thereby open our families to evil influences and dangerous temptations. We know there are enemies of the family that can destroy the vitality of our homes. We ask You to protect our families from evil and to hedge us about with Your gracious providence. May we be willing to live within Your will and purpose for our homes. Thank You for our families. The offerings we give now are the shared expression of our love and obedience to You. Amen.

Introduction. How do wise men and women walk? We walk in love, as Christ taught us to walk (Eph. 5:1–2). This is a high calling, but it is nevertheless exactly what the Lord expects of His people. When we fail, He is perfectly willing to work with us; He knows how to forgive. But make no mistake about it, God—though He is easily pleased—is hard to satisfy. He wants us to grow up in the fullness of life in Jesus Christ.

This may sound as though it is an admonition for personal Christian living alone; but because within the context of this passage is one of the lengthy passages on family relationships (Eph. 5:21–6:4), we should see these truths for the family, as well as for the individual life. We have spoken about friends of the family (sermon for May 22), but there are enemies of the family as well, and we must identify them. While it is true that television, motion pictures, and the influence of non-Christian minds are detrimental to the health of the family, these are not our primary enemies. We cannot isolate ourselves from the world if we are to have any impact upon it. The real enemies of the family are those which arise out of our own disobedience to the Word of God. These enemies can be named by looking carefully at our Scripture passage.

I. Enemy #1 is permissiveness (5:3–12).

The first enemy that will destroy a family is the permissive attitude which is popularly expressed as "anything goes." Sexual impurity, sexual filthiness, perversity, or dirty and immoral talk ought to be foreign to the people of God. When respect for the sexuality of the family is lost and no one sets standards for family attitudes toward sex, then the bond of trust that must hold families together becomes frayed and will soon break.

Children need to be taught the discipline that comes from obeying God. We do not have to do all the things we want to do. We are able to say no in order that at the right time and in the right way we can say yes. Young people, remember that the decisions you are making now in your dating relationships will determine to a great degree the moral authority you will have as a parent to give good counsel and encouragement to your children as to how they ought to use their sexuality.

Parental immorality always undermines parental authority!

II. Enemy #2 is drunkenness (v. 18).

This warning includes not only wine, but all liquors and drugs that alter the mental and emotional state and make us vulnerable to temptation and evil. A family is severely frustrated when one of its members becomes a different person because of what drugs have done to his or her mind. Alcohol is the worst drug problem in our nation. Adults prefer to talk about the drug problems of the young because they do not want to deal with the drug problem which they have installed in their own home bars. Pastors tend to be more vocal in their opposition to alcohol than most professionals because they are so often confronted in their counseling with families that have been destroyed by the effects of alcohol. As strong as peer pressure may be in the lives of young people, a consistent Christian lifestyle by the parents and fair and loving discipline can help to protect your family from this enemy.

III. Enemy #3 is selfishness (5:21–22, 25, 28–29).

Sermons on this text face one great difficulty. The men hear the part about how the wife should respect them and follow their leadership. The women hear the part about how their husbands should love them as Christ loved the church. The reason we hear the message that way is selfishness. We think first of ourselves, then later we think of the other.

We must hear both of the apostle's admonitions at the same time. In verse 21 we have the idea. The submission expected in a marriage is to be mutual, not a submission of the wife alone. First Corinthians 7:4 is a commentary on this very point. "For the wife does not rule over her own body, but the husband does; likewise the husband does not rule over his own body, but the wife does"(RSV).

In a Christian home there must be a willingness on the part of the wife and children to allow the husband and father to give leadership. He needs the respect of his family, not ridicule, if he is to be a successful leader of the family. Good leaders know how to listen. Good leaders are not tyrannical. Good leaders delegate authority and respect the decisions that others make. Good leaders are willing to give leadership and accept the responsibility of articulating the vision of what the goals for the group ought to be. Christian husbands are willing to let God make them into good leaders. Christian wives rejoice in helping God develop leadership in their husbands.

In a Christian home the wife is to be loved, not casually, nor haphazardly, but with thoughtful attention. A husband will love his wife with the kind of devotion and courage which marked Jesus' love for His church. Jesus loved the church and gave Himself up for her on the cross. No husband has begun to love his wife as God is calling him to if he is more concerned about his own welfare, self-esteem, and future than he is about his wife's welfare, self-esteem, and future. Jesus died to save His church. A husband must be willing to die for his wife . . . to give himself away for her well-being and growth. A wife has a right to be loved by her husband nobly, faithfully, and often. A daily prayer of gratitude to God for the wife He has given you will strengthen your love for your wife.

Wives are to be respected and husbands are to be loved. The admonition of the Scripture is not to reserve leadership for the husband nor love for the wife. Marriage is a blending of lives, and both husbands and wives are to be both respected and loved. Selfishness is the enemy. Thinking of one another and doing loving things for one another are ways to overcome this enemy!

IV. Enemy #4 is carelessness (6:4).

Fathers are instructed not to provoke their children to anger. That means, obviously, that discipline must be fair and just. But it also means that fathers must not be careless of their children. No one is so poor that he cannot pay attention to his child! Children know deep anger when they begin to realize that one or both of their parents are not really interested in them. A man said to his pastor, "My father was an excellent carpenter, but he never showed me how to do one thing. He could have helped me so much, but he never noticed me." The pastor was able to discern behind that complaint a latent anger which had blocked the son's emotional and spiritual growth for years.

Children know they have a right to be considered. They feel deep anger, which most often is repressed, when parents do not listen or set boundaries, or show interest, or expect excellence. It is important to heed this admonition to not be careless with your children, not only for their sakes, but also for your own. One way or another fathers have to pay attention to their children. Hopefully, it will be at the time in their lives when it can bring joy and growth. If not, it will come when it's too late to help, and all that is left to do is hurt!

V. Enemy #5 is ignorance of the Lord (6:4).

The greatest strength in any home is the knowledge of the Lord. The Jewish fathers were given the high task of being sure that their children learned of the Lord and the deliverance of their people from bondage (Deut. 6:1–9). Paul reminds us that children must be taught the "discipline and instruction" of the Lord. If they are not taught, they are ignorant. It is not because children are dumb or stubborn that they do not know God's way . . . it is because their parents have not taught them. It is not the school's fault nor the church's fault if children are spiritually illiterate; spiritual knowledge is the responsibility of the parents.

In godly matters one cannot teach if one is not experienced. If you are not on speaking terms with God, you will not be able to teach your children what they need to know.

Conclusion. Beware of the enemies that will destroy your family. Ask God to help you defend against permissiveness, drunkenness, selfishness, carelessness, and ignorance. If you must confess that you do not know the Lord well enough to teach your children, then He invites you to begin to walk with Him in faith that you may indeed be wise and successful in making the most of the time that you have with your family (5:16).

— *CRW*

* * *

SUNDAY EVENING, JUNE 5

TITLE: Questions About the Beatitudes

TEXT: **"And he opened his mouth and taught them, saying . . ." (Matt. 5:2).**

SCRIPTURE READING: **Matthew 5:1–12**

Introduction. Perhaps no sayings of Jesus are more familiar but less understood by the average Christian than the Beatitudes. Most congregations could be classified as belonging to one of three groups on the basis of their attitudes toward the Beatitudes.

A. *In one group there are those whose attitude is: "Come to think of it, I don't know what they mean. I've never tried to learn. And I don't care."* Not many of this group come to church, but there will be a few.

B. *In a second group there are those whose attitude is: "I have thought about the Beatitudes. I have wished I could have these qualities in my life, but this quest is not for me. These ideals are too high. I cannot attain to them."* A large percentage of the average congregation would fall into this group.

C. *In a third group are those whose attitude is: "The Beatitudes are idealistic. Only Jesus ever exhibited them perfectly.* This thing of being meek and merciful and pure in heart—don't you think these are the qualities we'll have in heaven, but they are not for now?" Not so! The Beatitudes are for the here and now. If Jesus had not wanted these qualities to be exhibited in our lives until we get to heaven, He would have waited until then to tell us.

What about the Beatitudes? What is the correct attitude toward these sayings of Jesus? Consider three questions about them taken as a unity.

I. What are the Beatitudes?

A. *The Beatitudes are plain, simple statements of fact, statements of truth, and not promises of reward.*

Jesus does not say that if a person is "poor in spirit" He will give him the kingdom in order to make him happy. The poor in spirit *are* happy "for theirs *is* the kingdom of heaven" (v. 3b). Jesus does not give gifts to make us happy. He creates conditions within us which enable us to find happiness everywhere. Jesus takes a person and gives him a character that radiates and creates happiness regardless of the outward circumstances.

B. *The Beatitudes describe not seven different classes of people, but seven different traits of character, or elements of Christian excellence, in one individual.*

Who is a Christian? A subject of the kingdom. Jesus is here describing what He came to create in the subjects of His kingdom. The whole Sermon on the Mount treats the character and conduct of members of the kingdom, those who become Christians. Here at the very outset we have the character Christ desires and requires of His followers sketched in these seven characteristics. These traits do not exclude one another. They are mutually dependent. If a person is "meek," he needs also to be "merciful"; if "merciful," he needs also to be "pure in heart."

II. What do the Beatitudes teach?

A. *The Beatitudes teach Christ's doctrine of the kingdom.*

The multitudes in Jesus' day, for lack of knowledge, degraded and materialized the teachings of the coming kingdom. They believed it to be a perpetual banquet where they would eat rich food and make merry. The more privileged classes were not more spiritual than the masses. They thought of the coming kingdom as a political revolution when the hated Romans would be overthrown. The Beatitudes, and the Sermon on the Mount as a whole, were a flat contradiction of both of these misconceptions. They taught, rather, that the kingdom is a spiritual realm which is not of this world, though in it. The kingdom of heaven is wherever the laws of heaven rule in the hearts of men. When Jesus speaks of His kingdom, He is speaking from a level of spiritual elevation whose condition He has tested, whose laws He has mastered, and into whose blessedness He would lead mankind.

B. *The Beatitudes teach Christ's doctrine of happiness.*

In this, the Beatitudes cut straight across the ideas of the world. Who are the happy people? The world says, "The rich, the famous, the powerful, those who live in ease and luxury." If carnal man would draw up a list of Beatitudes, they would go something like this: "Blessed are the rich, the famous, the well-born, the cultured. . . ." But not so Christ! Men look to outward circumstances for happiness, Christ looks to character. Happiness is decided not by what we have, but by what we are. Happiness is never dependent upon outward conditions but always upon an inward spirit. Therefore, Jesus says, "Blessed are the poor in spirit, . . . they that mourn, . . . the meek, . . . the merciful, . . . the pure in heart. . . ." All of these are inward qualities of heart and not outward circumstances.

III. How may we profit from a series of studies on the Beatitudes?

A. *Studying this perfect picture of Christian character, we will be able to see ourselves as we are.*

By this standard we will be able to take stock, to see how far short we fall. Are we poor in spirit, meek, merciful, pure in heart, peacemakers? We are not, but why not?

B. *Studying this perfect picture of Christian character, we may see ourselves as we could be, as Christ intended us to be.*

Seeing this let us "press on toward the goal" (Phil. 3:14a).

C. *Studying this perfect picture of Christian character, we may be challenged to make some progress toward bridging the gap between what we are and what we ought to become.*

If this quest is not for us, why should we preach? Why should we listen to sermons?

Conclusion. For the next eight Sunday evenings we will consider the Beatitudes. Seven of these are found in Matthew 5:3–9. The eighth, an often forgotten but authentic beatitude of Jesus is found in Acts 20:35. — *WTH*

* * *

WEDNESDAY EVENING, JUNE 8

TITLE: What Do You Think of Sin?

TEXT: "They say unto him, Master, this woman was taken in adultery, in the very act" (John 8:4).

SCRIPTURE READING: John 8:1–11

Introduction. A famous psychiatrist by the name of Karl Menninger wrote a book several years ago entitled *Whatever Became of Sin?* Menninger sounds like a preacher when he says that sin has virtually disappeared from the American vocabulary. Today sin goes by the names of "crime" or "sickness." Menninger called for a new emphasis on sin with the idea of responsibility, guilt, and even punishment.

Jesus had a lot to say about sin. Maybe our society would profit by taking an incident out of the life and ministry of Jesus and studying about sin. Such an example is furnished by Jesus' encounter with a sinful woman. Some scribes and Pharisees were going to stone her. Just before they were to stone her, Jesus stooped and wrote on the ground. The words and action of Jesus convicted the woman's accusers, and they left. "When Jesus had lifted up himself, and saw none but the woman, he said unto her, Woman, where are thine accusers? hath no man condemned thee? She said, No man Lord. And Jesus said to her, Neither do I condemn thee: go, and sin no more" (John 8:10–11). From this episode we may learn much about sin.

I. Sin is a universal problem.

"He that is without sin among you, let him first cast a stone at her" (v. 7b).

A. *Some people are guilty of sensual sins.* The woman was guilty of sin. The scribes and the Pharisees had caught the woman in the act of adultery. No one would deny that this woman was a sinner.

The world is filled with people who sin and express their sin with the sins of the flesh. Murder, adultery, stealing, and countless other sensual sins abound. But this is not the only kind of sinner.

B. *Other people are guilty of sins of the spirit or temperament.* The scribes and Pharisees were not guilty of adultery, but just the same they were sinners too. They were guilty of self-righteousness.

The world is filled with people who sin and express their sins with sins of the temperament. If we are not careful, we will overlook these sins and point only to the sensual sins. Jesus taught the universality of sin, which is expressed in many ways.

II. Sin is to be condemned.

A. *All types of sin are condemned by Jesus.* In the story of the woman caught in adultery, Jesus exercised condemnation. With skill the Lord made the Pharisees look at themselves. In some manner Jesus made these religious leaders look at their own sins instead of the sins of the woman. They felt that Jesus condemned their ways.

We must not see that Jesus was light on sin when He spoke to the woman. Jesus said, "Woman, where are those thine accusers? hath no man condemned thee? She said, No man, Lord. And Jesus said unto her, Neither do I condemn thee: go, and sin no more" (vv. 10b–11). In both cases Jesus condemned the sins, not the persons. The Lord dislikes sin, and He condemns its presence and action in every person.

B. *Sins are condemned for profound reasons.* The Lord denounced sin at every point because of what it does to an individual. It depraves a person. Continuing in the downward course of sin destroys the potential which every person possesses. Also, the Lord condemns sin because it brings guilt. Nothing can be more debilitating in a person's life than self-condemnation. Because of what sin does to the individual, Jesus condemns it.

III. Sin can be forgiven.

A. *Forgiveness is possible for everyone.* Sin need not destroy either religious leaders or the promiscuous person. Jesus constantly offered forgiveness to all people. In Jesus' time the religious leaders were in great danger, for they refused to look at their sin. Sin was destroying their lives, but they were blinded to its effects. Jesus offered forgiveness to a sinful woman. No person need remain in the condition of sinfulness. Forgiveness is available to anyone who repents.

B. *Forgiveness opens the door for new possibilities.* When Jesus forgave the woman caught in the act of adultery, new and wonderful possibilities were open to her. Think of just a few benefits: she was not condemned; she was challenged to a new lifestyle; she could have a new beginning in her life.

People are burdened with unforgiven sin. A newness of life will come to the person who repents and experiences God's forgiveness.

Conclusion. The text does not record whether the woman caught in adultery accepted God's forgiveness. I hope she did. I hope you will accept His forgiveness too.

— *HTB*

* * *

SUNDAY MORNING, JUNE 12

TITLE: You Can Have a Happy Family

TEXT: "But seek first his kingdom and his righteousness, and all these things shall be yours as well" (Matt. 6:33 RSV).

SCRIPTURE READING: Matthew 6:25–34

HYMNS: "Praise the Lord! Ye Heavens Adore Him," Anonymous
"God of Grace, and God of Glory," Fosdick
"Brethren, We Have Met to Worship," Atkins

OFFERTORY PRAYER:

Eternal and everlasting God, who was and is and ever shall be, Creator of the earth and all that is therein, Savior and Redeemer of our lives, and ever-present Spirit . . . we can scarcely take it in when we hear Jesus say that you are our Father, loving us even more than any parent could love us, desiring good things for us even more than they can.

You know us completely—where we go, what we do, when we cry, and when we laugh. You hear us when we pray, and You guide us in Your way.

It is our joy to live before You and to offer our gifts of praise now to You for Your work in this world. In our Lord's name. Amen.

Introduction. There might be a question in your mind as to the worthiness of setting before a family the goal of being happy. Happiness is certainly not the goal of the gospel for our lives. Obedience to God must always take precedence over "the fleeting pleasures of sin" (Heb. 11:25). But if we define happiness as a sense of well-being, of contentment, of joyful purpose in living, then happiness is, at least, what most people are looking for in life.

In this passage before us, Jesus has not dismissed that need as a superficial desire but here focuses on how an individual and a family can find true happiness. We don't have to be anxious about life . . . although we often are (vv. 25, 27–28, 31, 34). There is a way to find happiness in the midst of our living! And

Jesus wants us to find it. But first we need to recognize that we can miss happiness in a frantic effort to gain it for our family.

I. Ways we miss having a happy family.

A. *We miss having a happy family when we are never satisfied with what we have.* It is fine to be people of vision and anticipation for the future, but don't miss the taste of now and the colors of the present moment. Happiness is not some magical state of existence that we finally discover over the next mountain of life. Happiness is happening to you along the way, in the midst of life. People who seek happiness on the other side of the mountain are those who try to find the pot of gold at the end of the rainbow. They never will get there.

The tragic truth is that many families run right past happiness in the search for it somewhere else. Don't miss the gift of joy a child's smile can bring today. Don't miss the explosion of wonder a child's question can set off in your heart. Don't miss the gift of love your wife or husband would bring to you today. You will miss that moment if you are not paying attention!

B. *We miss having a happy family when we value happiness too much.* If you would rather be happy than committed to one another, if you would rather be happy than courageous, if you would rather be happy than responsible, if you would rather be happy than right, then you will never really be happy at all. Husbands and wives who value happiness more than sincere effort together in fidelity and love will not be happy for long. People who seek happiness in one marriage or affair after another are deceived into believing that happiness is a gift someone else can give when, in truth, happiness must come from within.

C. *We miss having a happy family when we are not willing to do the will of God.* If we will not seek first the kingdom of God and His righteousness, He cannot add to us the needs and desires of our hearts (6:33). The will of God does not always lead us to easy tasks or give us smiles and laughter. Sometimes we walk with Him through the darkness of suffering or in the outer reaches of rejection as we seek to follow Him. But the testimony of Christians has been that deep joy can be known in obedience and fidelity to His will. Hear Paul as he says, "I consider that the sufferings of this present time are not worth comparing with the glory that is to be revealed to us" (Rom. 8:18). This courage is also seen in the Spanish Christian's benediction, "And may God deny you peace, but give you glory" (Unamuno).

II. Ways we can have a happy family.

A. *We can have a happy family when we value each other* (Matt. 6:26). Our heavenly Father feeds the birds of the air. But what about us? He values us more than the birds of the air, so be sure He will care for you. We are given value by our Creator, and no one can take that from us if we refuse to let him. People are happy when each member of the family recognizes the value of every other member. People are unhappy in their homes when they do not treasure one another. We are each God's gift to the other members of our family. It is God who stands behind the value of every person and guarantees it. The next time you are tempted to ignore your children or shout at your spouse or ridicule someone's efforts, remember you are dealing with someone God loves and has created and shared with you for your joy and fulfillment.

B. *We can have a happy family when we understand that life is more than externals* (6:25). Life is more than food and drink, clothes and shelter. As important as they are, they are not the goal of life. It is ironic that in most Christian congregations talk about food, clothing, and houses is a discussion of status symbols, while in much of the world that same discussion is a debate about survival. It isn't just food, but dining at the "right" restaurants! It isn't just jeans, but designer jeans! It isn't just a house, but the address that we're interested in! God, save us from explaining our poor giving habits by pleading that our bills are so high, when much of our world does not have the luxury of even having bills!

A happy family puts sufficient emphasis on the necessities and desires of life to provide motivation for work and thrift, but it is not consumed by a passion for gadgets and expensive toys . . . nor by an anxiety about life's essentials. Jesus does not say don't worry about food and clothing because they are unimportant. Just the opposite. In verses 32–33, Jesus asserts the Father knows we need those things and He will provide them! They are so important, God will not leave their provision entirely up to us. He intends to provide for His own!

C. *We can have a happy family when we find the purpose in life God has for our family* (6:33).

When a family sees itself as a unit of love and service that can be offered to God for His use in blessing and redeeming His world, that family is on its way to happiness. Happiness is what happens to us on our way to doing the will of God! A wise pastor was able to raise four children who never felt it necessary to rebel against the church because their father helped them to feel all through his ministry that the family was a partnership in offering their lives to God for His service. There were spiritual and intellectual struggles with personal faith which were finally resolved, but never resentment toward the ministry their father sought to do, because they all considered themselves to be a part of it.

A family is happy when they are fully committed to seeking the kingdom of God *first*. This verse reminds us of the necessity of setting priorities for life. If God and His will are first, then nothing can be above or before Him. When God is at the center of life, everything else fits into place. Parents can help their children if by example and precept they teach them how to live loving God as they love nothing else and loving their neighbor as they love themselves.

Conclusion. You can have a happy family. It won't be easy, but it is possible. You won't be happy every day—there will be times when you are going through painful and difficult trauma—but by the grace of God even those moments can contribute to the growing joy and happiness you will find as you live and grow together within His will and loving care. — *CRW*

* * *

SUNDAY EVENING, JUNE 12

TITLE: The Poverty That Possesses

TEXT: "Blessed are the poor in spirit: for theirs is the kingdom of heaven" (Matt. 5:3).

SCRIPTURE READING: 2 Corinthians 8:1–9

Introduction. The person who is truly poor in spirit is blessed because such poverty enables him to possess the supreme possession of all, "the kingdom of heaven." For our sakes, Jesus set the example: "For ye know the grace of our Lord Jesus Christ, that, though he was rich, yet for your sakes he became poor, that ye through his poverty might become rich" (2 Cor. 8:9).

Poverty of spirit is the first character trait Jesus wants in His followers, the subjects of His kingdom. It is a trait that carries its own reward: "theirs *is* the kingdom of heaven." Note the tenses carefully here: "Blessed *are* the poor in spirit," not "have been," not "shall be," but "*are.*"

Two questions about this beatitude call for an answer.

I. What is this poverty of spirit?

Jesus says the ones who have it are blessed. How so? What does He mean? Consider the answer from two points of view.

A. *Negatively.*

1. Poverty of spirit does not mean *poverty of material possessions.* It is true that earthly poverty does sometimes produce conditions in which Christian virtues may thrive. It is also true that the Bible warns us against "the care of this world, and the deceitfulness of riches" (Matt. 13:22b), because of their power to distract us from the desire for heaven's treasure.

But happiness is a matter of character, not conditions. It issues from the rightness of our hearts, the relationships of our lives, and not from external conditions. A person may be a millionaire and yet be poor in spirit. One may be penniless but also proud and arrogant.

2. Poverty of spirit does not mean *poverty of native endowment.* No life was ever richer in natural endowment than Jesus', and yet He was poor in spirit.

3. Poverty of spirit does not mean *poverty of spiritual life* in the sense of being feeble and neutral in one's life. Jesus came to bring the abundant life (John 10:10b). He had patience with those of little faith, those weak in spirit, and those impetuous in actions. But He wanted to help them grow, to be of great faith, to be strong in convictions.

4. Poverty of spirit does not mean *pretension of humility.* Some are profuse in self-depreciation. Jesus had no patience with the sort of "worm in the dust" mock piety that is always saying, "I am nothing and nobody and not worth your notice." Often, deep down in their hearts, these are as desirous of the "chief seats and salutations in the marketplace" as the proudest of the proud. The pride that apes humility is more detestable than the pride that casts off all disguise.

B. *Positively.*

What then is this poverty of spirit which Jesus calls blessed?

1. Poverty of spirit is *that quality of spirit that accurately perceives that man, as he is, has no virtue inherent in himself, that each gift and each grace of the spirit comes from God.* That great expositor Alexander MacLaren said, "To me it means a just and lowly estimate of myself, my character, my achievements, based upon a clear recognition of my own necessities, weaknesses and sins."

When we see how completely dispossessed of virtue and grace and righteousness we are of ourselves, pride, self-esteem, and self-righteousness must fall away. When we see how rebellious against God and His righteousness have been our wills, we want to cry out with Paul: "Wretched man that I am!" (Rom. 7:24a). Poverty of spirit is the realization that spiritually we are dispossessed, bankrupt, and without merit of our own.

2. Poverty of spirit is *that quality of spirit that recognizes that, apart from God, man is forever incomplete, that the true center of life is God.* The world has little time and no admiration at all for such a person. Rather, it admires the self-sufficient man, the self-confident man, the self-made man (so called), the man who feels he is complete within himself. The Greek philosopher Plato, discussing the good man, the happy man, places one condition upon him. He must be "self-sufficient." Such was the spirit of Jean Jacques Rousseau in his impious boast that he would stand before the judgment bar of God with his "book of Confessions" in his hand and challenge anyone living to say, "I am a better man than that man." How much better to cry out with Augustus M. Toplady:

> Nothing in my hand I bring,
> Simply to Thy cross I cling;
> Naked, come to Thee for dress,
> Helpless, look to Thee for grace;
> Foul, I to the fountain fly,
> Wash me, Saviour, or I die!

3. Poverty of spirit is *that quality of spirit that longs for, that intensely desires, that God shall supply the true needs of the soul.* Jesus tells a story of "two men" who "went up into the temple to pray." One, a Pharisee, did not pray. He gave God a recital of his qualities and virtues. He was self-righteous, self-satisfied. This is exactly what poverty of spirit is not. The other, a Publican, was so conscious of his need, so full of the sense of his own shortcomings he would not even lift his head. But yet, so desirous was he of God's blessing that he cried out, "God, be thou merciful to me a sinner" (Luke 18:13b). This is poverty of spirit.

II. How does this poverty of spirit bless us?

In what sense is it true that the poor in spirit are happy in the blessing of possessing the kingdom? Here are five links in a chain that must not be broken.

A. *Poverty of spirit causes us to seek in Christ the grace we need.*

We need not mere conviction for sin, for conviction does not always lead to repentance and conversion. Poverty of spirit is that appraisal of our lack on the one hand and of our sins on the other that cause a person to seek salvation.

B. *Poverty of spirit conditions a man for receiving the gift of God.*

All of the prophets have realized this. Isaiah says, "Thus saith the high and lofty One that inhabiteth eternity, whose name is Holy; I dwell in the high and holy place, with him also that is of a contrite and humble spirit, to revive the spirit of the humble, and to revive the heart of the contrite" (57:15). David says in Psalm 51: "The sacrifices of God are a broken spirit: a broken and a contrite heart, O God, thou wilt not despise" (v. 17).

C. *Poverty of spirit releases the saving grace of God upon us.*

That is our only hope. This is effective only when we empty our hearts of self and throw ourselves like broken vessels upon His mercy.

D. *Poverty of spirit fits us for service in the kingdom.*

God loves to use the life that keeps self out of sight and honors only Him.

E. *Poverty of spirit opens the eyes of the heart* (Eph. 1:18) *upon the broad horizons of heaven's possessions.*

This vision says, "You are a child of the king. These things are yours."

Conclusion. Let's test ourselves. Let each one ask: "Am I poor in spirit, or am I self-satisfied, self-righteous, and arrogant?" An unknown poet has said:

He that is down, needs fear no fall,
He that is low, no pride:
He that is humble, ever shall
have God to be his Guide.

— *WTH*

* * *

WEDNESDAY EVENING, JUNE 15

TITLE: Christ and Time

TEXT: **"Jesus said unto them, Verily, verily, I say unto you, Before Abraham was, I am" (John 8:58).**

SCRIPTURE READING: **John 8:48–59**

Introduction. Once I gave a sermon entitled "Jesus Was the Greatest" to my secretary for typing. She responded, "Preacher, I think you have the wrong verb tense in the title." I looked at it again and said, "Mrs. Givan, that is grammatically correct." "It's not the grammar but the doctrine," she said. Looking at the title again, I reworded it to read, "Jesus Is the Greatest." Thank God for wise secretaries!

Getting the verb tenses correct about Jesus is a difficult task. You can say, "He was," for He lived in history. You can say, "He is," for He lives today. You can also say, "He will be," for He will always exist. Jesus is the eternal contemporary.

Think of the bewilderment of the Jews when Jesus said, "Before Abraham was, I am." There is a striking contrast in verb tense—*was* and *am*. This "I am" saying gives us insight into Christ and time.

I. Jesus is before time.

The Jews looked to the greatness of Abraham. They boasted of their kinship with Abraham. But Jesus claimed to be superior to Abraham. Over against Abraham's fleeting span of life, Jesus placed His timelessness. Jesus lived before Abraham and before creation. "In the beginning was the Word, and the Word was with God, and the Word was God. The same was in the beginning with God" (John 1:1–2). Jesus enjoyed fellowship with the Father before the sand went through the hourglass.

Because Jesus existed before time, this means that He is from everlasting to everlasting. Jesus is God in human flesh.

"Who, being in the form of God, thought it not robbery to be equal with God" (Phil. 2:6). Jesus is before time. He is God Himself.

II. Jesus is in time.

The Jews would not grasp the fact that God entered into time and space. They could not accept that a baby born in Bethlehem and reared by Jewish peasants could be the promised Messiah.

When Jesus entered into time, He did not cease to be God. He did not divest Himself of divinity. He entered into a new mode of being. The eternal God entered into our sphere of existence. "God was in Christ," Paul said.

When Jesus entered into time, He identified with our plight. He subjected Himself to life's trials and temptations. "For we have not an high priest which cannot be touched with the feeling of our infirmities; but was in all points tempted like as we are, yet without sin" (Heb. 4:15).

III. Jesus is supreme over time.

Jesus' words, "Before Abraham was, I am," describe Jesus' lordship over time. Oscar Cullman in the book *Christus und die Zeit (Christ and Time)* builds the idea that time finds its central thrust in Jesus Christ.

Jesus started the phenomenon of time. Because He created it and ordained it as a part of life, He is Lord over it.

Jesus will stop time. When Jesus appears for His final return, He will usher in the glorified kingdom. It will be timeless.

Conclusion. The greatest person is Jesus. He was before time. He was in time. He will be after time ceases. He is! —*HTB*

* * *

SUNDAY MORNING, JUNE 19

TITLE: Fathers and the Father

TEXT: **"But the father said to his servants, 'Bring quickly the best robe, and put it on him; and put a ring on his hand, and shoes on his feet; and bring the fatted calf and kill it, and let us eat and make merry; for this my son was dead, and is alive again; he was lost, and is found.' And they began to make merry" (Luke 15:22–24 RSV).**

SCRIPTURE READING: **Luke 15:11–32**

HYMNS: **"Great Is Thy Faithfulness," Chisholm**
"Faith of Our Fathers," Faber
"Lord, I'm Coming Home," Kirkpatrick

OFFERTORY PRAYER:

Father, in Your hands are all the fathers and mothers and children here today. We want to offer to You our families for Your blessing. All our dreams and plans we want purified and made holy by Your presence in them. All our fears and failures we ask You to redeem so that we can be the families and people You want us to be. Through Jesus our Lord, we pray as He taught us to pray . . . *(Lead into the Lord's Prayer).*

Introduction. Jesus called God "Father." In this intimate and intensely personal name, Jesus swept away all speculative attempts to name the Mystery. "Unmoved Movers," "First Causes," and "Grounds of Being" all suffer by comparison to Jesus' simple appeal to "our Father who art in heaven." In the story of the Prodigal Son, Jesus has given us a parable which can be mined again and again for its wealth of insight into God's way with His children. The story is the father's story. He is the central character when the story is heard as a whole (vv. 11–32). Jesus' point is clear: Your heavenly Father is like this earthly father who loves both his sons and waits eagerly for their return and reconciliation! On this Father's Day we can find helpful truths for fathers who would like to be like the Father. There are two great truths in this passage for us to see: (1) We learn how to be a father to our children by watching God's way with us, and (2) we enrich our understanding of God the Father from experiences we have as human fathers. The first truth helps us in a practical way to excel in the most important job a man has to do—to be an effective father. The second truth allows the insights gained from being a father to help us fulfill the most important privilege a man is ever given—worshiping and rejoicing in God the Father who has called us into being.

I. We learn how to be a father by watching God's way of fathering us.

A. *God the Father does not quit loving and neither should human fathers.*

The father in the parable waited and watched for his son to return. Jesus does not say how long, but it seems clear that he would have waited and watched for as long as the son was gone. Fathers and mothers sometimes go through repeated agony over the negligence and recklessness of their children. How long do you care? How long do you keep on looking? As long as it takes! God loves His people with an everlasting love, and fathers are called to love their children in that same manner (Jer. 31:3).

B. *God the Father balances freedom with responsibility and so should human fathers.*

The younger son was free to leave. The father does not forsake his own character and goals to chase after his son. The father must painfully allow his youngest son to find his way back. When the boy returns, broken and repentant, the father rejoices; but he will not let his boy back home on the son's terms: "Treat me as one of your hired servants" (Luke 15:19 RSV). The boy was born to be a son, and the father will not let him retreat from that responsibility. It's easier to be a servant than an heir. When a man or woman has been wounded and their self-confidence shaken, they are often willing to settle for security alone. But in God's loving acceptance of us there is His tough love which places the responsibility of sonship squarely on our shoulders. It is God's confidence that we can be sons and daughters that gives us courage to be just that.

C. *God loves all His children and so should human fathers.*

The elder brother was hurting with all the attention being lavished on "this son of yours" (v. 30). He would not call him his brother. "You never gave me so much as a kid goat, but for him you killed the fat calf! What's fair about that?"

The elder son's feelings are mirrored in millions of elder brothers who feel unjustly used, but the father's attitude is, "Son, you have been with me. We have shared together, planned together, worked together, laughed together. Meanwhile your brother has been absent from our joy. Look what he has missed. He's been hurt, rejected, shamed . . . we must try to make it up to him. He's home now and we need to celebrate."

Many Christians betray a deeply pagan view of the world when they secretly think that the people in the world are really the ones who are enjoying life and having all the fun. Living with the Father is what heaven is all about. Those who live in His presence now are tasting in advance what it will be like then. It is immaturity on our part to think we need more reward than His presence, and it is blindness to think that the sin of the world does not exact its own punishment from which a loving Father wants to redeem us. The father loved both his sons equally. Their different needs, however, required of him different expressions of that love. Wise fathers seek to be sensitive as well to the different needs of their children.

II. There are some experiences a human father has that help enrich his understanding of the heavenly Father.

A. *God cannot allow us to do everything we want to do.*

When a young father first has to deny his child a request and is unable to fully explain to the child the reason for his decision, he knows something of the dilemma God faces with His children. It is in moments like this that a father learns to be thankful that neither does the heavenly Father give us everything we ask for in prayer. Indeed, a prayer we might pray more often is, "Thank You, Lord, for not answering the prayer I prayed last year."

B. *God is quiet sometimes because His children aren't ready to listen.*

A father held his four-year-old child in his arms. She was angry and hurt. She could not understand why he would not let her do what she wanted to do. He knew he couldn't explain in a way she could understand. So for awhile he just held her as she beat her little hands on his chest. After awhile she fell asleep, her fury exhausted. He held her while she slept. When his little daughter awoke, she looked up and smiled, hugged his neck, said, "I love you," and ran off to play.

In that moment the father understood a little better why the heavenly Father sometimes stays silent to our bitter questions and angry accusations. We are not ready, maybe not yet able, to understand what God would like to say to us. So He holds on to us and waits. In His "not letting go" He speaks the most eloquent language of all!

C. *God wants His children to love one another.*

A pastor listened as a church member told him of observing two of his teenage children watching out for one another with an obvious sense of mutual love and pride in one another. The pastor felt a warm sense of joy and gratitude that it was that way for his children. Then he understood something more. God gains great joy and pleasure from the love and attention His children share with one another. On the other hand, He feels the sharp pain a father feels when His children turn on one another with divisive and bitter emotions. No wonder we are admonished in the Scripture to "love one another."

Conclusion. Jesus helped us to worship God with more understanding when He called Him "Father." He also helped us to be better fathers when He showed how the heavenly Father cares for His children.

All of us have been born into a natural family. We have a human father. But God also wants you to have a heavenly Father. He wants to be Your Father now and forever. He wants to help make up for what a human father did not or could not give you. He wants to build upon all the good experiences you have had with fathers to help you know fully how much you really are loved. No matter where you've been or how discouraged you may feel, He is ready to help you be a son or daughter in His glorious, eternal family. Come home to the Father! — *CRW*

* * *

SUNDAY EVENING, JUNE 19

TITLE: Joy Cometh in the Morning

TEXT: "Blessed are they that mourn: for they shall be comforted" (Matt. 5:4).

SCRIPTURE READING: Psalm 30:1–12

Introduction. Having never fully understood all that it means to be a Christian, we have never fully appropriated the full blessedness of the Christian life. "Blessed are they that mourn: for they shall be comforted" (Matt. 5:4). This is a plain statement of simple truth. Blessed is the man in whose heart the "consolation in Christ" (Phil. 2:1b) has been, is, and ever shall be effective. Blessed is the Christian, even in sorrow, grief and pain, because for him the comfort of God is sure.

As a child of God the psalmist of our Scripture reading—having passed through the fires of grief, pain, and trial—had found the balm of Gilead sufficient for his soul. His experience was this: "Thou hast turned for me my mourning into dancing: thou hast put off my sackcloth, and girded me with gladness" (v. 11). His faith was, ". . . weeping may endure for a night, but joy cometh in the morning" (v. 5). Any English translation must miss the picture of the word here rendered "endure." The figure is "to come in to lodge as a guest." The psalmist is saying, "Weeping may come in to lodge with us at eventide, but joy comes in as a guest in the morning." This is not a mere promise to a Christian, it is the unfailing result of being a Christian, the natural consequence of the Christian life.

Other than Christianity and its forebear, Judaism, every religion says that weeping, trials, and pain are things to be escaped; and those who do not escape them are unfortunate. Only Christianity knows any way of dealing with these unwelcome guests that does not involve arresting, perverting, or even abandoning life itself. In substance Buddhism says, "Sorrow and pain are universal. Therefore, endure for all must suffer." Cold comfort that! The Stoic seeks to become calloused in soul and therefore indifferent to suffering, a remedy worse than the disease. A dead heart is worse than a broken heart. Christian Science offers escape from the ills of life by denying and ignoring their reality, thus destroying their hold on human consciousness.

Opposed to all of these is Jesus' solution, which lies in the opposite direction in the abundant life, the happy Christian life, the eternal life that He came to give. Christianity would swallow up grief and pain in victory, mortality in life, and transmute the sorrows and trials of life into the joys and fellowship and love of heaven's own citizens. Only Christ can give "beauty for ashes, the oil of joy for mourning, the garment of praise for the spirit of heaviness" (Isa. 61:3b).

"Blessed are they that mourn: for they shall be comforted." These words are true to the facts, especially in three relationships.

I. These words are true to the facts of the conversion experience.

A. *The mourning of conviction for sin is comforted by the joy of forgiveness.*

Every Christian remembers the long "night" of weeping under sin's conviction before conversion came in the "morning." We were miserable and wretched; and then after weeping had endured for the night, the joy, the comfort, the peace of God came in the morning. Then we understood David's exulting words: "Blessed is he whose transgression is forgiven, whose sin is covered" (Ps. 32:1). We may paraphrase our text: "Blessed is the sinner who mourns because of his sin, for he shall be comforted as he finds the peace of God unto salvation."

B. *Not all mourning is blessed.*

1. There is the mourning of an ungodly sorrow that issues from our own folly. This is not blessed. There is a curse upon it.

2. There is the mourning over the failure of guilty schemes, the mourning of passion untamed, or of sensuality incapacitated, of the gray-haired miser over his vanished gold. This is not blessed.

3. There is the mourning of blasted ambition looking back over bloody battlefields and thwarted schemes of conquest. Upon none of these is the blessing attendant, but a sorrow and bitterness and misery unrelieved.

There is a sorrow of the world that worketh death, but there is also a godly sorrow that worketh repentance unto salvation. (*see* 2 Cor. 7:9–10).

C. *All mourning over sin is blessed.*

"Blessed are they that mourn." You can write that over sorrow for sin that issues in repentance unto God's pardon and peace. The New Testament abounds with illustrations. If the prodigal son was a sorrow-stricken sinner, his reception by his father represents the comfort God has ready for the sinner who mourns over his sin. The woman who wept scalding tears of repentance and gratitude upon the feet of Jesus was comforted when He said to her, "Thy sins are forgiven" (Luke 7:48b). The thief on the cross turned in his agony to cry, "Jesus, . . . remember me" (23:42b); and he was comforted, even in death. But the most telling illustration is not in the long ago, nor even in the Scriptures, but in the here and now, in your heart and mine where God's salvation has spoken comfort to our souls.

II. These words are true to the facts of a developing, enlarging, deepening Christian life.

In pressing on toward the goal of the Christian life, weeping often comes in to lodge as a guest for the night, but always, again and again, and in a more and more wonderful way, "joy cometh in the morning." As we grow toward "the measure of the stature of the fulness of Christ" (Eph. 4:13b), our capacity for life enlarges, our sensibilities to its wrongs and ills quicken, and our struggle with sin deepens into a conflict more and more desperate and deadly. It is also true that our capacity for the true joy of heaven's realm in like measure increases.

As the prophet had said, Jesus was preeminently "a man of sorrows, and acquainted with grief" (Isa. 53:3b). He was so because, as Adam Smith said, "He felt all the sin of man with all the conscience of God."

A. *Growth in Christ enlarges our capacity to live and therefore increases our capacity for either pain or joy.*

The biologist ranks living creatures in the scale of life according to their capacity for pain on the one hand or joy on the other. At the bottom of the scale lie the crystal and the clod registering neither, with no capacity for life. A little higher comes the earthworm, with few capacities for life. Then comes the turtle, whose hard shell guards it from suffering and whose cold blood makes it sluggish. Near the top of the animal kingdom is the horse, a finely coordinated, sensitive, spirited, intelligent animal. He lives much and suffers much. He is the mourner among the beasts. At the top of the scale stands man, the apex of creation. He rejoices in the richness of his mental and spiritual nature, and yet he is the mourner supreme.

However, man does not reach the summit until, in Christ, he becomes a new creature. Then his capacity for life is brought to its fullest. No one can suffer like the full-grown, mature man in Christ; but, on the other hand, no man can rejoice as he can. "Blessed are they that mourn," as only the true Christian can, "for they shall be comforted" with all the comfort of God which the world knows not.

B. *Growth in Christ quickens our sensibilities to the wrongs and woes and ills of the world.*

We cannot grow in the knowledge and likeness of Christ without taking to ourselves some of His love for the world and, therefore, some of His sorrow for its sins. Christ is a Man of sorrows because He loves the world and knows its sins. He feels all the sin of the world with all the heart of God. "Blessed are they that mourn" because of the sorrows and sins of the world, "for they shall be comforted" by being made ministering saints (*see* 2 Cor. 1:3–5).

C. *Growth in Christ deepens the conflict with sin in our lives.*

If we develop the power to resist sin, we sorrow all the more for our failures when we do stumble and fall. Here is the obvious fallacy of sinless perfection doctrine. Our sensitivity to sin, our hatred of sin, deepens as, through Christ, our power over it increases; and no mature Christian ever thought of himself as sinless and perfect. "Blessed are they that mourn" the deepest over their shortcomings and sins, "for they shall be comforted" to the full.

III. These words are, and ever shall be, true to the facts of eternity.

While I was a guest in the home of a man who was an excellent amateur photographer, I came in from visiting one afternoon to find him missing. When I asked his wife, "Where is Harley?" she replied, "He is in his darkroom. He will be out soon." In a few minutes he did come out, his prints developed, their images clear. The photographer always takes his negatives into a darkroom to develop them; and in the darkroom the image gradually appears clearer and clearer.

Isn't that, in part at least, what suffering and sorrow mean in our lives? Compared with the fadeless light of heaven's realm, this world is God's darkroom; but the great Artist of our souls is patient and little by little the image appears. One day He will take us out, the image clear, into the light of heaven's perfect day; and then shall come to pass the saying: "As we have borne the image of the earthy, we shall also bear the image of the heavenly" (1 Cor. 15:49). After earth's night of weeping is past, heaven's joy comes in the morning.

> Heaven's morning breaks, and earth's vain shadows flee—
> In life, in death, O Lord, abide with me.

Conclusion. Whence comes this comfort with which we are comforted? Not from ourselves, for we are like land-locked pools with limited reserves, but from the "God of all comfort" (2 Cor. 1:3b), as His power like a river flows through our lives.

The last scene of all is this: "And he shall wipe away every tear from their eyes; and death shall be no more; neither shall there be mourning, nor crying, nor pain, any more: the first things are passed away" (Rev. 21:4). There will be no weeping in heaven. We will enter heaven with the stain of tears on our faces. God, Himself, will wipe them away; and it will be for the last time. — *WTH*

* * *

WEDNESDAY EVENING, JUNE 22

TITLE: Distinctives of Discipleship

TEXT: **"Then said Jesus to those Jews which believed on him, If ye continue in my word, then are ye my disciples indeed" (John 8:31).**

SCRIPTURE READING: **John 8:30–59**

Introduction. What does it really mean to follow Jesus? Somehow in the latter part of the twentieth century people have lost sight of what it means to follow Jesus. Discipleship is linked to external observance of religion rather than a relational experience with Jesus Christ.

During the life and ministry of Jesus Christ many people sought to follow the Lord. "As he spake these words, many believed on him" (John 8:30). Many motives moved people to associate with Jesus Christ. Some were infatuated with the Lord's miracles and teachings. Others were just curious. Jesus did not want people to follow Him outside the motive of a genuine commitment. To distinguish the authentic followers, Jesus gave the distinctives of a true disciple.

I. A true disciple has continuance (John 8:31–33).

Jesus realized that some people made an impulsive decision to follow Him. At times in Jesus' ministry large crowds followed the Master. The Lord knew they followed just to hear His teachings, to observe His miracles, or to be a part of the crowd. He knew that many would decide not to follow Him. "After this many of his disciples drew back and no longer went about with him" (6:66 RSV).

Jesus pointed out that perseverance would be the sign of a true disciple. "If ye continue in my word, then are ye my disciples indeed" (8:31). Discipleship is not the excitement of one moment. It is a patient continuance in the footsteps of Jesus Christ.

Ignace Jan Paderewski started playing the piano at the age of three. He developed slowly, but he was determined to become a master of the piano. He practiced six hours almost every day of his life. By discipline and determination he reached his goal.

To a crowd of potential followers Jesus gave a sure sign of a disciple. A disciple is one who follows Jesus continuously. The genuine evidence is in the sustained effort.

II. A true disciple has freedom (vv. 34–38).

A. *Jesus taught of a freedom which led to bondage*. "Jesus answered them, Verily, verily, I say unto you, Whosoever committeth sin is the servant of sin" (v. 34). To a group of potential disciples Jesus taught about how sin leads to bondage. Going through life with self-will, self-trust, and self-assertion leads to a detrimental bondage. No one who follows Jesus can be a master to himself. This is the kind of freedom which binds an individual.

B. *Jesus spoke of a bondage which leads to freedom*. A true disciple is one who has renounced his way to the way of Christ. This kind of bondage to the Lord leads to authentic freedom. Jesus said, "If the Son therefore shall make you free, ye shall be free indeed" (v. 36). The true disciple of Jesus lives to please only one Person, and this Person is Jesus Christ.

A distinctive of Christian discipleship is freedom. A disciple of Jesus is not a slave to sin, but he is a slave to the Master.

III. A true disciple has a Christlike behavior (vv. 39–47).

The Jews made claims to be Abraham's children. By physical lineage this was true. However, Jesus taught that a true disciple was not one of mere physical descent. The Jews claimed to be disciples on pedigree and name. Many of these Jews lived lives that were contrary to Abraham's life. They sought to kill Jesus (v. 40). They slandered the name of Jesus (v. 41). Jesus said they were not God's children, for they did not reflect God's character. "Ye are of your father the devil" (v. 44a). To behave in the manner of the Jews was not characteristic of God's children but of the Devil's children.

God's children behave like His children. "If God were your Father, ye would love me" (v. 42a). Also, Jesus said, "He that is of God heareth God's words" (v. 47a). Nature will be true to itself. If one is born of God, then he or she will live in accordance with Christ's character.

IV. A true disciple honors Christ (vv. 48–59).

Many claimed to be disciples of Jesus, but they did not honor Him. Jesus said, "I have not a devil; but I honour my Father, and ye do dishonour me" (v. 49). The people dishonored Christ by saying that He was possessed with a demon. Also, they called Him a Samaritan. They could not be authentic followers and dishonor the Lord in this way.

True disciples honor Christ. Disciples honor the Lord by adoring Him. Also, disciples honor the Lord by obeying Him.

Conclusion. Are you a true disciple of Jesus Christ? The proof is not in mere externals. It is in continuance, freedom, the way one lives, and honoring Christ.

—*HTB*

* * *

SUNDAY MORNING, JUNE 26

TITLE: The Rich Rewards of Prayer

TEXT: "The prayer of a righteous man has great power in its effects" (James 5:16b RSV).

SCRIPTURE READING: James 5:13–18

HYMNS: "Have Faith in God," McKinney
"Open My Eyes That I May See," Scott
"Teach Me to Pray," Reitz

OFFERTORY PRAYER:

Holy and loving Father, thank You for being the Giver of Your love, Your grace, and Your mercy to us. Thank You for giving us the privilege of being Your children. Thank You for letting us come into the throne room to

thank You, praise You, and petition You. Help us this day to give ourselves to You in body and mind and spirit so that our lives will praise You and be a blessing to others. Accept our tithes and offerings today as emblems of our wish and hope to be completely in the center of Your good will. In Jesus' name we pray. Amen.

Introduction. It is the testimony of Holy Scripture that those who have the habit of prayer and then do not break that habit experience rich spiritual blessings in their hearts and lives.

It is the testimony of sacred Scripture and of contemporary Christian history that those who have served God significantly have been men and women with an earnest and sincere prayer life.

Today let us look at some of the rich rewards that come to those who have faith in God that expresses itself in a life of prayer.

I. A vivid awareness of the nearness of God.

"Draw near to God and he will draw near to you" (James 4:8a RSV).

When the grateful and humble child of God seeks to come into the throne room of the heavenly Father, one of the great benefits that will come to him is a vivid awareness of the nearness of God.

A. *To experience the nearness of God can be a frightfully disturbing experience to one who has not experienced genuine repentance, sincere confession, and the joy of being cleansed from the pollution of sin* (Isa. 6; Luke 5:8–10).

B. *Experiencing the nearness of God can also be very comforting* (Ps. 23:4). This is the comfort that gives strength and help in times of difficulty.

C. *Experiencing the nearness of God can be very exciting* (Phil. 4:13). When one has the assurance of the nearness of God, it can give great courage and joy as one faces the crises of life.

II. A vital experience of the dearness of God.

Jesus taught His disciples to approach the Creator God not on the basis of His being their Creator but in terms of His being "our Father who art in heaven" (Matt. 6:9). While He is the God who is in heaven, He is also the Father with whom we can have dialogue in the closet of prayer (v. 6). It is in the prayer experience that the Father communicates His nearness and His dearness to those who look to Him in faith and trust.

III. An enlightening experience of the wisdom of God (James 1:5–8).

Throughout the length and breadth of Holy Scripture and in the experience of the great saints we have testimony after testimony of how, as they prayed, God stimulated their thinking and caused them to have new insight that helped them to cope with the strains and pressures of life.

We have instance after instance in which God recalled to the memory of His discouraged children His goodness in the past and their experiences with Him in the past so as to encourage and help them face the pressures of the present.

IV. An enabling experience of the strength of God.

"He gives power to the faint, and to him who has no might he increases strength. Even youths shall faint and be weary, and young men shall fall exhausted; but they who wait for the LORD shall renew their strength, they shall mount up with wings like eagles, they shall run and not be weary, they shall walk and not faint'' (Isa. 40:29–31 RSV).

Time spent in the presence of God in harmony with Him, experiencing dialogue with Him, fills the child of God with the strength that comes from heaven.

Many are familiar with the famous cartoon character Popeye. Popeye faced many difficult and dangerous crises but was never adequate for these until he had eaten a can of spinach. With the eating of the spinach there came superhuman power to this comical character. I have often thought of how time spent with the heavenly Father brings to His child and servant a strength comparable to that which the spinach brought to Popeye.

The apostle Paul prayed for the believers at Ephesus that they might be strengthened with might through His Spirit in the inner man and that they might be filled with all of the fullness of God (Eph. 3:16, 19). He encouraged them to trust in and depend on the God who was at work within them and who was able to do far more abundantly than anything they had previously asked for or even thought about (vv. 20–21).

V. A cleansing experience of the forgiveness of God (1 John 1:6–7).

God is eager to forgive His sinful children. He is eager to cleanse us and make us as white as snow. Our heavenly Father does not delight in our being guilty of or burdened by sin. He is eager that we forsake those ways and attitudes that are destructive and come to Him for forgiveness and cleansing.

It is the testimony of Scripture that our God is a forgiving God who forgives fully and freely and forever when His children sit in judgment on their own sins and turn from the sin which disrupts their fellowship, destroys their influence, and deprives them of happiness and joy.

Prayer is the divine gift by which we can come into God's presence, receive His forgiveness, and experience both the cleanness that follows and the joy of a restored fellowship.

Conclusion. Do not rob yourself by neglecting to pray. Even when you do not feel like praying, that is all the more reason that you should give yourself to the habit and the practice of prayer.

Prayer is not a process by which you make ''brownie points'' with God. Prayer is not a magical means by which something happens automatically. Prayer was meant to be an experience in which a spiritual transformation takes place. This is why we are commanded to ''Rejoice always, pray constantly, give thanks in all circumstances; for this is the will of God in Christ Jesus for you'' (1 Thess. 5:16–18 RSV).

— *TTC*

* * *

SUNDAY EVENING, JUNE 26

TITLE: Rest Unto Your Souls

TEXT: ''Blessed are the meek: for they shall inherit the earth'' (Matt. 5:5).

SCRIPTURE READING: Matthew 11:25–30

Introduction. As Americans, our heritage has hardly prepared us for this beatitude. Our heritage is one that encourages contempt for what we understand to be "the meek" and admiration of the self-assertive. On the one hand, we have inherited, through the classics, the Roman ideal of greatness in which meekness has no place. On the other hand, we are the heirs of Anglo-Saxon self-assertiveness and insistence on personal rights and privileges. Under these influences we have come to admire power, domination, and personal success.

"Blessed are the meek: for they shall inherit the earth" (Matt. 5:5). On hearing this, the average American, if he is honest, will say, "To tell you the truth, I just don't admire that. Doesn't that mean a weak and spineless creature, a namby-pamby, milk-toast type of individual, flabby in character and lacking in self-respect?" Laboring under this false impression of what meekness is, they ask: "Who wants to be meek? More than that, the statement, 'They shall inherit the earth,' is ridiculous. Maybe some of them will go to heaven someday, but 'inherit the earth'? Forget it! I don't believe it!"

This beatitude meets with a poor reception by most people. Perhaps none in the list is as unpopular as this. To the popular mind this beatitude is unadmirable, undesirable, and unbelievable. But popularity is no reliable test of anything; and certainly not of things that pertain to Christ and His kingdom. The popular conception of Christian meekness is both erroneous and inadequate; and these ideas are therefore false. This is not a popular beatitude, because in its failure to understand what true meekness is, the world neither admires nor desires it.

But there are some other more reliable tests to apply to this saying of Jesus. "Blessed are the meek: for they shall inherit the earth." Jesus is stating a simple fact; and that fact is demonstrated to be true by three important tests.

I. There is the test of the Scriptures, the Word of God.

The word *meek* and injunctions to be meek are sprinkled throughout the Bible. Our attention is called to the profitableness of meekness. Moreover, meekness is enjoined as one of the most commendable traits of a saint. The psalmist says it will meet the test of survival: "But the meek shall inherit the earth; and shall delight themselves in the abundance of peace" (Ps. 37:11). Jesus took these words and expanded them into our beatitude.

A. *Paul urged the virtue of meekness upon those to whom he wrote.*

In a great passage in Galatians (5:22–23) Paul describes this fruit which the Spirit will plant in our hearts: "the fruit of the Spirit is . . . meekness." To the Colossians Paul describes how, as "God's elect," they are to clothe themselves: "Put on therefore, as God's elect, holy and beloved, a heart of . . . meekness" (3:12 ASV). To Timothy, Paul's own son in the faith, he says, "But thou, O man of God, . . . follow after . . . meekness" (1 Tim. 6:11).

B. *The apostle Peter also urged the virtue of meekness upon those to whom he wrote.*

In his first epistle he wrote, "Whose adorning let it not be the outward adorning . . . ; but let it be the hidden man of the heart, in the incorruptible apparel of a meek and quiet spirit" (3:3–4). Peter knew the mind of the world in these things, so he adds, " . . . which is in the sight of God of great price" (3:4b).

C. *The Bible, in general, demonstrates that the men most conspicuous for meekness are God's greatest men.*

1. In the Old Testament.

The outstanding example of meekness is not some person of colorless character without spirit, passion, or vitality, but Moses, one of the greatest men of all time. "Now the man Moses was very meek, above all the men which were upon the face of the earth" (Num. 12:3). And what a man he was: courageous, resourceful, able, high-spirited, strong. "Broken to God's bridle" (for that is what meekness is), amenable to correction, teachable in God's hands, learning of God, submissive to God's yoke. He was enduring, forbearing, suffering, not because of cowardice or fear, but for God's sake, His work's sake, His people's sake.

2. In the New Testament.

In his list of the Twelve Mark says of two of them: "James the son of Zebedee, and John the brother of James; and them he surnamed Boanerges, which is, Sons of thunder" (3:17). Think of it! John, the beloved apostle, who had once been described by Jesus as a "Son of thunder," became meek and lowly in heart, bowing to Christ's yoke, learning of Him.

Paul the persecutor, the blasphemer, became, by the Spirit's power, "all things to all men." Why? He says, ". . . that I might by all means save some" (1 Cor. 9:22b).

But above all there is the world's supreme example of meekness, Jesus Himself. He demonstrates His own beatitude to be true.

II. There is the test of the character and person of Jesus Christ.

What is meekness? In a word, meekness is Christlikeness. To become meek is to become like Christ. How do we attain it? In our Scripture reading, Jesus said, "Take my yoke upon you, and learn of me" (Matt. 11:29a).

A. *We become meek by submission to Christ.*

"Take my yoke upon you"—that was a figure the rabbis used for going to school, but it carried with it the idea of submission to the teacher. The actual word used to express the idea of meekness is the word used by the Greek writer Xenophon to speak of a horse, "broken to the bridle." Not some old "plug" without spirit, strength, or sensitivity, but a horse strong, sensitive, and high-spirited, but yet submitting to his master's bridle. One has translated this beatitude: "Blessed are the God-tamed." That is meekness. We may paraphrase our text: "Blessed are those whose strength is great, whose sensibilities are well developed, whose spirit is hot and quick, but who yet have taken Christ's yoke upon themselves, who have submitted to His bridle, who have become God-tamed."

The great Russian pianist and composer, Rachmaninov, had large and powerful hands. After one of his concerts, a critic wrote that he played as if "his hands were steel gloved in velvet." That is meekness—strength under control. Meekness is the courage to fear God, not men.

B. *We become meek by learning of Christ.*

"Take my yoke upon you and learn of me." The basis of Christ's appeal is not His power and wisdom, but the fact that He is "meek and lowly in heart." He wants us to imitate that, to cultivate it.

1. We are to learn *the unselfishness of Christ*—the unselfishness of the One who "came not to be ministered unto, but to minister, and to give his life a ransom for many" (Matt. 20:28b).

2. We are to learn *the gentleness of Christ.* Peter says of Him: "Who,

when he was reviled, reviled not again; when he suffered, he threatened not'' (1 Peter 2:23a). The greatest heroism is the strength of gentleness, to bear, to endure for Christ's sake.

3. We are to learn *the humility of Christ.* ''Lowly in heart'' means teachable, thoughtless of self, thoughtful of others, depending not upon self but upon God for strength. Humility is an inseparable corollary of meekness.

4. We are to learn *the courageousness of Christ.* At the bottom of the world's bravery lurks a miserable cowardice, the terrible fear that men will think we are afraid. Jesus had the courage to follow the will of the Father all the way to the cross, regardless of men or malice, of custom or convention.

5. We are to learn *the strength of Christ.* Paul caught the meaning of this when he said, ''For when I am weak, then am I strong'' (2 Cor. 12:10b). Dependence upon God releases His power upon us.

III. There is the test of results.

Jesus assures us that the power of meekness is vindicated by the results. ''Blessed are the meek: for they shall inherit the earth.'' Who owns the earth? Those who, like Jesus, are meek and lowly in heart and have found ''rest unto their souls.'' Do the meek inherit the earth? Many lines of testimony say they do.

A. *Biology says: ''The meek inherit the earth.''*

It seems that there would be more eagles and hawks than wrens, robins, and cardinals, but these birds of prey have recruited the opposition that has all but destroyed them. Why are there more house cats than Bengal tigers? It is the law of survival—the meek survive.

B. *History says: ''The meek inherit the earth.''*

Will our ''atomic muscles'' recruit the opposition that will one day destroy us? A great historian points out that the average age of the world's civilizations is 200 years. We observed our Bicentennial, July 4, 1976. ''The meek inherit the earth''—the strong destroy themselves. During the reign of Queen Victoria, the British empire spread from sun to sun; and during that time, 1819–1901, almost any Britisher would have been insulted if you had called him ''meek.'' And now what? The flag upon which, once, the sun never set is being hauled down all over the world. Kipling was a better prophet than he knew.

C. *Jesus says: ''The meek inherit the earth.''*

''And ye shall find rest unto your souls.'' We may understand the word *rest* in three ways.

1. Cessation from strife. The quiet and tranquillity of inward peace. The world belongs to the man with peace in his heart.

2. To rest upon something as upon a foundation. The meek man rests upon Christ. As Paul has said, ''For other foundation can no man lay than that which is laid, which is Christ Jesus'' (1 Cor. 3:11).

3. To rest in the sense of a legal term. The lawyer, having finished his plea for his client turns to the court and says, ''We rest our case.''

The meek man rests his case in the hands of Jesus; for if indeed he is meek, he has faith in the final vindication of the right, the triumph of love.

Conclusion. God help us to follow and to imitate Him who is ''meek and lowly in heart,'' for to Him heaven and earth belong. ''Blessed are the meek: for they shall inherit the earth.'' — *WTH*

WEDNESDAY EVENING, JUNE 29

TITLE: A Conversation About Suffering

TEXT: "And his disciples asked him, saying, Master, who did sin, this man, or his parents, that he was born blind?" (John 9:2).

SCRIPTURE READING: John 9:1–12

Introduction. When Robert Louis Stevenson first saw the twisted and diseased bodies of those who suffered from leprosy, he almost became an atheist. Later, he saw compassion in the leper colony in Malokai. Then his faith emerged triumphant. He wrote in the guest book at Malokai these words:

> To see the infinite pity of this place,
> The mangled limb, the devastated face,
> The innocent suffered smiling at the nod—
> A fool were tempted to deny his God.
> He sees, he shrinks. But if he gaze again,
> Lo, beauty springing from the breast of pain!
> He marks the sisters on the mournful shores:
> And even a fool is silent and adores.

Suffering is a fact of life. Its presence is always a mystery. Once the disciples of Jesus became perplexed over the suffering of a blind man. "And as Jesus passed by, he saw a man which was blind from his birth. And his disciples asked him, saying, Master, who did sin, this man, or his parents, that he was born blind?" (John 9:1–2). From this episode we get various insights about suffering.

I. Suffering provokes questions.

A. *The disciples wanted to know the cause of the blind man's suffering.* The traditional idea that prevailed in Jesus' day was that suffering was caused by some specific sin. The disciples could see many sufferers, and they could say that the cause was sin. But the blind man was a special case. He had been blind from birth.

B. *Suffering continues to provoke questions.* When people observe innocent persons suffering, they want to know the reason. Some suffering can be explained. Moral and physical laws have been violated, and the results are predictable. But yet other suffering cannot be explained. Natural calamaties, people with birth defects, illnesses, handicaps, and other maladies cannot be evaluated so easily. The questions continue, "Why?" "Why?" "Why?"

II. Suffering provides opportunities.

A. *Suffering provides an opportunity to find God.* The blind man had the opportunity to have an encounter with Jesus Christ. Some people will never stop to think about God if some suffering does not occur.

B. *Suffering provides an opportunity to live for God.* Being blind and then being healed gave the man the opportunity to testify to what God can do. Numerous sufferers have used their misfortunes to tell what God is doing to help them cope with their problems.

C. *Suffering provides an opportunity to help.* Jesus was not interested in explaining the reason for the man's blindness. The condition of the man provided

Jesus with an opportunity to help him. Sufferers in life provide numerous opportunities to help and minister.

III. Suffering produces benefits.

A. *Suffering gives a perspective on value.* Have you ever considered what was important to this blind man? Was it cash or clothes? I think not. It was his sight. During times of suffering we have the unique adventure of finding out what really matters.

B. *Suffering builds character.* The blind man's character had been built through stress. The time of trials not only demonstrates faith, but it is a time for faith to be developed.

C. *Suffering increases compassion.* The blind man was healed. After his healing he probably demonstrated compassion to other blind people. When one suffers, the compassion for other sufferers increases.

D. *Suffering drives us to God.* During the time of his blindness, the man must have called on God. He could not depend on himself. Jane Merchant, the invalid poet of Knoxville, once wrote:

> Full half a hundred times I've sobbed,
> I can't go on, I can't go on.
> And yet, full half a hundred times
> I've hushed my sobs and gone.
> My answer, if you asked me how,
> May seem presumptuously odd.
> But I think, what kept me on
> When I could not, was God.

Conclusion. Into every life the storms of suffering will come. Maybe the storm rages now. Jesus said a lot about suffering. Listen to His conversation and commit your life to Him. —*HTB*

* * *

SUGGESTED PREACHING PROGRAM FOR THE MONTH OF JULY

Sunday Mornings

Following a message that we hope will be appropriate for the observance of our national holiday, it is suggested that we use "The Seven Deadly Sins" as our theme in the coming weeks. These seven deadly sins are inward attitudes which affect not only conduct but character and human happiness. Through Jesus Christ and the power of the Holy Spirit, we can be delivered from these seven deadly sins.

Sunday Evenings

The Beatitudes, found at the beginning of the Sermon on the Mount, set forth vividly the inward spiritual characteristics of those who are ideal citizens of the kingdom of God. The suggested theme is "The Inward Attitudes of a True Disciple." Only when we are right in our inward attitudes can we be right in our outward conduct.

Wednesday Evenings

Continue the series of devotional messages based on the Gospel of John, using the theme "The Christ of John's Gospel."

* * *

SUNDAY MORNING, JULY 3

TITLE: Christian Citizenship: the Salt That Saves and Sweetens

TEXT: **"You are the salt of the earth; but if salt has lost its taste, how shall its saltness be restored? It is no longer good for anything except to be thrown out and trodden under foot by men" (Matt. 5:13 RSV).**

SCRIPTURE READING: **Matthew 5:13–16**

HYMNS: **"God of Our Fathers, Whose Almighty Hand," Roberts**
"He Leadeth Me! O Blessed Tho't!" Gilmore
"I Would Be True," Walter

OFFERTORY PRAYER:

Heavenly Father, we come to thank You today for Your blessings upon our nation. We thank You for our form of government. We thank You for the freedoms and liberties that we enjoy as citizens of this fine country. We pray, Father, that You will help us to be a godly people. Help us to serve You in such a way that we might become better citizens of this country in which we live. Help us to give ourselves supremely to You as we seek to be good citizens of our community. In Christ's name we pray. Amen.

Introduction. As we come to the anniversary of the signing of the Declaration of Independence, it behooves us to ask ourselves the question, "Are we being responsible citizens of our country?" In recent years there was a bumper sticker which read, "America: Love It Or Leave It." Christians would be wise to change that bumper sticker to read, "America: Love It and Lead It." We need to lead our nation to worship God and to be a responsible nation among the nations of the world.

Our text and Scripture reading emphasize the influence of the ideal followers of Jesus Christ. The text declares that we must function as salt; and the Scripture reading indicates that we are to serve as the light of the world.

A. *Dr. Foy Valentine has made some excellent suggestions and observations concerning a Christian's responsibility to be a good citizen within his community and country:* "Christian citizenship is applying the principles and values of the Christian faith in our world through appropriate involvement in the political process." As followers of Christ, we should be more than eager to apply spiritual and moral principles based on our faith in and obedience to God to the totality of American life.

It is possible for a person to take one of four different stances toward his country, his church, or his denomination.

1. One can be critical but not loyal. This person specializes in being perceptive in identifying problem areas but has no constructive suggestions to make in providing solutions.

2. One can be loyal but not critical. This person gives a blind but superficial loyalty to the group of which he is a part.

3. One can be neither critical nor loyal. Consequently, there is no real dedication in the heart of this person.

4. One can be both critical and loyal. In this instance, commitment is genuine. Love and respect will often demand discipline and rebuke.

We need a renewed faith in and obedience to God and service to our country and to its people.

B. *Dr. Valentine has also declared that "the first demand of Christian citizenship is involvement."* In his book *Citizenship for Christians* he gives some guidelines for responsible Christian citizenship.

1. Christians need to mix religion and politics. We must not eliminate religion from politics.

2. As Christians, we need to understand the real issues that confront us as citizens.

3. Christians need to be politically active.

4. Christians need to work with special-interest groups who are promoting worthy causes or interests.

5. Some Christians need to run for office.

6. All Christians need to vote intelligently.

7. To be a true Christian, one must always have a higher loyalty. Our loyalty to God takes precedence over all other loyalties.

I. Salt was and is a valuable item.

In the days in which Christ lived, salt was extremely valuable, so this sentence from the Sermon on the Mount really means, "You are extremely valuable."

When foods, especially vegetables, taste flat and need seasoning, more salt is the remedy. The tiny, white, crystalline cubes are necessary for the health of the human body. Throughout history salt has played an important part in life's drama. People living close to the sea could obtain a plentiful supply. Inland dwellers had to barter for it. Part of a Roman soldier's pay was given to him in salt and was called *salarium*. From this Latin word comes our English word *salary*.

II. Common salt was and is an essential part of the diet of man.

Salt is necessary for the digestion of food. Jesus said, "Man cannot live by bread alone." He was talking about the need for the spiritual as well as the physical. Man cannot live without salt. This is why salt pills are often given to those who perspire excessively in the heat of summer in order that they might maintain their strength.

Jesus was saying to His disciples that they are an essential part of a good society. Without Christians who live out their faith, no society can be what God meant for it to be.

III. Salt was a widely occurring and most useful substance.

This was true during the days of Jesus, and it is true today.

We can thank God for the followers of Jesus Christ who are truly His followers around the world. They serve as the salt.

IV. Salt was the substance used to prevent decay.

In the days before modern refrigeration, salt was used almost exclusively for the preservation of meat from decay. Most likely this was a primary thought in the mind of Christ when He spoke about His followers being the salt of the earth.

A. *Ideal followers of Jesus Christ prevent personal decay.*

B. *Ideal followers of Jesus Christ serve as salt in the home and preserve it from disintegration.*

C. *Ideal followers of Jesus Christ perform a valuable purifying function in their community and keep it from deteriorating.*

D. *The Christian citizens in a given nation preserve it from disintegration.*

V. Salt is used universally as a condiment to bring out the flavor of foods.

A. *One who is a true follower of Jesus Christ should bring sweetness and flavor into home life.*

B. *The business world needs the sweetening influence of those who love God and who are determined to do right at all times under all circumstances.*

C. *Teachers and students who are true followers of Jesus Christ can have a wholesome effect in the classroom, on the playground, and in the activities at school.*

D. *From the courthouse to the statehouse and on to the White House, followers of Jesus Christ are to serve as the salt of the earth, both preventing decay and bringing good taste into all of the activities of government.*

Conclusion. In the words of our text, our Lord points out the possibility of a terrible calamity: The salt can lose its distinctiveness and become worthless. The basic chemical nature of salt can be destroyed through erosion or pollution or contamination. What is true in the physical world can also happen in the spiritual realm.

What can we do to prevent this calamity from befalling us as the followers of Christ?

1. We need to recognize and respond to who we are and to what we are. We are the followers of Jesus Christ, and we are to function as the salt of the earth.

2. We should listen to the Scriptures as something not only to learn, but something to do and to be.

3. We should listen to the voice of the Holy Spirit as He leads us forward in commitment to God and in service to others.

4. We need to beware of the peril of drifting through life accomplishing nothing.

5. We need to respond to correction and chastisement in order that we might be pure and undefiled. —*TTC*

* * *

SUNDAY EVENING, JULY 3

TITLE: Delighting the Soul in Fatness

Text: "Blessed are they which do hunger and thirst after righteousness: for they shall be filled" (Matt. 5:6).

Scripture Reading: Isaiah 55:1–13

Introduction. It is a great blessing to desire earnestly and to receive the things of the Spirit which God will give to those who ask. Three things stand out about this beatitude.

A. *The universality of the figure in which it is conveyed.*

Hunger and thirst are elemental instincts known to all people, so Jesus' words strike a responsive chord in every heart. Taken together, hunger and thirst form a universal figure for an intense desire that is perpetual. The word translated "filled" is from a word that means "to fatten," as to fatten cattle on fodder, grain, or grass. Hence, Jesus' meaning is: "Blessed are those who desire, intensely and perpetually, what God has to give, for their souls shall be made fat on God's fodder." Long ago the prophet Isaiah quoted God as saying, "Hearken diligently unto me, and eat ye that which is good, and let your soul delight itself in fatness" (55:2b).

B. *The definiteness of the terms to which it is confined.*

Jesus speaks about those who are hungering and thirsting after righteousness. Upon no other desire does the blessing fall. Again the prophet said: "Wherefore do ye spend money for that which is not bread? and your labour for that which satisfieth not?" (Isa. 55:2a). There is a bread which is not the Bread of Life and drink that does not satisfy.

Like a coin too long in circulation, the word *righteousness* has so lost weight and value through years of misuse that it is almost too light and thin to convey Jesus' meaning. As Jesus uses it, righteousness means a right standing before God, a right relationship with God through Christ. Blessed are those who are longing to be right with God, for upon the atoning merits of Christ they shall be. But to a Christian, righteousness should also mean what it meant to Christ—to do the will of the Father (see John 4:34b). We are filled when the righteousness of Christ is imputed to us (2 Cor. 5:21) and when His Holy Spirit works the works of God through our lives.

C. *The quality of the condition that is called blessed.*

This beatitude describes a blessed alternation by which the soul grows to be like God. We hunger and thirst. We eat and drink and are satisfied; but in a matter of hours hunger and thirst return, and we repeat the process. Blessed is the process of hungering and thirsting after righteousness and of being filled, for by this process we grow and develop as Christians. Blessed is the one whose appetite for spiritual food and drink is growing, for he will be filled again and again.

Consider three questions about this beatitude.

I. Wherein are these blessed?

How are those hungering and thirsting after righteousness blessed?

A. *By the freeness of God's invitation to be filled.*

This is a steady refrain in the Bible. "Ho, every one that thirsteth," cries the prophet after the manner of the water peddler in the arid, upland villages; "come ye to the waters, and he that hath no money; come ye, buy, and eat; yea, come, buy wine and milk without money and without price" (Isa. 55:1). Jesus says, "If any man thirst, let him come unto me, and drink" (John 7:37b). And the examples may be multiplied (see also John 4:14a; Rev. 22:17b).

The intensity of our desire to be filled can never exceed the freeness of His invitation to feed our souls on His righteousness, which is manna to the hungry heart and life and health and peace.

B. *In the bounty of God's supply.*

"They shall be filled." As we grow in God's grace, capacity enlarges, and hunger and thirst for righteousness intensify; but our desire can never exceed God's resources. He still says, ". . . My grace is sufficient for thee" (2 Cor. 12:9a).

C. *In the certainty of the result.*

"They shall be filled." Oh, the blessed certainty of the gospel. This note runs throughout the Bible and sings its way through the Gospels' pages. "Him that cometh to me I will in no wise [literally, not never] cast out" (John 6:37b). Paul assures us, "Whosoever shall call upon the name of the Lord shall be saved" (Rom. 10:13). John's gospel preserves Christ's picture not only of the initial experience of salvation, but also of the provision for the Christian that follows (John 10:9). "And [shall] find pasture." No hunger is too great, no thirst too deep. "They shall be filled."

II. Why are these blessed?

In our thinking the pain of unsatisfied desire is not a happy condition. But Jesus says it is—*if* that hunger and thirst is for righteousness. It is because of that of which it is a sign and seal, and because of that to which it leads.

A. *This hunger and thirst is a proof of spiritual life and health and vitality.*

This is true in every realm.

1. In the realm of *the mind.*

The child asks questions because his mind is hungry, healthy, and growing. This is proof that the child's mind is growing.

2. In the realm of *the physical.*

An ordinary beech tree will draw up sixty-five gallons of water in a single spring day. Just how we don't know, but we do know it is because the tree is thirsty.

3. In the realm of *the spiritual.*

Above all, this is true of the hunger and thirst after righteousness. To desire intensely the things of the Spirit is a sign of spiritual life and vitality and health. The man alive unto God and righteousness, and vitally in touch with God, wants spiritual food. Sometimes we are too easily satisfied about the spiritual condition of other people, their standing before God. Just because they make some motion toward professing religion, we have no further concern about them. When no hunger and thirst for the things of God are apparent, there is cause for alarm.

B. *This hunger and thirst is a means of spiritual growth.*

When your child refuses to eat, from an economic standpoint you should congratulate yourself (groceries are expensive), but you do not. You become alarmed, fearing the child is sick, that he is not growing. True principles carry over from one realm to another. In the realm of the spiritual, we maintain vitality and growth as we take spiritual food and drink.

How wonderful to watch a growing Christian hungering and thirsting after righteousness, yea, whetting his appetite by exercising in the works of God—taking the tonic of His Word, breathing the pure atmosphere of prayer, and, at the same time, delighting his soul in the fatness of heaven's fare.

C. *This hunger and thirst carries the promise of maturity.*

Have you ever been a guest in a home and noticed marks on a door facing with names and dates by those marks? Someone was charting the growth of a child. Are we growing as Christians? In Philippians Paul calls attention to his own growth chart: "Brethren, I count not myself yet to have laid hold" (3:13a ASV). He is not satisfied, for he goes on to say, "I press on toward the goal unto the prize of the high calling of God in Christ Jesus" (3:14 ASV). The end and promise of the Christian life is maturity. We reach maturity in Christ as we press on, as we hunger and thirst after righteousness and are filled.

III. When are these blessed?

Wonderful is the word of our beatitude, matchless is the blessing, but when does it apply? When shall they be filled?

A. *The answer is* now; *this applies in this life.*

1. This blessing is *subjective,* within the heart and life now. This is the blessedness of advancing toward maturity, the blessedness of joy and peace in Christ in the mind and heart.

2. This blessing is *objective.* It is apparent to the world surrounding the Christian. Those men of science and education and letters whose work has blessed the world are those whose hungry minds did not stop short of fulfillment. They hungered again and continued onward. This is true of Christians. Those who have been the saving salt of the earth, lights upon a hill, have been those whose hearts have hungered and thirsted after God again and again and were filled.

B. *The answer is also* hereafter.

Our ideas of heaven as a time when all limitations will be removed is true. The Bible teaches that. But it also teaches that there will be growth in heaven, and that our capacity to enjoy it will grow forever and forever.

This is certainly true, but it is also true that we will have more ability to enjoy it, and heaven therefore will be a more wonderful place "than when we'd first begun."

Conclusion. One description of heaven is as a banquet where "many shall come from the east and west, and shall sit down with Abraham, and Isaac, and Jacob, in the kingdom" (Matt. 8:11b). Whatever else it means here is certainly the suggestion that, even then, the divinely blessed alternation of hungering and thirsting and being filled shall go on and on and on. —*WTH*

* * *

WEDNESDAY EVENING, JULY 6

TITLE: The Door

TEXT: "I am the door: by me if any man enter in, he shall be saved, and shall go in and out, and find pasture" (John 10:9).

SCRIPTURE READING: John 10:1–9

Introduction. Going through the wrong door can be an embarrassing and frustrating experience. One time my family and I dined in a Mexican restaurant. One of my sons went through a door labeled "Señoritas" instead of "Señores." Needless to say, he was embarrassed over his mistake.

People go through wrong doors seeking the meaning and significance of life. Their pursuits end in frustration.

Jesus said, "I am the door: by me if any man enter in, he shall be saved, and shall go in and out, and find pasture" (John 10:9). Jesus claims to be the access into genuine personhood and being. Let us notice the ways that Jesus is the Door.

I. Jesus is the Door to salvation.

Jesus opens the way to God. He introduces us to God in a unique manner.

Jesus is the only Door to salvation. All others claiming to lead people are "thieves and robbers." Many doors are marked "the Way to God," but Jesus is the right Door.

Jesus opens the door of possibilities. The term "saved" of John 10:9 presents two ideas. First, it means a rescue from real danger. Second, it means the healing from a disease. Only Jesus can rescue and heal.

II. Jesus is the Door of security.

Having gone through the door to salvation, the Christian can feel secure. Sheep feel secure because of the faithful, reliable shepherd.

We too can feel secure because of the presence of our Shepherd. Trials, tribulations, and threats will come our way. Our security lies in the continual presence of the Good Shepherd.

We can feel secure because of the fidelity of the Shepherd. Jesus is not fickle with His feelings. He seeks the highest good for His sheep. We can feel secure with a faithful Shepherd.

III. Jesus is the Door to satisfaction.

Jesus said, "I am come that [they] might have life, and that [they] might have it more abundantly" (10:10b). Others promise satisfaction but fail to bring it. Jesus brings genuine satisfaction.

Jesus brings the essence of life. Real life comes with the spiritual birth. Paul said, "For me to live is Christ, and to die is gain" (Phil. 1:21).

Jesus also brings the exuberance of life. The phrase used for "abundant life" means to have life in surplus. The Christian not only has the real life, but he has the superabundance of life.

Conclusion. Jesus is the Door. When we open our lives to Him, we understand ourselves, and we are able to relate to others. —*HTB*

* * *

SUNDAY MORNING, JULY 10

TITLE: The First Deadly Sin: Pride

TEXT: **"Pride goes before destruction, a haughty spirit before a fall" (Prov. 16:18 NIV).**

SCRIPTURE READING: **Proverbs 16:5, 18; 29:23**

HYMNS: **"Come, Thou Almighty King," Anonymous**
"The Rock That Is Higher Than I," Johnson
"Just When I Need Him Most," Poole

OFFERTORY PRAYER:

Loving Father, we approach Your throne assured of Your love and conscious of the rich gifts that You have bestowed upon us through faith in Jesus Christ, Your Son and our Savior. We thank You for Your generosity and thoughtfulness on our behalf. We come now to express our gratitude and our worship in the form of tithes and offerings. Accept these gifts as tokens of our love and as indications of our partnership with You in ministering to the world. Help us, our Father, to give ourselves totally to You and in service to others. We pray in Christ's name. Amen.

Introduction. Pope Gregory the Great (A.D. 590–604) divided all sins under seven headings. He believed that every sin a person commits can be classified under these seven categories. These seven words have come to be called "the seven deadly sins." Sometimes they are referred to as "the seven cardinal sins."

These seven sins are pride, anger, envy, impurity, gluttony, slothfulness, and avarice.

Although they are never found listed together in any single passage, they are continually condemned in Scripture. The outline of Dante's "Purgatory" follows the order of the seven deadly sins. Likewise, they are found in Chaucer's *Canterbury Tales* under the "Parson Tale." Carl Menninger gives a whole chapter of his book *Whatever Became of Sin* to these and other sins.

Thus, it would do us all well to spend today and the next six Sundays looking at each sin separately.

Today we begin with the sin of pride. Pope Gregory put this sin at the head of the list because he believed that all other sins grow out of this one.

Our Scripture readings for today each make a point about pride. I have chosen three verses from the Book of Proverbs, and each verse will make a point for the sermon.

I. Pride is often the source of our troubles.

In Proverbs 16:18, God says, "Pride goes before destruction, a haughty spirit before a fall" (NIV).

A. *Synonyms for "pride" are arrogance, haughtiness, insolence, contempt, snobbery, presumptuousness, rudeness, sassiness, audacity, disdain, and impudence.* Actually the list could be longer, but such endless listing would serve no purpose beyond that which has already been made, i.e., pride soon leads one to a multitude of sinful attitudes and actions.

B. *Pride that is unchecked alienates us from our fellow-man.* It may be a feeling of superiority based on racism, nationalism, intellectualism, social station, spirituality, or materialism. Regardless of its basis, smugness that causes one to swagger before mankind and strut in the presence of the Almighty is a harmful detriment to anyone's future.

C. *No one lives out his life without making mistakes.* Most of us make some serious error that requires our family's or our friends' support. When that happens, the boastful braggart is often left "to stew in his own brew."

II. Pride is hated by God.

"The LORD detests all the proud of heart. Be sure of this: They will not go unpunished" (Prov. 16:5 NIV).

A. *The pride that God hates is not a healthy self-respect.* Some Christians have the impression that it is a sin to believe in yourself, your talents, or your capabilities. These people try to develop an attitude of false humility that denigrates or belittles their musical talent, wealth, intellect, or spiritual maturity.

Such efforts are many times a kind of "reverse" pride. The more they play down their God-given abilities, the more others will heap praises on them. These people are playing at humility in order to get others to build them up.

B. *The pride that God hates is an arrogant haughtiness.* This is one who thinks more highly of himself than he really is. Believing that God has given one the wisdom to always be right in judgments or leadership is arrogance. Other members of the church are also guided by God's Holy Spirit, and their collective wisdom might be more true to God's will than one self-appointed leader.

C. *The punishment of God is promised to the conceited, self-inflated soul.* The latter part of Proverbs 16:5 says, "Be sure of this: They will not go unpunished."

The country expression I often heard as a boy was "the chickens come home to roost!" Whatever seeds one sows in life, he usually reaps (Gal. 6:7). Sooner or later there is a day of accounting.

III. Pride leads to humiliation.

"A man's pride brings him low, but a man of lowly spirit gains honor" (Prov. 29:23 NIV).

A. *Unhealthy pride is a form of self-deification.* Bertrand Russell wrote, "Every man would like to be God, if it were possible; some few find it difficult to admit the impossibility."[1] Adam and Eve's sin was one of a desire to be like God—knowing the difference between good and evil (Gen. 3:5).

Man's desire to control his own destiny leads him to believe—falsely—that

[1]Bertrand Russell, *Power, A New Social Analysis* (New York: Norton, 1969), p. 11.

he actually can control his emotions, attitudes, abilities, and intellect without God's help. Such faulty reasoning has led man to a secular humanism.

B. *Adam and Eve were brought low for their sin of pride.* God promises to do the same to all who do not accept their dependence on God.

I have seen such arrogance in the church. It is sad to say that some churches have such a well-oiled, institutional machine that they can keep the organization moving temporarily even without God's leadership.

C. *But the reverse is also true, i.e., a truly humble person is elevated to leadership.* If you are talented, you seldom—if ever—have to tell people. Admirable qualities usually find their way to surface.

This last verse tells us that the humble man gains honor. Jesus put it another way. He said, "Blessed are the meek, for they will inherit the earth" (Matt. 5:5 NIV).

Conclusion. Thus, we are able to see that the common sin of pride is abhorred by God. God detests such a sin and brings judgment on the one who lets pride become a lifestyle.

But for the one who is genuinely humble, God has many rewards.

True humility is found in Jesus Christ. He was a perfect example of intelligence, power, fame, ability, and leadership. Yet He never used these qualities selfishly or in conceit.

Consequently, we are encouraged to become "like Christ," and this is done by believing that He is God and that He alone can guide your life.

Will you accept Jesus as your Savior now? —*RGC*

* * *

SUNDAY EVENING, JULY 10

TITLE: As I Had Mercy on Thee

TEXT: "Blessed are the merciful: for they shall obtain mercy" (Matt. 5:7).

SCRIPTURE READING: Matthew 18:21–35

Introduction. The parable of the unmerciful servant illustrates in reverse the truth of this beatitude. To the debtor to whom the king would have forgiven all of his enormous debt, had he in turn been willing to forgive his fellow-servant a platry sum, the king said, "I forgave thee all that debt, because thou besoughtest me; shouldest not thou also have had mercy on thy fellow-servant, even as I had mercy on thee?" (Matt. 18:32b–33 ASV).

"Even as I had mercy on thee"—that is the moral of this parable; and in substance it may be phrased like this: "Woe unto the unmerciful: for they have not, nor can they receive the mercy of God." This is in exact reverse of our beatitude: "Blessed are the merciful: for they shall obtain mercy." This is a self-acting law of the moral realm that never fails, and from which there is no appeal. This is an absolute in the kingdom of God. If God's mercy does not awaken in our hearts some sense of mercy towards our fellow-man, let a man not deceive himself into thinking that he has received God's mercy, for he hasn't.

"Blessed are the merciful: for they shall obtain mercy." There are three things demanding our attention about this beatitude. Each can be stated in one word.

I. Mercy's explanation.

Remember: In these beatitudes Jesus is not speaking of seven different individuals; rather He is describing seven qualities of excellence He desires in one man. But before Jesus commended these qualities to others, He exhibited them Himself. His own life is the best commentary on them. In Him all of the strength and tenderness, all of the patience, long-suffering, and compassion, all of the love of a God of love was illustrated before men's eyes in His gracious life for our example and in His atoning death for our redemption.

A. *Christ was long-suffering with error, patient with failure, and kind with stupidity.*

How thankful we ought to be for that. He was gracious and generous in His appraisal of men who were sincere. Andrew brought Simon, his brother, to Jesus. Looking past the rough qualities, the impetuousness of that man as he was, Jesus spoke of him as he would become: "Thou art Simon the son of John: thou shalt be called Cephas (which is by interpretation, Peter)" (John 1:42b ASV).

To be kind, to be generous, to be gracious in our appraisal of our fellow-man, to look for the best rather than the worst—this is to be merciful.

B. *Christ was forgiving in spirit toward those who wronged Him and sinned against Him.*

His great love for the sinner overflowed in free pardon and forgiveness. On the cross He prayed for forgiveness for those who crucified Him, pleading, "They know not what they do" (Luke 23:34b). The only hindrance to His forgiving love was in the refusal on the part of the sinner to receive it. This is mercy—the forgiving spirit that longs to restore the fallen to his place.

C. *Christ was compassionate in heart and deed toward all those who needed the care of "the great shepherd of the sheep"* (Heb. 13:20b).

His heart went out in deeds of love toward the suffering, the sorrowing, the needy, the distressed, the bereaved. He was moved with compassion for the unloved, leaderless multitudes, "distressed and scattered, as sheep not having a shepherd" (Matt. 9:36b ASV). He helped them because He loved them. Peter's benediction on His life was that He "went about doing good" (Acts 10:38b). He had mercy on the sick, the halt, the lame, the blind. His word to His followers is: "Heal the sick, raise the dead, cleanse the lepers, cast out demons: freely ye received, freely give" (Matt. 10:8 ASV). Mercy is Christlikeness.

II. Mercy's demonstration.

Who are the merciful? Not those who can shed oceans of tears about the sins and woes of the world without ever harnessing their emotions to concrete action. Some who think they exhibit the quality of mercy are like Lincoln's steamboat, which had a four-foot boiler and a six-foot whistle; every time it blew the whistle, it had to pull over to the riverbank and get up steam again. They talk a lot, but by the time they get through blowing their whistle, they have no steam left to make progress against the world's woes. Being sentimental is not being merciful.

To be merciful is to exhibit, to some degree at least, the mind and spirit of Christ upon this hard and loveless world which knows so little of Him and has so little of His spirit. We are to do this, not for our own sakes or glory or reward, but for His sake and for His glory, that the world may come to know Him.

A. *If we are merciful, as Christ was merciful, we will exhibit the generosity of His judgments of others.*

Like Christ, we will search for the best, not the worst, in our fellow-man. Like our Master, we will be slow to condemn and quick to commend our brother, and this not out of a sense of duty, but as the natural expression of a loving heart.

B. *If we are merciful, as Christ was merciful, we will exhibit His spirit of forgiveness.*

We will be forgiving in spirit, refusing to hold a grudge, casting hate—by the Spirit's power—out of our hearts, blessing those who curse us, and praying for those who persecute us. How we need the compassion of Christ to flood our unfeeling hearts to send us out to give and forgive and serve for His sake.

C. *If we are merciful, as Christ was merciful, we will give ourselves for a world's need as He did.*

Is there any spark of His love for a lost and dying world in our hearts? Are there any of the tender mercies and compassions of Christ in us at all? Mercy is to have its demonstration in the minds and hearts and deeds of those who have received God's mercy and grace freely shed abroad in their hearts.

III. Mercy's benediction.

"Blessed are the merciful." What is the benediction pronounced upon the merciful? ". . . for they shall obtain mercy." The blessing upon the merciful person is that he shall receive in the same manner as that in which he gives. This is a self-acting law of the moral realm. It never fails. "They shall obtain mercy." The certainty of that blessing is based on the reciprocal law of life that Jesus stated so often, a law more dependable than the law of gravity.

It is true of general experience that persecution never produces tolerance, nor hate love, nor cruelty kindness. Life will pay off in like coin. As we give, we get. As we sow, we reap.

But in an infinitely higher sense this holds true. As between God and man, the merciful obtain mercy.

A. *To be like Christ in His judgments is to claim this blessing.*

To be gracious, generous, seeking and thinking the best—what if we are like that in our judgments? Jesus says, "For with what judgment ye judge, ye shall be judged: and with what measure ye mete, it shall be measured unto you" (Matt. 7:2 ASV). James tells us, "For judgment is without mercy to him that showeth no mercy: mercy glorieth against judgment" (2:13 ASV).

B. *To be like Christ in His forgiving spirit is to claim this blessing.*

To have an unforgiving spirit is to forfeit the same. Jesus tells us, "For if ye forgive men their trespasses, your heavenly Father will also forgive you. But if ye forgive not men their trespasses, neither will your Father forgive your trespasses" (Matt. 6:14–15). One of the petitions of the Model Prayer is: "And forgive us our debts, as we also have forgiven our debtors" (6:12 ASV). The unforgiving heart cannot receive forgiveness, nor the unmerciful, mercy.

C. *To be like Christ in deeds of compassion is to claim the blessing.*

In the story of the Good Samaritan Jesus answered the question, "Who is my neighbor?" When He had completed the story and asked, "Which of these three, thinkest thou, proved neighbor unto him that fell among the robbers?" His questioner was compelled to reply, "He that showed mercy on him" (Luke 10:36–37 ASV).

Conclusion. In that picture of judgment in Matthew 25, to whom did Jesus say, "Come, ye blessed of my Father, inherit the kingdom prepared for you from the foundation of the world" (v. 34b)? He said this to those who had exhibited mercy in their lives. To whom did He say, "Depart from me, ye cursed, into the eternal fire" (v. 41)? He said this to those who showed no mercy. — *WTH*

* * *

WEDNESDAY EVENING, JULY 13

TITLE: The Good Shepherd

TEXT: "I am the good shepherd: the good shepherd giveth his life for the sheep" (John 10:11).

SCRIPTURE READING: John 10:1–18

Introduction. Jesus took ordinary figures to describe the majesty of God. On one occasion He said, "I am the good shepherd." The pastoral figure was familiar. It communicated many wonderful truths about the Master.

Jesus used the word *good* with *shepherd*. It is not the usual word for good. The word means "winsome," "attractive," or "virtuous." There were many shepherds, but only Jesus deserved the name "good shepherd." Let us notice the reasons that Jesus deserved this name.

I. Jesus knows in a unique manner.

Shepherds of ancient Palestine knew their sheep. The sheep also knew their own shepherds.

Jesus knows people in a unique manner. He knows the name of every person. Once two young men agreed to read the Bible to a blind man. They planned to read through the New Testament. Beginning in Matthew, they encountered a long list of names in a genealogy. They wanted to skip it, but the old man insisted that they read each name. The blind man said, "God knew every one of those fellers by name, and He knows me!"

Jesus knows our needs. He knows sheep that have peculiar proclivities to sensual temptations. He knows those susceptible to discouragement. People vary in their needs, but Jesus relates to each need.

II. Jesus cares in a sacrificial way.

Shepherds often faced danger for the sake of their flock. Wild animals looked for sheep. Sheep-stealers waited to snatch a lamb.

The Good Shepherd put His life on the line for His sheep. "The good shepherd giveth his life for the sheep" (John 10:11b). Jesus gave His life sacrificially on the cross.

The Good Shepherd gives His life for the lives of others. He lays down His life for the sheep. Jesus died so that others may live. There is a winsomeness in what Jesus has done for others at the cross.

III. Jesus leads His flock in the right paths.

The shepherds of ancient Palestine led their sheep. They led them to green pastures and refreshing waters. They led them away from danger. A shepherd had to be a good leader.

Jesus leads in the right moral paths. When we obey His will, we go in the right direction.

Jesus leads us to our final destination. He leads us in the varied pilgrimages of life, but He also leads to a final destination.

Conclusion. Jesus is the Good Shepherd. No one compares to Him. —*HTB*

* * *

SUNDAY MORNING, JULY 17

TITLE: The Second Deadly Sin: Anger

TEXT: "He that is slow to anger is better than the mighty; and he that ruleth his spirit than he that taketh a city" (Prov. 16:32).

SCRIPTURE READING: Proverbs 16:32; Psalm 37:8; Matthew 5:21–22

HYMNS: "O Worship the King," Grant
"Guide Me, O Thou Great Jehovah," Williams
"Jesus, Lover of My Soul," Wesley

OFFERTORY PRAYER:

Thank You, Father, for the sunlight of this day. Thank You for the air that we breathe. Thank You for the food that nourishes our bodies. Thank You, Father, for the gift of eternal life through faith in Jesus. Thank You for the joy of fellowship in Your family. Thank You, Father, for the privilege that You granted to us of being earners and givers. Help us now, Father, as we come bringing tithes and offerings to indicate our love for You and our desire to see others come to know Jesus Christ as Savior. Help us to give ourselves totally to You. In His name we pray. Amen.

Introduction. The second deadly sin is a highly destructive sin; it is anger. Pride is at the head of this infamous list of sins, but following close on the heels of pride comes anger.

It is also a sin that seems to infect us all. No one appears to be immune. From the smallest child to the oldest adult, this sin stalks mankind like a predatory animal looking for an unsuspecting sheep.

Many parents are aware of the fierce temper of a small baby. It crys out until it is red with anger. Childhood sees the situation become no better. Fits of anger lead to bickering and self-centered fighting among siblings. Outward displays in childhood degenerate to sulking, pouting teen-agers. Anger causes a wife to develop a sick headache and a husband to slam doors. Older adults may suffer from ulcers, hypertension, and stress, which may be aggravated by violent outbursts of temper.

I. Uncontrollable anger is a sign of weakness.

"He that is slow to anger is better than the mighty; and he that ruleth his spirit than he that taketh a city" (Prov. 16:32).

A. *The majority of people are able to subdue their anger into a controlled reaction on most occasions.* However, all of us have had circumstances that have sorely tried our patience. During those stressful periods, we become different persons.

Excuses to downplay our temper tantrums are offered. We say that we were "just letting off steam" or that we were "temporarily insane."

The truth is that we lost control. We let our passion go unchecked. When this occurs, our personalities become repulsive, irrational, and border on being animalistic rather than human.

B. *Our Scripture passsage tells us that such conduct is the opposite of strength; it is a weakness of character.* It shows a lack of discipline. Anger that is uncontrolled motivates us to action. It leads us to say and do things we later regret. It is so highly destructive that a long-time friendship can be destroyed in a few minutes of unchecked fury.

C. *Our Scripture also implies that not "all" anger is evil.* It says, "He that is slow to anger," it does not say, "He that *never* gets angry."

The Bible indicates on more than one occasion that God became angry with both people and circumstances.

But God's anger is just, slow in coming, and usually tempered by a chance for one to be forgiven.

II. Uncontrollable anger leads to personal harm.

"Cease from anger, and forsake wrath: fret not thyself in any wise to do evil" (Ps. 37:8).

A. *Anger is such a strong emotion that when it subsides, it generally leaves a person emotionally drained.* Some people are better than others at getting over a fit of rage. It can be so upsetting that one does not feel like eating; sleep is interrupted or postponed; a headache results; indigestion may set in; elevation of blood pressure to dangerous levels can occur, as well as a multitude of other physical maladies.

At times the physical symptoms may disappear, only to reappear later when one sees the person who caused him to be angry. Anger in such cases soon becomes hatred, which leads to even more serious disturbance.

B. *Rage can rob one of self-esteem.* People get angry with themselves because they allowed themselves to lose control. They chastise themselves, which causes guilt, confusion, and frustration.

C. *Such uncontrolled anger leads one's thinking and attitudes to be marred.* Our Scripture passage says, "Fret not thyself in any wise to do evil."

Fretting causes us to think in evil ways of how to get even. Plotting evil makes us more like Satan than like God.

III. Uncontrolled anger leads to evil activity.

"But I tell you that anyone who is angry with his brother will be subject to judgment. Again, anyone who says to his brother, "Raca," is answerable to the Sanhedrin. But anyone who says, 'You fool!' will be in danger of the fire of hell" (Matt. 5:22 NIV).

A. *Jesus explains in this passage that the sin of murder begins in anger.* For those who take "temper tantrums" lightly or excuse their emotional displays of fury as being "just my fiery nature" need to realize that they have broken one of the Ten Commandments. Jesus does not take it so lightly. He counts it as disobedience.

B. *One who goes a step further by calling someone "a stupid fool" or "Raca!" (which means "You good-for-nothing") has progressed further in his degeneration.* God's judgment is dangerously close. Jesus reminds us that he is dangerously close to hell-fire.

Conclusion. Pride and anger are the first and second deadly sins. Anger that is out of control is as dangerous as murder. Anger causes physical harm to oneself and can lead to physical harm to others.

Mankind can seldom change his nature by personal resolve. He needs outside help.

Jesus Christ was able to change the Gadarene demoniac from a wild, rampaging beast into a calm, quiet, effective witness (Mark 5:1–20), and He can do the same for your temper.

If you would like to change, we invite you to come to Christ. —*RGC*

* * *

SUNDAY EVENING, JULY 17

TITLE: The Hill of the Lord

TEXT: **"Blessed are the pure in heart: for they shall see God" (Matt. 5:8).**

SCRIPTURE READING: **Psalm 24:1–10**

Introduction. Psalm 24 is often given the title "The Hill of the Lord," because the verses containing this expression form its very heart (vv. 3–5). The question "Who shall ascend into the hill of the LORD?" (v. 3a) is equivalent to asking, "What is true religion?" The psalmist answers, "He that hath clean hands, and a pure heart" (v. 4a).

True religion is more than a matter of having clean hands; it is first of all a matter of a pure heart. True religion is not a matter of deeds or observances or worship at all, except as these outward appearances, which are seen, are a sincere expression of a pure heart within, which is not seen. If the heart is pure in the sense Jesus wants it to be pure, the rest will take care of itself. Mixing our two Scripture passages, we might paraphrase our beatitude thus: "Blessed are the pure in heart: for they shall ascend into the hill of the Lord, and stand in His holy place; they shall receive the blessing fresh from the Lord Himself."

A. *How complimentary this beatitude is to humankind:* ". . . for they shall see God."

Created as he is, in the image of God, man has the faculty of spiritual sight (Eph. 1:18a). He *can* see God.

B. *How beautifully this beatitude expresses the deepest longing of the human heart:* ". . . for they shall see God."

The desire to see God, to look upon His face, is a longing as old as man, as contemporary as physical hunger. Throughout the ages man has cried out with Job: "Oh that I knew where I might find him! that I might come even to his seat!" (Job 23:3). And the better a man comes to know God, the deeper does this yearning become.

C. *How truly this beatitude tells us our deepest need:* ". . . for they shall see God."

Spiritual blindness is a great tragedy in our world. Sin and self-seeking, lust and pride, have put cataracts over "the eyes of the heart"; and our world cannot see God. But the blessing is available to all who will look. "Blessed are the pure in heart: for they shall see God."

This sixth beatitude brings us face to face with the nature and the demands of true religion, which is first of all a matter of the heart. Four questions demand an answer if Jesus' words are to mean anything to us.

I. What is the purity of heart of which Jesus speaks?

It is important to heed exactly what Jesus said.

A. *Jesus did not say, "Blessed are the pure."*

That would have gone straight into our minds with an exact meaning; and many have so understood this beatitude. But Jesus did not say, "Blessed are the pure." Neither did He simply make a parallel statement of the seventh commandment: "Thou shalt not commit adultery" (Exod. 20:14). Purity in our relationships with others is only one of the fruits of a pure heart.

B. *Jesus did not say, "Blessed are the perfect."*

That would have ruled out all of us; and this beatitude would not touch our lives at all. It is true that perfection is the only standard worthy of Jesus, and that He did say: "Ye therefore shall be perfect, as your heavenly Father is perfect" (Matt. 5:48 ASV). But He did not say that we shall never be happy this side of perfection.

C. *Jesus did say, "Blessed are the pure in heart: for they shall see God."*

The word *pure* here means unmixed, without alloy, unadulterated. To speak of your watch as a "gold watch" is not technically correct. The case is probably ten-karat gold, which means that it is alloyed with another harder metal to give it better wearing qualities. Thus the pure heart is a single heart, a heart devoted to the purposes of God. According to Jesus' meaning, a pure heart is an unmixed heart, unadulterated, with no cross-purposes, no crosscurrents in loyalty, no reservations in devotion. There is no true happiness for the one who says, "I will follow thee, Lord; but first . . ." (Luke 9:61b ASV).

II. How may we attain to the purity of heart of which Jesus speaks?

Purity of heart, in the sense Jesus has in mind, is attainable for every Christian who desires it with all his heart. This beatitude is not only for some aged saint in the late winter of life, nor simply for some exalted servant or prophet of God, some choice soul here and there. Purity of heart is a prize of supreme worth within the reach of every heart willing to receive it. But how do we attain it?

A. *By surrender.*

A surrender to Christ, full and entire, brings the cleansing power of God's forgiveness flooding through the heart to cleanse and purify. An Old Testament beatitude throws light on this beatitude of Jesus. Out of his experience the psalmist cries, "Blessed is he whose transgression is forgiven, whose sin is covered" (Ps. 32:1). This beatitude is not for the sinless but for forgiven sinners, not for the perfect but for the purified in heart. No sinner is excluded in the sweep of its possibilities. "Wash you, make you clean," says the Old Testament prophet (Isa. 1:16a) and he continues, "Come now, and let us reason together, saith the LORD: though your sins be as scarlet, they shall be as white as snow; though they be red like crimson, they shall be as wool" (1:18).

How do we become pure in heart? By a full surrender to Christ to be cleansed by His power. But that isn't all of the answer.

B. *By a complete consecration of the life to God.*

Not all Christians are pure in heart. Too many are borderline Christians; and, like the Israelites settling in the Promised Land, many of us stop before we drive out all our enemies. The pure in heart must drive out every Canaanite and every alien thought and purpose to give Christ full possession. Too many of us have mixed motives and desires. Our hearts need to be single, set on Him and on Him alone. To such is the vision promised.

III. What blessing does Jesus pronounce upon the pure in heart?

"Blessed are the pure in heart: for they shall see God." In this, the highest faculties of human nature are exercised; the deepest yearnings of the soul are gratified; the most compelling needs of the human heart are met.

What is the issue of a heart pure before God, a heart unmixed, without alloy, unadulterated by love for the world, and single to His service? "They shall see God," Jesus says. They shall see Him now; they shall see Him in hours of worship in God's house; they shall see Him in the circle of family worship; they shall see Him in holy hours of private prayer and meditation upon His Word. Behind the dark background of the world's confusion and misery, they shall see God as the one, single, sovereign, unifying purpose in the world and in history.

The promise is that one day the pure in heart shall look upon Him, not by implication, not indirectly, not "through a glass, darkly" (1 Cor. 13:12a), but face to face. The pure heart is the enlightened heart; and the promise is that those hearts, thus enlightened, shall see God.

IV. What are the abiding results in human personality of this vision of God?

A. *This vision of God causes us to see the unseen resources of God.*

Paul saw Jesus on the Damascus road and found the strength to carry through every trial. In his death agony Stephen saw "the Son of man standing on the right hand of God" (Acts 7:56b). This gave him the martyr's courage to die for Christ. Of Moses, the writer of Hebrews says, "For he endured, as seeing him who is invisible" (11:27b). Think of all Moses endured. How steadfast he was! How courageous! How dauntless! What was his secret? "He endured, as seeing him who is invisible."

B. *This vision of God causes us to see the infinite needs of mankind and gives us a sense of personal obligation.*

Having seen the infinite resources of God and the infinite needs of the world, this vision causes us to see that we are to be used to bring the two together. Moses, Isaiah, and Paul each saw the resources and the need, and each volunteered. The vision of God that does not send us out to serve is a spurious vision.

C. *This vision of God causes us to see what will one day be consummation of the Christian life and undergirds our lives with hope.*

Paul tells the Corinthians, "For now we see through a glass, darkly; but then face to face" (1 Cor. 13:12a). John promises those to whom he wrote; "We shall be like him; for we shall see him as he is" (1 John 3:2d).

Conclusion. What a blessed hope is this! In that day it will be fulfilled, vindicated.

— *WTH*

* * *

WEDNESDAY EVENING, JULY 20

TITLE: You Are in Good Hands With God

Text: "And I give unto them eternal life; and they shall never perish, neither shall any man pluck them out of my hand" (John 10:28).

Scripture Reading: John 10:27–30

Introduction. The Allstate Insurance Company has a captivating slogan. In their advertisements they claim, "You're in good hands with Allstate." This statement attracts people, for there is within every human being the need and desire for security. People want their houses, cars, and especially their lives to be protected.

Jesus made a security claim for believers: "And I give unto them eternal life; and they shall never perish, neither shall any man pluck them out of my hand" (John 10:28). The Lord gave a graphic picture of security. He pictured the believer as resting in the hands of the heavenly Father. Think of the amazing security one has by being in the Father's hands. Yet Jesus did not speak these words for security's sake alone. The words of our Lord suggest other truths. A person is "in the hands of God" for more reasons than just security. Let us notice the implications of being in God's hands.

I. God makes a person.

A. *There was a time when one was not in God's hands.* Those who refuse to submit to the Good Shepherd stand outside the fold of safety. Human beings want to take over their own lives and live as they please, rather than as God wants them to live. Every person on earth has gone astray like a rebellious sheep. Human beings have looked to the mirage of greener pastures and strayed like sheep only to find that they are alienated from God, abandoned to the wrong cause, and have abused every gift God gave.

B. *When a person responds in faith to Jesus Christ, God begins a great work within him or her.* "I am the door; if any one enters by me, he will be saved, and will go in and out and find pasture" (v. 9 RSV). Two words in the verse help to describe God's work in a believer. First, there is the word *saved.* It means a rescue operation. Second, there is the expression "find pasture." This describes God's daily care. Not only is there a rescue operation, but there is nourishment and growth.

Paul said, "For I am confident of this very thing, that he who began a good work in you will perfect it until the day of Christ Jesus" (Phil. 1:6 ASV). When a person trusts the Lord, God begins a good work. The Lord will continue this work until the day of Jesus Christ.

II. God uses a person.

A. *God does not put a person in His hands just to save; He intends to use that person.* Human beings do not enter into a relationship with God to sit and wait for the Judgment Day. No, God desires that the saved work in His service. Out of Elisha's ministry there comes an illustration of service. Elisha told a young man to put out his hand and "take . . . up" the lost axe head. It was not just to be rescued from a watery grave; it was to be restored to useful service again.

B. *We may be weak instruments, but in God's hands we may be used to do much.* God has the amazing power of choosing ordinary human beings and using them in His service. "But God hath chosen the foolish things of the world to confound the wise; and God hath chosen the weak things of the world to confound the things which are mighty'' (1 Cor. 1:27).

A golf club in my hands may mean a high score. But that same golf club in the hands of a professional golfer may mean a low score. The difference is in the one who uses the club. When we put our lives into the hands of God, He uses us for His service.

III. God keeps a person.

A. *The security of the believer depends upon the nature and character of God.* After we open our lives to God in faith, our security depends upon God. It does not depend on our power to hold on to God. Rather, it depends upon God's power to hold on to us. ''For I know whom I have believed, and am persuaded that he is able to keep that which I have committed unto him against that day'' (2 Tim. 1:12).

B. *The security of the believer does not mean a license to sin.* If one uses the concept of the security of the believer to practice sinful ways, then one does not really comprehend the idea of being in God's hand. In God's hand a person gradually experiences change. The Lord changes a person, and his or her life moves away from practicing sin.

Charles Haddon Spurgeon was asked, ''Do you believe in the perseverance of the saints?'' He replied, ''No, but I believe in the perseverance of the Savior.''

Conclusion. Are you willing to put yourself in God's hand? A party of inexperienced mountain climbers were facing a yawning crevasse which had to be crossed if they would reach the top. Their guide went over nimbly. Reaching back, he asked each member of the climbing party to give him his hand. One man came repeatedly to the edge, and each time he retreated. Finally, the guide reached for the man's hand once more and said, ''For thirty years I've been helping men and women across that gap, and I've never let one go yet.'' Will you reach out to the Lord? He has not let one go yet! —*HTB*

* * *

SUNDAY MORNING, JULY 24

TITLE: The Third Deadly Sin: Envy

Text: "A heart at peace gives life to the body, but envy rots the bones" (Prov. 14:30 niv).

Scripture Reading: 1 Peter 2:1–3

Hymns: "Holy Ghost, With Light Divine," Reed
"God Will Take Care of You," Martin
"Does Jesus Care?" Graeff

Offertory Prayer:

Blessed Father, for all of the influences that have combined under Your guiding hand to bring us to this place of prayer and worship, we thank You. Here with Your people we are reminded of the many blessings that You have bestowed upon us, both in the past and in the present. Today we would respond to Your grace with joy and gratitude and praise. We come bringing

the fruits of our labors in the form of tithes and offerings as expressions of our love and as indications of our partnership with You in ministering to a needy world. Through these offerings bless the preaching of the gospel to the ends of the earth that others might come to know Jesus Christ and worship You as Father. Minister to the needy, and help us always, our Father, to give and serve and be Your blessing to others. In Jesus' name. Amen.

Introduction. Envy and jealousy are identical twins. They walk hand in hand through our lives. Like the sins of pride and anger, envy is an all-too-common sin. Few of us escape its clutches. It creeps into our relationships and destroys our confidence in ourselves and in others.

Some claim to be exempt from this third deadly sin. "I don't have a jealous bone in my body" is more often talk than reality.

There are many examples of envy and jealousy in the Bible. King Saul was jealous of David's growing popularity. In 1 Samuel 18:28–29 the Scripture says, "When Saul saw and knew that the LORD was with David, and that all Israel loved him, Saul was still more afraid of David" (RSV).

Joseph felt the jealousy of his brothers. Genesis 37:11 records, "And his brothers were jealous of him" (RSV).

Jesus also was a victim of jealousy. " 'Do you want me to release to you the king of the Jews?' asked Pilate, knowing it was out of envy that the chief priests had handed Jesus over to him" (Mark 15:9–10 NIV).

I. Envy is the least understandable of the seven deadly sins.

A. *It has no rewards!* Envy does not make one's position or status more secure. Jealousy destroys relationships without insuring that one's status can be enhanced. It is never gratified and does not gain a profit.

B. *Envy grows out of fear.* Jealousy fears that someone else's success will be the beginning of one's own demise. Mistrust and suspicion are the beginning of an evil attitude.

Such fear invades marriage, family, the marketplace, school, professions, and the church. Christianity's history is littered with the ugliness of coveting. Church history reveals persecution and death by those who felt their status was threatened.

C. *Envy creates a grudging spirit.* Doubt gives way to bitterness. A person who has a happy marriage, successful employment, and intelligent children may be the target of jealousy. A sister may hate a brother because he does well in school. An employee may dislike another employee who gets a promotion. A church member may resent another Christian's being selected for the office of deacon.

And when all of the jealousy is combined, not one person has profited by letting such a bitter spirit enter his or her life.

II. Envy needs no justification.

A. *This point is seen continually in the Scripture.* David did not seek or pursue the throne of King Saul, yet Saul let envy grow to the point where it blinded his judgment and his relationship to God.

David was willing to be a loyal and faithful servant. Even when David had the chance to kill Saul, he didn't. If David had killed Saul, most would have called it self-defense. There was no justification for Saul's jealous rage.

B. *Jesus would have willingly spread the Christian message through the Pharisees.* Their religious knowledge could have been as useful as the apostle Paul's was to Him. Yet their jealousy kept them from becoming the tools of God.

Eventually the ugly envy in the hearts of the religious leaders led them to contrive false charges against Jesus and deliver Him to Pilate. Yet Jesus loved the Jewish leaders and would have rejoiced in their salvation. He meant them no harm. Their jealousy was unjustified.

C. *Therefore, let us remember that jealousy is seldom a proper response.* Coveting destroys spiritual health. It attacks its opponent with vengeance.

III. Envy takes away the joy of living.

A. *Envy isolates one from other people.* It sows the disposition that causes people to see life in a begrudging manner.

The Book of Esther tells the story of jealousy. It is the history of a man named Haman whose jealousy of the Jews centered on the Jewish leader Mordecai.

Haman became obsessed with hatred. His hatred led to deceit and a desire to enhance his own status with the king.

By the strange twist of God's hand on history Haman was hanged on the very gallows he built for Mordecai. Haman was trapped by his own envy.

B. *King Saul became a madman.* Finally, with his son dead and his enemies surrounding him, Saul fell on his own sword. The joy of life had long since departed.

C. *Happiness and contentment are two qualities all of us seek in life.* Yet our Scripture text in Proverbs 14:30 tells us that the opposite of such peace is envy.

Conclusion. Since envy and jealousy constantly stalk humanity, we must constantly guard our souls against its destructive power. It does not enhance our status and often causes us to lose more than we gain.

Jesus Christ is the way to peace. "A heart at peace gives life to the body" (Prov. 14:30). Since He is the Prince of Peace, He alone is capable of putting the mind at peace. If jealousy is one of your major sins, I bid you to turn to Jesus for help. —*RGC*

* * *

SUNDAY EVENING, JULY 24

TITLE: The Children of God

TEST: "Blessed are the peacemakers: for they shall be called the children of God" (Matt. 5:9).

SCRIPTURE READING: 1 John 3:1–10

Introduction. No work is more definitely in imitation of God's work than that of making peace, for God is a "God of peace." No one is more clearly demonstrated to be a child of God than the peacemaker, the man who by his own character and example and testimony is a reconciling influence in the world.

"Blessed are the peacemakers." How strange these words sound in our world today. For nearly 2,000 years men have been honoring these words of Jesus with their lips while their hearts have been far from Him. By our lives, our actions, and our words we have said, "Blessed are the sowers of discord, the fomenters of strife. Blessed are the warriors, the munitions makers." But, to paraphrase, Jesus says, "Blessed are the peacemakers: for they are, they shall be called, they are acting like the children of God." All of these described in Jesus' beatitudes are the children of God, for Jesus is describing seven facets of one character. Yet nothing demonstrates more clearly the character of Christ, the nature of God, than the effort to make peace.

Three observations will set forth the truth of this seventh beatitude.

I. The need for peacemakers.

Why are peacemakers needed so desperately in our time?

A. *Because of the enmity and strife on every hand.*

1. There is the enmity that exists between man and God.

This strife is as old as the human race and dates back to the Garden of Eden. Because of sin, man became unreconciled to God, an enemy and an alien. Our enemies fall into three classifications: enemies according to the natural order, enemies by virtue of certain relationships that exist, and enemies because of the acts and words of our lives. Until we are reconciled to God through Christ, His Son, we are enemies of God on all three scores.

2. There is the enmity that exists between man and his higher nature.

When a man is unreconciled to God, civil war exists within his own soul; and his heart is a house divided against itself. In *The History of Mr. Polly,* H. G. Wells said of one of his characters: "He was not so much a human being as a civil war." This is true of every man before he is reconciled to God.

3. There is the enmity that exists between man and man.

Men glare at and fight one another as individuals. Group rises up against group; race hates race; and nations hate and war against one another. Oh, the need for peacemakers!

B. *Because enmity and strife are so costly.*

1. Think of the cost of man's being unreconciled to, an enemy of, God.

Jesus tells us plainly, "Except ye repent, ye shall all likewise perish" (Luke 13:3b). Enmity against God is the source of all wretchedness. A personality divided against itself is unhappy and ineffective; and it means eternal death in the end.

2. Think of the cost of hatred and strife between man and man.

Hatred works havoc to the hated and more seriously damages the one who hates. Many a church has had its work all but nullified by the petty but bitter hatreds of a few. How infinite is the cost of hatred between nation and nation. No good can come out of war, and its cost is beyond calculation. Peacemakers are needed.

C. *Because someone must take the initiative.*

This is true if enmity and strife are ever to cease, if enemies are ever to be reconciled. The heart of the gospel is that "all things are of God who reconciled us to himself through Christ" and that "God was in Christ, reconciling the world unto himself" (2 Cor. 5:18–19 ASV). God took the initiative that we might be at peace with Him.

Christ is the great peacemaker in our hearts because, as Paul says, "He is our peace" (Eph. 2:14a). He keeps in perfect peace those whose hearts are stayed on Him (Isa. 26:3).

II. The identity of the peacemakers.

A. *Negatively.*

1. Peacemakers are not appeasers who love peace, or think they do, and seek after it in the cowardly fashion of leaving things alone, or of giving in to wrong and injustice. Like all virtues, peacemaking has its counterfeits. It is not the same thing as cowardice or love of a quiet life. One can let the other fellow have his way because he is bigger or shouts louder. This may be human and prudent, but it is hardly peacemaking. The peace-at-any-price people who cry, "Peace! peace! when there is no peace," may be the real foes of peacemaking.

2. Peacemakers are not meddlers.

Many times people think they are making peace when they are just sticking a finger into somebody else's pie, meddling in some quarrel that is really none of their affair. Peacemaking is often thought of as intervening in a quarrel; it ought to mean preventing a quarrel from arising in the first place.

3. Peacemakers are not the indifferent.

The peace of indifference is counterfeit. Some "couldn't care less" that there are millions of homeless refugees and displaced persons in the world. Some take for granted the need of the sick and lonely around them as the rich man in Jesus' story accepted the beggar, Lazarus, as a part of the street scenery. From his self-contained vantage point of plenty, he simply ignored him. His was a peace of soul that was dead like the peace of a stagnant pool with a green scum on top.

4. Peacemakers are not compromisers.

A formula of compromise may end an immediate controversy, but compromise is not peace. Among men Jesus alone never accepted any terms or agreed to any truce in the warfare for truth and righteousness.

B. *Positively.*

1. Peacemakers are those whose work is grounded in the reconciling work of Christ.

Isaiah refers to Him as "Prince of Peace" (9:6b). At His birth angels sang, "Glory to God in the highest, and on earth peace" (Luke 2:14a). He lived as a Man of peace. He spoke of His own peace, which He would bestow upon men (John 14:27). He went to the cross to pay the price of peace. Well did the prophet say centuries before, "The chastisement of our peace was upon him" (Isa. 53:5b). In retrospect, Paul said, ". . . having made peace through the blood of his cross" (Col. 1:20).

2. Peacemakers are those whose work stems out of an experience whereby the peace of God, in Christ, has become effective in their own lives.

Listen to Paul: "Therefore being justified by faith, we have peace with God through our Lord Jesus Christ" (Rom. 5:1). No man can be a peacemaker, either between God and man or between man and man unless he is first at peace with God Himself.

3. Peacemakers are those whose work finds its imperative and authority in a divine commission.

In that great fifth chapter of 2 Corinthians Paul speaks of God's "having reconciled us to himself and gave unto us the ministry of reconciliation" (v. 18b

ASV). He goes on to say, "Having committed unto us the word of reconciliation" (v. 19b ASV). In the next verse he states the business of a Christian: "We are ambassadors therefore on behalf of Christ" (v. 20a ASV). After the close of World War II one of America's top executives said, "We have been making the implements of war in great abundance and in great perfection; but the tools of war are not my company's real business. Peace is our business." Let every Christian say, "Peace is our business."

4. Peacemakers are those whose lives exhibit, in some measure at least, the character and likeness of God whose children they are.

III. The blessing pronounced upon the peacemakers.

At first glance this seems the strongest in the list: "For they shall be called the children of God." But when the meaning of those words sink in, this is also the most wonderful of them all. Two blessings or results follow.

A. *The first result is recognition.*

Not only are the peacemakers the children of God, they are recognized as being so. This is not a self-recognition, nor necessarily a recognition by the world—which is more apt to persecute them and call them traitors (Matt. 5:10–11)—but by God Himself. In his First Epistle John says, "Behold, what manner of love the Father hath bestowed upon us, that we should be called the children of God" (3:1a ASV). Who calls the peacemakers "children of God"? God does.

B. *The second result is realization.*

The peacemaker realizes in his own heart that he is a child of God when, by the Spirit's leadership, he is used by Him to lead another into peace with God in his heart.

Conclusion. A pastor was seeking to win a thirteen-year-old girl to Christ in her home when her mother interfered. The pastor asked that mother, "Are you a Christian?" "Well," she said, "I have a hope." She had five children. Not one of them was a Christian. All were in danger of hell, while she mouthed pious phrases. How could she have known? Had she tried to be a peacemaker between any one of her children and God, and had she succeeded, she could have said, "Now are we children of God, and it is not yet made manifest what we shall be" (1 John 3:2a ASV).

— *WTH*

* * *

WEDNESDAY EVENING, JULY 27

TITLE: The Grave Robber

TEXT: **"Jesus said unto her, I am the resurrection, and the life: he that believeth in me, though he were dead, yet shall he live" (John 11:25).**

SCRIPTURE READING: **John 11:1–53**

Introduction. Crimes take diverse directions. This is especially true with robbery. Thieves steal numerous items with different techniques. One of the most unusual kinds of burglaries is grave robbery. Intruders go inside a graveyard and steal valuable jewelry from graves.

Jesus stole bodies from graves. He commanded some people to return from the dead. One of these persons was Lazarus. At the graveside of Lazarus, Jesus claimed to be the Prince of life itself. Jesus said, "I am the resurrection, and the life: he that believeth in me, though he were dead, yet shall he live" (John 11:25). This is another great "I am" of the Bible. Let us notice why Jesus claimed to be the Prince of life.

I. Jesus is the first of life.

Jesus is the only one capable of creating physical life. He is responsible for the first of physical life.

Jesus is also responsible for the first of spiritual life. When a person opens his or her life to Jesus Christ, he or she begins to live. Jesus is the beginning of life.

II. Jesus is the fullness of life.

Jesus often spoke of living an abundant life. By this Jesus meant that He brings life to the fullest.

When we accept Jesus, we can have victory over the sins of life. We can live victoriously each day with the power of the indwelling Christ.

When we accept Christ, we can have deliverance from the fears and frustrations of life. Jesus brings meaning to life. He brings a better life. It is life in the fullest!

III. Jesus is the future of life.

Trust in Jesus Christ results in continued life beyond the grave. Jesus opens the door of death for the continuation of life.

Many people today are talking about life after death. The most forceful influence is Dr. Elizabeth Kubler-Ross's book *On Death and Dying*. An article in *McCalls* (Kenneth L. Woodward, "There Is Life After Death" [August 1976]) asserts that there is scientific proof for existence beyond the grave.

Conclusion. Jesus assures us not just a future life. He tells us about the fabulous, future life for His children. When we accept Jesus, we begin a life that continues forever. —*HTR*

* * *

SUNDAY MORNING, JULY 31

TITLE: The Fourth Deadly Sin: Impurity

TEXT: **"But a man who commits adultery lacks judgment; whoever does so destroys himself" (Prov. 6:32 NIV).**

SCRIPTURE READING: **Proverbs 6:32–33**

HYMNS: **"Love Divine, All Loves Excelling," Wesley**
"Let Others See Jesus in You," McKinney
"I Would Be True," Walter

OFFERTORY PRAYER:

Our heavenly Father, we are aware of our debts to You and to others. We come asking Your forgiveness and, at the same time, thanking You for the gift of forgiveness. Today we come bringing tithes and offerings as

expressions of our love and gratitude. Accept them and bless them in ministries that will honor Your holy name. In Jesus' name. Amen.

Introduction. The fourth deadly sin was labeled "impurity" by the ancient fathers. We know it better by the word *lust.* It is the category of sin that deals with the immorality of sexual sins. Lust, premarital and extramarital sex, prostitution, pornography, homosexuality, incest, and rape are all sins that may be classified as "impurity."

I. Lust demonstrates a lack of maturity.

A. *Our Scripture text for today makes this point.* "But a man who commits adultery lacks judgment" (Prov. 6:31a NIV). A lack of judgment indicates a lack of maturity.

The world declares otherwise, and unfortunately even some Christians have been fooled. The world calls some movies "adult movies" or rates them "For mature audiences only." When one sees such a movie, the Christian should rightly ask, "If this is maturity, then what would be immaturity?"

B. *Lust is built on the world of fantasy, not reality.* Lust dreams of activities that either are impossible or require the misuse and disregard of another's personal rights. It is selfishness in its lowest form. Impure sexual thoughts seek and desire self-gratification to the exclusion of anyone else.

C. *Lust is not the admiration of physical beauty.* It is perfectly natural to appreciate an attractive person. But real maturity does not let such "appreciation" become an obsession. That is the essential difference.

Lust is coveting. It is a craving that is out of control. It is unleashed passion. It is an animal unchecked—and man is more than an animal. He is a creature made in the image of God.

II. Lust demonstrates a lack of good judgment.

A. *Our Scripture text makes a second point about sexual depravity.* It states clearly that "adultery lacks judgment." Adultery, fornication, incest, rape, homosexuality, masochism, and all the other sexual sins demonstrate a lack of wisdom.

It is readily apparent that such actions do not take into consideration the consequences. On the other hand, if one does know the consequences of such activity and still proceeds, then he or she is indeed lacking in good judgment.

B. *"Sincerity" and "responsibility" are two qualities of good judgment.* "Free love" or "doing your own thing" are opposite qualities. Yet these latter two expressions permeate pornographic and base literature. Hiding under the guise of enlightened intellectualism, these people actually demonstrate an emotional level that is childish.

Babies demonstrate almost total selfishness and self-centeredness. This is necessary for their development, and hardly anyone expects them to act otherwise. They cry to gain our attention and have temper tantrums to express their feelings of frustration. The only way to end such behavior is to *completely* mold our world around their needs and desires.

The lustful person is quite similar. He resents any restrictions on his behavior and lacks the judgment to be able to understand that he cannot always have what he wants when he wants it.

III. Lust produces self-destruction.

A. *Our Scripture text says that anyone "who commits adultery lacks judgment; whoever does so destroys himself"* (Prov. 6:32 NIV).

There are so many ways this verse proves true. Ministers, doctors, lawyers, psychologists, and social service personnel see evidence of this weekly (and some see it daily).

Many lives are destroyed by so-called "free spirits." Sexual sins cause grief, destruction of trust, guilt, divorce, anger, frustration, jealousy, deceit, murder, physical injury, wrecked futures, loss of friendships and jobs, failure to receive promotions—the list seems endless!

B. *So many believe that it is their life and they should be allowed to live it as they choose.* Perhaps if one lived in a vacuum, such logic would make more sense. But because "no man is an island," such logic is absurd.

Nearly every one of the professionals listed above can tell you how adultery, incest, homosexuality, and the whole list of sexual sins has crushed and destroyed other lives.

Policemen in churches I have pastored have told me of the bitterness and hatred that such sins have caused.

C. *If you think you can violate the laws of God to your own selfish desires with impunity, you are wrong.* "Do not be deceived: God cannot be mocked. A man reaps what he sows. The one who sows to please his sinful nature, from that nature will reap destruction; the one who sows to please the Spirit, from the Spirit will reap eternal life" (Gal. 6:7–8 NIV).

Conclusion. Therefore, let us try to see our sexual appetite as a good gift from God to be used wisely and for enhancing marriage. By viewing our sexuality in a Christian and wholesome manner, we will honor God, demonstrate maturity, and contribute to a dependable and responsible society.

Failure to harness our sexuality will cause our culture and society to falter and disintegrate. It demonstrates a lack of maturity and good judgment.

If you are already a Christian and are having difficulty here, then turn back to Christ. I bid you to return to the basics of following Christ and His teachings for a rich and satisfying view of your sexual needs. —*RGC*

* * *

SUNDAY EVENING, JULY 31

TITLE: The Forgotten Beatitude

TEXT: ". . . remember the words of the Lord Jesus, that he himself said, It is more blessed to give than to receive" (Acts 20:35b ASV).

SCRIPTURE READING: Acts 20:17–35

Introduction. An experienced pastor tells of hearing both the pastor of his college church and the pastor of his seminary church preach a series of sermons on the beatitudes of Jesus. Neither included this beatitude that Paul preserved for us. Later, in a pastorate of his own, this pastor also preached a series on the Beatitudes, and he did not include this beatitude either. In preparation for the series he read six books on the Beatitudes, and none of them included it. Why not? His testimony was, "I forgot it." Then he added, "I suppose the two pastors I heard and the authors of the six books I read forgot it also." Ask almost any Christian, even the most careful Bible student, to name the beatitudes of Jesus, and he will name those listed in Matthew 5. Not one out of a hundred would name the one given in Acts 20.

So, to call this "The Forgotten Beatitude" is not only fair, it is also true to the facts. Why?

A. *There is no question as to the authenticity of this beatitude.*

That this is a genuine saying of Jesus there can be no doubt. Beyond doubt, this was a current saying of Jesus with which the Ephesian elders were familiar. Moreover, the writer, Luke, who heard Paul's address to these pastors and preserved it, also wrote the gospel that bears his name; and his gospel preserves, in slightly varied form, Jesus' beatitudes (6:20–23).

B. *There can be no doubt that Jesus demonstrated this beatitude in His life and ministry and death.*

Just as surely as He demonstrated meekness, mercy, and purity of heart, so did Jesus demonstrate that "It is more blessed to give than to receive."

C. *There can be no fault found with the form in which this beatitude is given.*

Paul prefaces his statement of the beatitude with a twofold caution: "Laboring," he said, "ye ought to help the weak, and to remember the words of the Lord Jesus, that he himself said, It is more blessed to give than to receive." His caution "to remember" is certainly in place for us, for this is the forgotten beatitude.

Let us discuss three questions about this problem.

I. Why is this beatitude the forgotten beatitude?

A. *We have never understood it.*

Taken together, the full impact of these words has never hit us as Jesus intended that they should. We tread lightly on the first half of this saying and let our minds dwell on the latter half. But the emphasis of our Lord is the other way around: "It is *more blessed to give* than to receive." This turns the normal attitude of the carnal mind upside down. This beatitude does not fail to recognize what some call "the lower blessings." There is a blessedness in receiving, and our Lord does not discount the fact. None of us could live for ten minutes apart from what we receive. It is blessed to receive, but it is more blessed to give.

B. *We have never believed it.*

If we doubt that this is the most disbelieved truth in the Word of God, we need but to look first at the average church treasury and, after that, into the faces of the average congregation when the offering is being received, or when the pastor mentions money. Many look upon giving to the church as a necessary nuisance, a bother, a thing to be dreaded. It isn't so at all if our hearts are right. The sense of our text then is this: "It is a far happier experience to give than to receive." And it surely is if our hearts are right with Him and if any portion of His Spirit is in us.

But, by and large, this is not so. Few are offended if they are overlooked in a tithing campaign or the every-member canvass. Why do we always have music when the offering plates are being passed? It has been suggested that this is a sort of anesthetic so it won't hurt so much. A certain pastor had to go back to his church a second time for an offering that had to be raised. He was so apologetic and so long-winded in his appeal that the organist caught on and played Mendelssohn's "Consolation" as an offertory. "It is more blessed to give than to receive." We flatly disbelieve this!

C. *We have never actually tested it out.*

Oh, a few have! And their testimony tells us that it is the very Word of God. They say, "It *is* more blessed to give than to receive." Those who love the most give the most. But the great mass of those called Christians cannot testify one way or another. They haven't tried it out! We are prone to forget things that are not ours by experience, so we relegate this beatitude to some pigeonhole in our minds and hearts. We forget it.

II. What results from this beatitude's being the forgotten beatitude?

A. *We have missed the main emphasis of the teachings of Jesus.*

This beatitude stands supreme among all the beatitudes of the Bible. It is the center of the Bible's teaching, the supreme emphasis of Jesus. To give was the purpose of His coming: "The Son of man came not to be ministered unto, but to minister, and to give his life a ransom for many" (Matt. 20:28). Selfishness is self-destructive; giving is redemptive, creative, permanent. We lose what we keep and keep forever what we give to God.

B. *We have missed the greatest joy, the supreme blessing of Christian living.*

What is Christian living? Just doing our level best to give more than we receive for Christ's sake because we love Him and because we love a lost world. What is the Christian philosophy of life? Just believing and trying to live by this Word of the One who redeemed us: "It is more blessed to give than to receive."

Men are more than animals and therefore cannot be satisfied by merely possessing the things of the physical world. No amount of earthly things can ever satisfy that spiritual part of us that God made to be blessed by giving. The writer of Ecclesiastes tells us: "He that loveth silver shall not be satisfied with silver; nor he that loveth abundance with increase: this is also vanity" (5:10).

C. *We have missed the boat in the conquest of the world by the gospel.*

Why has the gospel made such slow conquest of the world? Why have missions and evangelism lagged and dragged? For one thing it is because preachers have been so slow and so timid in preaching the glorious and joyous truths of the Bible about giving. And because people have been so rebellious and unbelieving when they have presented it.

There is no danger of exaggerating the measure in which this beatitude has been discredited in the world and even by Christ's own people. Selfishness is the dominant note of humanity, the cancer of society, the mud on the chariot wheels of God's army; and selfishness finds its supreme expression in man's attitude toward money. The world believes it is more blessed to get than to give; and therefore, for nearly twenty centuries, we have not carried the gospel to all the world.

III. What blessings would follow a wholesale recovery of this beatitude?

A. *There are the blessings that would fall on us as individuals.*

"It is more blessed to give than to receive." That is true for each one of us as individuals. We love our Lord because there was no trace or selfishness in Him at all. He gave and gave and gave; and it was His joy to give. The writer of Hebrews says of Him: "Who for the joy that was set before him endured the cross" (12:2). Jesus demonstrated the truth of this beatitude, as He did all of the others. We are to be like Him.

When a pastor persuades his congregation to give "not grudgingly, or of necessity" (2 Cor. 9:7b), but joyfully and liberally, he is doing a real service to their souls.

B. *There are the blessings that would fall upon our churches.*

It would mean that our churches would have the means, the resources, but above all the spiritual power to attempt to carry out the Great Commission.

A young seminary graduate was in his first pastorate in a rural setting. Both the church and his salary were small. With three small children he was having a hard time. One kind farmer in his church brought him a fine milk cow and the feed to feed her. "Pastor, milk this cow. She'll give all the milk your children need." Some weeks later when the farmer asked about the cow, the young pastor replied, "She went dry. I don't know why. We were very careful. We milked only the milk we had to have." That is bad for a cow. It is bad for a church. Because of their failure to give liberally, most of our churches have gone spiritually dry.

C. *There are the blessings that would fall upon an unsaved world.*

"It is more blessed to give than to receive." If they would only heed these words, churches would challenge an unsaved world by an exalted testimony and witness. The churches would begin to do the thing they were brought into existence to do. They would start knocking on the doors of the world with the gospel; the world would heed, and some would be saved.

Conclusion. This beatitude of Jesus is not a hyperbole, a deliberate exaggeration just for effect. Like all of the other beatitudes this is a plain statement of fact. The Beatitudes describe the traits of character of a happy Christian; and this one, so often forgotten, is the most joyous of them all. — *WTH*

* * *

SUGGESTED PREACHING PROGRAM FOR THE MONTH OF AUGUST

Sunday Mornings

As we conclude the series on the seven deadly sins, let us use the theme "Finding Victory Over the Seven Deadly Sins."

Sunday Evenings

"The Master's Recipe for Effective Praying" is the suggested theme for a study of the petitions found in the Model Prayer which our Lord gave to His disciples.

Wednesday Evenings

We continue with the theme "The Christ of John's Gospel."

* * *

WEDNESDAY EVENING, AUGUST 3

TITLE: The Eleventh Commandment

TEXT: **"A new commandment I give unto you, That ye love one another; as I have loved you, that ye also love one another" (John 13:34).**

SCRIPTURE READING: **John 13:31–35**

Introduction. Charles Templeton, in his book *Life Looks Up,* said that the history of the world has been affected by two events which took place in two small rooms, separated by thousands of miles and thousands of years. One room is found in a drab flat over a dingy laundry in the Soho district of London. In this small room Karl Marx wrote *Das Kapital*. It was a book which affected communism. The other room was in Jerusalem. It was the place where Jesus ate the Passover with His disciples and spoke some meaningful words.

Just as Jesus was about to go to the cross, He bequeathed to His disciples a badge they would need to wear. It would be a sign that they were His disciples. "A new commandment I give to you, That ye love one another; as I have loved you, that ye also love one another. By this shall all men know that ye are my disciples, if you have love one to another" (John 13:34–35). Jesus called the exhortation to love "a new commandment." This may be labeled "the eleventh commandment." Let us examine the various facets of this command.

I. The supreme place for love.

A. *Jesus gave a supreme place to love in His teachings*. Love was the central theme of the Master's teaching. "Ye have heard that it hath been said, Thou shalt love thy neighbour, and hate thine enemy. But I say unto you, Love your enemies, bless them that curse you, do good to them that hate you, and pray for them which despitefully use you, and persecute you; That ye may be the children of your Father which is in heaven; for he maketh his sun to rise on the evil and on the good, and sendeth rain on the just and on the unjust. For if ye love them which love you, what reward have ye? do not even the publicans the same?

And if ye salute your brethren only, what do ye more than others? do not even the publicans do so?" (Matt. 5:43–47).

B. *Jesus gave a supreme place to love in His life's relationships.* Love was the basis of a relationship with God and with other human beings. "And he answering said, Thou shalt love the Lord thy God with all thy heart, and with all thy soul, and with all thy strength, and with all thy mind; and thy neighbour as thyself" (Luke 10:27).

C. *Jesus gave a supreme place to love with His actions.* The Lord loved without recommendations, without restrictions, and without reciprocation. He always sought the highest good of human beings.

D. *Jesus wants His followers to give love a supreme place.* "Though I speak with the tongues of men and of angels, and have not charity, I am become as sounding brass, or a tinkling cymbal. And though I have the gift of prophecy, and understand all mysteries, and all knowledge; and though I have all faith, so that I could remove mountains, and have not charity, I am nothing. And though I bestow all my goods to feed the poor, and though I give my body to be burned, and have not charity, it profiteth me nothing" (1 Cor. 13:1–3). Love has the prominent place for a modern follower of Jesus.

II. The unique pattern for love.

If love is so important, how are we to love? Jesus gave the pattern for love: "That ye love one another; as I have loved you, that ye also love one another" (John 13:34). The pattern of love is not to be determined by our standard but by the pattern of Jesus Christ.

A. *Jesus loved inclusively.* He included the entire human race in His love. He loved outsiders and insiders; tax collectors, harlots, and other sinners were included in His love.

To be in God's family is to include all people within our love. No one can obey the eleventh commandment and exclude anyone from his love.

B. *Jesus loved indescribably.* There is no way in all the world to describe the lofty height of Jesus' love: "Greater love hath no man than this." Jesus went to the limit of self-giving love, even to the extent of giving His life on a cross.

C. *Jesus loved selflessly.* Jesus never loved anyone for what it could do for Him. He loved thinking what it would do for others.

III. The distinct purpose of love.

A. *The purpose of love is to identify true disciples* (John 13:35a). Loving as Jesus loved distinguishes disciples from the world. The identity of a Christian is not the creed he or she recites or the church to which he or she belongs, but the love which the Christian has for Jesus and other people.

B. *The purpose of love is to attract lost people.* The world will be attracted to those who love. In a popular song we are reminded that what the world needs now is "love, sweet love." The world will be attracted to people who love each other.

Henry Drummond, in his classic sermon *The Greatest Thing in the World,* suggests that by putting a small piece of iron in the presence of an electrified body, that piece of iron for a time becomes electrified. Putting a committed life in the presence of Christ would mean that Christ's nature could be seen in that life.

Conclusion. The world desperately needs love. Christ enables people to love. Will you not obey the eleventh commandment? It will mean that you will love one another.

— *HTB*

* * *

SUNDAY MORNING, AUGUST 7

TITLE: The Fifth Deadly Sin: Gluttony

TEXT: "If anyone has material possessions and sees his brother in need but has no pity on him, how can the love of God be in him?" (1 John 3:17 NIV).

SCRIPTURE READING: 1 John 3:17–18

HYMNS: "O Worship the King," Grant
"Grace Greater Than Our Sin," Johnston
"Blessed Assurance, Jesus Is Mine," Crosby

OFFERTORY PRAYER:

Our heavenly Father, we would offer to You our thanks for Your blessings upon us. We come bringing gifts which are but indications of the generosity of Your provisions for us. We remind ourselves that every beast of the forest is Yours and the cattle upon a thousand hills are Yours as well. We come bringing gifts that we might share in the work of Your kingdom in proclaiming the gospel to the ends of the earth and in ministering to the needs of the unfortunate about us. Bless these gifts and multiply them to Your honor and glory. In Jesus' name. Amen.

Introduction. Gluttony is not a sin we hear much about today, and, when we do, it is usually in reference to overeating. However, the sin of gluttony is more than just overeating, obesity, and overindulgence in food or drink. It is the sin of excess and intemperance. It is overdoing, unrestraint, self-indulgence, and inordinate extravagance.

Thus, gluttony covers a large number of sins. Certainly in our affluent society, we can readily see the extent of this sin and the many heartaches it causes. Gluttony seeks to satisfy our senses and our greed while disregarding the needs of others.

I. Gluttony is the sin of the affluent.

A. *The possession of wealth is not a sin.* Occasionally, ministers and churches may have given people the impression that affluence in and of itself is a sin. This is certainly untrue.

There are many wealthy people in the Bible who used their material blessings to serve God. However, there are many more illustrations in the Scripture about how prosperity became a stumbling block. As a matter of fact, the Bible generally tends to be skeptical of the use of great wealth by those who have it.

B. *In our Scripture text found in 1 John 3:17, the author is pointedly condemning those who have much but are stingy toward sharing a portion of their affluence with the needy.* If you have no pity, how can you say that you are a reflection of God? How can you say God's love is in you? John implies that this is impossible.

C. *Holding on too tightly may insure that you will always have possessions, but it will not insure friendship or God's approval.*

Most churches have benevolence programs—either through their local congregations or through their denomination (or sometimes both). It is also true that these are usually exhausted early or are funded by token amounts in comparison to needs.

Even churches find they must be judicious in the distribution of benevolence money, clothing, and food. Unfortunately, there are those who prey on a church's generosity or gullibility. But we must not let this keep us from doing as much as possible. Jesus does not promise us that people will not take advantage of us; frankly, He says they will try. But again, "let us not love with words or tongue, but with actions and in truth" (1 John 3:18 NIV).

II. Gluttony is a sin of sensual gratification.

A. *Gluttony is a gratification of our fleshly appetites.* It is often based on pleasure, amusement, excitement, comfort, and personal leisure. Drugs, alcohol, food, and tobacco are representative of this point. But this point of selfishness to the exclusion of others' needs can also be seen in our use of the world's natural resources.

It appears that many Americans believe somehow that it is our divine right to use water for irrigation, oil for heating and fuel, and coal for electricity without regard to future generations or to pollution or to the extinction of parts of God's creation.

B. *I do not doubt that God abhors a godless communism, but I strongly suspect He also hates a greedy Americanism.* In Philippians 3:19 the apostle Paul reminds us: Woe to those "whose end is destruction, whose god is their belly, and whose glory is in their shame, who mind earthly things."

What about the poor and poverty-stricken souls of our land? What compassion do we have for the senior adults who retired or were forced to retire on restricted incomes in a highly inflationary society?

It is true—our country went through a period of depression; but in order to remember how bad those times were, you must be over fifty years old. People younger than that would not have been old enough to remember it clearly.

C. *Most new automobiles cost more than some have paid for their houses.* I recently saw a new automobile priced at $17,500. It was a very small compact car. I remembered how in 1969 my wife and I had paid $16,250 for a new house, which had two full baths, wall-to-wall carpet, a garbage disposal, a dishwasher, and central heat and air. A man told me the other day that he had bought a new car, and it was the first time in his life he had ever paid that much for anything that did not have a lawn or shrubs.

III. Gluttony is the sin of too much without sharing.

A. *Too much, too often, too expensively, too soon is another way to define gluttony.*

Most people in Jesus' day were relatively poor. The average daily wage was one denarii—about sixteen to eighteen cents. A yearly income was about fifty to sixty dollars. In one's adult lifetime he had only two coats (or outer garments worn for warmth and protection from the elements).

Thus, what John the Baptist says in Luke 3:11 has more meaning if you understand how rampant poverty was among his hearers. He admonished, "The man with two tunics should share with him who has none, and the one who has food should do the same'' (NIV). Please notice that John does not admonish us to give away all that we have. He simply commands us to share part of our prosperity.

B. *James, the half brother of Jesus, writes in his epistle a similar thought:* ''Suppose a brother or sister is without clothes and daily food. If one of you says to him, 'Go, I wish you well; keep warm and well fed,' but does nothing about his physical needs, what good is it?'' (2:15–16 NIV).

In answer to the question of James, the implied answer is, ''Nothing! It is no good! It is useless!'' Having a lot or too much is not a sin. But having a lot or too much and not sharing is a sin.

Conclusion. Gluttony is not a sin we hear much about these days. Such preaching and Bible teaching would sound more like meddling than ''gospel preaching.'' But most of the prophets and the followers of Jesus had a lot to say about gluttony.

The Lord Himself warned His followers not to be overanxious about food and clothing, but to seek first God's kingdom (Matt. 6:25–34). —*RGC*

* * *

SUNDAY EVENING, AUGUST 7

TITLE: Our Father

TEXT: ''After this manner therefore pray ye: Our Father which art in heaven, Hallowed be thy name'' (Matt. 6:9).

SCRIPTURE READING: Matthew 6:1–15

Introduction. If we are to come boldly to the throne of grace to receive help in our time of need, we must know who sits on the throne. We must know who God is. We must know what kind of Person He is.

We can learn much by considering our Lord's most basic instruction on prayer. What we have commonly called the Lord's prayer contains some of the most profound thoughts on prayer found in all of the Bible. Every word in that pattern prayer is important. The prayer was given again in Luke's Gospel in response to a specific request from the disciples concerning prayer. They felt their inadequacy in prayer and wanted Jesus' aid. He responded by giving this beautiful pattern to follow.

How are we to understand the prayer? It was not given just to quote as a prayer to God, even though it is useful for this. All of us have experienced some beautiful moments with God as we uttered these words to Him. Dr. Martyn Lloyd-Jones contends that the prayer is actually meant to be an outline for prayer. It is to guide us in our prayers even as an outline guides a speaker in his sermon. The prayer presents two major concerns that we may present to the Father. The first three petitions are concerned with the glory of God: His name, His kingdom, and His will. The last four are concerned with our needs. This should always be the order of our concern when we come to present ourselves to the Father in prayer.

First, we will gather from it only the light it gives about the God to whom we pray. He is to be addressed, according to our Lord Jesus, as ''Our Father which art in heaven.''

I. We must know that God is our Father.

There were a few scattered references to God as Father in the Old Testament; but it was Jesus, our Lord, who really gave meaning to this address. Jesus came from the bosom of the Father, speaking of God as Father in very personal terms. What am I admitting or affirming when I address God in prayer as "our heavenly Father"?

A. *The resourcefulness of God.*

It is an acknowledgment of the resourcefulness of God. The root of this word translated *Father* includes the idea of originator. It points to a source, a cause, a point of origin. God is the Source.

The God who is the source of our physical life is also the God of all mercy and grace. As such, He is the source of our eternal life. The relationship we have with Him is at His initiative. He is the originator of the relationship. Every address of God as Father by a person in worship should be an acknowledgment of this. It is an affirmation that the relationship that each has with Him is His work, His creation.

B. *The responsibility of God.*

This address makes another suggestion. It speaks of being responsible. Some of us who are parents have felt our hearts skip a beat when a voice on the other end of the telephone line has asked about one of our children. The tone of voice suggested that the person wanted to know if I was the one responsible for him or her. To be a child's father is to bear some responsibility for him or her. Since God is our heavenly Father, the clear indication is that He is the one who is responsible for us. None of us would have dared to push off on God this responsibility, but fortunately He Himself made it so. Since God has revealed Himself as the One who accepts responsibility for us, it is not presumptuous for us to bring our joys and our needs into His presence. This is exactly what He expects and even encourages.

C. *The responsiveness of God.*

The other word that is suggested by this title of God is responsiveness. To address God as Father is to affirm that He is the responsive God of love that we know Him to be. Do you remember that helpful word about the Father that Jesus gave? He assured Thomas that "he that hath seen me hath seen the Father" (John 14:9). It is safe to assume that God is just as responsive to our needs as Jesus was to need wherever He met it. If you will read the Gospels with discernment, you will be reassured that Jesus was always accessible and responsive.

II. We must know that God is our Father in heaven.

The phrase that our Lord added to "Our Father" is significant. It reveals some things about the God to whom we pray, things that we need to know if we are going to pray confidently.

A. *His position.*

First, it is surely an affirmation that God is separate. It separates Him from all earthly fathers and personalities. Some people mistakenly approach deceased human beings in prayer. They select the great saints of the past and address prayers to them. This is surely a mistake. There is no need to come to some mere mortal, though he be dead, if you can come before the living God Himself. Furthermore, it separates Him from all living fathers. He is the one in heaven in contrast to all of those on earth. Whether they be our physical or our spiritual fathers, prayer is not to be addressed to them.

Secondly, related to this is the affirmation that God is sovereign. The heavens were understood to be the very seat of God. God is seen as the Ruler over all things. All things are under His control. So, to approach God as the heavenly Father is to approach the One who has the right to do whatever pleases Him. There is no other in all of the universe who has this kind of authority.

B. *His power.*

This title also points to God as powerful. "Our Father which art in heaven" addresses God as the One who has the power to do whatever needs to be done. "Father" would indicate that He would want to do it, but this indicates that He has the power to do it. Some of the titles with which people approach God today fail to acknowledge this. Some refer to Him as the "man upstairs." This is not the same thing as saying, "Our Father which art in heaven." A man, even though he might be "upstairs," is still a man. The "Father in heaven" is the One who has the power to do all things.

The apostle Paul surely caught hold of this truth. He affirmed in a prayer, "Now unto him that is able to do exceeding abundantly above all that we ask or think, according to the power that worketh in us" (Eph. 3:20). When you address God as "Our Father which art in heaven," this is what you are acknowledging.

Conclusion. Your prayer life is going to grow as your knowledge of God grows. Prayer has no meaning apart from this personal knowledge of Him. The great essential in a growing knowledge of God is fellowship with God. One of the greatest means of fellowship with God is prayer. Do you see where this leads? If you want to become more effective, more bold, more confident in your prayer life, then pray more. The more you pray, the better you will know the God who answers prayer, the more your sonship in His family will mean to you. The more He means to you, the more you will enjoy the experience of prayer. This will be true for eternity. So, brethren, let's go pray! —*DLL*

* * *

WEDNESDAY EVENING, AUGUST 10

TITLE: Going in the Right Direction

TEXT: "Jesus saith unto him, I am the way, the truth, and the life: no man cometh unto the Father, but by me" (John 14:6).

SCRIPTURE READING: John 14:1–6

Introduction. Going down a one-way street in the wrong direction is a frustrating experience. It happened to me during rush hour in a large southern city. Meeting irritated drivers and trying to turn around added to my misery. For the rest of the time I was in that city, I carefully noted each subsequent turn to see if I was going in the right direction.

Jesus talked about the direction of His life. It involved a cross. Yet, He taught the disciples that the cross was the way of life for the world. Thomas was not sure that he knew the right direction, so he asked, "Lord, we know not whither thou goest; and how can we know the way?" (John 14:5). Jesus replied, "I am the way, the truth, and the life" (v. 6a).

Going the right direction through your life is important. It is a joyful experience. Let us learn the instructions of how to travel the pilgrimage of life.

I. Take the only way.

Thomas knew of many other claims to be "the way." There have been many such claims. Philo called his philosophy "the Royal Way." Buddha claimed to be the discoverer of the "right path." Confucius called his teaching "the Way."

Jesus' claim goes beyond the philosophies. He says, "I am the way." He does not show or direct us to the right way. Jesus points us in the right direction and goes with us. He walks with us to lead us. He guides us as we travel. He does not tell us *about* the way. He *is* the way.

II. Believe the truth.

If we wish to go in the right direction, we must believe the truth. Many people have told truths. There is an element of truth in the varied philosophies.

Jesus said, "I am the truth." This claim goes beyond the idea of a truth. Jesus did not just tell truths; He embodied the truth. Many truths can be conveyed with words only. Anyone can teach truths about love, forgiveness, and humility. But only Jesus embodies these truths.

When we open our lives to Jesus Christ, we can live the good life. He is the perfect pattern of what life should be. To be open to Jesus, the Truth, means we are going in the right direction.

III. Live the life.

Going in the right direction means more than mere existence. Many philosophies offer an existence-style, not a real lifestyle. People search desperately for that which will make their days meaningful and worth living.

Jesus gives life. He gives more than the breath which animates our bodies. He makes existence worthwhile. He fills life with meaning.

When a person encounters Jesus Christ, he is introduced to God. Other philosophies offer temporary solutions to life's great riddles. Jesus offers permanent solutions.

Conclusion. You can go in the right direction. On your journey, Jesus is the Way. To know the truth is to encounter Jesus. To experience the life is to have real life.

— *HTB*

* * *

SUNDAY MORNING, AUGUST 14

TITLE: The Sixth Deadly Sin: Slothfulness

TEXT: **"If a man will not work, he shall not eat" (2 Thess. 3:10 NIV).**

SCRIPTURE READING: **2 Thessalonians 3:6–10**

HYMNS: **"Love Divine, All Loves Excelling," Wesley**
"At Calvary," Newell
"Love Lifted Me," Rowe

OFFERTORY PRAYER:

Our loving heavenly Father, we thank You for the warmth of the sunlight, for the refreshing breezes that blow, and for the beauty of the world in which we live. We thank You for life, for health, and for friends.

We thank You for Your grace and mercy toward us which You have revealed in Jesus Christ. Today we bring tithes and offerings to You because we want others to experience Your love. Bless these gifts to the proclaiming of the Good News around the world. Bless these offerings toward the relief of suffering. Bless these offerings for the coming of Your kingdom in the hearts of men. In the name of our Lord, we pray. Amen.

Introduction. Slothfulness is not a common word today. We use other words to describe the attitude of slothfulness. We speak of idleness, listlessness, lifelessness, apathy, indifference, goofing off, wasting time, good-for-nothing, sluggishness, procrastination, and laziness. Actually, there are even more synonyms and adjectives which describe this human condition, but the listener should understand the breadth of the problem by this meager listing.

The sloth is a lethargic animal with coarse hair. It builds no nest or home, sleeps eighteen hours a day, and wakes very slowly. The sloth is so inactive that a green algae grows in its hair.

Sloth permeates schoolwork, the marketplace, the home, friendships, and Christianity. Almost no area—except leisure—seems to be immune. Laziness is soundly condemned in the Bible. Proverbs 21:25 says, "The sluggard's craving will be the death of him, because his hands refuse to work" (NIV).

Our text is very explicit: "If a man will not work, he shall not eat" (2 Thess. 3:10 NIV).

I. Laziness is the neglect of duty.

A. *This is really a sin against ourselves as much as it is a sin against society.* It shows the difference between the person you are and the person you could be.

Paul's letter to the people at Thessalonica indicates that while he was with them, he and his companions did work. They accepted no gifts of food or other things without paying for them. Indeed, they worked "night and day" in order to keep from being a financial drain on anyone and to be a model for them (2 Thess. 3:8–9).

B. *God expects us to work.* It is our duty. When God put man in the Garden of Eden, He charged him to work and care for the garden (Gen. 2:15). Work is not punishment for Adam's sin; work is the privilege of man to serve God.

Laziness is the opposite of God's plan for mankind. A child should learn minor chores that prepare him for major responsibilities later. A husband is to work at marriage, being a parent, and a job. Likewise, a wife is to work at marriage, being a parent, and her home. If both husband and wife work outside the home, then household chores should be shared.

C. *To do less is to neglect your duties.* Some are too lazy to care. Some children are allowed to practice sloppiness at home because it is easier to let them alone than to correct and follow through with teaching. Then, as they grow into adulthood, they carry their laziness with them.

II. Laziness is a violation of Christian living.

A. *Some might ask, "How can doing nothing be a sin?"* In theology there are basically two kinds of sins: sins of commission and sins of omission. The first category contains those sins that we do, and the second category is the sin of not doing the things we ought to do.

For instance, if you do absolutely nothing, you will be lost. In the parable of the talents the servant who went and hid his talent in the ground was chastised because he did nothing with his talent.

B. *Some Christians are slothful in their prayer life, Bible study, church attendance, witnessing, financial support, and Christian service.*

The reason our world does not have an effective Christian witness in every country can be directly traced to laziness and inactivity by Christians throughout Christian history. There is a neglect of Christlikeness. We do not work as hard as we should to live as Christian examples.

C. *The Christian should be preparing for the return of Jesus.* Five of the ten virgins failed to prepare for the return of the bridegroom because of laziness (Matt. 25:1–13). Whatever else this parable may mean, it demonstrates that the Lord is going to come again and we as Christians must prepare for His return.

III. Laziness is a threat to God's plan.

A. *God does not intend for a person to be idle.* The author of Proverbs draws on nature to illustrate God's plan for man. In Proverbs 6:6–11 he graphically draws the analogy of the ant as a picture of how diligent one should be about living.

The ant has no commander, overseer, or ruler per se, but still he knows to work. He works because without it he will perish. He works hard in summer in order to enjoy the fruit of his labor in winter.

B. *Mankind must do the same.* God never intended for other humans to support the lazy. Welfare programs are wonderful for the disabled, infirm, and unfortunate in society. Many souls are severely limited by physical, emotional, and mental handicaps that prevent them from working side by side with the healthy and able-bodied.

But social programs that encourage one who is not disabled or mentally incompetent to remain unemployed should be eliminated.

Such plans build resentment among people that spills over against the deserving. To reward laziness is a sin.

Conclusion. Slothfulness is found in job performance, school, church, and politics. Every Christian should do his or her best at all times. We should labor as though God were our employer (Eph. 6:5–8).

Jesus Christ has commanded us to be an active and effective witness for Him. To do less is wrong. If you want to have the joy of solid biblical living, one of the things you must do is obey the command of Christ.

If you are not a Christian, I challenge you to serve and accept the only One who can bring joy to your work. —*RGC*

* * *

SUNDAY EVENING, AUGUST 14

TITLE: Hallowed Be Thy Name

TEXT: "After this manner therefore pray ye: Our Father which art in heaven, Hallowed be thy name" (Matt. 6:9).

SCRIPTURE READING: Luke 11:1–13

Introduction. We have called it the Lord's Prayer, but it is really the Model Prayer. It is a useful guide for the disciple to follow in his prayer life. It gives him some priorities by which to establish his prayer life. Most of us have quoted this prayer since childhood, but we have not looked carefully at what it really says.

What should be the primary burden of your prayer when you approach the heavenly Father? In this prayer, Jesus sets forth seven petitions. The first three are concerned with the things of God. The last four are concerned with the things of man. This reflects God's priority that should be observed in prayer. The first concern must always be with God's name, God's kingdom, and God's will. Then you can become concerned about daily bread and the like.

The first petition is "Hallowed be thy name." The biblical use of "name" is a little strange to modern ears. In understanding the Bible you cannot separate the name from the person. Maclaren said, "Name is character so far as revealed." To "hallow" something means to count it as holy. Literally, it means "to make holy." Since it is related to God in this text, we know that it carries the force here of regarding or acknowledging something as holy. There is no way that the name of God can be made holy, for He is the eternal Holy One.

I. A petition for a revelation of God.

A. *The spirit of the petition.*

This first petition can almost be understood as a confession. While it is voiced as a specific, urgent appeal, it has beneath it a confession. The only reason we would be moved to pray for God's name to be hallowed among men would be a recognition that it was not being done. So, it can be seen as a confession for mankind. As unthinkable as it may seem, mankind is guilty of not regarding God as holy, or of treating the name of God as a common, ordinary thing. It is an acknowledgment that it is not always so in my life. There are times when I walk without any regard for the name of God, and also times in which the name of God was represented through me as a very common thing.

B. *The burden of the petition.*

It is primarily through a petition that God will make Himself known, that God will confront man with the truth about Himself. It is a petition that God will reveal Himself to mankind as He revealed Himself to Moses at the burning bush. God so unveiled His holiness to Moses that he was compelled to remove his shoes and bow himself in the presence of God. It is a petition that God will unveil Himself to mankind like He did to Isaiah in the temple.

The conviction behind this petition is that only such a knowledge of God can meet the deepest needs of man. The first petition is not that man may have the strength to do what is right, but rather that he may know God. The conviction is that if man can come to know God, all of these other needs will be cared for in his life. Man's deepest problem is ignorance of God. Though the evidence for God is all about him, and God desires to make Himself known to man, still man walks on in ignorance. You find this priority in the prayers of Paul for himself and for others. He was moved to pray that "I may know Him, and the power of His resurrection." He longed for a deeper and fuller knowledge of God in his life. He prayed for other Christians that they might be "filled with all the fulness of God." This should also be the priority in our prayers for others.

II. A petition for a recognition of God.

The petition goes deeper than just a petition that men may know God as holy. They must not only know what Moses, Isaiah, and Peter knew, they must do what these men did. When they knew God as holy, they responded to Him accordingly. This is a petition that man's response to God will acknowledge and recognize Him as being holy.

A. *A missionary petition.*

It may be a missionary petition. As we look upon the world in its sin and ignorance, no prayer is more appropriate than a petition that God may be known and acknowledged by sinful man. It should be the passion of every Christian heart to see God reverenced by the nations of the earth.

B. *A personal petition.*

But it may also be, and must be, a personal petition. It must be a prayer that says, "Hallowed be thy name . . . in my life." We will be powerless in seeing the Name hallowed in the earth until it first be hallowed in us. What does this involve?

It will be seen in our speech. Our lips should speak the name of God with a sense of awe and reverence. If we really know who He is, we should speak of Him accordingly. The Old Testament people of God did this. They had such respect for the name of God, such an awareness of the holiness of God, that they would not write His name, and were even reluctant to speak His name. They often spoke of Him simply as "the Name." This stands in sharp contrast to the irreverent familiarity that has crept into our lives. We speak of God flippantly. Some even use His name blasphemously. That means that they associate the name of God with things that God would have nothing to do with. They are constantly using His name to call curses down on things, when He does not act so toward men.

This petition also includes our personal thoughts of God. Irreverent speech really begins with irreverent thoughts. The mouth can speak only what has been conceived in the heart. What are your thoughts of God? This would include those secret thoughts which you would not openly express. Do you harbor resentments toward God? Do you resent His claims upon your life? Do you resist His purposes for your life? Do you insist on having your own way rather than following His way? This petition is that God may be reverenced, acknowledged, and adored in your heart. It is a prayer that in your deepest heart there will be nothing except submission, adoration, and praise toward God.

But this petition also includes our personal conduct. "Hallowed be thy name." The name of God can be seen in the conduct of God's people. The conduct of our daily lives can be a blasphemy of the Name as well as our speech. Paul leveled such a charge against the Israel of his day. What is your conduct saying about God to those who watch? Is it speaking to them of a God of love, kindness, truth, and honesty? Or is it suggesting that God means very little to you? Does your conduct say to the world that God is worth knowing?

Conclusion. Jesus made the petition in a tense that suggested urgency. He felt that this should always be the urgent appeal of His people. He knew our needs better than we could ever know them. He felt it to be our greatest need—to know God and to walk day by day with reverent awareness of Him in everything we do. This can be so in your life if you will begin to give this proper priority in your prayer life.

—*DLL*

* * *

WEDNESDAY EVENING, AUGUST 17

TITLE: The Promise of the Holy Spirit

TEXT: "And I will pray the Father, and he shall give you another Comforter, that he may abide with you for ever" (John 14:16).

SCRIPTURE READING: John 14:15–31

Introduction. Saying "good-by" can be a hard task. I have noticed that people struggle with words when a friend or family member will be going away for a long period of time.

The disciples had a hard time bidding farewell to the Master. Jesus had prepared them for the fact of His death, but they were not willing to accept this reality. The closer the time came for Jesus' departure, the more they recognized the reality. The Lord and His disciples had a difficult time leaving each other.

Jesus told the disciples that the departure would be only for a short time. "Yet a little while, and the world seeth me no more; but ye see me: because I live, ye shall live also" (John 14:19). He promised that He would be with His disciples in the power and presence of His Spirit. In other words, Jesus Himself would be present with His disciples in another manner. Maybe believers need to examine the promise which Jesus gave to His disciples about the Holy Spirit.

I. The Holy Spirit is a personal presence.

A. *The personal presence of Jesus meant much to the disciples.* Think of the numerous times they were bewildered and afraid when Jesus was not present. First, the disciples were afraid when a storm arose quickly on the Sea of Galilee. Jesus was not with them. Second, think of their frustration as they tried to heal a man's son while Jesus was on a mountain with Peter, James, and John. The absence of Jesus brought a sense of loneliness to the apostles. His presence was a blessing to their lives.

B. *The personal presence of Jesus is promised to future disciples.* "And I will pray the Father, and he shall give you another Comforter, that he may abide with you for ever" (v. 16). When Jesus said "another," He suggested another of the same kind. The Comforter would be no other than the presence of God in a life. This means that the Holy Spirit is not some impersonal force or energy. It means that the Holy Spirit is not a doctrine alone. The Holy Spirit is God's personal presence with His disciples.

II. The Holy Spirit is a helpful Teacher.

A. *The earthly teaching ministry of Jesus meant much to the disciples.* In the solitude of Galilean and Judean hills, Jesus taught His men. He taught them many facts about life, character, interpersonal relationships, and numerous other truths.

B. *The continuing presence of the helpful Teacher is promised.* "Howbeit when he, the Spirit of truth, is come, he will guide you into all truth: for he shall not speak of himself; but whatsoever he shall hear, that shall he speak: and he will shew you things to come" (16:13). Jesus had taught numerous truths during His earthly ministry, but the apostles failed to understand them.

The Holy Spirit leads into new understanding of truth. Think about how

Peter did not understand the universal nature of the gospel. He had a prejudice against non-Jews. Throughout Jesus' ministry He rebuked this attitude in Peter, but Peter failed to grasp the universal scope of the mission of the Jews. The Holy Spirit led Peter to this truth.

III. The Holy Spirit is an authoritative guide.

A. *The guidance of Jesus meant much to the disciples.* Jesus was an authoritative guide for the disciples. It was hard to bid farewell, for they were bewildered about life's journey. Jesus had told them where to go, how to serve, what to say, and what to do. They felt the absence of Jesus would leave them bewildered about which route to take in life.

B. *The guidance of God is promised with the Holy Spirit.* "But the Comforter, which is the Holy Ghost, whom the Father will send in my name, he shall teach you all things and bring all things to your remembrance, whatsoever I have said unto you" (John 14:26). There is a daily struggle in the life of every believer. The believer does not have to be bewildered over the way to go. The Holy Spirit lives within each Christian, and He guides in the right direction.

IV. The Holy Spirit is a dynamic resource.

A. *Jesus lived alongside the apostles as a dynamic resource.* Think of the numerous times Jesus walked alongside these men to encourage them. They were going to feel helpless when the Lord left.

B. *Jesus promises the continuous presence of a divine resource.* The word *comforter* means "someone called alongside to help." It could mean a counselor who lends help. It could mean someone who pleads a legal case.

Conclusion. We need not be discouraged because the physical presence of Jesus is not with us. He is present in the Holy Spirit. Celebrate His presence! — *HTB*

* * *

SUNDAY MORNING, AUGUST 21

TITLE: The Seventh Deadly Sin: Avarice

TEXT: "Then he said to them, 'Watch out! Be on your guard against all kinds of greed; a man's life does not consist in the abundance of his possessions'" (Luke 12:15 NIV).

SCRIPTURE READING: Luke 12:15–21

HYMNS: "Come, Thou Almighty King," Anonymous
"He Leadeth Me! O Blessed Tho't!" Gilmore
"Have Thine Own Way, Lord," Pollard

OFFERTORY PRAYER:

Holy Father, it is impossible for us to express our thanks adequately for the abundance of Your blessings upon us. You are so gracious to grant to us the privilege of being Your children. We thank You for the gift of eternal life. We also thank You for lesser gifts that are present in the world about us. We would make our gratitude tangible by bringing tithes and offerings

to Your altar. Bless the use of these gifts in communicating the wonders of Your love and the measure of Your mercy. Bless these gifts to the relief of human suffering and to the enrichment of the human spirit, and may Your name be honored and glorified in it all. Amen.

Introduction. *Avarice* is much like the word *slothfulness* we had last week. It is not a word we use very often today. We speak more often about *greed.*

This is the last of the seven deadly sins, and it is also related to the last sin listed among the Ten Commandments: "You shall not covet . . ." (Exod. 20:17 NIV). Coveting is the beginning of greed. It begins with an inordinate desire to grasp and possess material goods. It can lead to deceit, theft, envy, jealousy, murder, war, and selfishness.

"The Midas touch" has become a desirable virtue, rather than a detestable and seriously sad sin. Many wish they had the "Midas touch." Forgetting the fable that was composed to teach the folly of greed, some Christians are hooked on materialism. It has become an obsession to gain more expensive possessions to add to or replace other possessions.

Jacob wanted Esau's birthright; Ahab wanted Naboth's vineyard; Judas sold Jesus for thirty pieces of silver; and Ananias and Sapphira held back land because of greed.

In our text for today we read Jesus' words from the introduction to the familiar parable of the rich fool who tore down his barns to build bigger ones—all because of greed.

I. Greed usually means someone else must suffer.

A. *Whatever it takes to make a dollar becomes all right.* Greed is a morality based on expediency. A criminal who traffics in illegal drugs believes only in caring for himself and his own comfort. He does not care about the lives that are destroyed or the thievery it takes for a junkie to maintain his habit.

Alcohol dealers seldom show concern for traffic victims, broken homes, battered wives and children, alcohol-related crimes, or the fact that alcoholism is the third major medical problem in this country.

B. *Car thefts, burglaries, embezzlement, assaults, shoplifting, robbery, and most murders have their origin in greed.* All of these crimes cause someone else to suffer.

Gambling is based on greed. To their shame, some professing Christians flock to gambling centers—casinos, race tracks, tourist areas, county or state fairs—all hoping to gain more with little effort.

C. *Suffering is caused by cheating, lying, and the deceit necessary to really be good at greed.* Confidence games are played on the elderly every year. Police departments report a growing number of older or more trusting Americans being taken in by con men.

II. Greed is a quest for more than just necessities.

A. *There are at least five items we need in order to live a reasonably happy life.* They are food, clothing, shelter, medical care, and a means to get enough money to purchase the first four.

To have the best-tasting food, the finest clothes, the nicest home, and the most expensive medical specialist is not necessary for living a full and happy life.

B. *Advertising tries to create desires that may not be necessary at all.* The sleekest sports car is hardly a necessity to life. Jewels, gold, and certain brand-name clothes can all become traps of greediness.

Jesus says in our text that "a man's life does not consist in the abundance of his possessions" (Luke 12:15). Most of us—preachers included—believe He was speaking to others and not to us.

III. Greed is a sophisticated form of idolatry.

A. *Most Christians would destroy a man-made figure of some god that was worshiped by a member of their family.* We do not believe in idolatry. Yet, greed is a man-made god that commands our money, time, and even that we sacrifice our families to it.

Some people will eventually give up friends, parents, wives, husbands, church, and Jesus Christ in the pursuit of possessions. Parents allow youth to take jobs that require them to work on Sunday and thus miss church. A father will work on Saturday, Sunday, and late nights in order to have extra money for Christmas—the birth celebration of Jesus—and will thus neglect his children and spouse. Some wives will push their husbands to earn more money in order for them to keep up with friends or their own selfish goals. Amos the prophet condemned wives who pushed their husbands toward greed (Amos 4:1).

B. *Credit and credit debt is out of hand.* Many Christians are deeply in debt—more deeply than what is reasonable. Credit debt has put these people of God on an endless treadmill.

Some churches are so deeply in debt that they cannot provide enough money for necessary programs, missionary giving, or evangelistic thrusts.

Conclusion. The seven deadly sins rob us of the "good life." At first they each seem to offer us a good and abundant life. Yet, it is a subtle satanic lie.

The good life is found only in Christ. God does not condemn these seven attitudes because He does not want us to have fun. He forbids pride, anger, envy, impurity, gluttony, slothfulness, and avarice because these pursuits destroy life.

Let us return to God. Let us lay aside these sins that so easily beset us, and let us return to Jesus Christ—His teachings, His plan for living. Will you turn to Jesus and receive the rich, full life He intended for you? —*RGC*

* * *

SUNDAY EVENING, AUGUST 21

TITLE: Thy Kingdom Come

TEXT: "Thy kingdom come. Thy will be done in earth, as it is in heaven" (Matt. 6:10).

SCRIPTURE READING: Romans 14:13–23

Introduction. The Gospel of Matthew presents Jesus as the King of the Jews. It is truly the gospel of the kingdom. This whole sermon that we call "the Sermon on the Mount" is to be seen in this relationship. In the midst of the sermon our Lord gives this Model Prayer, which His disciples are to pray. The second petition in the prayer is "Thy kingdom come."

What does He mean? "Thy" kingdom calls our attention to the nature of the kingdom. It is the kingdom that belongs to and comes from God. It is to the heavenly Father that we pray "thy kingdom come." The word *kingdom* is to be seen in a dynamic sense. It does refer to a realm in a primary sense. The primary thrust is that of reign or rule. The kingdom of God is the dynamic reign of God as king.

Jesus spoke of the kingdom of God in different ways. He speaks of the kingdom in the present. He affirmed to His disciples, "The kingdom of God is within [or among] you" (Luke 17:21). Whether you understand the preposition to mean that the kingdom was present in their hearts or present in the midst in the person of the King of heaven, it makes little difference. Jesus surely taught that the kingdom of God had come to earth in His ministry. He pointed His critics to His miracles as a sign that the kingdom of God was near at hand. But Jesus also spoke of the kingdom of God as something future. He spoke of the coming of the kingdom. To which aspect of the kingdom then does this prayer relate? Surely, it must include both aspects. Let us see how it might relate to our prayers.

I. A petition for the present rule of God in human hearts.

A. *A confession of need.*

The petition makes an important admission to God. It can be understood as a confession. A prayer for the coming of the Father's kingdom is surely the admission that there is another ruler in charge now. The world of mankind has never been without a ruler. Since the fatal act of man in the Garden of Eden, man has been in the kingdom of darkness which has Satan as its prince. He is the active ruler in this kingdom. So this prayer is a petition for the replacement of the rule of Satan with the rule of God through His Son, the Lord Jesus Christ.

B. *A missionary appeal.*

This then has strong missionary implications as we pray it in the present. Those men and women who accepted Jesus Christ as Lord and Savior are removed from the kingdom of darkness and placed under the rule of the Lord Jesus Christ in the kingdom of God. The kingdom of God is present in their hearts in a spiritual way in the present moment. According to what Jesus told Nicodemus, a spiritual birth is necessary for man to be transferred from the kingdom of flesh into the kingdom of God. So, a prayer for the coming of the kingdom of God can be understood as a prayer that the rule of God may be extended to other hearts through their heeding the gospel of God's dear Son through repentance and faith.

C. *The personal.*

This prayer, "Thy kingdom come," also has some important personal implications as it relates to the present. When the children of God receive Jesus Christ as Lord of life, and begin to know His saving power in their lives, it brings them other insights. They become progressively aware of the incompleteness of the rule of God in their lives. While they have acknowledged Jesus as Lord, they find themselves struggling with the application of His lordship. They find a sinful inclination to withhold parts of their lives from His rule. They find a resistance to His rule. This prayer is personal acknowledgment of this. It is a prayer that His rule will be imposed in a more complete way in our hearts. It is a prayer of submission to His rule. "Thy kingdom come—in my heart, in my business, in my home, in all of my affairs."

II. A petition for the future rule of God in the affairs of the universe.

A. *The dethronement of evil.*

Jesus never deceived His disciples. He never encouraged them to believe that they would ever successfully dethrone the alien ruler in the universe. He always made it clear that this would be done by God Himself. The coming of the kingdom of God will involve an invasion by the sovereign King Himself. This is the great theme of the last book in our New Testament. God is going to intervene in the affairs of men through His Son, and the mighty kingdom of evil over which Satan rules will be destroyed. It will be crushed by the mighty Son of God. So this is a prayer for Him to act in that way. It is a prayer for the King to come and to bind Satan and put him in the bottomless pit, to dethrone every enemy of God and to make them His footstool, and to close down every power that is opposed to God.

B. *The enthronement of Christ.*

This kingdom's coming will also involve the enthronement of the Lord Jesus Christ and His people. He is to exercise rule over the earth with the rod of iron. He will truly be the crowned Prince of Peace!

If we could begin to comprehend what this will mean, we would make it our earnest appeal day after day. We would ever be praying, "Thy kingdom come!" The coming of the kingdom is the hope of the whole creation. Paul tells us in Romans that the whole creation is groaning like a woman in childbirth in anticipation of that day! The coming kingdom will mean the removal of the curse and the restoration of the earth. It will be a beautiful experience of redemption and healing for the earth. It will truly become a Garden of Eden again under the rule of God's kingdom.

C. *Our hope.*

This coming of the kingdom is the hope of the nations of the earth. Nations will continue to be troubled with wars and rumors of wars until this kingdom comes. Nations will continue to destroy one another until that day. But under the rule of Jesus Christ, they will turn their destructive weapons into instruments to make man's welfare better. They will stop even the study of war. There will truly come a peace into the relationships of earth under the rule of the kingdom of God.

This coming of the kingdom is the hope of the individual Christian. Until that kingdom comes in the glorious person of the King, our personal struggles will continue. Death will continue to hold sway over our families. Corruption will continue to express itself. Our struggles with the flesh will continue until we see the King face to face. But then, we shall reign with Him.

Conclusion. Are you ready to pray this petition? Are you ready to pray it for your personal life? Are you ready for Jesus to be the rightful, fully crowned King over all of the affairs of your life right now? Are you ready to pray this as a missionary prayer? Are you ready to make this your prayer for the coming of the kingdom in its ultimate expression? May God give us a heart for the coming of the King.

—DLL

* * *

WEDNESDAY EVENING, AUGUST 24

TITLE: Becoming a Christian

TEXT: "Abide in me, and I in you. As the branch cannot bear fruit of itself, except it abide in the vine; no more can ye, except ye abide in me. I am the vine, ye are the branches: He that abideth in me, and I in him, the same bringeth forth much fruit: for without me ye can do nothing" (John 15:4–5).

SCRIPTURE READING: John 15:1–17

Introduction. Do you have a desire to be a better Christian? Most Christians sincerely want to be better. How then can you actually be a better believer? Some say that practicing academic exercises, such as reading the Bible or other good books, will make one a good Christian. Others advocate that benevolent services make a person a better Christian. Actually one does not *begin* the Christian life in faith and *continue* it through academic exercises and benevolent services. Genuine faith *results in* academic exercises and benevolent services.

Jesus used the illustration of the vine and the branches to describe the Christian life. Jesus said, "I am the true vine." His followers were known as the "branches." Using this analogy we can learn more about the Christian life.

I. A vital union with Christ.

A. *Many people have mistaken concepts about how to become a Christian.* The Jews considered themselves branches because of birth, nationality, and race. Yet they refused to have a vital union with Jesus Christ.

People take many measures to be united with God. However, union with the Lord does not come by belonging to a church. Nor does union with the Lord come by being born into a Christian home. Nor does it come by observing rules and regulations.

B. *Becoming a Christian is to be united with Christ.* How does a branch receive life? It receives life by a vital union into the life of the branch. The life of the vine then comes into the branch.

How then does one become a Christian? One becomes a believer by opening one's life to Jesus Christ. The Lord comes into a person's life and brings His type of life. Paul's favorite expression for a Christian was a person "in Christ."

II. A constant abiding in Christ.

A. *To grow as a Christian abiding in Christ is a necessity.* "Abide in me, and I in you" (John 15:4a). A branch cannot bear fruit of itself. This says you cannot be a better Christian by your own power. The branch must abide in the vine. The word *abide* means to keep in constant contact.

B. *To abide in Christ will result in Christlikeness.* "He that abideth in me, and I in him, the same bringeth forth much fruit: for without me ye can do nothing" (v. 5b). The resources for fruit-bearing (Christlikeness) come from depending on Jesus Christ. One does not attach a branch of grapes to a vine and expect them to receive nourishment. One who is not attached to Jesus Christ will not bear fruit.

Abiding in Christ results in God's kind of character. "But the fruit of the

Spirit is love, joy, peace, long-suffering, gentleness, goodness, faith, meekness, temperance'' (Gal. 5:22–23).

III. A reaching out for Christ.

A. *Christians are chosen for a divine purpose.* The figure of the vine and branches had been a significant symbol of the mission purpose for Israel. When Israel failed to fulfill God's intention, the prophets applied the analogy of the vine. Isaiah pictures Israel as a vineyard run wild (cf. 5:1–7). Jeremiah described Israel as a ''degenerate . . . vine'' (2:21). Hosea called Israel ''an empty vine'' (10:1).

B. *Christians can reach out and bless the world.* They have been chosen for joy. ''These things have I spoken unto you, that my joy might remain in you, and that your joy might be full'' (John 15:11). They have been chosen for love. ''This is my commandment, That ye love one another, as I have loved you'' (v. 12). Also, believers have been chosen to be ambassadors. ''Ye have not chosen me, but I have chosen you, and ordained you, that ye should go and bring forth fruit, and that your fruit should remain: that whatsoever ye shall ask of the Father in my name, he may give it you'' (v. 16).

Once a German ruler wished to possess a Cremoni violin. He offered an enormous price. It was published at marketplaces throughout the region. For months there was no success.

One day an old man appeared at the castle gate. The man was poorly dressed and had a worn violin case under his arm. The servants refused to admit him.

Finally, the old man insisted that the servants carry a message to the master. He asked them to say, ''Heaven's music is waiting at your door.''

The prince ordered him to be admitted immediately. The old man took a perfect violin from the worn case. He made marvelous music and won the prince's praise.

''The violin must be mine. Name your price!'' the prince said.

''I want no money,'' said the old man. ''The violin may be yours on the condition that I pass my life within your house and use the instrument every day.'' The prince accepted the old man's offer.

Conclusion. God wants to enter life. If you allow Him, He will enter and make your life meaningful.

—*HTB*

* * *

SUNDAY MORNING, AUGUST 28

TITLE: The Deliverer From Sin

TEXT: ''Wretched man that I am! Who will deliver me from this body of death? Thanks be to God through Jesus Christ our Lord!'' (Rom. 7:24–25a RSV).

SCRIPTURE READING: Romans 8:31–39

HYMNS: ''O Worship the King,'' Grant
''Christ Receiveth Sinful Men,'' Neumeister
''Thou, My Everlasting Portion,'' Crosby

Offertory Prayer:

Loving Father, thank You for the gifts of light and love and life. Thank You for hope and health and all of the help that You have given to us. Thank You for the privilege of being in Your house with Your people today. As we bring our tithes and offerings, we pray that You will accept them and bless them to the end that Your name will be honored and glorified. In Jesus Christ our Lord. Amen.

Introduction. Romans 7 pictures the tragic failure and disappointment of a believer who tries to find peace of heart through human strength and effort to keep the holy law of God. Paul would declare that he who seeks to overcome the seven deadly sins in willpower and human effort alone will experience the despair of one who finds a fatal flaw within that produces repeated failure.

There are two powers that would claim the right to rule in the heart of man. Paul described these as "flesh" and "Spirit." By the term "flesh" he is referring to our human nature which is defiled by sin. It is that portion of ourselves which remains unregenerate and does not experience the new birth. It is that part of our human nature which provides a bridgehead for sin. It is the inward tendency that we all have to drift downward rather than to move upward.

When Paul speaks of "the Spirit," he is speaking of the indwelling Holy Spirit, who came to live within the believer at the moment of conversion and who makes it possible for the child of God to grow in Christlikeness.

Romans 7 describes the pain and disappointment, the failure and despair of one who tries to live a Christian life without a conscious dependence on the living Christ and the gift of the Holy Spirit. Yielding to the unregenerate nature described as "flesh" is the road to ruin. Recognizing and responding to "the Spirit" is the road to life and peace.

Romans 8 begins with "no condemnation" and closes with "no separation." The contents of Romans 8 declare that there need be no defeat in the Christian life. However, it should be recognized that Christian victory over the seven deadly sins is not automatic and inevitable. We must accept responsibility for our spiritual response to the indwelling Spirit. Romans 8 contains twenty references to the person and the work of the Holy Spirit in the life of the believer. It is through this living, present power of the Holy Spirit that we are to be delivered from the tyranny of sin.

From Romans 7 into Romans 8 we move from the prostration of defeat to the promise of victory. We move from spiritual depression to spiritual delight. We move from a sigh to a song. The indwelling Holy Spirit makes possible spiritual victory and high ethical conduct that reflects the grace and the glory of God.

I. The indwelling Spirit sets us free from the law of sin and death (Rom. 8:1–4).

The Holy Spirit of God liberates us from the law of sin and death and makes it possible for the believer to live righteously. When sin would serve as an oppressing tyrant, the Holy Spirit comes in to deliver us with a strength greater than the law as a governing principle had for Old Testament believers.

II. The indwelling Spirit would deliver us from the weakness of the flesh (8:5–13).

Even after a person has come to know Jesus Christ as Savior, he is still plagued by the power of an inward tendency to sin. This is where the devil seeks to do his work in the heart and life of the believer. Paul is affirming that through the power of the Holy Spirit, we can have victory. In his Epistle to the Galatians, he affirms that instead of living for the flesh, we can reap the harvest of the Spirit if we will trust in Him and walk in Him and obey Him (5:16–25).

III. The indwelling Spirit provides leadership for the children of God (8:14).

The Holy Spirit wants to lead us in thought and word and deed. By faith we are to recognize and obey these divine impulses that could have no source except the heart of a loving God. The Holy Spirit is the Creator of a quality of life in which the will of God is loved, accepted, and obeyed.

IV. The indwelling Spirit gives testimony to our divine sonship (8:15–17).

The Holy Spirit communicates with the believer that he is now a child of God and a member of the family of God.

As Satan tries to defeat us by tempting us to fall into any of the seven deadly sins, we need to firmly grasp our new relationship with God in order that we might overcome evil and achieve victory.

V. The indwelling Spirit is God's pledge of our final and complete redemption (8:18–25).

In Romans 7, Paul describes the despair of one who finds it impossible to overcome the seven deadly sins by human strength alone. Here in these verses, he describes the glorious expectation and the assurance of the final victory that God has provided for those who trust Jesus Christ as Savior. He promises us victory not only over our evil nature in the present, but He promises us final and ultimate and complete redemption beyond history.

VI. The indwelling Spirit aids us in our efforts to pray according to the will of God (8:26).

All of us have difficulty praying properly. Paul tells us that it is the ministry of the Holy Spirit, who wants to deliver us from the seven deadly sins, to aid us in our prayer life.

VII. The indwelling Spirit makes intercession for us according to the will of God (8:27–28).

No one can overcome the flesh in human strength alone. No one can overcome an evil nature by trying to obey the law.

The Holy Spirit of God not only seeks to aid us in our prayer efforts, but He intercedes in heaven for us according to the will of God.

Conclusion. Who is to deliver us from the power and presence of sin? Let us thank God that through Jesus Christ and the precious gift of the Holy Spirit we can have deliverance now from the power of sin, and ultimately we shall have complete redemption and salvation from the very presence of sin. —*TTC*

* * *

SUNDAY EVENING, AUGUST 28

TITLE: Thy Will Be Done

TEXT: "Thy kingdom come. Thy will be done in earth, as it is in heaven" (Matt. 6:10).

SCRIPTURE READING: Luke 22:39–46

Introduction. "It is God's will." These words are used so often to interpret the tragedies of life. In legal language, "an act of God" is used to explain the great catastrophes that bring so much suffering and ruin. And yet Jesus instructs us to pray, "Thy will be done." Does this mean that we are praying for catastrophes and tragedies to befall us?

Such tragic events are not what we find associated with the will of God in the Bible. God wills to create a world, to create man, to redeem man, to send His Son. This will of God is an expression of His eternal purpose and will be accomplished. There is really no need for us to pray for the accomplishment of these eternal purposes of God. But the will of God is also defined as including the commands of God. God's will includes the pattern that we will follow in the daily conduct of our lives. We need to pray that this might be done in our lives and in the lives of others.

But the concern of this particular petition is about how we do it. We are to do the will of God, but we are to do it in a particular way. His will is to be done "on earth as it is in heaven." This means that we are to look to heaven for our pattern of response. Even though we do not know as much about heaven as we would like to know, we do know enough to give us some helpful instruction at this point.

I. Submissively.

There is only one Lord in heaven. Every creature there bows before Him in worship, adoration, and submission. In the Revelation, John saw the saints bowing before Him and casting their crowns at His feet. Isaiah saw the angelic beings with six wings. Two of their wings were used to fly with speed to carry out His every wish. Two of their wings were used to cover their faces as an act of reverence in His presence. John described the saints as those who "serve Him day and night." He is absolute Lord over everything there, and everyone is completely submissive to His will.

There is a form of obedience in which submission may be lacking. One little fellow expressed it eloquently to his mother. She made him sit in the corner as a form of discipline. He didn't like it so he tried to stand up. But she was firm and insisted that he be seated. As he took his seat, he replied, "I may be sitting on the outside, but I am still standing on the inside." She could make him respond physically, but she could not make him submissive in spirit. Some of us respond to the will of God in this way. We give in to the insistence of God, but we do not really submit to Him as Lord. This is a prayer that we would have the very spirit of heaven as we approach the will of God.

This indicates that our attitude in doing the will of God is just as important as the act itself. Is your obedience a true submissive act to the Lord?

II. Completely.

A. *Completely—not selectively.*

In heaven, the will of God is done completely. The angels are not selective in their obedience to the will of God. Whatever God says, they do. Those who refused to give to the Lord God complete obedience, and chose to exercise their own will in opposition to His will, have been excluded from heaven. They are no longer privileged to enter into the presence of God.

Jesus teaches us to pray that the will of God may be done this way in our lives and in our world. There is an evident tendency to be selective in our response to the will of God. We pick which of His precepts will guide us. As an example, a man may choose to follow the will of the Lord about his attendance in public worship, but he may choose to ignore the will of God as it relates to stewardship. He may choose to follow his own ideas about giving. Another man may be very careful to follow the will of the Lord about stewardship. He may be more careful than a Pharisee when it comes to calculating his tithes and offerings, but he may ignore the will of the Lord as it relates to his marriage. He may choose to follow the lust of the flesh rather than the will of the Lord in these matters. In heaven it is never so! There, the will of God is done completely!

B. *Completely—not partially.*

We may also be partial in our obedience. We may go only as far as seems right to us. We may reserve the right to determine exactly how far we will go in our response to the will of God. But we need to remember that partial obedience is actually disobedience. There must be no selectivity or partiality in our response. Whatever He says, we must do.

III. Joyfully.

A. *Like the angels.*

Joy would be one of the most obvious marks of the heavenly response. Heaven is a place of joy. The angels are singers. There are many references in Scripture to angelic songs. Their songs mark them as they do the will of the Father in heaven.

B. *Like the Son.*

This was evident in the life of the Lord Jesus Himself. In a great Messianic psalm, Jesus says, "I delight to do thy will, O my God; yea, thy law is within my heart" (Ps. 40:8). He did not do the will of God out of a sense of duty, but rather with great delight. This explains His statement about the will of God in Sychar. "Jesus saith unto them, My meat is to do the will of him that sent me, and to finish his work" (John 4:34). He found a real joy in doing the will of His Father. It was bread to His spirit.

Your response to the will of God is to be one of your first concerns when you bow before Him. You need to be concerned that you might know His will fully and do His will joyfully.

IV. Constantly.

This never changes in heaven. There is no record of there ever being a need for a revival in heaven. No angel ever wavers in his devotion to the will of God. No angel ever withdraws his support from the program of the Lord. He is there all of the while. Day after day he is there to do whatever God commands. Years and millenniums go by but they still obey with the same joy and delight. They are ever at the task of doing whatever God assigns.

Our Lord provides us with a beautiful example. Jesus allowed nothing to turn Him from doing the will of the Father. He did not allow the response that others made to Him discourage Him. He did not even allow the difficulty involved in doing the will of God to deter Him. When the will of God took Him to the cause, He set His face steadfastly to do the will of God. With a willing heart and delight in His God, He went all of the way!

Conclusion. Are you giving consideration to the will of God in your life? It should be one of your first considerations when you come to pray. It is more important that you know and do the will of God than that you have even your daily bread. God makes this a matter of first concern. Will you? —*DLL*

* * *

WEDNESDAY EVENING, AUGUST 31

TITLE: The Joy of Living

TEXT: "These things have I spoken unto you, that my joy might remain in you, and that your joy might be full" (John 15:11).

SCRIPTURE READING: John 15:11–17

Introduction. Talking about joy and happiness in today's world is a difficult task. John Steinbeck, in his book *Travels with Charlie,* tells of traveling across the United States in his camper with his dog, Charlie. Traveling incognito, not as a Pulitzer-prize-winning novelist, Steinbeck met many people. Almost everyone he met was unhappy with his or her vocation and where he or she lived.

Joy seems to have vanished from our world. Study the faces of people you see around you, and you will see expressions of gloom. Listen to people, and you will learn how widespread misery really is. There seems to be a fanatic search for whatever will bring joy to living.

Jesus wanted people to have joy. "These things I have spoken to you, that my joy may be in you, and that your joy may be full" (John 15:11 RSV). Perhaps our joyless world needs to examine the joy about which Jesus spoke.

I. It is an independent joy.

A. *Some would make happiness depend upon circumstances.*

1. They think good conditions bring happiness.
2. They think power or fame makes one happy.
3. They think adequate financial resources make one happy.

B. *Jesus gives a joy which does not depend on external circumstances.*

1. At what point in Jesus' ministry were the words of the text spoken? Jesus said these words about joy on the day before He was to die. Yet even then Jesus could talk about joy.

2. The joy that Jesus gives is an inward joy. It does not depend on external circumstances. Irrespective of the conditions of life, Jesus' joy makes a person happy.

II. It is a resultant joy.

A. *Some make the pursuit of happiness the energy of their existence.*

1. Happiness eludes us when this is the sole reason for its search.

2. Happiness results as a product of a relationship with the Lord. Albert Schweitzer said, "One thing I know. The only ones among you who will be really happy are the ones who have sought and found how to serve."

B. *Jesus gives a joy which results from a service to Him.*

1. Jesus possessed joy because He was obedient to the Father. "Looking unto Jesus the author and finisher of our faith; who for the joy that was set before him endured the cross, despising the shame, and is set down at the right hand of the throne of God" (Heb. 12:2). For Jesus, joy resulted from doing the wishes of the Father. Joy to a believer is doing what the Lord wishes. It is a result of obedience.

2. Jesus possessed joy because He trusted the Father. Jesus believed that no matter what happened the providence of God would prevail. God will never lose control. Joy results from a profound trust in the Lord.

III. It is an abiding joy.

A. *Some think they have happiness, but it does not seem to abide.*

1. There is an element of pleasure in the world. Many people seem to have momentary pleasure when they get a salary increase or some other monetary gain.

2. The pleasure which the world gives does not satisfy long.

B. *Jesus gives an abiding joy.*

1. Nothing can destroy the joy which Jesus brings.

2. The joy of the Lord will prevail through all kinds of crises.

IV. It is a full joy.

A. *Some think they have true happiness, but it is really a surface happiness.*

1. Abraham Maslow, a Jewish psychologist, has identified several needs of human beings. The first two needs are survival and safety. People need food and shelter, and they need a feeling of security. Yet, according to Maslow there are much deeper needs. A person could have the basic needs met and still he could be unhappy.

2. Some people never move beyond basic physical needs to discover the joy of finding meaning for life.

B. *Jesus gives a joy which satisfies to the fullest.*

1. He desires His disciples to have a "full joy." This means a joy which goes to the depths and reaches to the heights.

2. Jesus alone is adequate to give a joy which can satisfy every element of a human being.

Conclusion. You do not have to be miserable any longer. Jesus wants to give you joy. Don't be fooled by the world's temporary joy. Let Jesus fill you with His satisfying joy.

— *HTB*

* * *

SUGGESTED PREACHING PROGRAM FOR THE MONTH OF SEPTEMBER

Sunday Mornings

Flowing out of the emphases on the seven deadly sins and the need for victory over them, we are suggesting the theme "Recognizing and Responding to God's Gift of the Holy Spirit" for the morning messages throughout the month of September.

Sunday Evenings

We continue and conclude the series of messages based upon the Model Prayer, using the theme "The Master's Recipe for Effective Praying."

Wednesday Evenings

"Amen and Amen" is the theme for a series of studies in Psalm 119, as we find the psalmist giving voice to prayers with which we can concur today.

* * *

SUNDAY MORNING, SEPTEMBER 4

TITLE: The Gift of the Holy Spirit

Text: **"And I will pray the Father, and he will give you another Counselor, to be with you for ever, even the Spirit of truth, whom the world cannot receive, because it neither sees him nor knows him; you know him, for he dwells with you, and will be in you" (John 14:16–17 RSV).**

Scripture Reading: **John 14:15–19**

Hymns: **"God, Our Father, We Adore Thee," Frazer**
"'Tis So Sweet to Trust in Jesus," Stead
"Holy Ghost, With Light Divine," Reed

Offertory Prayer:

Heavenly Father, thank You for granting to us the privilege of coming to Your house to meet with other members of Your family that we might rejoice together in Your love and that we might commit ourselves more completely to Your purposes for us. Today we thank You for the gift of Your Holy Word. We thank You for the gift of eternal life which causes us to love You and to love others. We come, thanking You for the privilege of worshiping You with our substance, and so we bring tithes and offerings. Accept these gifts, and bless them to the good of our community and our world and to Your glory, we pray. In Jesus' name. Amen.

Introduction. We all like to receive gifts. Parents enjoy receiving gifts from their children, and children enjoy receiving gifts from their parents.

Husbands enjoy receiving gifts from their wives, and wives enjoy receiving gifts from their husbands.

People enjoy receiving gifts from their friends.

Employers occasionally receive gifts from their employees, and employees enjoy receiving gifts from their employers.

There are times when we give gifts to strangers, and there are times when we receive gifts from total strangers.

God is the greatest Giver of gifts. James declares, "Every good endowment and every perfect gift is from above, coming down from the Father of lights with whom there is no variation or shadow due to change" (1:17 RSV).

Our Lord contrasted the good gifts of God with the ability of fallen man to give good gifts to his children: "If you then, who are evil, know how to give good gifts to your children, how much more will your Father who is in heaven give good things to those who ask him" (Matt. 7:11 RSV). The only gifts that God bestows are good gifts.

I. God always gives His good gifts with the right motive.

All of us have had experience in receiving gifts which did not come with the highest motives. When God gives a good gift, it is always with the proper motive.

A. *God's gifts come as an expression of His love.* God's gifts are not substitutes for His love. God's gifts never come as a bribe. God's gifts never come as a payment.

B. *God's gifts are an indication of His hope for us.* We should recognize His gifts as an affirmation of our worth. His gifts come to us as an expression of His divine confidence in us.

C. *God's gifts to us are always chosen by His wisdom.*

1. God's gifts are practical.
2. God's gifts are good.
3. God's gifts are helpful.

II. God's good gifts are always appropriate.

Someone remarked concerning a gift of money, which came in the form of greenbacks, "The color of the gift is always appropriate."

God's gift of the Holy Spirit to each believer as an indwelling presence is a gift. It is unmerited, and it does not come as an expression of gratitude or as some kind of a payment for service rendered.

A. *The Holy Spirit is a gift of unknown value to the recipient at first.* The value of this gift to the new believer is far beyond anything that he could possibly evaluate.

B. *The Holy Spirit is a gift of unsuspected value to everyone.* There is not a single person who receives this gift from God who has any idea before receiving the gift concerning its significance to them.

C. *The Holy Spirit is a gift of undiscovered value to most believers.* Have you ever received a gift without understanding its value or recognizing its significance? This is true in every instance concerning the gift of the Holy Spirit.

D. *The Holy Spirit is a gift of unappreciated value to most of us.* How long has it been since you have expressed sincere gratitude and thanksgiving to God for His gift of the living presence of His Holy Spirit?

E. *The Holy Spirit is a gift of great value.* The Holy Spirit is in reality the living gift of God's presence.

1. This gift has great practical value.
2. This gift can have great sentimental value.
3. This gift can have great emotional value.
4. This gift can have great spiritual value.
5. This gift has great teaching value.
6. This gift has great permanent value.

III. We need to recognize and appreciate God's gift of the Holy Spirit.

A. *The Holy Spirit is God's gift.*

1. The Holy Spirit is not a reward for hard work.
2. The Holy Spirit is not a prize to be won.
3. The Holy Spirit is not a property to be purchased.
4. The Holy Spirit is not a treasure to be stolen.

B. *The Holy Spirit is a gift from God to each of His children.*

1. The Holy Spirit is a present gift.
2. The Holy Spirit is a purposeful gift.
3. The Holy Spirit is a powerful gift.
4. The Holy Spirit is a precious gift.
5. The Holy Spirit is a personal gift.

C. *It is interesting to note how the promise of the gift of the Holy Spirit is translated in modern versions of the Bible.* The variety in the manner in which this verse, John 14:16, has been translated provides us with a key to the significance of this great gift that God has given to us.

1. The King James Version translates this verse, ". . . give you another *Comforter.*"

2. The Revised Standard Version translates this verse, ". . . another *Counselor.*"

3. Charles B. Williams translates this verse, ". . . another *helper.*"

4. Phillips translates it, ". . . give you *someone else.*"

5. The New English Bible translates it, ". . . to be your *advocate.*"

6. The Holy Spirit is all of these: Comforter, Counselor, Helper, Someone Else, Advocate.

Conclusion. God gave the gift of His Son, who came to die for us.

God has given to us the gift of His Spirit to live within us.

Christ came and died on a cross to save us from the penalty of sin.

God's gift of the Holy Spirit came to live within us to work the works of God within us that we might be delivered from the power of sin in the present.

If you are not yet a believer in Jesus Christ, the Holy Spirit invites you to come to Him today that you might receive the gift of forgiveness and the gift of eternal life.

If you have already received Jesus Christ as Savior, the Holy Spirit is a gift that you should recognize, appreciate, and respond to fully. — *TTC*

* * *

SUNDAY EVENING, SEPTEMBER 4

TITLE: Our Daily Bread

TEXT: "Give us this day our daily bread" (Matt. 6:11).

SCRIPTURE READING: Psalm 146

Introduction. Prayer begins with Godward concerns, but it does not end there. The first three petitions of the Model Prayer make petitions for the name, kingdom, and will of God. These must be the first concerns in our prayer life. But then Jesus gave us four petitions to cover our personal needs.

The last four petitions are inclusive. "Give us our daily bread" touches on the needs of the body. "Forgive us our debts" includes the needs of the soul. "Lead us not into temptation, but deliver us from evil" speaks to the spiritual needs of the person. This reminds us that whatever concerns us can be brought to the heavenly Father as a matter of concern.

"Give us . . . our daily bread" would seem to be a rather simple statement of need. Yet many attempts have been made to set forth different interpretations of the request. Some have drawn back from thinking of it as a simple request for "daily bread." They have changed it to mean spiritual bread from the Word of God or Christ the Bread of Life; and some have even referred to it as the bread of the Lord's table. There is no need for such spiritualization of the request. Our God is just as concerned that the basic necessities of life be supplied as He is with the spiritual bread for the spirit. Our God is concerned about the total person. What can we learn here?

I. The petition for daily bread acknowledges God as the source of bread.

A. *The explanation.*

What does the petition for "bread" include? The word should be understood as including all of our material needs. Whatever is necessary to sustain our physical life in the world is included. We are to come to God with our petitions for those necessities of life. Such a petition is an acknowledgment of God as the source of the necessities of life. This is an important acknowledgment for the Christian. Later in this same chapter Jesus rebukes worldly anxiety over the necessities of life. He declares that we are denying God when we become anxious over what we will eat or what we will wear or where we will live. He affirms that God knows that we need all these things.

B. *An example.*

God gave to His people a lesson on this truth rather early in their national history. Their food supply ran out soon after they left the land of Egypt. In the desert toward Sinai there were no other supplies available. They became very anxious about the situation and began to murmur loudly about it. But God graciously began to supply them all of the food that they needed. They learned that the God of creation and redemption has supplies of bread. He feasted them on angel's food every day. They called it "manna" because it came directly from God.

C. *The application.*

Modern man is likely to forget the source of His bread in this day. There seems to always be the middle man to make us forget. Some seem to see the government as the source of bread. Everything seems to be controlled by and granted by the government. So, any discussion of the instability of the government naturally causes anxiety about the necessities of life. Governments have always been uncertain and undependable. This is not a new situation. Jesus wanted us to know that the real source of bread is always there. God never changes. He is behind every secondary source of supply. Without His sunshine and rain, without His creative presence in nature, there would be no food, shelter, or clothing.

This creates another problem for some of you. You have always accepted responsibility for providing your own bread. You have not felt any need of asking God for assistance in this. You have had plenty to eat and plenty to wear without asking. Do not be deceived! The bread you have been eating and the clothing you have been wearing have come to you as a gift from God. God has been merciful to bestow them upon you even though you have neither asked nor acknowledged Him. A little thoughtful consideration on your part will make it clear that ultimately God is the source.

II. The Prayer for daily bread affirms God's method of supply.

A. *"This day."*

In this simple petition there are some important lessons about how God supplies our needs. "Give us this day our daily bread." "This day" points to one of them. God's regular method is to supply our needs as the needs occur. Literally, it is a cry for bread for "today." We are not to be praying about bread for next year or in our old age, but for today.

The wisdom of God in this is rather clear. If He gave us all that we would ever need for life at the beginning of life, we would have a tendency to forget the Giver as we went about using up the gift. But since He is pleased to give it to us daily in response to our prayers, there is no opportunity to forget that we are dependent upon Him to meet every need of our lives.

B. *"Daily."*

Another indication of the method of God is in the word translated "daily." This word has given the translators some problems. It was thought for many years that the Gospel writers had just coined a word. No instances of its use could be found in any other Greek writing, but in recent years other instances have been found. What is indicated means more than just the reception of the supply daily. It includes the idea that we receive that which is needful and necessary. It is really a petition for just what is necessary to meet the need that you have. This speaks a word of caution to my heart. I need to be careful about asking God for material things. I should only ask Him for whatever is necessary to meet the basic needs of my life. If He is pleased to give me more than enough to meet my basic needs, I should be grateful and generous with others. But if he gives me only enough to meet my basic needs, I should also be content. The apostle Paul counsels us to be content with food and clothing.

III. The petition for daily bread expresses concern for others.

A. *Explanation.*

There is no place for selfishness when we come before the heavenly Father in prayer. The Model Prayer makes this clear by making the pronouns plural. Here it stands out. "Give us this day our daily bread." "Our" expresses this concern. When I come before the Father, I must bear a concern for any in the family who have personal, material needs.

B. *Application.*

Do your prayers reflect this? Selfishness is a hindrance to effective prayer. God will not hear you if you are only concerned about bread for yourself. He is Father over the whole family. "Ye ask, and receive not, because ye ask amiss, that ye might consume it upon your lusts" (James 4:3).

Conclusion. This petition for daily bread surely mandates a practice of daily prayer. God wants you to come before Him daily with the concerns of your life. It surely mandates daily thanksgiving as well. If He faithfully supplies the necessities of our lives each day, it would be a crime not to express genuine thanksgiving before Him. Let me call on you to replace your anxieties about all such matters with prayer. If it is a real need in your life, you know that He will hear and will answer. —*DLL*

* * *

WEDNESDAY EVENING, SEPTEMBER 7

TITLE: Prayers That We Need to Pray

TEXT: "With my whole heart I seek thee; let me not wander from thy commandments!" (Ps. 119:10 RSV).

SCRIPTURE READING: Psalm 119:9–16

Introduction. It is altogether appropriate for us to say, "Amen," either audibly or inaudibly, when we listen to the prayers of others and those prayers express the deep desires of our heart. The Hebrew word *amen* means "let it be so." It is an affirmation of concurrence and agreement. Each of us can participate more meaningfully and more profitably in the public prayers uttered by others if we listen intently and appropriately say, "Amen."

With great benefits coming to us, we can study the written prayers of others. Often they verbalize the prayers that we would like to utter, and we can then say, "Amen," as we read written prayers.

Psalm 119 is an artistic record of the psalmist's devotions and dialogues with God. The psalm contains many prayers that we could profitably pray as our very own prayers.

Tonight we look at the second stanza of this acrostic poem, which is composed of twenty-two stanzas. It contains some prayers that each of us needs to pray.

I. "Let me not wander from thy commandments" (v. 10).

The psalmist recognized the human tendency to wander away from the proper path. He offers a prayer that he might be saved from a life of aimless wandering. Why does man wander away from God's truths?

A. *Perhaps it is because we have a fallen nature.*

B. *Perhaps it is because we are forgetful.*

C. *Many of us are preoccupied with other things, and we find it easy to drift.*

D. *We can be tempted by the promises and the possibilities of what the world has to offer.*

E. *Some of us wander because of weariness.*

The psalmist prays that God will so work in his life that he will be saved from wandering away, straying, from God's precious commandments.

II. "Teach me thy statutes" (v. 12).

Repeatedly throughout this longest psalm in the Bible, we hear the psalmist repeating this petition, "Teach me thy statutes." Each of us should repeat this prayer and mean it with all of our heart.

In this petition the psalmist is saying, "I want what God wants." God's grace had worked within the innermost being of this man to cause him to want to follow God's statutes.

We need to remember that our Savior was thought of as the great Teacher (Matt. 5:1–2; 7:28–29).

Only as we understand the teachings of God through Jesus Christ can we truly walk in His ways and do the things that He wants us to do.

III. Putting feet on our prayers.

For prayer to be meaningful and productive, we must do more than just talk to the Father God. We must cooperate with Him as He works to bring about the fulfillment of the desires we have expressed in the petitions that we have offered.

A. *We can keep our lives pure by bringing our thoughts and actions under the searchlight of God's Holy Word* (Ps. 119:9).

B. *We can avoid a life of sin by storing up God's Word in our hearts that it might serve as both a restraint and as a challenge* (v. 11).

C. *We can verbalize the great truths and the great insights that come to us from God's Word in our conversations with others* (v. 13).

Conclusion. If we would pray effectively, we need to delight ourselves in God's precepts, His ways, His statutes (vv. 14–16).

Devotional Bible study can be the listening side of prayer. God will speak to our needs through His Word if we study it with trust and with a willingness to be obedient.

Let us consider the prayers that the psalmist has given voice to in this stanza, and let us say, "Amen," from the heart to the prayers that we need to pray for our own spiritual good. — *TTC*

* * *

SUNDAY MORNING, SEPTEMBER 11

TITLE: The Holy Spirit: A Living Gift

TEXT: ". . . even the Spirit of truth, whom the world cannot receive, because it neither sees him nor knows him; you know him, for he dwells with you, and will be in you" (John 14:17 RSV).

SCRIPTURE READING: John 14:15–20

HYMNS: "Holy, Holy, Holy," Heber
"Serve the Lord With Gladness," McKinney
"Holy Spirit, Faithful Guide," Wells

OFFERTORY PRAYER:

Father in heaven, thank You for being so wise and generous. Thank You for being so great and good. Thank You for offering to us so many spiritual blessings and opportunities. Today we come offering ourselves to You. Accept our tithes and offerings as indications of our love and as symbols of our desire to participate with You in Your ministry of mercy and helpfulness to a needy world. In Jesus' name we pray. Amen.

Introduction. There are many different options open to someone who is eager to bestow a gift on someone he or she loves. Some gifts are inanimate in nature. They may be described as gadgets. Some gifts, like cut flowers, are perishable and have only temporary value. There are also living gifts—perhaps a puppy or a kitten or a lovely growing plant. Some gifts are perishable while others are of a permanent nature. Some gifts are very precious and personal.

God our Father has seen fit to bestow a living gift within the mind and heart of each of His children at the moment of their conversion. We refer to the gift of the Holy Spirit, who is the living gift of the presence of God Himself.

I. The Holy Spirit is a living gift.

The Holy Spirit is not a mere influence that comes from God. The Holy Spirit is more than a force, like gravity or magnetism or electricity.

Jesus uses the personal masculine pronoun in our text to describe this living gift from God.

A. *The Holy Spirit speaks as a Communicator.*

"He who has an ear, let him hear what the Spirit says to the churches. To him who conquers I will grant to eat of the tree of life . . ." (Rev. 2:7 RSV).

B. *The Holy Spirit intercedes as a divine Intercessor in the interest of those who have received Jesus Christ as Savior.*

". . . the Spirit helps us in our weakness; for we do not know how to pray as we ought, but the Spirit himself intercedes for us with sighs too deep for words" (Rom. 8:26 RSV). The Revised Standard Version has translated this verse correctly, whereas the King James speaks of "the Spirit *it*self."

C. *The Holy Spirit testifies regarding Jesus Christ.*

". . . the Spirit of truth, who proceeds from the Father, he will bear witness to me" (John 15:26 RSV).

D. *The Holy Spirit leads the servants of Christ in service; Philip is a classic illustration.*

"And the Spirit said to Philip, 'Go up and join this chariot'" (Acts 8:29 RSV).

In his Epistle to the Romans Paul describes the leading of the Spirit. "For all who are led by the Spirit of God are sons of God" (8:14 RSV).

E. *The Holy Spirit functions as a Guide into an understanding of divine truth.*

"When the Spirit of truth comes, he will guide you into all the truth; for he will not speak on his own authority, but whatever he hears he will speak, and he will declare to you the things that are to come" (John 16:13 RSV).

F. *The Holy Spirit appoints spiritual leaders for the churches.*

"The Holy Spirit has made you guardians, to feed the church of the Lord which he obtained with his own blood" (Acts 20:28 RSV).

A pastor needs something in addition to a majority vote of a congregation to be an effective minister. He needs to be appointed simultaneously by the Holy Spirit.

G. *That the Holy Spirit is a living gift can be perceived by virtue of the fact that He can be grieved by improper conduct on the part of those who are within the body of Christ.*

"And do not grieve the Holy Spirit of God, in whom you were sealed for the day of redemption" (Eph. 4:30 RSV).

II. The Holy Spirit is a divine Person.

When God bestows the gift of the Holy Spirit within the heart of His child, He is bestowing a living gift who is at the same time a divine Person. "And because you are sons, God has sent the Spirit of his Son into our hearts, crying, 'Abba! Father!'" (Gal. 4:6 RSV). God is Spirit. God is not localized in a body as man is. God in Spirit comes to dwell within the body of each believer as a living presence.

A. *This living gift of the divine presence comes into our lives in order to purify us and to cleanse us and to reproduce within us the character and the personality of the Lord Jesus Christ.* ". . . how much more shall the blood of Christ, who through the eternal Spirit offered himself without blemish to God, purify your conscience from dead works to serve the living God" (Heb. 9:14 RSV).

B. *This living gift of the Holy Spirit is all-powerful.* This power was demonstrated in the miraculous conception of the Christ when the Holy Spirit came upon Mary in great power (Luke 1:35).

C. *This living gift of the Holy Spirit knows all of the things of God as well as the things of man.*

"God has revealed to us through the Spirit. For the Spirit searches everything, even the depths of God. For what person knows a man's thoughts except the spirit of man which is in him? So also no one comprehends the thoughts of God except the Spirit of God" (1 Cor. 2:10–11 RSV).

This divine Person who has come to dwell within us knows all about us and, at the same time, has perfect understanding of the mind of God. He seeks to lead us to think the thoughts of God.

D. *The Holy Spirit, which God has given to us as a living gift, is spoken of as God in the Scriptures.*

". . . Ananias, why has Satan filled your heart to lie to the Holy Spirit and to keep back part of the proceeds of the land? . . . You have not lied to men but to God" (Acts 5:3–4 RSV).

This is also seen in Paul's statement to the Corinthians. "And we all, with unveiled face, beholding the glory of the Lord, are being changed into his likeness from one degree of glory to another; for this comes from the Lord who is the Spirit" (2 Cor. 3:18 RSV).

Conclusion. The Holy Spirit of God invites each nonbeliever to put faith in Jesus Christ and to receive Him as Lord and Savior. He uses the Bible, the church, your family, your friends, and the emptiness of your heart to communicate this.

If you will receive Jesus Christ as Savior, the Holy Spirit will enter within you to work God's good work within you. He will work for your eternal welfare.

"Therefore, as the Holy Spirit says, 'Today, when you hear his voice, do not harden your hearts as in the rebellion'" (Heb. 3:7–8a). —*TTC*

* * *

SUNDAY EVENING, SEPTEMBER 11

TITLE: Forgive Us Our Debts

TEXT: "And forgive us our debts, as we forgive our debtors" (Matt. 6:12).

SCRIPTURE READING: Mark 11:20–26

Introduction. Jesus instructs us to make all of our felt needs a matter of prayer. The needs of our body are to be a matter of prayer. This is the message of the petition, "Give us this day our daily bread." But the felt needs of our mind are also to be made a matter of prayer. A part of the soul of man is his conscience. God placed within us a little voice that protests when we violate our sense of right and wrong. What do you do when you feel guilty? You should pray. You should not carry guilt through even one day. You should pray, "Forgive us our debts as we forgive our debtors."

Let me remind you that this is a prayer for disciples. Some have been teaching that once you become a Christian you never need to confess or seek forgiveness again. But Jesus taught His disciples to pray this prayer daily.

I. The petition makes a personal confession.

A. *The possibility of sin in the Christian.*

"Forgive us our debts." That is a confession of a felt need in one's life. The person praying this petition is admitting to the heavenly Father that he is indebted to Him. This brings before us an important question about the Christian life. Does a person sin after he becomes a Christian? Is he still responsible for his sins after he becomes a Christian? Both the Scriptures and the Christian experience answer the first question. The Scripture assures us that it is the will of God that we not sin, but that God has made provision for our sin (1 John 2:1–2). It warns us that if we deny that we have sinned, we are just playing games with ourselves and seeking in futility to deceive God (1:8, 10). We will ever be aware that we are still coming short of the glory of God. In our honest moments, we will have to admit that we have not given to God and our fellow-man all that we owe them.

B. *The response to sin in the Christian.*

This petition is a personal confession. It grows out of a person's taking sin seriously in his or her personal life. This word *debts* is an interesting word. In the giving of the same prayer in the Gospel of Luke, the word *sin* is used. The word *sin* means "to miss the mark" or "to come short." The interchange of these words indicates that when we come short of God's ideal, or God's purpose for our lives, that we run up a debt with God. Each act of sin puts us into debt with God, and we have nothing with which to pay the debt. I owe to God a life of complete love, service, worship, and devotion. When I fail to give it to Him, I have a debt that I cannot pay. The same is true in my relationship to my fellow-man. I owe to him love, concern, and care. I am to be as concerned for his welfare as I am my own. A failure to have this kind of ministering concern runs up a debt.

II. The petition expresses an urgent appeal.

The appeal is "forgive us." It is expressed in the most urgent way. The appeal assumes that God is a forgiving God. From all that Jesus taught and revealed about God, we know this to be a safe assumption. The holy God, who has been offended by our sins and to whom we have become deeply indebted, is a generous, forgiving God.

A. *Because of the nature of sin.*

The heart of this appeal is an acknowledgment of our inability to pay the debt we have run up on His books. The essence of the appeal is that God will cancel out all that is on the book against us. The word *forgive* means to "cancel," "dismiss," "send away." When we make this kind of appeal, we know that we are unable to do anything about the debt that we owe, so we ask God to cancel it. It is really an appeal for God to bear the cost Himself. Although there is no mention of it here, we know that God is a forgiving God because He has been willing to pay the price. This is what took place at the cross. Christ died in our stead, and thereby paid the price so that God could forgive.

B. *Because of the broken fellowship.*

But how does this relate to the life of a Christian? Did not forgiveness come when we received Christ as Lord and Savior? The answer is an obvious yes. But this is a family prayer. Your receiving Christ as the Lord of your life put you in the family, but you can lose the joy of being in the family if you do not continue to practice this confession and make this appeal for forgiveness. While the sins in your life do not cause you to lose your place in the family, they do interrupt your fellowship with the Father. He cannot and will not have fellowship with you as long as you are keeping sin in your life unconfessed. The conscious communion we experience with God flows out of a cleansed heart. This cleansing comes only as we ask God daily for forgiveness. So the urgency of this appeal comes out of the sense of sin and the burden of broken fellowship.

III. The petition includes a testimony.

A. *The inevitable wrongs.*

The appeal is of no value unless it is accompanied by this testimony, "as we forgive our debtors." Behind this testimony is a helpful insight into life. Life is so constructed that we must anticipate that we will be wronged by others along the way. Sometimes the wrongs may be verbal. We may be falsely accused, or we may be the victim of misrepresentation, or our good name may be misused. The wrongs may be material. Sometimes we may be the victims of dishonesty or deceit. The wrongs may be physical, or they may be legal. Injustice is just a fact in our world. The wrongs may be emotional or psychological. When we come to God to ask Him for forgiveness, we must be able to give testimony that we have forgiven those who have wronged us.

B. *"Full of mercy and forgiveness."*

This does not mean that we are making our actions toward others a basis for our appeal. Our exercising forgiveness toward someone else does not build up some merit on which we can base our appeal. We are no more deserving of God's forgiveness after we forgive the other person than we were before. It is our duty to be a forgiving person. This does not make the forgiveness a legal matter.

What does this mean? It means that we are in no position to receive or experience God's forgiveness as long as we have unforgiveness in our hearts. Jesus emphasized this: "For if ye forgive men their trespasses, your heavenly Father will also forgive you. But if ye forgive not men their trespasses, neither will your Father forgive your trespasses" (Matt. 6:14).

We are not truly repentant until we have come to the place where we can forgive. So, this testimony gives evidence of a broken spirit and a contrite heart.

There is one other question that we need to consider. Can I forgive a person until he seeks my forgiveness? The answer is no. God cannot forgive us until we seek His forgiveness, but there is always in the heart of God a readiness to forgive. God will take the initiative in seeking to bring us to a place where we will ask forgiveness. He will keep showering us with evidences of His goodness even though He must withhold from us the joy of His fellowship. This is designed to bring us to repentance where we will confess our sins. So we must not use this to excuse what is basically an unforgiving and bitter spirit. We must have a purity of heart in this matter when we come before the Lord. Our testimony must be genuine, for God knows our hearts.

Conclusion. Are you ready to pray? Do you have your confession ready? Is it specific? Are you ready to make your appeal—"Forgive me"? Are you ready with your testimony? Can you say to God, "I have forgiven those who have wronged me"? This must be the daily pattern of your prayer life. —*DLL*

* * *

WEDNESDAY EVENING, SEPTEMBER 14

TITLE: A Prayer for Eyes That See

TEXT: **"Open my eyes that I may see wonderful things in your law" (Ps. 119:18 NIV).**

SCRIPTURE READING: **Psalm 119:17–24**

Introduction. In this third stanza of the longest chapter in the Bible, we find more prayers that we can profitably pray along with the psalmist.

I. The motive behind our praying is important (Ps. 119:17).

Jesus had much to say about praying with the proper motive (Matt. 6:5–8).

James declares that an unworthy motive can deprive us of an affirmative answer from God when we pray (4:3).

The psalmist prayed for the abundance which God is able to provide. The Revised Standard Version translates his petition, "Deal bountifully with thy servant, that I may live and observe thy word" (Ps. 119:17). Today's English Version translates it, "Be good to me, your servant, so that I may live and obey your teachings." This saint of long ago was requesting that God deal generously with him in order that he might be able to live a life of obedience and helpfulness to others.

A. *He could have prayed for riches.*

B. *He could have prayed for acceptance and popularity.*

C. *He could have prayed for that which would be pleasurable to his appetites.*

D. *He could have prayed for that which would have contributed to his comfort.*

The psalmist prayed with a proper motive. We should examine our motives and try to bring them into conformity with the character and will of our Father God.

II. A prayer for spiritual sight.

"Open my eyes, so that I may see the wonderful truths in your law" (v. 18 TEV).

It seems as if sin and selfishness create a film over our eyes that makes it difficult for us to see anything except that which is physical, tangible, material.

Paul taught that it was the strategy of Satan to put a blindfold on the minds of unbelievers so that they could not see the truth of God as it was revealed in Jesus Christ (2 Cor. 4:3–4).

Throughout the ministry of Jesus He was seeking not only to cure those who were physically blind, but He sought to open the spiritual eyes of His disciples that they might see the truth of God. It is significant that, following His resurrection, ". . . he opened their minds to understand the scriptures . . ." (Luke 24:45 RSV).

Every time we open up God's Word, we need to pray for eyes that truly see the marvelous things that spring up out of God's truth.

A. *We need eyes to see God as we study His Word* (cf. Isa. 6:1).

B. *We need eyes that will enable us to see ourselves as we read God's Word* (cf. Isa. 6:5).

C. *We need eyes that see the needs of others as we study God's Word* (Matt. 9:36–38; John 4:35b). In our praying we should ask the Lord, "Take the veil from over my eyes and help me to see what You want me to see."

III. A prayer of gratitude (Ps. 119:24).

In verses 21–24 the psalmist speaks of troubles and of enemies who were plotting to bring about his downfall. During this time of great travail of soul, he found strength, comfort, and help by listening to the great truths of God's Word. He had discovered that studying God's Word could be a listening experience. It is more important that we hear what God has to say than to give voice to our petitions.

Conclusion. Do you want God to deal bountifully with you? Then examine your motives as you pray.

Do you understand all of the mysteries and problems that perplex you? If not, then pray that God will open your eyes as you study His Word.

As you read God's Holy Word, listen to the voice of His Spirit. —*TTC*

* * *

SUNDAY MORNING, SEPTEMBER 18

TITLE: Using the Gifts of the Holy Spirit

TEXT: "As each has received a gift, employ it for one another, as good stewards of God's varied grace" (1 Peter 4:10 RSV).

SCRIPTURE READING: 1 Peter 4:7–11

HYMNS: "All Hail the Power of Jesus' Name," Perronet
"Holy Spirit, Faithful Guide," Wells
"Make Me a Channel of Blessing," Smyth

OFFERTORY PRAYER:

Holy Father, thank You for the gift of Your Son to us that we might know You and experience Your salvation. Thank You for the gift of Your Holy Spirit to dwell within us as Teacher, Guide, Counselor, and Helper. Thank You for the gifts which the Holy Spirit has imparted to us that we might minister effectively in the name of Christ for Your glory in and through the church. Help us now as we come bringing gifts to You to be used in the advancement of Your kingdom's work. We pray in Jesus' name. Amen.

Introduction. God is the great Giver. He has given to us the gift of His Son, Jesus Christ, to be our Savior, Teacher, Friend, Lord, and Helper.

God has given to us the gift of the personal presence of His Holy Spirit to dwell within us permanently. He is to enable us to do God's work.

The Holy Spirit was given on the Day of Pentecost to accomplish a number of significant purposes. The Holy Spirit came to identify Jesus Christ as the risen, living Lord and Messiah.

The Holy Spirit was given to unite the followers of Christ into a living body in which the Christ could dwell and continue His work of redemption in the world.

The Holy Spirit was given to identify the church to the Jewish people as the New Israel through whom God would carry forward His eternal redemptive purpose.

The Holy Spirit was given to enable and to empower the church to succeed in preaching the gospel to the ends of the earth.

The Holy Spirit was given to impart and to plant the confession "Jesus Christ is Lord" at the very center of every person's being.

The Holy Spirit was given to produce within each believer the nature and character and personality of Jesus Christ as He is permitted to produce His fruit.

The Holy Spirit was given to the church and to individual Christians in order that the church might function effectively in making the gospel known to the world. While the Holy Spirit is the great gift of God to each believer, the jscriptures teach us that the Holy Spirit imparts spiritual gifts to every member of the church that each one might fulfill the function God has for him.

I. The gifts of the Holy Spirit.

References are made to the variegated gifts of the Holy Spirit for ministering in the church and through the church to the world are listed in several different books of the New Testament.

A. *Paul listed some of the gifts of the Spirit in his letter to the church at Rome* (12:3–8).

B. *One of the major sections in Paul's First Epistle to the Corinthians is found in chapters 12–14*. In this passage Paul is seeking to deal with a problem that was divisive and that was hindering the church. There was an exaggerated emphasis on the value and the use of the gift of speaking in ecstatic languages and an almost total absence of recognition that the supreme gift of the Spirit was love, followed by the gift of prophecy and many other gifts. The gift of speaking in tongues was the last on the list and evidently the least of the gifts, yet some of the Corinthian believers were making it to be the most important of the gifts.

C. *In Paul's Epistle to the Ephesians, there is another list of some of the gifts of the Spirit* (4:11f.).

II. The nature of the gifts of the Spirit.

A. *The gifts of the Spirit are all "grace gifts."* They are bestowed by the Holy Spirit, rather than merited or earned for outstanding service. They may take the form of talents, but in reality they are gifts from the Holy Spirit.

B. *The gifts of the Holy Spirit are His sovereign gifts.* "But it is one and the same Spirit who does all of this; as he wishes, he gives a different gift to each person" (1 Cor. 12:11 TEV).

C. *The gifts of the Holy Spirit are functional gifts.* The gifts of the Spirit are not decorative ornaments to be worn. The gifts of the Spirit are not like boxes of candy to be enjoyed. These gifts enable believers to minister as the body of Christ. These gifts are intended to produce harmony and effectiveness in service (14:5c).

D. *The gifts of the Holy Spirit are primarily for the congregation, that is, for the good of the church* (v. 12). This is not to imply that the individual is not edified or built up by receiving a gift from the Holy Spirit.

E. *To every believer there is given a gift from the Holy Spirit.* "So we are to use our different gifts in accordance with the grace God has given to us" (Rom. 12:6 TEV). So far as we can observe, the Scriptures teach that each believer has received at least one gift from the Holy Spirit.

III. Discovering and using your spiritual gift.

How is one to be certain concerning his or her spiritual gift? Is there a way by which we can discover what our spiritual gift is?

A. *We should study the scriptural lists of the gifts of the Spirit and then examine ourselves sincerely and honestly to see if we have some talent, gift, or inclination that would indicate that God has placed upon us the blessing and the burden of a particular gift.*

B. *We should experiment in acts of faith in the direction we feel led, trusting the Spirit for guidance.* We can do this by identifying needs about us that we believe we can meet and then do what we can to meet those needs. It is possible that we discover that we have the gift after we have met a particular need.

C. *We should examine our spiritual satisfactions.* If we get a particular joy out of doing a certain type of Christian service, it could be that we are working in the area in which the Holy Spirit has given us a gift.

D. *We should evaluate our effectiveness in service.* Certainly it would follow that if we are a monotone who cannot carry a tune, we do not have the gift of singing solos or being a part of a singing group. The gifts of the Spirit are for the building up of the church. If what we attempt to do does not build up the church, then it probably follows that that is not the area in which we have a gift.

E. *Recognize the affirmations of other believers.* Many times others who are more mature in the faith will recognize your gifts before you do. When others commend you for a service that is rendered, they may be giving you a clue concerning what your gift is.

Conclusion. God has given to mankind the gift of His Son. Have you received this Gift into your heart? Have you let Him become your Savior, your Teacher, your Friend, and your Helper?

If you have received His Son, Jesus Christ, as your Savior, you have also received the gift of His Holy Spirit. When we become the children of God, God sends the Spirit of His Son into our hearts (Gal. 4:6).

If you have received God's Son and Spirit, then there is a gift or gifts that the Holy Spirit has given to you in order that you might be a living, vital, functioning part of the body of Christ. May God bless you and use you greatly as you recognize and respond to the gift which the Holy Spirit has bestowed upon you for ministering in the world. — *TTC*

SUNDAY EVENING, SEPTEMBER 18

TEXT: Lead Us Not Into Temptation

TEXT: "And lead us not into temptation, but deliver us from evil" (Matt. 6:13).

SCRIPTURE READING: James 1:1–14

Introduction. The battle with temptation is a continuing battle in all of human life. It is "common to man." This prompts our petition for today, "Lead us not into temptation."

Doubtlessly, the Teacher intended for each of these petitions to be repeated daily. Even one day of relaxation in the battle with temptation can be spiritually fatal. While Jesus did not experience the need voiced in the second of the petitions, "Forgive us," He did experience this one. Since He never succumbed to any temptation, He never had to request forgiveness. You may question whether He really knew the power of temptation, since He never responded to it. The truth is that the only person who ever knows the full power of temptation is the person who resists it. Jesus knew more about the power of temptation than any of us.

This petition lends itself to some deeper meditation.

I. This petition affirms the sovereignty of God.

We must not forget that all of this prayer is addressed to "Our Father which art in heaven." We begin the prayer by addressing God as the sovereign, almighty Father in the heavens. In a sense, each petition affirms this of Him in some way, but this does so in a special way.

"Lead us not into temptation." "Lead us" translates the Greek word that is commonly translated "bring us." It is usually used with reference to a person's moving or bringing something from one place to another. It probably even expresses the Hebrew idea of causing it to be brought or led. So this petition affirms that God is in a position to cause things to happen, to bring us or lead us, as it may please Him. He is affirmed to be the Sovereign One.

A. *Over circumstances.*

Since temptation can come from finding oneself in the wrong circumstance, this affirms that God has control over circumstances. It addresses Him as the One who orders the steps of His people. Do you believe that God can actually order the circumstances of your life to protect you from the allurements of evil?

B. *Over spiritual forces.*

Since temptation forces usually come from spiritual forces outside of our lives, this affirms that God has ultimate and sovereign control over all of the spiritual forces in our world. Satan and his agents do not move outside the realm of God's control. While God does not cause them to do the things that they do, He does still have them under His sovereignty. They are not God's equal in power and sovereignty.

C. *Over us.*

Since many temptations are of our own making, this petition affirms that God has sovereignty over our lives. "Lead us, bring us!" It personalizes the sovereignty of God. It is so easy to see God as having control over everything except your life. It is easy to slip into an attitude that sees all of life as being out of control. This petition affirms God as being the one in control, the Sovereign One.

II. This petition acknowledges the significance of temptation.

You may become confused about temptation from reading the Bible. At times God is presented as the source of temptations, but at other times the devil is presented as the source. Which is right? Actually, both are true. The confusion comes from the meaning of the word *temptation*. The root meaning of the word is "to try" or "to test." It came to mean also to tempt one to do something evil or sinful.

A. *Temptation as testing of character.*

Whenever the Bible speaks of God's "tempting" a person, it is always in the sense of putting one through a trial or a test. This is what He did to Abraham when He instructed him to offer Isaac as a sacrifice. The Bible says that God tempted him (Gen. 22:1). The New International Version correctly translates the word "tested." God was not tempting Abraham to do something sinful, but He was testing the depth of his commitment and the strength of his faith. Whenever God puts a man to the test, it is to give him the opportunity to prove himself. Of course, there is always the possibility of failure, but the test will not create the weakness of commitment—it will only reveal it. Just as a test given to a student does not create his ignorance, it only reveals it. All of us know that it is not uncommon for the student to blame the test for his failure, but deep inside we know better.

The Bible assures us that God never tempts anyone to do evil. He Himself cannot commit sin, nor can He tempt anyone to commit sin (James 1:13). It is always a mistake to blame God for our temptation to do something that is wrong. God is in no way responsible for the temptation.

B. *Temptation as allurement to sin.*

Whenever the word *temptation* is used in connection with sin, another besides God is responsible. Ultimately Satan himself must bear the responsibility, but obviously he will work through our own evil nature, through others, and through circumstances. It is this type of temptation that is referred to in this petition. It is a prayer that we may escape a confrontation with a temptation to sin. Only a fool flirts with temptation. There is always the possibility that he will succumb to the allurement of evil.

What can I expect if I pray this prayer? Can I expect that God will protect me from the influence of the tempter? Can I expect immunity from temptation? No! Even our Lord Himself, who surely knew how to pray this prayer, did not totally escape confrontations with temptation. We can expect that we will not be stumbling into temptation unprepared. We can expect that God's provisions to resist temptation will always be available and adequate.

III. This petition announces the surrender of life.

"Lead me not into temptation." This is a prayer of surrender. It is a personal surrender to the lordship and leadership of God in one's life. It is a renunciation of the lordship and leadership of self. Behind this expression of surrender there are two important things.

A. *The motivation to surrender.*

1. The desire to avoid sin. This petition expresses a real desire to avoid sin. The location of this petition in the prayer is significant. It follows the petition

for forgiveness. Whenever a man experiences release from guilt through forgiveness, it leaves him with a desire never to sin again. Unless this desire is present, you may question whether the person has experienced God's forgiveness. Instead of wanting to go back to the old scene of sin, the person is left with a desire to avoid sin at all cost. He wants to be through with sin forever.

2. The depth of the surrender. This control is to be complete. Just consider what will be involved in this. Where does temptation occur? It occurs in certain circumstances—so this means that you are surrendering to the Lord to guide you into whatever circumstances might please Him and keep you from sin. It occurs through certain friends—so this is a surrender to the Lord of even the right to choose your own friends. This is a request that He give you only friends who will help you avoid sin. It occurs when you go to certain places and involve yourself in certain amusements—so this is a surrender to the Lord of even your free and recreational time. He can choose the places you go and the things you do. It occurs when you read certain books or watch certain television shows—so this is a surrender to the Lord concerning the books you read and the television programs you watch. It occurs when riches or poverty come to a man—so this is a surrender to the Lord of the whole financial scene. You are ready for Him to determine how much of this world's goods you may enjoy. Sometimes it may occur with success or failure in certain ventures—so you surrender these questions to the Lord, too. Everything must be surrendered to His lordship and leadership.

Conclusion. For this to be your daily prayer, it must become the desire of your heart. You cannot pray this petition unless you consider the question of personal sin to be a serious matter. As long as you take sin lightly, this will never be your earnest prayer. It could be the beginning of a new freedom and new walk with God in your life. Try it! Your life could move upward to a new moral plane if you make this your daily prayer. —*DLL*

* * *

WEDNESDAY EVENING, SEPTEMBER 21

TITLE: Prayer and the Word of God

TEXT: "Make me understand the way of thy precepts, and I will meditate on thy wondrous works" (Ps. 119:27 RSV).

SCRIPTURE READING: Psalm 119:25–32

Introduction. Psalm 119 is an acrostic poem composed of twenty-two stanzas, each of which uses and emphasizes one of the letters of the Hebrew alphabet. It is a poem which exalts the law, the testimonies, the ways, the precepts, the statutes, the commandments, the words, and the promises of God.

One of the finest ways to pray effectively is to pray the prayers of biblical characters. We can pray the same prayers that the psalmist prays with great profit. Let us look at some of the prayers in this stanza of Psalm 119 that we might have some assistance in our prayer life.

I. "Revive me according to thy word!" (v. 25b RSV).

We hear the psalmist praying for a revival or for a renewal in his innermost being. He is discouraged and depressed. He feels as if he is down in the very dust of life. He cries out to God for a revival and a restoration of the vital energies of life.

There are times when each of us needs to pray this prayer.

II. "Make me understand the way of thy precepts" (v. 27a RSV).

The psalmist is here praying for insight into the inner meaning of the teachings of God's Holy Word.

We can discover truth by research. We can discover truth by reason and logic. But the greatest discovery of truth comes through divine revelation. The psalmist is crying out to God for inward spiritual understanding so that he will then be able to speak of all of God's wondrous works.

III. "Strengthen me according to thy word!" (v. 28b RSV).

The psalmist was aware of his weakness and his inability to do what he needed to do. He felt overwhelmed with heaviness and grief and sorrow. He stood in need of divine spiritual resources. He cried out to God for strength to face life.

A. *In the New Testament we are encouraged to be strong in the Lord and the power of His might* (Eph. 6:10). The implication is that we have no hope of overcoming evil and achieving what we need to achieve apart from the strength which comes from God.

B. *Paul found strength through Jesus Christ and was confident that he could make all adjustments in all of the things that he needed to do through faith in Jesus Christ* (Phil. 4:13).

There is not a day that goes by when we, as the children of God, do not need to say, "Amen" to this petition offered by the psalmist.

IV. "Put false ways far from me" (v. 29a RSV).

The psalmist was eager to have removed from him the ways of falsehood, the ways of untruth that would lead to the wrong kind of destination in this life and to failure as far as the next life was concerned. He felt a need to be delivered from deception, falsehood, and untruths.

This is a prayer that we need to pray so that we might be able to see through the sham of much that is presented in our world today. We need to be delivered from falsehood and deception. The psalmist was eager to enjoy the grace of living according to God's truth rather than being destroyed by falsehood.

V. "Let me not be put to shame!" (v. 31 RSV).

The psalmist had a healthy fear of failure. He did not want to experience humiliation and embarrassment. He did not want to cast reflection upon his God. He prays that he might be saved from failure.

A. *Paul warned the followers of Christ at Corinth against the danger of failure and expressed his determination that through discipline and dedication he would avoid personal disappointment and failure* (1 Cor. 9:24–27).

B. *When Paul wrote to the Roman Christians, he expressed great confidence in the power of the gospel to save*. He declared that the gospel had never disappointed him up to this point.

Conclusion. In the words of this stanza in Psalm 119 we find many petitions from the heart of the psalmist that we can and should concur with. As we read this prayerfully, we should be able to say a sincere "Amen" to each of these petitions. The psalmist has prayed our prayer for us. —*TTC*

* * *

SUNDAY MORNING, SEPTEMBER 25

TITLE: Obeying the Command of the Holy Spirit

TEXT: "And the Spirit said to Philip, 'Go up and join this chariot'" (Acts 8:29 RSV).

SCRIPTURE READING: Acts 8:26–40

HYMNS: "Rejoice, Ye Pure in Heart," Plumptre
"Guide Me, O Thou Great Jehovah," Williams
"Jesus, Savior, Pilot Me," Hopper

OFFERTORY PRAYER:

Holy Father, thank You for the blessings of the past. Thank You for the blessed privilege of being alive today and being with Your people. Thank You for letting us rejoice in Your grace and mercy. Thank You for giving to us the privilege of giving ourselves to You and to others in service. Accept our tithes and offerings as symbols of our desire to be totally at Your disposal. In Jesus' name. Amen.

Introduction. Philip, the deacon, provides us with a dramatic illustration of what it means to make a personal response to the Great Commission of the Lord Jesus Christ.

Some believe that they are obeying the Great Commission when they attend the Bible school and the worship services of their church.

Some people believe they are obeying the Great Commission when they sing in the choir.

Some believe they are obeying the Great Commission when they teach a Sunday school class.

Some believe they are obeying the Great Commission when they give a tithe of their income plus offerings.

Some believe they are obeying the Great Commission when they offer prayers for missionaries.

All of these are but partial responses to the Great Comission of our Lord.

Philip provides us with a dramatic demonstration of how we are to obey the Great Commission on a one-to-one basis in our individual, personal lives.

I. Philip was sensitive to the Holy Spirit's indwelling presence.

Many of us never respond to the Holy Spirit because we do not recognize that He is within us and that He is seeking to do the work of God in us, to us, and through us.

II. Philip was listening to the voice of the Holy Spirit.

A. *"But an angel of the Lord said to Philip, 'Rise and go toward the south'"* (Acts 8:26). The remarkable thing is that Philip arose and went (v. 27). He was obedient to the messenger of God.

B. *"And the Spirit said to Philip, 'Go up and join this chariot'"* (v. 29). The Scripture then reads that Philip ran to him. Philip received an impulse from the Holy Spirit and had the wisdom to be responsive.

III. God's love was active in this whole experience.

A. *God loves all people.*

B. *God guides His people who will obey Him to witnessing opportunities.*

C. *God furnishes interested seekers for salvation to those who will be obedient.*

D. *God gave to Philip a proper approach to share the Good News with this needy man.*

E. *God gave to Philip a message—the Good News of God's grace.*

F. *God brought about conviction of sin and need and conversion.*

G. *God won a great victory.*

Our God is the seeking God. He seeks the sinner; and when a sinner seeks God, they get together—particularly when one of God's children is listening and obedient to the Spirit.

IV. Philip had a heart surrendered to God.

A. *Philip believed that God is love and that you can trust Him without fear.*

B. *Philip had a sensitive spirit that was open to God.*

C. *Philip had his spiritual receiving set turned on.*

D. *Philip had a heart that was obedient because of love.*

E. *Philip shared the Good News.*

V. The Ethiopian official became spiritually rich!

A. *As the representative of his queen, he was*

1. Privileged
2. Powerful
3. Popular

B. *As a human being, the Ethiopian official had*

1. An empty heart
2. A hungry heart
3. A needy heart
4. An open heart

C. *The Ethiopian official responded with a believing heart and experienced happiness and joy through faith in Jesus Christ.*

Conclusion. A loving God and a needy heart got together because one of God's children was sensitive to the presence of the Holy Spirit and responsive as the Holy Spirit moved Him to witness.

What if Philip had been too busy?

What if Philip had been spiritually lazy?

What if Philip had been untrusting and consequently too fearful?

What if Philip had been spiritually dull and disobedient? God would have missed the privilege of saving a man, and a man would have missed the privilege of coming to know Jesus Christ.

May God help each of us to recognize and respond to the presence of God's precious, powerful, personal Spirit who has come to dwell within us. We will bring glory to God, and we will be the means by which the Good News will be proclaimed on a one-to-one basis to other members of our family, to our friends, and even to strangers that God sends into our lives.

If today you have not received Jesus Christ as Savior, the Holy Spirit invites you to trust Him, to receive Him, and to receive the gifts of God in the form of forgiveness and the gift of eternal life. —*TTC*

* * *

SUNDAY EVENING, SEPTEMBER 25

TITLE: Deliver Us From Evil

TEXT: "And lead us not into temptation, but deliver us from evil: For thine is the kingdom, and the power, and the glory, for ever. Amen" (Matt. 6:13).

SCRIPTURE READING: Matthew 6:1–15

Introduction. Seven is the number for completeness in the Bible. It is of special interest that the Master of prayer gave us just seven petitions in the Model Prayer. This could indicate that He felt that the seven petitions covered every need that man might bring to God.

"Deliver us from evil." This is the last of the petitions. It voices a cry that comes from the heart of the children of God as they live in this world. It is a cry expressing great urgency. Surely, it is appropriate as we assemble for worship in the midst of a troubled world. Consider with me some important implications set forth by this simple petition. There is an urgent need for us to be taking this petition to our heavenly Father daily.

I. The reality of evil.

Translators are not agreed about how this is to be translated. There has been much discussion about the proper understanding of these words. The Greek text has the definite article before "evil." How is the noun then to be translated? Is it to be translated as a neuter as in the King James Version? If so, then we would understand it to mean all of the evil things that are in the world and all of the evil things that happen to people. Or should it be translated as a masculine as in the New International Version? If so, then it is to be understood as a reference to the Evil One or Satan. Bible scholars have been divided quite evenly over the translation. While I know that some kind of choice must be made in the translation, does it really make that much difference in the interpretation? My honest feeling is that it does not. The petition is surely a cry for rescue from all evil—evil persons and evil things.

A. *The presence of evil.*

But one thing is clear. This petition does affirm the presence of evil in the world. The reality of evil in the world is one of the great issues that has occupied theologians and philosophers of all persuasions. Our Lord did not hide His face from the reality of evil in the world. He affirms the reality of an Evil One. Around the turn of this century learned men had just about excluded any idea of a supreme person of evil from their thinking. They attributed all such ideas to superstition and ignorance. But the events of the twentieth century have forced man to reconsider. How do you explain the senseless injustice and violence in our world apart from some kind of demonic influence? In some cases the students of human behavior have been ahead of the teachers of the Bible in affirming the reality of this Evil Person in the world.

B. *The experience with evil.*

This petition goes even deeper. It comes out of a life that has been personally confronted with the presence and the power of evil. This is not the prayer of a proud and arrogant man who sees himself as the captain of his own ship, the master of his own fate. It is rather the prayer of a broken man who has had his eyes opened to the nature of the world in which he lives, and has seen just how powerful evil can really be. He has beheld the shame, sorrow, and suffering that are present in the world and has been made to drink of the cup himself.

II. The responsibility for evil.

A. *God is not responsible.*

This petition clearly assigns the responsibility for evil. Who is responsible for evil in the world? Clearly God is not! If God were responsible for the evil that is in the world, then this would be a petition for God to deliver us from His own creation. While it is wonderfully true that God makes the evil in the world serve His ultimate purpose, it is a serious mistake to assign responsibility for the evil in the world to God. Whatever evil you may encounter may be used of God to perfect holiness in your life, but God does not accept ultimate responsibility for it.

B. *Satan is responsible.*

If God is not responsible, then who is? Without speculating about his origin, the Bible assigns responsibility to the Evil One for the evil that is in the world. While man shares the responsibility with him because of his joining him in Genesis 3, Satan is still presented as the great adversary of God and enemy of man. He is the ultimate source of evil. So this prayer to God is ultimately a prayer against the Evil One, Satan.

Can we lay the ultimate blame on Satan? Yes! Ultimately, he is to blame for all of the physical evil in the world. All of the famines, earthquakes, tornadoes, plagues, diseases, and the like are ultimately the responsibility of the Evil One. The world God originally created did not include these. They came only after the evil design of the Enemy prevailed over man.

The same is also true of moral evil. While man is a sinner who creates his own shame, sorrow, and sadness, Satan has an ultimate responsibility for the whole thing. Murder is his idea. Robbery is his idea. Drugs are his idea. Divorce is his idea. Rape is his idea. Adultery is his idea. All of the moral evils that beset man on every side come from the Evil One. There is a basic unity to all of the evil that confronts us in the world.

This petititon will help you keep this straight in your thinking. You will quit blaming God and your fellow-man. You will begin to lay the blame where it belongs. It belongs on the shoulders of the great master-mind of evil who forsook his God-appointed place to lead an open rebellion against the rule of God, and thereby brought evil into being.

III. The rescue from evil.

Deliver is a strong word. It means to save, to rescue, to preserve. This is a request that God will do what only God can do. It is an acknowledgment that we cannot keep or preserve ourselves from the presence, power, and person of evil. Only God can do this. But what does it include?

A. *The present rescue.*

It is a prayer that God will daily deliver us from the design that the Evil One may have upon our lives. It is a prayer that we might escape the shame and sorrow that he would impose on us through sin. It is renunciation of evil in every form and a genuine petition to be kept by God from evil in every form. This petition looks to the heavenly Father for His daily protection and intervention on our behalf. Only He can be our salvation from evil!

B. *The future rescue.*

However, it may well be that the primary thrust of this petition is future. It is a petition for the ultimate, final, complete deliverance from evil. It is a prayer for the new heaven and the new earth. It is a prayer for the final binding of Satan and the coming of the day when God shall wipe away all tears and establish a world in which there will be no more sickness, no more sorrow, and no more pain. It is a prayer for God's final act of salvation, which will be inaugurated by the second coming of our Lord Jesus Christ.

Conclusion. Have you become too content with our world as it is? Have worldly pleasures so sedated you that you no longer feel the weight of evil that is in the world? Can you sleep peacefully at night in the midst of the sickness, sin, sorrow, and suffering that is in our world? There is so much of it that it almost drives you to despair. If you are spiritually in touch with the Lord and His world, surely you must be moved to pray, "Deliver us from evil!" The need of the hour is for a company of praying saints who will pray until deliverance comes.

—*DLL*

* * *

WEDNESDAY EVENING, SEPTEMBER 28

TITLE: Amen and Amen

TEXT: "Teach me, O LORD, the way of thy statutes; and I will keep it to the end" (Ps. 119:33 RSV).

SCRIPTURE READING: Psalm 119:33–40

Introduction. *Amen* is a transliteration of the Hebrew word into both Greek and English.

"Amen" is used of God, His testimonies, and His promises as meaning "faithful."

There are cases where the people of God used "Amen" to express their assent to a law and to their willingness to submit to the penalty attached to the breach of that law (cf. Deut. 27:15; Neh. 5:13).

"Amen" is also used to express acquiescence to another's prayers (1 Kings 1:36). "Amen" is also used by some when another is offering thanks to God (1 Chron. 16:36). These verses would suggest that we need to let others help us with our prayers. That is, when someone else prays a prayer that expresses the deep desires of our heart, it is permissible and proper that we say, "Amen," either audibly or inaudibly.

There are many petitions offered up by the psalmist to which we can say "Amen and amen."

I. A prayer of agreement and affirmation (Ps. 119:33).

The psalmist was praying to God, saying, "Teach me, O LORD, the way of thy statutes; and I will keep it to the end."

Today's English Version translates this last phrase, "And I will obey them at all times." This is a prayer in which all of us should participate.

A. *To pray this prayer is to make the law of God personal.*

B. *To pray this prayer internalizes the law of God and writes it on the walls of our hearts.*

II. "Lead me in the path of thy commandments" (Ps. 119:35 RSV).

A. *The psalmist in the Great Shepherd Psalm says, "He leadeth me in the paths of righteousness for his name's sake"* (23:3b). This does not mean that God leads us in the paths of righteousness for God's sake. It means rather that He leads us in the paths that are right because the character of God is at stake. The only way that God can lead us is in paths that are right.

In this petition the psalmist is praying for divine leadership that he might walk in the right paths throughout life.

B. *Through Jeremiah God spoke and said, "Stand ye in the ways, and see, and ask for the old paths, where is the good way, and walk therein, and ye shall find rest for your souls" (6:16).*

III. "Incline my heart to thy testimonies, and not to gain!" (Ps. 119:36 RSV).

A. *Feelings of insecurity pull us toward the desire for profits in the economic world.*

B. *Greed can capture our minds and hearts, and we can become the servants of mammon.*

C. *The psalmist was praying that God would deliver him from the lure of the material and lead him to that which was eternal and permanent.* He was eager that God would help him guard his heart, because out of the heart come the issues of life. This verse has been translated, "Bend my heart to your will and not to the love of gain."

This is a prayer to which all of us should say, "Amen and amen."

IV. "Turn my eyes from looking at vanities" (Ps. 119:37 RSV).

Today's English Version translates this verse, "Keep me from paying attention to what is worthless; be good to me as you have promised." This verse has also been translated, "Keep my eyes from what is false by your word, give me life."

The writer of the Book of Ecclesiastes came to recognize that many of the things that we look upon with desire produce emptiness and despair once they are obtained. The psalmist is here praying that he might be delivered from all the pursuits and ambitions which lead to emptiness and disappointment.

All of us need to join with the psalmist in praying this prayer.

V. A prayer for deliverance from failure (Ps. 119:39).

Today's English Version translates verse 39, "Save me from the insults that I fear."

A. *A healthy fear of failure can be positive and helpful.*

B. *This verse has been translated, "Keep me from the scorn I dread, for your decrees are good."*

The psalmist is earnestly praying that God will so work in his life that he will be saved from making decisions and choosing ways that will lead to disappointment and shame.

Conclusion. These petitions are very personal. The psalmist is giving voice to a strong cry for deliverance from subtle dangers.

To his petitions we can say, "Amen and amen." —*TTC*

* * *

SUGGESTED PREACHING PROGRAM FOR THE MONTH OF OCTOBER

Sunday Mornings

On every Lord's Day the pastor should share the Good News of God's love in and through Jesus Christ. There are times when the messages should focus on nourishing the family of God and other times when the purpose should be to instruct the family of God. The suggested focus for the Sunday mornings of October is on evangelism—sharing the Good News with a sense of urgency, seeking to persuade the noncommitted and nonbelievers to put their faith in Jesus Christ. The suggested theme is "Today Is the Day of Salvation."

Sunday Evenings

"The Church Which Is His Body" is the suggested theme for a series of expository sermons based on texts from the Book of Ephesians. It is through the church that the Lord is seeking to carry on His work in the world today.

Wednesday Evenings

Continue the devotional study of the Psalms using "Amen and Amen" as the theme.

* * *

SUNDAY MORNING, OCTOBER 2

TITLE: The Holy Spirit Invites You

TEXT: **"The Spirit and the Bride say, 'Come.' And let him who hears say, 'Come.' And let him who is thirsty come, let him who desires take the water of life without price" (Rev. 22:17 RSV).**

SCRIPTURE READING: **Hebrews 3:7–11**

HYMNS: **"God, Our Father, We Adore Thee," Frazer**
"Christ Receiveth Sinful Men," Neumeister
"Softly and Tenderly," Thompson

OFFERTORY PRAYER:

Heavenly Father, thank You for offering to us the gift of eternal life through Jesus Christ. Thank You for offering to us the gift of Your living presence in the Holy Spirit. Thank You for the gift of membership in Your family through the church. Thank You for the opportunity You give to us to serve You and to minister in Your name in our world. Bless these tithes and offerings that they might be used to exalt Your name and minister to the needs of a needy world. In Jesus' name we pray. Amen.

Introduction. Man's greatest need is to know God through faith in Jesus Christ.

Because man's deepest need is spiritual, God sent His Son, Jesus Christ, to die on a cross to show His love for us and to conquer death that He might demonstrate to us the reality of eternal life.

Following this great redemptive activity accomplished by Jesus Christ, God sent His Holy Spirit into the church and into the world to invite all nonbelievers to come to Jesus Christ through faith that they might receive the gift of eternal life and become the children and servants of God.

If you are still a nonbeliever, you may be shocked to learn that the Holy Spirit of God is in the world today in order that He might invite you to become a believer in Jesus Christ.

The words of our text declare that the purpose of the church and of the Holy Spirit is to invite you to come to Jesus Christ, who is the fountain of living waters. He alone can quench the thirst of your soul.

The primary thrust of our Scripture reading urges us to listen attentively and responsively as the Holy Spirit of God speaks to our innermost being.

In the closing days of our Lord's ministry, He detailed some of the activities of the Holy Spirit who would come on the Day of Pentecost. One of the primary functions of the Holy Spirit was to bear personal and powerful testimony to the conscience of men regarding who Jesus Christ was and is and what he came to do (cf. John 14:26; 15:26; 16:7–11).

I. Listen to the Holy Spirit because of His divine Person.

The Holy Spirit is more than just an influence. The Holy Spirit is more than just a power like magnetism or electricity or gravity. The Holy Spirit is the divine Person of God. He uses various means of communicating with you.

A. *The Holy Spirit uses the Scriptures.*

B. *The Holy Spirit uses the church as a communicator.*

C. *The Holy Spirit uses individual believers as His spokesmen.*

D. *The Holy Spirit uses the events of life to interrupt your thoughts and to speak to you if you have ears to listen.*

II. Listen to the Holy Spirit because of His divine purpose for speaking.

A. *He speaks to those of you who are unsaved.* He comes to convince you that the sin of unbelief is the sin that separates a man from God (John 16:7–11). The Holy Spirit alone can convince a person of his sinfulness and of his need to cease rejecting God's love and His claims.

The Holy Spirit does not come to convict you and convince you of your unsaved and lost condition merely to make you feel negative about yourself and experience inward misery and depression. He comes to convert you from unbelief to belief and from rejection to acceptance. Only the Holy Spirit can take an x-ray of your heart and soul and reveal to you your lost condition. He does this that He might attract and persuade you to receive Jesus Christ as Lord and Savior.

B. *He speaks to those of you who are saved.* The Holy Spirit speaks words of comfort and assurance to the new convert (Rom. 8:15-16). It is the plan of the Father God to communicate the new relationship that follows faith to each believer.

The Holy Spirit comes to speak words of encouragement and to provide assistance for living the Christian life when one becomes a believer. It is not the plan of God for one to attempt to live the Christian life in human strength alone. The Holy Spirit provides the power that is needed to overcome evil and to reap the harvest of the Spirit (Gal. 5:16-23).

The Holy Spirit will also speak to the saved about the needs of those who do not yet know Christ as Savior. The Holy Spirit will seek to enlist us in His activity of trying to lead men to become believers in Christ.

III. Listen to the Holy Spirit because of His divine power.

A. *Only the Holy Spirit of God has the power to produce the miracle of the new birth in the believer* (Titus 3:3-7).

The new birth is a divine and miraculous work wrought by the Holy Spirit.

B. *The Holy Spirit has the divine power to enable us to develop a Christian disposition and character.* He begins His good work within us at the moment of conversion and will continue this work of seeking to produce within us the very character of Jesus Christ throughout our lives (Gal. 5:22-23).

C. *The Holy Spirit has been given to us to assure us of our victory over death and the grave* (2 Cor. 5:5). The indwelling gift of the Holy Spirit is God's guarantee that one day we shall have ultimate and complete victory over death and the grave.

Conclusion. Let me urge you to listen to the Holy Spirit now. He invites you to receive Jesus Christ today. Nowhere in all of God's Word do you find an encouragement to believe in Christ for the forgiveness of sin and the gift of new life *tomorrow*.

Today is the day of salvation (2 Cor. 6:2). Today is the day God wants to forgive your sins. Today is the day God wants you to become His child. Today is the day Christ wants to give you the gift of eternal life. Today is the day the peace of God can be yours.

The Holy Spirit invites you. Come to Him now while you have time and opportunity. — *TTC*

* * *

SUNDAY EVENING, OCTOBER 2

NB

TITLE: The Church—the Body of Christ

TEXT: "Now you are the body of Christ and individually members of it" (1 Cor. 12:27 RSV).

SCRIPTURE READING: 1 Corinthians 12:12-31a

Introduction. Centuries ago the psalmist said, "I will praise thee; for I am fearfully and wonderfully made" (139:14a). And this insight was ages before our modern knowledge of anatomy. We *are* "fearfully and wonderfully made." For all its wonderful advances science has no system of communication to compare with the nervous system of the human body; it has developed no pump to compare with the human heart; it can devise no receiving set like the ear; and it has developed no mechanical device that can exactly reproduce the human voice.

But for all that, the human body is a marvelous example of unity in diversity. There are dozens of organs performing dozens of different functions, yet in such harmony that we must make a deliberate effort to think of the human body in any way except as a unity.

In the church at Corinth there had been jealousy, envy, and strife among the members. Some had gifts that the others did not have and, as a result, they thought of themselves more highly than they should have. This provoked the less gifted to jealousy. The result was discord and strife among the members. In substance Paul is saying to them, "You do not realize your relationship to one another and to Christ. You are joined to one another and dependent upon one another just as the members of the body are joined to one another and dependent upon one another. You are the physical expression and instrument of Christ in this world just as the body is the physical expression and instrument of the mind."

"You are the body of Christ and individually members of it" (1 Cor. 12:27 RSV). Several practical suggestions about the church are called out by this text.

I. Each member of the church is different from every other member.

This is the suggestion of diversity in unity—one body composed of many different members, each of which is different from the other. The church is neither a dead mass of similar particles like a heap of sand, nor a living swarm of antagonistic individuals like a cage of wild beasts. It has the unity of a living organism, the unity of a living body. No two parts are alike. All discharge different functions for the good of the whole. The unity of the church is not that of inorganic nature, a monotonous collection of similars like a pile of bricks. It is the oneness of a living organism, no member of which exercises the same function as another. Some inescapable, practical implications follow:

A. *Every member of Christ's church has some place of service cut out for him.*

Sometimes we wonder about the function of an appendix or tonsils, but, all in all, there are no useless members or organs of the body. They each have a function to perform, and unless they do, the whole body suffers. No two members of the church have equal abilities. Some have great gifts. Others are not gifted at all. But every member has a function to perform for the common good. Under the leadership of the Spirit it is his privilege and duty to discover what that place is and to fill it.

B. *Every member of Christ's church must fill his own place, perform his own function in the church.*

As Paul says, "And the eye cannot say to the hand, I have no need of thee: or again the head to the feet, I have no need of you. Nay, much rather, those members of the body which seem to be more feeble are necessary" (vv. 21-22 ASV).

Every pastor has had members of his church say to him, "All I can do is just go to church and sit there." The majority of those who say this could do more if they would. But even so, granting that this is all a member can do, he needs to do that! If every resident member of every church would only fill his place at every service, what a difference it would make!

C. *No place of service is so low as to be despised or looked down upon, and no place is so high that it justifies conceit on the part of the one filling it.*

Some members at Corinth were discouraged. Their attitude was: "We don't amount to much in the church." Paul says to them, "If the foot shall say, Because I am not the hand, I am not of the body; it is not therefore not of the body" (v. 15 ASV). Some at Corinth had too high an estimate of their own worth. To them Paul says, "The eye cannot say to the hand, I have no need of thee" (v. 21a ASV). To the Romans Paul is even more specific, "For I say, through the grace that was given me, to every man that is among you, not to think of himself more highly than he ought to think; but so to think as to think soberly, according as God hath dealt to each man a measure of faith'' (12:3 ASV).

II. Each member of the church is to be devoted to the best interests of every other member.

This is the suggestion of devotion to the common good. Someone has said, "In brute creation it is the stomach that rules the world." Selfishness rules. The law of the jungle is "Every man for himself and the devil take the hindmost." But in Christ's church the ultimate aim is the well-being of one's fellow members and therefore of the whole church. Since the church is a living organism, each member is to be devoted to the highest good of every other member.

Paul tells these Corinthians, ". . . the members should have the same care one for another" (1 Cor. 12:25b ASV). He gives two reasons for this:

A. *"And whether one member suffereth, all the members suffer with it"* (v. 26a ASV).

When one member is the victim of half-truths or untruths, when any member is the prey of cheap gossip, all the church is the loser. When one member falls into sin, all suffer. Sinning on the part of one member of the church is like putting poison in the public reservoir. Sooner or later all the members are the worse for it.

B. *When "one member is honored, all the members rejoice with it"* (v. 26b ASV).

Since the church is a body, what is for the good of one is for the good of all. Paul urges the Romans, "In love of the brethren be tenderly affectioned one to another; in honor preferring one another" (12:10 ASV). The members of a church are to be devoted to one another's good to the building up of the body in love.

If only we followed that ideal—if only we were truly concerned about our brother's welfare—how different things would be in our churches.

III. Each member of the church is dependent upon every other member.

This is the suggestion of mutual dependence. In the human body the whole body is dependent upon the functioning of each organ. When one organ is diseased and unable to perform its function properly, the whole body is sick. The proper use of the hands and feet is dependent upon the health of the nervous system. The welfare of the nervous system is dependent upon proper circulation. If the kidneys become diseased, the heart may be affected. No part of the body is independent of any other part.

In like manner, no member of the church is independent of any other member in the worship and service of Christ. "A single man," says Poor Richard, "is an incomplete animal. He resembles the odd half of a pair of scissors." So it is in the church. No member is the whole of himself; his fellow members complete him. If the church is to go forward, if the church is to grow, every member must fill his place and perform his function because every other member is dependent upon him for it.

Conclusion. Consider a sober question: What is the function of the whole body, each member performing his individual part? "Now you are the body of Christ," our text says. What the physical body is to the mind and soul, the church is to Christ—the physical instrument by which He works His will in the world.

— *WTH*

WEDNESDAY EVENING, OCTOBER 5

TITLE: Prayer and the Promises of God

TEXT: "Let thy steadfast love come to me, O LORD, thy salvation according to thy promise" (Ps. 119:41 RSV).

SCRIPTURE READING: Psalm 119:41-48

Introduction. Again we look at some of the prayers prayed by the psalmist. We would let his prayers become our prayers. As we read these prayers from Holy Scripture, it is entirely appropriate that we say, "Amen," to his prayers, and thus we make them personal.

We should base our prayers on the promises of God as did Abraham, Moses, and Jeremiah.

We should listen to the promises of our Lord and claim these promises in prayer.

As we look at these petitions, let us sincerely say, "Amen," from our hearts.

I. A prayer for the exertion of God's love (119:41).

The King James Version translates this verse, "Let thy mercies come also unto me, O LORD, even thy salvation, according to thy word."

The Revised Standard Version translates it, "Let thy steadfast love come to me, O LORD, thy salvation according to thy promise."

The New International Version translates it, "May your unfailing love come to me, O LORD."

Here the psalmist is asking God to demonstrate His love for him.

Perhaps we ought to pray that the Lord will open our eyes and help us to see the continuous exertions of His love toward us.

II. A prayer for adequate speech at all times (v. 43).

Often we find ourselves speechless when we have opportunity to witness or to help someone. Later we say to ourselves, "Well, why didn't I think of it at the time?" The psalmist had similar experiences.

A. *He speaks of those who taunt him because of his faith in the Word of God* (v. 42). The people of God have had enemies who would taunt them and criticize them through the years.

B. *There are those who would intimidate us* (v. 46). There are some people to whom we are afraid to speak as we ought. The psalmist prays that God will give him adequate speech.

The King James Version translates verse 43, "And take not the word of truth utterly out of my mouth; for I have hoped in thy judgments."

The New International Version translates it, "Do not snatch the word of truth from my mouth, for I have put my hope in your laws."

Today's English Version puts it in the positive: "Enable me to speak the true message at all times, because my hope is in your judgments."

Let us pray that God will help us to always speak for Him as He would have us do.

III. Prayers of affirmation.

A. *"I will always obey your law"* (v. 44 TEV).

B. *"I will live in complete freedom, because I have tried to obey your rules"* (v. 45 TEV). The New International Version translates the result of obeying God's law as, "I will walk about in freedom."

C. *"I will also speak of thy testimonies before kings"* (v. 46 RSV). "I will announce your commands to kings, and I will not be ashamed" (TEV).

D. *Expressions of love and praise:* "I find pleasure in obeying your commandments, because I love them" (v. 47 TEV); and "I respect and love your commandments; I will meditate on your instructions" (v. 48 TEV).

Conclusion. In each of these great affirmations, we should be able to unite with the psalmist in petition to God. Let us join him in prayer and say from our hearts, "Amen and Amen." —*TTC*

* * *

SUNDAY MORNING, OCTOBER 9

TITLE: The Lostness of the Lost Man

TEXT: "For the Son of man came to seek and to save the lost" (Luke 19:10 RSV).

SCRIPTURE READING: Luke 15:1-7

HYMNS: "Amazing Grace," Newton
"He Included Me," Oatman
"The Way of the Cross Leads Home," Pounds

OFFERTORY PRAYER:

Holy Father, we pray today that You would open our eyes and help us to see more completely the evidences of Your grace to us. Help us to accept life as a gift. Help us to recognize that every day is a gift from You. Help us to accept this hour of worship as a divine appointment. Give to us the faith that we need to experience the living presence of the Christ in this service. As we come now to bring tithes and offerings, help us to place them in the hands of Him who gave Himself for us on a cross. In His precious name we pray. Amen.

Introduction. It is the clear message of the New Testament that God so loved a lost and needy world that He gave His Son Jesus Christ to die on a cross that the lost world might be saved (John 3:16).

It is clear on every page of the four Gospels that Jesus Christ was concerned about the lostness of lost people; he wanted to rescue and restore them to the Father.

The lostness of lost men was such a pressing burden upon the heart of the apostle Paul that it caused him to become a spiritual "workaholic" for God, seeking to evangelize the world (Rom. 10:1).

Why is it that the modern-day Christian has no sense of urgency to help save lost men from the fate that follows a life of no faith in Jesus Christ? Have we accepted a materialistic way of life that eliminates the spiritual?

Is it possible that we have let the devil do to us what he has done to the minds of nonbelievers so that they would not become the children of God (2 Cor.

4:4)? Surely if Satan can blind our minds to the lostness of lost men, we will not urgently press upon them the claims of Christ or point out to them their need to trust Him as Savior.

Let's consider some of the losses that the lost man experiences because he is lost from and to God in unbelief.

I. The lost man loses the very life of God.

When one becomes a believer, he receives in the miracle of the new birth the very life of God. He receives eternal life, which is more qualitative than quantitative. Jesus says, "I give them eternal life, and they shall never perish, and no one shall snatch them out of my hand" (John 10:28 RSV). He who spends his life in unbelief loses the very life of God.

II. The lost man loses the nature of God.

The miracle of the new birth brings with it the very nature and character of God in embryonic form. Through faith we become partakers of divine nature (2 Peter 1:4). In the new birth we become the children of God (1 John 3:1-2). He who rejects Jesus Christ as Lord, or he who neglects to receive Jesus Christ as Savior, loses the privilege of receiving this nature of God.

III. The lost man loses the presence of God.

The disciples were greatly strengthened and blessed by the presence of Jesus Christ during His earthly ministry. He encouraged them with the promise of His abiding presence as they would seek to carry out the Great Commission (Matt. 28:20). He does this by means of His own indwelling presence in the person of the Holy Spirit (John 14:16-18).

IV. The lost man loses the guidance of God.

Isaiah described the nonbeliever as a sheep who has gone astray, having turned to his own way (Isa. 53:6). He urges the nonbeliever to seek God while He may be found and to return to Him so that he might obtain pardon and mercy (55:6-7).

The psalmist, speaking from experience and out of a heart of great faith, speaks of the guidance of God: "He leadeth me in the paths of righteousness for his name's sake." God is pictured as a Shepherd who leads His sheep along the paths of life that lead to abundant living in the here and now.

Through the Holy Spirit God wants to guide us and give us directions throughout life.

V. The lost man loses the comfort of God.

Sooner or later we all experience the pain of separation from those near and dear to us through death. It is possible to be comforted by the precious promises of God which are found throughout the Scriptures. Only those who are of faith can really claim these precious promises of God concerning the house not made with hands, eternal in the heavens. Paul speaks of the grief of those who have no hope (1 Thess. 4:13). No doubt he is referring to those who have either rejected Christ or neglected to trust Him. One loses this comfort when he neglects Christ.

VI. The lost person loses the privilege of going to the Father's home at the end of the way.

Heaven is being prepared for those who receive and believe in Jesus Christ as Lord and Savior (John 14:1-6).

It is not the will of the Father God that any should perish but that all should repent and receive the gift of forgiveness and eternal life (2 Peter 3:8-9).

The losses which the nonbeliever experiences in this life are too numerous to list. He who shuts Jesus Christ out of his life robs himself and impoverishes himself throughout eternity.

God the Father loves you but will not compel you to return to Him. Jesus Christ loved you so much that He went to a cross and died there for you. He was so powerful that He conquered death and the grave. He is so gracious that He offers to you forgiveness that is full and free forever.

Conclusion. Today is the day when you should turn from a life without faith and ask Jesus Christ to forgive your sins and to receive you into the family of God. You have already lost much. Don't take a chance with losing your soul forever. He waits for you today. Come to Him now. — *TTC*

* * *

NB

SUNDAY EVENING, OCTOBER 9

TITLE: Walking Worthily As a Church Member

TEXT: "I therefore, the prisoner in the Lord, beseech you to walk worthily of the calling wherewith ye were called" (Eph. 4:1 ASV).

SCRIPTURE READING: Ephesians 4:1-6

Introduction. *Walking* is often used in the Bible as a figure of speech to describe a certain manner of life. This is true of the seven passages where it is used in the Epistle to the Ephesians. In these Paul is both describing and contrasting the walk of the believer and the unbeliever.

In chapters 1–3 of Ephesians, Paul describes the height and depth, the glory and wonder of the Christian calling. It is a glorious privilege to be a Christian. In chapters 4–6, he urges these Christians to walk worthily of such a privilege. Paul is urgent: "I therefore, the prisoner in the Lord, beseech you to walk worthily of the calling wherewith ye were called" (4:1 ASV). Paul is saying, "You are members of *His* church. You are representatives of Christ in this world. Let your manner of life be such that it will not be a reproach to your master. 'Walk worthily of the calling wherewith ye were called.'"

Three things about this worthy walk, all hinging on our text, are suggested in Ephesians.

I. The manner of the worthy walk.

Paul says, ". . . with all lowliness and meekness, with longsuffering, forbearing one another in love; giving diligence to keep the unity of the Spirit in the bond of peace" (4:2-3 ASV). Let us measure ourselves by these two verses of Scripture. How far short we fall!

A. *First, he says, "with all lowliness and meekness."*

More exactly, this reads, "with all modesty and humility of spirit." We need these qualities of spirit. The weeds of pharisaism spring up so quickly in our hearts. How easily we feel ourselves to be the spiritual superior of our brother, but we are not to do so. This is not the worthy walk.

B. *Again, he says, "with longsuffering."*

Freely rendered, this reads, "enduring with unruffled temper." Sometimes we hear a person say, "I can endure what they say about me if it's true; but if it's not, I just can't stand it." That is not in imitation of Christ. That is not His spirit. Peter tells us of our Lord, "Who did no sin, neither was guile found in his mouth: who, when he was reviled, reviled not again; when he suffered, he threatened not" (1 Peter 2:22-23). James tells us, "Let every man be swift to hear, slow to speak, slow to wrath" (1:19b). How often we turn these around.

"Endure with unruffled temper." What a difference it would make if we did. The whole point is that we ought not to be so easily offended. We are supposed to be Christians who are growing up to be men and women in Christ.

C. *Again Paul says, "forbearing one another in love."*

Freely rendered, he is saying, "Putting up with one another in a spirit of love." But what if some brother in the church can't "endure with unruffled temper"? Paul says, "Put up with that brother. Bear with him." As long as people are human, there will be a need for Christian forbearance. Any pastor will tell you how many times members of his church call for all the forbearance he can command; and surely the opposite is true. Why are we short on Christian forbearance? Perhaps it is because we are short on Christian love.

In our homes this is true. Ask any man about his wife, or any wife about her husband. Our patience wears thin. But most of the time we do forbear one another in love in our homes. How do we do it? Why? Because we love one another. In like manner we are to love one another as members of Christ's church.

D. *Still again, Paul says, "giving diligence to keep the unity of the Spirit in the bond of peace."*

No member of any church is to do or say anything to mar or destroy the fellowship of the church. To be guilty of such a thing is a grievous sin with which few can compare; and the penalty is terrible (1 Cor. 3:17).

But this is not a negative command. It is positive, something we are to do. We are to work diligently at the job of keeping "the unity of the Spirit in the bond of peace."

II. The direction of the worthy walk.

We do not become worthy, mature Christians in a moment. We do not grow "unto a fullgrown man, unto the measure of the stature of the fulness of Christ" (Eph. 4:13b ASV) in the twinkling of an eye. We must walk in that direction.

A. *We must walk in the direction that leads out of death into life.*

"And you did he make alive," Paul says in the second chapter of this epistle, "when ye were dead through your trespasses and sins" (v. 1 ASV). A Christian is a person who is now alive to God.

There are thousands in the world who are alive to worldly ambitions, pleasures, business, politics, and to all of the world's interests and demands; but they are dead toward God, "dead in trespasses and sins." Every Christian can remember when he had no interest in the things of the Spirit because he was dead to them. But if we are walking in the direction that leads out of death into life, we ought to be growing away from the fleshpots of the world and into the things of Christ. John tells us that we cannot love things that are at opposite poles (1 John 2:15). We cannot walk in two directions at the same time.

B. *We must walk in the direction that leads from sin to holiness.*

Also in Ephesians 4 Paul says, "This I say therefore, and testify in the Lord, that ye no longer walk as the Gentiles also walk, in the vanity of their mind" (v. 17 ASV). Paul describes the Gentile walk in the verses that follow (vv. 18-19). "That is the way you were," Paul is saying, "but there is to be a difference now. 'Ye did not so learn Christ' " (v. 20). It is tragic to see those who profess to be Christians but in whose lives you can tell no difference. They go to the same places, do the same things, desire the same things; and apparently they are the same.

If we are walking in the direction that leads from sin to holiness, we ought to reach the point in our pilgrimage that we no longer relish our old sins, but rather the things of God.

C. *We must walk in the direction that leads from darkness to light.*

In the fifth chapter of Ephesians Paul says, "Ye were once darkness, but are now light in the Lord: walk as children of light" (v. 8 ASV). What a powerful figure! Christ is the Light of the World (John 8:12), and we are to walk toward Him.

Two people walking in opposite directions may be at the same spot for just an instance, but their destinations are different. If we walk toward the darkness of sin, the darkness grows darker and darker. The opposite is also true. "If we walk in the light, as he is in the light, we have fellowship one with another, and the blood of Jesus his Son cleanseth us from all sin" (1 John 1:7).

III. The results of the worthy walk.

A. *There is the result of good works.*

In Ephesians 2 Paul says, "For we are his workmanship, created in Christ Jesus for good works, which God afore prepared that we should walk in them" (v. 10 ASV). Good works are the crown, the result, the proof, the test, the product of a Christian life; but they do not produce it.

B. *There is the result of growth in God's love.*

Paul says in the fifth chapter of Ephesians, "Be ye therefore imitators of God, as beloved children; and walk in love, even as Christ also loved you, and gave himself up for us" (vv. 1-2 ASV). "Walk in love." That is what we need to do. Walk in the love of God, realizing more and more the constraining power of the greatest force in the world (2 Cor. 5:14a).

C. *There is the result of maturity as a Christian.*

In one of the great verses in Ephesians Paul says, "Till we all attain unto the unity of the faith, and of the knowledge of the Son of God, unto a fullgrown man, unto the measure of the stature of the fullness of Christ" (4:13 ASV). That is the goal of it all, the destination of the Christian walk. He goes on to say, "that we may be no longer children, tossed to and fro and carried about with every wind of doctrine, by the sleight of men, in craftiness, after the wiles of error; but speaking truth in love, may grow up in all things unto him, who is the head, even Christ" (4:14-15 ASV).

Conclusion. As we apply this injunction of Paul to our lives, there is both a caution and an injunction. The caution is this: Let no man sit in judgment upon his brother. Let no man attempt to judge whether someone else is walking worthily or not. The injunction is this: Let every man ask himself, "Am I walking worthily or unworthily of the calling with which I was called?" — *WTH*

WEDNESDAY EVENING, OCTOBER 12

TITLE: The Prayers of the Psalmist

TEXT: "Thou art my portion, O LORD: I have said that I would keep thy words" (Ps. 119:57).

SCRIPTURE READING: Psalm 119:57–64

Introduction. "Amen and Amen" is the theme for this series of studies of Psalm 119, as we look at some of the great prayers uttered by the psalmist.

I. Prayer and positive self-esteem.

The psalmist rejoiced as he took a spiritual inventory and recognized that God was his greatest and dearest possession. The Revised Standard Version of the Bible says, "The LORD is my portion, " while the King James Version is more personal and says, "Thou art my portion." Today's English Version translates it, "You are all I want, Lord." As the psalmist talked to God, recognizing that he belonged to God and that God was committed to him, he was spiritually enriched and felt better about himself.

II. Prayer and sincerity.

"I entreated thy favour with my whole heart (v. 58a). Today's English Version translates it, "I ask you with all my heart; have mercy on me." Faith and sincerity are essential if we would pray effectively.

III. Prayer and God's promises.

"Be merciful unto me according to thy word" was the petition offered by the heart of the psalmist (v. 58b). The RSV translates it, "Be gracious to me according to thy promise." The psalmist was in the habit of clinging to and claiming the promises of God when he prayed. This is a habit that we should form.

IV. Prayer and repentance (v. 59).

Repentance is not just the beginning point of the life of faith and discipleship. The life of faith is to be characterized by continuous repentance. The psalmist says it in beautiful words: "I thought on my ways, and turned my feet unto thy testimonies" (KJV). The New International Version translates this, "I have considered my ways and have turned my steps to your statutes." A French translator puts it this way: "I have pondered over my ways and returned to your will."

Each time we pray, we are to search our hearts and let God help us so that we might turn from evil.

V. Prayer and praise to God (v. 62).

Most of us think of thanking God and praising Him when prosperity comes. Some of us think of praising and thanking Him when we go to church. In this verse the psalmist tells us that midnight is a good time to arise and give thanks to the Lord because of all of His righteous judgments.

The psalmist suggests that when we have difficulty getting to sleep, it might be wise to thank God for the many blessings He has bestowed upon us and praise Him for His goodness to us. This might help us to relax and get a better night's sleep.

VI. Prayer and the recognition of God's love.

The psalmist was rejoicing over the fact that the earth was full of God's mercy and steadfast love. He was rejoicing over the fact that God's love was a never-failing, never-ending love. This is a truth that all of us need to recognize and respond to positively.

The closing line in this stanza of this great acrostic poem closes with words of petition: "Teach me thy statutes." To these prayers of the psalmist, let each of us say, "Amen and Amen." — *TTC*

* * *

SUNDAY MORNING, OCTOBER 16

TITLE: Harvest Time

TEXT: "Do not be deceived; God is not mocked, for whatever a man sows, that he will also reap" (Gal. 6:7 RSV).

SCRIPTURE READING: Galatians 6:7-10

HYMNS: "The Kingdom Is Coming," Slade
"Must I Go, and Empty-Handed," Luther
"To the Work," Crosby

OFFERTORY PRAYER:

Precious Father, You have invited us to come to Your house that we might worship You in Spirit and in truth. We thank You for the presence of Your children as we come to bow before You in gratitude and praise. We rejoice in Your kindness to us. We thank You for Your blessings to us. We come now, thanking You for the privilege of letting us share in Your kingdom's work through tithes and offerings. Bless these gifts to the end that Your kingdom might come into the hearts and lives of the people in this community and to the ends of the earth. We pray in Jesus' name. Amen.

Introduction. Our text declares in definite terms that while we may not be farmers, all of us face a harvest in the future.

The apostle Paul paints a picture of life as an opportunity to plant in one of two fields:

1. We all have the opportunity to do our planting in the realm of our fleshly nature (cf. 1 John 2:15-16).

2. We all have the opportunity to plant in the realm of our spiritual nature (cf. v. 17).

Paul pictures life as an opportunity to reap a harvest.

1. We will reap a harvest in the area of our fleshly nature if that has been the area in which we have done our planting (Gal. 5:16-17).

2. We can reap a harvest in the realm of the Spirit if we have been sowing to the Spirit (vv. 22-23). It is highly possible that many of us have not interpreted the words of our text as fully and completely as we should have. The apostle Paul is not speaking primarily to nonbelievers in this text. He is warning believers against the peril of living only in the dimension of their earthly and fleshly nature. Many of us may be sowing only in the realm of the flesh and may be totally neglecting the Spirit.

The words of our text should speak loudly, both to the unsaved person who sows only in the realm of the flesh and to the saved who faces the peril of neglecting the Spirit while sowing to his fleshly nature.

I. We harvest exactly what we plant.

This is both a law of nature and a law of God. When you sow wheat, you do not reap oats. When you plant cotton, you do not reap turnips. When you plant beans, you do not reap popcorn. When you plant potatoes, you do not reap pumpkins.

If you have neglected or rejected Jesus Christ as Lord and Savior, you are sowing in the realm of your flesh. If you have received Jesus Christ as Savior, it is still possible that you are neglecting to sow in the Spirit as you could and should.

II. We reap the harvest where we plant.

A. *If your life is spent sowing to your fleshly nature, you shall reap a harvest only in the realm of the flesh.*

B. *If you recognize and respond to the spiritual, you can reap a harvest in the realm of the Spirit.* Many of you have recognized that you are something more than intelligent animals. You have recognized that you are made in the image and likeness of God and that you have the potential for fellowship with God. You can be in partnership with God. To the degree that you cultivate this part of your life you will reap a harvest in the realm of the Spirit.

III. We harvest more than we plant.

It is interesting to see how many tomatoes grow on one tomato vine, which was produced by a single tomato seed. It is interesting to see how many grains of wheat are produced by a single grain. It is interesting to see how many grains of corn are on an ear of corn produced by one grain of corn.

In the realm of the flesh, you reap more than you sow.

In the realm of the Spirit, you reap more than you sow.

If you want to reap an abundant harvest, then plant many seeds in the realm of the Spirit.

IV. We harvest later than when we plant.

No farmer expects to reap a harvest the same day he plants his seed. The harvest comes later. There are some seeds that produce fruit in a matter of six weeks, like radishes and lettuce. There are other seeds that produce a harvest which takes years to mature.

We can reap the harvest of the flesh as well as the Spirit during our lifetime. Many of the fruits come to us here and now.

We can also reap the harvest of the Spirit in the life beyond. What we are and do lives on and bears fruit after our lips have become silent and our hands stilled by death. God rewards His children for the total impact of their lives; and, consequently, it is possible to sow seeds that will produce fruits after our earthly life is over.

Conclusion. Harvest time is coming. What will the harvest be? Are you sowing only to your flesh? If so, you need to turn from the life of no faith and the life of selfishness which leads to destruction. You need to come to God through faith in Jesus Christ and begin to live as God meant for you to live.

If you have already received Jesus Christ as Savior, you would be wise to cooperate fully with God's Holy Spirit as He seeks to work the work of God within you.

There is a harvest day coming, and the harvest will be determined by the sowing that is done in the present. —*TTC*

* * *

SUNDAY EVENING, OCTOBER 16

TITLE: The Goal of the Church

TEXT: **"Till we all attain unto the unity of the faith, and of the knowledge of the Son of God, unto a fullgrown man, unto the measure of the stature of the fulness of Christ" (Eph. 4:13 ASV).**

SCRIPTURE READING: **Ephesians 4:7–16**

Introduction. The total impression of this passage is that Christ has a goal, a supreme standard for His church, and that goal is so high, so exalted that it taxes the imagination to comprehend it. Nonetheless, here and now, in the body of this flesh we are to strive to attain it.

Specifically, this passage leaves three impressions upon the mind and heart: (1) Christ has given us the *grace* whereby we may reach the goal. (2) The *means of growth* for reaching the goal are at hand. (3) We must *not stop nor be satisfied* short of the goal, no matter how high the standard nor how great the difficulties in the way.

The first impression then is *grace*.

I. Grace for reaching the goal Christ has for His church.

We must never take our eyes away from the grace of God. We are always to remember that we are not Christians because we deserve to be. We have not been brought "out of death into life" (1 John 3:14b) because of any merit of our own. The whole Christian transaction, whereby we cease to live unto sin and begin to live unto God, is all of grace—God's grace.

Two things strike us about this grace, this free gift of Christ toward those who are His own.

A. *First, there is its impartiality* (Eph. 4:7).

"But unto each one of us was the grace given"—not to just a few out of the church, not just to the pastor or the leaders, "but unto each one of us. . . ." Although "according to the measure of the gift of Christ," the capacity of one member might exceed that of another, no member of His church is left completely dispossessed. His gifts are measured not by any favoritism on God's part, for His love is everywhere and toward all the same. God's grace is impartial.

B. *But second, there is its individuality* (v. 11).

God's gifts are specifically fitted to the capacity of each individual to receive them. It follows, therefore, that each person in the church has a task cut out for him "according to the measure of the gift of Christ" in equipping him to do that task. Paul says, "And he gave some to be apostles; and some, prophets; and some, evangelists; and some, pastors and teachers" (v. 11 ASV). And this is not a complete list.

That Christ's churches are not challenging our sin-sodden society and moving this needy world toward God is not His fault. He has given His people the grace to move toward the goal of "the measure of the stature of Christ."

The second impression is *growth*.

II. Growth toward the goal Christ has for His church.

Paul says in this passage that we "may grow up in all things into him, who is the head, even Christ" (v. 15b ASV). Paul calls some in the church at Corinth who had not grown "babes in Christ" (1 Cor. 3:1b). He was saying to them, "You haven't grown a bit as Christians since the day you were converted. You are baby Christians, wholly immature."

How may Christian growth be attained? What are the means? Paul gives several suggestions.

A. *We grow by stability of Christian convictions* (Eph. 4:14).

In typical fashion Paul mixes his metaphors here, using first the unstable nature of the child and then an unanchored ship driven about in a turbulent sea to describe their instability.

Instability of Christian convictions is one sure sign of immaturity of Christian character, while stability is a sure means of growth. There is such a thing as Christian certitude—as "the rock of ages" (Isa. 26:4) for our feet; as a standard in religion, God's Word; as an anchor and stay for our faith. Apart from certainty of faith and stability of convictions we don't grow very much.

B. *We grow by sincerity of Christian love* (Eph. 4:15a).

"But speaking truth in love" (ASV). The marginal reading has it, "But dealing truly in love." The problem is we have no verb for truth in English, while the Greek does. Literally Paul says, "But truthing in love." The import of his words is that our manner of life is to be sincere and true, thinking truly, speaking truly, dealing truly, and all in a spirit of genuine love, without diversions to divide our allegiance, without hypocrisy to deny our witness, without divisions to hinder our purpose in Him. "Truthing" in love—love for Christ, for one another, for those who are lost.

C. *We grow by the solidarity of the Christian community* (Eph. 4:15b-16).

Again Paul uses the figure of the human body, "from whom all the body fitly framed and knit together through that which every joint supplieth" (v. 16). All the members of the church are knit and joined together. Every member is joined to every other member. What is for the good of one is for the good of all, and what causes the hurt of one is for the injury of all. Where there is not solidarity of purpose and unity of spirit in the church there cannot be growth.

The third impression is *greatness*.

III. The greatness of the goal Christ has for His church.

How great and how high is it? Heed how Paul takes us step by step to the top. After naming the gifts that Christ through grace gives to individuals in the church (v. 11), he tells why:

A. *"For the perfecting of the saints"* (v. 12a).

The word translated *perfecting* means "mending," the same word that is used where we are told of fishermen "mending their nets." Where members of the church may be quick-tempered, gossips, busybodies, and empty-headed, Paul calls us to "mend these things." Why?

B. *"Unto the work of ministering, unto the building up of the body of Christ"* (v. 12b).

This is to the end that Christ might have a fit and usable instrument through which He can nurture His saints, grow His children, and save the lost.

C. *He goes on, "Till we all attain"* (v. 13a).

Christ's ideal for His church is not for just a few choice souls who excell, not for just a few who reach the top but for every member of His church, all of His own.

D. *But Paul moves higher yet, "Till we all attain unto the unity of the faith, and of the knowledge of the Son of God, unto a fullgrown man"* (v. 13a).

Paul is saying, "Till we all attain to His standard of unity and maturity, full grown and united. No differences of opinion in the Lord, no divergences of conviction, no divisions of spirit." We say, "Surely that is the top! We could come no nearer to perfection than that." But not yet! The goal is one step higher. Listen to the grand and soaring height of the goal:

E. *"Unto the measure of the stature of the fulness of Christ"* (v. 13b).

Man can move no nearer God's likeness than that. Thinking like Christ in our minds, loving like Christ in our hearts, resembling Christ in our lives, giving ourselves to the purposes of God as He gave Himself, reminding men of God because we are fashioned in the likeness of His Son.

Conclusion. Do we see the point of this great passage? Paul lays tremendous emphasis upon the church, the body of believers, not on its size but on its soul quality. He had a burning desire to win souls, but he believed with all his heart that exalted Christian character within the church was the surest means of doing this.

This comes home to us, and we cannot avoid it. We emphasize quantity but not quality. We glory in reports but we do not demand repentance. We have width and breadth but neither height nor depth. Our churches grow in size but our members do not grow spiritually. It is useless to add members who do not grow in Christ. We are cursed with a low ideal. We are plagued with an unworthy contentment. We are satisfied far short of the goal. Let us pray over this passage until the blaze kindles in our hearts. — *WTH*

* * *

WEDNESDAY EVENING, OCTOBER 19

TITLE: The Prayer of a Depressed Saint

TEXT: "How long, O LORD? Wilt thou forget me for ever? How long wilt thou hide thy face from me?" (Ps. 13:1 RSV).

SCRIPTURE READING: Psalm 13:1-6

Introduction. The Psalms present to us a record of the life of God's people in all of its dimensions. In the Psalms we find records of high worship experiences in which praise is being offered to God. We find records of sorrow and grief. We find records of perplexing questions. We find expressions of faith. But we also find expressions of despair.

Psalm 13 presents to us the prayer of a man in deep depression.

Today we know that depression may be the result of many different factors. Some have a tendency toward depression because of heredity. Others experience deep depression because of a chemical imbalance. One may go into depression because of mistreatment by someone near and dear to him. One may also experience depression because of a negative way of thinking. Depression is often the result of weariness and physical collapse. Some experience deep depression because of their utter helplessness. Depression often accompanies illness. Others experience depression as death approaches. All of us experience some depression because of impatience. Divine chastisement is also a cause for depression. Maybe this was the reason David was so depressed and gave voice to this psalm.

I. A prayer during a time of depression.

A. *Have you ever prayed to God when it seemed as if He had forgotten you* (13:1a)? Does God really forget His children?

B. *Have you ever prayed when it seemed as if God had turned His face away from you* (13:1b)?

C. *The psalmist was depressed by the length of the suffering he was experiencing in his soul* (13:2a).

D. *The psalmist was so depressed that he experienced sorrow in his heart throughout the day* (13:2b).

E. *The psalmist was depressed because of the victory of his enemy over him* (13:2c). Many have experienced depression because of the victory of Satan over them.

II. A cry for help while in a state of depression (vv. 3-4).

It is exceedingly difficult to pray effectively when one is in the depths of despair, suffering the pains of depression. In such a time one needs to pray a prayer of confession, asking for cleansing; and yet it is difficult to pray this kind of a prayer if one is experiencing certain forms of depression.

The psalmist continued to pray even in the midst of his despair. In times like these we need to study God's Word and recognize our relationship to Him and continue to come before Him as needy children (Heb. 4:16).

III. The faith of the psalmist in depression (Ps. 13:5-6).

A. *The psalmist was able to continue to trust in the steadfast love of God* (13:5a). Many times a person suffering depression finds it impossible to believe that God continues to love him or her.

B. *The psalmist had faith to believe that he would yet rejoice in the great salvation of God* (13:5b). Perhaps the psalmist had this assurance because he believed that God would forgive him and cleanse him.

C. *The psalmist decided to sing unto the Lord because he was confident that God would deal bountifully and graciously with him* (13:6).

Conclusion. Depression in one form or another will be the experience of all of us somewhere along the road of life. Depression must be dealt with or one will live a life of misery.

God is good. He loves us. He works for good in everything that life brings to us (Rom. 8:28).

If our depression is due to the discipline of our heavenly Father, let us rejoice rather than giving way to discouragement. Let us look up because something good is going to happen (Heb. 12:5-13). —*TTC*

* * *

SUNDAY MORNING, OCTOBER 23

TITLE: The Joy of Knowing Jesus Christ As Savior

TEXT: **"For by grace you have been saved through faith; and this is not your own doing, it is the gift of God—not because of works, lest any man should boast" (Eph. 2:8-9 RSV).**

SCRIPTURE READING: **Ephesians 2:11-22**

HYMNS: **"Great Redeemer, We Adore Thee," Harris**
"Jesus Is All the World to Me," Thompson
"We Have Heard the Joyful Sound," Owens

OFFERTORY PRAYER:

Heavenly Father, we come to You as the great Giver of Your grace. We worship You because You are of supreme worth to us. We come today praying for the assistance of Your Holy Spirit that we might give ourselves completely to You as we bring tithes and offerings for the advancement of Your kingdom's work. Bless these gifts in a tangible way so that Your Word can be preached and Your truth taught. May Your blessings be upon the unfortunate who stand in need of ministries of mercy. In Jesus' name we pray. Amen.

Introduction. As Paul wrote his Epistle to the Ephesians, he was rejoicing over the blessings of God that had come upon these people as a result of their faith in Jesus Christ as Savior.

Ephesians 2 points out some of the new relationships which make joy indescribable possible in the heart of each one who receives Jesus Christ as Savior, Lord, Teacher, and Friend.

I. Through Jesus Christ we are made alive with a new kind of life (Eph. 2:1, 4-6).

A spiritual resurrection takes place when one receives Jesus Christ as Savior. Up to this moment the individual is in spiritual death and darkness because of sin. He or she does not have the divine life of God. Physically the nonbeliever is a walking, living, spiritual corpse in need of a spiritual-life implant. This new life comes in the miracle of the new birth when we respond to Jesus Christ with faith. To be alive from the dead is a joyous experience for those who know Jesus Christ.

II. We are brought near to God and to others through the blood of Jesus Christ (vv. 11-13).

Man in his natural state is alienated from God. Alienation from God results in alienation from other human beings. Sin not only separates a man from his better self and from his higher nature, but it also serves to separate him from his fellowman. Paul speaks of Gentiles who were separated from Christ as being "alienated from the commonwealth of Israel . . . and strangers to the covenants of promise, having no hope and without God in the world" (v. 12 RSV).

Man is a lonely creature unless he has established a relationship that makes fellowship possible with other human beings. Paul was rejoicing over the fact that now those "who once were far off have been brought near in the blood of Christ" (v. 13 RSV).

III. Through Jesus Christ we experience the peace of God and peace with God (vv. 14-15).

In repentance we yield to the rule and the will of the Creator God. By faith we put our trust in Him and signify that we are no longer rebels. Following this response of faith, we experience the peace of God and peace with others. We are no longer the enemies of God, and ideally we do not have an enemy in the world.

The child of God, through faith in Jesus Christ, can know an inward peace that passes all human understanding.

IV. Through Jesus Christ we now have access into the presence of God through the Holy Spirit (v. 18).

Until one comes to know Jesus Christ as Savior, he is an outsider and does not feel close to God. He does not have access to the throne room of the Eternal where it is possible for him to address God as "our Father." Paul rejoices in this new relationship that he and all of us have through faith in Jesus Christ. This is one of the supreme joys of being a follower of Jesus Christ.

V. Through Jesus Christ we become citizens of the kingdom of God (v. 19).

The privilege of citizenship in a great country is not properly appreciated by those who live there. The same can be said concerning those who are no longer strangers and sojourners but are now fellow citizens with the saints in the kingdom of our dear Lord and Savior. Paul speaks of this transfer of citizenship in his Epistle to the Colossians. He praises God and says, "He has delivered us from the dominion of darkness and transferred us to the kingdom of his beloved Son, in whom we have redemption, the forgiveness of sins" (1:13-14 RSV). The joy of citizenship is one of the joys that comes as a result of knowing Jesus Christ.

VI. Through Jesus Christ we become members of the family of God (v. 19b).

It is one thing to be a creature made in the image and likeness of God. It is wonderful to have the potential of being Godlike. Yet it is even more wonderful to experience a spiritual birth which makes us the sons and daughters of God and brothers and sisters to each other through Jesus Christ.

Membership in the family of God is a joyous experience around the world. You can meet total strangers who have something intensely wonderful in common with you. The joy of being a member of God's family comes to us through faith in Jesus Christ.

VII. Through Jesus Christ we become a part of the living temple of God (v. 22).

Salvation is something more than a legal relationship with God. It is a dynamic experience in which God Himself comes to dwell within the heart of each believer individually and in all believers collectively. We become a living temple in which God dwells. We become the meeting place where others can come to know God and where God comes to minister to a needy world.

Conclusion. Rich beyond words is the person who comes to know Jesus Christ as Savior. Joyous indeed is this privilege.

If you have not yet opened the door of your heart to let Jesus Christ become your Savior, I would encourage you to do so without delay. There is great joy for you through knowing Jesus Christ. —*TTC*

* * *

SUNDAY EVENING, OCTOBER 23

TITLE: Christ—the Head of the Church

TEXT: "He is the head of the body, the church" (Col. 1:18a RSV).

SCRIPTURE READING: Colossians 1:9-23

Introduction. Paul was concerned about making clear the relationship of Christ with His people. Sometimes his emphasis was on Christ's people—His church—as His body. At other times Paul's emphasis was on Christ as the Head or Lord of His church. The latter emphasis is true of our text.

"He is the head of the body, the church." This simple but profound text has three down-to-earth meanings for us.

I. The absolute primacy of Christ in His church.

Christ's people must understand this, subscribe to it, and glory in it. His interests are supreme; His cause comes first; His will is primary. To the world the church is a convenient group of respectable people to be used, when the occasion arises, to serve the interests of the world. But the church is to serve only the interests, purposes, and will of Christ, to put Him first.

A. *When in the church we put our own interests ahead of the interests of Christ, we dishonor Him as Head.*

The question we need to ask ourselves is not "How will this affect me?" but "What will be the result for Christ's cause? Will this promote or injure? Will this serve His best interests or defeat them?"

B. *When in the church we put human sentiment ahead of the interests of Christ, we dishonor Him as Head.*

Sometimes we conduct certain types of services that have little to do with the gospel, but make a powerful appeal to sentiment. To these appeals we respond in numbers and enthusiasm that shames our response to the simple appeal of the gospel. This is not to decry the place and power of sentiment in our lives; but when we let human sentiment become a more powerful force in our church life than our love for and loyalty to Christ, we are not putting Christ first; we are not letting Him be the Head of His church.

C. *When in the church we put the interests and claims of the world ahead of Christ, we dishonor Him as Head.*

The world's interests do have some claim upon us, but not first claim (Matt. 6:33). Christ's claims are first always. Yet the hue and cry of the majority of our church members is, "Don't you know I've got to make a living?" What they are really saying is, "I am only in this world on a business trip. If I can find a little time to spare, I'll use it to serve the Lord." To a man who put a worldly claim first, Jesus said, "No man, having put his hand to the plough, and looking back, is fit for the kingdom of God" (Luke 9:62b).

D. *When in the church we put the desire to please people ahead of the desire to please Christ, we dishonor Him as Head.*

Genuine harmony in a church is a vital necessity. Paul tells the Thessalonians, "Be at peace among yourselves" (1 Thess. 5:13b). Yet there is a spurious, superficial sort of harmony in the church, bought at the expense of pleasing men instead of Christ, that doesn't mean a thing except the defeat of the highest purposes of the gospel. Some in the church are childish in their emotions. Their feelings will be hurt anyway. In Christ's church we are not to be slappers of backs and dispensers of sugar sticks. We are to serve the interests of Christ.

II. The absolute authority of Christ over His church.

Christ is the supreme Ruler of His church on earth. No one else is nor could be. Since His authority is supreme, since His church is answerable only to Him, three inescapable implications follow.

A. *A New Testament church must be a pure democracy, a democratic body.*

This is inescapable. Answerable only to Christ, who is the Head, every member must be equal in rank, privilege, and power with every other member. This doesn't commend, it condemns orders in the ministry. Jesus said, ". . . one is your teacher, and all ye are brethren" (Matt. 23:8b ASV). There are no official boards in a church, nor could there be. There can be no ruling person or group either within a church or without.

B. *A New Testament church must be independent and self-sufficient.*

Since Christ is the Head of the church, the doctrine of the autonomy of the local church not only makes sense, it is necessary. Since churches owe their supreme and undivided allegiance to Christ, they could not accept rule from one another or any other earthly rule of any sort. If Christ is the Head of His church, no one else can be. This denies all ecclesiastical systems that would substitute the rule of man for the rule of Christ. This denies that the church could be subservient to or united in any way with the state. The sphere of the church is entirely spiritual and answerable only to Christ.

C. *New Testament churches, though independent of one another, must cooperate with one another in Christ's program.*

Since Christ is Head of the church, He is Head of every local New Testament church. He has a program. He can direct these churches in that program. The churches working together under the leadership of Christ, the Head, do not surrender their sovereign rights in cooperating with one another; they exercise them. The whole program, therefore, both within and among the churches ought to be characterized by harmony, unity, and purpose.

III. The absolute dependence of Christ's church upon Christ.

Just as the human body is helpless and lifeless apart from the head, so the church is helpless and lifeless apart from Christ. The last night before His crucifixion Jesus gently warned His disciples, "Apart from me ye can do nothing" (John 15:5b ASV).

Do we not devise and promote and try to carry on programs that are of men and not of Christ? In our modern day we speak of "the program of the church."

But apart from Christ the church has no program and no power to conceive or to execute a program. The church is completely dependent upon Him.

Conclusion. How can this text, this message, strike home in our hearts? "He is the head of the body, the church." The body is composed of members. He must be the Head of every member of the body. Let each one of us ask himself: "Are His interests primary in my life? Is His rule over me complete? Is my faith in Him implicit? — *WTH*

* * *

WEDNESDAY EVENING, OCTOBER 26

TITLE: A Prayer for Divine Correction

TEXT: **"Search me, O God, and know my heart! Try me and know my thoughts! And see if there be any wicked way in me, and lead me in the way everlasting!" (Ps. 139:23-24 RSV).**

SCRIPTURE READING: **Psalm 139:1-12, 23-24**

Introduction. A devotional study of the Psalms can be particularly helpful in nourishing our faith and assisting us in our prayer life.

Psalm 139 emphasizes the unlimited knowledge of God (vv. 1-6). This psalm also emphasizes the fact that God is always and everywhere present (vv. 7-12). This great psalm celebrates the truth that God is our Creator (vv. 13-18). The psalm closes with a prayer against the wicked and a prayer for divine correction as the psalmist faced the present and the future.

I. A prayer for divine probing (v. 23).

The psalmist is positioning himself upon the physician's examining table. He is requesting God to examine the motives of his heart and the thoughts of his mind. He recognizes that the source of actions and conduct is found in the thoughts and emotions of the inward man.

Perhaps David was motivated to pray this prayer for divine probing because he was being severely tested by his enemies. He considered himself to be the enemy of those who were the enemies of God (vv. 19-22). Perhaps he was disturbed by some of his hostile thoughts toward these ungodly enemies of God who were also his enemies.

II. A prayer for divine directions (v. 24).

The psalmist brought his mind and heart under the searchlight of God's watchful eye, not merely in order that he might be informed about himself, but that he might correct his way.

We read in the Book of Proverbs, "Every way of a man is right in his own eyes" (21:2). We also read, "There is a way which seemeth right unto a man, but the end thereof are the ways of death" (14:12).

God speaks through Isaiah and urges the wicked to forsake his way and the unrighteous man his thoughts (55:7). God speaks further and says, "For my thoughts are not your thoughts, neither are your ways my ways. . . . For as the heavens are higher than the earth, so are my ways higher than your ways, and my thoughts than your thoughts" (vv. 8-9).

A man may be quite sincere and yet be thinking the wrong kind of thoughts and walking in the wrong way. The psalmist recognized this truth and urged God to reveal to him whether there was some wicked way within his heart.

The psalmist prayed, "Lead me in the way everlasting." He wanted to forsake any false paths that would lead to the wrong destination. He wanted to be delivered from self-deception. He wanted to be saved from inaccurate thought processes and decision making.

He prayed that God would guide him into paths that would be pleasing to God and that would bring peace to his own heart and mind.

Conclusion. How long has it been since you have had a thorough physical examination? How long has it been since you have taken your temperature in order to see whether or not there was some undetected infection in your body? How long has it been since you looked into your mouth to see if you had a red spot in your throat? These are some of the techniques that are used to detect the presence of infection or illness.

How long has it been since you have brought yourself into the presence of God for a spiritual examination? It might be a painful experience, but it could be highly profitable.

We would be exceedingly wise if day by day we would pray, "Search me, O God, and know my heart! Try me and know my thoughts! And see if there be any wicked way in me, and lead me in the way everlasting!" (vv. 23-24 RSV).

— *TTC*

* * *

SUNDAY MORNING, OCTOBER 30

TITLE: Salvation in the Present Tense

TEXT: ". . . work out your own salvation with fear and trembling; for God is at work in you, both to will and to work for his good pleasure" (Phil. 2:12b-13 RSV).

SCRIPTURE READING: Philippians 2:12-13

HYMNS: "O Worship the King," Grant
"More Like Jesus Would I Be," Crosby
"Since Jesus Came into My Heart," McDaniel

OFFERTORY PRAYER:

Thank You, Father, for the gift of Your love revealed in Jesus Christ. Thank You for sending the gift of Your Holy Spirit to dwell within our individual hearts to abide within Your church. Thank You for the promise of our Lord to come and be with us today as we meet together in His name. We come bringing tithes and offerings that we might honor You and that we might show to You our love and gratitude. Accept these gifts and bless them to the end that others shall come to experience Your love and know Jesus Christ as Lord and Savior. In His name we pray. Amen.

Introduction. There are three days on everybody's calendar: yesterday, today, and tomorrow. Many people miss today because they are living in yesterday. Others miss the present because they are worried about tomorrow.

Let us look at salvation both in the past and future tense, and then concentrate on salvation in the present tense.

I. Jesus Christ came to save us from the past.

As the Lamb of God, Jesus Christ came to take away the sin of the world (John 1:29). Jesus came and lived and loved and served and suffered upon a cross that He might die in our place under the penalty of our sins (1 Peter 1:18-19; 2:24; 3:18). There are many passages of Scripture that confront us with the glorious truth that Jesus Christ died for our sins that He might save us from all we have done in the past or are doing in the present or will do in the future (1 Cor. 15:3-4). Through faith in Jesus Christ, we gain a position of acceptance with the Holy God (Rom. 5:1). Through faith in Jesus Christ, we pass from under the wages of sin and receive the gift of eternal life (6:23).

As we look at the great redemptive acts of Jesus Christ and our new relationship with God on the basis of faith in Christ, we need to beware lest we think in terms of salvation only in the past tense.

II. Jesus Christ came to save us in the future.

One of the dominant motives that many people have for trusting Jesus Christ is so that they might be prepared for the future. The Scriptures tell us and observation verifies the fact that it is appointed for men to die (Heb. 9:27). This passage of Scripture also informs us of the fact that after death occurs we meet God in judgment. The following verse informs us of the fact that Jesus Christ, who has already borne the penalty of our sins, will appear the second and final time, not to deal with our sin, but to save us from the very presence of sin. Paul speaks to the Philippians about the fact that the day will come when we shall be raised from the dead and be fashioned after the likeness of our glorified and risen Lord (Phil. 3:20-21). Jesus speaks to His apostles and encourages them not to have an agony of anxiety about the future because He will not only go to prepare a place for them, but He will return to receive them unto Himself. In the final Revelation we find a brief description of the house not made with hands, eternal in the heavens, which God is preparing for those who love Him (21:3-5).

III. The present-tense salvation experience through Jesus Christ.

Jesus the Savior came into this world to do something more than just save us from the sins we have committed in the past.

Jesus Christ came into this world to do something more than save us from the presence of sin in the future.

Jesus Christ came into this world to save us from the power and practice and downward pull of sin as a present-day experience. Our text gives to us the gospel of our present-tense salvation: "God is at work in you, both to will and to work for his good pleasure" (Phil. 2:13 RSV).

Jesus Christ died on the cross under the penalty of our sin. Jesus Christ conquered death and arose triumphant and victorious that He might deliver us from the power and practice of sin in the present.

The conversion experience is one in which we open ourselves to let the living Christ come to dwell within us in the person of the Holy Spirit.

The Holy Spirit dwells within each of us in order that we might experience a great salvation in the present. Jesus wants to do this as He functions as the Teacher come from God, who has come to teach us how to relate to God and to our fellow-man.

Jesus was not only the Savior, but He was also heaven's infallible Teacher.

A. *Our Lord would save us in the present from hate and hostility toward other human beings* (Matt. 5:43-48). In His teachings regarding Christian love, our Lord wants to deliver us from destructive and hurtful relationships with other people.

B. *Our Lord would save us in the present from anxiety about the necessities of life by encouraging us to have a great faith in our Father God* (6:25-33). Our Lord encourages us to seek first and foremost the rule of God in all of our relationships and to trust the Father to provide for us the necessities of life.

C. *Our Lord has bestowed upon each of us the gift of His Holy Spirit in order that we might be enabled to live a Christlike life in the present* (Gal. 4:6-7; 5:22-23).

Conclusion. The great salvation that Jesus Christ brings to us relates to the past and to the future, but also very much to the present. It is not His will that you live in weakness and defeat. If you will come to Him and trust Him, not only for the gift of forgiveness but for victory in the present, you can be sure that He will assist you. He is not a Savior who is limited to the past. He is not a Savior whose power is to be revealed only in the future. Jesus Christ wants to give you victory over the evil within and the evil about you in the world in the present. — *TTC*

* * *

SUNDAY EVENING, OCTOBER 30

N B

TITLE: The Peace of the Church

TEXT: "Be at peace among yourselves" (1 Thess. 5:13b).

SCRIPTURE READING: 1 Thessalonians 5:1–13

Introduction. In 1946, a pastor-evangelist was in a series of meetings in a small, rural Kentucky community, where he was a guest in the home of one of the oldest families in that area. To his delight he discovered that some member of that family had been the clerk of that church for more than one hundred years. Moreover the book containing the minutes of all items of business back to 1839, when the church was organized, was in their care. For the visiting pastor that book was interesting reading. In the minutes of almost every business conference this entry appeared: "The peace of the church was called for."

The visitor was told that the formula was this: The moderator of the conference would ask, "Brethren, are we at peace?" No one knew what might follow. No doubt their business meetings were interesting and well attended, because almost any kind of gathering would have been hard-put to match these sessions in human interest, emotion-packed drama, and pure "slapstick" comedy. But whatever might have been the shortcomings of our fathers, in whatever respects they may have failed, they sincerely tried to carry out the literal words of our text. They meant to have peace if they had to fight with one another to obtain it. If our forefathers were too strict in the matter of church discipline, perhaps our churches today are too lax. It was easy to get out of their churches, but hard to get in; now it's easy to get into our churches, but you can hardly get out.

Three preliminary considerations should be noted concerning this text.

A. *The spirit of this text cannot be enforced by force.*

No peace of any sort can be either secured or maintained in that way. Our forefathers tried to enforce "the peace of the church," and they had "confusion worse confounded"; and I daresay they permanently wounded as many saints as they converted sinners.

B. *This text presupposes an autonomous, independent, democratic body.*

The words "be at peace among yourselves" addressed to any other group would make no sense. Who else besides a plain, simple, New Testament church, where every member is equal in rank and privilege with every other member, a pure democracy, would even have the privilege of being at war among themselves?

C. *The status of peace, the degree of fellowship within a church, is difficult to analyze.*

Sometimes a church is like a shallow, clear mountain stream where every ripple may be seen. Again, a church may be like a deep, muddy river, calm and placid on the surface, but torn by dangerous undercurrents.

"Be at peace among yourselves." This text provokes three pertinent questions.

I. What does this text mean?

The answer should be considered both negatively and positively.

A. *Negatively.*

1. Peace is not the painlessness of inertia and lifelessness. A church may appear to be at peace when in reality it is dead. Peace is a living thing—positive and dynamic, fruitful and productive.

2. Peace is not the stupor of indifference and unconcern. To have the spiritual senses stupefied is not to be at peace.

3. Peace is not the negative spirit of let alone. (The French have a word for it, *laissez-faire*—"let it drift.") In every church there are those who retreat to the safety of a judicial position, refusing either to be quoted or to get involved. But a cowardly retreat is not peace. "Be at peace among yourselves."

B. *Positively.*

1. This means the peace of a good conscience, resulting from a faithful and consistent walk before God as a Christian. Paul enjoins this in several epistles (Gal. 5:16; Eph. 4:1, 17; 5:8b). John shows us the exact parallel between a worthy walk and peace; "If we walk in the light, as he is in the light, we have fellowship one with another" (1 John 1:7a). But if we walk after the manner of carnal men in jealousy and strife (1 Cor. 3:3), we violate "the peace of the church." If the Christian doesn't have the peace of a good conscience, what else matters?

2. This means the peace of an undivided heart. Jesus said, "Blessed are the pure in heart" (Matt. 5:8a). That means pure in the sense of being undivided, entire, without alloy. "Blessed are the undivided in heart."

3. This means the peace of a contented mind resulting from the knowledge of having done our best for Christ as we serve Him in His church. People who work together get together and stay together. They have to because even a mule cannot kick when he is pulling nor pull when he is kicking.

II. Why is this text so necessary to a church?

"Be at peace among yourselves." Any other state of affairs in a church is a terrible blow, both to the church as a body and to the individual members. Why?

A. *For the sake of our growth in the grace and knowledge of Christ.*

We are commanded to grow (2 Peter 3:18a). We do not grow while on a spiritual hunger strike. The first thing a pouting child does is to leave the table. Several years ago in India a man named Mohandas K. Gandhi led his nation in their struggle for independence from Great Britain. His weapon was the hunger strike. The British could not persuade him to eat. They dared not let him die. He won. Some in the church try this weapon on God. He is not impressed. They hurt only themselves.

B. *For the sake of our witness as a church before the world.*

It is unthinkable that a child of God should have no resemblance to his Father. Paul tells us, "For God is not a God of confusion, but of peace" (1 Cor. 14:33 ASV). Jesus said, "Blessed are the peacemakers: for they shall be called sons of God" (Matt. 5:9 ASV). Not only are true peacemakers "sons of God," they are also recognized as such. For peacemakers not to be at peace among themselves is an unthinkable contradiction.

C. *For the sake of the effectiveness of the church as a soul-winning agency.*

To whom was Christ's Great Commission given? To His church. To whom did our Lord commit the task of winning men to Him? To His church, only to His church. Paul asks the Corinthians, "For if the trumpet give an uncertain sound, who shall prepare himself to the battle?" (1 Cor. 14:8). How less likely is the world to hear if the notes are discords?

III. How can we apply this text to our lives?

How can we be at peace among ourselves in the church?

A. *We can be at peace with God within ourselves as members of the church.*

In the church at Philippi there were two women—Euodia, meaning "fragrant," and Syntyche, meaning "fortunate"—who had some sort of disagreement; and this seems to have been more than a personal matter. Paul is impartial. He says simply, "'I exhort Euodia, and I exhort Syntyche, to be of the same mind in the Lord" (Phil. 4:2 ASV). This was necessary to the peace of that church for these women had been useful members (v. 3).

B. *We can have a consciousness of Christian love and brotherhood that will rule out strife by putting our brother first.*

Jesus said, "One is your teacher, and all ye are brethren" (Matt. 23:8b ASV). Paul's admonition to the Philippians that they "be of the same mind, having the same love, being of one accord, of one mind" (2:2b ASV) would bring peace to any church anywhere. "We know that we have passed out of death into life," John tells us, "because we love the brethren" (1 John 3:14 ASV).

C. *We can be at peace through a common loyalty to the supreme Head, even Christ* (Col. 1:18a).

Jesus said, "For one is your master, even the Christ" (Matt. 23:10b). Christ is the only true touchstone of fellowship. If we walk with Him, we will be at peace (1 John 1:7).

Conclusion. If our fathers were too concerned about "the peace of the church" and how to maintain it, we are too unconcerned. Paul's injunction still applies. This text is as relevant and important as it ever was. — *WTH*

* * *

SUGGESTED PREACHING PROGRAM FOR THE MONTH OF NOVEMBER

Sunday Mornings

November is the month of Thanksgiving. In this month we think of God's generosity. We should respond to Thanksgiving with thanksliving. "Thanksgiving to God and Thanksliving for God" is the suggested theme.

Sunday Evenings

"The Past Speaks to the Present" is the suggested theme for a series of messages based upon the lives of the patriarchs.

Wednesday Evenings

We should be in a process of being changed into the image of the likeness of Jesus Christ. Jacob, who was originally a crook, had a life-changing experience with God. "Lessons From a Changed Man" is the suggested theme.

* * *

WEDNESDAY EVENING, NOVEMBER 2

TITLE: Selfishness Separates Families

TEXT: "Now therefore, my son, obey my voice; and arise, flee thou to Laban my brother to Haran" (Gen. 27:43).

SCRIPTURE READING: Genesis 27:30-45

Introduction. Jacob and Esau, twin sons of Isaac and Rebekah, differed from the start. Esau, the older, was a man of the field, while Jacob was a "home boy." Twice during their days at home, Jacob took advantage of Esau. First, he enticed his older brother to sell his birthright to him for a mess of pottage. The second time he and his mother, Rebekah, deceived Isaac and tricked him into giving the major family blessing to Jacob rather than Esau.

Because of this, Jacob had to flee and spent twenty years in a distant land waiting for Esau's wrath to cool. Even when he returned, he was still not certain that he was safe from his older brother's wrath. Some valuable lessons come to us from this story.

I. Parents should never "play games" with their children.

One of the saddest scenes in contemporary family life is to see one parent take the side of one child and another take the side of the other. This can lead to domestic suicide. Of course, parents do not always "play the game" the same way Isaac and Rebekah played it. There are variations in this quest for popularity with our children. Sometimes one parent bestows secret and even lavish gifts upon the child with the instructions, "Don't let the other one know it." This is a fatal game also. Usually when parents play games, it is because there is something lacking in their personal relationship with each other. The old cliché still shouts loudly, "The best thing a father can do for his children is to love their mother." This applies the other way also.

II. There are no shortcuts to realizing our life's goals.

Jacob tried to "con" his way upward, but it didn't work. We never gain for ourselves when we take advantage of another person's weakness or shortsightedness. When the morning of reality arrives, the consequences are terrible.

III. To gratify our appetites immediately can be dangerous.

We do not always need what we think we do at a given moment. Years of regret and grief can come because we make a foolish bargain on impulse.

IV. A divided family is tragic.

Look at the terrible result of the competitive nature that was present in the parents. On the surface it appears that Rebekah was more at fault than Isaac, since she was the aggressive one. Isaac, however, should have shown more awareness. He seems to have allowed the dominating spirit of his wife to have full sway. Regardless of how we assess the blame, both parents suffered tremendously. Esau married Hittite women; and although Jacob married Leah and Rachel, Semitic girls from Rebekah's family background, it was twenty years before Jacob returned with the grandchildren. We are not even sure that Rebekah ever saw Jacob's children since we have no record of when she died. What a terrible price to pay for sowing seeds of discord by showing partiality to children.

Conclusion. Let's not end on a negative note. How can we have a united family? The best way is for a mother and father to keep love meaningful and vital with each other. The greatest security children will ever have and the thing that will bind them closer together than anything is to know that their mother and father genuinely love each other. With the divorce rate so high today and with many other couples staying married in name only, how necessary it is for us to take inventory of our homelife and make the necessary adjustments. The greatest help to family solidarity and marital unity is to let Jesus Christ be the Lord of our home.

—*FMW*

* * *

SUNDAY MORNING, NOVEMBER 6

TITLE: Give What You Have to God

TEXT: **"What is that in thine hand?" (Exod. 4:2).**

SCRIPTURE READING: **Exodus 4:1-8**

HYMNS: **"Hark, the Voice of Jesus Calling," March**
"I'll Go Where You Want Me to Go," Brown, Pryor
"Ready," Anonymous

OFFERTORY PRAYER:

Our Father, You have proved Yourself to be the "giver of every good and perfect gift" in many ways, but most of all in the sending of Your Son. The world needs to hear the message of a crucified and risen Savior. Part of the money that we give this morning will go to tell people in other lands about the Savior. Some of it will be used here at home to preach the gospel, and some of it will be used in our own church program. Bless each gift that is

given. We magnify Your name through our stewardship of resources, and thank You for the privilege of giving. Bless this part of the service and make it both worshipful and meaningful. We pray in Jesus' name. Amen.

Introduction. What a comedown Moses suffered! At one time he enjoyed the possibility of sitting upon the throne of Egypt. In this Scripture, he is looking after sheep in the desert, far removed from civilization.

What had caused it? He tried to run ahead of God. Can you picture the mother of Moses, during those early formative years, whispering to him that he should remember he was a Hebrew and someday God would raise up someone to deliver the Hebrews from bondage? As the years passed, Moses felt the deepening impression that he was the one God had chosen to do the job. The mistake he made was that one day when he saw an Egyptian oppressing a Hebrew, he killed him and buried his body in the sand. Later, fearing discovery, he fled the land. What a terrible price we often pay for our impatience and hot-headedness!

God had not forgotten Moses, however; and here before the burning bush He is ready at last to thrust Moses into the service He had planned for him. God works all things together for good to those that love Him, and even the forty years' discipline in the desert served as a great school for the man who would later lead his fellow Hebrews throughout this very area.

I. God needs people to do His work.

Of course, God could have reached down with His strong hand and rescued His chosen people any way He desired. There is no limit to what God can do! Likewise, God could send angels to herald His message of salvation through the sky if He wished. But he doesn't want to do it that way! God uses people to do His work. Aren't you glad? An old story tells in creative imagination how, when Jesus returned to heaven, all of the hosts turned out to greet Him. He explained to them the plan of salvation, how He had died and had risen from the grave, and that now salvation is possible for all the world. They were all rejoicing until one angel said, "But, Jesus, how will the world know what You've done?" He replied, "I told My friends to tell others. Then they will tell still others, and the message will be told around the world." The angel said once more, "But suppose they don't do it? Suppose they're too busy or too careless, what then? How will the world know about You?" Jesus paused a moment, looked down, then raised His eyes and said, "But they're My friends. They will not disappoint Me. I have no other plan!"

Stewardship is man's accepting the responsibility to do with his life what God has planned for him. Of course, it involves material possessions. We cannot do everything that needs to be done or that we would like to accomplish ourselves. We can, however, give our money in order that those who can give full-time service may be able to devote themselves completely to the Lord's work. This does not exempt us from volunteer work, but it does enable us to have a share in the full-time work of those whom God has chosen for this ministry.

II. God supplies answers for our excuses.

Most of us are much like Moses. We hold back from accepting responsibility. Notice the excuses Moses set forth and how God answered them. When the call first came, Moses had, or at least seems to have had, an identity crisis. He asked, "Who am I, that I should go unto Pharaoh, and that I should bring forth the children of Israel out of Egypt?'' (Exod. 3:11). God did not tell him who he was but rather promised to be with him and guide him. How true today! We will never discover the full truth about ourselves until we commit to the Lord the abilities that we possess.

Next, Moses wanted to be assured of authority for his work. God gave him a new revelation of Himself (3:14), insisting this was all of the credentials he needed.

When Moses insisted further that the people would not believe him or listen to his voice, God worked two miracles for him. Let us learn a lesson about miracles at this point. God will provide the miracle if we need it, but He will only do for us what we cannot do for ourselves. When Moses pled his lack of eloquence, God promised to be with him, which He had already assured him He would do in a previous statement.

The final excuse of Moses was simply that God send somebody else. At this point, Aaron suddenly appeared. An interesting, almost amusing, scene takes place. God promises Moses that Aaron will be his spokesman. The curtain of charity is drawn over the rest of the scene. One wonders if perhaps Moses suddenly realized that if he did not accept God's call, God might turn to Aaron. This is not stated in the text, of course, but it may have crossed Moses' mind. At any rate, Moses was now ready for the task.

Excuses are seldom, if ever, the real reasons why we hold back and refuse to accept God's will for our lives. The chief problem involved with stewardship is that it means we accept responsibility, and few people are anxious to do it.

III. What is in your hand?

The rod of Moses has become a symbol. Like David's small sling, what we have, little though it may be or seem, can be used tremendously if we will give it unreservedly to the Lord. The small boy had only five loaves and two fishes, but he gave them to the Master. Someone has suggested that the boy went home and told his mother of the miraculous feeding. When he had finished, he said, ''Mother, I wonder if He could do the same if I gave Him everything I have?'' Of course, God can do with us far more than we can ever do with ourselves.

> Give God a chance
> Before you choose the path your life shall go.
> Seek earnestly his will for it to know;
> And if he says, ''I want it all,''
> Do not delay but heed the call.
>
> Give God a chance
> For when he calls he'll surely show the way
> Not all at once but guidance day by day.
> Trust him, he is the living Lord.
> Have faith and take him at his word.
>
> Give God a chance.
> The harvest fields are white and lost in sin
> Are those whom God could use your life to win.
> Before you choose what you will do,
> Give God a chance to speak to you.

Conclusion. What motivated Moses to a life commitment? Two things seem to have merged. First, he saw the need. Second, he knew that, in God, he had resources available. These two things will likewise lead us to discharge our stewardship. God will take care of us if we are faithful in doing our duty, whether it be the bringing of financial gifts for God's work to be carried on or by laying ourselves on the altar for service—or both. —*FMW*

* * *

SUNDAY EVENING, NOVEMBER 6

TITLE: Getting Guidance From God

TEXT: "And Isaac brought her into his mother Sarah's tent, and took Rebekah, and she became his wife; and he loved her: and Isaac was comforted after his mother's death" (Gen. 24:67).

SCRIPTURE READING: Genesis 24:1-67

Introduction. Each day thousands of airplanes fill the skies all around the world. Traveling by airplane has become one of the easiest and safest methods of travel. Learning about how airplanes are guided is a phenomenal discovery. Each airplane is guided by a team of traffic controllers. The pilot or copilot tells them where he wants his craft to go, and the traffic controllers plan a route. As the airplane takes off, climbs in altitude, and lands, a guidance system directs it. Pilots depend upon the guidance system.

There is a character in the Old Testament who represents a person under the guidance of God. Isaac's story is picked up with Abraham. He was the son of Abraham and Sarah. He was born late in the lives of his parents according to God's promise. When Isaac grew into a young man, he was still a bachelor. Abraham sought to find a wife for Isaac. Getting a wife for Isaac represents a good example of getting guidance from God. Let us examine the steps of getting guidance from God.

I. Determine to follow God's will.

A. *Isaac was confident that God wanted a wife for him.* She would share his faith and be sympathetic with his purpose. He knew that the marriage would work better if there was some similarity of family background. Consequently, Abraham sent back to his old home in Mesopotamia where such a person was likely to be found. Isaac was willing to do the Lord's will.

B. *If you are going to receive God's guidance, you must have a willingness to do His will.* We cannot follow God's will when we have determined within ourselves to do what we please. If you refuse to open or yield your will to the will of God, you cannot find the guidance you are seeking.

II. Use your rational powers.

A. *The servant of Isaac used his rational powers to seek a wife.* At the bidding of Abraham, the servant took ten of his master's camels and all sorts of choice gifts and set out. He reached the city of Nahor late in the afternoon when the women went to the well for water. The servant then reasoned, "Behold, I stand here by the well of water; and the daughters of the men of the city come out to draw water: And let it come to pass, that the damsel to whom I shall say, Let down thy pitcher, I pray thee, that I may drink; and she shall say, Drink, and I will give thy camels drink also: let the same be she that thou hast appointed for thy servant Isaac; and thereby shall I know that thou hast shewed kindness unto my master'' (Gen. 24:13-14). The servant knew that Isaac needed a self-reliant and outgoing woman for his wife. Choosing a wife was not a matter of mere chance. It was the deliberate use of rational powers.

B. *God wants people to use rational powers of the mind in seeking God's will.* Some people use chance to seek for God's will. It is much like flipping a coin and saying ''heads'' or ''tails.'' Others expect some miraculous intervention from heaven. They expect God Himself to appear, to speak audibly, and to tell them exactly what He wishes them to do. Still others use strong emotional feelings about God's will.

God wants you to use your head in seeking His will. Examine both the positive and negative sides of the issue in a rational manner. This will help you clarify your thinking. Think of every possible angle of the decision. God wants you to use your mind as you seek His will.

III. Pray about the matter.

A. *Isaac's servant prayed for the right woman for his master.* ''And he said, O LORD God of my master Abraham, I pray thee, send me good speed this day, and shew kindness unto my master Abraham'' (v. 12). The servant believed in the power of prayer. If he wanted light from the Lord, he had to look in that direction.

B. *Prayer is a useful means of receiving God's guidance.* Jesus sought God's will, and He prayed constantly. One example of Jesus' praying to the Father was in Gethsemane. He talked honestly to God, telling Him He wanted to find some way other than dying. Three times He asked God to remove the cup, yet He was moving to the place of submission. Finally He said, ''My Father, if this cup may not pass unless I drink it, thy will be done.'' Jesus used prayer to arrive at the right decision.

IV. Wait on the Lord!

A. *The servant of Abraham waited on the Lord.* ''And the man wondering at her held his peace, to wit whether the LORD had made his journey prosperous or not'' (v. 21). Rebekah came to the well to get water. After she had done so, she offered the servant of Isaac some water. ''And she said, Drink, my lord: and she hasted, and let down her pitcher upon her hand, and gave him drink. And when she had done giving him drink, she said, I will draw water for thy camels also, until they have done drinking'' (vv. 18-19). Rebekah gave both the servant and his camels water. Without a doubt it was an immediate answer to his requirement for Isaac's wife. Yet he did not want to act impetuously. While Rebekah went for more water, he waited for the feeling of certainty.

B. *In getting guidance from God, make sure you give His leadership time.* God guides deliberately. He does not lead recklessly. Therefore, one needs to be careful in making quick decisions. ''But they that wait upon the LORD shall renew their strength; they shall mount up with wings as eagles; they shall run, and not be weary; and they shall walk, and not faint'' (Isa. 40:31).

Conclusion. Are you trying to go through life directing yourself? This could lead to frustration or even disaster because you do not know where you are going. You need to follow God's guidance. To follow His guidance, make up your mind to follow His will, use your rational powers, pray about the matter, and wait on the Lord.

— *HTB*

WEDNESDAY EVENING, NOVEMBER 9

TITLE: Finding God For Yourself

TEXT: "Surely the LORD is in this place" (Gen. 28:16).

SCRIPTURE READING: Genesis 28:1-22

Introduction. Do you find God or does God find you? In a sense it works both ways. When an outstanding evangelist asked a young boy, "Have you found Jesus?" the lad replied, "Mister, I didn't know Jesus was lost." Of course, that's true. On the other hand, God is lost to us if we do not know Him.

This Scripture study tells how a young man, away from home for perhaps the first time, discovered God for himself—an experience that surpassed any previous knowledge he may have had of the Lord.

Jacob may have made it all the way to Bethel the first night away from home. Remember, he was fleeing from Esau and was a young man. He probably traveled light and fast. The spot he chose to spend the night was the site of an old Canaanite worship place. God, however, used this location as a sanctuary for His glory. Our Lord can always give new meaning to old things, and He delights in transforming the ungodly into something or someone that will bring praise to His name. Jacob had a marvelous dream that night and awoke to find that his life had new meaning. For perhaps the first time in his life, God was real to him. This firsthand experience transformed him and set him on his way to Haran with a new attitude toward life and changed goals. Some great lessons come to us from this experience.

I. We often find God in unlikely places.

Moses found God in a burning bush, but Jacob found Him in an old Canaanite sanctuary. We usually associate one's being saved with a formal church meeting, a revival, or some other religious assembly. Indeed, this is a good place. On the other hand, people have been convicted of their sins even while they were at a place that was seemingly not conducive to spiritual encounters. Of course, a previous experience at worship or a previous testimony by a friend may have paved the way for the experience occurring in an unlikely place. The point is, however, that God can speak to anyone anywhere He chooses. We cannot limit God nor circumscribe rigidly how He will do His work in this world.

II. Sometimes it helps to get away from home.

Jacob's family environment was not the best. His mother, as best as we can understand the biblical record, tried to do his thinking for him. When this occurs, a young person often needs to get away for a while and become his own person. We should remember, of course, that this is not necessary for all children because all parents do not "operate" the same way. In Jacob's case, however, he needed to "find out who he was"; and what better way than a quiet place where God could speak to him!

III. A "too hasty" commitment can be immature.

One does not like to find fault with the great biblical characters, but the Bible presents them as they were, "warts and all." We must be honest enough to admit that Jacob's vow was not a completely mature Christian commitment. For instance, it was too "iffy" and was based on the fact that God would bless him.

He said, "*If* God will be with me, and will keep me . . . and will give me bread . . . and raiment . . . so that I come again to my father's house in peace; *then* shall the LORD be my God" (vv. 20-21). Mature Christians know that you do not "bargain with God" in promising to be dedicated. God does not always give us the things we want and think we need. Our promise to tithe should not be based on the fact that God gives us plenty. Some great Christians have been called on to suffer tremendously, but have still maintained their faith in God. If we take Jacob's vow literally, he would not have been obligated to serve God or bring the tenth to Him until God brought him back safely to his father's home, which actually did not occur until twenty years later. We should watch carefully our promsies to God.

IV. God accepts us as we are.

The glorious thing about Jacob's experience and our own is that God is willing to receive us and bless us even when our understanding of Him is inadequate and even immature. Someone has said that becoming a Christian is surrendering as much of ourselves as we understand today to as much of Jesus as we understand today. How true! God blessed Jacob even though his understanding of divine things lacked much of being at the highest level.

Conclusion. All of our motives are mingled. A lost person cannot expect to understand everything about the Christian faith at the beginning. The birth experience in the spiritual life requires growth as much as the one in the physical realm. Jacob learned much about God at Bethel, but he had more to learn as he faced the experiences before him. So do we! —*FMW*

* * *

SUNDAY MORNING, NOVEMBER 13

TITLE: Such As I Have

TEXT: "Silver and gold have I none; but such as I have give I thee" (Acts 3:6).

SCRIPTURE READING: Acts 3:1-16

HYMNS: "Something for Thee," Phelps
"All Things Are Thine," Whittier
"Trust, Try, and Prove Me," Leech

OFFERTORY PRAYER:

Our Father, how vast is Your creation! When we think of the birds of the air, the fish of the sea, and every creeping thing on the earth, we sing again, "How great Thou art!" We thank You for loving us as we are, men and women who are sinful, and we praise You for providing redemption through Jesus Christ. Help us to be still and know that You are God. Send Your Spirit to arouse us from dullness and coldness. Help us to keep afresh in our spirit the thrilling thought of Your unspeakable love for us. Make us diligent in Your work and use these gifts this morning to further the glorious work of spreading the gospel. We pray in Jesus' name. Amen.

Introduction. The Book of Acts takes up the story of Christianity where the Gospels leave off. After Jesus ascended to heaven, the Holy Spirit came in a unique way, and the apostles moved forward dynamically and daringly to tell the story of the risen Christ.

Of course, the Book of Acts tells only a few of the many wonderful events that must have occurred. The Holy Spirit led Luke to record the visit of Peter and John to the temple, where they healed the man who had been lame from birth. How strange Peter's words must have sounded when he said, "Silver and gold have I none"; but how exciting Peter's deed when he took the man by the right hand, lifted him up, and, through the power of the Holy Spirit, healed him. A double miracle occurred that day! The man learned to walk and leap at the very moment he was healed.

A great stewardship lesson is present in this story. We are to do "what we can with what we have where we are for Jesus' sake today" and never wait for a greater opportunity nor for a time when we have greater abilities and resources.

I. Money isn't everything.

Too often when we speak of stewardship, we think of money. How thrilling to see a story where money is not set forth as the most important thing. In fact, Peter even came close to minimizing it. He said plainly, "Silver and gold have I none" and then proceeded to work the miracle.

Does the time ever come in the life of a church or a religious organization that money can actually be a stumbling stone? Thomas Aquinas, an outstanding religious leader of another generation, once visited the pope and was shown all the treasures of the Roman Church. The pope said to Thomas, "Well, Thomas, no longer can the church say, 'Silver and gold have I none.'" Thomas replied, "Yes, Holy Father, but have you ever thought that the church is in danger of also not being able to say, 'In the name of Jesus Christ of Nazareth rise up and walk"? We must be careful, in our day, not to evaluate our local churches and even our mission boards in terms of budgets alone. Pastors and missionaries of other days were not nearly so concerned about a "cost of living" raise as they were a "cost of loving" raise. Let us be careful, very careful, to keep our priorities correct!

II. But money is important.

The preceding paragraph is true, but something else is true also. It takes money—cold, hard cash—to carry on God's work in today's world.

God's Word says much about the stewardship of possessions, the giving of money. In his Second Letter to the Church at Corinth, Paul devoted two chapters (8 and 9) to the matter of giving. He said, "Therefore, as ye abound in everything, in faith, and utterance, and knowledge, and in all diligence, and in your love to us, see that ye abound in this grace also" (2 Cor. 8:7). He pointed out that our supreme example in giving is the Lord Jesus Christ who, though rich, became poor in order that through His poverty we might become rich.

God has given to some people the ability to make "big money." Their duty is to set aside an even larger part of that money to the work of the gospel. In Old Testament days, the tenth was the minimum. Certainly a Christian would not want to give any less to the spread of the Christian faith than the Old Testament Jew gave for his faith. In fact, counting all of the special offerings and supplementary tithes, the Old Testament saint was commanded to give far more than a tithe.

Money is important! We live in a world far different from that of Peter, John, and Paul. There was, of course, a monetary system in that day, but money is far more essential as a means of exchange than it has ever been before in the world. And more than ever before, the importance of propagating our faith is clear. We must lead people to Christ, and soon; or our way of life, as we know it, is in serious jeopardy.

III. What do you have?

A generation ago the emphasis was on "talents and abilities," but today we speak of "gifts" when we speak of what we have to offer God in service. There may be a fine distinction between the two, but we are not interested in that distinction at this moment. Rather, the question comes to all of us, "What do I have to offer my Lord?" Another question follows closely, "Am I willing to give myself—including my talents, abilities, and gifts—to be used any way that God sees fit?" When General Pershing landed in France with the American Expedition Force in World War I, he presented himself and his army to General Foch, Commander of the Allied Forces, and said, "Our men, our equipment, our resources, all that we have are yours. Use them as you see fit." God is certainly waiting to hear every Christian say, in essence, the same thing. Stewardship is giving "such as we have" to our Master unreservedly for use in the service of His kingdom.

Conclusion. Everyone who believes in Christ and is dedicated to Him actually has great possessions. They are, however, spiritual resources. He should find his greatest joy in sharing with others the gospel by lip and by life. This, however, does not relieve him from the responsibility of supporting God's work financially. A true believer in Christ should be a liberal person with large sympathies and great compassion. We cannot evade our responsibility in financial things by rationalizing that we are "spiritual" and, therefore, are not required to bring financial gifts. In the Old Testament, even the Levites gave tithes of the tithes. On the other hand, giving money does not release us from the duty of serving in other ways. Stewardship involves both finances and lifestyle. It is not a case of "either/or" in relationship to stewardship. We are obligated to the "both/and" principle. Time, talent, tithe, influence—all that we have belongs to God!

—*FMW*

* * *

SUNDAY EVENING, NOVEMBER 13

TITLE: Watch Your Weak Moments

TEXT: **"And Esau said to Jacob, Feed me, I pray thee, with that same red pottage; for I am faint: therefore was his name called Edom. And Jacob said, Sell me this day thy birthright. And Esau said, Behold, I am at the point to die: and what profit shall this birthright do to me?" (Gen. 25:30-32).**

SCRIPTURE READING: **Genesis 25:18-34**

Introduction. Each person experiences weak moments when decisions should not be made. Dieters see appetizing desserts when they are at a weak moment, and they yield. Sometimes when people are tired, they make decisions in driving which can be costly, even deadly. Character can leave a person as a result of a weak moment.

Esau had a lot of advantages. He was the oldest son of Isaac and Rebekah. He had a love for life with the skill of a hunter. However, the greatest blight of Esau's life was that he could not handle the weak moments. This was especially true when he sold his birthright to Jacob out of the desire of a passing hunger.

The story of Esau is one to teach us some valuable lessons about the weak moments of life. Let us look at these lessons and heed them.

I. Physical desires must be tamed.

The first lesson to learn from Esau's life is that physical desires must be tamed. Esau allowed physical impulses to go unchecked, and he lived to regret his carelessness in one of his moments of weakness.

A. *Observe the occasion of Esau's weak moment.* Esau had been in the field hunting. When he returned home, Jacob was cooking some red pottage. He was hungry and tired, and that was his favorite dish. He quickly proposed that Jacob give him some of the pottage. Jacob declined. Under one condition would Jacob give him food, and that was to sell his birthright. Listen to Esau: "Behold, I am at the point to die: and what profit shall this birthright do to me?" (Gen. 25:32).

B. *Weak moments come in our lives.* Weak moments come to every person. These are the times when our reserves and resources are depleted. That which is the expedient matter we think is to satisfy the particular appetite that seeks satisfaction.

J. Wallace Hamilton wrote a book which he titled *Ride the Wild Horses.* The thesis of this work is that God gave us every desire we have. No desire is bad within itself. But it must be controlled by God. So, the first lesson is to allow God to tame your physical desires. But there is another lesson.

II. Privileges need to be treated responsibly.

The story of Esau teaches believers another valuable lesson. This is the idea of treating God's entrusted gifts with a great degree of responsibility.

A. *Look at the great gift Esau possessed.* Esau was the first-born son of Isaac and Rebekah. This was a distinctive possession, for the first-born son observed the law of primogeniture. He was to be supreme or ruler over the other children. Privileges of inheritance belonged to this son. Esau had a marvelous privilege which he could have never attained by human achievement.

Unfortunately Esau disdained his great gift during a moment of weakness. Feeling the pains of hunger and thinking about his birthright forced him to look carelessly at his great privilege.

B. *Great privileges need to be treated responsibly.* God endows all of His believers with one or more gifts. The Lord desperately desires that we acknowledge and use His gifts. Do not neglect to treat responsibly those God-given abilities. Do not treat them as lightly as Esau did. Let us learn to cherish our privileges and to treat them responsibly. We have learned valuable lessons from Esau's life, but there is another lesson.

III. Decisions need to be considered carefully.

Perhaps the greatest lesson Esau learned is the crucial importance of moments of decision. The decisions you make influence the rest of your life.

A. *Think about Esau's crucial decision.* Esau's decision was a momentous one at the time. Stated simply, it was the decision whether to remain hungry and in possession of his birthright or to satisfy his appetite and live without his birthright. At the moment the decision seemed obvious to Esau. Later he lived to regret that decision, for the retrieving of his birthright from Jacob was impossible. That decision in a moment of weakness turned out to be a blight on the rest of his days on earth.

B. *Treat the decisions of life with great care.* Life brings all kinds of decisions. There are big ones and little ones. Without a doubt, we should be ever conscious of God's leadership in our lives. He leads us during the moments of strength, and He leads us during our moments of weakness. He will never lead us to ultimately regret a decision.

Conclusion. Do you have a resource for the weak moments of life? All of us have those times, and we need Someone greater than ourselves. Invite Christ into your life. He will join His life with yours. —*HTB*

* * *

WEDNESDAY EVENING, NOVEMBER 16

TITLE: We Reap What We Sow

TEXT: "What is this thou hast done unto me? did not I serve with thee for Rachel? wherefore then hast thou beguiled me?" (Gen. 29:25).

SCRIPTURE READING: Genesis 29:16-28

Introduction. The eager lad went with exuberance on his journey. His steps must have been lighter as he anticipated the experiences of a new country. With the help of the Lord Jacob immediately found the country where his mother's kinfolk lived. The adrenaline must have been flowing in his system because when he saw Rachel, he was able, by himself, to roll the stone from the well's mouth, a task that usually required several men. When he identified himself to Rachel, she was delighted to know him and ran to tell her father.

Jacob the schemer met his match in Laban, his mother's brother. Jacob remained as a guest for a month, but after that Laban suggested that a contract be drawn up for work. Jacob proposed that he work seven years for Laban's daughter, and at that time she would become his wife. However, Jacob did not count on Laban's craftiness.

The wedding feast was a great one, with all the customs of that day. The next morning, after the wedding had been consummated the night before in the darkness of the tent, Jacob discovered he had Leah, the other daughter of Laban, rather than Rachel. Of course, he raised great objections, but Laban showed him the "small print in the contract" by telling him that it was a custom of their country never to give the younger daughter in marriage until the first-born was wedded. As a result, Jacob had to serve another term for Rachel. Naturally, Jacob loved Rachel more than Leah. However, God blessed Leah with many children. But it was a long time before Rachel bore even one child, and then she died giving birth to the second one. Some great lessons stand out for us from this story.

I. God leads His children along.

Jacob had set out on a dangerous journey, and many things could have happened to him. However, God was with him, and the text indicates that he came quickly to the country where his mother's people lived. In fact, on first inquiry he found Rachel. This seems to have been more than coincidence. God was working in Jacob's life.

How refreshing for us to know that in spite of our shortcomings and sins, God can use us. The Lord had chosen Jacob as the channel through which the Messiah would come. If we had been choosing, no doubt, we would have picked Esau, for in many ways he was a more likeable character. Yet, Jacob, with all of his undesirable traits, had a nature sensitive to God's will. He did not always act in accordance with his knowledge, but he genuinely loved God in spite of his personal ambition and inconsistent nature. Esau, on the other hand, was a worldly-wise sophisticate who felt no need for religious affiliation or divine support.

God blesses us when we are earnestly trying to do His will. He will lead us if we will only keep ourselves in tune with Him. He does not count our mistakes, but only our good intentions. His mercy is always ready to wipe the slate clean and give us a fresh start. The land of Laban was the place of "beginning again" for Jacob. We, too, can know the joy of starting afresh if we will honestly seek the Father's face and His will.

II. The web of deception is a tangled one.

One of our poets put it succinctly:

> Oh, what a tangled web we weave,
> When first we practice to deceive.

Jacob learned this firsthand. He started out as a supplanter. Nothing mattered to him except getting what he wanted. He did not care whom he hurt in securing the things he felt he must have at a given moment. Then he met someone who operated from the same base. Experts do not agree as to whether or not we inherit emotional qualities, but we cannot help but wonder if the "craftiness" was not from his mother's side of the family. After all, she aided him in deceiving Isaac, and now we find that her brother has the same characteristics. When Jacob and Laban met each other, it was an "irresistible force hitting an immovable object." Laban, however, had more resources to work with and, therefore, had Jacob at a disadvantage.

What do you imagine Jacob thought the morning after his wedding when he saw Leah? Do you suppose he saw any relationship between the darkness of the tent the night before and the darkness of his father's eyes when he tricked him? The similarities are too great to go unnoticed. Jacob must have had at least a moment of remorse, probably much longer. We do not, however, see any repentance coming forth at this moment. Sin has stalked its victim! Jacob was now getting a "dose of his own medicine."

III. God always sends compensation.

The relationship between Jacob and his wives is an interesting one. God blessed Leah with children, which was the greatest honor that could come to a woman of that day. I remember talking to a Jewish guide in Israel several years ago. He no doubt reflected the feeling of his people even to this day as he suggested that Rachel was the "beauty queen" who did not want to work, while

Leah was the better of the two. We do not have dogmatic evidence of this, but the implication seems to be in the text. Also, Rachel died earlier and was buried by the side of the road near Bethlehem. She never enjoyed the blessings and fruits of old age. Leah, however, lived a long time and was finally buried in the cave of Macphelah with Jacob, her husband, and the other two patriarchs and their wives. Nearly forty centuries have passed, but the grave of Leah is still honored. Also, God sent the Savior through one of Leah's sons, Judah. Life indeed has a strange way of sending compensating blessings for our inadequacies and adversities.

Conclusion. Jacob's life is a strange mixture, a paradox, a dilemma. On the one hand he was crafty and suffered for it. On the other hand, however, God stood within the shadows and kept watch over Jacob. He overruled Jacob's mistakes and sin and blessed him in spite of them. Aren't you happy that we serve a God who, because of His mercy, forgives our sins! —*FMW*

* * *

SUNDAY MORNING, NOVEMBER 20

TITLE: Give Yourself in Service

TEXT: **"I beseech you therefore, brethren, by the mercies of God, that ye present your bodies a living sacrifice, holy, acceptable unto God, which is your reasonable service" (Rom. 12:1).**

SCRIPTURE READING: **Romans 12:1-9**

HYMNS: **"Serve the Lord With Gladness," McKinney**
"Our Best," Kirk
"To the Work," Crosby

OFFERTORY PRAYER:

Our Father, soothe the anxieties of Your children. Bring calm where there is disorder and buoyancy where there is burden. Send peace for our distractions. Touch, guide, encourage, and empower us in order that we may commit ourselves afresh to the great task of living the Christian life in a world where there is so much opposition to Your purposes. Give us the strength to bear the pettiness of people and resolve the misunderstandings of incompatible natures. We know that the spirit is willing but the flesh is often weak. Rescue us from ourselves and from our sins. Keep us unspotted from the world. As we bring our offerings this morning, may it be not only a duty to be discharged but a privilege to be utilized and enjoyed as we invest in the spreading of God's Word to the world. We pray for Jesus' sake. Amen.

Introduction. When we come to chapter 12 in the Book of Romans, we are standing at the watershed of this great letter. There is, in Canada, a place where one can see the Great Divide, where one is on the "roof of the world"—from it water flows in two opposite directions. Our text for today is like that. When Paul says, "Therefore," he looks back at the first eleven chapters of his letter, where he had stressed a systematic theology that presents all of the essential facts about man's relationship to God from a doctrinal standpoint.

When Paul says, "I beseech you . . . that ye present your bodies a living sacrifice," he looks at the practical side of religion, the true test of one's orthodoxy. Not what man says he believes, but what he does proves the genuineness of what he says he believes. Unless one puts into practice in daily living what he professes to believe, he does not truly believe it.

I. How is your doctrine?

Paul began the Roman letter by clearly outlining man's depraved condition before God. After a few introductory words about himself, the Roman church's reputation, his thwarted plans to come to them, and the nature of the gospel he preached, he tackled the sin problem.

In the latter part of chapter 1, he dealt with the gentile world. Although they did not have the Mosaic Law, they had a law within their own hearts, which they had violated, failing to live up to the truth they possessed. For that reason, the Gentiles stood as sinners before God. In chapter 2, Paul dealt with the Jewish people who had religious privileges but failed to realize their possibilities, violating God's law and refusing to live up to the light which had been revealed to them. Paul ties all the strings together in chapter 3, climaxing with the great statement that "all have sinned, and come short of the glory of God" (v. 23).

Chapter 4 deals with salvation by faith. Man has always been saved by faith, even in Old Testament days—it was Abraham's faith that God counted for righteousness. In chapter 5 the glorious results of faith are outlined; and in chapter 6, Paul made clear the obligations of one who has been justified by faith, concluding with the timeless declaration that the "wages of sin is death; but the gift of God is eternal life through Jesus Christ our Lord" (v. 23). Chapter 7 pictures the struggle between the old man and the new man in the life of the believer; while chapter 8 shows the victory that comes to those who are in Christ and the security they enjoy because of His constant presence and unfailing power. Paul concludes chapter 8 with a glorious statement that nothing is able "to separate us from the love of God, which is in Christ Jesus our Lord" (v. 39).

Chapters 9 through 11 deal with the Jewish people and are, in a sense, a transition between the doctrinal section and the practical section. We should, however, note that God loves Israel and stands ready to receive them unto Himself when they come to Jesus Christ for salvation.

II. How is your dedication?

Notice the expression "a living sacrifice" which Paul uses to express his concept of dedication. The people to whom he was writing—Jewish Christians who had accepted Christ on the Day of Pentecost probably made up most of the group—were steeped in the Old Testament Scriptures. They understood the sacrificial system whereby an animal was slain as an offering to God. Paul suggests that the Christian does not bring a dead sacrifice to the altar but rather brings himself as a "living" sacrifice.

Most people despise the word *sacrifice*. To them it suggests asceticism, negativism, and narrowness. Paul, however, put the word *living* in front of it and thus removed the stigma of Jewish law and set forth an innovation. Someone translated it, "Put your bodies at God's disposal as a living thank-offering." The Christian faith does not teach distortion or repression of the body. Rather, the body is to be made available for God's service. He alone knows best how to use it to His glory and to our growth. In this context, the word *body* means the total person. Our hearts, minds, and physical energies should be brought to God for Him to use as He sees fit to accomplish His redemptive purpose in this world.

III. How is your devotion?

Actually, we will never be any more dedicated to God than the measure of our love for Him. Whether we wish it, seek it, or realize it, God loves us. Even when we devote our minds, hearts, and bodies to selfish ends, He still cares deeply for us and makes His sun shine on the just and unjust. When we refuse to love God, we are cowardly and selfish. No shame is equal to that of refusing to love the One who loves us so greatly.

Stewardship is more than the giving of money. It involves a proper attitude toward our material resources and giving a proper share to God. One can give without loving; however, he can never love without giving. What a revolution would take place in Christian work if God's people would, first of all, love Him and then support God's work in this world.

When Paul says that the presenting of ourselves to God is our "reasonable" service, he uses a word that can best be translated "spiritual." Of course, supporting God is reasonable and rational, but Paul meant even more. We serve God because our spirits are in tune with His Spirit. Even as God's Spirit bears witness with our spirit that we are the children of God (8:16), so our spirit testifies by our devotion and dedication that we have been transformed by the Holy Spirit of God.

Conclusion. The work of the Lord waits on two things—men and money, persons and purses! It takes both to do the Lord's work—someone to go and someone to "hold the ropes" while the other seeks to serve. All of it, however, goes back to what we believe about Christ, about sin, about salvation, and consequently about service. Paul writes later in this same chapter concerning the fact that we are one body in Christ and everyone a member of another. He points out that since we have gifts differing according to the grace that is given to us, we should exercise those gifts in harmony with His will. How is your doctrine? How is your dedication? How is your devotion? Each of the three is important! Each one builds on the other; but the climax, the top rung of the ladder, is our devotion to God based on our love for Him. *—FMW*

* * *

SUNDAY EVENING, NOVEMBER 20

TITLE: A Name Change

Text: **"And he said, Thy name shall be called no more Jacob, but Israel: for as a prince hast thou power with God and with men, and hast prevailed" (Gen. 32:28).**

Scripture Reading: **Genesis 32:22-32**

Introduction. Occasionally people become dissatisfied with the names their parents have given them. Several years ago the country and western singer Johnny Cash popularized a song entitled "A Boy Named Sue." You could not blame a boy given the name of Sue for wanting to have his name changed.

Names were significant in the Old Testament. Often they described a person's character. The name *Jacob,* for example, meant "deceiver" or "supplanter." Without a doubt he needed a name change. The story of Jacob is one of a person getting a new nature and then receiving a new name to describe his new nature. "Thy name shall be called no more Jacob, but Israel: for as a prince hast thou power with God and with men, and hast prevailed" (Gen. 32:28). Let us examine the insights into Jacob's story of a change.

I. All of us need a name change.

The story of every human being is one of rebellion against God. Therefore, everyone needs a name change.

A. *Jacob's story is an exposure of a sinful nature.* The reality of Jacob's character is first reflected in his name. Throughout his life he lived up to the reputation of being a trickster. He cheated his brother, Esau, out of his birthright in a moment of great weakness. Then Jacob tricked his father, Isaac, into blessing him rather than Esau. When Jacob had tricked Isaac and Esau had been robbed of the blessing, he had to flee to his uncle Laban in Haran. But Jacob continued with his deceptive nature.

B. *Jacob's sinful nature is an exposure of every human being's character.* Though we might not have been as deceiving as Jacob, our nature is still sinful. Once a French writer said: "I never examined the heart of a wicked man. I once became acquainted with the heart of a good man: I was shocked." Looking at our sinful nature causes us to conclude, "All have sinned." A new nature is desperately needed.

II. All of us can have our nature changed.

The story of the Bible is that every human being may have a new nature. No one need remain the way she or he is. Your character can be changed.

A. *Jacob's story is one of being brought to submission.* Jacob's being brought to submission happened in an unusual manner. On his return to Canaan from Laban's home in Haran, he came to a stream called the Jabbok. He knew that he would encounter Esau, thus he made preparations to appease his brother. Jacob sent flocks ahead as gifts for his brother.

Having sent everyone ahead, he spent the night alone beside the Jabbok. During the night the most important event of his life took place. "And Jacob was left alone; and there wrestled a man with him until the breaking of the day" (32:24). The thought came to Jacob that his real antagonist was not Esau or Laban but the Lord. The Lord wrestled with Jacob until Jacob was submissive. When Jacob met God, he got a new nature and a new name.

B. *Jacob's change is an indication of what can happen to every human being.* Harry Emerson Fosdick, pastor for many years at Riverside Church in New York City, preached a sermon entitled "No Man Need Stay the Way He Is." If you do not like yourself the way you are, then you can change. That is what happened to Jacob at Jabbok—a deceiver became a good man.

Changing our nature results as a submission to the will of God. Instead of trying to run your life, allow God to control your life. When you submit to God's will, your nature will be changed.

III. All of us are changed to serve the Lord.

Having our natures changed is not just a passive transaction. It means a change in lifestyle. When we are changed, we are led to service.

A. *Jacob's story reflects a new lifestyle.* Jacob became a new man when the Lord prevailed over his life. His name was changed from "Jacob the deceiver" to "Israel," which means "prince or perseverer with God." He changed his relationship with Esau, his brother. In previous years he had done everything to exploit Esau; but after Jacob's encounter with God, he did everything to seek reconciliation with Esau.

B. *Jacob's service indicates that every life-changing encounter should lead to service.* The business of serving belongs to the experience of being saved. Serving others keeps a person from excessive preoccupation with himself.

Life can change for you. There was a man named John Newton who went to Africa where he could be free to sin to his heart's content. There he became involved in the slave trade. Then John Newton had an experience with the Lord and wrote the words to "Amazing Grace."

Conclusion. Jacob desperately needed a change. His change of nature came when he allowed the Lord to prevail in his life. When the Lord prevailed, Jacob became a profitable servant of the Lord.

Do you acknowledge that you need a new nature? Will you allow God to change your life? —*HTB*

* * *

WEDNESDAY EVENING, NOVEMBER 23

TITLE: Struggling for Our Faith

TEXT: "I will not let thee go, except thou bless me" (Gen. 32:26b).

SCRIPTURE READING: Genesis 32:22-32

Introduction. Jacob's life with Laban was a stormy one. Surely Laban did not completely despise his son-in-law since he presented him with a number of grandchildren. Yet the scheming between the two went on constantly, and finally Jacob left the country. Even then, there was a stormy scene. But they "mended their fences," and Jacob was on his way back to the land of his father and mother.

The scene at Jabbok is a strange one. Jacob sent his company on before him and was left alone. He was greatly disturbed because he did not know how Esau would receive him. Jacob did some earnest praying that night, and this experience with the "mysterious stranger" was, no doubt, a great part of his encounter with God. We cannot dismiss this episode as a dream. Even though we cannot understand it completely, the account is historical. Who was this "mysterious stranger"? Jacob later said concerning the incident that he had "seen God face to face," and we must leave the account there. However, some valuable lessons stand out for us.

I. Old sins still haunt us.

Twenty years had passed. Surely Esau had mellowed! This thought must have gone through Jacob's mind, but he was not sure. After all, he had treated his brother shabbily; and Jacob, crafty soul that he was, was afraid that Esau possessed similar characteristics.

One of the worst things sin does is to punish us itself. God has, in His own way, arranged things so that many times sin punishes the sinner. God is not required to do it. He has created a moral world. The law of sin and retribution often dishes out its own reward and punishment.

II. God can enter directly into the affairs of men.

None of us understands God's workings. Paul said, "And without controversy great is the mystery of godliness" (1 Tim. 3:16). He does not choose to intervene directly on all occasions, but when His redemptive program needs His personal attention, He gives it. Jacob needed to learn a great lesson. If we count his experience at Bethel as the beginning of his "saved life," we must look on this one at Jabbok as the time when he made a complete surrender of himself to the Lord with the full knowledge of what it cost. Ideally, of course, when we accept Jesus as Savior, we receive Him also as Lord. Unfortunately, however, it is often later in our Christian life that we understand enough about God to accept His full claim upon us. Jacob needed to be completely subdued by the Lord. Pride, greed, ambition, and all of the accompanying vices still held sway in his life. God refused to give up on Jacob. He had chosen him for Himself and insisted on keeping him as a special person in His redemptive program.

III. Jacob met the test.

In the New Testament, we are taught that salvation comes by grace through faith and "that not of works." In some of these Old Testament stories, we must be careful not to push too far in order to find an analogy of "salvation by grace" in the experiences of the great men God chose and used. The simple point of this story is that Jacob hung on doggedly and literally "fought for his faith." He felt unworthy, subdued, frustrated. The years at Haran had taken a toll on his life. If he once felt that God had a great purpose for him, he was not so sure now. Yet he was not willing to give up the experience at Bethel. He would not let God cast him off. He continued to grapple although perhaps he did not understand the exact nature of the conflict.

How like our lives is this experience! Sometimes we fight the fight of faith when we do not understand the true nature of the battle. Sometimes God nudges us with adversity in order to humble us and make us useable in His service. Although we must accept this story as literal history, many spiritual lessons emerge. As God touched Jacob, so He has touched us many times. When we come through the conflict, we understand God in a greater way. We need the storms of life as much as we need the blue sky.

Jacob was never the same after the Jabbok experience. He still had touches of the old life, but something happened by the brook that refined and mellowed him, making him able to cope with the remaining years and the problems they would bring. —*FMW*

* * *

SUNDAY MORNING, NOVEMBER 27

TITLE: What Is Your Life?

TEXT: "For what is your life? It is even a vapour, that appeareth for a little time, and then vanisheth away" (James 4:14).

SCRIPTURE READING: James 4:13-17

HYMNS: **"We Give Thee But Thine Own," How**
"Serve the Lord with Gladness," McKinney
"To the Work," Crosby

OFFERTORY PRAYER:

Our Father, You have told us that You are the Alpha and Omega, the beginning and the end. You have also promised, "Lo, I am with you always." As we come to the time of offering, help us to remember that You are indeed the beginning of life for us and the One who stays with us until the very end. Help us to beware of feeding our safety deposit boxes and starving our souls. Help us to understand that when Jesus said, "It is better to give than to receive," He was expressing one of the most profound truths of life. Help us to realize we can be "labourers together with God" by sending people to preach the gospel where we cannot go ourselves. Grant that as we have received many generous gifts from You, we may now count it a joy to bring to You the accumulated bounties of our lives in order that Your work may be carried on. Help us, above everything else, to seek a fuller life with You and to attain a closer walk with the One who loved us and gave Himself for us. We pray in Jesus' name. Amen.

Introduction. The Epistle of James is probably the most practical writing of the New Testament. The author, a half-brother of Jesus, stressed conduct and behavior as the true test of whether or not one is a genuine Christian. Some have called his book "the Proverbs of the New Testament," while others have pointed out its similarity to the Sermon on the Mount.

Writing to Christians who were scattered throughout the Roman Empire, James emphasized the necessity for patience, especially as related to the tongue, warning that one of the worst sins a Christian can commit is that of failing to carefully watch his words. In this particular section of Scripture, James is emphasizing the uncertainty of the future, which was certainly a relevant fact in the lives of the Christians who lived in a world that was hostile to the members of the new faith.

I. A worldly goal.

Man has always sought to further his own interests. First, of course, is self-preservation, but most people seek an added security sufficient to protect them from all contingencies. Of course, we too often think of security only in material terms. When one adopts this philosophy, he is never quite certain that he has enough financial resources to protect him from the hidden dangers that lurk in today's society. James pictures a man as planning a business, confident that he can secure enough gain from it to immunize himself from any inevitability.

Such an attitude begins with materialism, but it leads to a complete epicurean approach to life. Self-indulgence becomes the order of the day, and all goals are interpreted in terms of enjoying the things of life which appeal to the lower nature. While the materialist is heaping up gains for security, he is also indulging in things opposed to the spirit. This may, at first, sound contradictory, since a person should provide for himself and his family; but this lifestyle usually emerges from one who sets his goals primarily in terms of things rather than deeper and more meaningful values.

II. A timely truth.

James hurls forth a warning much needed by all people and especially essential for those who make worldly goals their aim in life. He compares human existence with a vapor, joining the many other figures of speech in the Scriptures that describe our pilgrimage on this earth. For instance, various writers refer to life as a swift ship, a handbreadth, a thread cut by the weaver, a dream, a sleep, a shadow, a weaver's shuttle, water spilled on the ground, and wind. All of these express the idea of brevity. When David complained to Jonathan that "there is but a step between me and death" (1 Sam. 20:3d), he expressed a truth that applies to all of us, even though an evil king is not pursuing us with intent to kill. Life has been called a "little gleam of time between two eternities" and "scarce the twinkle of a star in God's eternal day."

III. What is life all about?

Since uncertainty exists everywhere concerning our tenure upon earth, the wise person will seek to make the most of his days. The old cliché that says, "The best use of life is to invest it in something that will outlast it," contains tremendous truth. When one lives for self alone, he will come to the end of his way with few friends. When one adopts a "shaken reed" of life and dwadles through it, shifting from one goal to another, he will end up with no accomplishments because he had no real purpose in living. If one seeks to exploit others, somewhere down the line he will become cynical and distrust everyone else because he has unconsciously transferred his own character to the ambitions of others.

The best approach to life is to live it with what the old timers called "an eye single to God's glory," which means exactly what James said, "For that ye ought to say, If the Lord will, we shall live, and do this, or that" (4:15). In days when the emperors were crowned at Constantinople, a royal mason came to the new ruler and set before him a number of marble slabs. He was asked, at that time, to choose one for his tombstone. Those who have picked out cemetery plots and made prearrangements for their funerals testify that is is an awesome experience. Yet all of us need to keep before us the fact that our times are in God's hands.

Stewardship steps in at this point and says, "All that you have comes from God. To rejoice in your own boastings is evil. If you know to do a good thing and refuse, it becomes sin." Whether in the realm of material possessions or other investments of life, we face daily the matter of how we shall utilize our resources. To choose goals is a dangerous thing because most of us will probably come close to reaching them. Therefore, we should be certain they are worth the effort. The only aims in life that are worthwhile are those related to the advancement of God's work in this world.

Conclusion. When you come to the end of your way, will you be glad that you've lived? Certain guideposts stand on the path to such a feeling. Have you used your possessions for more than your own self-interests? Have you despised nothing in the world except falsehood and wickedness? Have you feared nothing except cowardice? Have you been governed by your admirations rather than your disgusts? Have you coveted nothing of your neighbor's except his kind heart, gentle manners, and compassionate attitude? Have you sought to spend much of your time in personal communion with the Lord but never forgetting the practical world that needs your help?

Life is for living! True living, however, means service, which has been called the "rent that we pay for living on this earth." When life is lived in harmony with God's principles, we can find a little heaven here on this earth.
—*FMW*

* * *

SUNDAY EVENING, NOVEMBER 27

TITLE: A Godly Man

TEXT: "So now it was not you that sent me hither, but God: and he hath made me a father to Pharaoh, and lord of all his house, and a ruler throughout all the land of Egypt" (Gen. 45:8).

SCRIPTURE READING: Genesis 45:1-15

Introduction. Thomas Mann told the story of Joseph in three lengthy volumes. Indeed, Joseph is one of the most exciting characters in the Bible. He was blessed with natural endowments which deserve our admiration. His life was beset with misfortune and adversity which evokes our sympathy. Joseph was blessed with godly qualities which demand our imitation.

The biblical writer told the story of Joseph in thirteen chapters (Gen. 37–40). The story begins in the land of Canaan. Joseph was his father's favorite son. His brothers became jealous over their father's favoritism and Joseph's egotism. The brothers intended to kill Joseph, but they decided instead to sell him to some Ishmaelite merchants. Joseph became a slave in Egypt. His story continues in a mixture of sorrow and happiness. The story of Joseph concludes with a great reunion with his family. Let us notice the godly qualities of Joseph's life.

I. A godly man forgives injustices.

A. *Joseph had numerous injustices directed his way.* Let us observe several illustrations of injustices against Joseph. First, Joseph's brothers mistreated him. They put him in a large pit, threatening to leave him to die. Later they sold him to some slave traders, and these traders in turn sold him to an officer in the Egyptian government. Second, Joseph was treated unjustly by Potiphar's wife. She accused him falsely of an illicit sexual affair. Joseph was thrown into prison. Third, while Joseph was in prison, he did a favor for the pharaoh's baker. The baker promised to help Joseph get out of prison, but he forgot Joseph. The story of Joseph contains one injustice after another.

B. *Joseph forgave each injustice directed against him.* Joseph did not have an agenda of retaliation. In each case he sought the highest interest of the person or persons who treated him unfairly. The scene of Joseph forgiving his brothers furnishes a glorious picture of one who forgives injustices. "Moreover he kissed all his brethren, and wept upon them: and after that his brethren talked with him" (45:15). The opposite spirit would have been a spirit of retaliation. This proves that the way to overcome injustice is to return good.

II. A godly man withstands adversities.

A. *Joseph knew the problems of adversity.* The story of Joseph is one of physical and mental hardship. Ambition for the future was frustrated when he was sold as a slave. Joseph knew the agony of disappointment. His brothers failed him. A baker forgot his favors. Joseph could have easily turned from his optimistic attitude to negative feelings against people. He lived life as a prisoner and as a slave. This man knew the meaning of hardship.

Believers are not exempt from adversities. Study the Bible carefully, and you will read about the adversities of godly people. The godly person is one who learns to withstand his or her adversities.

B. *Joseph judged the adversities in the light of God's plan.* Listen to his estimations about his hardships: "Now therefore be not grieved, nor angry with yourselves, that ye sold me hither: for God did send me before you to preserve life. . . . And God sent me before you to preserve you a posterity in the earth, and to save your lives by a great deliverance. So now it was not you that sent me hither, but God: and he hath made me a father to Pharaoh, and lord of all his house, and a ruler throughout all the land of Egypt" (vv. 5, 7-8).

God's people need to evaluate hardships in the context of their relationship to God. Listen to Paul: "And we know that all things work together for good to them that love God, to them who are called according to his purpose" (Rom. 8:28).

III. A godly man resists temptations.

A. *Joseph resisted the solicitations of Potiphar's wife.* Another reason that one can consider Joseph a godly man is because of his resistance in the presence of strong temptation. Joseph had been promoted from a slave to the manager of Potiphar's household. Joseph was handsome, therefore, Potiphar's wife was attracted to him. Without a doubt she made herself extremely attractive to Joseph. She asked him to have an affair with her, but Joseph refused. In the presence of her attractiveness and her earnest solicitations, Joseph refused.

Temptations comprise a part of life. The satanic solicitor seeks to draw each believer from God's intended direction. God wants us to have His power to resist these solicitations. You can only resist the temptations of life by having God's power within to say no.

B. *Joseph had reasons for resisting the woman's temptations.* Several sources caused Joseph to resist. First, he had respect for Potiphar. "But he refused, and said unto his master's wife, Behold, my master wotteth not what is with me in the house, and he hath committed all that he hath to my hand; There is none greater in this house than I" (Gen. 39:8-9a). Second, Joseph had a great sense of responsibility to God. "How then can I do this great wickedness, and sin against God?" (v. 9b). Third, Joseph respected himself as well as Potiphar's wife. He knew the damage an illicit sexual act would do. He wanted to be able to live with himself. Joseph had the resources to resist temptation.

Conclusion. Would you like for someone to say about you, "He or she is a good person"? You have a good model. Studying the life of Joseph provides an adequate example for you. If you seek to imitate his life, you will know how to be a good person. But greater than following his example is having a relationship with Joseph's God. If you will open your life to God, you will have the resources to be good! —*HTB*

* * *

WEDNESDAY EVENING, NOVEMBER 30

TITLE: Start Over Where You Began

TEXT: "And God said unto Jacob, Arise, go up to Bethel . . . make there an altar unto God, that appeared unto thee when thou fleddest from the face of Esau thy brother" (Gen. 35:1).

SCRIPTURE READING: Genesis 35:1-10

Introduction. To Jacob, Bethel was more than a geographical location. It was the place where he had first come to know the Lord in a personal way. All of us have our Bethels. For some of us, it is where we accepted Jesus Christ as personal Savior. This certainly ought to be the most hallowed spot. We may also have "smaller Bethels" in our lives—those times when we awakened to a more meaningful relationship with God. Whatever Jacob may have known about God before his Bethel experience, we do not know. We can be certain, however, that this was the dearest place on earth to Jacob because there he entered into a relationship with the Lord that, though clouded over at times by sin, remained his moment of inspiration that sent him forth with a song in his heart.

Now God wants him to follow up the Jabbok experience with a time of fresh dedication. He calls upon him to go back to the place of spiritual origin. The text does not tell us that God commanded him to do it, but Jacob took his household with him and told them to put away the strange gods they had become attached to during the days in Haran, to purify themselves, and put on fresh clothes as a symbol of a new spiritual beginning.

How Jacob's heart must have beat faster when they handed him all the various pieces of jewelry which stood for dedication to foreign gods and practices. He hid them and, most likely, never went back to secure them. Some great teachings are found in this account.

I. We all need periods of fresh beginning.

The world is "too much with us." We cling, too often and too long, to the superficial things that a secular way of life offers. Even though we have surrendered to Jesus, our dedication is far from complete. We do not bow down to gods as the pagans did, but we often incorporate their value system into our lifestyle. Although technically, we cannot "rededicate" something that has once been dedicated, we can reaffirm our dedication and loyalty. We can ask God to help us make a fresh start. We can tell Him once more that we love Him and seek to lead our families into closer fellowship with Him.

II. A truly saved person never forgets.

If one has once experienced deliverance from sin, it will always remain as a special experience in his life. The New Testament doctrine of "once saved always saved" in the teachings of Paul is reflected, in some senses, in this story. Jacob had been delivered by God at Bethel and he never forgot it. Years of sinning and selfishness had driven a wedge between him and proper fellowship with God, but the relationship was still there. We cannot always find perfect analogies between the Old Testament and New Testament in spiritual experiences, but here we can see enough to make a comparison. God delivered Jacob at

Bethel from fear and distress. At Calvary, He paid the price to deliver us from the fear of sin and the distress of guilt. We need to come back often to our initial experience in order to secure renewed grace for living and strength for service.

III. For maximum happiness, sin must be put away.

Even though we are saved from the guilt of our iniquities by the atonement made at Calvary, the influence of worldliness is an ever-present threat. How much Jacob was personally influenced by the gods of Laban's family we cannot be sure, but his family seemed to have picked up the habit of idol worship. Perhaps Jacob did not personally indulge, but his influence was not strong enough to keep his family from this sin. How often this is true of us! Our lives are not so much terrible as they are empty. There is not enough spirituality in our homes to lead our children to faith in Christ. We need to go back to the Bethel experience and secure fresh motivation. We need to clean out the cobwebs and eliminate the trash. God had given Jacob a new name at Jabbok. He renews this truth at Bethel. He expects a new direction from now on in Jacob's life.

Conclusion. Do you need the Bethel experience? What would it do for you if you genuinely returned to the eager desire to serve Christ that you had on the day you were saved? Why not spend some moments by yourself reviewing the time you were saved and reaffirming your faith in the Savior? Would this not lead you to a deeper dedication in your Christian life? We all need to do this from time to time.

— *FMW*

* * *

SUGGESTED PREACHING PROGRAM FOR THE MONTH OF DECEMBER

Sunday Mornings

"God's Affirmative Action" is the suggested theme for a series of Advent sermons celebrating the coming of God into human flesh.

Sunday Evenings

"Go Tell It on the Mountain" is the suggested theme for messages which emphasize the need for modern-day followers of Christ to publish the Good News that was proclaimed dramatically at the time of His birth.

Wednesday Evenings

The patriarch Joseph continues to speak powerfully to those who read the Book of Genesis. "Lessons From Joseph" is the suggested theme.

* * *

SUNDAY MORNING, DECEMBER 4

TITLE: God's Affirmative Action Program: the Reason

TEXT: "In him was life, and the life was the light of men. And the light shineth in darkness; and the darkness comprehended it not" (John 1:4, 5).

SCRIPTURE READING: John 1:1-5

HYMNS: "Come, Thou Almighty King" Anonymous
"Joy to the World!" Watts
"Go Tell It on the Mountain," Work

OFFERTORY PRAYER:

Our Father, as we come on the first Sunday of this month in which we give attention to the birth of Jesus Christ, Your Son, help us not to lose the Christ in the trappings of Christmas. So much can divert our attention from You; help us to be attentive to the main event of the Christmas season.

The Christmas season makes us think of giving. As You have given so much for us, notably Your Son who came to earth and died on the cross for us, may we not slight You in the giving of our gifts. Make us generous to Your causes as You have been generous to us and our needs. Accept our gratitude for Your generous mercy to us. Accept and bless our gifts as we give them to You. And forgive us our sins, we pray. In Jesus' name. Amen.

Introduction. With words we say, "I love you." With words we communicate grief, sorrow, joy, and happiness.

When God wanted to communicate with humankind, He did it with a word. John 1:1, with words reminiscent of Genesis 1:1, expresses it, "In the beginning was the Word. . . ."

In recent years we have heard a lot about Affirmative Action Programs. The federal government has been interested in Affirmative Action Programs to see that businesses right some wrongs, balance some imbalances, correct some faults—to bring reconciliation. God also had an Affirmative Action Program. It, too, was designed to bring reconciliation—reconciliation between God and man. In these Sundays leading up to and including Christmas Day we will examine God's Affirmative Action Program as expressed in the prologue to John's gospel, John 1:1-18.

The first matter to consider is the reason for God's Affirmative Action Program. Why did God need an Affirmative Action Program?

Why did God have an Affirmative Action Program? Because humankind needed a new beginning in Christ and God had a word He wanted to say to us, a word of witness to the new creation in Christ.

I. God had an Affirmative Action Program because God had a word for us.

A. *This Word of God is communicative.*

When the writer of the fourth gospel wanted to tell us of God's Word to us, he chose a concept that would communicate to all the people who would receive this gospel. The concept was "Word." To Jews, Greeks, Christians, and the world at large this was a concept that would communicate what God had done in Christ Jesus.

1. Power. To the Jews the Word of God meant power. God spoke a word and the world came into being (Gen. 1). The Word of God could burn like fire or shatter like a hammer (Jer. 23:29). The Word of God could accomplish divine purpose (Isa. 55:11). The Hebrews who would read this gospel would immediately understand the power of God when they understood that the Word was in the beginning with God and was God.

2. Principle. But to the Greek reader "the Word" would mean a rational principle. It had to do more with philosophical thought than personal power. The Jewish apologist Philo had adopted this Greek philosophical concept to refer to the projected thought of the transcendent God, the clue to the meaning and purpose to life.

3. Proclamation. The early Christian church viewed the preaching of the gospel as a "ministry of the word" (Acts 6:4). The entire event of Christ's life was a divine declaration, a redemptive proclamation. We are told in Revelation that "his name is called The Word of God" (Rev. 19:13). In preaching the Word, the early Christians were proclaiming the redemptive message of Jesus Christ.

4. Person. The unique conviction of the prologue to John's gospel is that the Word of God became a Person. It was not just power or principle or proclamation but person. When truth becomes personal, it becomes meaningful to us.

God had a word for us, a word that communicates to us in a personal way that we can be made right with God.

B. *The Word of God is comprehensive.*

1. It relates to God. The Word is identical with God. It is not just that the Word is identified with God; it is identical with God. When you want to see God and know what God is like, you look to Jesus Christ. He is related to God in being. He gives us an accurate communication of God.

2. It relates to the world. The Word of God relates to the world in that it was the agent of creation. God is always known by His creative activity. John and Paul both wanted to make sure that we know that creation was as much the

work of Christ as was redemption. God relates to the world in creativity.

3. It relates to humankind. But the comprehensive Word which God spoke also relates to all of humankind. It is expressed in two terms: life and light. These translate to redemption. Jesus Christ is related to humankind redemptively.

So the reason for God's Affirmative Action Program is that God had a Word for us, a Word that was both communicative and comprehensive. By this Word God spoke the last Word to us. Listen to the opening words of the Book of Hebrews: "In many and various ways God spoke of old to our fathers by the prophets; but in these last days he has spoken to us by a Son, whom he appointed the heir of all things, through whom also he created the world" (Heb. 1:1-2 RSV).

II. God had an Affirmative Action Program because God had a witness to us.

If the Word which God has spoken to us shows us what Christ, the Word, is, it also shows us what Christ does. Through this Word that had become flesh, God gave a witness to Himself in this world. Christ came into the world to reveal God and to redeem persons. That witness is expressed in two key words in John's Gospel: life and light.

A. *Life.*

In Christ there is life. One thing Jesus did was to impart life to persons who lived with no hope of eternal life.

For all the hopeless, helpless, wondering, wandering people in the world Jesus gives the promise that there is life—life with worth and meaning. Jacob Timmerman was a Jewish newspaper publisher in Argentina. In 1977 he was taken prisoner by the revolutionary government due to his writing. Placed in a prison and subjected to torture, he has told his story in a book entitled *Prisoner Without a Name, Cell Without a Number*. One night the guard failed to close the peephole in his door. When he looked out the peephole, he saw that the peephole in the door facing his was also open. Then he saw an eye behind it. Looking through the peephole was forbidden. Thinking it was a trap he stepped back, waited, then returned to the peephole. The eye on the other side of the hall did the same. Through that night they looked through the peephole at one another. They never knew who the other was. But that blinking, that flutter of a movement proved to Timmerman that he was not the last human survivor on earth amid that universe of torturing custodians. They invented games that night, moving away, then returning, creating movement in their confined world. And there was the blink, the acknowledgment that there was life. That night in the solitude he knew there was life (condensed in *Reader's Digest,* Nov., 1981, pp. 233-234).

In the Word God has a witness to us that there is life.

B. *Light.*

This life is also described as light.

Christ brings light into the world—light about our darkened ideas about sin, about self, and about salvation. The light of God's love shines about us in Jesus Christ. Twice in John's gospel Jesus made the claim for Himself, "I am the light of the world" (John 8:12; 9:5).

Notice something about this light. The darkness cannot put it out. The light of God's grace shines with such power that the depths of the darkness cannot put it out. The light of God's love shines with such power that the darkness cannot even dim it. God's light in Jesus Christ is brighter than all the accumulated darkness of the world's sin and refusal to come to the light.

God's witness to us is that the Word has become flesh and lived among us. This gives witness to both what we can know about God and what we can experience with God—life and light.

Conclusion. When you have something to say, you use a word to express it. God expressed His love for us, His life in us, and His light to us in a Word—Jesus Christ. That Word became flesh and dwelt among us. Through it we see God and respond to His love in faith. —*JEC*

* * *

SUNDAY EVENING, DECEMBER 4

TITLE: Telling the Good News

TEXT: **"And the angel said to them, 'Be not afraid; for behold, I bring you good news of a great joy which will come to all the people; for to you is born this day in the city of David a Savior, who is Christ the Lord'" (Luke 2:10-11 RSV).**

SCRIPTURE READING: **Luke 2:8-14**

Introduction. It is significant that an angelic choir announced the birth of Jesus Christ to an astonished group of shepherds.

It has been the privilege and joy of the followers of Christ to sing and speak of His coming since that significant night.

It is the privilege of present-day followers of Jesus Christ to join that angelic choir and tell the Good News with joyful sound.

The early followers of Christ were "going" witnesses, and as they went, they told the Good News. It is interesting to note where they shared this Good News.

I. **They shared the Good News in the city of Jerusalem where Jesus had been crucified** (Acts 2:5-8).

II. **They shared the Good News in the temple area which was dedicated to worship** (v. 46a).

III. **They shared the Good News from house to house** (vv. 43-46; 20:20).

IV. **They shared the Good News in the streets and marketplaces** (5:15; 14:8-10).

V. **They shared the Good News in the synagogues** (cf. Acts 6:9-10).

VI. **The Good News was shared with an Ethiopian eunuch on a desert highway** (8:26-38).

VII. **Peter and others shared the Good News in the house of Cornelius the Gentile** (10:22-48).

VIII. **Paul and Silas shared the Good News while confined to a prison cell** (16:25-32).

IX. **Paul shared the Good News while aboard a ship at sea** (27:22-25).

X. **Paul shared the Good News before governors and kings** (24:1-27; 26:1-32).

Conclusion. We can see that under all kinds of circumstances and in a great variety of different places, the early disciples of our Lord joined the angelic choir in communicating not only the birth but the miraculous life, the substitutionary death, and the victorious resurrection of Jesus Christ.

We should follow the suggestion of the poet who said,

Go tell it on the mountain,
Over the hills and everywhere;
Go tell it on the mountain,
That Jesus Christ is Lord.

—*TTC*

* * *

WEDNESDAY EVENING, DECEMBER 7

TITLE: Dream, But Don't Make Dreams Your Master

TEXT: **"And they said one to another, Behold, this dreamer cometh" (Gen. 37:19).**

SCRIPTURE READING: **Genesis 37:1-28**

Introduction. Joseph, like Jacob, stands out as one of the most delightful and exciting characters of the Old Testament. Unlike Jacob, he had brothers of different mothers. This contributed to the diversity of interest and intensely competitive spirit among the children, leading to actual hostility. Although Jacob and Esau had their differences, they shared the same parents; and, in the end, they seemed to have become reconciled to the point that they did not seek harm for one another.

On the other hand, Joseph, although he forgave his brothers, remained a possible threat to them, at least in their own minds, until the very end. Although he had forgiven them and given them positions of privilege in Egypt, they feared that after their father Jacob died, he would still retaliate for the evil they had done to him.

The Scripture here concerns the early years of Joseph. He dreamed dreams, and it appears certain that God was in them. On the other hand, this youthful lad talked glibly about them. Even though we recognize that Joseph was chosen of God for a great mission, he was still a human being, and it is not irreverent to point out certain things about his immaturity.

I. Dreams are important.

The prophet Joel said that young men "see visions." How true! Youth is the time when we perceive with piercing distinctness because our faculty of vision is fresh. The true test of a man's ability to cope with life is his vision. Man, unlike other creatures, can see and evaluate the future. No one but man can watch the stars with intelligent curiosity or seek to read the future with God's help.

Men live by visions. Foolish people laugh at ideas and concepts they cannot understand. Dreams are not, as they have been called, "the vaguest things we know." They represent ideals, and we cannot dismiss a matter by saying, "It's a very good thing, but it's only an ideal." The world owes much to good men who have dreamed and then worked hard to make their dreams come true.

II. Dreams can be dangerous.

If it is wrong never to dream, it can also be wrong to dream and then act unwisely and indiscreetly with reference to the dreams. We should be careful about telling others all of our secrets. Some things are too intimate to be shared. When we feel that God has revealed something to us privately, we should deliberate carefully before we say too much about it to other people. For one thing, we may be wrong. What we feel God is saying to us may merely be our subjective egotism, a projection of our own desires. Then, too, even if we are correct in discerning God's will, others are perhaps not ready to learn all that we know. God has revealed the truth to us because it is something He wishes to share with us. We need to consider carefully when other people are ready and able to hear our "word from the Lord."

Joseph let it be known that he considered himself a man with a "great future"; and, no doubt, the implication of his words was that God had spoken to him in the dreams. This irritated his brothers, a fact that does not surprise us.

III. To make dreams come true requires hard work.

Many years ago I heard a message entitled "Dreams Plus," which I have never forgotten. I cannot remember all of the outline nor the illustrations the speaker used, but I do remember that he suggested the things we need to add to our dreams in order to make them become a reality. The one I remember most was "hard work," which he emphasized more than any other point. God helps us when we are in His will, but God does not do for us the things we can do for ourselves.

Let it be said to Joseph's credit that he added hard work to his dreams. As we shall see in other studies of his life story, he kept himself morally pure, waited patiently, and took advantage of every opportunity. These things are necessary if we are to see our dreams become realities.

Conclusion. Although we cannot agree with all of the theology in the popular song of many years ago, two lines, if separated from their context, are certainly true. The song says,

> If your heart is in your dream
> No request is too extreme.

If we apply this to a Christian context, we can accept the truth of it. God will give us the strength, if we will be faithful to Him, to realize our ambitions—provided, of course, they are worthy of His help. We all need to be dreamers, for without vision either an individual or a nation perishes; but we must not let our dreams master us. We need to "stay on top of them" and never cease until the dream of yesterday becomes the fact of tomorrow. This is what faith is all about. One writer said that faith is "an affirmation and an act that bids eternal truth be present fact."

— *FMW*

* * *

SUNDAY MORNING, DECEMBER 11

TITLE: God's Affirmative Action Program: the Revelation

TEXT: "He was not that Light, but was sent to bear witness of that Light" (John 1:8).

SCRIPTURE READING: John 1:6-8

HYMNS: "Send the Light," McCabe
"Come, Thou Long Expected Jesus," Wesley
"Christ Is the World's True Light," Briggs

OFFERTORY PRAYER:

Our Father, accept our gratitude for this day, this life, and all these blessings you have given to us. Make us as excited to be human beings as You were to become one of us. Help us to know the light that Jesus, the Christ, can bring into our lives. Allow us to open all the dark places of our hearts and lives to the sunshine of the Savior's love. Shine into our lives, and give light and life, we pray.

Into Your hands we give the money that is representative of our lives. May we be just as free to give our lives into Your hands and to Your will. Forgive us our sins and assure us of Your continued presence. In Jesus' name and for His sake we pray. Amen.

Introduction. Someone is always telling.

There hardly seems to be anything a person can do without its getting out. Someone always leaks the news. Lyndon Johnson once warned Henry Kissinger to read the newspaper columnists and see which of his associates they were saying nice things about, then fire him. That would be the staff person who was leaking secret news to the press.

Whatever the secret is, it can't be kept. Someone always knows. And someone always tells.

Revelation is one of the words that we use to express this. A revelation is a making known; it is the opening up and the showing out of a truth.

God's Affirmative Action Program had a revelation. It became known. But the revelation of what God was doing in the world through Jesus Christ, His Son, was not an accidental exposure. It was by design.

I. The revelation in God's Affirmative Action Program uses an instrument.

A. *Commission.*

John was the instrument of God's revelation of what He was doing in the world. That John was born was no accident. Notice how the gospel expressed it: "There was a man sent from God, whose name was John" (1:6).

John was a person under commission from God Himself. We move from eternity into time. The first verse of the prologue (1:1) tells us that Jesus existed throughout all eternity. This sixth verse tells us that into time as we know it there came one with a commission: to reveal to us the Promised One sent by God. God sent a man to tell us that He had sent His Son. This was John's commission.

B. *Mission.*

But John was also a man on a mission. Commissioned by God, he had a mission to men. That mission was to give witness to the light that would shine in the world.

Notice that the gospel makes a clear distinction between Jesus Christ, the Light of the World, and John the Baptist who bore witness to the light. His mission was to introduce persons to the One whose light could lead them into life.

C. *Submission.*

The purpose of the witness of John was that people might submit themselves in faith to Jesus Christ as personal Savior. The Scripture expressed it through the words, " . . . that all men through him might believe" (v. 7).

"Believe" is used in the Gospel of John as "faith" is used in other gospel accounts. "Believe" is the verb; "faith" is the noun. Verbs, as you will remember, express action. *Believe* is the action you take toward Jesus Christ when you realize that He has brought the salvation of God to you.

We are also to be instruments of God in giving this witness.

II. The revelation in God's Affirmative Action Program has an illumination:

Light always indicates illumination. John the Baptist was not the light that would illuminate the world. But he would bear witness to the true light that would illuminate the darkened life of every person. Have you ever stood on a dark night, trying to get your bearings, when suddenly a flash of light illuminated the area sufficiently for you to see where you were? God's light flashes into our lives in Jesus Christ. William Barclay has suggested three areas where the light of Jesus Christ has illuminated the shadows of life.

A. *Doubt.*

People have often doubted that they could know God. God seemed so unreal and so unknowable to them. But the coming of Christ into the world has removed that shadow. We do not have to wonder if God is or what He is like. We have Jesus Christ to show us the character of God. Since the Word was with God from the very beginning and the Word was God Himself, then the Word is what God is. The doubts that we have about God are gone.

When Christ came into the world bringing light, He dispelled the doubts about God. We can know God.

B. *Despair.*

The world into which Jesus came was filled with despair. The Greek philosopher Seneca said, "Men are conscious of their helplessness in necessary things." But Jesus gave hope. With Christ there can be forgiveness, strength, and help for living. The light Christ has shed into lives dispells despair. Persons no longer have to live in despair with no hope or help. Christ gives both hope and help. He gives salvation.

C. *Death.*

The ancient world feared death. At best, death was annihilation. At worst, death was torture by whatever gods there were. People were afraid of those possibilities. But Jesus—by His coming, His life, His death, and His resurrection—showed that death was only the way to a larger life. Death did not have to be feared any longer. Christ defeated death. And we can live in that victory.

With the coming of Christ into the world, there was light in the world. This light illuminated all the dark places of life to shine with God's glory and grace.

III. The revelation in God's Affirmative Action Program is inclusive.

Notice how inclusive is this revelation of God: " . . . that all men through him might believe . . . which lighteth every man that cometh into the world" (vv. 7-9).

The ancient world was rather exclusive. The Jews hated the Gentiles and taught that the Gentiles were created for no other purpose than to be fuel for the fires of hell. The Greeks never dreamed that their knowledge was for every person. The Roman world looked down on the other peoples whose language they did not understand and called them barbarians. But Christ came to give light to every person. The love of God is inclusive.

Notice the implications of this fact.

A. *Witness.*

John's witness was for all persons. He was to witness to the world that Jesus Christ gave both life and light. God's love and forgiveness are for all persons.

Edwin Markham, the poet, came to the age of retirement after a long and successful career anticipating a life of ease and rest. Then he made the shocking discovery that his life savings had been mishandled and fraudulently appropriated by a banker friend. He found no legal recourse, so he was a pauper at retirement.

Bitterness filled his soul as he tried to restructure his life. He attempted to write again, but he was so obsessed with the injustice that had been done him and the bitterness that he felt toward his former friend that he could not write.

Markham sat one day drawing circles—doodling. Finally, he cried out, "I must forgive him or I shall die!" He knelt and prayed that God would help him, and immediately the peace of God came into his life.

B. *Missions.*

If God's love encircles everyone, this also implies missions. No person or nation is outside the circle of God's love. The Christmas season is a perfect time to think about missions because the coming of Christ into the world assures us that the love of God and the salvation from God is intended for all the world. It is a worldwide work that God has begun in Christ Jesus.

A missions volunteer once testified that one of the things that sharpened her call to missions was observing a door with an electric eye in a department store while doing Christmas shopping. She noticed that the door opened for anyone who came to it. Any person who broke the beam of the electric eye had entrance into the store. Similarly, she realized, the doors to the kingdom of heaven open to any person who approaches them. God's love is for everyone. That is the basis for missions.

Conclusion. During the Christmas season we remember God's Affirmative Action Program. God took an affirmative action in sending His Son, Jesus, into the world to make Himself known to us and to die on the cross to redeem us from our sin. He had a witness to that. John revealed what God had done as He pointed to the Christ. As this revelation has been made known to you, will you respond in faith?

—*JEC*

* * *

SUNDAY EVENING, DECEMBER 11

TITLE: The Motive for Telling the Good News

TEXT: "Now those who were scattered went about preaching the word" (Acts 8:4 RSV).

SCRIPTURE READING: Acts 8:1-8

Introduction. The angels hung out over the battlements of heaven to announce the good news that Jesus Christ was born. It is interesting to study the Book of Acts and discover the dynamic enthusiasm with which the early followers of Christ had an inner compulsion that would not be silenced, giving testimony to Him.

It might be revealing to discover that there were a number of different motives that moved them to share the Good News.

I. The painful shock of persecution motivated them to move out into new areas of witnessing.

At first the church was completely Jewish in its constituency. Jesus came to a group of people who were rather clannish and restricted in their world view. They found it impossible to believe at first that God loved the whole world.

It was the pain and shock of persecution that thrust them out of the city of Jerusalem into areas beyond. And our text tells us that as they went, they announced the Good News.

The fact that they did not necessarily go because of a great love for a lost world may comfort us. But let us not allow this fact to move us to complacency.

II. They shared the Good News because they discovered the joy of being bearers of good news (Acts 2:41-47; 5:42).

It is always a burdensome task to be the bearer of sad news. No one likes to convey the information that someone has died or is terminally ill.

It is joyous to bring good news. The gospel is not good advice. The gospel is good news from God concerning what He was seeking to accomplish in the life, teachings, death, and resurrection of Jesus Christ.

This was such wonderful news that once it was understood, the early church could not remain silent. They were motivated by the joy that they experienced within their hearts in the privilege of being communicators of the Good News.

III. The early followers of Christ shared the Good News as a personal response to the authority of their crucified but risen and living Lord (Matt. 28:18-20).

To the early apostles, the lordship of Jesus Christ was real.

A. *They recognized Him as Lord over nature.*

B. *They recognized Him as Lord over the demoniac.*

C. *They recognized Him as Lord over disease.*

D. *They recognized Him as Lord over death.*

E. *They recognized Him as Lord of their very lives.* To them bearing witness for Christ was not an elective, it was an imperative.

IV. The early Christians were sharers of the Good News because they responded to the leadership of the Holy Spirit.

The Book of Acts is a success story. It declares the success of these early followers of Christ as, under the leadership of the Holy Spirit, they communicated the good news of the birth, life, and great redemption that is available through Jesus Christ.

V. **These early Christians shared the Good News about the Christ because they believed that all men away from Christ are lost from God and do not know the way home—there is salvation in no other** (Acts 4:12).

VI. **The early Christians shared the Good News because it is most natural, normal, and proper for a Christian to want others to become followers of Jesus Christ also.**

Conclusion. Because of compassion and the command of Christ, we should do with great joy as the chorus tells us:

Go tell it on the mountain,
Over the hills and everywhere;
Go tell it on the mountain,
That Jesus Christ is born.

—*TTC*

* * *

WEDNESDAY EVENING, DECEMBER 14

TITLE: Without Purity, We Cannot Please God

TEXT: **"How then can I do this great wickedness, and sin against God?" (Gen. 39:9c).**

SCRIPTURE READING: **Genesis 39:1-20**

Introduction. Whatever immaturities Joseph may have had as a young lad, his dedication and genuineness of character more than made up for them. When he arrived in Egypt as a slave, Potiphar, Pharaoh's chief executioner, bought him. Immediately Joseph advanced in position and, within a short time, was trusted with great responsibilities. His trouble, however, began when his master's wife sought to entice him. Joseph refused, but she would not give up. Later, the wicked woman accused Joseph of doing the very thing he had consistently refused to do.

This incident, the refusal of Joseph to compromise his moral integrity, is perhaps the most remembered fact about his life in Egypt. The event certainly stands as a "watershed" in his career. If Joseph had yielded to Potiphar's wife's advances, the history of his life would probably have been far different. He stood firm on his convictions and was forced to go to jail, but he emerged victorious a few years later. One interesting sidelight to the story is that Potiphar probably did not actually believe his wife's story. If he had, Joseph would have been executed immediately. When Potiphar placed him in jail, he was actually showing mercy. If the chief executioner of the land had felt his slave was trying to seduce his wife, he would have had him killed. Interesting lessons speak to us from this story.

I. You can't keep a good man down.

Quality of life will show wherever we are. Joseph must have performed his tasks well in Potiphar's home. We do not know exactly how long it took for him to be recognized as a person of responsibility, but the text suggests that it was soon. We read, "And it came to pass from the time that he had made him overseer in his house, and over all that he had, that the LORD blessed the Egyptian's house for Joseph's sake; and the blessing of the LORD was upon all that he had in the house, and in the field" (Gen. 39:5). The Scripture continues by saying that Potiphar left all that he had in Joseph's hands and did not know what he had except the bread which he ate. Likewise, Joseph was not boasting but simply stating a true fact when he said, "There is none greater in this house than I; neither hath he kept back any thing from me" (v. 9). God's blessing was upon Potiphar's house, but we are safe in saying that part of the fact that Potiphar's business prospered was that Joseph was a good administrator.

II. Sin of any kind is against God.

When Potiphar's wife insisted that Joseph yield to her advances, he said to her, "How then can I do this great wickedness, and sin against God?" (v. 9b), which shows Joseph thought first in terms of his relationship to God. He knew that it would be wrong to take another man's wife, but he also kept before him the fact that it was God's moral law, first of all, that must be obeyed.

All sin is against God. This is because God has ordained the moral law. When we mistreat another person, we mistreat one of God's creatures. When we abuse our body, we abuse the temple in which the Lord dwells. So-called "sins against society" are, first of all, sins against God.

III. Personal purity is essential for successful living.

No sin known will blight a young person's life and cripple his chances for happiness in the future as much as sexual immorality. When one crosses the line of physical indulgence and allows himself to become impure in this realm, something happens to his life. Things are never the same. Even if we are saved and forgiven, we carry with us the crippling effects of the deed. More than a century ago, a young man led a young woman into a passionate indulgence. As a result, she became weaker and went from one promiscuous experience to another, ending up as a broken piece of feminine humanity. Later, the young man had a genuine experience of salvation, and the Lord called him to preach. He carried with him the memory of what he had done to this young woman. He could not rest until he searched and found her. He pled with a broken heart for her to forgive him and sought to lead her to forgiveness in Christ and the beginning of a new life, but she was weak and unable to "come back" as he had done. This man carried a broken heart to the grave.

Conclusion. Guard your personal purity! Like the little white ermine that protects its white fur even at the cost of its life, remember that purity is the dearest thing you possess. When one compromises the sanctity of his body, he usually, if not always, will compromise in other areas, too. Paul said it simply but succinctly to Timothy, "Keep thyself pure" (1 Tim. 5:22). —*FMW*

* * *

SUNDAY MORNING, DECEMBER 18

TITLE: God's Affirmative Action Program: the Response

TEXT: "He came unto his own, and his own received him not. But as many as received him, to them gave he power to become the sons of God, even to them that believe on his name" (John 1:11-12).

Scripture Reading: John 1:9-13

Hymns: "Hark, the Herald Angels Sing," Wesley
"Awake, My Soul, Awake," Keach
"What Wondrous Love Is This," American Folk Hymn

Offertory Prayer:

Our Father, we stand truly amazed at Your love for us. When we consider the message of the Christmas season, that Jesus Christ, Your Son, was born into the world for the forgiveness of our sins, we are breathless. But help us, O Lord, that we will not be so breathless that we cannot give witness to this great event and its meaning to our own lives. And help us, O Lord, that we will not be so unresponsive to the great gift of grace that we will not give our gifts to You in love this day. Please accept our gifts, forgive us our sins, and guide our lives. We pray in Jesus' name. Amen.

Introduction. When the Word that existed from the very beginning became flesh and came to earth to dwell among us—when the light that illuminated the life of every person came to the world that He had created—He was not always well received. The response was not generally positive.

God's Affirmative Action Program affirmed the need of persons for salvation. He sent His Son, described in John's gospel as the Word, to earth for the dual purposes of revealing God and redeeming humankind, expressed in John's prologue as life and light. But the response was not always good.

After a three-verse description of the person who came to bear witness to the light, John the Baptist, and a disclaimer that John the Baptist was not the light himself but was instead a witness to the light, the prologue returns to the description of the Word that became flesh. This portion of the prologue, John 1:9-13, describes the response that the world of persons gave to the light of God. Generally, it was a negative response. Coming to His own earth and to His own people, He was rejected by them. But there was also a positive response. Some accepted Him. To them He gave the privilege of becoming the very children of God.

Notice, then, the response to God's Affirmative Action Program. And consider carefully your own response to it.

I. In the response to God's Affirmative Action Program we see particularity.

A. *Nothing is ever universal until it is first local.*

Particularity is expressed in this passage. The universal light that could light up the life of every person in the world became a particular person—Jesus of Nazareth. The One who existed from before the beginning of the world came into this world at a particular place on the globe and at a particular time in history.

It is one thing to talk about the great universals such as light and life, but they become real to us when those universals are made local. Then we can really know them as they are put into a single life.

God has always made the universal known by showing us the local and particular.

1. God loves all peoples and all races, but through a particular people—the Jews—God revealed Himself.

2. God loves all families of the earth, but in a particular family—the family of Abraham, Isaac, and Jacob—God worked out His love.

3. God delivers all people from the bondage of sin, but in a particular event—the Exodus event—God showed His power of deliverance.

4. God existed for all time, created the world, and sought to reconcile sinning, rebelling humankind to Himself; but in a particular Person—Jesus Christ, the Word who became flesh—God made this known to all people.

B. *Nothing is ever known until it is first experienced.*

What God had been trying to get across to all of humankind was experienced in Jesus Christ. Then it became known by persons. People could see the light that shone brightly in our world by the coming of Christ into the world. Each person had the potential of having his own life illuminated by that light. Then only what had been known intellectually of acceptance, forgiveness, and family could be experienced. Then it would really be known.

The particularity of God's love, grace, mercy, forgiveness, and acceptance became evident when the light that was the Word entered the world that He had created in the particular person of Jesus of Nazareth. That is what we celebrate at Christmas.

II. In the response to God's Affirmative Action Program we see personality.

A. *The personality shows continuity.*

John is careful to show the continuity of the Word that existed from the very beginning and the personality that we know as Jesus of Nazareth.

The Christ who was born into the world at that first Christmastime was not different from the God who had existed always. He was that God. There was a continuity in His existence. He was in the world already; in fact, He had always been in the world. But in the birth of the baby in Bethlehem the One who had always been in the world took on a particular personality that we could see and know.

B. *The personality shows creativity.*

Not only was this personality one of continuity—the same God who had always been in the world had come into His world as a baby—but it also showed creativity. This was the same God who had created the world.

The God who created that world came into it by the birth of Christ. No wonder the angels sang! No wonder the star shone brightly! It was a time for joy and wonder: the Savior was born!

C. *The personality shows closeness.*

The Word who had always been in the world, who had in fact created the world, was now introduced to the world. He was close to us. He could be seen by us. He could be touched by our hands.

That was one of the emphases that John wanted to make. There was a belief in his day that matter was evil and that the God who was good could not have created a world composed of matter. So they came up with the idea that there was a series of emanations from God down to one who was so far removed from God that he could deal in the evil stuff of matter. John, on the other hand, went to great lengths to show that the ever-existent God not only created matter, He took on human flesh; He *became* matter. When He had a body and a personality, He could be seen, touched, and really known. God was personified. God took on a personality. And God had taken on the personality of Jesus when the Word became flesh.

III. In the response to God's Affirmative Action Program we see practicality.

There is a very practical result from God's taking on human flesh and becoming a person in Jesus Christ: everyone is confronted with the Christ and forced to make a choice. The light that can illuminate every life in the world has to be received. God did not force Himself in the world, nor does He force Himself into human lives. A practical decision has to be made.

A. *Negative: rejection of Christ.*

One response that a person can make to Christ is to reject Him. One can turn away from the light. One can refuse the life that He offers through faith.

This is what the prologue of John's gospel expressed. Christ came into the world that He had created, but the world did not receive Him. He came to the people whom He had made and to whom He had made himself known, but His own people did not receive Him. One could face the practical matter of deciding for or against Christ and reject Him.

B. *Positive: acceptance of Christ.*

But some accept Christ. In three repetitious phrases John makes it known that those who accept Christ are given the right (NEB, NIV) to become the children of God. Notice that those who become the children of God do so by the miraculous means of new birth, not by human will or effort. It is through God's grace that persons can know redemption. They become a part of God's family by grace through faith.

Conclusion. There must be a response to God's Affirmative Action Program. Why not make it a positive response and accept the Christ who has affirmed you by coming into your world and giving His life for you? —*JEC*

* * *

SUNDAY EVENING, DECEMBER 18

TITLE: Sharing the Good News

TEXT: ". . . and you shall be my witnesses in Jerusalem and in all Judea and Samaria and to the end of the earth" (Acts 1:8 RSV).

SCRIPTURE READING: Acts 1:6-11

Introduction. There are many ways in which we can follow the words of encouragement given to us by the poet who said,

> Go tell it on the mountain,
> Over the hills and everywhere;
> Go tell it on the mountain,
> That Jesus Christ is born.

I. The Good News can be communicated in a sermon.

Every time the pastor stands in the pulpit, he should have some good news from God for those who are listening.

II. The Good News can be communicated through a song.

Some people have the talent for singing. This should not be so much a display of musical ability as a time for sharing some good news about God.

By our participation in the song portion of our worship services, we can share the experience that is in our hearts about what God has done in us, to us, and for us.

III. The Good News can be communicated in a Bible lesson that is taught.

Every teacher in Sunday school should see himself or herself as a communicator of the good news regarding Jesus Christ. We are not merely to teach the Bible. We are to communicate the Good News from God which is contained in the Bible.

IV. The Good News can be communicated in the form of a personal testimony to a group.

If we are sensitive and alert, we will have opportunities from time to time to share the good news about what Christ means to us. This should be done in such a manner as not to create the impression that we are overly pious.

V. The Good News can be communicated in a personal conversation.

One should be no more hesitant about sharing the good news of what God means to him than about how he enjoys a good meal.

VI. One can even use the telephone to share the Good News with others.

There are times when people are unavailable, but it is possible to be in touch with them by telephone. We can use the telephone to register our concern and to indicate our hope for their spiritual welfare.

VII. The Good News can be communicated in a letter or Christmas card.

God can use a written as well as a spoken message to help someone come to have faith in Jesus Christ.

VIII. The Good News can be communicated through a book presented as a gift to one who is interested in reading.

IX. The Good News can be communicated through the investments we make in the work of God.

X. The Good News can be communicated through causes that we support.

Conclusion. There is no limit to the manner and forms that are available to communicating the Good News that Jesus Christ is born.

We need to share this Good News personally.
We need to share this Good News prayerfully.
We need to share this Good News in the present. — *TTC*

* * *

WEDNESDAY EVENING, DECEMBER 21

TITLE: Ingratitude Is a Marble-Hearted Fiend

TEXT: "Yet did not the chief butler remember Joseph, but forgat him" (Gen. 40:23).

SCRIPTURE READING: Genesis 40:1-23

Introduction. Even while he was in prison, Joseph's sterling character shone forth. The keeper of the prison recognized Joseph's integrity and put him in charge of all the prisoners. Like Potiphar, the warden gave Joseph free reign, and God caused everything he did to prosper.

Once more dreams entered into Joseph's life. The royal butler and the royal baker were both in prison, and both dreamed dreams. Joseph interpreted their dreams correctly. The baker was killed, and the butler was restored to his position. Joseph refused to take credit for the wisdom but gave it to God. Also, he requested the butler to remember him kindly and make mention of him to Pharaoh. The butler agreed; but after he was restored to favor, he failed to keep his promise. Oh, the tragedy of ingratitude! Let us look at the story closely and glean some truths.

I. God keeps His eye on His chosen ones.

We must never forget, even in these beautiful "character stories," that the most important message of the Old Testament is the fact that God was working redemptively through the nation He had chosen. Although our Savior did not come through the line of Joseph, God used Joseph to preserve the Israelites, and, at this time, he was the "key person" in the messianic story.

Of course, not all of us are chosen for such a strategic mission, but we all are important to God. He has a place for each of us in His service; and if we show Him we intend to do His will and perform that which He has chosen for us to do, He will take care of us. An old truism says that every Christian is divinely protected as long as he is in the will of God and doing what God has mapped out for him. In spite of all the opposition of the wicked people he encountered, Joseph continued to prosper because he was faithful in his living and loyal to the things God had planned for him.

II. Evil people respect good people.

If a person today will live right and stay humble, wicked people will be impressed and show a proper attitude toward him or her. Of course, both righteous living and a proper attitude are important. If we are overbearing in our righteous deeds, we can easily hurt our cause and even bring the wrath of others down on us. Joseph stayed humble even when great responsibility was given to him. When he was called on to interpret the dreams, he gave credit to God. Wisdom is a great virtue, but to give credit to the Lord for our wisdom is the zenith of it all.

Some have criticized Joseph for seeking to extract a promise from the butler, claiming that he was not trusting God sufficiently. This is not a fair accusation, however, because God expects us to use every legitimate means of advancing ourselves as long as we do not violate Christian conscience or employ unchristian methods. Joseph was doing what any of us would have done under the same circumstances. He was patient, but he also saw a chance to better himself and took advantage of it. No one can blame him for what he did. In fact, he gives to us an example of using constructively every opportunity that comes to us.

III. Selfishness and ingratitude are Siamese twins.

Very few statements in the Bible are as sad as the words, "Yet did not the chief butler remember Joseph, but forgat him" (Gen. 40:23). Before we condemn the butler too much, however, we need to look at our own lives and ask whether we have been fair with people who did favors for us. In fact, the greatest kindness ever shown to anyone is when Jesus Christ died on the cross for us. Have we been faithful to Him? Have we kept the vows we made in the early days of our salvation experiences when our hearts were tender and grateful?

Of course, the butler did remember Joseph later, but it was when he saw a chance to impress the Pharaoh. How often our good deeds are mingled with selfish motives! If Satan cannot get us to do a bad thing, he will lead us to do a good thing with the wrong spirit and from the wrong motive. This also is a part of ingratitude.

Conclusion. Take a good look at yourself! Recall friends who have helped you along the way. Perhaps it was the person who led you to Christ as Savior. It may have been a person who helped you secure a job or a teacher who opened up new areas of truth to you. What about your parents who made sacrifices for years in order to give you a good education? —*FMW*

* * *

SUNDAY MORNING, DECEMBER 25

TITLE: God's Affirmative Action Program: the Reality

TEXT: "And the Word was made flesh, and dwelt among us, (and we beheld his glory, the glory as of the only begotten of the Father,) full of grace and truth" (John 1:14).

SCRIPTURE READING: John 1:14-18

HYMNS: "It Came Upon a Midnight Clear," Sears
"Angels, From the Realms of Glory," Montgomery
"Silent Night, Holy Night," Mohr

OFFERTORY PRAYER:

Our Father, on this day that we celebrate the birth of Jesus Christ, Your Son and our Savior, into the world, give us the grace to truly celebrate. We celebrate Your loving concern for us. We celebrate Your willingness to share life with us. We celebrate Your identification with us. We celebrate Your salvation to us.

On this day when so much attention is given to gifts, may we think primarily of Your gift to us of Your Son who gave life . . . of His sacrifice which gives eternal life . . . of Your abiding presence in the Holy Spirit which gives meaningful life. . . . We give our gifts to You. Please accept them, bless them, and strengthen each one of us with Your great gift of grace. In Jesus' name we pray. Amen.

Introduction. God's Affirmative Action Program became a reality on a cold winter's night when Jesus was born in Bethlehem. At that time the preexistent, eternal Word took on human flesh and came to live among us. From this point on John no longer calls Him "the Word" but lets out the secret and gives us His name—Jesus Christ.

God took affirmative action toward us. Jesus Christ had come into our world. What people had hoped for and looked toward had become a reality.

I. In the reality of God's Affirmative Action Program there is exaltation.

A. *Before exaltation, there is limitation.*

John 1:14 shows three ways in which the Word was limited; the self-limiting aspect of the Incarnation is expressed in these terms.

1. A limitation of time. The preexistent Word who had existed from the very beginning became a Person, who lived at a certain time in human history. He who had transcended all time was born at a specific time.

2. A limitation of temperament. The Word became flesh. He actually became a human being. He took on the full temperament of a person. Jesus' appearance in history was not a theophany but an incarnation. The appearance of God to Moses at the burning bush was a theophany, an appearance of God. The burning bush was commandeered for its purpose—it was used and abandoned. But Jesus' appearance was an incarnation. He was not commandeered but surrendered His will to the Father's purpose. His human nature was not marginal but central to His mission. The biblical record tells us that the child grew, that He increased in wisdom. He was authentically human. As any child grows physically and matures mentally, so did Jesus. To make Him anything else makes Him less than human. He was truly human, and He suffered the limitations of time and place and family.

3. A limitation of temporariness. The passage declares that Jesus dwelt among us. Literally, that word is "tabernacled." The tabernacle, you will remember, was the tent that was used as the place of worship in the wilderness. Jesus "pitched His tent" among us. It reminds us of the tabernacling presence of God with His people. But a tent also indicated temporariness. While one will enjoy living in a tent for a camping trip, few people want to live in a tent permanently. Christ Jesus showed His limitation when He became a real Man who was born into history to spend some time with us.

B. *Beyond limitation, there is exaltation.*

1. Exaltation comes through His glory. Glory is a word used throughout the Scripture, especially by John. As you go back to its Old Testament roots, you are reminded again of the tabernacle. There the glory of God was perceived. It is even given a name *Shekinah*. It means "that which dwells." The glory of God dwelt in the tabernacle. So the glory of God really means the presence of God. In Christ there is exaltation because the very presence of God is there in all His glory.

2. Exaltation comes through His Sonship. Jesus was called the "only begotten son of God." That word literally means "the only one of a kind." Jesus is not simply another son of God; He is the only-one-of-His-kind Son of God. There is no other to whom He can be compared.

3. Exaltation comes through His character. Two aspects of his character are outlined for us:

Grace we understand to be the unmerited favor of God. It is the divine compulsion of God to give us more than we deserve. But William Barclay points out that there is another meaning to grace. From the same root word as grace also comes our English word *charm*. There is not only the unmerited favor of God but the charm, the winsomeness, of God that is seen in Jesus Christ.

Truth shows us that God is determined to be predictable, consistent, trustworthy. In Christ we see that truth that is thoroughly trustworthy. It is a truth that liberates us, setting us free from all those things that would bind us down.

II. In the reality of God's Affirmative Action Program there is evaluation.

A. *Evaluation in terms of the witness.*

1. A witness of priority. This Word that had become flesh and lived with us was the very One John the Baptist had announced. He was the witness of the Christ. Christ was the object of his witness.

2. A witness of presence. With the coming of Jesus, we could know the fullness of God. With Christ we can know assuredly that God was not just something or even someone "out there." He is right beside us and shares life with us fully. Ernest Shackleton said that on his thirty-six-hour march over the ice to the South Pole with his two comrades, it seemed to him that often there were four of them, rather than three. One of his companions said to him, "Boss, I had a curious feeling on the march that there was another person with us." The third companion confessed to the same idea (*Interpreter's Bible,* 8, p. 474). God is indeed always with us as we march through life.

3. A witness of purpose. The fullness of the presence of God with us is experienced "grace for grace." Literally, this expression means grace exchanged for or replaced by more grace. Today's English Version translates it well, "one blessing after another." We never exhaust the blessings of God. Instead, they come rolling upon us one blessing after another.

B. *Evaluation in terms of the winner.*

To Jewish minds Moses was the great hero of the faith. Moses had led them from captivity in Egypt. Moses had led them on the wilderness wanderings. Moses had led them to the Promised Land. Moses had given them the Law. Through Moses had come the law of God that directed their lives and determined their relationship to Him.

If Moses gave the Law, what did Jesus give? Jesus gave grace and truth. In any evaluation, then, Jesus would be judged superior. Through Him came the realization of the grace of God and the reality of the truth of God.

III. In the reality of God's Affirmative Action Program there is explanation.

A. *Jesus, the seen, explains the unseen.*

No one has ever laid eyes on God physically. There is not a person who has actually seen God.

But Jesus—the only-one-of-a-kind Son of God who has an intimate relationship with God (that is what is meant by "in the bosom of the Father")—has declared Him to us. From the seen, Jesus Christ, we can know of the unseen, God.

The word *declared* can here be transliterated "exegeted." When a passage of Scripture is exegeted, it is made known; it is explained precisely and clearly. That is exactly what Jesus Christ has done for us concerning God: He has made Him known to us precisely and clearly. By His life, His teachings, and His actions, we can know what God is like. Jesus has explained the unseen by the seen.

B. *Jesus explains the Father by the Son.*

The life of Jesus is the divine disclosure of God. When we want to know about God, we look to that Word who was from the very beginning with God, who was God Himself. From the Son we can see the Father.

Conclusion. God's Affirmative Action Program worked. Through that action God reached out to show and share His love with each one of us. Its reality is seen in the Incarnation. The eternal Word took on temporal flesh and shared life with us. From that and His death we receive and have life. —*JEC*

* * *

SUNDAY EVENING, DECEMBER 25

TITLE: The Content of Our Testimony

TEXT: ". . . I bring you good news of a great joy which will come to all the people; for to you is born this day in the city of David a Savior, who is Christ the Lord" (Luke 2:10b-11 RSV).

SCRIPTURE READING: Luke 2:1-20

Introduction. The angels sang a song concerning the birth of the Savior. Christmas is the time when we hear more sacred music than at any other time of the year. Jesus Christ came and put a song in our hearts. He can put a song in the hearts of others if we will share the good news of His coming. We need to explain in terms that can be understood that Jesus Christ is indeed a wonderful Savior.

The angels could sing about His birth. We can sing over the fact that he has come and brought the blessings of God into our hearts and lives.

We can tell the good news of what Jesus Christ means to us.

I. We can sing of the joy of forgiveness.

Jesus Christ came into this world to deal with our sins. He dealt with the penalty of our sins on the cross. He paid the wages of our sins which is death (Rom. 6:23).

Through faith in Him, we are assured of the gift of divine forgiveness (Acts 10:43). This means that before the Father God we are no longer condemned. This should bring a great joy to our hearts—the joy of forgiveness.

II. We can sing of the joy of eternal life (John 3:16).

God did not send His Son into this world to condemn us to death but to give us the reality of life eternal.

Jesus came into this world to give us eternal life (John 10:27-28). This eternal life is more qualitative than quantitative. It is something much more than mere existence. It is the very life of God. Eternal life is the life of the Eternal.

III. We can sing of the joy of friendship with Jesus Christ (John 15:15).

One of life's greatest treasures is the treasure of a genuine friend. Jesus identified with those who live by the principle of love as a friend.

Jesus is the friend that we need.

Jesus is the best friend any of us can have.

Those of us who have come to know Him not only as Savior but as friend have something to sing about.

IV. We can sing of the joy that comes through the help of the Holy Spirit.

The Holy Spirit came to be a counselor, a comforter, a helper (John 14:16; Acts 1:8). Those of us who have achieved some degree of spiritual maturity need to bear testimony to others concerning the blessings of allowing the Holy Spirit of God to aid us and lead us in ministry to others. As we do so, this can be the means of encouraging others to trust Jesus Christ as Savior.

V. We can sing of the joy of our Lord's leadership in the time of uncertainty (Matt. 28:20).

Our Lord has promised to those who obey Him the blessing of His personal presence. He leads and guides those who trust Him and obey Him.

Those who have experienced the fulfillment of that promise have a joy to sing about. We need to share the Good News of this Christ who was born and who has continued to live.

Conclusion. We have many items of good news to communicate to the world in which we live regarding the Christ who came long ago.

It is not enough to just sing about the birth of a baby. We need to sing about the significance of this One who was born in Bethlehem.

> Go tell it on the mountain,
> Over the hills and everywhere;
> Go tell it on the mountain,
> That Jesus Christ is born.

Tell it with joy.
Tell it with expectancy.
Tell it expecting God to bless and use your testimony for the good of others.

—*TTC*

* * *

WEDNESDAY EVENING, DECEMBER 28

TITLE: To Err Is Human, to Forgive Divine

TEXT: "Now therefore be not grieved, nor angry with yourselves, that ye sold me hither: for God did send me before you to preserve life" (Gen. 45:5).

SCRIPTURE READING: Genesis 45:1-13

Introduction. One more story remains in this series from the life of Joseph. Events moved rapidly after the butler finally told Pharaoh about the prisoner who had such wonderful ability because of his God. The Pharaoh's dream was interpreted by Joseph. The Hebrew lad was made "prime minister" of the land, second only to the king himself. Later his brothers came to Egypt to buy grain during the famine. Joseph played "cat and mouse" with them for a short period, but at last he revealed himself to them.

No nobler statement can be found anywhere in God's Word than the words of Joseph to his brothers. Not only did he forgive them for what they had done, but he went so far as to say that God was actually using them in His plan when they did the dastardly deed. Of course, this did not lessen their guilt, but it was a charitable interpretation of events by this noble soul who knew nothing of vindictiveness and had no desire for revenge. The story points out some tremendous truths for our consideration.

I. God has His own way of doing things.

God knew exactly when to bring Joseph out of the dungeon. Often we do not have nearly as much problem with God's will as we do with His timetable. We want Him to act on our schedule, not His! God sent the dream to Pharaoh at exactly the correct time for Joseph to step in and interpret it.

How much better off we all would be if we simply trusted God to open doors for us. Our "politicking" often gets us into trouble because sometimes it lands us in places that God does not intend for us to be. This does not mean that we should never put forth any human effort, but it does mean we should be cautious, trusting God's leadership and realizing that He will cause a thing to happen to us and for us at the time He knows is best.

II. Sin haunts us constantly.

Notice how the brothers said to each other while they were in Egypt buying grain, "We are verily guilty concerning our brother, in that we saw the anguish of his soul, when he besought us, and we would not hear; therefore is this distress come upon us" (Gen. 42:21). Many years had passed since they had sold Joseph into bondage, but their consciences were awakened when their brother, unknown to them, acted harshly with them concerning their younger brother, Benjamin. Surely this was not the only time during the years that they had talked about the terrible thing they had done to Joseph.

III. Forgiveness is Christlike.

The heart of the gospel is the merciful love of our heavenly Father. In Jesus Christ He sets us free from both the guilt and power of sin. Paul says, "For scarcely for a righteous man will one die: yet peradventure for a good man some would even dare to die. But God commendeth his love toward us, in that, while we were yet sinners, Christ died for us" (Rom. 5:7-8). This is the ultimate in forgiveness!

Joseph's refusal to retaliate against his brothers was not merely because he did not want to hurt his father. Years later, when Jacob died, the brothers became frightened. They came to Joseph, afraid that he would seek revenge; once more, they begged for forgiveness. Joseph wept as he said to them, "Fear not: for am I in the place of God?" (Gen. 50:19). He said to them basically the same thing he did when he first revealed himself to them. They proposed evil against him, but God meant it for good. He assured them that he would continue to nourish them and their little ones.

Conclusion. How do you handle your desire for revenge? Even though all of us have sinned against other people, perhaps all of us have also had times when someone has sinned against us. Jesus said, "Blessed are the merciful: for they shall obtain mercy" (Matt. 5:7). Someone described revenge as the "costliest morsel that has ever been cooked up in hell"; while someone else called forgiveness "the odor which a flower yields when trampled upon." Charles Spurgeon once said, "Cultivate forbearance until your heart yields a fine crop of it. Pray for a short memory as to all unkindness." —*FMW*

* * *

MISCELLANEOUS HELPS

* * *

COMMUNION SERVICES

TITLE: Making Ready

TEXT: "And the disciples did as Jesus had appointed them; and they made ready the passover" (Matt. 26:19).

SCRIPTURE READING: Matthew 26:17-29

Introduction. In the early days of our country, the Quakers were scorned and considered strange because of the ways in which they quietly, in prayer and meditation, conducted their periods of worship. They sat silently until someone in the group felt moved by God to sing a hymn or deliver a message. This was their way of preparing themselves for an encounter with God, for an experience of worship. They understood and practiced the exhortation of the prophet: "The LORD is in his holy temple: let all the earth keep silence before him" (Hab. 2:20).

This is not the pattern most evangelical Christians follow today, however. We have confused frivolity with joy—and there is all the difference in the world. There is a time and a season for everything, according to the writer of Ecclesiastes. There is a time to laugh and a time to cry, a time to keep silence and a time to speak. There is something special about a "holy stillness." It is fraught with expectancy, with anticipation.

Today we have come to the Lord's Table. There was probably nothing Jesus did with the disciples before His crucifixion which was more deeply moving, more unforgettable, than this experience in the Upper Room. And part of the reason for the impact it made on the disciples was that *it was prepared for*. Jesus had told His disciples to "make ready" for it, and they did. There are three basic preparations Christians ought to make before they come to the Lord's Table.

I. First, there ought to be physical preparation.

It is obvious that Jesus had made previous arrangements privately for the Passover meal with the disciples. He told them that as they entered the city, they would see a man carrying a pitcher of water. They were to follow him to a house, and they were to go to a particular "upper room." Jesus took care that the proper physical preparations were made.

One of the cherished memories of my childhood is that of the preparations our family made on Sunday mornings in order to get everyone ready and off to church and Sunday school on time. Our father helped to get the three of us children ready, while mother was busy with the major chores. He put on our socks, tied our shoes, and combed our hair. It was a cooperative venture. My parents believed in the right kind of physical preparation on Sunday morning. Many times when tempers flared, father would lecture us on the uselessness of going to God's house with a wrong attitude. I am grateful because my parents taught me the importance of making the proper physical preparation for worship in the Lord's house. Certainly it is especially important to be physically prepared for the sacred experience at the Lord's Table.

II. Second, there must be the proper mental preparation.

The prophet Isaiah gives us one of the most precious promises in the Bible in regard to one's relationship with the Lord: "Thou wilt keep him in perfect peace, whose mind is stayed on thee: because he trusteth in thee" (Isa. 26:3). It is with the mind that one concentrates and focuses his attention on something. What about the "mental preparation" for worshiping God and for coming to the Lord's Table? Peter, in his first epistle, exhorts us to "gird up the loins of [our minds]" (1 Peter 1:13). He means for us to learn the art of concentration by allowing the Holy Spirit who indwells us to control our minds.

How often have you had the experience, before or during the worship hour, of having your thoughts wander into some areas of unusual sensitivity for you? Perhaps there has been a misunderstanding with a fellow worshiper, and you see that person sitting across the way. Immediately you begin to be uncomfortable. You start to remember certain things which have happened. Soon you are angry and upset and totally unable to enter into the spirit of worship.

How can we overcome this? Isaiah told us. We must "stay our minds" on Jesus Christ. Open God's Word, and let it speak to you. It is "sharper than a two-edged sword," and the Holy Spirit will empower it to excise those offending thoughts and prepare you mentally to worship God at His Table.

III. Third, there must be spiritual preparation.

In 1 Corinthians 11:26-34 Paul speaks clearly about the Christian's conduct in regard to the Lord's Table. He deals plainly with our spiritual preparation. He tells us that the ordinance of the Lord's Supper is not a meaningless, perfunctory "ritual" in the church. It should never be something we "tack on" to the end of a worship service.

So what do we do? It is exceedingly simple: "Let a man examine himself." In the presence of God, in the light of His Word, we must examine ourselves as to whether or not we are spiritually prepared to come to the Lord's Table. First, we must see if we have repented of all known sin and confessed those sins before God. There is no experience as sublime and glorious as the sense of sins forgiven and of full acceptance into the presence of God. With that sense of spiritual well-being, one can come to the Lord's Table truly with "joy unspeakable." "If we confess our sins, he is faithful and just to forgive us our sins, and to cleanse us from all unrighteousness" (1 John 1:9).

Second, consistent Christian living is an essential part of proper spiritual preparation for the Lord's Table. If the Holy Spirit convicts us of wrongness in our hearts toward God or toward our fellow-man, then it must be righted. We cannot enjoy the Lord's Table when there is a wrong spirit within us. John tells us plainly that the proof of our sonship under God is whether or not we love one another.

Conclusion. The Lord's Supper ought to be a precious and unforgettable experience every time we come to His Table. Why? Because we are "showing forth the Lord's death till he comes." We must be *clear reflectors,* cleansed of all known sin. And to do this requires that we be *physically prepared*—our bodies, which are temples of the Holy Spirit, must be tuned physically for this worship experience. We must be *mentally prepared*—we must "stay our minds" on the Lord and ask Him to help us, by His indwelling Spirit, to focus our thoughts on the Lord Jesus. Then, we must, of all things, be *spiritually prepared*. Then, when these basic preparations have been made, we come with joy to the Lord's Table; and we leave, having truly experienced His presence. — *DLJ*

TITLE: The Discipline of Discipleship

TEXT: "And he said to them all, If any man will come after me, let him deny himself, and take up his cross daily, and follow me" (Luke 9:23).

SCRIPTURE READING: Luke 9:23-27

Introduction. As we prepare to come to the Lord's Table for this high and holy experience of remembrance, I would like for us to consider two words: *discipline* and *discipleship*. Actually, discipleship means "discipline." The disciple is one who has been taught and trained by the Master; he is one who has come with his ignorance, superstition, and sin to find learning, truth, and forgiveness from the Savior. Without discipline, we are not disciples, even though we profess His name.

It is doubtful that any generation has resented and rebelled against discipline any more than our own. In fact, ours has been labeled "the permissive generation." Liberty and license have replaced law and order. Furthermore, the spirit of permissiveness has become a lifestyle with most people—even Christians. This lack of discipline is the avowed enemy of faithfulness to God. It weakens compassion, for it places the first and primary emphasis upon "self."

But just what do we mean by "discipline"? The dictionary defines it as "training that corrects, molds, or perfects the mental faculties or moral character." And without difficulty, we can translate this definition into the spiritual realm. For the growing, maturing, developing Christian, there must constantly be correction and molding, all leading to the ultimate perfection which we shall experience when we come to stand in the presence of Christ.

I. Discipleship requires the discipline of conversion, wherein we recognize our lost estate, our rebellion against God, and then come repenting to the Savior.

"Conversion" takes two forms in the Christian's life. First, it is the initial experience that comes when one realizes he is lost and without hope, and, repenting of his sins, recognizes Jesus Christ as Savior. This is the most difficult discipline of all, for it is the deathblow to pride, the basic and parent sin spawned by Satan himself. It is never easy for anyone to humble himself to the point of admitting that he is a sinner. But when this happens, the miracle of conversion takes place. It is all God's doing. It is "not by works of righteousness which we have done, but according to his mercy he saved us" (Titus 3:5).

But "conversion" takes yet another form in the Christian's life. There are the daily conversion experiences the Christian has as he turns from "sins," from immaturity and childishness, and begins the difficult but glorious journey of Christian growth. As the Christian walks with the Lord, he is daily being subjected to the discipline of change, of conversion, and he is being "conformed to the image of God's own dear Son." How are you reacting to the discipline of *daily conversion?*

II. Then, discipleship requires the discipline of cost.

Jesus said, "He that loveth father or mother more than me is not worthy of me: and he that loveth son or daughter more than me is not worthy of me" (Matt. 10:37). And on a later occasion, He expanded that statement: "If any man come to me, and hate not his father, and mother, and wife, and children, and brethren, and sisters, yea, and his own life also, he cannot be my disciple" (Luke 14:26).

What did Jesus mean by those statements? The quality and intensity of love we have for God, because of this great salvation through His Son, should be so superior to even our love for our closest kin that the comparison would be like "love versus hate"! There is only one person who is qualified to sit on the throne of our hearts, and that is the Lord Jesus. We should abhor anything or anyone who would vie for that place.

It is always difficult to truly make Christ *Lord* of one's life and allow Him to remain in that position. Total lordship of Christ in our lives is costly. It means that one has submitted every waking hour to Him and that there has come to exist within a constant and continuing awareness of His presence.

III. Finally, discipleship requires the discipline of cross-bearing.

Three things seem to be necessary for us each day: our daily food (for which we are told to pray, "Give us this day our daily bread"), our daily work (in which we are to be faithful, "if any would not work, neither should he eat"), and our daily cross. What *is* the cross we are to bear daily? It is not the cross of our Savior, who suffered for our sins upon the tree, for we can add nothing to the price of our redemption. Least of all is it the bearing of some burden, some inconvenience. Rather, it is the denial of oneself, in the deepest meaning of that word. It is full surrender to the will of God. It is a daily saying "No!" to the desires and demands of self and saying "Yes!" to the loving commands of Christ.

The cross is an instrument of death. There is no such thing as "sinless perfection" for the Christian in this life. Therefore, every day that we live we must, in the power of the Spirit of Christ, deal a "deathblow" to self. *That is cross-bearing*. And furthermore, it is not a morbid, long-faced experience. There is no joy as deep, as permeating, as that which comes to the Christian who has placed self under the control of God and has acquiesced to the lordship of Jesus Christ.

Conclusion. As we prepare to come to the Lord's Table to partake of these precious emblems, let us consider seriously this matter of discipline of discipleship. Are we experiencing daily the discipline of conversion—are we letting God change us, correct us, mold us, perfect us? Have we dealt with the discipline of cost—are we willing to relinquish all in order that Christ might inhabit the throne of our hearts? And what are we doing about the discipline of cross-bearing? Are we letting God deal that "deathblow" to the ugliness of self every day, thus becoming more and more like Jesus, who is our pattern? —*DLJ*

* * *

TITLE: A Labor of Love

TEXT: **"I have glorified thee on the earth: I have finished the work which thou gavest me to do" (John 17:4).**

SCRIPTURE READING: **John 17:1-11**

Introduction. Today we shall sit as a family of believers in the Lord Jesus at His Table. These elements of which we shall partake speak both simply and eloquently of the mission and purpose of our Lord on earth. One of the many facets of His life and ministry had to do with His own concept of His mission in regard to the will of His heavenly Father. When Jesus spoke the words recorded in our Scripture passage for today, He had come to a very lonely moment in His life. Peter, James, and John—the "inner circle" of His disciples—had gone to sleep in the Garden of Gethsemane. They could not stay awake to watch and pray with Him. But His heavenly Father was near, and in this great High Priestly Prayer, Jesus poured out His heart to Him.

One statement in the prayer stands out in particular: "I have glorified thee on earth: I have finished the work which thou gavest me to do" (v. 4). Had not Jesus accomplished what He implied here, all else would be lost.

I. How did Jesus "glorify the Father"? He did so by His teachings and by His miracles.

God is glorified before man when man comes to know what God is like—who He is. This was the first part of Jesus' mission on earth. When Jesus came, according to the apostle Paul, "in him dwelleth all the fulness of the Godhead bodily" (Col. 2:9). God dwelt in a perfect, sinless human body. With human emotion, understanding, and interaction, Jesus showed man God—and thus God was glorified in the person of His Son. His teachings brought to maturity, fulfillment, and perfection the Word of the Law.

In the incomparable Sermon on the Mount Jesus laid down with unmistakable clarity how His people are to live. In those words He set forth the most difficult spiritual obstacle course imaginable. In fact, the only way one can "live" the Sermon on the Mount is in the Spirit of Christ who indwells every believer. And we yield to Him as we die to self. This is the paradox of our faith: Life and victory come through death and defeat!

Jesus also glorified the Father through the miracles He performed. He overruled the known laws of nature and, with divine power, healed broken and diseased bodies. Yet Jesus never intended for His healing ministry to become an end in itself. Sometimes God chooses to use physical infirmity and adversity as a means of refining our faith. In such times of trial and testing, a Christian learns to concentrate on Christ more completely. We cannot always know the mind of God in these matters. When it is His will to exercise His miraculous healing power, we give Him all the praise, for He does so always to glorify Himself and not man.

II. Jesus also glorified the Father in that He finished the work which God gave Him to do.

It is not by accident that the sacrifice of Christ on the cross is called by theologians "the doctrine of the work of Christ." Jesus said, "I have finished the work which thou gavest me to do." On the cross He cried, "It is finished!" The work of redemption which He had come to do had reached its decisive conclusion. He had endured the cross because there was set before Him the joy of a completed task.

Thus the Bible indicates that Jesus found joy in this work assigned to Him. How *could* Jesus "enjoy" a mission or task so fraught with opposition and rejection, with misunderstanding and cruelty? He did so because, having been "one with the Father," He had experienced from before the beginning the divine thrill at the conception of the plan of salvation. Before God laid the foundations of the world, He knew man would choose evil instead of righteousness. Because of that foreknowledge, He planned for man's salvation. Certainly it broke the heart of God when man acted out in his time what God in His omniscience saw him do before he was even created.

Therefore, when Jesus was born—God incarnate in human flesh—intermingled with the love that caused it was the joy of bringing to completion *in time* this great salvation! It had been conceived and incubated in the mind of God; it had been symbolized and typified in the Old Testament; and now it was *actualized* in the life, death, and resurrection of Jesus. Indeed, it was a "labor of love" when Jesus finished the work which God gave Him to do.

III. Christians can glorify the Father as they allow the risen Christ to shine forth from their lives.

The miracle of God's grace ought to be a constant announcer to the world that Christ lives in us. Jesus said to His disciples, "Ye are the light of the world." The flickering light of an inconsistent Christian testimony can be disastrously misleading to one who is trying to find the way. What a glorious anticipation to be able to say at the end of life's day, "Father, I have finished the work which thou gavest me to do." Paul was able to say it: "I have fought a good fight, I have finished my course, I have kept the faith" (2 Tim. 4:7).

Conclusion. As we partake of these blessed emblems today, let us remember that our Lord's life, from Bethlehem to Calvary, fulfilled the purpose of His heavenly Father. That purpose was "to glorify the Father" and to finish the work God gave Him to do. That, to Jesus, was "a labor of love." Let us, during these sacred moments, commit ourselves anew to glorify our Lord and Savior through *our* lives.

—*DLJ*

* * *

FUNERAL MESSAGES

TITLE: The Beauty of Death

TEXT: "O death, where is thy sting? O grave, where is thy victory? The sting of death is sin; and the strength of sin is the law. But thanks be to God, which giveth us the victory through our Lord Jesus Christ" (1 Cor. 15:55-57).

SCRIPTURE READING: Ecclesiastes 1:1-11; 1 Corinthians 15:51-58

Introduction. Sometimes, out of the darkness of our sorrow in the face of death, we find ourselves asking, "Is there anything logical about death? Why do we die? Is death just a tragic waste?" The apostle Paul tells us that death is the means whereby we shed our bodies of corruption in order to receive bodies which are not subject to decay. When man sinned, his body became subject to disease, pain, decay, and the ravages of time. God did not intend that man should live forever in such a body. Suppose man could *not* die, but was fated to live forever in a body which grew ever older, weaker, and more painful, an eternal victim of disease and corruption? So, while death is an enemy, God causes even this enemy to serve us for our good. In this sense, therefore, death is a blessed release, offering the anticipation of a resurrection body that is incorruptible and immortal.

The great problem with human life, for those of us who remain, is our ability to see only one side of it. In a sense, we see the "underside" of life.

Truly, we "see through a glass darkly," and we "know in part." But in the midst of these human questions and doubts, we hear this promise buried in the ancient Book of Ecclesiastes, "[God] hath made every thing beautiful in his time" (3:11).

I. In God's own time and in His own way, He gives us the perspective to see things as they truly are, and as He intended them to be.

A. *This principle operates in nature.* Consider the seed as an example. A seed looks dry and ugly and dead—shriveled and lifeless. Could you imagine a person giving a packet of flower seeds in memory of a departed loved one or friend? And yet, the seed contains within itself all the beauty of the flower. In the orderly processes of nature, the seed puts forth the shoot, the shoot becomes the plant, the plant bears the bud, and the bud breaks open into glorious blossom. "God makes all things beautiful in his time."

B. *Notice, also, the beauty in the cycle of our seasons.* We naturally enjoy the beauty of the springtime, as all nature seems to throb with returning life. In the summer, the fields are golden with their ripening grain. Then the season moves on to autumn. The trees turn to scarlet and gold, and we bow our heads in humble thanksgiving for the harvest of the earth. But then the winter comes, with the glistening magic of icicles and snow. Each part of the year has its own beauty—how can we compare them? We can only agree that "God makes all things beautiful in his time."

C. *The same principle can be seen in human life.* Which of the ages of mankind is most beautiful? We think of the dimpled smile of the tiny babe in its helplessness and innocence. Then there is the schoolgirl with her hair in pigtails and braces on her teeth, running down the walk to meet her dad. Or the young man dressed in his academic cap and gown. Then the time moves on to motherhood and fatherhood and to the busy years of building a home and family. Finally the wrinkles of old age appear—the face is creased with lines drawn there by love. Every age seems to offer a greater beauty than the age before. "God makes all things beautiful in his time."

D. *But then, one day long ago, an ugly cross was raised on the outskirts of an ancient city.* Upon that instrument of torture was nailed the mangled body of a young Galilean prophet who had been stripped and beaten. A crown of thorn branches was crushed down upon His head and a sarcastic inscription placed above Him: "This is the King of the Jews." Could anything change such a picture into a thing of beauty? Yet three days later His tomb was empty! God made Him both Lord and Christ, this Jesus who was crucified. Today, lives are devoted in humble and loving service in the name of this same Jesus. Even His cross has become a thing of beauty to us. "God makes all things beautiful in his time."

II. In the face of this, we can grasp something of the challenge of Paul's words: 'O death, where is thy sting? O grave, where is thy victory?" (1 Cor. 15:55).

A. *Where* is *the sting of death?* It is the terror of the person who approaches God unforgiven of his sins. It is the fearful anticipation of an unknown and mysterious future.

B. *What* is *the victory of the grave?* It is the eternal claim upon the soul unsurrendered to God—the hopeless, endless imprisonment in a Christian eternity. Apart from God, death is indeed a fearful state; there is an awesome finality about it.

C. *But, thank God, Paul does not leave us there*. To learn the secret of his courage and the courage and strength of every child of God, we must consider these words: "But thanks be to God, which giveth us the victory through our Lord Jesus Christ" (v. 57). Paul anticipated death—not with a morbid desire to escape from life, but realizing its inevitability (for the Scriptures declare that "it is appointed unto man once to die"). Paul delighted in the fact that Christ had removed from death all the fearful and chilling aspects which once accompanied it. He came back from death not only to tell us that there is more beyond, but to promise us: "In my Father's house are many mansions: if it were not so, I would have told you. I go to prepare a place for you. And if I go and prepare a place for you, I will come again, and receive you unto myself; that where I am, there ye may be also" (John 14:2, 3).

Conclusion. Certainly every living Christian anticipates the return of Christ. This is the abiding hope of the New Testament. But our human bodies grow tired and weak. Jesus comes for His children also in death. And there, in the presence of God, they no longer "see through a glass darkly," and they no longer "know in part." The mysteries of life which perplex *us* are revealed to them. If they could speak to us today, no doubt they would echo the words of Paul: "Therefore, my beloved brethren, be ye stedfast, unmoveable, always abounding in the work of the Lord, forasmuch as ye know that your labour is not in vain in the Lord" (1 Cor. 15:58). —*DLJ*

* * *

TITLE: Ready!

TEXT: "For I am now ready to be offered, and the time of my departure is at hand. I have fought a good fight, I have finished my course, I have kept the faith: Henceforth there is laid up for me a crown of righteousness, which the Lord, the righteous judge, shall give me at that day: and not to me only, but unto all them also that love his appearing" (2 Tim. 4:6-8).

SCRIPTURE READING: Psalm 121; Romans 1:16

Introduction. In his farewell address to the Congress of the United States of America following his recall, General Douglas MacArthur quoted these lines which have been made all the more immortal because of his dramatic use of them: "Old soldiers never die; they just fade away."

Whereas that may hold true for earthly soldiers, it is *not* true of soldiers of the Cross. There is no "fading away" for those who have faithfully served the Captain of their salvation. Rather, a far more fitting epitaph for them would be the words of Paul as he anticipated his departure from this life (2 Tim. 4:6-8).

I. Note first that the great apostle made a victorious declaration: "I am now ready to be offered, and the time of my departure is at hand" (v. 6).

"I am ready!" What a victorious, electrifying declaration! Yet it is a statement every member of God's family should be able to make at a moment's notice. It does not mean that every single thing in one's life that should have been done *was* done, nor that every milestone of maturity in the faith which should have been passed *had* been passed. Rather it describes the believer who has grown daily, steadily, consistently in the faith.

Then, to be "ready" means also to accept firmly and irrevocably the sovereign will of God. The committed Christian, though he may and should love this earthly life filled with opportunities to serve his Lord, sees no conflict in saying, "I am ready" for the moment of homegoing. Certainly the dedicated believer wants to fill every minute God allots him on this earth with "sixty seconds' worth of distance run" (Kipling). But still, he believes that the "time of departure" for every person is always at hand, always imminent. Thus, he sees to it that his attitude is one of readiness.

II. Then, after Paul made his thrilling declaration, he did a bit of reflecting: "I have fought a good fight, I have finished my course, I have kept the faith" (v. 7).

A. *"I have fought a good fight."* Paul did not mean that he had always fought at his best or that his ministry had always been at "peak performance." Rather, the word *good* does not describe the manner of "fighting," but the fight itself. The warfare in which God's people are engaged is a good one because victory is assured. No earthly general, however convinced he might be of the ability and proficiency of his troops, could ever say, "Go forth to battle, men; but have no fear, you have already won!" That would be the height of presumption. But this *is* what the Lord says to *His* soldiers. For on the cross the battle between good and evil *was* won, for time and eternity. We are simply "attending to the details" here on earth according to the will and purpose of an all-wise and sovereign Lord.

B. *"I have finished my course."* Paul was not saying that he had done perfectly and without flaw every single thing that was included in God's will for his life and ministry. Though he was a giant among God's servants, Paul was still subject to the frailties of humanity, and he would have been the first to admit that fact. But what he was saying was that God has set out a course for His people, and His desire is to leave them here until they finish it. They will not perform it perfectly, but they will finish it.

C. *"I have kept the faith."* By this, Paul meant that he had guarded the truth of God's Word. He had not let his emotions run away with his common sense and with the spiritual discernment God had given him to comprehend and to apply God's Holy Word to his life. He had received his orders, and he had not tampered with them. He merely sought to carry them out in accord with the instructions God had given him. He was true to his calling.

III. Finally, Paul states, with thrilling overtones, a glorious fact: "Henceforth there is laid up for me a crown of righteousness, which the Lord, the righteous judge, shall give me at that day: and not to me only, but unto all them also that love his appearing" (v. 8).

"A crown of righteousness!" *Whose* righteousness? Paul's? No! The righteousness of Jesus Christ which had been given to him at the moment of his surrender to God in repentance and faith. Paul would have been the first to say that "in me there is no good thing." He would have agreed fully with the prophet who stated: "All we like sheep have gone astray; we have turned every one to his own way; and the LORD hath laid on him the iniquity of us all" (Isa. 53:6).

Thus the "crown" the believer shall receive in heaven is the crown of *Christ's* righteousness, which we have received *not* because of *our* goodness, but because of the unmerited grace of Almighty God.

Conclusion. So we can see that what Paul wrote to young Timothy about *his* anticipated homegoing is not so high and exalted a testimony that it should be reserved only for such spiritual giants as this illustrious apostle. Rather, he was describing the legacy *every* child of God should leave behind him. Thus the believer, like a true soldier of the Cross, is retired temporarily from the ranks. Yet, through his lingering testimony of faith, he continues to serve and praise God in his "heavenly retirement."

—DLJ

* * *

TITLE: The Legacy of the Good Shepherd

TEXT: "The LORD is my shepherd; I shall not want" (Ps. 23:1). "I am the good shepherd, and know my sheep, and am known of mine. As the Father knoweth me, even so know I the Father: and I lay down my life for the sheep" (John 10:14-15).

SCRIPTURE READING: Psalm 23

Introduction. During the years of our childhood we learn to quote this beautiful Shepherd Psalm. Then, in the middle years, when we grapple with the common problems of family and home and of our busy lives in general, we find ourselves returning to this psalm in moments of exasperation and frustration, finding a new sense of comfort and strength. We come to understand more about a Shepherd who will guide us through the difficult times. But then, as the years pass and the autumn and winter of life come upon us, the words of this lovely psalm become more meaningful than ever. Loved ones are taken away. The emptiness, the void that is left behind, is sometimes almost unbearable. Then we find ourselves quoting with an even deeper understanding: "Yea, though I walk through the valley of the shadow of death, I will fear no evil: for thou art with me. . ." (v. 4a).

There is little doubt that David wrote this psalm during the sunset years of his life. He is reflecting, thinking back on the countless ways in which the Lord God was a "shepherd" to him.

I. The key to the psalm is found in the first verse: "The LORD is my shepherd; I shall not want."

Who *is* the Lord? Let us allow Jesus Himself to answer for us with the words He spoke to those who listened to Him one day long ago: "I am the good shepherd, and know my sheep, and am known of mine. As the Father knoweth me, even so know I the Father: and I lay down my life for the sheep" (John 10:14, 15). Isn't this, in essence, what David was saying? Because the Lord was to him as a true shepherd is to his sheep, he would not want for that which is needful for his soul. When he walked through the dark valley of sorrow, he would not want for grace and strength to carry him through the long and weary days.

Furthermore, not only did the shepherd know his sheep in those Far Eastern lands, but the sheep also knew their shepherd; they would not follow a strange shepherd. Jesus said it like this: "But he that entereth in by the door is the shepherd of the sheep. To him the porter openeth; and the sheep hear his voice: and he calleth his own sheep by name, and leadeth them out. And when he putteth forth his own sheep, he goeth before them, and the sheep follow him: for they know his voice" (10:2-4). Indeed, "The Lord is my shepherd; I shall not want."

II. But that is not all: "He maketh me to lie down in green pastures: he leadeth me beside the still waters. He restoreth my soul" (Ps. 23:2, 3a).

Here, in essence, is the life story of a child of God. He begins life with the morning and the labor and toil of the day. But then come the resting periods, the times for communion with God, for getting in touch afresh with heaven. "He *maketh* me to lie down." Could it be that this is what weariness is for—perhaps even illness? In the hustle and bustle of life, we sometimes forget how to relax, to have time to think, to enjoy the God who created us to serve Him.

Then David tells us that God is able to transform the most difficult situation into "a green pasture" and the most violently tossing waves into "still waters." Green is the most restful of all colors and, at the same time, the most hopeful. The "green pasture" requires clouds and showers and then the sunshine. The storm clouds are often necessary to bring the rain; but there always comes the sunshine.

Inevitably God leads us "in the paths of righteousness for his name's sake." By this, David means "straight paths," paths with direction, leading somewhere. Life, when it is directed by God, is never without direction. It is always moving toward a goal. Likewise, when God calls one of His own to be with Him, He is fulfilling His plan and completing His purpose in that person's life.

III. "Yea, though I walk through the valley of the shadow of death, I will fear no evil: for thou art with me; thy rod and thy staff they comfort me" (v. 4).

Note that the refreshing time beside the still waters and in the green pastures came *before* the most difficult part of the journey with the Shepherd—that part which leads "through the valley of the shadow of death." Tests of life—the hard stretches on the road—do not often come in the morning years of our living. Rather they come in the afternoon, after we have had time to become acquainted with our God as Friend and Lord, as well as Savior. We have had time to walk and talk with Him, and to hear Him tell us that we are His own.

IV. The last two verses of this delightful psalm prepare us for the journey's end.

Here the imagery changes abruptly from that of the Shepherd leading His sheep through the wilds of life's wilderness to that of a kindly Host providing lovingly and generously for His guests.

The Good Shepherd has brought His flock home, and the idea of home is made all the more appropriate by the picture of the spread table and the lavish provisions made ready by a most fatherly Host. The sheep are safe in the fold; the enemies are outside, glaring but helpless. Truly, one's "cup of joy" overflows at the prospect of our Good Shepherd's thoughtful and loving care for His sheep.

Conclusion. Not only is our Shepherd the One who leads and guides us and goes before us to smooth the rough path and lighten the dark way, He also sees to the "rear guard." He takes care that we shall not be "ambushed" from behind by evil. For His twin courtiers, "goodness" and "mercy," are following us all the days of our lives; and in the end, we are assured of "dwell[ing] in the house of the LORD for ever."

—*DLJ*

* * *

WEDDING CEREMONIES

TITLE: What God Hath Joined Together

Minister (as the bride and her father, or the person giving her away, stand before the minister): Dearly beloved, we are now about to hear the wedding vows of _____ (Bride) and _____ (Groom). May I ask who presents the bride?

Thank you, _____ . You are to be commended for bringing your lovely daughter, _____ , to the altar so that, before God, her marriage might be solemnized.

Let us pray. "Our Father, look down upon us with Your smile of approval. May Your Son and our Savior, the Lord Jesus Christ, be present to add His blessing. May the Holy Spirit attend and seal these vows in love. In our Savior's holy name we pray. Amen."

When God created man, He saw that it was not good for him to live alone. Thus He prepared for him a helpmeet, a beloved companion. He took not the woman from Adam's head, lest she should rule over him; nor from his feet, lest he should trample upon her; but from his side, that she should be equal with him. He took her from close to his heart, that he should love, cherish, and protect her.

Marriage was honored by the presence of Christ at the marriage feast in Cana of Galilee, and used by Him as the emblem of that great day when He, the Bridegroom, adorned in all His glory, shall come for His church, whom He has purchased with His blood, and who shall be dressed in the spotless garment of His righteousness.

Marriage was commended by the apostle Paul who, speaking under the inspiration of the Holy Spirit, declared that it was "honorable in all things." A marriage made in heaven is a union of two lives—two hearts that beat as one—so welded together that they walk together; they work and labor together; they bear each other's burdens; they share each other's joys.

I want to remind you both that you are to cultivate the habit of being congenial, loving, and tenderhearted. You must always receive each other, just as you are, in love, remembering that the vows you are about to take are as binding in adversity as they are in prosperity, and that these vows are to be broken only by death.

I will ask you now to join hands.

Groom's vow

Will you, _____ , take _____ as your wedded wife, to live together after God's ordinance in the holy estate of matrimony? Will you promise to love her, comfort, honor, and keep her, and forsaking all others, remain only with her so long as you both shall live?

Answer: I will.

Bride's vow

Will you, _____ , take _____ as your wedded husband, to live together after God's ordinance in the holy estate of matrimony? Will you promise to love him, honor and keep him, and forsaking all others, remain only with him until death parts you?

Answer: I will.

Vows to each other and ring ceremony

Minister addresses the couple together: Do you solemnly promise before God and in the presence of these witnesses to receive each other as husband and wife, pledging yourselves to love each other, and to make every reasonable exertion to promote each other's happiness until the union into which you are now entering is dissolved by death? *(They answer together:* "We do.")

I will ask you then to seal the vows which you have just made by the giving and receiving of rings. The circle is the emblem of eternity, and gold is the symbol of all that is pure and holy. Our prayer is that your love and your happiness will be as unending as these rings. They are tokens of remembrance, and in the years to come they will remind you of this happy hour. My prayer is that you will be as happy then as you are now.

Minister directs groom to place ring on the bride's finger, and then to repeat after him: With this ring I thee wed. I take thee, _____ , to have and to hold, to love and to cherish, in sickness and in health, for richer or for poorer, for better or for worse, so long as we both shall live.

Minister directs bride to place ring on the groom's finger, and then to repeat after him: With this ring I thee wed. I take thee, _____ , to have and to hold, to love and to cherish, in sickness and in health, for richer or for poorer, for better or for worse, so long as we both shall live.

Then the couple declare in unison: "Whither thou goest, I will go; and where thou lodgest, I will lodge; thy people shall be my people, and thy God, my God."

Minister: And now, according to the laws of this great country in which we live, and by my authority as a minister of the gospel, I pronounce you husband and wife, in the name of the Father, and of the Son, and of the Holy Spirit. What God has joined together, let not man put asunder.

Let us pray: "Our Father, send Thy blessings upon these Thy servants, this man and this woman whom we bless in Thy name. Help them always to keep the vows and the covenant they have made with each other today. May their lives be crowned always with the benediction of Thy love and grace, and may they share Thy peace, which passes all human understanding. Fill them with Thy grace. Through Jesus Christ our Lord we pray. Amen."

Recessional —*DLJ*

* * *

TITLE: Marriage Ceremony

PROCEDURE: Organ prelude
Lighting of the candles
Seating of grandmothers and mothers
Processional
Solo (Father remains with bride before the minister)

Minister: There is no human relationship as high, as holy, or as beautifully rewarding as that which exists between a Christian man and woman in the bonds of marriage. Marriage is one of three "carry-overs" from the Garden of Eden. The Sabbath day of rest for the body, mind, and soul and the dignity of labor are the other two. Thus, marriage is an experience which God intended to bear the primeval blessings of Eden upon it.

_____ and _____ share already the highest possible relationship with each other because of their faith in Jesus Christ. They are a handmaiden and a servant of the Lord. When they are united in holy matrimony, the light of God in their lives will be fused into one light; the music in their hearts will blend into one beautiful symphony of love.

Who gives this woman to be married to this man? *(Father answers,* "Her mother and I," *and places the bride's hand on the groom's arm. He returns to be seated beside the bride's mother. Bride, groom, minister, maid of honor, and best man ascend steps to platform.)*

Minister: (Reads 1 Corinthians 13.) After God had made Adam in the Garden of Eden and observed this solitary man attending to the task in the garden which had been assigned to him, God said: "It is not good that the man should be alone; I will make an help meet for him." Then Moses, in recording the incomparably beautiful account of the Creation, stated: "And the LORD God caused a deep sleep to fall upon Adam, and he slept: and he took one of his ribs, and closed up the flesh . . . thereof: and the rib, which the LORD God had taken from man, made he a woman, and brought her unto the man. And Adam said, This is now bone of my bones, and flesh of my flesh: she shall be called Woman, because she was taken out of Man. Therefore shall a man leave his father and his mother, and shall cleave unto his wife: and they shall be one flesh."

So we can see that the beautiful institution of marriage is a product of the Garden of Eden. And further, the sanctity of the marriage vows was guarded in one of the Ten Commandments God gave to Moses and to the world on Mount Sinai.

I think it is far beyond the level of coincidence that our Lord's first miracle was performed not in the hallowed and sacred precincts of the temple or in a synagogue, but upon the joyous occasion of a marriage feast in Cana of Galilee.

Thus we are assembled here to witness the pledges which _____ and _____ are now to make to each other, and to assure them of our prayers for their happiness and joy in this new and sacred relationship. What marriage was in the Garden of Eden, it can be now. Marriage, as a holy institution, has never fallen. It is that part of Paradise which still continues to soothe troubles and comfort sorrows. _____ and _____ , it can, and will, be this to you, if you will guard it with your tender care, with your attention to little things, and, most of all, with your patience and understanding toward each other and your continued devotion to God. These things I charge you here, in God's name, to remember.

The marriage vows

(Pastor addresses the groom.)

_____ , wilt thou have _____ to be thy wedded wife, to live together after God's ordinance in the holy estate of matrimony? Wilt thou love her, comfort her, honor and keep her, in sickness and in health; and, forsaking all others, keep thee only unto her so long as you both shall live? *(Groom answers,* "I will.")

With what token do you wish to seal this vow? *(Groom takes ring from best man and, handing it to pastor, says,* "With this ring.")

The ring is a symbol of eternity. In its perfect roundness, it has neither beginning nor ending. It is made of gold, which is a symbol of purity. Our prayer for you, _____ and _____ , is that your love for each other may be symbolized in these rings which you shall wear as tokens of your love for each other—that it will be lasting and will grow deeper and deeper as long as you both shall live on this earth.

_____ , will you take this ring and place it on _____'s finger as a token of the vow you have made to her and before God and all of us—and hold it in place as you repeat to her the following vow:

"I, _____ , take thee, _____ , to be my wedded wife; to have and to hold from this day forward; for better, for worse; for richer, for poorer; in sickness and in health; to love and to cherish till death do us part. With this ring I thee wed, and with all my worldly goods I thee endow. In the name of the Father, and of the Son, and of the Holy Spirit."

(Pastor then addresses the bride.)

_____ , wilt thou have _____ to be thy wedded husband, to live together after God's ordinance in the holy estate of matrimony? And wilt thou love, honor, and keep him, in sickness and in health; and, forsaking all others, keep thyself only unto him, so long as you both shall live on this earth? *(Bride answers,* "I will.")

With what token do you wish to seal this vow? *(Bride takes ring from maid of honor and says,* "With this ring," *and gives it to the pastor.)*

Then, _____ , as _____ has placed on your finger this token of his love for you, will you do likewise for him? Now, will you hold the ring, as you repeat after me the following vow: *(Identical vow made by groom).*

"And Ruth said, Entreat me not to leave thee, or to return from following after thee: for whither thou goest, I will go; and where thou lodgest, I will lodge: thy people shall be my people, and thy God my God. Where thou diest, will I die, and there will I be buried. The LORD do so to me, and more also, if aught but death part thee and me."

Forasmuch as _____ and _____ have consented together in holy wedlock, and have witnessed this committal before God and all of us, having pledged and sealed their vows with these rings, I pronounce that they are husband and wife, in the name of the Father, and of the Son, and of the Holy Spirit. What God hath joined together, let not man put asunder.

Prayer

God the Father, the Son, and the Holy Spirit bless, preserve, and keep you; the Lord graciously and with His favor look upon you and fill you with all spiritual blessings and love. May He cause His face to shine upon you, and grant you the peace that passes all understanding. In the name of His Son and our Savior, the Lord Jesus Christ, we pray. Amen.

The recessional

—DLJ

* * *

MESSAGES FOR OLDER CHILDREN AND YOUNG PEOPLE

TITLE: The Poor Little Rich Man

TEXT: "And when Jesus came to the place, he looked up, and saw him, and said unto him, Zacchaeus, make haste, and come down; for to day I must abide at thy house" (Luke 19:5).

SCRIPTURE READING: Luke 19:1-10

Introduction. Zacchaeus—could we call him "the poor little rich man"? Zacchaeus' name, ironically, means "pure." He was a man whose shortness of physical stature has come to symbolize the littleness which characterized him in other ways. He was a cheat, a traitor, a turncoat to his own people. He was selfish and self-centered; he was greedy and totally uncaring in his attitude toward others.

And yet, as has been true in so many other cases, Jesus saw something in Zacchaeus. Through all of those outside layers of ugliness and sin, Jesus saw *potential*—He saw what this man could become. Everybody else had long since given up on Zacchaeus—but not Jesus. This little man was one of the last persons Jesus gathered to Himself before He went to the cross. For when He passed through Jericho this time, He was on His way to Jerusalem and to the cross.

I. The condition of Zacchaeus.

In one verse, we have Luke's description of him: "And, behold, there was a man named Zacchaeus, which was the chief among the publicans, and he was rich" (Luke 19:2).

That sounds like a note you would put on a man's application for the loan of a large sum of money! It tells us about his occupation—a lucrative one—and about his financial condition. He was "rich." His name, Zacchaeus, was purely Jewish, and as we noted earlier, it means "pure." Perhaps, when Zacchaeus was presented by his parents in the temple, they gave him that name to express their hope and desire for him. And if that were true, and if either or both of his parents were still living, I am quite sure they were heartbroken. For Zacchaeus had become everything else *but* "pure" in his manner of living.

Luke tells us that Zacchaeus was a "chief publican." That meant that a whole district was under his supervision. His position came as an appointment from Rome. The tax rate for the people was fixed by Rome, and then the schedule of taxes was given to the chief publican. He was left free to add to the taxes as much as he dared to pay himself and the tax collectors working under him. Thus Zacchaeus and his fellow tax collectors were hated by the Jews not only because they had betrayed their people by selling out to Rome, but also because the taxes they assessed were unbelievably high.

Consequently, in spite of his great wealth, Zacchaeus was banned from any social life with his people, and he was excommunicated from the temple and the synagogue. In a very real sense, he was "a man without a country."

II. The curiosity of Zacchaeus.

Listen again to Luke: "And he sought to see Jesus who he was; and could not for the press, because he was little of stature. And he ran before, and climbed up into a sycomore tree to see him: for he was to pass that way'' (vv. 3-4).

It is almost like a breath of fresh air to discover that Zacchaeus was curious. A healthy curiosity is always a hopeful sign about a person. Curiosity and the urge to investigate, to find out, indicate that a person is in a good state of mental health. So Zacchaeus ''sought to see Jesus who he was.'' Some have thought that Zacchaeus was already convicted of his sins and was running to Jesus. They say that Zacchaeus had been waiting for Jesus to come, and that he knew this was his ''big moment.'' I doubt that. Rather, the situation was simply that a great crowd of people surged down this Jericho street, and Zacchaeus was overcome with a natural curiosity to see what it was all about.

But he was also *determined* to satisfy his curiosity. He was a short man, and he could not see easily over the heads of the people. So he found a sycamore tree with a low-hanging limb, and he boosted himself up among the leaves of the tree, right over the roadway where Jesus was to pass. The Holy Spirit often takes advantage of a person's natural, inherent curiosity to bring him to an awareness of his lostness and of his need for a Savior. Likewise, the Holy Spirit took advantage of *Zacchaeus'* curiosity.

III. The encounter Zacchaeus had with Jesus.

''And when Jesus came to the place, he looked up, and saw him, and said unto him, Zacchaeus, make haste, and come down; for to day I must abide at thy house. And he made haste, and came down, and received him joyfully'' (vv. 5-6).

Note the phrase, ''And when Jesus came to the place, he looked up.'' Most of us, walking along that street with hundreds of people crowding around us, would easily have missed a man looking down from the limb of a tree overhead, especially if he was hidden among the leaves! But Jesus looked up because He knew there was someone ''lost'' up in that tree, and He ''came to seek and to save that which was lost''! Always the compassionate, loving eyes of Jesus were searching the crowds, the multitudes, for those who were candidates for His kingdom.

There is no doubt that Jesus stopped when He came beneath that overhanging limb where Zacchaeus was perched. He called Zacchaeus by name. Could they have met before? Probably not. Because He was the Son of God, Jesus knew who Zacchaeus was before He ever saw him! So Jesus commanded Zacchaeus to come down and informed him that He would be a guest in his house that very day. Only one other time did Jesus ask for some gesture of hospitality—from the Samaritan woman at Jacob's well when He said to her, ''Give me to drink.'' Isn't it strange that *both* of these persons were ''outcasts,'' from the standpoint of their acceptance by others?

The people were aghast that Jesus would be seen in the company of Zacchaeus. Before Jesus' visit in Zacchaeus' home was over, a radical change had taken place in that tax collector's life. His sins were forgiven, and his heart was changed. Whereas once his life had been characterized by getting, he was now saying, ''I give.'' That is the way of Christianity. Before he met Jesus, he was mastered by *greed;* afterwards he was mastered by *grace*.

Conclusion. What, then, was the glorious ending to this story? ''And Jesus said unto him, This day is salvation come to this house'' (v. 9). This was Jesus' mission. ''For the Son of man is come to seek and to save that which was lost'' (v. 10).

—*DLJ*

TITLE: The Man Who Wouldn't Give Up

TEXT: "And when he heard that it was Jesus of Nazareth, he began to cry out, and say, Jesus, thou son of David, have mercy on me. And many charged him that he should hold his peace: but he cried the more a great deal, Thou son of David, have mercy on me" (Mark 10:47-48).

SCRIPTURE READING: Mark 10:46-52

Introduction. Bartimaeus—a begger in Jericho. It is sad to be a begger *anywhere,* but the tragedy was even worse with Bartimaeus, for he was also blind. Clustered around the gate leading out of Jericho toward Jerusalem were the usual beggars. Among them was Bartimaeus, ever raising his sightless eyes in response to the sound of footsteps passing his way, begging for money to buy food.

As Jesus and His disciples were going out of the city of Jericho, it was necessary to pass by these beggars. One of them seemed particularly interested in getting Jesus' attention.

I. The encounter between Jesus and this blind beggar by the Jericho roadside.

Apparently Bartimaeus and his father were well known in Jericho since Mark is careful to name him, and then to translate the name, "son of Timaeus." When I was growing up, there was such a "character" in my hometown. He was always downtown with his cup and pencils which he sold. All of the children knew and loved Jake, for he was a kind and jovial man who had been blind from birth. His face was covered with large warts, and until you got to know him, there was something a bit repulsive about his appearance. He played a harmonica, and he played amazingly well. The children would gather around him, and he would play the "fun tunes" we liked so well. Everybody knew Jake, the blind man. Likewise, everybody in Jericho seemed to have known Bartimaeus and his father.

On this particular day in Jericho, the crowds were larger because great numbers of people were passing through on their way to Jerusalem for the Passover. But there seemed to be something else going on, a sort of high tension in the air. Immediately the sensitive Bartimaeus knew this. He may have grabbed the cloak of a passerby and asked him, "Man, will you tell me what is going on? Something is happening! Somebody unusual is in the crowd. Tell me, who is it? What is happening?" And apparently someone told Bartimaeus that it was "Jesus of Nazareth" who was causing all of the commotion.

No doubt Bartimaeus had already heard about Jesus. Being a Jew, he was familiar with the words of the prophet Isaiah and others who had prophesied that a Savior would come, who would be of the line and tribe of David. Immediately the Holy Spirit helped Bartimaeus make this connection in his mind. For he cried out, "Jesus, thou son of David, have mercy on me!" The people who were talking with Jesus tried to hush Bartimaeus, "but he cried out the more a great deal." Maybe Bartimaeus felt that this was his last chance, we don't know. Anyway, ignoring the protests of the people, Bartimaeus kept on crying out in order to get Jesus' attention.

II. The conversation between Bartimaeus and Jesus: "And Jesus stood still, and commanded him to be called. And they call the blind man, saying unto him, Be of good comfort, rise; he calleth thee" (Mark 10:49).

It is significant that we read, "And Jesus stood still." Instantly, Jesus knew all about Bartimaeus. He knew that there had been a "countdown" going on inside him. When he called out, "Jesus, thou son of David, have mercy on me," Jesus knew that the moment of transformation had come for that blind beggar. So Jesus "commanded him to be called." The people who had been trying to hinder Bartimaeus from getting Jesus' attention caught the urgency and felt the authority in Jesus' words. Quickly they did an about-face. "Be of good comfort, rise; he calleth thee," they said to the beggar. With no hesitation at all, Bartimaeus, "casting away his garment, rose, and came to Jesus."

Jesus asked him, "What wilt thou that I should do unto thee?" Certainly Jesus knew what the man wanted more than anything else in the world. He was blind; he wanted to see! But Bartimaeus needed to state his need before the Lord. God knows that we are sinners; but still He wants us to state that fact with our own mouths. So Bartimaeus said, "Lord, that I might receive my sight."

III. Jesus' accommodation of Bartimaeus.

The climax of the story is wonderful. Jesus accommodated the physical need of Bartimaeus; that is, He healed his blindness. But far more important is the fact Jesus added Bartimaeus to His spiritual family, for we read, "And immediately he received his sight, and followed Jesus in the way" (v. 52b).

Jesus' answer to Bartimaeus was thrilling: "Go thy way; thy faith hath made thee whole." Jesus did not heal sick people indiscriminately. It was not His purpose to heal all of the sick people and open the eyes of all of the blind people. But when the healing of a sick body, or the opening of blind eyes, would open the way for a spiritual victory, for the salvation of a soul, He did it gladly and enthusiastically.

Thus, Jesus "accommodated" the physical need of Bartimaeus; that is, He healed his blindness. But the greatest blessing that came to Bartimaeus that day was that he also received salvation.

Conclusion. Bartimaeus became a traveling companion with Jesus and His disciples as they left Jericho and went to Jerusalem. Most probably Bartimaeus was in Jerusalem when Jesus was arrested, tried, and crucified. He may well have been among the one hundred and twenty believers who were instructed by Jesus, after His resurrection, to wait in the Upper Room in Jerusalem until the Holy Spirit came.

The story of Bartimaeus is another in a long succession of miracles Jesus performed. And these miracles continue to this day, for whenever a person, recognizing his spiritual blindness, calls out, "God, have mercy on me!" Jesus stands still, bids that person come, and changes his darkness into light. —*DLJ*

* * *

TITLE: A Father and His Son

Text: "And straightway the father of the child cried out, and said with tears, Lord, I believe; help thou mine unbelief" (Mark 9:24).

Scripture Reading: Mark 9:14-29

Introduction. Under normal circumstances, few human relationships are as special as that which exists when there is a strong bond between a father and his son. And yet, when the son is the helpless victim of an incurable disease, and the parents must watch him suffer without being able to do anything to relieve his suffering—that is a scene that will break the hardest heart! Such is the case with this moving story Mark has recorded for us.

The setting in which this incident took place was one of breath-taking beauty. An artist could have a field day with this, for in the background there was the majestic and towering Mount Hermon, silent, snow-capped, and regal on the horizon. Somewhere on that mountain Jesus had just been transfigured before three of His disciples and had appeared before them, along with Moses and Elijah, in the stunning brilliance of His glorified body.

Therefore, as our story opens, we find it is

I. A scene of extremes (vv. 14-19).

Let's imagine for a moment that we have been waiting with the other nine disciples down in the valley, somewhere at the base of Mount Hermon, for Jesus and the other three disciples to return. A serious problem had developed while they were away. A father had just brought his demon-possessed son to the nine disciples on the reputation that Jesus could cast out demons. Instead of detaining him until Jesus could return to deal with the problem, they proceeded to deal with the matter themselves. They had watched Jesus perform many miracles, including the casting out of evil spirits. They had heard the words He had spoken, and they thought they "knew the formula."

There is every possibility they could have thought within themselves: "Here's our chance! When Jesus is here, we are always in the background. No one ever pays any attention to us. Why don't we cash in on a little of this glory for ourselves!"

How many times have you and I taken some matter into our own hands, foolishly thinking that we were capable of handling the situation in our own strength? We knew the "magic formula"; we could say all the right words. *And we fell on our faces!* Why? Because we forgot that we can do nothing effectively for God apart from the power of the indwelling Christ. The disciples failed miserably because they tried to heal the disturbed boy in *their* power and for *their* glory.

When Jesus appeared, the father of the demon-controlled boy related to Jesus what had happened. Jesus' reply was one of the saddest statements that he made: "O faithless generation, how long shall I be with you? How long shall I suffer you?" (v. 19). When He said this, He was including not just the disciples who had failed, but the scribes who also were there, *and* this suffering father and his son. Jesus was saying that He lived in the midst of a people without faith.

But then, for a few moments, the situation grew worse. We have seen that it was a scene of extremes. Now we see it as

II. A scene of tragedy.

"And they brought him unto him [Jesus]: and when he saw him, straightway the spirit tare him; and he fell on the ground, and wallowed foaming" (v. 20). Do you remember what happened when Jesus and the disciples approached a wild man who lived in the region of Gadara? He came screaming down the cliffside, begging Jesus to go away and not torment him "before his time." The demons knew what was about to take place. So it was with the boy in this story. For while Jesus and the boy's father were talking, the evil spirit in the boy seized him, and he lapsed into what may have been the worst convulsion he had ever had.

The father said to Jesus, "If thou canst do any thing, have compassion on us, and help us" (v. 22). He might have been saying, "Lord, I came with my boy hoping that You could heal him. But You were not here, and Your disciples were helpless. Does this mean that *You* cannot help us either? But still, Lord, if You can, please help us!" Jesus saw a tiny flicker of faith in what the father said, and He seized upon it. "If thou canst believe, all things are possible to him that believeth" (v. 23). The father cried, "Lord, I believe; help thou mine unbelief" (v. 24).

III. A scene of victory.

And Jesus "rebuked the foul spirit, saying unto him, Thou dumb and deaf spirit, I charge thee, come out of him, and enter no more into him. And the spirit cried, and rent him sore, and came out of him: and he was as one dead; insomuch that many said, He is dead. But Jesus took him by the hand, and lifted him up; and he arose" (vv. 25-27). Realizing that he was about to be disembodied, the evil spirit made one last, violent attempt to hurt the boy. Then the boy lay "as one dead." The experience was so utterly exhausting, both physically and spiritually, that he appeared to have no life in him at all. Then Jesus took his hand and lifted him up. Luke, in his account of the incident, adds, "He gave him back to his father."

Conclusion. Why had the disciples of Jesus failed so miserably? In fact, they were still perplexed about it, for as they were leaving the scene, they asked Jesus, "Why could not *we* cast him out?" (v. 28). Jesus answered them plainly: "This kind can come forth by nothing, but by prayer and fasting" (v. 29). In effect, He was saying, just as He would say to you and me when we fail in our Christian witness and testimony, "You don't live close enough to God!" God's power was available for their use, but what activated that power was a close and intimate relationship with God.

Paul once said, "I can do all things . . ."; and if he had stopped there, we would be justified in calling him an egotist. But he said, "I can do all things through Christ which strengtheneth me" (Phil. 4:13). That's the secret. Like the boy in the story, we "believe," but our belief is often weak, unsupported by prayer and obedience toward God. The disciples became overconfident, and they failed. May God help us to be certain that our confidence is always in *Him,* and not in ourselves. —*DLJ*

* * *

TITLE: Pilate—a Man on Trial

TEXT: **"Pilate saith unto him, What is truth? And when he had said this, he went out again unto the Jews, and saith unto them, I find in him no fault at all" (John 18:38).**

SCRIPTURE READING: **John 18:28-40**

Introduction. Pontius Pilate—the only reason we know his name is because of his encounter with Jesus Christ. Had he never come in contact with the Son of God, history would have ignored him, passed him by. But what *do* we know about him?

He was a man who had a haughty disposition. He loved his authority; he was cold and without compassion. His whole attitude toward Judea, and toward the Jews, was that of scorn and hatred. The only reason he made any attempt to quell uprisings and riots and bloodshed was because of Caesar's insistence that the famed "Roman peace" be maintained in the Empire.

Pilate was a contemptuous man. When the Jewish priests brought Jesus to him, the first question he asked was couched in satire and contempt. If Pilate had lived in our day and had spoken to them in the vernacular of our generation, he would likely have said, "Oh, it's *you* again! *Now* what?"

Yet, in all fairness, when we read between the lines of Pilate's story on the pages of the New Testament, we find that Pilate understood justice. He had a passion for the observance of the Roman law. He did everything he could except the one final thing that he *could* have done, to save Jesus. In fact, he probably would much rather have had Caiaphas crucified that day than Jesus!

But let's move a bit closer to this complicated and strange man and see if we can follow just what happened to him as he came under the spell of Jesus Christ.

I. First, Pilate was *annoyed* when the priests brought Jesus to him: "Then said Pilate unto them, Take ye him, and judge him according to your law" (v. 31a).

Probably this is the first time Pilate had ever seen Jesus. He may not even have looked closely at Him at this first encounter. For this was not the first time these troublesome and hypocritical Jewish priests had brought prisoners to him for arraignment. Then perhaps he whirled around with a swish of his judicial Roman robes and said over his shoulder, "Don't bother me with your religious disputes! *You* have *your* law in these matters! Take Him, and judge Him according to *your* laws. Now, get out of here!"

But Pilate was stopped cold in his tracks when Jesus' accusers said, "But, Governor, *our* court is not permitted to put a man to death. *You* know that." In a moment, Pilate saw that these Jews were not seeking for justice. They wanted blood! It was then that Pilate walked back to the center of the judgment hall and "called Jesus." This prisoner was not like the usual rabble-rouser they brought to him.

II. So, in the progression we are following with Pilate, we find now that he was *arrested* by this prisoner, this Jesus, whom the Jews had brought to him.

The first question Pilate asked Jesus as they stood aside in the Praetorium was, "Art thou the King of the Jews?" Jesus' answer was interesting: "Sayest thou this thing of thyself, or did others tell it thee of me?" Or, in other words, "Is this an original thought with you, or are you just repeating what you have heard others say?" This obviously was uncomfortable ground for Pilate, for he quickly changed the subject.

It is at this point that Pilate apparently abandoned his "cat-and-mouse" game. With obvious sincerity and judicial decorum, he asked Jesus, "What have You done? Why have they brought You here to me? Why do they want the death sentence?" Pilate was amazed all the more when he heard Jesus say, "My kingdom is not of this world; if my kingdom were of this world, then would my servants fight, that I should not be delivered to the Jews: but now is my kingdom not from hence" (v. 36).

Then quietly, incredulously, Pilate asked Jesus, "*Are* You, then, really a king? Did I hear You correctly? You spoke of a 'kingdom.' Does that mean that

You *are* a king?'' And with no hesitation, Jesus answered Pilate: ''Thou sayest that I am a king. To this end was I born, and for this cause came I into the world, that I should bear witness unto the truth. Every one that is of the truth heareth my voice'' (v. 37).

III. Now the progression moves yet farther along for Pilate: From annoyance, to being arrested by this strange man, Pilate is now ***astounded*** **by what he hears.**

After Jesus had spoken, Pilate exclaimed, ''What *is* truth?'' In all of this, we can see how rapidly Pilate was being brought to the point of facing himself, of facing the God of truth, of making a decision about life and destiny. This is the same progression any individual follows when he is about to reach a point of decision. Before one can come to receive Jesus Christ as Savior, he must become thoroughly disenchanted with himself. He must realize that there is one source of truth, and it lies in God, expressed in His Son, the Lord Jesus Christ.

Then it was that Pilate went out and faced the Jews, saying to them, ''I find in him no fault at all. But ye have a custom, that I should release unto you one at the passover: will ye therefore that I release unto you the King of the Jews?'' (vv. 38c, 39). By this time, Pilate likely was the most confused and bewildered man in Jerusalem. But he did the cowardly thing. He submitted Jesus to the dreaded Roman scourge. He had Jesus beaten. After the inhuman beating, and after the mocking soldiers had placed the crown of thorns on his brow and the mock robe about his bleeding shoulders, Pilate brought him forth before the mob. ''What shall I do then with Jesus which is called Christ?'' was his question (Matt. 27:22).

IV. There is one last, tragic, hopeless step in this progression with Pilate: We have seen him annoyed, arrested, and astounded; now, we see Pilate ***defeated.***

Pilate stalled for time. He called Jesus before him again, but Jesus would not answer him. Then, in spite of the accusations of his conscience, he bowed to the evil wishes of the mob. And in the final analysis, it was not Jesus who was on trial, but Pilate! A choice was being forced upon him. Throughout that bleak and stormy day, there was one clear issue before him. The same issue is before every person who is faced with the truth about God and His Son, Jesus. ''What shall I do then with Jesus which is called Christ?''

Conclusion. As to what ultimately happened to Pilate, we do not know. We do not know what happens when a person violates his conscience and slams the door for the last time in the face of God. But we *do* know that today is the day of salvation. Now this moment, is the acceptable time. It may be *your* time. —*DLJ*

* * *

SENTENCE SERMONETTES

1. ''Love is the golden thread that ties the heart of all the world.''
2. ''The visions of God are seen only through the lens of a pure heart.''
3. ''The conversion of a soul is the miracle of a moment.''
4. ''Love does not dominate, love cultivates.''

5. "Those who bring sunshine to the lives of others cannot keep it from themselves."
6. "Never hold on to the failures of yesterday."
7. "Worrying is like a rocking chair. It will give you something to do, but will get you nowhere."
8. "Fear can be used as a springboard."
9. "Do you have invisible means of support?"
10. "You cannot get anywhere today if you are still mired down in yesterday."
11. "Defeat must be faced, but it need not be final."
12. "Lord, help me remember that nothing is going to happen to me today that You and I can't handle."
13. "Tomorrows are only todays waiting to happen."
14. "Happy hearts make happy homes."
15. "Patience endures today, while it works for tomorrow."
16. "A house is built by human hands; a home is built by human hearts."
17. "God helps the helpless."
18. "When you are hemmed in, the only way to look is up."
19. "We must nourish the roots of faith before we can expect the fruits of action."
20. "The impossible is often the untried."
21. "Worry never robs tomorrow of its sorrow, it only robs today of its strength."
22. "So live that those who know the most about you have the greatest confidence in you."
23. "The Lord gives us talents, but we have to develop them."
24. "There is no better exercise for the heart than reaching down and lifting someone up."
25. "God's assurance gives us endurance."
26. "God does not love you because you are important. You are important because God loves you."
27. "Don't be weakened by too much week end!"
28. "Good friends are sunshine on a rainy day."
29. "We can measure our likeness to Christ by our sensitivity to the pain, trials, and loneliness of others."
30. "Prayer is the key, but faith turns the knob that opens the door to heaven's blessings."
31. "Walking with the Lord is the best exercise to build a healthy soul."
32. "Success is not measured by heights attained but by obstacles overcome."
33. "Every day brings a child of God one day nearer home."
34. "The safest hiding place in the world is in the center of God's will."
35. "What we weave in this world, we shall wear in the next."
36. "There is only one place in which success comes before work—that is in the dictionary."
37. "You can never do a kindness too soon because you never know when it will be too late."
38. "God still speaks to those who take time to listen."
39. "Kind words never die."
40. "You will live as long as God lives—either in heaven or in hell."
41. "Fear and faith travel the river of life, but only faith should be allowed to anchor."

42. "Worry pulls tomorrow's clouds over today's sunshine."
43. "When God gives burdens, He also gives shoulders."
44. "He is no fool who gives away that which he cannot keep in order to gain that which he cannot lose."
45. "The Lord washes away our faults with a soap called Forgiveness."
46. "When troubles assail you, turn to God—He will never fail you."
47. "When praying, do you give instructions or report for duty?"
48. "The word which God has written on the brow of every man is Hope."
49. Formula for living: "Keep your chin up and your knees down."
50. "There is nothing so kingly as kindness, and nothing so royal as truth."
51. "Love is the master key that opens the gates of happiness."
52. "A world without a Sabbath would be like a man without a smile or like a summer without flowers."
53. "Regret and fear are twin thieves who would rob us of today."
54. "God in our heart can mean the difference between despair and victory."
55. "The true measure of love is loving without measure." —*BCC*

* * *

TOPIC INDEX

SCRIPTURE INDEX

Sermon texts are in bold type